Blue Texas

Justice, Power, and Politics

COEDITORS
Heather Ann Thompson
Rhonda Y. Williams

EDITORIAL ADVISORY BOARD
Peniel E. Joseph
Matthew D. Lassiter
Daryl Maeda
Barbara Ransby
Vicki L. Ruiz
Marc Stein

The Justice, Power, and Politics series publishes new works in history that explore the myriad struggles for justice, battles for power, and shifts in politics that have shaped the United States over time. Through the lenses of justice, power, and politics, the series seeks to broaden scholarly debates about America's past as well as to inform public discussions about its future.

More information on the series, including a complete list of books published, is available at http://justicepowerandpolitics.com/.

Blue Texas

The Making of a Multiracial Democratic Coalition in the Civil Rights Era

MAX KROCHMAL

The University of North Carolina Press
Chapel Hill

Published in association with The William P. Clements Center for Southwest Studies, Southern Methodist University, by The University of North Carolina Press, Chapel Hill

This book was published with the assistance of the Authors Fund of the University of North Carolina Press.

© 2016 Max Krochmal
All rights reserved
Set in Adobe Text Pro by Westchester Publishing Services

The University of North Carolina Press has been a member of the Green Press Initiative since 2003.

Library of Congress Cataloging-in-Publication Data
Names: Krochmal, Max, author.
Title: Blue Texas : the making of a multiracial Democratic coalition in the Civil Rights era / Max Krochmal.
Other titles: Justice, power, and politics.
Description: Chapel Hill : University of North Carolina Press, [2016] | Series: Justice, power, and politics | Includes bibliographical references and index.
Identifiers: LCCN 2016004007 | ISBN 9781469626758 (cloth : alk. paper) | ISBN 9781469661513 (pbk. : alk. paper) | ISBN 9781469626765 (ebook)
Subjects: LCSH: Electoral coalitions—Texas—History—20th century. | Minorities—Political activity—Texas—History—20th century. | African Americans—Political activity—Texas—History—20th century. | Mexican Americans—Political activity—Texas. | Political participation—Texas—History—20th century. | Civil rights movements—Texas—History—20th century. | Texas—Politics and government—20th century.
Classification: LCC JK4889 .K76 2016 | DDC 324.2764/0609045—dc23
LC record available at http://lccn.loc.gov/2016004007

Cover image: Farm workers marching along ridge in south Texas (n.d.); courtesy, Mexican-American Farm Workers Movement, Special Collections, The University of Texas at Arlington Libraries, Arlington, Texas.

For Courtney

Contents

List of Abbreviations Used in the Text, xi

Prologue, 1

Chapter 1 People Are Power, 14
  The Mass Uprising and the Maverick Coalition

Chapter 2 Segregation Is an Economic Problem, 56
  Black Workers Win the Right to Vote

Chapter 3 Forcing Us Together in Self-Defense, 87
  The Cold War, the Black Vote, and the Liberal Movement

Chapter 4 Minorities Combine, 133
  G. J. Sutton, Albert Peña, and the Democrats of Texas

Chapter 5 Unions Are Needed So Desperately Here, 171
  The Rebirth of the Labor Movement and the Seeds of the Bexar Coalition

Chapter 6 We Shall Be Heard, 194
  Civil Rights in Black and Brown from the Sit-ins to Viva Kennedy

Chapter 7 Trying to Reach Substantially Unanimous Agreement, 232
  The "Latin Vote" and the First Democratic Coalition

Chapter 8 Separating the Wheat from the Chaff, 276
  Intraracial Divides Give Way to Interracial Unity

Chapter 9 They'll Never Separate Us Again, 315
  The Multiracial Democratic Coalition on the March

Chapter 10 New Power for Texas Minorities, 360
  Winning the Battles, Losing the War

Epilogue, 398
　　The Multiracial Marcha

Acknowledgments, 423
Notes, 429
Bibliography, 493
Index, 513

Illustrations

George P. Lambert in San Antonio, 15

Roadster pickup truck with slogans supporting pecan sheller strike, 24

Latane Bartlett Lambert, 30

Moses LeRoy, 60

Attorney W. J. Durham, 68

Mrs. Erma DeLoney LeRoy, 84

Liberal activist Chris Dixie speaking at the 1964 Texas Democratic Convention, 111

Mrs. R. D. (Frankie Carter) Randolph, leader of the Democrats of Texas, 119

Garlington Jerome (G. J.) Sutton after his 1948 election victory, 136

Rev. Claude W. Black Jr., 141

Albert A. Peña Jr., with Senator John F. Kennedy, 156

Cluster of union balloons used in Tex-Son strike, 183

H. S. (Hank) Brown speaking at the Texas State AFL-CIO Convention, 187

Rev. Claude W. Black Jr. and others confronting police outside a Handy Andy store, 205

Moses and Erma LeRoy with labor leader Jerry R. Holleman, 227

Don Yarborough greets supporters at Austin airport, 270

Rev. Claude Black and G. J. Sutton picketing San Antonio City Hall, 286

"A Giant Awakening," PASO cartoon, 301

Booker T. Bonner displaying receipt for appointment with Governor John Connally, 332

"Freedom Now" March in Austin, 343

Crowd at Woolridge Square Park following march, 345

Francisco F. "Pancho" Medrano with Dallas African American activists during poll tax repeal campaign, 364

Moses LeRoy speaking to a farmworkers' rally in Corpus Christi, 399

A multiracial crowd at farmworkers' Labor Day, 1966, march at the capitol in Austin, 400

Maps

Major cities and regions of Texas, 11

Houston neighborhoods and landmarks, 88

San Antonio neighborhoods and landmarks, 146

Communities visited by Mrs. Erma D. LeRoy, 1959–62, 261

Approximate route of Gilbert Garcia, December 1961 to January 1962, 263

List of Abbreviations Used in the Text

ACWA	Amalgamated Clothing Workers of America
ADA	Americans for Democratic Action
AFL	American Federation of Labor
AFL-CIO	American Federation of Labor—Congress of Industrial Organizations
AGIF	American G.I. Forum
AIFLD	American Institute for Free Labor Development
BSRC	Brotherhood of Steamship and Railway Clerks
CAC	Civic Action Committee
CCBG	Citizens Committee for Better Government
CIO	Congress of Industrial Organizations
CIO-PAC	CIO Political Action Committee
COPE	Committee on Political Education
CTM	Confederación de Trabajadores Mexicanos (Mexican Workers Confederation)
DOSA	Dallas Open Shop Association
DOT	Democrats of Texas
FEPC	Fair Employment Practices Committee (Committee on Fair Employment Practice)
FIA	Freedom in Action
GGL	Good Government League
HA-YOU	Huntsville Action for Youth
HCCL	Hod Carriers and Common Laborers
HCCO	Harris County Council of Organizations
HCD	Harris County Democrats
HUAC	House Un-American Activities Committee (House Committee on Un-American Activities)
ILA	International Longshoremen's Association

ILGWU	International Ladies' Garment Workers' Union
IUE	International Union of Electrical, Machine, and Radio Workers
LAD	Loyal American Democrats
LDF	Legal Defense Fund
LNPL	Labor's Non-Partisan League
LULAC	League of United Latin American Citizens
LULACer	Member of the League of United Latin American Citizens
MAPA	Mexican-American Political Association
MDTA	Manpower Development and Training Act
NAACP	National Association for the Advancement of Colored People
NAPE	National Alliance of Postal Employees
NFWA	National Farm Workers Association
NLRB	National Labor Relations Board
NMU	National Maritime Union
NNC	National Negro Congress
ORIT	Organización Regional Interamericana de Trabajadores (Inter-American Regional Workers' Organization)
OVL	Organized Voters League
OWIU-CIO	Oil Workers International Union
PAPA	Pan American Progressive Association
PASO	Political Association of Spanish-Speaking Organizations
PVL	Progressive Voters League
PYA	Progressive Youth Association
SACO	San Antonio Chicano Organizers
SCL	Students for Civil Liberties
SCLC	Southern Christian Leadership Conference
SDA	Students for Direct Action
SDEC	State Democratic Executive Committee
SDS	Students for a Democratic Society
SNCC	Student Nonviolent Coordinating Committee
STFU	Southern Tenant Farmers Union
TCLU	Texas Civil Liberties Union

TCV	Texas Council of Voters
TFC	Texas Federation Club
TLD	Texas Liberal Democrats
TOLD	Texas Organization of Liberal Democrats
TSFL	Texas State Federation of Labor
TSLC	Texas Social and Legislative Conference
TSU	Texas Southern University
UAW	United Auto Workers (International Union, United Automobile, Aerospace and Agricultural Implements Workers of America)
UCAPAWA	United Cannery, Agricultural, Packinghouse, and Allied Workers of America
UE	United Electrical Workers
UMW	United Mine Workers of America
UPO	United Political Organization
UPWA	United Packinghouse Workers of America
VOTE	Voters of Texas Enlist
WAA	Workers Alliance of America
WAD	Women's Activities Department
WPA	Works Progress Administration

Prologue

On August 28, 1963, while much of America nervously watched the March on Washington, nearly one thousand demonstrators gathered in the all-black neighborhood of East Austin, Texas, to march toward the state capitol in 102-degree heat. Their two-mile route wound its way down crumbling streets, passed run-down houses and segregated schools, and finally crossed over into the white section of town, with its gleaming, pink granite capitol and lily-white Governor's Mansion. Veteran activists of all colors from across the state flanked several hundred local black teenagers, while groups of white college students and Mexican American activists joined the procession. Picket signs calling for "Freedom Now" competed with a dizzying array of homemade placards. One linked Texas governor John Connally to the infamous segregationist George Wallace of Alabama. Others carried slogans that connected civil rights to labor: "No more 50¢ per hour," read one, and "Segregation is a new form of slavery." Still another praised the president while adding some Spanish flair: "Kennedy sí, Connally no." The marchers sang movement songs lambasting the governor, who flatly refused to meet with them despite the fact that, hours earlier, President Kennedy had received a delegation of activists at the White House. Under the Texas sun, the demonstrators approached the capitol but could not stop there as planned. State police had turned on the lawn sprinklers to keep the marchers off the grounds while the governor continued working inside.

The weary protestors instead assembled under the live oak trees at a nearby park, listening and cheering as movement leaders gave speeches before the eager state press corps. The orators called for the passage of federal and state civil rights acts, but they did so in an unusual manner. "They'll never separate the Latin-American and Negroes again in politics," thundered W. J. Durham of Dallas, an African American attorney, state leader of the National Association for the Advancement of Colored People (NAACP), and president of the all-black Texas Council of Voters. "They'll never separate the independent white man and the Negro again. They'll never separate labor and the Negro again. We're going to march on the street, pray on the streets, sit in the streets, walk on the streets. We're going to fight at the ballot box and in the courts. I believe that's the last message I've got for my governor." Henry Muñoz, a printer and union activist from San Antonio, delivered a similar message on behalf of the Political Association of Spanish-Speaking Organizations (PASO), the state's most militant Mexican American civil rights organization. "The Negro today asks justice," Muñoz said. "We do not answer him ... when we reply to the Negro by asking 'Patience.' Along with the Negro and in many instances worse off, patiently waiting is the Mexican-American. ... To ask for patience from the Negro is to ask him to give more of what he has already given enough. In this hour, it is not our respective races which are at stake—it is our nation."[1]

The unprecedented march was decades in the making. Strange as it may seem now, beginning in the 1930s, African American, Mexican American, and white labor and community activists gradually came together in a broad struggle for democracy in Texas.[2] Separate local organizing efforts in the barrios, ghettos, union halls, and storefront campaign offices of the state's major cities gradually gave way to local experiments in multiracial collaboration. By the mid-1960s, the activists created a formal, egalitarian, statewide alliance in support of liberal politicians and an expansive, multiracial civil rights agenda. The protestors in Austin represented just the tip of a much larger iceberg—a vast network of black, brown, and white activists in all of the urban areas and many of the country crossroads of Texas. They demanded not just integration for blacks but also an end to discrimination against Mexican Americans. More boldly, they called for labor rights, economic justice, and real political power for all. They called their partnership simply the "Democratic Coalition."

This book is about the *other* Texas—not the state of big hair and cowboy conservatism, but the hidden Lone Star traditions of community organizing, civil rights, trade unionism, and liberal, multiracial coalition building. It tells the story of how an otherwise ordinary group of diverse activists first organized their separate bases, then crossed the color line to find one another, and together connected their freedom struggles to the labor movement and electoral politics. It follows the tumultuous, decades-long process of developing a common agenda and building a multiracial coalition, detailing the circuitous manner in which people who were initially unfamiliar with one another came to act as one. And it shows how building bridges between cultures became the crucial weapon in destroying Jim Crow and Juan Crow—and in transforming electoral politics in Texas and the nation.

For the past half-century through the present day, the eyes of America's pollsters and pundits have been fixed upon the Lone Star State. Three presidents began their careers in the cauldron of Texas politics, an unstable mixture that included a former U.S. senator, a member of Congress, and a governor. The state's shifts from a bulwark of the white supremacist Solid South to the home of the liberal Great Society to the foundation of red state conservatism continue to confound most observers. The most recent swing proves especially perplexing. How could the nation's second most populous state, with a burgeoning minority population, remain reliably Republican? What could Democrats do to win it back? And what would American politics look like if Texas were to turn blue?

The March 4, 2008, Democratic primary offered party activists some indication of their future. More than half of the nearly 3 million Texans who cast ballots in that election voted for then-senator Hillary Clinton, who bested her rival, then-senator Barack Obama, by 100,000 votes. That same evening, hundreds of thousands of those voters returned to their neighborhood schools, libraries, post offices, and other polling sites to participate in the second half of the "Texas two-step," a relic of local democracy in which voters held Iowa-style caucuses to elect pledged delegates from every precinct in the state. For decades, the evening meetings had been the province of only a handful of dyed-in-the-wool Democrats, but in 2008, new faces overwhelmed the party regulars. More important, the hundreds of on-the-ground organizers from the upstart Obama campaign succeeded in turning out legions of their supporters, dwarfing those of the former first lady. Despite facing opposition from the state party brass, Obama carried the precinct caucuses, then the county gatherings, and finally the statewide convention. Looking ahead to the Democratic National Convention in Denver, the nation's soon-to-be first black president left Texas with a majority of the state's delegates in his pocket, curiously winning the primary after losing the election itself.[3]

Even more surprisingly, Obama won Texas over the objections of most of the party's other nonwhite activists. For the past decade, the Mexican American Democrats and Tejano Democrats clubs had kept the candle burning in the dark night of Republican dominance—the GOP held every statewide office since the election of 1996 and all but one since George W. Bush's surprise defeat of Ann Richards, a liberal Democrat, two years earlier. Clinton had courted the state's Mexican Americans since her first political visit back in 1972, when she roamed the wilderness of South Texas with seasoned labor and civil rights activists and gave speeches at countless *mexicano* honky-tonks on behalf of George McGovern's disastrous bid for the presidency. Now in the twenty-first century, few Mexican American activists dared abandon a proven ally for a long shot. After all, nobody, not even the masses of black Texans who chanted "Yes, We Can" at the state convention, really believed that the United States would elect an African American to its highest office.[4]

The rest, as they say, is history. Obama rode the momentum of his victory in the Texas two-step to a series of primary victories, the nomination, and finally, the presidency. Reversing their antipathy toward Obama at the Texas convention, the state's Mexican Americans joined Latinos nationwide in rallying behind the Democratic nominee. Latinos nationally deepened their support four years later, when some 71 percent of the record number of Latinos who made it to the polls in the 2012 general election voted to reelect the president. Observers noted that the addition of Latinos to the president's coalition of young people, college graduates, union members, and African Americans pushed him to victory nationwide.

Liberals felt the same could hold true in Texas, where Obama garnered nearly 3.3 million votes in 2012, a staggering number despite the fact that it represented only 40 percent of the total ballots cast. Still, those mixed results proved good enough to convince a senior campaign staffer to come to the state to set up Battleground Texas, a new grassroots organization aimed at turning the state blue over the next decade. The AFL-CIO, the nation's leading labor federation, likewise announced plans to focus its new organizing efforts in the state. National news outlets such as NPR, the *New York Times*, and the *New Republic* all ran series or feature stories on the future of Texas liberalism.[5]

Virtually all commentators agreed that the growing Latino vote would represent the key to the futures of both political parties. Yet the history of that vote and, most critically, its relationship to African American politics remain unexamined. Was Latino support for Obama a fluke or evidence of a deeper bond between the nation's two largest minority groups? Can black-brown solidarity be counted on again in the next election? How and why can white candidates confront racism? Will winning that next campaign prove sufficient to uplift America's black and brown communities, or must political change be accompanied by grassroots protest?

The story of the making of the Democratic Coalition of Texas helps to answer these questions. By the 1960s, following decades of experimentation, the most militant African American and Mexican American activists formed a tight alliance with one another as well as with the white leadership of the state's organized labor movement and white liberal activists. Their combined agenda was rooted in broad-based social movements with expansive agendas that combined race with class and approached electoral politics as a means for change rather than an end in itself. They sought nothing less than the democratization of all aspects of life in their communities, cities, state, and nation.

Each constituent part of the coalition worked separately, first organizing in their own communities to meet their own needs. But gradually, through a process of trial and error, the organizers of each group approached like-minded activists across the color line. They did so out of desperation and self-interest, with each of them needing help to outflank the more conservative members of their own ethnic groups. Over time, the occasional foray to an interracial meeting across town led to more regular gatherings, then to marching on each other's picket lines, and, finally, to concerted action in the streets and at the ballot box.

Coming together across racial lines did not erase difference, nor did it subsume one group's agenda for another's. Rather, the coalition consisted of independent parts that worked together for a common cause despite disagreement and tension. The alliances built sometimes fell apart and then had to be reorganized. Coalition building, or "coalitioning," as one participant called it, remained a contested and contingent process.

This history does *not* suggest that African Americans and Mexican Americans were "natural allies," nor were they, as many assume, inveterate antagonists. They were simply different. When they worked together in politics, they made a series of agreements and compromises that held them together for a time and then came apart. Crucially, this meant both that black-brown cooperation could not be taken for granted—and also that black-brown conflict was *not* an insurmountable obstacle that precluded interminority coalitions. When it did occur, multiracial collaboration took place because of the human relationships forged experientially among the activists. Their work together had slowly produced bonds of friendship and trust. It was not rhetoric or vaguely "similar histories of oppression" that brought the disparate groups together, but years of struggling side-by-side in the trenches. Or, as another activist put it some years later, "Working unity is better than talking unity."[6]

More generally, the coalition succeeded because it both recognized and transcended racial difference. It prioritized the needs of its most vulnerable partners. It did not treat all members as atomized individuals, nor did it deploy "color blindness" to avoid thorny issues of racial inequality. Rather, it developed a deliberately democratic internal structure that allowed for discord and disagreement while still guaranteeing to each of its constituents an equal voice and fair representation. African Americans could veto any initiative that advocated gradual or "voluntary" rather than immediate integration, while organized labor could block a candidate who wasn't pledged to repeal the state's despised "right-to-work" law. The coalition worked because its most privileged members—labor and white liberals—plunged headlong into the fight for black and brown civil rights. The whites backed up their words with actions, hiring community organizers in the barrios, sitting in, and getting jailed alongside black student demonstrators. The more liberal, the more explicitly integrationist, the more militant the tactics, the more effective the coalition became.

At the same time, the history of the coalition suggests that racial solidarity only went so far in predicting a group's political inclinations, including how they voted. In fact, *intra*racial conflict frequently begot efforts to forge *inter*racial coalitions. The activists learned this lesson experientially: over several decades, after countless flare-ups and disagreements with their co-ethnic "social betters," they painstakingly separated themselves from their conservative counterparts. Distinctions of class, ideology, strategy, and tactics all mattered at least as much as did ties of race or ethnicity. Black, brown, and white activists all arrived at some version of this common conclusion, and they turned to one another in response. Slowly and unsteadily, they built lasting relationships of mutual need and support and, finally, trust. To be sure, their differences did not disappear, and each partner maintained its independence. Still, the creation of the coalition gave each of its members an unprecedented sense of support, growing political power, and new opportunities to advance and broaden their separate agendas.

Indeed, over time the causes of civil rights and political liberalism grew inseparable. African American, Mexican American, and white labor and community activists all rallied around the Democratic Coalition's promise of small-d democracy in Texas. They demanded "Freedom Now," but they also aimed to overthrow the oligarchy that had long oppressed the state's black, brown, and white working people. They fought for both goals by working together.

And they forever transformed politics in Texas. Although the assassination of President Kennedy soon after the March on Austin undermined the multiracial movement, the coalition still carried out an unprecedented voter registration and mobilization drive and staged numerous direct action demonstrations that finally brought democracy to the state. Just decades removed from the reign of the white primary and the border bosses that had restricted black and brown votes, African Americans and Mexican Americans and their white labor and liberal allies permanently enlarged the electorate and broke down the doors of the Democratic Party. The veteran organizers finally overthrew Jim Crow and Juan Crow and achieved a degree of economic justice and political power in Texas that was scarcely imaginable just a few years before. At the same time, the activists hit a ceiling that limited how much power they could wield, leaving work that remains to be done today—and a blueprint for how to do it.

———

This book thus speaks to the present and future by exploring models from the past. It starts from the dual premise that race remains one of the central dividing lines in our culture and that progressives cannot hope to bring together America's diverse amalgam of working peoples without first finding a way to build coalitions across the nation's multiple color lines. The word "multiple" is key. Much of the scholarship and public debate surrounding race in America has been implicitly based upon one of two binary formulas, either "black vs. white" or "Anglo vs. Mexican." Yet the nation's racial mixture is no longer defined in black and white. Looking through a multiracial lens makes the black and brown civil rights movements look different, connecting each to the other and both to broader currents in the nation's political life.

While many Americans associate the two civil rights movements with leaders such as Dr. Martin Luther King Jr. and César Chávez, and both with the policies of Presidents John F. Kennedy and Lyndon B. Johnson, historians have increasingly turned toward examining the grassroots organizing traditions of ordinary people of color. Rooted in autonomous community institutions as well as scattered pockets within the house of labor, "local people" gave the black civil rights movement its esprit de corps. They provided the foot soldiers of the struggle and gave direction to the young activists of the Student Nonviolent Coordinating Committee (SNCC). The young activists' daily "spadework" created the crisis that forced politicians to dismantle Jim Crow, while their belief in ordinary people challenged the nation to truly embrace its democratic promise.[7] The Mexican American civil rights movement likewise transcended the famous strike and boycott launched by farmworkers in California. Across the Southwest and, indeed, the nation, Mexican Americans challenged the laws and customs that segregated them into inferior schools, confined them in low-wage work and overcrowded neighborhoods, and denied them the right to freely exercise the franchise. In the barrios of urban America as well as in nearby factories and fields, *mexicano* "local people" also demanded that the nation live up to its creed of liberty and justice for all. They did not simply imitate the black freedom struggle but instead developed their own vision for the country's democratic future.[8]

Both groups of activists did so through community-based freedom struggles as well as in labor and electoral politics—subjects that themselves remain poorly understood in American culture. Coming of age in the Great Depression, the U.S. labor movement emerged as a democratic response to the inequities of big business. Wages and working conditions mattered, as most workers of all colors lived in poverty and were maimed or killed in industrial accidents at alarmingly high rates. Yet labor was anything but a special-interest group. It was a mass movement that boldly demanded a voice on the shop floor and a seat at the table in the nation's politics and emerging regulatory agencies. Just as "local people" advanced the civil rights movements, ordinary workers—men and women of all races and creeds, in every region—propelled the expansion of unions to address the specific issues that they and their communities faced. They secured a permanent foothold in industry by arming the "arsenal of democracy" during World War II, and they laid the foundation for the country's postwar prosperity.[9]

Along the way, the labor movement realized that electoral politics should no longer remain the province of the elites but rather that America's working people could counteract the special interests of their employers by taking action at the ballot box. For union activists, as for the "independent liberals" who joined them in forming local Democratic clubs across the country, politics was not a cynical game in which the goal was simply to win. Instead, they believed that public policy should benefit all people, that government was capable of doing good if only it could be wrested from the hands of selfish elites. For many working people, as for the organizers of the black and brown civil rights movements, politics represented the last best hope that America had a place for ordinary people to share equally in its riches.[10]

Acquiring formal political power likewise remained a chief goal of the African American and Mexican American civil rights and liberation movements. Black and brown activists did not desire power for its own sake, nor did they simplistically or naively seek to elect black or brown faces to high places. Rather, electoral politics was part and parcel of the broader fight for democracy and dignity, a key tool in the struggle, but not the ultimate goal. For civil rights organizers in countless locales, the power to elect independent representatives for their communities went hand in glove with the fight for economic opportunity and the more abstract goal of empowering their constituents. Politics was not a sideshow but a central objective as the freedom struggles demanded the recognition of new voices and new communities on the American stage. Each group had always exercised agency, but the mass movements of the mid-twentieth century destroyed the old systems of Jim Crow and Juan Crow and allowed African Americans and Mexican Americans to make new claims for first-class American citizenship.

The decades-long story of coalition building in Texas reflects this larger national history of ordinary people transforming the meaning of American democracy. Turning the focus to the connections between the separate struggles foregrounds the critical roles played by African American, Mexican American, and white labor and community organizers. These otherwise ordinary people propelled their distinct agendas by building bridges, connecting the battles against racism with the fights for economic justice and real, independent political power.

The tale told in these pages invites readers to reinterpret and reimagine the study of American politics and social movements. It recasts black-brown coalition building as a *process* rather than making totalizing claims about inherent cooperation or mutual discord.[11] It shows both continuity and change across the several decades of the "long civil rights movement," detailing the economic underpinnings and working-class nature of the modern black freedom struggle among "local people."[12] It recovers militancy, interracial partnerships, and the mobilization of a nonwhite racial identity among members of the

"Mexican American Generation" of activists after World War II, a group long discounted in Chicano/a-Latino/a Studies as conservative, assimilationist, and even at times anti-black.[13] It reveals raging conflicts surrounding class, ideology, tactics, strategy, and even race and ethnicity *within* the so-called black and brown communities. It questions the assumptions of bureaucratization and self-defeatism that predominate in studies of postwar organized labor and instead reveals alternate paths available during the crisis of U.S. liberalism in the 1960s.[14] It reconnects the black and brown struggles for liberation to the realm of formal electoral politics, tying the grassroots bottom-up story to the familiar top-down narrative. Above all, it highlights the ways in which deeply pragmatic civil rights activists took the promise of postwar liberalism and made it their own rallying cry, joining with organized labor to weave together new combinations of race and class even as leaders of the national, white liberal-labor alliance proved unable to do so.

The two civil rights movements often developed separately, but they did not proceed down "parallel tracks," as one historian has asserted. Nor was their coming together a series of exceptions to a general rule of black-brown conflict.[15] Rather, beginning in the 1930s, African American, Mexican American, and white labor activists built and consolidated their bases, at times coming together in fleeting moments of cooperation. They then survived the onslaught of the Cold War by redirecting their efforts into new channels. White liberal political organizers likewise found their own footing and developed their constituency, but they remained limited because they attempted to do so without talking about race.

The renewal of labor militancy in the late 1950s, along with the rise of direct action protests and a distant ally in Washington in 1960, recalibrated the political scene, forcing white liberal and labor leaders to engage their black and brown counterparts as equal partners for the first time. Efforts to come together proceeded in fits and starts, in part because the most militant black and brown activists struggled to free themselves from the constraints imposed by their more conservative race leaders, and in part because white liberals continued to cling, often unconsciously, to their own sense of superiority.

Finally, after years of trial and error, many of the key players in the numerous civil rights, labor, and political struggles throughout Texas sat down together in a sprawling Dallas hotel ballroom in the summer of 1963. With careful preparation, they drew on their decades of experience to deepen their liberal electoral alliance by committing themselves, as a group, to the fight for civil rights. This book tells the story of how each of the principal members of the Democratic Coalition that they formed raised their own voices, organized their communities, found each other, and finally stood together for a common cause.

The Setting: Texas on the Eve of the New Deal

But all of that was still to come in the early 1930s. Indeed, in the previous half-century all vestiges of democratic politics had been exorcised from the civic life of Texas. The state's founding fathers had withstood the "horrors" of Black Reconstruction and then repelled the greatest mass movement in American history, an agrarian uprising and a People's Party that threatened to rewrite the rules that governed the nation's financial system. White terrorism, race baiting, and economic coercion cut the struggle short.[16] A land grab in South Texas then fueled social banditry and plans for another armed revolution among the area's *mexicano* residents, while unrestrained industrial capitalism in East Texas brought black and white timber workers together—at times in collaboration with some of the Populist farmers who had led the revolt a generation before. Still, by the end of World War I, these social experiments had succumbed to the censorship of their journals and the imprisonment and killing of their leaders.[17] Even the narrowly focused, lily-white craft union movement that took the place of these utopian schemes proved too radical for the business and governing elite of the Lone Star State. Working under the banner of the Texas Open Shop Association, founded in 1919, visionaries among the state's leading entrepreneurs systematically crushed the trade unions. Any business that was not overtly hostile to organized labor was boycotted.[18]

After the dust settled and victory was secured, politicians continued to make entreaties to the common folk, but the latter did not respond. Most stayed home on Election Day. They didn't, in the Texas vernacular, "go fishing" because they didn't like the candidates. Rather, they had long ago lost the franchise. The poll tax passed in 1902 all but guaranteed that most citizens would not participate in the biennial American ritual of walking to the county courthouse, grabbing a leaflet or two from the zealous supporters of one man or another, and pulling a lever to show their support for the best candidate.

The invention of Jim Crow in the early twentieth century added an even greater obstacle to the practice of democracy in Texas. Even if they had money and paid their poll taxes in January, black voters were not allowed to vote in the all-important, all-white Democratic primaries of spring and summer. They waited instead until November to choose between the businessmen's Democrat (a virtual lock) and a white Republican.[19] Most African Americans who farmed did so as sharecroppers, but over time they fell further and further behind and ultimately fled from debt peonage, migrating to become wage workers in the state's growing cities. In Houston, Dallas, San Antonio, and dozens of smaller towns, those who could find work were confined to the dirtiest, lowest-paying jobs. There were no opportunities for advancement. A handful of ministers, lawyers, doctors, undertakers, and educators gained status within

Major cities and regions of Texas

the segregated black neighborhoods, but the independent political power to which their fathers and grandfathers had aspired during Reconstruction and the Gilded Age was barely imaginable. Some self-styled race leaders happily settled into their new roles as diplomats, dispensing patronage as cogs in white-led urban political machines. Yet the best that black men who worked with their hands could hope for was a steady job digging ditches or shoveling coal for a railroad or steel foundry, sweeping floors in a factory or hotel, trudging through oil fields, or loading cotton into the hulls of cargo ships. A lucky few waited on white passengers on Pullman trains or sorted and delivered the mail. Many black women worked as servants in white households, at times facing the threat of sexual assault by their employers, while many others washed clothes or cooked and cleaned in offices, restaurants, and hotels. Black women who were teachers and the wives of the ministers, lawyers, doctors, and undertakers built churches, schools, sororities, and a wide range of community service clubs and associations. Yet they too could scarcely envision the world that their grandmothers had sought to create.[20]

In South Texas, Jim Crow helped the comparatively few Anglo farmers displace the many Tejano ranchers, recasting the region's longtime inhabitants as "dirty Meskins" unfit for anything but stoop labor. Through the consolidation of mass quantities of land, the remapping of county lines and political jurisdictions, and the disenfranchisement of average citizens, a handful of Anglo commercial growers built a series of feudal fiefdoms over which they exercised near-absolute control. Most of their subjects did not vote. Those who did had their poll taxes paid by their foremen, who then piled them into the back of a truck and told them how to vote "the right way." The Tejanos of the nineteenth century (Texans of Mexican descent) increasingly shared space and rubbed shoulders with thousands of Mexican immigrants who fled the revolution south of the border in the three decades after 1910. Many of these immigrants wished to return home some day, but others suspected that the home they knew no longer existed. In the meantime, most *mexicanos*, whether citizens or immigrants, traveled from farm to farm, working different harvests on an annual rotation. Over time, their seasonal migrations took them to San Antonio and Corpus Christi and later to the fields of the American Midwest. At times they found casual work in light industrial factories in the cities along the way. The work of packing fruits, nuts, and vegetables, of turning cotton into textiles, or of sewing cheap clothes generally remained reserved for "Meskin" women, workers whom employers believed would work hard, not complain, and in any event accept pay far below that of anyone else. *Mexicano* men built railroads in the countryside or, in the cities, found the same dirty, low-paying jobs that were available to their African American counterparts. As in the black community, a few *mexicano* professionals gained prominence in the barrios, and in some cases they served as intermediaries between the working masses and the urban allies of the old feudal bosses. Some of the immigrants still longed for revolution. But most who resisted Jim Crow in South Texas—*Juan Crow*—encountered imprisonment, deportation, or violent attack at the hands of the Texas Rangers.[21]

Hard times were not new for the multiracial working-class majority of segregated Texas in the early twentieth century. The onset of the Great Depression certainly made hard times harder, but it was the election of Franklin Delano Roosevelt and the long reach of the New Deal that created the first crack in the state's white supremacist structure. Although the "Establishment" in the Lone Star State attempted to thwart the president's initiatives at nearly every turn, poor Texans of all colors seized the opening created by the New Deal and began to chip away at the rocks of Jim Crow and Juan Crow.

Their task would prove challenging. In Dallas, union organizers and radical political activists would run headfirst into the full might of America's leading corporations. In San Antonio, workers would build a mass movement in the face of fierce repression, upsetting the local balance of power and laying the groundwork for decades of fruitful multiracial coalition building. And in Houston's Fifth and Third Wards, black men and women who grew up amidst a terrible race riot would find new opportunities in the factories born out of the oil boom and World War II. They would soon translate their experiences on the shop floor into a powerful and expansive civil rights movement that would break open the state's political process.

Few of the activists in these early struggles would emerge completely unscathed. Some would be fired from their jobs, blacklisted, beaten, brutalized, or jailed. But the organizing skills and experience they acquired along the way would ultimately last longer than their wounds, priming them to lead the next wave of upheaval.

Chapter 1

People Are Power

The Mass Uprising and the Maverick Coalition

In early 1938, nearly ten thousand *mexicano* workers walked off their jobs hand-shelling pecans in dismal warehouses scattered across the West Side of San Antonio. Organized block-by-block throughout the city's sprawling, impoverished barrios, the general strike quickly took on a larger meaning. Activists and police authorities alike talked of "a mass uprising." Union members and organizers clashed with police and filled the local jails for nearly two months. Strikers and the unemployed converged on City Hall, rallying for change. Soon the entire neighborhood was up in arms, fighting for better living conditions in addition to higher wages on the job. A "revolution" was taking place.

Against all odds, the *mexicano* workers won. Although the victory on the shop floor would prove fleeting, the larger impact of their movement could hardly be overstated. The following year, a maverick New Dealer would ride the wave of the insurgency to the mayor's office, bringing the Mexican American pecan shellers into common cause with white labor activists, liberals, and the city's first independent African American voting bloc. The rise of a newly militant faction on the all-black East Side would prove especially transformative, laying the foundation for a generation of civil rights struggles and multiracial collaborations across the city and state. More immediately, the loose coalition behind the mayor would weave demands for economic justice and calls for civil rights into a powerful mixture that would break the back of San Antonio's political machine. Although the mass movement would eventually succumb to external pressures, it would first plant the seeds of a decades-long, broad-based struggle for democracy. Politics in Texas would never be the same.

George P. Lambert and the Reds in Dallas

At the middle of the coalition in San Antonio stood George Lambert, a young idealist from the coalfields of West Virginia. A slender man with dark, combed-back hair, thick eyebrows, and an intense, piercing gaze, Lambert came to the Alamo City via Dallas after stops across the American South. He was born in 1913 in Bluefield, West Virginia, and became a socialist, pacifist, and trade unionist while working his way through the state's flagship university in the

A young George Lambert, the student socialist turned union organizer and lifelong civil rights and political activist, outside near a factory in San Antonio in the late 1930s. Courtesy George & Latane Lambert Papers, Special Collections, The University of Texas at Arlington Library, Arlington, Texas, AR127-19-6.

early 1930s. A professor introduced him to the Young People's Socialist League and the Student League for Industrial Democracy, both of which pushed him into the Socialist Party then led by Norman Thomas.

Lambert gained vital hands-on knowledge in 1934, when he took a summer job at a nearby garment factory. He didn't last long, getting fired along with several of his coworkers for contacting a union organizer. The union helped Lambert get a job in an area coal mine, where he joined the United Mine Workers (UMW) and remained for the rest of the summer. Still, he continued to learn on and off the job, soaking up the class struggle firsthand. One day on his free time, he visited a picket line of white women striking another garment factory in the area. Lambert watched in awe as the women dove into the muddy streets outside the building, laying their bodies on the line to block trucks from approaching the plant. Around the same time, Lambert began tagging along with a UMW staffer as the union tried to reorganize the coalfields of northern West Virginia. Talking to wizened old miners, he gained still more on-the-ground experience before heading back to Morgantown to return to school.

Lambert didn't make it long in the stuffy confines of the university. More than ever, he believed in unionism, socialism, and peace among the world's working people. When he refused to enroll in mandatory ROTC classes that fall, he was duly expelled.[1] News of his defiance traveled, and the Quaker-affiliated

People Are Power   15

Guilford College in North Carolina stepped in to offer the courageous pacifist a scholarship to continue his formal education. But even after he moved to the Tar Heel State and again enrolled in school in 1935, the labor movement and the Socialist Party continued to pull him away.

A disastrous industrywide strike had devastated North Carolina textile workers the previous year. Signs of violent clashes abounded. In Greensboro, the gates at Cone Mills were adorned with mounts for machine guns. A single organizer of the textile workers union was now responsible for the entire state, so he gladly assigned several cities to the eager young volunteer from West Virginia. Near Durham, Lambert later remembered, a group of "people obviously connected with the mill owners" pulled him and his collaborators off the train platform and threw them in jail overnight. Surviving arrest intrigued rather than rebuffed the young activist, who "got so interested in the labor movement" that he "lost interest in getting a college degree."[2]

Lambert became more active than ever in the Socialist Party, an avocation that took him to Tennessee, Arkansas, and Georgia. Along the way, he gained his first, life-changing exposure to the struggle against Jim Crow. In 1936, the college dropout helped coordinate the gubernatorial campaign of Kate Bradford Stockton, one of a handful of Tennessee "mountain socialists" who helped launch the Highlander Folk School, a soon-to-be legendary training ground for labor and civil rights activists.[3] While crisscrossing the state with various socialists, Lambert attended some of his first interracial meetings. On one occasion, H. L. Mitchell, the head of the Southern Tenant Farmers Union (STFU), brought him to a lively rally of African Americans on the courthouse steps of Earl, Arkansas. Gathering under the watchful eye of hostile deputy sheriffs known for arresting black dissidents and hiring them out as convict laborers, the ordinary tenant farmers, black and white, astounded Lambert with their courage. He was especially impressed by the black unionists that came to the rally despite risking being forced into "slave labor" for the cause. Around the same time, Lambert traveled to Memphis, where he worked with a local branch of the Workers Alliance of America, a group of the poor and unemployed that advocated for expanded relief from the New Deal and local agencies. He again saw the inside of a southern jail cell after being arrested for showing a film without a license at a Memphis STFU meeting.[4]

Lambert drifted on the Socialist Party circuit following Stockton's defeat. Late in 1936, he went to Atlanta to support a group of autoworkers who had sat down at their machines and refused to work. One month before the months-long sit-in in Flint, Michigan, the Atlanta workers were offering a glimpse of the ultimate solution to the age-old problem of how to truly shut down a company. The North Carolina women had lain down in the streets, while the Atlanta men sat down on the job to prevent the hiring of scabs. Lambert was exhilarated by the fight, joining the picket soon after the men left the plant. He drove around town drumming up support for the workers from a bright red truck equipped with a billboard on the roof and a megaphone blaring old labor songs such as the "Internationale."

While in Atlanta, Lambert attended his first integrated luncheons and dinners at the all black Morehouse College and joined the local chapter of the NAACP. He met with and brought a Jewish fraternal order into the local union movement. His brief interracial forays in Tennessee and Arkansas led Lambert toward deeper contact and even closer relationships across lines of race and ethnicity. Attending a single rally with African Americans was one thing, Lambert knew, but blacks and whites eating together and joining the same associations represented a powerful slap in the face to white supremacist culture of Dixie. Transgressing those barriers proved an important experiential lesson for the blossoming southern dissident.[5]

In the summer of 1937 the party asked Lambert to go to Dallas, Texas, a city whose growing working population they hoped to organize. By early August Lambert had joined Socialist organizer Herb Harris and Texas party chief Carl Brannin in projecting political films at various venues around town, hoping that the impromptu screenings would attract a few party members. The trio of activists took turns performing various tasks—advertising the venue, hitting the streets to recruit attendees, dealing with local authorities, setting up the projector, introducing the films, and finally asking participants to join the cause. They staged a screening outside City Hall and might have attracted a few converts, but other, more hostile audiences around Dallas also took notice.

A few days after the event downtown, the activists advertised another film screening at a park across the street from the South Texas Cotton Mill. This time it did not go as planned. The agenda included a double feature of Pare Lorentz's *The Plow that Broke the Plains*, a history of the Dust Bowl sponsored by the New Deal, and *Millions of Us*, a Socialist propaganda piece. The first film proceeded without incident, but Lambert grew increasingly nervous as a number of "big husky fellows" who were "obviously not textile workers" began to gather around them. As Harris loaded the second film, "somebody shouted, 'Get the goddam Communists. We don't want any reds in Dallas!'" Between fifty and one hundred of the "husky" men stormed the organizers, scattering the crowd. "The next thing I knew, I had been knocked to the ground, and I could hear and see the sound truck being pitched over and the motion picture projector being shattered," Lambert later recalled. The young West Virginian was beaten until he lost consciousness; Brannin fled and managed to escape. The attackers kidnapped Harris, beat him, coated him with a tarlike substance, and rolled him in feathers. Then they deposited him in an alley behind the *Dallas Morning News*. Photographers from the paper, whom the attackers had already tipped off, waited to take pictures, one of which ran on the front page the next day. City police were nowhere to be found.[6]

The assailants seemed to emerge out of thin air, but it soon came to light that officials of the Ford Motor Company plant in East Dallas had orchestrated the attack. By that time, Ford remained the lone nonunion holdout among the Big Three American automakers. The previous winter, the United Auto Workers (UAW) in Flint, Michigan, had used the sit-down strike pioneered in Atlanta to bring General Motors to its knees. Chrysler soon flinched as well, agreeing to recognize the union in order to avoid a similar strike. Ford alone continued to resist. It's unlikely that the firm's small Dallas plant figured prominently in its strategy to combat the influence of organized labor at its larger factories in and around Detroit. Still, local company officials—like their counterparts across the country—moved to combat the rising tide of unionization on their shop floor and the larger community. Drawing on the strength of the Dallas Open Shop Association (DOSA), an antiunion business alliance leftover from the 1920s antilabor offensive, local Ford leaders enlisted an army of "goon squads" to intimidate, harass, and, when all else failed, beat the tar out of any and all subversives in town. The latter group included both the "outside agitators" like Lambert and the local people who sympathized with them. The goons coordinated their attacks with the city's antiunion newspaper as well as with the police, who agreed not to interfere with the plans of a leading manufacturer.[7]

Such was the atmosphere for organizing in Dallas—and indeed, in much of Texas—during the long, hot, and mostly forgotten summer of 1937. Lambert and his colleagues had stumbled right into the trap. The activists' film screening had no connection to the Ford plant, and the organizers had no Communists in their ranks. Still, local Ford management, with help from corporate headquarters in Detroit, offered a handful of workers lucrative jobs in the "outside squad," a company of goons who specialized in roaming around town beating down all labor and leftist efforts. Hundreds of other Ford workers were forced to join the "inside squads," which normally were confined to spying on their colleagues within the plant. Those that declined to serve in this capacity were threatened with losing their jobs.[8]

But the real power lay not in the half of the working class that Ford hired to kill the other half, to paraphrase the words of nineteenth-century robber baron Jay Gould.[9] Rather, merchants and industrialists across the city coordinated their actions through DOSA. The trade group shared "an interlocking directorate" with the Dallas Chamber of Commerce that in turn dominated local politics. The chamber made appeals to outside industry by claiming that it was free from the labor agitation that plagued the Northeast, Midwest, and West Coast. For its part, the association threatened to levy a $3,000 fine against any business that knowingly hired a card-carrying union worker. Ford led the charge, but it remained part of a broader, coordinated campaign to stymie industrial unionism and political radicalism.[10]

Still, despite this massive effort, Dallas remained riddled with labor organizing. Two years before the beatings at the park, in 1935, white, black, and Mexican American women joined the International Ladies' Garment Workers' Union (ILGWU) and went on strike at all thirteen garment factories in the city. Representing approximately 40 percent of the industry's workers in the state, the unionists voted overwhelmingly to walk off the job in protest of "sweatshop-like conditions" in the plants. When employers hired replacement workers during the industry's all-important "Market Week," the union maids confronted the scabs on the street and stripped off their clothes using pin hooks, the small blades attached to thumb rings that were a mainstay of the seamstresses' craft. The spectacle "stripping party" represented a declaration of independence for Dallas's long-invisible working women, a feat that earned not just local media coverage but also international publicity. Each of the unionists was fined twenty-five dollars and sentenced to three days in jail. A "don't buy" campaign promoted by the Texas State Federation of Labor failed to bolster the union's cause significantly, and the conflict fizzled out nine months after it began. Nonetheless, the garment manufacturers still made good on their pledge to the DOSA by blacklisting the strikers, leaving them unable to find new jobs in Dallas.[11]

Such repression, combined with the weakness of local American Federation of Labor (AFL) unions, gave Dallas the reputation of "the worst open-shop center in the United States."[12] By 1937, the Ford Motor Company and the local open shop association clearly hoped to preserve that hard-won reputation. Just days before the attack on Lambert in the park, Mike Bierner, a local owner of a hat factory, called Ford managers to ask for help with his own labor problem. Members of the "outside squad" kidnapped millinery union organizer and vice president Max Baer and beat him nearly beyond recognition before throwing him into a field to die. A passing motorist found Baer unconscious, with one eye hanging from its socket, and took him to a hospital, where he didn't wake up for nearly two weeks. The goon squads beat more than fifty workers that summer. Some of them were union supporters, others leftist political activists, still others caught in the crossfire. The staged newspaper image of organizer Herb Harris's tarred-and-feathered body conclusively drove the message home.[13]

In the end, the Chamber of Commerce's campaign of terror succeeded in stifling the efforts of labor and political activists, but it did not, ironically, prevent the unionization of the Dallas Ford plant. Management disbanded the "outside squad" late in 1937 and ended the "inside" espionage program in 1938. With the union scare over, the company either fired the former thugs or forced them back into their old jobs—and their correspondingly reduced pay scales. By 1940, many of the former goons turned against Ford and cooperated with investigators from the National Labor Relations Board (NLRB), which held a widely publicized hearing on the violence and condemned the company's antiunion activities. As union members across the country continued to battle the company on multiple fronts, the UAW at Dallas Ford won a contract in 1941.[14]

Blacklisting and beatings aside, the labor movement was on the march—even in the open shop stronghold of Dallas. While it came too late for the striking garment workers, the passage of the National Labor Relations Act (or Wagner Act) in 1935 enabled the federal government for the first time to directly intervene in private industrial conflicts. The Wagner Act created the NLRB, the first federal agency with the necessary teeth to force companies like Ford to refrain from intimidating their workers in order to prevent unionization. The board's early willingness to support working people and to end Dallas-style firings and beatings clearly represented a New Deal for working people in Texas—at least for those who were fortunate enough to hold formal jobs in private industry. Unfortunately for everyone else, including most working women and people of color, the Wagner Act, like the Social Security Act and other New Deal legislation, categorically excluded agricultural laborers, domestic servants, and public employees, effectively and intentionally limiting its reach.[15]

These inequities notwithstanding, the federal government's support for working people and the labor movement created a sense of optimism and authority for organizers who sought to democratize Texas and America. George Lambert recalled the mood of the times, invoking a frequently repeated line of union activists in the 1930s: "Boys, the President wants you to organize."[16] For a brief moment, working people in Dallas and throughout Texas heeded the call. DOSA could no longer punish its members for signing a union contract. Workers increasingly took the risky steps of talking to one another and to "outside agitators" like Lambert. Labor had come to stay. Liberal politics and advances in civil rights would not be far behind.

For his part, after facing the Ford goons in Dallas, Lambert paused for reflection. He wrote an article on the state of labor in the city and sent it off to the *Nation*. After a brief trip to North Carolina, he moved on to Houston, where he campaigned for the Socialist Party while working part time for the Steel Workers Organizing Committee. There he looked on as local leaders from the newborn steel and oil unions formed a statewide branch of the national Congress of Industrial Organizations (CIO), the upstart challenger to the stolid AFL. Lambert helped build the fledgling steel workers local at the Hughes Tool Company and other plants and got to know the officers of the new statewide body. In early February 1938, the heads of the Texas CIO asked him to go to San Antonio to conduct a brief investigation into what they thought was a minor disturbance among the *mexicano* workers who shelled nuts on the Alamo City's West Side. They expected him to return within two days, but history had other plans.[17]

"A Mass Uprising"

Across the nation the nascent grassroots labor movement opened the door for hundreds of experiments in mass organization among the disenfranchised. In most cases, workers plunged through the threshold and confronted their bosses with a deceptively simple demand: an acknowledgment of their right to bargain collectively. Their desire to make their voices heard fundamentally challenged the existing power relations in American industry—and the authority of big business in society writ large. Occasionally, the unity forged on the shop floor translated into heightened levels of cooperation in other community affairs, including electoral politics and the black and brown struggles for civil rights.

By the time Lambert arrived in San Antonio, the famed "cradle of Texas liberty," the struggle was already well underway. Years of quiet organizing among a handful of *mexicano* workers at the bottom of the state's economy had led to first an industrywide general strike and then a mass movement that quickly spread across the city's West Side barrios. Although he had gotten ever deeper into the labor movement and radical politics over the past three and a half years, Lambert was overwhelmed by what he saw.

The pecan shellers' strike was no ordinary trade union conflict. Strikers and sympathizers held nightly meetings, on some occasions simultaneously at two or three locations. Crowds that "numbered in the hundreds and sometimes thousands" would spill out of the mass meetings and onto the sidewalks and streets. The police often lurked outside, waiting to beat the workers and their allies or to arrest them for obstructing the right-of-way, gathering illegally, "carrying a sign without a permit," or some other trumped-up cause. And yet the workers—seemingly unintimidated by their surroundings—kept striking, continued to attend the mass meetings, and didn't flinch at going to jail.

Living conditions in the barrio also seemed otherworldly to the young Lambert. The predominately *mexicano* West Side bore some resemblance to the gritty mining camps of Appalachia and the mill towns of North Carolina's Piedmont, places with which he was already familiar. Yet the San Antonio barrio had even more in common with the still poorer ramshackle hamlets of the sharecroppers Lambert had visited in the rural Arkansas Delta. Life in the Alamo City's four-square-mile *mexicano* enclave remained almost premodern. Large portions of the neighborhood flooded after nearly every rain, the bulk of the streets remained unpaved, and many of the packed houses lacked electricity and indoor plumbing. Unemployment was rampant, public sanitation virtually nonexistent. Yet as work disappeared in the countryside, the West Side's population swelled. Two-thirds of the city's 100,000 *mexicano* residents had crowded into the West Side's barrios by the start of the 1938 strike.

The residents of the West Side included recent immigrants who had fled Mexico in the bloody decades after the 1910 revolution as well as the descendants of old Tejano families from across South Texas. The distinction between the native- and foreign-born was often lost on local Anglos. As the Depression deepened, local charities and administrators in the rising New Deal all but categorically denied assistance to *mexicanos*, whether or not they were citizens. Government and private welfare agencies both deemed the *mexicanos* foreign, lazy, and unworthy of relief. Some of the *mexicanos* took on odd jobs and tried to eke out a living in the city year-round. More often, they migrated in and out of the city seasonally, traveling to the beet fields of Michigan or Wisconsin each summer and returning to Texas to work its late fall and spring harvests. In the cold winter months, both the migrants and the more sedentary *mexicanos* took jobs shelling pecans for pennies a pound, working all day and all week on piece rate to cobble together paychecks of just a few dollars. Initially, the occupation was dominated by women, but men joined their ranks as they became ever more desperate for work. Whole families sat side by side on wooden benches in rustic sheds that held fifty, sixty, or as many as two hundred workers. The work was dirty, strenuous, and poorly compensated. Still, some twelve thousand desperate *mexicano* workers labored in more than one hundred such sheds by 1938.

Mexicanos lacked any political power to speak of. A few Mexican American professionals enjoyed positions of high status in the barrio but not substantial incomes or influence in the world beyond. The bulk of neighborhood denizens rarely voted, and when they did so, they tended to vote at the behest of the city's powerful downtown machine. Life was bleak.

Then, the poorest *mexicanos* launched a mass movement.[18] The pecan shellers, or *nueceros*, had gone on strike as early as 1934, before the Wagner Act, but the industry contained that earlier rebellion and recognized only a company union at the conclusion of the strike. The CIO-affiliated United Cannery, Agricultural, Packinghouse, and Allied Workers of America (UCAPAWA) chartered a local union in San Antonio in late 1937, but the organizing effort stalled, attracting less than one hundred members. The union's ranks spiked in January 1938 when a pair of veteran UCAPAWA organizers arrived from the Rio Grande Valley and made contact with a twenty-one-year-old Tejana activist named Emma Tenayuca. The firebrand organizer, later dubbed *la pasionara* for her passionate defense of San Antonio's *mexicano* workers, was already a five-year veteran of the struggle. She had learned the power and limitations of collective action by participating in the failed strikes of cigar and garment workers in 1933 and 1934. In their wake, Tenayuca helped organize a series of sit-ins and other protests against local officials' exclusion of *mexicanos* from many New Deal relief programs. She joined the Communist Party, not out of adherence to party dogma, but rather because it was the only group in the state that supported improvements in the civil rights and working conditions of ordinary *mexicanos*. She became an officer of the party, married its state president, and spearheaded the local branches of the affiliated Unemployed Councils and the Workers Alliance of America. She proved to be an extremely effective organizer. Under Tenayuca's direction, the Workers Alliance grew to fifteen branches with over three thousand members by the time the UCAPAWA organizers arrived. A series of events soon added urgency: the recession of 1937, an early frost in the Valley that displaced countless farmworkers and brought them to San Antonio, a new reduction in the relief rolls, and a sharp wage cut by the Southern Pecan Company's "King" Julius Seligmann all precipitated the mass strike of 1938.

On January 31, six thousand to eight thousand *nueceros* working in 170 different packing sheds walked off the job. As many as three thousand were members of the Workers Alliance, and most were women. The rest followed their lead and joined the union en masse, swelling the membership of UCAPAWA's Local 172 and resulting in the election of Tenayuca, who was not a union member, as the "honorary strike leader." Most of the packing sheds closed their doors immediately, allowing the union to focus its pickets on just a handful of shops.[19] Thousands of workers gathered each evening in vacant lots near the job sites, where they listened to the fiery oratory of Tenayuca, her husband and party chief Homer Brooks, and other speakers. Soon the workers were joined by other *mexicanos* from a wide range of occupations across the West Side, as sympathetic small businessmen, other migrant farmworkers, the few lucky ones who managed to receive relief, and the unemployed all rallied behind their cause. Tenayuca set the tone, attacking not only the pecan bosses and their poverty wages but also the city's miserly public assistance, the refusal of firms to hire *mexicano* workers into skilled jobs, and the terrible living conditions on the West Side.

Lambert arrived on the scene in early February, during the first week of the strike, and quickly made contact with Tenayuca and UCAPAWA officials. The union put him on the payroll and charged him with coordinating the strike's public relations efforts. He soon found himself beside Tenayuca, speaking at the mass meetings (with the help of an interpreter) and walking the picket lines along with ordinary *nueceros*. He also participated in private strategy meetings with Tenayuca, Brooks, international union president Donald Henderson, and countless rank-and-file activists.

A 1927 Ford Roadster pickup truck with handpainted slogans in support of the pecan sheller strike. The newspaper caption noted that an "Unidentified policeman is steering the car as it is being towed down the street following arrest of owner for violating a city sign ordinance" in San Antonio, February 25, 1938. Courtesy *San Antonio Light* Photograph Collection, UTSA-ITC, Image L-1769-C, San Antonio Express/ZUMAPRESS.com.

Lambert was impressed by what he saw. "I think it wasn't the fact of a strike in itself," he later recalled. "The pecan shelling industry wasn't that important economically.... But it had at its inception taken on the aspect of a mass uprising among the Mexican-Americans in the entire West Side of San Antonio, and it was being participated in actively by hundreds and perhaps thousands who didn't themselves make a living in the pecan industry." Some participants were members of other unions, or political radicals like Lambert, but many others had no such orientation. As Lambert put it, "They were not interested in anything except improving on the poor conditions on the West Side."[20]

The lines between the union and the community blurred, as did the divide between a simple labor conflict and a more general push for civil rights. Lambert remembered a "big *hombre*" named Cisneros who was a migrant farmworker with a large family and a big car that he used for their seasonal journeys. Despite having "no connection at all" to the pecan industry, Cisneros provided transportation for union members and served as a bodyguard for Tenayuca. Likewise, Lambert recalled, a number of Works Progress Administration (WPA) workers who were also members of the Workers Alliance labored on the relief rolls during the day but joined the pecan shellers in attending movement meetings at night.[21]

The massive strike rattled the city machine. Politics in San Antonio had long been dominated by a small handful of white businessmen, but unlike its counterparts in many other contemporary American cities, the San Antonio machine "had no colorful boss at the head." Instead, as Lambert wrote soon after the strike, "a composite bossism made up of the city's commissioners" had long perpetuated itself by winning the support of Anglo businessmen, "the vice and gambling element vote," and "a portion of the middle class vote." Charles Bellinger, the leading African American entrepreneur in the fields of vice and gambling on the city's black East Side, "delivered the Negro vote in a block . . . in return for concessions" that included public works projects, jobs, and other patronage. Meanwhile, the *mexicanos*, "their vote not organized and therefore receiving no concessions," sold their votes individually for the remaining crumbs and thereby "had their votes regularly delivered" to the machine. The result was "a machine known far and wide to be reeking with graft and corruption" that was abnormally "certain of its tenure."[22]

The emergence of the New Deal had forced the machine to offer at least the illusion of reform and some semblance of caring about the poor. Mayor Charles Kennon (C. K.) Quin, who had led the city since 1933, publicly advocated a cleaner city government while still quietly enjoying the machine's solid support. Quin promised to end corruption, but after winning reelection in 1935 he instead consolidated the power of the machine in his own hands. "Since all pay checks made out to those working in the administration . . . had to be signed by him," Lambert noted, the mayor "found it a comparatively simple matter to bring recalcitrants into line. Instead of a 'reform' government, the citizenry of San Antonio soon found . . . a worse city administration [than] they had before."[23]

A well-organized West Side threatened to disrupt this misbalance of power. Worse, a Communist-led uprising along class lines threatened to unite the city's *mexicanos* with its poor whites and possibly, in the city fathers' worst nightmare, with its African Americans. The threat of such a coalition was not lost on Quin or on police chief Owen Kilday, who responded to the strike with an iron fist.

City Hall swiftly moved to squash the strike, combining brute police force and mass arrests with virulent anti-Communist rhetoric. Immediately after the first walkout, police arrested Tenayuca and other organizers on charges of communist agitation. That evening the *San Antonio Light* declared, "So serious did Chief Kilday consider the situation that he mobilized 150 officers for riot duty and stationed radio squads, armed with riot guns and tear bombs, at strategic points on the West Side, where most of the factories are located."[24] In the days and weeks that followed, Kilday's forces engaged in a series of violent skirmishes with union members. Officers clubbed men, women, and children alike with axe handles and tear-gassed pickets at least eight different times. In response, picketers threw tacks on the streets to blow out the tires of police cars and vandalized incoming shipments of raw pecans.[25] Police arrested more than one thousand strikers and sympathizers, including men, women, and children—as many as three hundred were jailed on a single day and crammed into a space designed for sixty prisoners. Lambert lost track of how many times he was taken to jail, but he recalls being "picked up twice for having blocked the sidewalk where there wasn't a sidewalk and had never been a sidewalk ... [and] there [is] still no sidewalk." When the jails overflowed, the police at times took strikers fifteen to twenty miles outside of town, dropped them off, and made them walk home.[26] Inside the jail on one occasion, Lambert wrote down the words to a handful of labor movement songs, including "We Shall Not Be Moved" and "Solidarity Forever." A colleague translated them into Spanish and led the crowd in song, adding in traditional Mexican labor ballads and *corridos*. In another case, when the detained strikers protested the jail's overcrowded conditions, their keepers shut them up by spraying them with fire hoses. Police violence grew so acute that the Mexican consulate protested the treatment of its expatriate citizens to the U.S. State Department.[27]

Open warfare raged between the city's white elites and its *mexicano* workforce—the strikers and their detractors alike could agree on that much. When the union sought an injunction against the Police Department six weeks into the conflict, Chief Kilday swore under oath that he "did not interfere with a strike." Rather, he said, "I interfered with a revolution."[28] Throughout the struggle the *San Antonio Express* carried similar statements in which Kilday linked a larger "revolution" to the pecan shellers' "communistic" strike.[29] While he may have exaggerated the union's connection to the global Red Menace, Kilday was sincerely rattled. The pecan sheller uprising posed a serious, existential threat to the city machine.

In truth, the Communist element remained relatively minor in the strike's daily operations. Telesforo Oviedo, the president of the strike committee, told a local Spanish-language newspaper that the Communist threat had been overblown: "It is inexact to say that the workers' movement is headed by communists. Senora Emma Tenayuca Brooks, who is accused of being a communist by Kilday, is not the only one responsible for the movement ... up to now the police have tried to break up the strike, but the strike committee has decided to continue with the worker movement."[30] Lambert, a committed Socialist who often disagreed with many Communist Party officials, likewise recalled that leftist ideologies played a small role in the strike's leadership. "The only reason that [Tenayuca] identified herself as a Communist was because as far as she could see there was nobody else in this country who were [*sic*] in the least interested in doing anything about the economic situation on the West Side of San Antonio or among the Mexican-Americans in those days. . . . [H]er interests were with the people there."[31] Lambert added that the strike was not "a completely Communist-run thing and was worthwhile in terms of the good that would come out of it for the pecan shellers, whether or not the Communists had anything to do with it. Basically it was just a trade union operation."[32] For many ordinary *mexicano* pecan shellers, neither communism nor socialism had any bearing on the strike. Their movement was simply about improving conditions at work and at home on the beleaguered West Side.

The tale of Alberta Zepeda Snid broadly reflects the experiences of the thousands of ordinary *mexicanos* who became part of the strike. Interviewed in 1979, Snid recalled traveling to the sugar beet fields of Michigan and following the cotton harvest across Texas throughout her childhood. Her parents emigrated from Mexico's northern mining region shortly before she was born in April 1919, and throughout the 1920s and 1930s the family migrated along with the crops. The Zepedas made their permanent home in a barrio in San Antonio's West Side. Like many of their neighbors, they felt the sting of the Great Depression, when the few job opportunities they depended upon became even fewer, so they augmented their meager income by spending the winter months working in the pecan sheds. Snid's mother entered the industry first, and her father soon joined her.[33] Eighteen years old when the strike began, Snid did not remember exactly how it started, but she recalled that it was her mother who took an immediate interest in the union and then brought the rest of the family into the movement. Unlike many labor disputes, the pecan sheller strike did not feature an internal union structure that mirrored the organization of the industry, Snid recalled. Rather than identifying and appointing rank-and-file leaders on each shift in each shed, UCAPAWA organized by neighborhood and block, grafting the union on top of networks that the Workers Alliance had already established. The elder Mrs. Zepeda became first a block captain and then the vice president of her neighborhood council, the key building block of the Alliance, the union, and the larger pecan sheller movement. Snid's father was initially hesitant to support the strike, but Mrs. Zepeda brought the entire family to the picket lines and to the mass outdoor meetings at Cassiano Park on Zarzamora and Laredo Streets. Mr. Zepeda soon joined the effort in his own right, inspired by Tenayuca and the ongoing local Communist Party meetings. Mrs. Zepeda became a leader of the local union. The entire family spent time in jail during the conflict.[34]

Snid's tale underscores what the strike meant for many rank-and-file participants. Snid watched and learned from her parents' passion for the cause, and she credits the conflict with raising her own political consciousness. She remembers interacting with the Communist Party officials, other *mexicano* leaders from the Workers Alliance, and a number of white UCAPAWA organizers. "We learned that through organization we could do something," she recalls. "Maybe we didn't win that much as far as money was concerned, but we learned that being united is power regardless. It is power. A single person cannot do anything. Alone we could not do anything. People are power."[35]

From relatively well-off migrants to WPA workers to the poorest of the poor pecan shellers, there were few people on the West Side who did not participate in the uprising. Block by block, neighbor by neighbor, the pecan shellers of San Antonio formed an expansive, inclusive organization deeply rooted in the West Side barrio. Women like Mrs. Zepeda were its on-the-ground leaders, and empowered women like Mrs. Snid, who would later become a leader in the garment workers union, were among its many legacies.

One group was conspicuously absent from the pecan sheller movement: the Mexican American middle class. Lambert recalled that a variety of *mexicano* organizations donated the use of their halls to the union, as did many of the sympathetic pecan shed operators who worked as subcontractors for "Pecan King" Seligmann, the head of the employers' association and the dominant force in the industry. But the local chapters of the League of United Latin American Citizens (LULAC), the state's largest Mexican American civil rights organization, did not. In fact, many of its leaders joined the police department, the machine at City Hall, the Mexican Chamber of Commerce, and the Catholic Church in publicly opposing the strike, denouncing it as dominated by Communists. Their allegations were not entirely without merit. Yet as the observations of Snid, Oviedo, Lambert, and even Chief Kilday make plain, tens of thousands of the city's *mexicano* residents overlooked the Red Menace and flocked to the fight against the racial division of labor and the poverty it produced. Meanwhile, instead of joining the workers' struggle, the small group of professionals who appointed themselves leaders of the *raza* (the people, referring to *mexicanos*) staged their own mass meeting at Cassiano Park. There they asked the workers "to divorce themselves from their 'Communistic leaders'" and attempted to form a separate anti-Communist pecan sheller union. Their efforts failed, and they watched helplessly as the workers passed them by, sticking to the UCAPAWA and the larger movement.[36]

Finally Governor James V. Allred intervened. The publication of images of peaceful pickets being bludgeoned and gassed and the very real possibility that the strikers would return the violence combined to make inaction impossible. Allred, a supporter of the New Deal, sent the state Industrial Commission to investigate the conflict. The stolid City Hall machine refused the governor's delegates permission to meet on city property, but, even so, the investigation managed to turn the tide against the employers. The pressure of national and international publicity, the ongoing solidarity of the *nueceros*, and Allred's personal entreaty together persuaded Seligmann to submit to arbitration with the union. After a thirty-seven-day strike, on March 9, 1938, the "Pecan King" caved to the most of the union's demands.[37]

As many as twenty-five thousand people attended a victory dance on the West Side, filling the barrios with revelry. The fear was gone, and the power of unity affirmed for countless *mexicanos*. "We learned a whole lot," Snid later reflected, speaking for all of the city's pecan shellers. "I think we learned how to even defend ourselves more. I think we forgot a little bit of the fear that we had, because we couldn't say nothing, we couldn't talk, period. Afterwards it was entirely different."[38]

A "Comradely Union"

For Lambert and other organizers, the struggle was just beginning. The strikers and activists had endured beatings and arrest and yet had come out the other side relatively unscathed. The union had survived the police department's efforts to whip up a wave of anti-Communist hysteria. The workers had earned a hard-won victory. Still, movement leaders understood that the forces of repression and reaction that emerged so forcefully during the conflict would not go quietly into remission with the signing of the union contract. After all, the struggle had signaled a "revolution" to the leaders at City Hall, and nobody would reasonably expect the machine bosses to simply sit tight and watch as the ground shifted beneath their feet. It would not be long before the city fathers and the major pecan employers would attempt to regain their lost authority. Lambert and other movement organizers were at once elated and daunted as they looked to the future. It was now more pressing than ever that they continue to expand their base of support in preparation for the unknown fights ahead.

Lambert hoped to position San Antonio as a critical battleground in the larger war to extend the New Deal and the labor movement into the South. Remaining on the union payroll, he mailed out pamphlets on the movement and wrote articles for the Federated Press, a left-wing wire service friendly to organized labor, as well as the *Nation* and other publications. Between daytime meetings and late into the evenings, he sat at his typewriter and fired off letters on the local situation to friends and colleagues across the country, hoping that any one of them might bring more resources and energy to the pecan sheller movement. One of those letters reached a student activist from North Carolina who would soon become Lambert's closest ally and companion in the struggle, not just in San Antonio but in countless battles for decades to come.

Latane Bartlett spent much of her time in college working in North Carolina's local labor movement and radical political clubs. Born in 1916 in Zebulon, near

Latane Bartlett Lambert, a young idealist from North Carolina who came to Texas during the pecan sheller strike and would become one of the state's best-known liberal and labor leaders. Photograph dates to the mid-1930s. Courtesy Joe Lambert, digital photograph in author's possession.

Raleigh, Bartlett moved to Greensboro when she was six years old. Her father worked in the insurance and real estate business, but that did not shield the family from the ravages of the Great Depression. Soon after the stock market crash in late 1929, the thirteen-year-old Bartlett accompanied her father to hear a speech at the county courthouse by Norman Thomas, a Presbyterian minister and the Socialist Party's perennial presidential candidate (he ran six times beginning in 1928). "He talked just like a preacher," she later recalled. The Depression exposed her firsthand to people all around her who were going hungry, while her father railed against Wall Street's exploitation of the South and introduced her to politicians like Thomas and the populist Huey Long of Louisiana.

By the time she enrolled at the University of North Carolina Woman's College in her hometown in 1934, Bartlett recalled, "I had convinced myself that I was socialist" and "wanted some kind of utopian society." She became interested in the peace movement, started a student socialist club just off campus, and joined the left-wing American Student Union. Bartlett went to meetings with her counterparts at the all-black, all-female Bennett College nearby and traveled to Washington, D.C., to protest American militarism. In 1936 or 1937, around her junior year, Bartlett joined the Communist Party, not because she was all that interested in Russia but because she "saw them as more effective than the socialists in terms of what was going on in the South . . . what [was] happening locally."[39]

At the same time, Bartlett gained a reputation as a talented performance artist, singing, dancing, and acting in theater troops—all roles that were made easier by the fact that she was impossibly beautiful. "Said to be one of North Carolina's most attractive and popular girls," as one newspaper put it, Bartlett boasted beautiful, wavy light brown hair that was always perfectly bobbed and pinned above her tall, fair-skinned forehead, a style that showcased her large, round, inviting eyes and tempting flash of a smile. She began studying ballet when she was around eight years old, kept at it, and during college she picked up extra cash teaching children how to dance. Beginning in her freshman year she joined the Playlikers theater group on campus, "one of the outstanding college dramatic organizations in the country," in which she appeared in several leading roles. Her performances won laudatory reviews from critics, who noted that she possessed "a most pleasing voice" and was also "easy to look at it." The building that housed her ballet class was also home to a radio station, WBIG, which soon became a new platform for the budding artist. Bartlett first hosted a children's amateur hour and then a "fashion program" that, in the words of one observer, "created a great deal of local and national comment." The station then made her its chief promoter of a new Shakespeare series and other programs targeting women and children. She started making rounds addressing school audiences, women's organizations, and the luncheon meetings of local civic clubs, leaving "a decidedly favorable impression" at each stop.[40]

Surprisingly, these high-society affairs complemented rather than detracted from her more idealistic pursuits. Ballet lessons and speaking engagements took Bartlett to rotary clubs and chambers of commerce, but they also put her in touch with women's political associations and local labor unions. She got to know the children of textile-mill workers, and then their parents. Soon, she took another part-time job as the educational director of the local Central Labor Council. She learned that she could use the arts to interact with working people and that poor people could use the arts to rally support for political causes. A "strikingly lovely young woman," Bartlett lit up rooms wherever she went. Once inside, she used her many talents to help create the distinctive working-class popular subculture that became the heart of the labor movement across the South.[41]

Bartlett entered her senior year of college in the fall of 1937, but soon the excitement of the workers' struggle overtook the importance of her studies. She spent more and more of her time off campus at WBIG or the Labor Council. Like George Lambert, she grew impatient with school. The two young activists had first met in 1935, and for the next year they ran in overlapping activist circles in Greensboro. They sometimes attended a meeting together or showed up on the same picket line, and soon they became friends in the struggle. When Lambert left for Tennessee and finally made his way to Texas, the two stayed in touch but remained distant, platonic correspondents. Then just before he made his way to San Antonio, around Christmas of 1937, Lambert briefly returned to North Carolina to pay Bartlett a visit.

To her great surprise, he kissed her. And then he left, returning to Texas before either of them knew what their romance might produce. Discovering the pecan shellers' mass movement already underway in San Antonio, Lambert sent Bartlett a series of letters telling her all about it. "It just seemed like to me that it was the most tremendous thing that was happening in the country," Bartlett later recalled, "and I decided I had to come out and see what it was all about." The thought of reconnecting with Lambert was intriguing, she added, "but mostly, he got me up to Texas because there was excitement, that was fun, that was an adventure." Politics came first, but romance was a not-too-distant second. When her school's Easter break rolled around in early April 1938, the twenty-one-year-old Bartlett went to San Antonio.[42]

By the time she arrived, the strike had ended in victory, but the struggle was still underway. Taking advantage of her talents as a fundraiser for the arts, Lambert got Bartlett a job with the union soliciting contributions for UCAPAWA, earning just over ten dollars a week. Her wages added up to less than half of what Lambert earned for similar work, a difference that reflected the era's assumption that men should be in charge and garner enough pay to serve as family breadwinners while women ostensibly labored for fun, or perhaps for extra cash. In practice, neither young activist could count on a regular paycheck, as their wages came out of whatever money they managed to raise. Still, the uncertainty didn't matter much to either of them—they were committed radicals, and here they were, in the middle of a revolution![43]

With little hesitation, Bartlett moved in with Lambert soon after her arrival. They shacked up in a room at the Gunter Hotel downtown and quickly became part of a "gang" of local revolutionaries and union activists. All of its members were involved in the pecan workers movement, and they spent all of their time together, both on and off the job. Luisa Moreno, who was organizing the nation-wide Congress of Spanish-Speaking Peoples (El Congreso de Pueblos de Habla Español) in addition to her duties for UCAPAWA, became a close friend, as did union organizers James and María Solís Sager and union business agent Santos Vasquez. Communist journalist Peggy Vance and a houseful of radicals and artists on the West Side rounded out the group. The whole scene resembled the lofts and salons that had emerged among bohemians in New York's Greenwich Village, or the cafés and bookstores that would soon pop up among the beatniks of San Francisco's North Beach. And yet, here, in Depression-era San Antonio, was an equally vibrant network of idealists, dreamers, and organizers, working and partying side-by-side, all in their twenties, and all committed to living and breathing the cause. In the middle of all of it, Lambert and Bartlett fell hopelessly in love.[44]

Just a week or two into their Texas romance, however, someone tipped off the local newspapers. Two of the union's staffers, both "outside agitators" from North Carolina, were not only stirring up communism in San Antonio but were also living in sin. The free-love culture of the Popular Front gave the union's opponents powerful ammunition to discredit it, so UCAPAWA urged the duo to resolve the situation. As the newspaper planned a big story on their tryst out of wedlock, the two activists came up with a plan. "Hell, we'll just fool them," Bartlett remembered deciding alongside Lambert. "We'll get married."

Without much planning or deliberation, they took out a license, found a Congregational minister, and bought a pair of cheap, gold-plated rings. The next evening, a Saturday, Bartlett and Lambert each returned to the union hall after a day of routine meetings with union members and supporters. In front of a large audience of pecan shellers and fellow travelers, Bartlett appeared stunning "in a tailored suit of navy blue woolen" and a corsage of gardenias, and even the normally stoic Lambert became overwhelmed by the moment. The two professed their love for each other as well as for the movement, pledging to remain independent equals in matrimony and promising to forge a sexually open life-and-work partnership they would later call a "comradely union." A month after the strike victory, on April 9, 1938, the newly minted Mr. and Mrs. Lambert celebrated their marriage with another massive dance party, flanked by their "gang" of radicals and countless *nueceros*.[45]

For the next couple of months, the Lamberts carried on, working for the union, writing pamphlets and press releases, and raising money for the movement. Their personal and professional lives continued to blend, as they would for decades. They joined Brooks and Tenayuca, union staffer Vasquez, the gang's Moreno, and other leaders for strategy meetings, working to develop the union's responses to the growing crisis of automation and planning another strike for the coming fall. For a while, Latane took notes at union meetings and maintained the local's sketchy membership records. She and George operated independently by day, putting out bulletins or meeting with the pecan shellers in their homes or at neighborhood corner stores. Latane wandered the West Side with abandon despite the fact that she stuck out like a sore thumb, a sole Anglo woman alone in the barrio. She resisted the efforts of some union leaders to assign a guard to protect her and slipped away from her escorts whenever possible. She later remembered the neighborhood as a "friendly, warm place" in which she always felt comfortable. The newlyweds didn't think twice about settling into an apartment on the West Side. Still, when the rent came due, the Anglo landlord kicked them out because, as Latane later recalled, "He said we had too many Mexicans come and see us." They found another place on Commerce Street, this one owned by an old Jewish radical. He liked their politics and their gang of visitors and was happy to let them stick around. The young couple remained dirt poor, but life was good. They ate beans and chalupas and *pan dulce* from the grocery across the street, while Latane sold her best North Carolina fur coat and even pawned her fancy watch to pay their bills. They managed. Overall, nothing mattered but the movement.[46]

As spring transitioned into summer, the Lamberts redoubled their efforts to spread word of the strike far and wide. George penned an article for the *Nation* in which he cast the pecan sheller conflict in terms of civil liberties, contrasting the workers' right to organize and strike with the brutal police repression meted out against them. Around the same time, he coauthored and edited a sixteen-page tabloid for the Texas Civil Liberties Union. Devoted entirely to the pecan sheller strike, the pamphlet featured an illustration of the iconic Alamo chapel above a sketch of the entrance to San Antonio City Hall, surrounded by the title: "San Antonio: The Cradle of Texas Liberty . . . And Its Coffin?" Lambert, the union, and the TCLU circulated the publication across the nation, using its details of rampant police brutality, mass jailing, and violations of free-speech rights to raise funds for the pecan shellers' ongoing fight and other liberal causes around the state. Soon the American Civil Liberties Union responded by listing San Antonio as one of the four "worst" cities in the nation, "where repression is so continuous as to clearly stand out."[47]

In early July, three months after the strike ended, the union and its allies extended the public relations campaign across the border. They invited Vicente Lombardo Toledano, the general secretary of the Confederación de Trabajadores Mexicanos (Mexican Workers Confederation, or CTM), to speak at an open-air rally at Cassiano Park on the West Side. As the event neared, the city machine refused to grant a permit. Denied the use of public property, organizers defiantly moved the event to a vacant lot at Trinity and San Carlos Streets, a site of many mass meetings during the strike. There, some three thousand *mexicanos* again ignored the city's repression and assembled to hear the "John L. Lewis of Mexico."[48] Meanwhile, the city machine struggled to regain the power it had lost in the strike.

A Maverick against the Machine

San Antonio's political bosses focused on the one local official who had come out publicly in support of the pecan shellers' movement, U.S. congressman Fontaine Maury Maverick. "Maury," as he was usually known, was the grandson of Samuel Augustus Maverick, a founding father of the Texas Republic and iconoclastic politician and rancher. The elder Maverick came to Mexico's northernmost province in 1835, thrust himself into the Lone Star revolution, and signed the Texas Declaration of Independence the following year. He rode the winds of change to a series of prominent political posts, becoming mayor of San Antonio in 1839, a member of the Texas Congress in the 1840s, and a legislator of the new state in the 1850s. He worked to make the land laws fairer for his German and *mexicano* constituents, and he battled against secession from the Union until it became inevitable. Still, the Secession Convention appointed him to a prominent commission, and he returned to serve in elected and appointed offices after the Civil War. Throughout these pursuits, he amassed over 300,000 acres of land in West Texas in the county that now bears his name, where he became a successful if careless cattle rancher. A slur describing an unbranded calf from his always-wandering herd engendered the term "maverick," while his political exploits added to its iconoclastic present-day meaning.[49]

Samuel Maverick's grandson Maury inherited the trademark family name, a penchant for holding political office, and a tendency to be guided by his brash, relentlessly independent spirit. A veteran of the Great War and a committed civil libertarian, the younger Maverick abhorred the city machine's wanton buying and selling of votes and aligned himself with San Antonio's middle-class movement for municipal reform in 1930. The reformers elected an entire slate of candidates to office, including Maverick, who became the county tax collector. This seemingly innocuous position actually carried great power, especially in the political arena, since it oversaw the collection of poll taxes. Maverick used the post to combat voter fraud and charged his employees with serving all citizens instead of handing out patronage to political friends.

The deepening devastation of the Depression drove Maverick to confront the city's sweeping poverty directly. He immersed himself in relief efforts, cofounding a voluntary group that aided military veterans and their families and coordinating the finances of the municipal Central Relief Committee, a task that included managing funds from the Reconstruction Finance Corporation as well as soliciting private donations. He also established and directed the Diga Colony, a utopian self-help camp offering shelter and training for unemployed transients, and he carried out a statewide study of "hobo jungles" as a participant-observer (who only occasionally snuck away to his hidden car to get a warm meal or hot shower). He returned convinced that only massive federal programs could relieve the poverty he encountered, anticipating in his conclusions both the structure and the form of many forthcoming New Deal initiatives.[50]

Maverick knew how to drive that message home. Seeking to extend his relief efforts in Washington, in 1934 he jumped into the fray to represent the new Twentieth Congressional district of San Antonio and surrounding Bexar

County (pronounced "bear"). His principal opponent was none other than the machine's sitting mayor, C. K. Quin. Perhaps riding the wave of the liberal ascent nationwide, and with the aid of a powerful congressman in the next district to the south, Maverick defeated Quin by a sizable margin. One observer noted that Maverick's victory "cracked the San Antonio machine" for the first time, even though Mayor Quin maintained his dominance in municipal politics.[51] When Maverick arrived in Washington in 1935, according to his biographer, he "attracted national attention as the organizer of a group of 'maverick' congressmen who tried to 'out-New Deal' the New Deal." He helped pass a series of liberal measures, including the Patman Bonus Bill, neutrality legislation in foreign affairs, and new federal support for local public utilities such as the Tennessee Valley Authority.[52]

Back home in San Antonio, Maverick openly supported what he saw as the "right" of workers to organize into labor unions and championed the expansion of local relief efforts. A steadfast supporter of civil liberties, he had long defended the free-speech rights of all people, including Communists and other radicals. Thus the presence of the admitted Communist Emma Tenayuca among the city's mostly *mexicano* women in the cigar and garment workers unions in 1934 did not prevent Maverick from endorsing their organizing efforts. During the pecan sheller uprising of 1938, Maverick did not hesitate to send the union a telegram in which he offered his unconditional support. In his message, addressed to a UCAPAWA organizer but intended for public consumption, the congressman wrote, "I stand for the protection of the right of peaceful picketing of any and all groups over the United States. That includes my friends the Latin American population of San Antonio which numbers nearly ninety thousand." The civil libertarian argument established, Maverick also added his concern for the material conditions of the working poor. "I hope the people of San Antonio will fight for better living conditions," he wrote. "To the Latin American population must be given the Constitutional right of civil and religious liberty, the right to speak, and the right to organize and picket peacefully. More they are entitled to a decent standard of living [*sic*]."[53] Echoing the "four freedoms" of Roosevelt's New Deal, Maverick added that "a decent standard of living" was also a right to which workers were "entitled," and that they should also be free to bargain collectively at work and speak their minds in political affairs.

Maverick's support for the striking pecan shellers was not merely rhetorical. His telegram bolstered the workers' spirits, encouraging them to keep fighting. On a more concrete level, it was at the congressman's urging that Governor Allred asked the state Industrial Commission to hold a hearing on the strike, an intervention that quickly led to a settlement.[54] Maverick also cofounded the Texas Civil Liberties Union and underwrote the publication of Lambert's "Cradle of Texas Liberty" pamphlet.

City officials did not take kindly to Maverick's meddling in the conflict. They understood that the congressman's support for the movement threatened to erode the machine's already shrinking local power, particularly if the ordinary *mexicanos* that had risen up on the West Side now began voting in large numbers, independent of the old bosses. The machine had tried and failed to unseat Maverick in the 1936 primary, but the chaos of the strike added new urgency to the task. Paul Kilday, the brother of the machine's overbearing police chief, announced soon after the strike that he would run against the two-term liberal congressman in the 1938 Democratic Party primary.

The battle lines were soon drawn. Kilday appealed to conservative white voters by promising to restore law and order. He branded Maverick and his supporters as radicals, arguing that the sole issue of the election was "Communism vs. Americanism," with Maverick representing the former and Kilday the latter. Such a tack was not entirely new, as Maverick's opponents had attempted to paint him Red in each of the previous two elections. Still, as George Lambert put it in a piece for the *Nation*, this year the challenger could marshal new evidence. Maverick had supported the CIO, and Kilday brashly claimed that "mass unionism—spells communism." Maverick also visited the Russian ambassador in Washington, a not outlandish act of diplomacy that Kilday nonetheless claimed was further proof that the congressman was taking orders directly from Soviet Moscow. Such framing helped Kilday secure the endorsements of the city's Chamber of Commerce, "most of the bankers and industrialists," and "the hierarchy of the Catholic Church." The conservative, craft-oriented AFL also announced its support for Kilday at both the national and local levels, reflecting both local politics and the enmity between the AFL and CIO across the country.[55] Kilday also drew a line between the "communist" CIO and the purportedly all-American AFL. In mid-July, just ten days before the election, the machine candidate urged a crowd on the Anglo North Side to "resent the inference that San Antonio is a community of pecan shellers." Asking his listeners to read between the lines, Kilday contrasted those unskilled *mexicano* strikers who embraced radicalism with the city's truly "great American labor element"—"American" being synonymous with both "white" and anticommunist.[56] Of course, Kilday also enjoyed the support of the city machine, with all of its many devoted patronage recipients and other followers, including the machine's African American wing on the East Side.

For his part, Maverick had long depended upon what a writer in *Survey Graphic*, a contemporary left-leaning magazine, called "'hell-and-high-water votes'—votes that went to him in spite of anything because he was so well known and well liked."⁵⁷ Lambert added that Maverick could count on "the votes of the working people of San Antonio" thanks to his support for the pecan shellers and other labor causes over the years. The CIO unit's political arm, Labor's Non-Partisan League (LNPL), appointed Lambert, business agent Vasquez, and Willie Garcia, another UCAPAWA organizer, to serve as the local chapter's screening committee for candidates. The LNPL endorsed Maverick and prioritized his campaign, promising to deliver the vote mobilized by the pecan sheller movement, including both union members and the strike's legions of supporters on the West Side. Local members of the AFL also supported Maverick, despite the federation's formal endorsement of Kilday. Lambert reported that a straw poll among members of the Blacksmith's Union at local railroad shops awarded Kilday only nine out of seven hundred votes cast. Lambert also projected that Maverick would win "the Army vote, that portion of the voters who are directly dependent" upon the city's massive Fort Sam Houston and its many suppliers, not because those voters leaned liberal but because of the congressman's success at winning appropriations for the district. Finally, Maverick expected a sizable vote from "a heterogeneous, more or less independent portion of the middle class who have their doubts about Maverick's labor leanings" but "believe he is fundamentally sincere." He had emerged from a larger movement for municipal reform, and many of his longtime collaborators remained in his column.⁵⁸

The Lamberts and their gang of activists dove headfirst into Maverick's campaign, but they faced an uphill battle from the start. Texas law required citizens to register by paying their poll taxes by the end of January each election year, so the window expired the same day the strike got underway. Consequently, despite its close ties to the thousands of newly active union members and West Side residents, the union's LNPL was no longer able to add the workers and their supporters to the voting rolls for that year. The effort had to depend instead upon convincing the many *mexicanos* who were already registered to eschew the machine and then making sure they showed up at the polls to vote for Maverick. The activists set up a campaign headquarters and went to work. Days before the election, George Lambert was confident that "The West Side with its 90,000 'mexicans' is almost solidly behind him [Maverick]. Even those who will vote down the line for the machine on every other candidate will vote for Maverick because Maverick has kept his promises to the Latin-American people—something new in San Antonio politics."⁵⁹

Lambert's observation bears repeating. Maverick was the first candidate to actively court the *mexicano* vote independent of the downtown machine, an act that signaled a new departure in local, state, and even national politics. The present-day "Latino vote" did not yet exist, and most *mexicanos* who voted did so at the direction and expense of local political bosses of both the urban and rural varieties. The term "Latin American" was itself a relatively new descriptor of Mexican-descended people who wished to exercise the full rights and responsibilities of citizenship in the United States. But the group was not yet well known as a political force or even as an ethnic group beyond the American Southwest. Maverick's own famous definition of a "Latin American" as "a Mexican who has paid his poll tax" said it all.[60]

Less than two weeks before the election, Kilday again charged that Maverick was a radical, but this time he did so on personal terms. Kilday singled out a recent visit to San Antonio by the national head of the CIO's political division, charging that the shifty union staffer came to the city unannounced and met behind closed doors with Maverick and known radicals. Chief among the latter was Latane Lambert, who, Kilday explained, "is the wife of George Lambert, a CIO organizer who is now in charge of things on the West Side and she is a full paid-up member of the Communist Party." By overstating George's influence in the barrios, Kilday made extra hay out of Latane's political preference and her role in the campaign. The duo made for great political theater.[61]

The final tally of votes largely broke along the established battle lines, but the result was unexpected. Despite Kilday's charges, the local LNPL campaign succeeded in convincing an unprecedented number of West Side residents to vote against the city machine. Maverick carried the sixteen precincts targeted by LNPL in the barrios by some one thousand votes.[62] But Mayor Quin padded the city payroll by hiring four hundred new city workers, whom he paid a total of more than $3,000, probably as a quid pro quo for votes against Maverick.[63] Police chief Owen Kilday added icing to the cake by mobilizing his troops to fan out across the West Side to intimidate voters on a scale unseen since the conclusion of the strike.[64] In the end, his brother carried the district by 493 votes out of 49,151 cast.[65]

It was a stinging, narrow defeat. "Everyone here knows the election was stolen," Lambert wrote a few days after the election, but Maverick did not contest the final count.[66] The inertia of bossism, the toxic mix of racial resentment with anticommunist fervor, and the ongoing disfranchisement of most of the city's *mexicanos* proved too much for Maverick and his allies to overcome.

The loss devastated the leaders of the pecan sheller uprising. The machine overpowered their one prominent advocate, leaving them more vulnerable than ever to future attacks. Lambert had written a colleague that the movement could not "afford to lose him [Maverick] because he is the only consistent friend of labor in the South today."[67] Yet lose him they did. Although the strike had temporarily called the machine's authority into question, the political order of San Antonio was now seemingly restored.

On a personal level, the setback added insult to injury for the Lamberts. Latane had left town a week before the election to take a job teaching drama and music at the Southern Summer School for Workers, a residential institute for emerging labor leaders from across Dixie, in Asheville, North Carolina. For the next few months, the two activists sent letters and postcards to each other on an almost daily basis. Their messages combine the banalities of married life with all that is sacred and profound. Passionate declarations of love and lust mix with perfunctory expense reports, while excited updates on the movement dovetail with mundane commentaries on finding new jobs. At once painfully practical and deeply emotional, the letters reveal two kindred souls desperately working to make a difference in the world, to live their radical values, and above all, to find a way to reunite with one another.[68]

The Lamberts' discussion of Maverick's defeat displayed all of these traits. The night of the election, Latane wrote to George, "I can't wait until I see the morning papers. God, I hope Maury wins by a huge majority.... Please write me a detailed account of the election." She closed on a more personal note. "Sweet, I am missing you more than I thought it possible to ever miss anyone. I can't imagine what it will be like two or three weeks from now.... I am, at the moment, in a desperate mood. I want to see you, touch you, love you." She then quickly returned to business, signing off with the initials of her maiden name. "But no more of that. My regards to the comrades—and to the union. All my love, L. B."[69] George sent her the information she wanted the following day. "Bartlett, darling," he wrote; "It looks like Maury is licked. Most of us here can't realize it's true even yet ... I'm in a blue funk about it. I haven't had any sleep since about five o'clock Saturday morning, and I feel like hell." In the end, "Machine organization plus money beat Maury," he reported, adding that the "silk-stockinged North Side Districts came in so goddamned heavy that they wiped out our West Side margin."

For George, the implications of Maury's defeat were enormous. "What happened here today [sic] is going to be a stunning blow all over the nation," he wrote. "It's perhaps no more than can be expected though. Maury was too good for San Antonio." He concluded with some personal remarks, noting that he planned to mail her two dollars and a bag of avocados, asking about life in Asheville, and signing off: "I love you with all my heart, George."[70] Latane took the election results more personally. "I am heartbroken," she wrote two days later. "It [is] so tragic that rat Kilday should win over a good man. The damn would-be blue noses and their lesser lights should fry in hell.... I can't believe it's true. I am so disgusted. God damn them." Then her letter turned sugary sweet. "Short letter. Adore you. Pining for you. Bartlett."[71]

As the campaign came to a close, George also feuded with UCAPAWA president Henderson and eventually lost his job with the union. Although it made the couple's dire financial situation worse, the change did not significantly alter George's daily activities. He continued organizing the pecan shellers and

WPA workers without pay and publicized their plight as a freelance journalist.[72] Latane carried on at the summer school, but the couple was simply too broke to make any definite plans for the future. Instead they continued to share their news, resources, hopes, and dreams through their love letters. "Enclosed please find two dollars ($2.00) for which please send two big kisses," George wrote playfully, adding that he was using his most business-like tone in writing the letter. "I should appreciate your prompt attention to this matter."[73] Another note on union letterhead read simply, "Please be informed that I love you dearly."[74] A few weeks later, Latane could not contain her passion. "Darling, I want you so much I could die," she wrote. "I want you—I want you like all hell. I am coming home to you sometime soon and when I do you had better be ready for me. I'm warning you in plenty of time. I am going to kill you. . . . Every god damn bit of my love, L. B."[75]

Interspersed with such pronouncements, George also reported that there remained much work to be done in San Antonio. The sense of looming danger that the organizers had felt after the strike victory had turned into a series of full-fledged threats to the movement.[76] George wrote days after Maverick's defeat that "the union is in the doldrums."[77] A mass meeting on July 31 confirmed the fact that the strikers had achieved their goals of union recognition and increased wages only to see the industry begin hemorrhaging its workforce. After the strike, Pecan King Seligmann moved to consolidate and mechanize the shelling process. Work in the scattered West Side pecan sheds—which always slackened for the seasonal migration to the cotton fields—appeared to be drying up at alarming rates. Efforts to organize union "shop committees" proved difficult as the workers moved from one factory to another or out of the industry entirely. Lambert and other union activists hurried to help their members negotiate the rapid changes in the pecan industry and respond to the growing layoffs.[78] The masses of unemployed *mexicanos* and WPA workers who had joined the movement instead encountered new cuts to the relief rolls, leaving the former pecan shellers even worse off than before. Some 5,500 WPA workers faced renewed unemployment thanks to an announced layoff that was set to take place on September 1.[79]

Lambert, the union, and the Workers Alliance responded by again rallying the West Side. Lambert returned to his old tactic of showing films around town. A screening of WPA movies at the same vacant lot at Trinity and San Carlos Streets on August 3, an otherwise typical Wednesday night, drew a crowd of two thousand people. A few days later, the UCAPAWA and WAA held a joint Executive Board meeting to chart a strategy, including plans for demonstrations downtown. Two weeks later, the Mexican CTM also joined in the effort. Lambert was hopeful that his efforts to add sympathetic clergy and small businessmen to the chorus of citizens opposing the mass layoff would soon pay off. By the end of the month, Alliance members went to City Hall at least twice to directly confront Mayor Quin and the rest of the city machine's commissioners. In the end, the Bexar County government sponsored a series of new projects and rehired the city's laid-off WPA workers, keeping the movement alive at least temporarily.[80]

At the same time, the union laid plans for another pecan industry strike to take place that fall. While the details remain hazy, it is clear from the Lamberts' correspondence that the pecan shellers' local was ready for another round of battle. As the employers attempted to revive the old company union, UCAPAWA launched a drive to rebuild its membership, and it also resumed its outreach to community allies. George wrote to Latane that the organizers "have already talked with the Mexican Consul about getting food in from the surrounding small towns if we need it in a strike." The industry's transiency and changes notwithstanding, the WPA layoff fight had proven that the movement could still mobilize large numbers of people. "We're going to be able to really put on a show here in November if they force us to strike," Lambert added.[81]

Such optimistic projections proved fleeting. The union's plans dissipated when Seligmann and other employers announced that the new federal minimum wage established by the Fair Labor Standards Act would cut so deeply into the industry's profits that the old factories would be forced to shut down and reopen with fully mechanized operations. When the law took effect on October 24, the union had little choice but to join the bosses in asking the U.S. Department of Labor for an exemption from the act's minimum-wage requirements.[82]

In a twist of fate, at the same time that the pecan shellers lost ground, the Lamberts' fortunes improved. George received a job offer from the CIO-affiliated Amalgamated Clothing Workers of America (ACWA). He accepted it, but only on the condition that he could remain in San Antonio long enough to assist the pecan workers' struggle into the new year. Latane soon returned to Texas to join her husband in ACWA's worker education program, but the movement's steady decline cast a pall over the couple's long-anticipated reunion.[83]

For their part, many pecan shellers were reduced once again to seeking aid from stingy local relief agencies, while the union continued mobilizing for improved welfare provisions. With winter approaching, the Lamberts organized a relief committee that helped the shellers avoid starvation and lobbied for government assistance. A local newspaper credited the union with serving three thousand meals per day across the West Side. A large photo of an elderly *mexicano* dining at one union kitchen carried a simple but sympathetic caption: "This aged worker eats by grace of C. I. O." The union petitioned city, county, and state officials for the most basic charity, including "$183 to pay for the shipping of a $5000 carload of beans." In response, Governor Allred invited a committee of workers to visit with him in Austin and received them cordially with cookies and coffee, yet no substantial aid followed. Reality hit hard later that day when a restaurant on Congress Avenue refused to serve the predominately *mexicano* delegation.[84]

In the end, public relief remained miserly, and UCAPAWA could not keep it going on its own. When the joint labor-management request for an exemption from the minimum-wage law failed in early 1939, the pecan manufacturers responded by completing the process of automation. Industrial reorganization accomplished what brute police force could not—it busted the union and sent the *mexicano* workers home from the steps of City Hall and back into obscurity on the West Side. From more than six thousand members at the height of the strike, Local 172 would claim fewer than eight hundred by 1940, just two years later, and less than one hundred by the end of World War II.[85] Still, the former pecan shellers would flex their collective muscle one last time, returning again to the political arena in the spring of 1939. In so doing, they would change the state of Texas forever.

G. J. Sutton and the New Maverick Coalition

For all the painful defeats movement leaders had endured in the second half of 1938, they were about to assert their place in San Antonio's civic life once again. Their old ally, liberal ex-congressman Maury Maverick launched an improbable comeback bid, confronting the city machine head-on by announcing that he would run for mayor against the machine's multiterm incumbent, C. K. Quin. His strategy centered on rallying his old allies and finding new ones in unlikely places. The liberal *Survey Graphic* reported that Maverick had "learned that only careful organization could defy a powerful machine." Following his defeat in the previous year's primary, Maverick "set out to build a strong political coalition of his own," a new alliance that "organized all the elements which were friendly to his progressive views: youth, women, middle class reform groups, Mexicans and labor." He organized a slate of candidates called the "Fusion Party," with his name on the top of the list, and opened a handful of campaign offices, including one on the *mexicano* West Side. His diverse supporters swung into action.[86]

Contemporary reports and latter-day historians assumed that San Antonio's African Americans would continue to vote as instructed by the city machine. Despite the fact that Maverick had garnered a reputation as a racial liberal, conventional wisdom held that black voters would remain loyal to downtown.

Yet for the first time, a well-organized contingent of black voters on the East Side would rebuff the machine and cast their votes for an independent, liberal candidate. Discarding decades of paternalistic tradition, a sizable portion of the city's African Americans would come together to chart a new course, one that demanded rights rather than requesting patronage. That shift, so subtle that it remained all but unnoticed at the time, in fact represented a watershed moment in both the city's and the state's political history. A new bloc emerged that would make its presence felt for decades to come.

At the dawn of 1939, however, even Maverick could not have anticipated the support he would garner on the city's all-black East Side. As one black civil rights leader would later put it, "Maverick had a problem" when it came to winning African American votes.[87] The former congressman's opposition to the city machine dovetailed with his commitment to combat vice—these two Progressive Era causes went hand-in-hand and allowed him to win the unfaltering support of the white middle-class reform and women's groups. Yet these stances placed him in direct opposition to Charles Bellinger, the black gaming, saloon, and political boss who had regularly delivered as many as eight thousand promachine votes from the city's African Americans until his death in 1937. For years, Maverick had unleashed a steady stream of often quite personal criticism at Bellinger, at times using language that "carried racial overtones," in the words of a leading local historian. Moreover, the rivalry with the African American boss led Maverick, who had voted for the federal antilynching law and supported other civil rights causes, to endorse Bexar County Democratic Party officials' use of the all-white primary as well as the end of nonpartisan voting in municipal elections. His reasons were local. All-white, partisan elections stood to undermine the power of Bellinger's black bloc vote, Maverick believed, thereby undermining City Hall and paving the way for greater efforts at reform. Furthermore, Maverick remained personally averse to "social equality" with African Americans and maintained that the best route to racial uplift was through economic improvement. Like many southern liberals, he assumed that whites understood the path to progress better than their politically unsophisticated black counterparts. Such paternalistic logic and the realpolitik of the white primary led Maverick to abandon his general defense of civil liberties, souring more than a few African Americans to his cause. In contrast, Bellinger's close ties to the machine meshed unusually well with a stance in support of civil rights, a position that helped him rally his base of poor black voters.

Whatever the limits of Maverick's racial liberalism, the more important factor was that he remained incapable of delivering the jobs and other patronage that Bellinger had secured from the machine for decades, or that his son Valmo Bellinger continued to offer after his passing. The Bellingers' connections to City Hall had helped both father and son become key contributors to the "upbuilding" of black schools and community centers—essential institutions that represented sources of pride among San Antonio's black residents and that mitigated the worst indignities of Jim Crow in significant, material ways. Even without his stance on the white primary, then, Maverick's frontal attacks on the Bellingers and the patronage system had ensured only minimal black support for the white crusader in his several previous campaigns.[88]

Yet the deepening of the Great Depression meant that the East Side of the late 1930s was not the East Side of decades past. Organized in the local branch of the NAACP, a group of black reformers began moving away from Bellinger and finally broke from the machine completely.[89]

One key leader of this shift was a community leader named Samuel J. Sutton. Born into slavery in Virginia in 1863, he attended Armstrong Normal College in Richmond after Emancipation, moved to Texas, and became the principal of San Antonio's "old Riverside school" for African Americans in 1891. He married Lillian Viola Smith, and both husband and wife soon became leaders in the city's rich network of black self-help associations. A fierce advocate for educational improvements, Sutton pointed out the flaws of machine dominance, especially after Depression-era fiscal woes curtailed the city's largesse. His careful attacks forced Bellinger to recognize the principal's leadership and incorporate him into the machine.[90] He also forced some concessions from the city. A new black high school opened in 1932, and Sutton himself was appointed to several local health and welfare boards.[91] The Suttons' leadership in public was matched by the remarkable example of their private lives—at the height of the age of Jim Crow, all twelve of their children who survived to adulthood earned college degrees. By the 1930s, the family stood as the scions of black progress in San Antonio, a widely respected, tight-knit clan whom postwar civil rights activists would describe as the city's "black royalty."

Principal Sutton had gained a seat at the table, but he did not break away from the machine in the political arena. That task was left to his eighth child, Garlington Jerome, known within the family as "Dee" and to everyone else by his initials, G. J. For the next forty years, G. J. Sutton would represent one of the most outspoken, militant, and effective black leaders in the city and across Texas. At times strategic, at other moments uncompromising, the junior Sutton would spend decades carefully hammering out the local partnerships that would become the foundation of the statewide Democratic Coalition of the 1960s. In the depth of the Great Depression, he stood at the center of the new uprising of young African Americans against the machine. His calls for civil rights and economic improvements were not new, but his approach was innovative. Rather than depend on patronage, Sutton advocated the organization of black voters as an independent political force. And he hitched his wagon to the burgeoning labor movement and unfolding liberalism of the New Deal.

Born in San Antonio in 1909 and raised in the family home on Cherry Street on the East Side, G. J. came of age expecting to be treated with the level of respect that accompanied his family's high status. When G. J. left his hometown to attend Wiley College, his self-confidence collided head-on with the customary domination of African Americans in rural East Texas. It "was an awful place," Sutton later remembered. "Nobody respected black people. Blacks even had to get off the sidewalk when whites passed." One day while Sutton was shopping downtown, a white man grabbed him and put a hat on his head, chastising him for the disrespectful act of going bareheaded in public. The man also began rifling through Sutton's pockets, grasping for his money. "I was enraged," he recalled, "and I beat the heck out of him." Sutton understood that no act of self-defense in the face of white violence would go unpunished, so he ran back to campus seeking refuge. A few hours later, the school president called the student into his office, where local law enforcement officers told Sutton that they were going to arrest him for assaulting a white man. Rather than submit to arrest, he promised to fight back. "I told them I'd do it again if I had to and if anything happened to me, the NAACP would take the case to court." They left without arresting him, but Sutton was asked to withdraw from Wiley before the coming semester. He soon left Texas for Ohio, where he enrolled at Wilberforce College, the nation's first historically black institution. Still, Jim Crow followed him. Another racial incident in the nearby town of Xenia, Ohio, resulted in Sutton's arrest in 1935. Again, he survived the encounter, finishing school and graduating soon afterwards before taking another degree at the Cincinnati College of Embalming.[92]

G. J. Sutton returned to San Antonio in 1938, where he took over his brother's funeral home, founded two years earlier. Still less than thirty years old, G. J. soon found an outlet for his inchoate anger toward racial injustice. Joining the junior chapter of the local NAACP, he became part of a crop of new young leaders who embraced a more confrontational political style. One of his collaborators was the barber John Inman, a self-employed activist who had made his mark protesting against the unfair treatment of black service men at nearby Camp Travis. As local historian Kenneth Mason has written, Inman began working with various "progressive and liberal coalitions that sprang up in the city, and established working relations with white unions, and Mexican leaders such as Emma Tenayuca." In 1932, Inman worked unsuccessfully to elect the first black candidate for city council, a campaign that earned the endorsement not only of black reformers but of Mexican Americans as well. Although many such efforts proved unsuccessful, Inman learned experientially that African Americans in San Antonio "could win greater support by creating alliances across the color line." Along the way, Inman's "many activities brought him into contact with Maury Maverick."[93]

Joining with Inman, G. J. Sutton aimed to follow in his father's footsteps but to do so more aggressively. He "questioned the viability of racial separation" itself and instead advocated integration and full equality. While his father had served on local boards and been incorporated into the machine, G. J. maintained complete autonomy from downtown and became a fierce critic of the patronage system. His occupation as an undertaker serving an all-black clientele also gave him a degree of economic independence that his father lacked as a public school employee. The "defection" of G. J. Sutton from the Bellinger apparatus, historian Mason concludes, "was a great loss" that "provided a sense of legitimacy to the anti-machine movement . . . [and] symbolized the growth of a conscious intellectual class."[94]

Like many black activists across the country, Sutton also joined Popular Front organizations that included Communists and other radicals. He became the head of the San Antonio branch of the National Negro Congress (NNC), a coalition of militant African American civil rights, labor, and religious groups initially led by A. Philip Randolph, president of the all-black Brotherhood of Sleeping Car Porters.[95] Sutton's older sister, the future Lillian W. Sutton-Taylor, also became active in the NNC. At the same time, two of their younger siblings served as some of the first "colored" delegates to Popular Front–affiliated national youth conventions held in Washington, D.C. San Antonio's black royal family was on the march.

Together G. J. Sutton and Inman turned the NAACP youth branch into a militant civil rights group. Demanding nothing less than integration, their immediate goal centered on building a new constituency that could act independently of the downtown machine and its East Side wing. Electoral politics represented a means rather than an end in itself. In order to win civil rights, they needed to gain control of the East Side. And in order to do that, they needed to find allies across the color line and the entire political spectrum.

Maury Maverick became the beneficiary of the young activists' search for allies. Sutton secured the NNC chapter's endorsement for the ex-congressman's 1939 mayoral campaign. Although the customarily nonpolitical NAACP did not endorse, Sutton and Inman mobilized individual members from the branch to work in Maverick's campaign.[96] For his part, Maverick hoped that his liberal racial credentials would bring African Americans into the fold. He had voted for the federal antilynching law and gave much-needed support to the Texas State Conference of Branches of the NAACP by speaking at their first meeting during the Texas Centennial Exposition in Dallas in 1936. His mayoral bid three years later captured the attention of African American newspapers across the state, and the black weeklies of Waco, Houston, and Dallas all endorsed him despite their geographic distance from the campaign. At the local level, Maverick's antimachine stance meshed well with Sutton and company's aspirations. The civil rights activists rallied behind the white liberal despite his earlier support for the white primary—itself a positioned informed by local antimachine politics.[97]

The battle lines on the East Side came into focus. Following the death of boss Charles Bellinger in 1937, his son Valmo carried on the family machine by turning out votes for Kilday in the 1938 general election. He promised to again deliver the bulk of the black votes to incumbent Mayor Quin in the 1939 mayoral race. Sutton and Inman's independent camp stood ready to campaign for Maverick. What remained unclear was how many votes the reformers could mobilize and whether it would make any difference in the outcome of the larger election.

Like Sutton, the other members of Maverick's coalition of "youth, women, middle class reform groups, Mexicans and labor" came to his candidacy with their own agendas. Many middle-class women's groups looked to Maverick to finally rid the city of the pervasive gaming and extensive alcohol trade that had earned Bexar County the epithet "beer county" during Prohibition. The revelation of Quin's widespread vote buying on behalf of Kilday in the 1938 congressional primary took an additional toll, helping Maverick attract the votes of many self-styled progressives.[98]

For their part, neither the city's Mexican Americans nor union members were universally supportive of Maverick, and often the two categories blurred together. Both groups remained divided internally. *Mexicano* working people in and around the pecan sheller movement remained organized enough to throw their collective weight behind Maverick's campaign, and soon the mostly *mexicano* ILGWU, an affiliate of the AFL, joined them. The ILGWU's international president, David Dubinsky, gave Maverick $1,000, a quarter of which the candidate redirected to the union's local affiliates to get their two thousand members to the polls.[99] After the initial layoffs and fights for relief in the pecan industry, George Lambert and other organizers managed to secure work on the new pecan shelling machines for some two thousand union members, and their newly increased wages filled the union coffers with dues that could be used for political purposes. Other union leaders and unemployed pecan shellers became full-time political operatives for LNPL, the CIO's political arm.[100] Although both Lamberts were away from the city for most of the spring, George returned on Election Day and described LNPL's effort as an "excellent" precinct-level "organizational job."[101] As historian Richard A. Garcia summarized it, "The Mexican laboring class was striking out against the bosses and working for the liberal Maverick."[102]

Despite the fact that Maverick had kept his promises to the city's *mexicanos*, he attracted the support of only a handful of prominent Mexican Americans.[103] Although a pair of leaders aggressively organized some LULAC members to support Maverick, most of the upwardly mobile Mexican American middle class voted their pocketbooks and sided with the incumbent downtown. *Mexicanos* differed along class lines, the historian Garcia adds, as "politics and ideology superseded ethnicity."[104] Still, the *mexicano* workers' numbers ultimately triumphed. No exact breakdown is available for the West Side, but observations of "heavy turnout" in favor of Maverick abound.[105]

When Election Day rolled around on May 9, 1939, Maverick won, in what the newspaper declared was "one of the most bitterly-fought election battles in San Antonio political history." Turnout was heavy, dwarfing by nearly four thousand votes the previous record for a city election set in 1931. The liberal ex-congressman tallied 18,375 votes, a margin of 3,501 over C. K. Quin, and nearly seven thousand ahead of a third candidate, Leroy Jeffers, who gained support from conservative but antimachine white voters on the North Side. Garcia concludes that "The election, consequently, was an anti-Quin vote by the Anglo community, but a pro-Maverick vote by many in the Mexican community."[106]

The breakdown on the East Side proved equally revealing. Maverick carried more than one-third of the section's black vote, more than any antimachine candidate ever. The efforts of G. J. Sutton's group translated to 1,107 votes, or just over 35 percent of the total votes cast in the African American precincts, while Bellinger's machine helped Quin draw 1,665 (53%), and Jeffers garnered the rest.[107] These seemingly small numbers nevertheless represented a sea change in local politics. Even as the mayor carried all of the black precincts, the defection of a substantial number of black voters gave Maverick a sum equal to nearly one-third of his total margin. Sutton and company must have been elated. The antimachine forces did not yet control the East Side, but they had clearly succeeded in creating a new, independent bloc. The returns not only validated their approach but also promised more progress in the future.

Maverick needed both a sizable victory on the *mexicano* West Side and a significant narrowing of his deficit on the African American East Side. He accomplished both goals and won the race, not because of his "hell and high water voters," but due to a new coalition among the city's black and brown citizens.

"Maury won!" George Lambert declared in a letter to Latane the morning after the election. "And his entire ticket won with him!" The couple's work for ACWA had taken them north to Fort Worth, and Latane had since left to teach music and theater at another labor school in the mountains of Arkansas, but George had returned to San Antonio on Election Day to help with voter turnout on the West Side. UCAPAWA leader Santos Vasquez and the other pecan shellers "really did a swell job," he declared. "Last night we stuck around at the Fusion Party Headquarters almost all night making sure there would be no hitches in the majorities Maury and his crowd started piling up from the first. . . . About half the people I know in town were also there." He reunited with the couple's gang of radical friends and gave reports on each of them. He also broke down Maverick's sizable margin: "The West Side went solid. The Negroes went for Quin. Jeffers ran a poor third. All in all, it's swell."[108]

The morning's newspaper likewise reported that Quin "led in negro boxes." For most observers at the time and since, the more than 1,100 black votes for Maverick remained unnoticed and unremarkable. The culture of paternalism and machine patronage was sufficiently engrained among San Antonio's white population that the work of Sutton and company went undetected or remained a footnote at best. Even Maverick overlooked the shift, as did most of his allies. Decades later, the Lamberts would reunite in coalition with Sutton, but for the moment, George's "swell" mood did not extend to the city's black activists.

Nonetheless, black support for the Maverick campaign in fact represented a crucial development that would forever change San Antonio and Texas politics.[109] In adding independent African Americans to his loose coalition of "reform groups, women, Mexicans and labor," Maverick unwittingly laid the groundwork for decades of multiracial political and community organizing in the city and state—efforts in which working-class black and brown people would play critical roles. Labor's left wing, white liberals, and unprecedentedly large independent factions of Mexican Americans and African Americans all coalesced around Maverick's campaign. It was a winning formula, even if Maverick and Lambert and many of their allies remained blind to the critical changes taking place on the East Side. G. J. Sutton, for one, would not soon forget the experience of organizing that first independent black vote, including the all-important lesson that he managed to pull it off only by crossing the color line. Over time, Sutton would continue to organize his base and demand and win a seat at the table. For the moment, however, black, brown, and white members of the Maverick coalition would all discover that wielding power would prove even more difficult than gaining it.

The Counterrevolution

The emerging multiracial, liberal, and majority working-class coalition evidenced in the Maverick campaign represented a realignment of the state's decades-old Jim Crow political environment—but not only on the left side of the aisle. The San Antonio pecan sheller uprising and its political outgrowth also reshaped the nature of the conservative opposition. To nobody's surprise, the machine and its allies fiercely contested Maverick's tenure from its first days. At the same time, the liberal mayor's ambitious reform agenda produced many enemies, and he failed to maintain or extend his electoral coalition once in office. The combination would prove disastrous to the mayor and the city's nascent liberal coalition.

Maverick delivered on his promise to impose progressive reforms in the city, but his actions had unintended consequences. He brought vast improvements to the city public health system, passed new meat inspection ordinances, reformed the assessment and collection of property taxes, created new parks and tourist attractions, and zealously combated the vice business as well as corruption in local government. This last item included a wholesale purging of the police and fire departments, a near-collapse of their pension systems, and the removal of countless blue- and white-collar patronage employees throughout the city. Maverick believed in the virtues of a professional, apolitical civil service, but his many supporters were accustomed to the practices of San Antonio's urban politics and expected the spoils that should rightly come to the victors. To make matters worse, Maverick had little taste for appointing his minions to even the most aboveboard posts, and, in any case, he often traveled around the country in support of sundry liberal causes.[110]

Maverick's distaste for patronage had devastating consequences. First, after he ignored a hiring recommendation from the head of the local garment workers union—a key supporter of his campaign among labor's CIO wing and ordinary Mexican Americans on the West Side—the spurned union leader helped the machine-allied district attorney bring charges against Maverick for having used campaign funds to pay the union members' poll taxes. The practice remained customary among South Texas *patrones*, but it was also a potential felony, and the mayor was indicted on a total of twenty-six counts. The case went to court in December of 1939, when the presiding judge quickly determined that the attacks were politically motivated and dismissed all of the charges.[111]

The mayor's commitment to progressive good government had even more deleterious effects on African Americans. Historian Judith Doyle observes that while the administration increased the total number of black city employees, the gains remained limited to blue-collar occupations. In contrast, African American white-collar appointees who had been hired by the machine government and had served as health inspectors, librarians, and nurses were all removed from their posts. The number of black city nurses dropped from three to one, even as African Americans gained more positions as garbage collectors, janitors, and maids. At the same time, black workers in the police and fire departments were swept out along with the rest of the machine appointees. Both the machine's Valmo Bellinger and the antimachine G. J. Sutton protested the mayor's actions, and the dispatched white-collar workers formed new organizations in opposition to Maverick. The peddlers of vice doubtlessly took a hit from the mayor's crackdowns as well. Black discontent with the administration grew even more acute in 1940, when Maverick offered his support for a reform to the city charter that would replace the extant form of government in which commissioners were elected at-large with a city manager arrangement in which city council members would be elected from single-member districts. On the surface, the proposal appeared a democratic impulse and mirrored proposals that independent black activists would make throughout the 1960s and 1970s. Yet the reformers drew up the plans without the participation of any black representatives, and the proposed district lines promised to split the black vote apart. The plan would break the back of the machine, but it would also destroy all black political power in the city. Sutton protested the plan to the mayor privately, but Maverick took no action. Meanwhile, much of the East Side campaigned against the charter amendment and helped secure its defeat. Historian Doyle concludes that Maverick remained blind to the fact that he had won unprecedented black support in the 1939 election and therefore willfully overlooked the needs of his African American constituents, including the entreaties of the loyal Sutton and even the national leaders of the NNC.[112]

Such missteps mattered, but the conservative counterrevolution to the Maverick miracle probably proved more decisive in bringing down the coalition. It found its most extreme expression in a mob that stormed the City Auditorium after Maverick refused to bar the local Communist Party, led by Emma Tenayuca, from holding a meeting there on the evening of August 25, 1939. Maverick, ever the civil libertarian, maintained that the First and Fourteenth Amendments to the U.S. Constitution made it illegal for him to prohibit any group, regardless of ideology, from using a municipal facility. Veterans' organizations, the Catholic Bishop, conservative and machine politicians and columnists—all opponents of the pecan sheller movement and Maverick's coalitions in both 1938 and 1939—held a different view. A mob of eight thousand, led by American Legion officers, a well-known "Ku Kluxer," and a former Republican gubernatorial candidate, rushed past nearly two hundred city policemen wielding tear gas and fire hoses—who in another great irony had been ordered there this time by the Maverick administration to protect the Communists!

George Lambert was not present for the meeting but described the scene in the *Nation*, noting that the mob "smashed into the auditorium," despite the fact that the Communists had already escaped through a side door. The rioters then held their own mass meeting. One speaker who addressed the mob from the dais clarified the vigilante group's legal philosophy: "When they joined the Communist Party they wrote themselves out of the Constitution, and they aren't entitled to free speech or anything else." Later that evening, members of the mob raised an effigy of the mayor in front of City Hall, "with a placard attached which read, 'Hanged that Americanism might live.'" Fifteen hooded

Klansmen rounded out the night by visiting Maverick's ranch outside town, but they "withdrew when they found he was not there."[113]

The mob's exploits were just the most visible expression of the counterinsurgency taking place in San Antonio and across Texas and the South. Led by C. K. Quin, the machine and its reactionary allies denounced Maverick ad nauseum, again branding him a Communist and a "CIO-lover." Owen Kilday, the machine's former chief of police and brother of the congressman who had unseated Maverick in 1938, rebounded from his dismissal early in the new administration to win election to the far more powerful post of county sheriff. Developments in state and national politics made matters worse for the embattled mayor. In 1940, Vice President John Nance Garner, a Texas conservative from nearby Uvalde, emerged as the southern Democratic alternative to Roosevelt, whom liberals hoped would seek an unprecedented third term. Maverick joined with the liberal mayors of Houston and Austin to back the president, while the Garner faction worked to secure the support of the Texas Democratic Party. Prior to the state party convention in Waco, Maverick's allies cut a deal that would ultimately secure Roosevelt's renomination, but the mayor felt betrayed by his erstwhile allies and ended up punching one of them in the entrance to the hall. Garner then won a symbolic vote and secured control of the state party, while the incensed Maverick was forced to take solace in the fact that his efforts had prevented a serious challenge to Roosevelt at the party's national convention. Still, Maverick's partisanship and politicking had also succeeded in alienating more than a few swing voters on the city's affluent, white North Side.[114]

After two years of chaotic reign, Maverick faced the voters in 1941 and asked to be reelected as mayor. His opponent remained the same as in the contest two years earlier, but the terrain had shifted in critical ways. Quin ran for the machine and mobilized the city's white conservatives as well as Bellinger and the other anti-Maverick black organizations. Sutton again organized independents on the East Side on behalf of the liberal coalition, and white reformers returned to the mayor's "hell and high water" voters. Yet two groups remained conspicuously absent: the "Mexicans and labor" on the city's South and West sides.

Perhaps no amount of political acumen could have saved Maverick from one undeniable fact: he took office at the very moment that the pecan sheller movement was crumbling, stripping him of the largest, most dynamic wing of his mass base. His rift with the ILGWU combined with the anti-Communist riot at the Municipal Auditorium to further estrange him from the city's surviving CIO unions, while the AFL remained openly hostile. His reluctance to spread patronage and his attacks on the police and fire departments certainly didn't help. In the end, Quin regained critical ground on the *mexicano* West Side, and neither the CIO nor Tenayuca's Workers Alliance could stem the tide.[115] Maverick failed to account for these losses, leaving his fate all but sealed.

Close attention to his black constituents on the East Side might have saved Maverick, but the mayor's years of ignoring the city's African Americans resulted in few additional votes. Thanks to Sutton's efforts (as well as incumbency), the liberal increased his total from 35 percent of the city's black vote in 1939 to 38 percent in the first round of balloting in 1941. Maverick narrowly trailed Quin overall, but a new state law now required a runoff. The liberal mayor had one last chance. With his back against the wall, Maverick abruptly changed course, shifting from ignoring the city's African Americans to openly attacking them while wildly chasing the white supremacist vote. He chastised black voters for wielding the vote independently. Then, at a rally in the white working-class Denver Heights neighborhood, he exclaimed, "If Quin goes into city hall, Bellinger will be the most important man there. . . . Even your cook would be more important than you. We can't afford to have San Antonio dominated by the colored race." Despite such pronouncements, in the runoff Maverick actually added almost one hundred African American votes to his total, even as his share of the black vote slipped to 36 percent. Overall, Quin won the close election by a margin of three percentage points, or almost twelve hundred votes out of more than forty thousand cast. It was an ignominious end to the electoral career of a nationally renowned racial liberal. And for his constituents, the more pressing fact remained that the machine had returned to power once again.[116]

Thus a mass movement in San Antonio emerged and faded, leaving behind not only many wrecked lives and several stunted political careers but also vivid memories of the democratic possibilities that just might be obtainable through labor organizing in coalition with diverse campaigns for civil rights. Organizers like George and Latane Lambert and G. J. Sutton would not soon forget their maverick uprising, and neither would the countless *mexicanos*, white liberals, and black civil rights activists who participated in it. Sutton in particular must have been both encouraged and dismayed, bolstered by his ability to disrupt the Bellinger machine and regularly mobilize a sizable portion of the black vote and simultaneously disheartened by the political ignorance and philosophical betrayal of his white former ally. The lessons were clear: in the years ahead, he would need to continue to organize his base in order to build future alliances from a position of greater strength. For her part, the Communist firebrand Tenayuca would soon disappear from the scene, blacklisted from employment in the Alamo City, driven underground by anti-Communist repression, and ultimately forced to flee to California to restart her life as a humble laborer.[117]

Maverick's electoral coalition proved fleeting and not altogether substantive. It represented a loose tactical alliance between white middle-class reformers, *mexicano* workers, East Side insurgents, and Popular Front radicals—all centered on the politician himself. Once Maverick arrived in office, all of these groups except the reformers faded from the mayor's agenda, and he failed to notice that his mass base had evaporated, while his greatest new opportunity had failed to materialize. The pecan shellers' movement had destabilized the old regime and produced new bonds, but it had disappeared just as rapidly as it emerged. It would take many more years for a new coalition to again challenge the powers that be. Yet a pattern and example now existed that would reappear in altered form in the decades to come.

Chapter 2

Segregation Is an Economic Problem

Black Workers Win the Right to Vote

The contributions were small—a nickel here, a few pennies there, maybe a dime or quarter once in a while. Members of the Houston NAACP's Labor Committee stood on street corners and outside factory gates asking the city's poorest for a few cents and a moment of their time, all for the cause of freedom. Churches passed extra collection plates, mailmen spread the word on their routes, and railroad workers carried the message down the lines. A wealthy club owner, a barber, a dentist, and other businessmen gave major donations that could be measured in whole dollars. Even a few white folks joined the effort.

All the hard-earned wages went to support a quixotic court case that nonetheless promised to win for African Americans the simplest and most sacred role in a democratic society: the right to vote. Most people, black or white, thought it was crazy. Although they participated in municipal politics, African Americans remained excluded from the Democratic Party primary, the key contest in the Solid South. Many black working people could not imagine anything else, and they scoffed at the activists' efforts to collect their pennies or more. The leader of the local party, who of course was white, likewise did not believe change was possible. One donor to the cause who worked as a shoeshine boy at the county courthouse was polishing the chairman's boots when a prominent black activist passed through the building. The party chief looked up and exclaimed that "as long as he lived, [Black folks] would never vote in a primary." Instead, the U.S. Supreme Court would soon deliver a landmark decision in *Smith v. Allright*, striking down the white primary and extending the franchise so dramatically that one activist called it "a Second Emancipation."[1]

As World War II raged in Europe and the Pacific, black workers in Texas and across the country fought another pitched battle on the home front. They demanded an end to racial discrimination, expanded economic opportunities, and real political power. In Houston, they launched a series of efforts to counter discrimination on the shop floor and in their unions and then carried those experiences home into their communities in the Third and Fifth Wards. They infused new militancy into older race organizations like the NAACP and aimed high, sponsoring a series of court cases that targeted core tenets of

Jim Crow. The vote was first; education would come quickly on its heels. And black workers were at the center of the civil rights storm.

African American workers and their allies became advocates of what has come to be called civil rights unionism, a combined push for racial and economic justice in which, in the words of one eminent historian, "neither race nor class trumped the other, and both were expansively understood." With black workers swelling its ranks, the Houston chapter of the NAACP became the second largest local unit in the country, growing from just over one hundred members in 1939 to 12,700 by the end of the war. The expanding rolls both reflected and fueled the branch's success in the courtroom, where it would win a pair of cases that reverberated across America. Soon after, many of the local leaders would join with white radicals and union activists to mount a potent third-party challenge to the South's all-white antilabor political oligarchy—a campaign that included the city's first integrated political rally of the twentieth century.[2]

Houston's black workers built a booming civil rights movement in the city in the 1940s. They gave the struggle its purpose and meaning, swelled its ranks, and provided its leadership. Although the movement would eventually succumb to external pressures, civil rights unionism in Houston would first recruit a new cohort of activists and imbue them with a broad agenda and invaluable practical experience. Newly emboldened, the activists—both men and women—would survive the chill of the Cold War and carry the struggle forward into the decades ahead.

Black Workers and the New Unions

Throughout the 1930s and 1940s, a quiet revolution had begun in Houston and all along the Texas Gulf Coast. Working people of all hues flocked to join a rapidly expanding and often dynamic new labor movement. Although white workers shied away from using the new unions as a force to combat Jim Crow, black Texans voted with their feet—for the union. African Americans workers jumped at the opportunity to join a struggle that promised to upend the city's and the state's traditional arrangements of political and economic power, even as they understood the shortcomings of their white counterparts. Organized labor might not have the answer for every problem in the broader battle, but the unions represented a tool that could be wielded in the larger struggle for jobs and freedom.

After the gusher at Spindletop in 1901 led to a rush for black gold, Houston quickly became the center of the world's oil industry. The opening of the Houston Ship Channel in 1915 connected the city to the gulf, adding a critical piece of infrastructure. Houston had long been a hub in the exporting of raw materials, but the addition of oil and a viable port now made it the region's undisputed transportation headquarters. The city grew from a population of 44,000 in 1900 to over 292,000 in 1930.[3] Black and white working people from rural East Texas and Louisiana flocked to find jobs in Houston's new industries, as did smaller numbers of *mexicanos* from both sides of the South Texas border. Still, like their counterparts in Dallas and San Antonio, the new arrivals in Houston did not initially receive a sizable share of the dividends created by big oil and related industries.[4]

That arrangement first began to change among the stevedores. Nearly dormant in 1931, the International Longshoremen's Association (ILA) became the bedrock for a reinvigorated labor movement in Houston, but it did so within the confines of Jim Crow. Since 1914, the two segregated Houston locals of the ILA had split the available work using a "50-50 agreement" under which black and white crews alternated unloading the fore and aft halves of each boat in port. The division was neither perfect nor uncontested, but across the board, relations between the segregated locals proved cordial. Ironically, complete separation allowed the all-black locals to flourish, electing talented, often outspoken African American union leaders who advocated racial justice inside the all-black union hall while partnering with white labor leaders on job-related issues on the docks. The black unionists did not demand the integration of the unions, but they expected and received fair representation on the job. Segregation meant that local black leaders could retain their autonomous base instead of competing for scarce positions in a single, biracial, and in most cases majority-white union.[5]

From that imperfect foothold along the waterfront, African American workers in and around Houston gained entry into unions in the railroad, shipbuilding, oil, and steel industries. They remained confined to the lowest-paying, least-desirable jobs, as the growing, industrial unions of the CIO—though formally integrated—tended to defer to the Jim Crow custom of all-white leadership. Some unions in the AFL followed the ILA's lead in creating segregated locals for African Americans, but in most cases the black workers lacked the power to shape union policy or direct the work in an equal manner akin to the "50-50 arrangement" on the docks. Other AFL unions joined the Railroad Brotherhoods in either excluding black members entirely or offering them second-class membership in all-black, nonvoting union auxiliaries that permitted little power to shape union or employer policy.[6]

Whatever form the new unions took, African Americans jumped at the opportunity to join. Despite the varied inequities, collective bargaining agreements at times entitled black workers in the South to some degree of fair treatment and racial egalitarianism on the job even as they were denied equality with whites in other areas of life. For example, the democratic processes of some interracial unions allowed African Americans, who were often unable to participate in formal electoral politics, to vote in internal union elections and to partake in creating organizational policy. In addition, unions across the nation challenged the autocratic independence of white foremen, who for decades had arbitrarily hired, fired, directed, and disciplined workers of all races. Union contracts instead required foremen to follow specific procedures for promotions and transfers and only permitted disciplinary action in cases of just cause. Contracts further established grievance procedures that allowed black workers to demand a hearing with upper management. In the Jim Crow South, such provisions added up to a deep symbolic challenge to white supremacy, undermining a system that sanctioned reprisals against African American attempts to improve their conditions both inside and outside the workplace. Most important, unions offered black workers job security. Labor's record on the racial front was checkered, to say the least, but participation in unions still afforded some African American workers an unprecedented degree of shop-floor democracy. As historian Robert Korstad has put it, union contracts replaced the "racial etiquette, paternalism, [and] personalism" customary under Jim Crow with "a new language of rights and obligations" understood by workers and managers alike.[7]

Black workers in Texas, like their counterparts across the South and nation, joined the labor movement en masse as part of a broader effort to improve their economic standing and gain access to first-class citizenship. They hoped to use the unions to gain access to the highly skilled, lucrative positions that had long been reserved exclusively for white workers. Such an agenda often compelled black workers to confront both hostile employers and antagonistic or indifferent white union leaders, but confront them they did.[8]

The Education of Moses LeRoy

No individual epitomized the newfound militancy of the black masses more than railroad worker Moses LeRoy. Born in Abbeville, in southern Louisiana, in 1897, Moses was raised by his single mother, Melissa Ferry, a domestic servant. He was short and dark-skinned, stocky and sturdy, without being overweight. His rich laughter and warm, knowing face, ringed with tightly cropped salt-and-pepper hair, gave him an appearance that was welcoming, wise, and seemingly ancient, even as a young man. Although descended from slaves and a child of humble beginnings, he had the good fortune to receive a formal education at a small boarding school run by Baptists in nearby New Iberia. Still, LeRoy recalled having "one heck of a time trying to eke out a living," so he left school as a teenager to work alongside other black men in the sawmills located in the northern portion of the state. An economic downturn

Civil rights unionist Moses LeRoy witnessed the Camp Logan Riot of 1917, became a leader in Houston's segregated labor movement in the 1920s, and emerged as a key organizer of the city's booming black freedom struggle during World War II. Photograph ©Houston Chronicle. Used with permission.

in 1914 pushed LeRoy west to Houston, where he found casual jobs digging sewer ditches and performing unskilled tasks for contractors in the city's affluent southwestern section. He moved around a lot until he finally landed a job as a "handy-man chauffeur" for a doctor and his family. The position led him to take up residence alongside other black house servants in a pocket neighborhood near the Fourth Ward.

In 1917, LeRoy was driving home from dropping the doctor off at the train station downtown when black soldiers at nearby Camp Logan rose up in mutiny and a race riot engulfed the city. "I don't know why I wasn't killed in that riot," LeRoy recalled over sixty years later. He hid his boss's car and set out on foot. "I didn't see any Blacks. I wondered what was happening so I went down to Milam and Prairie [streets]. I saw a mob down there. They broke into Carter's hardware store and took all the ammunition and every one of the whites marched by me and all of them was going to kill a Nigger." LeRoy managed to hide in his home as the authorities imposed martial law on the city. With "a [white] soldier on every street car" and "a soldier on every corner" downtown, he eventually returned to work, driving his doctor around the eerie, abandoned city.[9]

While Houston leaders today speak with pride of the city's relatively moderate history of race relations, LeRoy's experience belied their claims. The

Camp Logan riot surely remained on the forefront of his mind as he looked for a better job and a place to settle permanently in the city. He narrowly avoided service in the Great War by leaving his post as a chauffeur to find work in a war-related industry, toiling at a sawmill on the edge of the bayou in town. Life was stable. He met and married a woman named Grace, and the couple had a daughter, Coral, in 1919. At some point, Moses's mother joined him in Houston, moving in with the young family in a house in the Third Ward, a predominately African American area that featured the city's premier black business district. Yet their peaceful existence was disrupted by tragedy when Grace died from bronchitis and a weak heart in September 1921, just weeks after her twenty-first birthday. Moses's mother helped him raise Coral and picked up extra work as a hairdresser. Times were tough, but the multigenerational family got by and even managed to build a house at 3017 Bremond Street.

It helped that LeRoy had found work at the Southern Pacific Railroad yards, where he would remain for more than forty-seven years. The railroad gave him the most stable employment a black man could find, even if it offered little room for advancement. Black workers were confined to hazardous, dirty jobs and classified as unskilled labor. "Irrespective of how much expertise a Black had," LeRoy recalled, "he was assigned to the labor designate." The whites held skilled positions such as "checkers" of incoming cargo or tradesmen who fixed broken railroad cars, while blacks served as freight handlers, stevedores, porters, and other common labor positions. A few were "breakout men, like if the truck broke down and you had to push it on, [you were] considered a breakout man."[10]

The racial division of labor at the railroad yards was a given, and black workers like LeRoy responded accordingly. In 1922, skilled white workers struck the Southern Pacific, and black workers eagerly, if temporarily, replaced them. The company attempted to circumvent the white pickets by running a special train to transport the black workers to the far end of the Fifth Ward, but the white workers aggressively pursued the scabs before and after work. "And then the hell would break out," LeRoy recalled. "The whites would run them to fair thee well." When the whites eventually returned to work, the blacks resumed their old jobs. More than a decade later, sometime in the 1930s, LeRoy joined an all-black freight handlers auxiliary to the all-white Brotherhood of Steamship and Railway Clerks. He was "harshly criticized for going into that type of union" since the auxiliary had no bargaining or voting rights, leaving black workers to be represented solely by their white Brotherhood counterparts. Yet LeRoy's decision was economically motivated and at least in part coerced: joining the auxiliary was the only way that black workers could enter the "Reserve Department," which was probably a new guarantee against future layoffs created by the white Brotherhood. All of the maneuvering paid off for LeRoy, who became an informal foreman or "gang boss" by 1940. More important, he gained their respect and soon became an officer of the union auxiliary.[11]

Around that same time, LeRoy began to believe that breaking down the racial barriers in the workplace was both necessary and possible. He attended a commencement ceremony at Jack Yates High School, the city's second-oldest all-black secondary institution, where he witnessed a powerful address by preeminent African American historian Rayford Logan. LeRoy remembered the historian's speech vividly, so well that he claimed he could "probably quote him verbatim" decades later. LeRoy recalled Logan saying, "We must have peace in the world. . . . We must have a just peace, a lasting peace. Not a peace as we had in World War I signed behind closed doors by the world's three great dictators. . . . It must be a people's peace." As LeRoy pondered the meaning of that lofty idea, Logan added, "What are you willing to contribute?" LeRoy later recalled, "As I sat there and listened to that master sermon I made myself a promise. . . . If from tonight I can make a contribution irrespective of how minute, I would try."[12]

LeRoy credited Logan with calling him to action, but in fact his deepening passion for justice may have stemmed from his heart rather than his head. He attended the commencement along with his new wife, the former Erma DeLoney. Born in 1913 in the rural hinterlands of Fort Bend County to the city's southwest, DeLoney came to Houston as a teenager to live with her aunt and uncle in the Third Ward, just a half-mile down Bremond Street from the LeRoy family home. She graduated from Yates High, probably in 1931, and went to Prairie View College, at the time the state's sole public institution of higher learning for African Americans. She earned a bachelor of science degree and later did graduate work in counseling, but she worked only intermittently outside the home. She instead adopted the air typical of an educated, middle-class black woman of the time—she dressed well, carried herself properly, spoke the King's English, joined book clubs, attended coffee klatches, and volunteered at the all-black Blue Triangle Branch of the Young Women's Christian Association (YWCA). She was six feet tall and strikingly good looking, "a beautiful, stately woman," with light skin and long hair pinned high above her head. Her presence lit up the room around her, and her "very articulate" speech brought her extra attention. DeLoney was roughly fifteen years LeRoy's junior, and she towered over him in charisma as well as height. She was, in short, way out of LeRoy's league.[13]

Such differences did not stop the pair from dating beginning in the late 1930s, marking the start of what observers would later call a "civil rights love story." While no early correspondence between the couple has survived, their passion for each other is evident in dozens of testimonial letters addressed to the couple later in life. One read, "You know, Moses, I have observed that progressive-minded men are more dependably liberal if their wives have common interests in understanding. Thus, in honoring you we also honor Erma." Another added that "she was the one who first encouraged and inspired you." Erma and Moses married in December 1938, just a week after his forty-first birthday. She was barely twenty-five. In spite of the age gap, Moses LeRoy found in Erma DeLoney a partner and "helpmate," a kindred spirit who would stand at his side and propel him forward in the labor and civil rights movements for decades to come. They became universally known as "a team," a dynamic duo in the city's emerging black freedom struggle.[14] Whether it was love or intellect, both of the newlyweds came away inspired when Dr. Logan addressed the Yates High School graduation around 1940. They moved in with a brother-in-law on Jones Street in the city's working-class Fifth Ward, not far from the Southern Pacific yards, and quickly got to work.[15]

The LeRoys drew upon their experiences of racism and economic exclusion and plunged headlong into the city's growing civil rights and black labor movements. The two issues became inseparable: "Segregation and discrimination is [sic] an economic problem," Moses later reflected. "They didn't discriminate against me because of my color but in the final analysis it paid a hellacious dividend." A simple allegory that LeRoy recited told a much larger tale. "The industrialist would give the poor white worker maybe a dollar . . . and give the poor Black fifty-five cents. And they would pay the poor white worker so bad he'd go back to the industrialist and say, 'Boss, can't you do a little better? . . . My old lady and I can hardly make it.' But he was told, 'I'm giving you a dollar now because you're better than those niggers. . . . I can get these niggers for 55 cents and they could do as good a job as you can.'" The moral of the story was clear for the industrialist and the workers alike. "He kept this 'nigger' dangling over their heads," LeRoy concluded. "You might not believe it, but if the poor white worker . . . could get with that darky, both of them could get a dollar and a half. It's that simple."[16] Armed with this vision, drawing upon a life of exclusion, and motivated by the oratory of Dr. Logan, LeRoy challenged the racial division of labor on the job. He became more active than ever in his union auxiliary. "I was more or less interested in breaking down the barrier that barred blacks from integration and high-paying jobs, because of the group system," he recalled.[17] Although he fought "doggedly" and "desperately" against the ongoing segregation of jobs at the Southern Pacific, LeRoy learned that he and his all-black auxiliary union ultimately had little power to change the situation in the face of a hostile employer and the white Brotherhood of skilled workers. "I tried to take action . . . but it fell on deaf ears," he later recalled. "I couldn't do anything—not until we were sort of given a legal weapon."[18]

While progress at the worksite remained elusive, the LeRoys increasingly turned their attention to the larger civil rights movement in the community. They found both an outlet for their energy and a new source of inspiration and strength in the local branch of the NAACP. There the struggle for dignity and economic opportunity dovetailed with another front in the movement: the fight for the right to vote.

Civil Rights Unionism and the Fight for the Vote

It began with a nightclub owner, a barber, and a couple of lawyers. In 1932, the mixed group came together in Houston to found the Harris County Negro Democratic Club, a group dedicated to winning the right to vote for the area's black citizens. The Terrell Election Laws passed thirty years earlier had removed most African Americans from the state's voter rolls through the imposition of a poll tax, literacy tests, and other restrictions to the franchise. Still, the task of foreclosing the right to vote proved incredibly difficult. It required that extrajudicial violence be meted out against any holdouts, especially in rural areas, and soon it necessitated the creation of a new legal subterfuge known simply as "the white primary."[19]

Its genius was its simplicity. When the biracial populists were vanquished at the turn of the century, virtually all white voters across the South had rallied behind the bloody shirt of the Confederacy and thereafter remained stalwart members of the Democratic Party. With most black voters removed from the picture thanks to disfranchisement, and the Republican Party identified with the hated North, general elections quickly became uncompetitive. The real action took place when the white Democratic voters made their selection in the party's primary. Yet, much to the dismay of the architects of Jim Crow, black voters continued to organize as a bloc and sought to swing close primary elections in favor of their preferred candidates. The white primary represented the perfect solution. The state of Texas (and others across the South) considered the party a private entity, so it was free to violate the constitutional amendments borne out of Reconstruction—namely, the Fifteenth Amendment, which holds that states may not restrict the right to vote based on race or color. Like any other private association, state leaders maintained, the Democratic Party could define its own rules for membership. Threatened by a still ominous, if diminished, black vote, the party duly excluded African Americans from its ranks and consequently from voting in the all-important primaries. Using the party that they themselves ran, Democratic state officials added an extra layer of insurance, finally ensuring that even the best-educated, wealthiest African Americans who could read and pay their poll taxes still would not be able to vote in the state's most significant elections. The party's goal of enduring white supremacy appeared all but assured.

Nonetheless African Americans continued to wield the power of the vote whenever and wherever possible. Many battled for influence in the Republican Party, but there too they lost out to lily-white southern Republicans who accepted white supremacy as the sine qua non of politics. In San Antonio, African Americans consistently voted in nonpartisan municipal elections, but they tended to do so under the direction of the city machine (at least until the Maverick election of 1939). In contrast, in Houston, white officials feared that the city's larger black population could become a powerful swing vote in tight races, so they sought to exclude black voters from the political process at the local level in addition to state and national races. Local elections in the Bayou City thus remained partisan contests, so the few black citizens that defied the odds and managed to register and vote could still only cast their ballots in the general elections and remained unable to influence the primaries.

The activists that came together to form the Harris County Negro Democratic Club in 1932 understood all this and still believed they could carve out new space for participation in the political arena. Over the next two years, they joined the legions of African Americans nationwide who bolted the Republican Party of Lincoln to embrace the New Deal Democratic Party of Roosevelt. More important, the Democratic Party was the only party that mattered in the Jim Crow South, so the club focused on breaking into it as the path to power. Out in El Paso in the previous decade, a local NAACP member had twice sued the state after being denied the vote in the Democratic Party's white primary. In both cases, after years of legal wrangling, the U.S. Supreme Court maintained that the party was a private entity, and the system stood, with some minor amendments by Democratic officials. By 1934, after a series of failed local attempts to gain access to the right to vote, the Negro Democratic Club members decided that it was time to escalate the struggle. Represented by a pair of race lawyers, barber Richard Randolph "R. R." Grovey attempted to vote in Houston's Democratic primary, was rejected, and filed a new suit. This case was novel in that it asked for such small financial damages that the state appeals courts gave it no standing, so *Grovey v. Townsend* proceeded immediately to the U.S. Supreme Court. Still, the outcome was the same. Within months, in 1935, the nation's highest court again accepted the logic that the party discriminated privately without the state's legal imprimatur. National NAACP leaders were furious with the Houston activists' apparent failure, accusing them of setting back the cause of winning the ballot for years, if not decades. Still, the case brought new energy to ordinary African Americans in Houston and set the stage for a mass movement.

In fact, although the case against the white primary failed, the personnel and the tactics represented new departures in the larger struggle against Jim Crow. Like the LeRoys, R. R. Grovey combined the fight for civil and political rights with a broader commitment to labor organizing and economic justice. Born in 1890 in rural Brazoria County to the south of the city, Grovey went to college and became a high school principal before joining what one scholar calls "the other great migration" of African Americans to Houston in the early twentieth century. He secured a relatively good job at the Houston and Texas Central Railroad but left to attend barber school, opening a storefront on Dowling Street in the Third Ward. By the late 1920s, the shop had become a hub for "ongoing conversations . . . about the perpetual racial divide," leading Grovey to found the Third Ward Civic Club, a political action organization that brought the societies of the black middle class together with the city's nascent black labor unions and civil rights groups. Grovey described the target demographics and long-term goals of the club a few years later. "We didn't go out and organize school teachers and the doctors and write down a program for the "little" Negroes," he began. "We called the washerwoman, the maid, the ditch-digger, the businessman, the cook, the preacher, the hod carrier, the dentist, the bricklayer, the teacher, the longshoremen, and the gentleman of the press. It is our aim that in working out our problems, the doctor and washerwoman will sit down together; and the newspaperman will sit down with the hod carrier; and the dentist and the dock worker will join, all in a common cause that will free the Negro from the shackles of economic and political slavery."[20]

By deciding to take the white primary fight into his own hands, Grovey earned a reputation as a "troublemaker" among the city's respectable African American leaders. In response, Grovey only increased his use of militant tactics. In 1937 Grovey traveled to Washington, D.C., to denounce the nomination to the U.S. Supreme Court of Hugo Black of Alabama, a known segregationist senator and recent member of the Ku Klux Klan. Moses LeRoy later recalled standing on the neighborhood's street corners collecting nickels, dimes, and quarters to help Grovey finance the trip. The barber soon became an organizer for the CIO as well, using his barbershop to attract black workers to the growing labor movement.[21]

As the Great Depression grew deeper, even the city's older civil rights organizations turned their focus to economic issues, and the pace of the larger movement quickened. First established in 1913, the Houston chapter of the NAACP had fluctuated between small and dormant until 1937, when the men from the Negro Democratic Club took over the branch's leadership and brought with them new energy and an increasingly aggressive, militant style that demanded immediate change.

Most critically, the change in leadership opened up space for Mrs. Lulu Belle Madison White, the wife of nightclub owner and political activist Julius White, to leave her teaching job and become the branch's unpaid youth director. The change set in motion a period of unprecedented growth and relevancy for the NAACP. Although women were initially excluded from formal decision-making positions, Mrs. White's position as youth director gave her access to the group's "inner circle" of leaders. After branch president Clifton Richardson Sr. died in office in 1939, White briefly served as the chapter's acting president. Along with the new president, Rev. Albert A. Lucas, she then spearheaded a membership drive that grew the branch from just over one hundred to nearly two thousand members.[22]

The bulk of those members came from the city's burgeoning mass of black workers. Civil rights unionists like the LeRoys joined the branch and rallied behind White, helping her forge connections between the NAACP and ongoing labor and political organizing. She believed that the full integration of African Americans into industry would not only bolster their economic condition but would also advance the struggle for civil rights.[23] Like Grovey and the LeRoys, White embraced the labor movement despite the rising criticism concerning the role of Communists, particularly in the CIO. As her biographer explains, White defended her stance with a simple statement: "You take your friends where you find them."[24]

The rise of civil rights unionism within the local NAACP branch dovetailed with a new development in the war against the white primary. In 1940, chapter president Lucas recommended two of his parishioners at Good Hope Baptist Church to serve as plaintiffs for a new test case. Two longtime NAACP members—Sidney Hasgett, a part-time mailman, hod carrier, and local union official, and Dr. Lonnie Smith, a dentist from the Fifth Ward—agreed to take on the task. Both attempted to vote in the August Democratic primary runoff, along with veteran activists Grovey, Julius White, and Carter Wesley. As they expected, election officials refused to give them ballots, and they filed suit.

The newly founded NAACP Legal Defense Fund (LDF) led by Thurgood Marshall took charge of the proceedings, along with William J. Durham, the general counsel of the Texas State Conference of Branches. Born in 1896 in Sulfur Springs in East Texas, W. J. (Bill) Durham survived a 1930 race riot that burned his law practice in Sherman to the ground, and he soon began filing civil rights cases. He defended rural African Americans who were losing their lands and mineral rights by nefarious means, and he won an injunction against his own Grayson County that temporarily blocked the white primary there. After A. Maceo Smith, a NAACP leader in Dallas, successfully lobbied to create an all-black exhibition within the larger Texas Centennial Exposition of 1936, Durham joined Lulu White and association leaders from across the state in

Attorney W. J. Durham, originally from Sherman, Texas, photographed at his office in Dallas, 1966. Durham helped found the Progressive Voters League and the Texas Council of Voters, two key black political institutions, and served as the lead lawyer for the local and state NAACP bodies. He helped bring the *Smith* and *Sweatt* cases to the U.S. Supreme Court and defended the association in *State of Texas v. NAACP* in 1956. From the Marion Butts Collection of the Texas/Dallas History and Archives Division, Dallas Public Library, PA2005-4/2675.1.

founding the State Conference of Branches the following year. For more than three decades thereafter, Durham would serve as the civil rights movement's chief lawyer and one of its most eloquent spokesmen. His endorsement of the effort to overturn the white primary assured it a talented legal mind as well as the critical support of A. Maceo Smith, the Dallas branch, and the entire State Conference of Branches of the NAACP.[25]

With the blessings of Marshall and Durham, union leader Hasgett became the lead plaintiff. While local attorney and publisher Wesley had taken *Grovey* directly to the Supreme Court before suffering a resounding defeat, Marshall and Durham resolved to use *Hasgett* to build a large body of evidence against the state through a series of appeals. At each stage of litigation, they believed, the state would reveal more clues that the Democratic primary was in fact a public affair, that officials excluded citizens based solely on race, and thus that the denial of African American participation in the primary did, in fact, violate the Constitution.[26]

Knowing a lengthy appellate record would take years to construct, they began to build a war chest for the long, expensive legal battle to come. Once again, Grovey, LeRoy, and other union and community activists took to the streets, collecting pennies, nickels, dimes, and quarters for the cause. George Nelson, another barber turned CIO organizer, recalled that ordinary

African Americans did not believe the case could succeed, even as they turned over their hard-earned dollars. The opposition likewise thought it was a lost cause. The party's local chairman believed that black people would not vote in a primary "as long as he lived," and surely the bulk of his white constituents held similar views.[27]

An accident of history led Marshall and the other NAACP attorneys to abandon the *Hasgett* case in favor of a new, stronger suit led by the dentist Lonnie Smith. A case stemming from followers of the liberal Huey Long in Louisiana forced the Supreme Court to rule that the primary did in fact represent a public entity, subject to constitutional review. The association's lawyers realized that they needed to rewrite their briefs to respond to this new precedent, and they needed a watertight, fresh case featuring a plaintiff who had voted in the first primary election (not the runoff as had Hasgett). Combing the records, they discovered that NAACP member Smith had already voted in both contests in 1940 and could therefore become the new standard-bearer for the case without any further delay. After a vigorous debate in which the impatient Houston activists initially balked at starting over, Marshall scrapped *Hasgett* and convinced them to launch what would become *Smith v. Allright*.[28] Although the dentist became the face of the campaign, it continued to grow out of the branch's militant brand of civil rights unionism. "We used Lonnie Smith as a guinea pig," Moses LeRoy later recalled. "I wasn't on the firing line all the time but I helped to pass the ammunition."[29] The same could be said for Grovey, Nelson, Hasgett, and the thousands of black labor and NAACP activists who helped raise money and awareness for the case.

The branch prospered despite the many delays in the courtroom. In 1943, six years after she had become youth director, and four years removed from her stint as acting president, Lulu White accepted the post of executive secretary, the chapter's top staff position. Under her leadership, and with assistance from Rev. Lucas and countless labor activists in the Third and Fifth Wards, the Houston NAACP extended its reach and lived up to its reputation as a particularly aggressive branch. The branch grew from two thousand members to nearly 5,700 by the end of 1943, and just over 10,700 a year later.[30] At the same time, the chapter began mobilizing in the political arena even before *Smith* was settled. With White at the helm, it collaborated with the CIO's Political Action Committee (CIO-PAC), a successor to LNPL, which targeted and then defeated three conservative Democratic congressmen across Texas in 1943. The chapter's education and political action committees sponsored citizenship classes for black voters and encouraged members to pay their poll taxes and register to vote.[31]

Finally, the NAACP's efforts and organizing against the white primary were vindicated. In April 1944 the U.S. Supreme Court handed down its ruling in

Smith v. Allright, overturning and declaring wrong several decisions made just a decade earlier. The court "made up for decades of inaction and obfuscation with one of the most unambiguous decisions in its history," in the words of one historian. The justices declared simply that "the right to vote in such a primary for the nomination of candidates without discrimination by the state . . . is a right secured by the Constitution" and particularly the Fifteenth Amendment.[32]

To be sure, the court's politics were changing, yet credit for the hard-fought victory belonged elsewhere. For more than a decade, local activists led by Grovey, Wesley, and Julius White had carried forward the torch of full citizenship. Literally thousands of ordinary black Houstonians had rallied behind the cause, and talented lawyers from across the state and nation translated their aspirations into the legal language of the courtroom. For the Houston NAACP, this represented a crowning achievement.

It was Lulu White who declared *Smith* "a Second Emancipation."[33] Her statement aptly captured her peers' sense of jubilation, though perhaps it hinted at more than simple triumph. Just as the freedmen and women after the Civil War discovered that exercising the full extent of their newfound citizenship would prove tremendously difficult, so too the movement in Houston—as in Texas and indeed the entire nation—was just beginning.

Heman Sweatt and the Battle for Fair Employment

Civil rights cases in the courtroom developed hand-in-hand with the struggle for better jobs and equal employment opportunity. Between 1944 and 1948, civil rights unionists took advantage of wartime rhetoric and labor shortages to demand that the federal government come to their aid in advancing up the occupational ladder and in ending the worst indignities of Jim Crow. Once again, Lulu White and the Houston NAACP stood at the center of the struggle, while Moses and Erma LeRoy and many other rank-and-file civil rights unionists took the lead on the ground.

In March 1944, a month before the *Smith* ruling would be handed down, a letter carrier named Heman Marion Sweatt joined the legions of civil rights unionists nationwide who began protesting segregation on the job during World War II. He filed a written grievance against the post office, charging systematic discrimination against black workers in violation of the Civil Service Code, and demanding equal opportunity for African Americans in hiring and promotion. Although the petition itself was not unusual, it proved to be the precursor to an extraordinary series of events. Yet the struggle, which would end with the desegregation of higher education in America, began with a much simpler act: Sweatt's protest against Jim Crow at work.

Sweatt filed his grievance with the assistance of a lawyer and his union, the National Alliance of Postal Employees (NAPE), an all-black union that combined radical racial uplift with militant shop-floor representation. Black post office workers like Sweatt often practiced "dual unionism," joining the white-led craft unions of the letter carriers or clerks as well as NAPE, which included all African American workers at the post office. The white-led unions overlooked Jim Crow, so NAPE emerged as a kind of NAACP on the job. It lacked formal collective bargaining rights but made up for it by actively fighting against segregation both at work and in the larger community.

Sweatt's membership in NAPE was a family affair. Although the union was founded in Tennessee and had grown national in scope, the Alliance traced its origins to a series of discussions that took place in the home of Heman's father, postal worker James Leonard Sweatt, in Houston in 1913. The senior Sweatt and the other NAPE founders also helped charter the Houston NAACP chapter the same year, but the union became their main avenue for activism. While the broader civil rights movement had its ups and downs and changes in leadership, NAPE in Houston carried the torch for black postal workers for three decades without interruption.

Heman Sweatt, born a year before the union and the NAACP branch started, would soon emerge as a preeminent figure in both organizations. In 1944, his grievance straightforwardly challenged the longstanding practice in which African Americans could be promoted to become indoor clerks and were permitted to interview for supervisory positions, but were then always passed over in favor of white applicants. Like many union petitions, this grievance proved unsuccessful in the short term, but it produced one lasting legacy: it stoked Sweatt's interest in pursuing a legal career.[34]

As luck would have it, the following year, state and national NAACP leaders began searching for a plaintiff for another civil rights case focusing on higher education. Historians agree that Marshall, Durham, and other association attorneys believed that the court's ruling in *Smith* had not only reinforced the right to vote protected by the Fifteenth Amendment but had dramatically expanded the court's interpretation of the Fourteenth Amendment, which guaranteed all people equal protection under the law. For decades, the association and other civil rights activists had advocated for the creation of black schools that were truly on a par with white schools without challenging the "separate but equal" court doctrine established in 1896. Now, thanks to *Smith*, the time was finally right to launch a full-scale assault on that dubious principle.

Although their ultimate goal was the integration of schools for all ages, Marshall and other NAACP and LDF leaders decided to begin their nationwide campaign with several test cases focusing on graduate-level higher education. While younger black students could attend segregated primary, secondary, and even postsecondary schools within the confines of Jim Crow, it remained all but impossible for African Americans to pursue advanced degrees. "Colored" graduate and professional schools simply did not exist. At best, southern states offered black students scholarships to attend integrated schools in the North, but even that custom fell far short of equal treatment. Since the militant Houston branch chapters and the Texas State Conference of Branches retained the infrastructure and momentum created by the successful white primary fight, NAACP leaders again looked to activists in the Lone Star State to spearhead the struggle.

They did not have to look far for a target. Like its counterparts across Dixie, the law school at the University of Texas in Austin flatly refused to admit black students, and no alternative existed. Perhaps more important, unlike many of its southern neighbors, Texas could not possibly claim that the state could not afford to accept black students, as the university's endowment had swelled since the first of its many oil wells began producing in 1923.[35]

This legal logic and political strategy notwithstanding, the NAACP struggled to find a plaintiff who would bear the burden of carrying the case. Doing so would require great personal sacrifice: black litigants often faced a range of reprisals that at times included eviction from one's home or termination from one's job. It was no coincidence that Grovey and Smith were both self-employed and economically independent. Pursuing such a case also required a tremendous amount of time on the plaintiff's part, even, at times, money. Adding to the pressure, anyone who volunteered would become the face of the struggle and would thus need to stand firm for years of battle in the courtroom and in the arena of public opinion.

In October 1945, just as the association had all but given up its search for a plaintiff, Lulu White found him in an otherwise routine meeting at a church in the Third Ward. After detailing the planned strategy for the case, White again made an appeal for someone to volunteer to represent the race. A "hush" descended over the room, one historian writes. "The brothers and sisters present looked strangely at White and then searched the faces of their peers." A few moments later, Sweatt stood up and "with a soft but certain voice . . . said he would do it."

Sweatt represented both an unlikely candidate and the perfect person for the task. He had a good job at the post office, a position that was the envy of many hard-working African Americans. Although he had served as one of the thousands of NAACP members who had collected donations for the *Hasgett* and *Smith* cases, he was not yet a formal leader in the branch. On the other hand, the protections of the civil service and his union membership in the NAPE meant that although he was not self-employed, he was unlikely to face economic reprisals. Although not a stellar student, he had enjoyed the process of filing his grievance and had developed a nascent interest in the law. Most important, he could count on the support of not only the NAACP but also of his father and the entire leadership of the NAPE.[36] A committed civil rights unionist, Sweatt also understood that such discrimination in higher education thwarted the upward mobility of the state's entire black population—only thirty African Americans held Texas law licenses at the beginning of the white primary campaign. Even the most talented black students struggled to climb the professional ladder. Sweatt had personally confronted employment discrimination at the post office and had come up short. Taking the fight to the state's segregated professional schools represented the logical next step. He put in his application, was rejected, and filed suit. Everyone knew it would be a long fight, but Sweatt and the larger civil rights unionist movement were ready for battle.

As the *Sweatt* case worked its way through the courts, civil rights unionists across Houston extended the crusade against Jim Crow both on the job and in the community. Moses and Erma LeRoy, already active supporters of the NAACP, took on leadership roles within the branch. Erma became an aide to Lulu White, whom she later described as a close friend and political mentor. By 1947 she also served as assistant recording secretary for the Texas State Conference of Branches. By that date, White had become director of branches for the statewide body, and Mrs. LeRoy at times accompanied her as she traveled across Texas.[37] By the end of the war, Moses had been elected and reelected to the branch's Executive Board. He first supervised the chapter's youth activities and then chaired its committee to reach out to returning veterans. He also roamed the city organizing black workers into the Railroad Brotherhoods, the Hod Carriers, and other AFL unions, even as he remained a steadfast supporter of the CIO. At the same time, he urged black workers to join the NAACP and tagged along with his wife and Lulu White on organizing expeditions around the state. In one incredible case, Moses LeRoy and White traveled to assist a branch in rural East Texas, where they learned that a local black man was being held by a white farmer "as a slave," forced to work without pay and imprisoned in a chicken coop. Shocked, the duo liberated the captive and lived to tell the tale.[38]

With White at the helm and the LeRoys in the trenches, membership in the Houston branch grew exponentially, while new chapters popped up across Texas, and the state conference grew more powerful. The Houston NAACP added two thousand members in 1945 to reach its peak of 12,700, the second highest membership of all branches in the nation, trailing only Detroit, another hotbed of civil rights unionism. By 1948, White credited LeRoy and other "members of the labor division" he led with bringing more than one thousand members into the branch.[39]

Much of the membership increase could also be attributed to the fact that the Houston branch had actively taken up the cause of black workers who were fighting to end discrimination on the job. One critical tool was the newly created Committee on Fair Employment Practice (FEPC). In the face of black union leader A. Philip Randolph's threat to lead a 100,000-man March on Washington in 1941, President Roosevelt issued Executive Order 8802, banning racial discrimination in war-related federal contracts and establishing the FEPC to oversee the new measure. The *Pittsburgh Courier*, a leading black newspaper, called for a "Double V" campaign—a fight for victory against racism at home as well as fascism abroad.

In Houston, as across the nation, African American—and to a lesser extent, Mexican American—workers seized the promise of the new agency to demand promotions and access to skilled positions in the arsenal of democracy. Workers in the oil, steel, and aircraft manufacturing industries filed countless complaints with the FEPC, exposing their companies' systematic refusal, based solely on race, to promote them to lucrative, skilled positions. The agency held widely publicized hearings in Houston that embarrassed the executives of the city's and the Gulf Coast's oil refineries and manufacturing concerns, and black and brown workers jumped at the opportunity to share their accounts of segregation on the shop floor. Still, the employers ranged in their responses from openly hostile to quietly patronizing, and few promotions or changes were forthcoming.[40]

In the end, the lofty wartime rhetoric did not prove decisive, and the FEPC did not fulfill its promise of opening up America's defense industry. The agency lacked significant enforcement powers, and progress remained slow. To make matters worse, the executive order was a response to the crisis of the Second World War, so its mandate expired with the end of the fighting abroad. Civil rights unionists in Houston joined their counterparts across the country in calling on Congress to make the FEPC permanent. Moses LeRoy joined Randolph and March on Washington Movement delegates from thirty-seven states at a rally at the Capitol in support of a permanent FEPC bill. Lulu White wrote to her U.S. senator to urge him to vote for the measure, but he joined other conservative southern Democrats in rallying to kill the legislation.[41]

As government support remained elusive, black workers in Houston took matters into their own hands. They joined the national strike wave of 1946, the largest in U.S. history, and LeRoy, White, and other local NAACP labor activists rallied behind them. Some five thousand African Americans in Houston walked off the job as part of the nationwide steel walkout, while over seven hundred black workers joined a successful strike against the City of Houston.[42] For his part, Moses LeRoy continued to battle for influence within his white-dominated union, the Brotherhood of Steamship and Railway Clerks. He had joined his local auxiliary back in the early 1930s, but the Brotherhood refused to admit black workers until 1939 and continued to deny African Americans an equal say in union affairs. Each auxiliary was subservient to a white-led local, and black activists could do little more than carry dues and complaints to the white Brotherhood officers. "If you had a little grievance, they might handle it or not." Le Roy later recalled. "But there were no basic laws of guaranteeing anything from oppression or anything else." AFL and Brotherhood leaders at the national level perennially promised equal treatment, but it was only "lip service," LeRoy added. In reality, black workers could not even attend the Brotherhood's all-white conventions. In 1947, LeRoy and another longtime black member managed to present a resolution in absentia at the union's national convention in San Francisco that called for the elimination of race bars within the union. The white delegates ended up passing a revised version of the measure but still did not implement any changes at the worksite. Although LeRoy and his black colleagues remained confined to a second-class auxiliary, they viewed the passage of the resolution as a hard-won victory and a building block for the future.[43]

While each of these battles produced partial victories at best, they nonetheless helped to create a powerful movement culture in Houston's Third and Fifth Wards. Civil rights unionists had already broken open the political system, and they were in the thick of a protracted battle for access to higher education. Although progress was slow, they remained hopeful that they could also upend the many-decades-old barriers to economic opportunity. The sky was the limit.

Nowhere was this sense of optimism and progress clearer than in the case of Freeman Everett, the leader of the all-black longshoremen and hod carriers unions on the Houston waterfront. After a decades-long fight, black stevedores in ILA Local 872 had, by the 1940s, won half of the work coming through the Bayou City's bustling port. The backbreaking task of loading and unloading ships by hand offered the highest wages available to unskilled African Americans, but work remained sporadic, even during the labor shortages wrought by World War II. Black dockworkers responded by banding together to form the all-black Hod Carriers and Common Laborers Local 18, a union aimed at winning representation and wages for general unskilled construction jobs. Everett joined his fellow members in alternating between work on the docks and jobs in construction, so it made sense that he served as president of both Local 872 and Local 18.[44]

Everett soon became the most recognizable black labor leader in Texas in the 1940s, thanks to the concerted efforts of a statewide caucus of African American civil rights unionists. In 1946, Everett and other black delegates at the annual convention of the Texas State Federation of Labor (TSFL) in

Houston sponsored a resolution calling on the state labor body to appoint or elect a "Negro Vice-President at large and two organizers." The measure passed, but no action was taken.[45] A year later, the African American delegates to the TSFL convention at the Baker Hotel in Dallas were stopped at the door by the bellman, who refused to admit them through the building's front door. They gained access to the building lobby only when accompanied by a white TSFL official, who met the black men at the door on each day of the convention. Once inside, they proposed a constitutional revision that would create the post of twelfth vice president specifically for the election of the "Negro Vice-President at large," piggy-backing on the federation's earlier creation of an eleventh vice president for a white woman officer. The measure encountered fierce resistance and went down to defeat before being resurrected and passed in the final moments of the convention. Still, a motion to fill the newly created position was ruled out of order as the meeting adjourned.[46]

The real breakthrough came the following year, 1948, at the TSFL convention in Fort Worth. In the intervening months, twenty-five to thirty leaders of the ILA, the Hod Carriers, and other black unions from across Texas assembled and decided to walk out of the upcoming convention if they, as one member put it, "couldn't get into the hotels like any other delegate." Fort Worth's Texas Hotel again barred the men from entering through the front door, so they entered through a clean freight elevator around the back of the building, registered for the conference, and then retired to a nearby barber college for their own rump convention. They christened their group the Texas Federation Club (TFC), elected their own officers, resolved to boycott the remainder of the official TSFL gathering, and decided that they "would protest to the national [AFL] if this situation wasn't alleviated and something done about it real quick." A white TSFL official arranged to again escort the black delegates through the hotel lobby, but the newly emboldened TFC leaders refused to enter. So the two conventions continued to meet, separated by a few blocks, but connected by a courier service that ran messages between the hotel and the rump caucus.[47]

With the TFC members still outside, white delegates inside the TSFL convention debated the federation's racial future. A delegate from the ILA's white Houston Local 1273—which shared the work with black Local 872—stood to speak in support of the black delegates. "We are in a position that probably most of you people are not in," he said. "We have hundreds of good union colored men working on the same job we are every day. We learned a lesson a few years ago, that somebody's got to learn in Texas sooner or later. If we can't bring the colored worker up to us, he's sure going to hold us down to him." He urged the delegates to appoint Everett as the state federation's twelfth vice president, and Everett was soon elected by acclamation.[48] A subsequent row forced the white delegates to pass a resolution guaranteeing that the federation would only meet in hotels that provided nondiscriminatory "seating and servicing" for black delegates. As the meeting came to a close, Freeman Everett arrived on the convention floor, received a badge and credentials as Vice-President, and pledged to use his office to expand the federation's black membership.[49]

The dramatic actions of the black delegates over several years—their first resolutions, the rump convention, the formation of the Texas Federation Club, and the election of the TSFL's first black vice president—won them a degree of formal recognition that for the first time mirrored their presence on the ground. The all-black unions had secured an unparalleled degree of power at the worksite that in turn produced grudging acceptance among white unionists at work and at the highest levels of union governance. To be sure, such awareness of their demands did not immediately produce equal employment opportunities, but for the first time, the needs of black workers could no longer be ignored. And within Houston, Everett's Locals 872 and 18 would remain powerful bastions of "civil rights unionism" for decades to come.

The emerging movement culture in the Bayou City even, at times, led to new understandings of the role of women in American society. For example, Rannie Cook entered the broader movement by way of the National Alliance of Postal Employees (NAPE). Like Heman Sweatt, she worked at the post office and became active through the union's grievance procedure. After serving as a clerk during the war, Cook was dismissed following constant fighting with her white boss. She attempted to get her job back through the union but failed because she was classified as a temporary employee. Still, the experience made her an even more vocal advocate for her coworkers, culminating in her election to the presidency of the local ladies' auxiliary to the NAPE by 1947.[50] Active participation in the NAPE also led Cook into NAACP. She soon joined Mrs. Erma LeRoy as an officer of the Houston branch and attended the conventions of the state conference in 1947 and 1948. She became active in the chapter's membership campaign, was elected at least twice to its board, and served as acting secretary of the state conference's board of directors.[51] Cook also contributed as an organic intellectual of the movement. In addition to her work in the NAPE and the NAACP, Cook opened a small book and gift shop on Lyons Avenue, in the heart of the working-class Fifth Ward. The store remained more of a lending library than a for-profit enterprise. Texts included pamphlets on fair employment and civil rights produced by the CIO, the FEPC and other federal government agencies, and the NAACP. Readers likely would have also found copies of the *Postal Alliance*, the official organ of NAPE; the NAACP's *Crisis*; and the *Informer* and other black newspapers.[52]

Like Lulu White and Mrs. LeRoy, Cook engaged in a surprisingly high level of activism for a married woman of any race in the 1940s. Yet her own words on the role of women in the fight for racial and economic justice prove even more enlightening. As president of the local ladies' auxiliary to NAPE in 1947, Cook also served as a member of the executive committee of the national women's body within the union and as a diplomat to Houston's Alliance men. In a speech titled "What We, As Women, Owe to Our Group," Cook calls on the wives and daughters of postal workers to become better informed and to become advocates for NAPE members and all black people. "Until we become integrated into the scope of this political situation as to how it affects you, me, and my next door neighbor, we can not hope to survive," she wrote. Presenting a bold vision for black women's role in the civil rights unionist movement, she asked, "What can we do? Incorporate ourselves with militant organizations such as the NAACP. Come in to the Auxiliary to the NAPE. Cease to feel that darning socks and baking a pie constitutes being a good wife. . . . Our men need support, [and] we as fighting women can give it to him [sic] in the Auxiliary to the NAPE. Come out and hear the program."[53]

Working-class women like Rannie Cook and Mrs. Erma LeRoy are often absent in the historical record. Their voices prove even more elusive. Cook's plea combines motherly concern for family with militant advocacy for the race. Although she operates within the "separate sphere" reserved for women in the period, she does so as a radical proto-feminist. Her words shed light on the profound and diverse implications of the movement. While the struggle prioritized issues of race and class, it also created space for new discussions about gender. To be sure, black women's activism was not new. But Cook's statement highlights the radical connections being made among working-class women of color who became politicized during the heightened labor and civil rights uprisings of the 1930s and 1940s.

Overall, civil rights unionists could count a number of key victories during and immediately after the war. Despite the limitations of the FEPC and their failure to extend it, many black workers had taken advantage of wartime labor shortages and federal interventions to win raises and move up the occupational ladder, however slightly. The union movement had grown substantially, and black labor activists played critical roles in helping Lulu White expand the NAACP's membership and purview. The *Grovey*, *Hasgett*, and *Smith* cases had won them the right to vote, and *Sweatt* now gave them hope that school integration was on the horizon. For African American workers like Moses LeRoy, times had clearly changed since the dark days of the city's 1917 race riots. Expectations had skyrocketed during the war, and the movement had emboldened them to think that change was indeed possible. Freeman Everett had won a foothold for black workers in the staid TSFL. Women like Lulu White, Mrs. LeRoy, and Rannie Cook were taking on new leadership roles, and civil rights unionists were fostering a movement culture that percolated deep into black Houston. Although optimism abounded, an imminent conservative turn in national and state politics would soon threaten many of the activists' gains. More immediately, the challenge of wielding the vote would prove even more difficult than the battle to win it.

Erma LeRoy and the Progressive Party Challenge

For Moses and Erma LeRoy, the struggles for economic improvement, racial advancement, and political power remained inextricably intertwined. Upon learning of his reelection to the chapter's executive board in December 1946, Moses LeRoy wrote a rare letter to "My Dear Mrs. White." In one of the few documents in which his writing has survived, LeRoy accepted the position and added his thoughts on the challenges ahead. "Being constantly aware of the impending crisis threatening the masses and minority groups of all races, a problem to which I am gravely concerned," he wrote, "I hereby pledge myself to the aggressive task of this vital and noble responsibility." Service in the NAACP did not represent service only to African Americans, he suggested. Rather, he was committed to "the masses and minority groups of all races" and thus, to building coalitions across racial lines.[54]

Nowhere was this truer than in the political arena. In the first national primary elections following *Smith* in 1946, African Americans across the South organized to vote as a bloc, often for the first time since the end of Reconstruction. Conservative white Democrats pulled out all the stops, intimidating would-be voters from registering, exacting economic reprisals against African Americans who successfully added their names to the rolls, and, when all else failed, threatening violent retaliation. Such "paramilitary politics" had been a regular feature of electoral life from the Civil War on, and black voters after *Smith* knew all too well that extrajudicial factors could resurface at any time. As one leading Houston newspaper declared, "blood would flow in the streets" if African Americans attempted to vote after *Smith*. "Blacks were afraid," Moses LeRoy recalled. Members of his union planned to go vote after work, but "that article was haunting them." LeRoy accepted his "vital and noble responsibility" and ran for precinct judge in Box (Precinct) 47, at the Breckenridge School. He encouraged his coworkers to stare down what he hoped was an empty threat. They did so, casting their ballots without incident, and LeRoy garnered what he thought were enough votes to make him the new precinct judge. Yet he brought no election observers with him to the polling place, and a white family that had long run the mixed-race precinct for the Democratic Party announced that he had lost. He believed that some of the paper ballots supporting him had been stolen but had no way of proving it. Meanwhile, in neighboring Precinct 48, African Americans turned out en masse and helped to sway a tight local election. NAACP activist, CIO organizer, and barber George Nelson recalled, "Not only did we vote, but we had the biggest precinct in the state out there in Fifth Ward.... My brothers and sisters out there voted all day and half the night."⁵⁵

The sizable turnout notwithstanding, the LeRoys, Lulu White, and other black activists chafed at their ongoing exclusion from the local Democratic Party, as state and national political developments left them further estranged from the party of Roosevelt. Historian George N. Green writes that, beginning in 1938, the state Democratic Party split between New Deal liberals such as Maury Maverick and conservatives that represented the "Establishment," an uneasy alliance of oil barons and related industrialists, flamboyant ideologue candidates, and local-level elites. The "primitive years" of Establishment dominance commenced when W. Lee "Pappy" O'Daniel of Fort Worth used his "Pass the Biscuits, Pappy" radio program to pose as a populist through a remarkable four successful statewide races in as many years (1938–42). As governor in 1941, O'Daniel pushed for and signed the Anti-Violence Act, a law that made conflicts on picket lines or threats against scabs punishable as felony offences. He then abandoned his post to fill a vacant seat in the U.S. Senate, defeating in the primary then-congressman Lyndon B. Johnson, a moderate who was at the time identified as a supporter of the New Deal. Already distinguished as an enemy of labor, "Pappy" as senator now made it clear that he would not support the permanent FEPC bill nor the other demands of the civil rights movement.

Back in Texas, the Establishment continued its reign largely unabated. In 1946, following the *Smith* decision, most African Americans threw their support to New Dealer Homer Rainey, a former president of the University of Texas and renowned civil libertarian. Again, the Establishment cruised to victory. Rainey garnered only 25 percent of the vote in the first Democratic primary and then lost the runoff to an Establishment conservative by a two-to-one margin. The Rainey campaign represented a breakthrough for the black vote, but it also signaled the ongoing dominance of white supremacist oligarchs in the state party. In 1947, the legislature responded to the postwar upheavals in the steel, auto, and other basic industries by expanding upon the O'Daniel Anti-Violence Act and passing nine additional antilabor laws. One prohibited mass picketing, a practice it defined as two pickets standing within fifty feet of one another.⁵⁶

The tenor of the Democratic Party in Washington was not much better for civil rights unionists. In 1947, Congress overrode President Truman's veto of the Taft-Hartley Act, a bill that gutted labor's "magna carta," the Wagner Act, and replaced it with what union activists called a "slave-labor bill." Taft-Hartley outlawed a range of tactics that unions had used successfully since

1935, including the sit-down strike and mass picketing. It also allowed states to pass right-to-work laws, legislation that allowed workers to avoid paying union dues or joining the union at their workplaces even as they enjoyed the benefits of union representation. It also required union officers to sign affidavits pledging that they were not members of the Communist Party, a provision that then led to the mass purging of radicals and suspected radicals from the labor movement. While the Wagner Act had protected workers from employer reprisals, Taft-Hartley tipped the industrial relations balance decisively in favor of the bosses.[57] A year later, in 1948, Truman added insult to injury when he sent a watered-down civil rights bill to Congress that did not include a revived FEPC. Although civil rights activists considered it woefully inadequate, the president's weak legislation still died in the Senate, falling victim to a filibuster by southern conservatives such as O'Daniel.[58]

Truman's failure to defeat Taft-Hartley and his slow progress on civil rights led many African American activists and leftist whites nationwide to abandon the president during his reelection bid in 1948. Houston's civil rights unionists reacted not only to the onslaught of antilabor legislation and the inaction regarding Jim Crow at the federal level but also rose up in opposition to the intransigence of Establishment Democrats and the "Dixiecrat" rebellion brewing in Texas and across the South that spring. The LeRoys, Lulu White, and other activists "took a leave of absence from the Democratic Party and helped to blow life into the Progressive Party movement in this country," as Moses later put it. "We brought Henry Wallace along, the great vice-president of Roosevelt," he continued. A former secretary of agriculture, Wallace had served as the nation's vice president during FDR's third term, from 1941 to 1945, but he had been dropped from the ticket in 1944 in favor of Truman. Wallace was then appointed secretary of commerce, but Truman fired him after Roosevelt's death because Wallace advocated a "century of the common man" and world peace through rapprochement with the Soviet Union. By 1948, Wallace had become the standard-bearer for the left wings of the labor and civil rights movements, emerging as the presidential nominee of their new third party. For activists in Houston, Wallace brought a fresh perspective that forever changed the political landscape. LeRoy recalled that Wallace declared, "'Down with segregation! Down with racism!'" The contrast between the integrationist stand of Wallace's Progressive Party and the decades of obstructionism and exclusion at the hands of the Democratic Party in Texas could not have been clearer.[59]

The Progressive Party of Texas drew heavily upon networks the NAACP and black union activists had long worked to establish. At an organizational meeting in Austin on March 21, 1948, the multiracial Committee to Get Wallace on the Ballot in Texas elected a slate of officers that included Lulu

White as one of several vice chairmen. Leftist Houston labor lawyer Herman Wright served as the group's leader, while Austin writer and deposed professor J. Frank Dobie was elected honorary chairman. Wright's law partner, Arthur Mandell, and Harry Koger, a union organizer who succeeded George Lambert in the pecan shellers union in San Antonio, also served on the executive committee.[60] In late April, the statewide Progressive Party held its founding convention in Houston. San Antonio NAACP leader John Inman, a key leader along with G. J. Sutton in the Maverick mayoral campaign, was elected the party's chairman in the state's twenty-sixth senate district.[61] LeRoy credited the Progressive Party with holding the first integrated political meetings in the South. While his observation may be overstated, it still suggests the unprecedented nature of independent black participation in electoral politics in Texas. When Wallace visited the city for two days in late September, white mobs protested the interracial gatherings, hurled eggs at the candidate, and nearly forced him out of town with additional violence. By contrast, Lulu White held a tea for Wallace at her home, featuring the radical black actor and singer Paul Robeson. The party's slate for state offices was likewise integrated: the white attorney Wright stood for governor, while a black minister from Dallas ran as his lieutenant.[62]

The campaign proved energizing for many local civil rights unionists. After being denied control of Precinct 47 in the Democratic primary two years earlier, LeRoy now eagerly served as the precinct captain for the Progressive Party, heeding the party's call to organize black voters in his immediate neighborhood. Years later, he fondly recalled meeting Wallace personally. Around the same time, LeRoy was elected chairman of his union's legislative committee, a post that took him to a statewide meeting of mostly white Brotherhood members in Fort Worth and also led to an exchange of letters with his congressman, probably for the first time.[63] For her part, NAPE women's auxiliary leader Rannie Cook became the captain for the all-important black Precinct 48, and her name appeared on the ballot as one of the party's electors (she would cast one of its votes in the electoral college if Wallace were to carry Texas). Sidney Hasgett, one of the white primary plaintiffs, also appeared on a list of the party's supporters. Early gatherings were small but inspiring. Cook scribbled on a blank party form that Houston's Progressive Party campaign "reminds me of the beginners meeting of the NAACP—100 members."[64]

Despite such optimistic enthusiasm, the Progressive Party ultimately succumbed to the Democratic juggernaut in Texas and across the country. Wallace polled just under 2.4 percent of the national popular vote and failed to carry a single state. In Texas, the party won less than four thousand votes—less than one-half of 1 percent. At best, he may have competed in a handful of mixed-race precincts in Houston, but Truman easily carried the biggest black box, number 48.⁶⁵ In the final months of the campaign, Truman's camp won the endorsement of the national CIO, whose leaders worked tirelessly to bring rank-and-file union members back into the president's fold.⁶⁶ The national NAACP and African Americans nationwide likewise abandoned the Progressive challenger and rallied behind the president after Truman desegregated the military, commissioned a high-profile report on civil rights, and oversaw the inclusion of the best civil rights plank yet seen within the Democratic Party's official platform. The right-wing challenge of Dixiecrats in the States Rights Party led by Strom Thurmond of South Carolina doubtlessly compelled many white liberals and moderate Democrats to rally behind the president as well.⁶⁷

Outnumbered both nationally and locally, LeRoy and many other black Houstonians stuck with Wallace to the bitter end. On November 12, ten days after the election, LeRoy wrote a form letter thanking Progressive Party supporters for their "most sincere, [important], and untiring stand in the interest of and on behalf of social justice, equality of opportunity, and freedom for all men everywhere." Even in defeat, LeRoy remained optimistic: "In my opinion the New Party is by no means dissolved. We shall ever continue to fight for the ideas for which we deem right and just."⁶⁸

Although LeRoy's prediction about the party's future proved incorrect, the transformative effect of the Progressive movement on both grassroots black activists and future Democratic Party leaders remains clear. LeRoy later recalled that the third-party challenge "broke the gentlemen's agreement between the other parties" that they would remain lily-white. Whereas the Democrats and Republicans had both excluded African Americans for decades, the left-wing challenge to Truman forced the remaining white Democrats in Texas to recognize the power of the black vote and, over time, to seek the support of black voters. As LeRoy put it, "They began to holler 'Me too!' So if there's any liberality among either one of the parties, it's because of the frontal attack we made on them."⁶⁹

In the nearer term, the insurgent political movement continued. In a January 1949 nonpartisan special election, Mrs. Erma LeRoy ran for a vacant seat in the Texas House of Representatives, appearing on a ticket alongside Virginia L. Bell, who stood for a seat in the state senate. One black, the other white, both women maintained close ties to labor and the Progressive Party. The city's civil rights unionists represented their base, and other Progressive Party activists likely provided the nucleus of their field operation. Surviving literature from the campaign spelled out its platform without ambiguity: "You voted against Taft Hartley because that law was weakening your union," yet that fight "will be meaningless unless you also vote to kill the nine Texas anti-labor laws because they are each little Taft Hartleys." Only LeRoy and Bell "are pledged to the complete repeal of these laws."

Mrs. Erma DeLoney LeRoy, perhaps the first African American woman to seek a seat in the Texas legislature, photographed circa 1960 when she began serving as a special political representative for the Texas AFL-CIO. Courtesy Photographic Archives [Labor Collections], Special Collections, The University of Texas at Arlington Library, Arlington, Texas, PA-48-Leaders.

Both candidates broke from the custom of women appearing as political figures only in support of their husbands and instead ran on their own merits. Additionally, Mrs. LeRoy's candidacy likely represented the first bid for office by an African American woman in Texas as well as one of the earliest attempts by a black person to gain a seat in the Texas legislature in the twentieth century. LeRoy's run came less than five years after the fall of the white primary and more than a decade before Barbara Jordan first stood for office. At most, the duo carried a few precincts, and neither finished among the top contenders in crowded fields containing twenty candidates in each race. Still, their very presence underscores the lasting effects of the Progressive Party challenge.[70]

Nationwide, the Wallace campaign represented what one historian called the "high point and demise" of the civil rights unionist movement.[71] Still, although reactionary politicians were gaining power and the Red Scare was gaining steam across the country, the movement's eventual decline was not yet on the minds of most Houston activists as the 1940s came to a close. In fact, the local NAACP and the larger movement instead celebrated another signal victory in June 1950, when the U.S. Supreme Court ruled unanimously in favor of the plaintiffs in *Sweatt*, ordering the University of Texas to admit the letter carrier and union activist to its all-white law school. The court did not immediately overturn "separate but equal," but in *Sweatt* and two other cases it called out one of the central lies of Jim Crow by demanding that southern states create truly equal facilities for African Americans or face mandated integration. Civil rights activists across America rejoiced. "I think it is a milestone in the progress of applied democracy," Sweatt told the *Informer*, adding that he would finally enroll that fall.[72] For their part, Moses and Erma LeRoy must have gained some satisfaction that they had answered Professor Logan's call to contribute to the struggle for "a people's peace" at home and abroad.

New migrants to the boomtown of Houston in the first decades of the twentieth century, African American workers had gained a foothold in the city's industry and then in its social and political life by the 1940s. They gradually came to wield more influence within the labor movement, on the shop floor, and in their communities. Moses and Erma LeRoy, Rannie Cook, R. R. Grovey, Sidney Hasgett, George Nelson, Heman Sweatt, and countless others all helped Lulu White build a dynamic, militant branch of the NAACP and a larger civil rights unionist movement dedicated to the dual struggles for racial and economic justice. Lulu White, Mrs. LeRoy, and Rannie Cook all extended by example the role of women in American civic life. With its victory in *Smith v. Allright*, the movement destroyed the all-white Democratic primary, while the interracial Progressive Party challenge of 1948 forced the Democrats to finally open their doors to black voters. The movement in Houston won another crowning victory when *Sweatt* brought parity and limited integration to higher education and, in so doing, laid the groundwork for future campaigns aimed at the primary and secondary schools. Although there had been notable setbacks as well, as the 1940s came to a close there remained reason for hope among those who sought to bring democracy to the Bayou City and the Lone Star State.

The importance of winning the vote can hardly be overstated. Voting represented and continues to reflect the most important right in a democratic society. Without it, African Americans would be forever dependent on the charity of paternalistic white benefactors. The system of Jim Crow could be softened around its edges, but without the black vote, it could never be defeated. The vote held the promise, however elusive, that a fundamental shift in race relations might take place. For the first time, African Americans could speak for themselves in the electoral arena. The optimists among them believed that, with careful organization, they could exert real power in proportion to their numbers. Everything else would flow from there. Improved schools, equal access, and, above all, better jobs—all of these goals now appeared attainable through exercising the vote. The extension of the franchise to African Americans also renewed hope that America might be absolved of slavery, one of its original sins. The winning of the vote gave the nation a chance to truly fulfill its democratic creed. More immediately, it also offered white workers and *mexicanos* the possibility that their voices would be heard as well.

The multiracial working class of urban Texas had risen, stumbled, won, lost, and gone sideways. When all the tumult ended, one legacy was crystal clear: politics would never be the same. The white supremacist distribution of power, the Jim Crow hierarchies of race and labor, and even the relationship between men and women were all up in the air. African Americans had won the franchise, *mexicanos* had begun to organize independently of the *patrones*, and even white workers had started to discover the liberalizing effects of trade unionism. State Democratic Party leaders, like municipal politicians before them, took notice. Not since the Socialist Party that flourished prior to World War I had the white conservative domination of local and state politics been so fundamentally challenged. Now working people across Texas were on the march, joining unions, civil rights organizations, and neighborhood political campaigns. A hint of autonomous multiracial collaboration was evident in San Antonio, and interracial alliances had likewise bolstered the movement in Houston.

All this progress notwithstanding, Texas remained a far from democratic place. Most working people—whether they were black, brown, or white—still struggled to make ends meet. The prospects for improving their economic conditions remained dim. Very few went to the polls on Election Day. Despite the powerful challenges levied by civil rights and labor activists in the urban areas, white elites continued to dominate at both the municipal and state levels. The existing power relations of the 1920s had not been drastically altered. For organizers like Moses and Erma LeRoy of Houston, G. J. Sutton of San Antonio, and the omnipresent George and Latane Lambert, the struggle was nowhere near over. Each of them had, as a Hill Country rancher might say, "earned his spurs" in the labor and political campaigns of the Great Depression and World War II. What the future would hold was anybody's guess. But whether they knew it or not, the seeds of a larger struggle for democracy in Texas had already been planted.

Chapter 3

Forcing Us Together in Self-Defense

The Cold War, the Black Vote, and the Liberal Movement

On January 17, 1949, four African American men, led by barber and union organizer George T. "Pop" Nelson, convened a meeting at First Shiloh Baptist Church in Houston's working-class Fifth Ward. Organizers of the steel workers and laborers unions joined him in issuing the call, as did other NAACP, neighborhood, and union activists. Railroad worker Moses LeRoy came to the gathering, along with the president of his local union. Julius White and several of the city's leading black businessmen also attended, as did a group of upwardly mobile entrepreneurs who desired more influence in civic affairs.

On this Monday evening, the businessmen, well-dressed as always, and the labor leaders, clad in their Sunday best, filed in side-by-side to the church's hallowed sanctuary, their dark suits and ties spotting the vast hall's glossy cherrywood pews. These magnates, shopkeepers, and blue-collar workers had little in common besides their skin tone and a desire to do something to confront the indignities of Jim Crow.

Nine days earlier, Mrs. Erma LeRoy had run unsuccessfully for a seat in the state legislature. From this, and the several previous elections, the assembled men had learned that much remained to be done to unify the city's newly enfranchised black citizens. Despite their disagreements over strategy and tactics and their divisions along class lines, they resolved to bury their differences and form an alliance of community organizations that could advance the race through political action. They envisioned it as the electoral wing of the NAACP, a new body that could bring power and services to their overlooked neighborhoods. As the group's subsequent leaders would put it, it would "usher in economic stability, educational opportunity and political progress for all people in the African American community." They settled on a name that emphasized its function as a coalition while masking its mission of racial uplift: the Harris County Council of Organizations (HCCO).[1] By the end of the 1950s, the HCCO would become a force to be reckoned with in local and even state politics.

At the same time, the group's rise in stature coincided with the growth of two similar organizations: one, a group of white liberals who came together in the Harris County Democrats (HCD), the other, a small cadre of Mexican American professionals and union men who formed the Civic Action

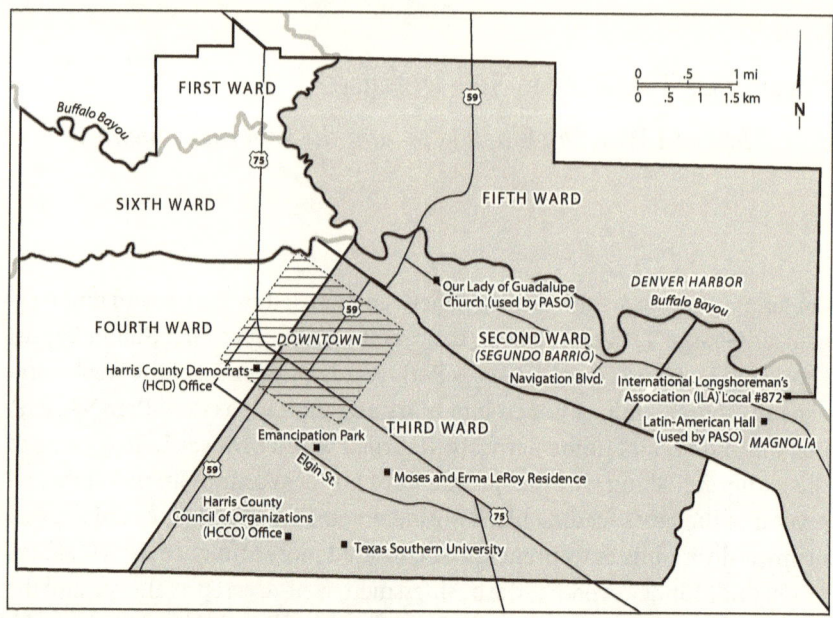

Houston neighborhoods and landmarks

Committee (CAC). The leaders of these groups believed that they, like the men of the HCCO, lacked a voice in the city's and the state's electoral affairs. They too needed new ways to unify and mobilize the people they represented, and they considered politics a means to an end rather than an end in itself. White liberals believed they were duty bound to use the resources of government for the betterment of all, that the oligarchy that had long dominated Texas politics had left all of the state's citizens impoverished. They sought to organize what they called simply "the liberal movement" in Houston and beyond. The Mexican American men of CAC agreed with the liberals' premise, but they also hoped to use politics to uplift their community by bringing new representation, power, and services to the city's scattered barrios. The three groups had only sporadic contact with one another throughout the decade, but each of them separately identified, organized, and consolidated their bases. Dramatic moments were rare and fleeting, but the daily "spadework" of organizing proved more than enough to occupy the city's black, brown, and white activists.[2]

The new organizations tackled their work in a radically altered context. The chill of the Cold War destroyed some of the new unions, and many of those that survived only managed to limp along. Communists and other radicals, who had proven themselves steady allies of African American and Mexican American working people from San Antonio to Houston, struggled to prove their patriotism and faced repression that drove them either underground or completely out of public life. The Ku Klux Klan began to ride again, and the defenders of white supremacy spread the word that the twin dangers of the Red Menace and civil rights threatened to topple the American way of life. When verbal intimidation failed, physical terror and legal injunctions served as effective tools to thwart black and brown ambition. Even white workers found their modest aspirations curtailed. Their unions made little headway in politics, new organizing was near impossible, and even small strikes became protracted struggles. Across Texas, civil rights unionists experienced the emerging Cold War like a noose slowly tightening around their necks.

Still, rather than retreat, veteran activists responded to this repression by redirecting their activism into new channels, often in the electoral arena. Black and brown political cultures in the postwar period remained far from moribund—in fact, they flourished, and they did so in conversation with one another and with white labor and liberal activists. African American and Mexican American organizers each experimented with different tactics and separately learned from both their victories and mistakes. Working from distinct bases, organizing in distant neighborhoods, and following their own leaders, black and brown activists developed not one but two civil rights movements, each of which linked the struggles for racial uplift with broader demands for economic justice and real political power. Although they appeared to have similar aims, the two movements pursued different agendas and remained separate even as they developed in tandem and even, at times, collaborated. Disagreements remained, but by the close of the 1950s, new forms of multi-racial alliances would gradually begin to take hold. Mutual suspicion would slowly give way to mutual trust.

The Cold War clearly took its toll on the civil rights unionist movement of the 1940s, but what would emerge in its place—quietly, and below the radar—was a trio of new institutions that would lay the foundation for a new wave of upheaval, not just in Houston but all across the state.

The Cold War on Labor and Civil Rights

The demise of the Progressive Party of Houston represented just one aspect of a larger trend in which the space for militant labor, civil rights, and political activism rapidly narrowed after World War II. The passage of the O'Daniel Anti-Violence Act prohibited mass picketing, the national Taft-Hartley Act ushered in the antiunion "right-to-work" epoch, and the nine "little Taft-Hartleys" passed subsequently by the Texas legislature imposed one of the most restrictive legal regimes in the nation. To make matters worse, the leaders of both organized labor and the black civil rights movement turned against some of their most militant members, including many effective, longtime organizers who may (or may not) have been sympathetic to the Communist Party. By the time the Red Scare was finished, the wartime civil rights unionist movement would be unrecognizable—even as many radical activists rededicated themselves to the struggle for the long haul.

Labor's purge of suspected radicals commenced even before the war was over. Since the founding of the Texas State CIO Council in 1937, organizers and local union leaders of various radical political persuasions had worked side by side, subsuming any sectarian agendas in service of a larger movement. The pecan shellers union had included countless Socialists, Communists, and other radicals, but all had focused their energies on aiding the indigenous *mexicano* uprising on San Antonio's West Side. Likewise in Houston, a handful of radicals joined the ranks of the National Maritime Union (NMU) and a few locals of the oil and steel workers unions, but their political persuasions generally remained subordinate to the larger struggle to organize new factories. Over time, however, a growing anti-Communist faction within the statewide labor federation grew suspicious of their Pink and Red counterparts. The need to rally together around the war effort delayed the reckoning, but with fascism on its heels in 1945, the anti-Communist forces came together and purged their radical colleagues from the leadership of the state council, completing the process some five years before the national CIO expelled its radical wing.

The removal of radical activists from the movement had a devastating effect. One of the principal recipients of the anti-Communists' wrath was Arthur Mandell, the Jewish labor lawyer, NAACP member, and Progressive Party officer who had become one of Lulu White's close friends and allies during and after the war. Believing that Mandell was one of the "pro-Communist" faction's ringleaders, the new anti-Communist leadership balked at paying his fees. Mandell, a longtime counsel for several oil worker locals and other unions, was effectively blacklisted, despite the fact that he had recently won a U.S. Supreme Court case overturning one of the nine despised Texas antilabor laws. Herman Wright also lost his labor clients after serving as the Progressive Party's candidate for governor, an act that made him a Communist in the eyes of most union leaders. Even the founding head of the Texas CIO Council was ensnared in the factional dispute, despite the fact that he too was not a Communist Party member. Distraught, he suffered a nervous breakdown and was confined to a state veterans' hospital, where he died soon thereafter. His successor, also not a Communist, still drew the anti-Communists' ire before suffering an industrial accident that "almost completely incapacitated him." He retired to his brother's farm in Mississippi and was never heard from again.[3]

The industrial unions continued to grow, for a time, but they did so having lost one critical source of their dynamism. After the war, the national CIO launched "Operation Dixie," an ambitious drive to organize the South in which Texas would play a leading role. While the campaign sputtered in the textile industry, it provided critical assistance to unionization efforts in the oil, steel, and related industries along the Gulf Coast. With the simultaneous organization of aerospace and auto workers and the affiliation to the CIO of the former company union of Southwestern Bell telephone workers, the Texas State CIO Council grew from a low point in 1946 of 31,410 members in 84 affiliated local unions to nearly 56,000 members in twice as many locals by 1950 and nearly 86,000 affiliated members by 1954. By that year, total CIO membership in the state hovered somewhere above 100,000. The AFL in Texas counted about three times that many members, while the independent Railroad Brotherhoods represented a virtually all-union industry. In sum, approximately 20 percent of the nonagricultural labor force in Texas was unionized by 1955, with even more workers covered by union contracts in the "right-to-work" state.[4]

Yet without the leftist commitment to racial justice, the leaders of Operation Dixie made the calculated decision to downplay race to avoid the Red- and black-baiting that integrated unions often provoked among white southerners. Texas labor leaders followed suit and focused most of their postwar organizing efforts on the unionization of white workers. The strategy backfired. The refusal to tackle Jim Crow dampened the enthusiasm of many black workers, who for the past decade had proven themselves the most committed advocates of unionism in the region. At the same time, employer propaganda convinced white workers that the unions promised integration and the end of their special privileges in the labor market. Operation Dixie sputtered in the predominately white textile industry and failed to hold back aggressive employer offensives in tobacco, rubber, and other leading southern enterprises. In Texas, the unions won recognition and new contracts and grew into the postwar era, but they did so with a predominately white membership with little commitment to racial justice on the shop floor. For their part, most black and brown workers were simply left out in the cold. Many continued to labor in agriculture or domestic work, both fields excluded from the collective bargaining rights guaranteed by the Wagner Act. Some of the oil refinery unions took baby steps toward meaningful integration by the late 1950s, but technological change undermined even their modest efforts. Most nonwhite industrial workers remained confined to the dirtiest, most dangerous, poorest-paid jobs—union or no union.[5]

One exception to the general rule of lily-white, anti-Communist union leadership was the United Packinghouse Workers of America (UPWA), based in Fort Worth. There the union developed a radical multiracial alternative to postwar business unionism, but it too was undermined by a toxic mixture of anticommunism and white supremacy. During their organizing drives soon after the war, the UPWA meatpacking locals had depended upon the strategic location and stalwart support of black workers on the killing floors. The Texas unions were still directed by a mostly white leadership, but dictates from the UPWA's national headquarters in Chicago, combined with aggressive organizing by local black and brown workers, resulted in significant power sharing among all racial groups. One black worker served as the union's delegate to the Texas State CIO Council and even became a vice president of that body. In 1952, following a directive from the national union, Armour & Company desegregated its shop floor, prompting a walkout of conservative white workers followed by a tense union meeting in which both sides were heavily armed. Black, brown, and white liberal union members responded to the conflict by forming an Anti-Discrimination Committee that organized over two years and successfully replaced the union's local and district officers with a new, multiracial slate. In 1954, Mary Salinas, a Mexican American woman, ascended to the presidency of the Armour local, and George Thomas, a black man, became the director of the UPWA's four-state southwestern district. The local and district unions then recommitted to the fight for civil rights, joining the national UPWA as exemplars of social unionism at the height of the Cold War.

Yet the story doesn't end there. Jilted former leaders of the local and district union bodies appealed first to a disgruntled national officer and then to the national CIO, claiming that the transition in leadership stemmed from Communist influences in the UPWA at all levels. Months of investigations ultimately uncovered no Reds in the union's ranks, but the UPWA's commitment to interracial democracy branded it as sufficiently Pink to warrant distrust in Jim Crow Texas. The state NAACP expressed concern about alleged Communist domination of the union, a stance that cut off the association from a potentially large membership base with substantial financial resources. Worse, the cowboys in the all-white Stock Handlers Union No. 59 led the charge as locals across the district disaffiliated from the UPWA in protest. District director Thomas charged that the unions' defection stemmed more from racial resentment than Red politics, and he successfully rallied black workers at the sugar refinery locals in Louisiana and Southeast Texas to prevent a wholesale flight from the union in the region. In contrast, the Armour local in Fort Worth remained a stalwart supporter of Thomas and an example of multiracial shop-floor democracy, aided by the support of the national union in Chicago. Civil rights unionism flourished at Armour and in the district office into the 1960s. But the damage had been done. Unionists across the state learned by the UPWA's example that if they moved too fast on the race issue, they would be branded as Communists and forced to fight for their lives as elected leaders. Most white unionists instead decided to walk a tightrope in which they feigned minimal compliance with national equal opportunity directives but conceded only gradual changes to the traditional patterns of discrimination on the shop floor. Even the most liberal among them blamed the deeply ingrained prejudices of their white rank-and-file memberships for their own inaction.[6]

Texas labor leaders did not entirely abandon their goal of reaching out to black and Mexican American workers, but the white supremacist anticommunism of the Cold War continued to dictate and narrow the parameters of their overtures. Even the locus of black power in the labor movement—the segregated all-black locals—faced setbacks. After becoming the twelfth vice president of the Texas State Federation of Labor (TSFL), longshoreman Freeman Everett received a stipend from the federation to travel across the state organizing African American workers. In town after town throughout the early 1950s, his efforts were rebuffed. Outside of Corsicana in East Texas, Everett, a silver-tongued orator, was midway through a speech to a group of brick makers when a county sheriff appeared "with one of these big Texas hats on—pistols and sidearms sagging down," as another organizer recalled it. "Which one of you Niggers is Freeman Everett?" the lawman called out. "By God . . . you Niggers from Houston coming up here are causing confusion. . . . Our Niggers are happy. . . . I'm going to take you across town and put you in jail." He took Everett and his companion to his car, drove them to the local lockup, and then, to their surprise, turned them loose. He added, "By God, get you some gas and get in that car, and don't come back up here disturbing our Niggers." Similar incidents befell Everett across the state, until finally the TSFL president pulled his funding for the campaign. In so doing, the TSFL sent a message, however inadvertently, to the state's African Americans. White supremacist violence had won, and labor's commitment to black workers simply faltered. In the cities, most black workers continued to languish in unskilled positions, and those few that paid union dues often lacked representation in union affairs. If black workers wanted to improve their condition, they were going to have to do it themselves, and they would need to look beyond the house of labor.[7]

Electoral politics offered little hope, as the state was plunging ever further rightward after World War II. To be sure, anticommunism wasn't new to Texas politics. East Texas congressman Martin Dies had launched the first iteration of the House Un-American Activities Committee back in 1938, and governor-turned-senator Pappy O'Daniel had flayed the alleged Communist menace in his campaigns throughout the 1940s. Historian George Green suggests that the two demagogues overplayed their hands, prompting the state's business Establishment to back less colorful if no less conservative candidates beginning in 1942. Although Maury Maverick and other liberals managed to keep the Democratic Party in line behind Roosevelt's bid for a third term in 1940, the archconservative "Texas Regulars" bolted the state convention in 1944 and temporarily withheld the state's Electoral College votes from the president, despite the fact that he had carried the popular vote overwhelmingly. Two years later, the Regulars threatened a secession movement before aiding the Establishment's businessmen in defeating the liberal Homer Rainey in the 1946 gubernatorial campaign.

The battle lines were clearly drawn: Rainey, the deposed former president of the University of Texas, continued to face charges from his opponent that he coddled Communists on campus—a charge first levied against him by Dies's committee in 1940. Worse, as African Americans and the CIO rallied behind Rainey, his detractors had little trouble painting him Red. As Green notes, the "three causes—academic freedom, labor union rights, and civil rights" became the focal points of the Establishment's campaign against Rainey. The combination of these causes on the far right became even more apparent in 1948, when the Regulars became the States' Rights Party and fell into line behind Dixiecrat Strom Thurmond. Even among the mainstream conservatives, the inseparable trio would serve as their imaginary enemy for the next decade.[8]

The possibility of a white supremacist backlash in their ranks notwithstanding, the leaders of the Texas State CIO Council attempted to fight the tide of reaction by building political coalitions with other liberal groups in the state, including a handful of black and brown organizations. Back in 1944 the council's leaders had launched the Texas Social and Legislative Conference (TSLC) as a front organization through which its member unions could funnel support from the CIO-PAC to candidates without making them appear too friendly to organized labor. The work of the TSLC quickly evolved beyond participation in elections to include advocacy for pension reform and other broad policy issues as well as lobbying against the onslaught of antiunion legislation after the war. Both sides in the CIO council's internal dispute on the Red issue endorsed the initiative, and the CIO was soon joined by the Railroad Brotherhoods and, briefly, the TSFL. The other major heavyweight in the coalition was the Texas Farmers Union, an association, by the mid-1950s, of some three thousand white liberal yeomen that wielded disproportionate political weight due to the state's still heavily rural population and the overrepresentation of the countryside in the state legislature. At its peak, the coalition counted twenty-one formal affiliates, including the all-black Progressive Voters League (PVL) and the American G.I. Forum (AGIF), an organization of Mexican American veterans. Under the leadership of Marion Storm, the TSLC helped prevent the Dixiecrat takeover of the 1948 state Democratic Convention. Labor leaders agreed that Storm uniquely "had the knack of reconciling the divergent interests and viewpoints of the component organizations making up the Conference, thus welding them into a unified and efficient force."[9]

Still, the TSLC had little to show for its organizing. When Storm died in 1950, the conference fell apart. It continued to lobby for liberal policies, but its voice of protest was a lone one. In 1951, for example, one TSLC leader tried to convince a conservative state senator to withdraw a bill that would make the union shop a violation of state antitrust law. The senator replied that he appreciated knowing the coalition's view "to guide me in my voting because whatever you are 'fer' I'm 'agin' and vice versa." The state AFL left the coalition soon thereafter, and the TSLC never regained its previous level of influence.[10] The leaders of the Farmers Union continued to correspond with CIO officers, as did the officers of the NAACP, PVL, and the AGIF. Occasionally throughout the 1950s, speakers from one group would address a convention of another. Yet, as the Cold War picked up steam, labor, civil rights, and farmers' organizations maintained a cordial coalition at best, staying in touch with one another, but keeping their erstwhile allies at arm's length and doing little else in concert.[11]

With no outlet in the electoral arena, real and perceived Communists faced persecution at the grassroots level as well. As historian Don Carleton has shown, the leadership of the small Texas Communist Party faced arrest, imprisonment, and deportation in the final years of the war and its immediate aftermath. Labor cleaned house and cut off lawyers Mandell and Wright. A final effort of the party to organize a youth chapter at the University of Houston in 1949 was curtailed before it got off the ground. The demise of the Progressive Party likewise foreclosed the electoral arena. The Communist Party ceased operations in 1950, but the Red Scare grew nonetheless, thanks to the efforts of the Minute Women, a group of housewives with particularly strong chapters in Houston and San Antonio. In the Bayou City, grassroots anticommunism reached its zenith when it forced the school board to dismiss a newly hired deputy superintendent of schools in 1953. San Antonio began imprinting red stamps on all the subversive volumes in its library, but it stopped short of setting the books alight.[12]

Such right-wing hysteria continued to reverberate in electoral politics. In 1949, the Establishment governor who had defeated Rainey died unexpectedly, elevating Lieutenant Governor Allan Shivers to the top post. Like his predecessor, Shivers hewed the Establishment line, but surprisingly that included increased funding for schools and other modernization efforts. Over time, he shifted from advocating this respectable conservatism to all-out anticommunist demagoguery in the tradition of O'Daniel and Dies. The NAACP, the CIO, and subversives in the university quickly became his favorite targets. He used the 1950 election cycle to replace the remaining liberals in the state Democratic Party leadership with his own appointees, consolidating his personal control of Texas politics to an unprecedented degree.[13]

The triumph and long reach of anti-Communist sentiment were never clearer than in 1951, when the TSFL invited Shivers to address its annual convention in Galveston. Carefully avoiding any discussion of what he called "partisan politics," Shivers instead focused on his vision of labor's role in solving the pressing public policy problems of the day. His job centered on balancing the demands of myriad "special interests," he began, including organized labor. Such groups must subsume their demands in favor of the "public interest," he added. "Then, and not until then, we will stop the sweep, or at least shorten the arc, of . . . the competition between labor and management. Note that I use the word 'competition' to describe the continuing struggle between these two elements of our American way of life. I am grateful that the labor movement in Texas is predicated upon *competition between equals* and not upon *class warfare*." The latter concept was wholly outdated in the context of postwar America, he added. The mythic community Shivers envisioned even extended into the political arena. There union men rightfully sought "the achievement of union ends—not for the advancement of an alien theory of government and economics that is antagonistic to the American way."[14]

The TSFL welcomed the governor's vision of "competition between equals" and harmonious labor relations. They also appreciated the fact that, to the surprise of no one in attendance, the governor said absolutely nothing about race. If the battle between labor and management was relatively insignificant, then the struggle of blacks and Mexican Americans for first-class citizenship was so unimportant that it didn't even warrant comment. States' rights and segregation were as American as apple pie. The movements of the Depression and World War II remained a distant memory, and the governor and his allied "Shivercrats" dominated Texas politics into the mid-1950s.

All that remained for black working people was the NAACP, but even that storied organization soon fell victim to white supremacist anticommunism and Shivercrat domination. Historian Merline Pitre reports that the Houston branch's fortunes paralleled those of Lulu B. White, the chapter's dynamic executive secretary and state director of branches. White lost influence in the branch soon after the Progressive Party campaign of 1948. For three years prior to the election, while *Sweatt* worked its way through the courts, she had feuded incessantly with newspaper editor Carter Wesley over the best means of pursuing better educational opportunities for African Americans. Both steadfastly supported Sweatt's bid to integrate the University of Texas, but they differed in their responses to the state's decision to postpone integration by establishing a black university and law school in Houston. White demanded complete integration of the flagship school in Austin and nothing else, while Wesley advocated both integration and the building of a separate black institution.

The dispute gradually escalated, with Wesley using his column to attack White in an increasingly personal manner. Most important, he publicly accused her of being a Communist, demanded that she resign from the branch, and hounded her until she finally did so. Wesley cited as evidence White's close relationship with white labor lawyers Arthur Mandell and his partner Herman Wright—even though both men were themselves members of the NAACP—as well as her association with the NMU, other CIO unions, and the Progressive Party campaign. By 1947, White and Wright shared a "close friendship," according to her biographer, and Wright attended White's twentieth wedding anniversary celebration. Wesley was incensed and charged guilt by association. "When a Communist is willing to go to Negro houses and drink liquor with them and call them by their first name, they know that as far as these white people are concerned, the race question is solved." In other words, black activists could not hope to make progress as long as they associated themselves with radicals who advocated not just political rights but "social equality." Their goal was not to dine or intermarry with whites, but to simply gain equal access. By 1949, Wesley grew "obsessed" with removing White from office, and she finally capitulated on June 13 of that year.[15]

White's departure from the post of executive secretary did not entirely remove her from the organization, but it did effectively gut the Houston branch. She remained the state director of branches, and, in 1950, she briefly worked as a field organizer for the regional office. She earned and received much of the credit for extending the NAACP across the state in the wake of the *Sweatt* case, and Erma LeRoy continued to travel with her on organizing forays.

Back in Houston, branch president Rev. L. H. Simpson elevated White's administrative assistant, Christia V. Adair, to the post of executive secretary, deepening the rift among branch leaders and accelerating its decline. White had first hired Adair in 1946 in hopes of grooming her to become her successor, but, as historian Pitre writes, "the two parted company after a few years because of personality conflicts and political and philosophical differences."[16] In particular, Adair resented White's pro-Communist sympathies as well as her meddling in branch affairs after her resignation.[17] The local executive board soon split into two factions, one loyal to White and the other to Simpson and Adair. Most civil rights unionists and indeed most ordinary members likely remained in White's camp as branch membership dropped from 6,975 in 1949 to 1,315 in 1950, the first year of Adair's administration. Even as NAACP lawyers continued to pile up victories in court, the local movement continued to suffer. In 1953, concerned national NAACP staffers investigated the situation and resolved that Adair was both "inefficient" and "incompetent," and they instructed White to lead a new membership campaign. White's effort in response proved successful, yet it further isolated Adair and Simpson. The local executive board soon ceased functioning. One staffer of the New York office attempted to sack Adair in the spring of 1955, but local president Simpson managed to save both her job and his own post. White remained a leader of the dissident faction, officially an outsider but informally synonymous with the

NAACP among many African Americans in Houston and across the state. Moses and Erma LeRoy and other civil rights unionists remained loyal to White until her death in 1957, after which her "close friend" Moses served as an honorary pallbearer. Formerly one of the association's largest and most active branches, the Houston chapter now lay in tatters.[18]

Yet the NAACP still awaited the second half of the Cold War's one-two punch. In September 1956, two years after the *Brown v. Board* decision, state attorney general (and Shivercrat) John Ben Shepperd declared war on the NAACP in a last-ditch effort to prevent the impending desegregation of schools that fall. Led by a former FBI agent, Shepperd's men conducted surprise simultaneous raids on the association's offices in Houston and Dallas, seizing the chapter and regional offices' files and financial records but generally failing to obtain membership lists. The attorney general's office soon secured "a temporary restraining order that barred the NAACP from doing business in Texas." Charging the association with barratry, or illegal solicitation of clients, Shepperd instigated a show trial near his hometown in Tyler, in faraway Northeast Texas, forcing the leaders of various local chapters to travel long distances to confront him on his own turf. There he surprised them, forcing them to undergo harsh interrogations by Texas Rangers, followed by a spectacle courtroom hearing as a mob of White Citizens Council members looked on.

Ironically, Christia Adair, who for years had frustrated her superiors with her poor record keeping and brash independence, now became the defense's star witness. She testified that she could not turn over the branch's membership list because she did not maintain one, and she demonstrated clearly that neither New York nor the state office in Dallas exerted control over activities in Houston. Just as she had previously refused to cooperate with Lulu White and national NAACP officials, she now defiantly resisted the state's questioning over sixteen days on the witness stand. Her intransigence gained her notoriety in the black press and among NAACP officials, reversing some of the damage done by her feud with White. Her own celebrity increased, but her remarkable testimony did not stop the state's war on the association. Rather, much to the chagrin of state conference attorney W. J. Durham, the presiding judge accepted every portion of the attorney general's suit and upheld the injunction banning the NAACP. The following spring, in consultation with the association's New York office, the court handed down a decision that allowed the Texas chapters to resume activity, but only under the close scrutiny of the attorney general's office. NAACP lawyers accepted the decision as a compromise by the state, and they further agreed that an appeal of the ruling would be impossible. Yet statewide membership had fallen by more than 50 percent, so the New York office appealed the case in order to make a public display of ongoing defiance. The group's Texas leaders temporarily resigned in protest, forcing the national officers to drop their appeal. Many of the leaders never returned, and others faced renewed repression. A. Maceo Smith, who founded the state conference and had guided it since its inception, was forced by his employer to resign his position. In 1962, one national NAACP staffer would remark that the association was then still recovering from the 1956 injunction. It would never be the same.[19]

The most important remaining institution of the civil rights unionist movement had been all but destroyed. The state conference would continue to limp along, as would the Dallas branch. Association attorney W. J. Durham would continue to press school desegregation lawsuits across the state. Back in Houston, when Lulu White died in 1957, the NAACP chapter all but died with her. Now, more than ever, civil rights unionists like the LeRoys would have to look elsewhere for allies in the ongoing freedom struggle.

Civil Rights Unionism Survives and Thrives

Although Houston no longer supported the mass mobilizations of the civil rights unionist movement of the previous decade, African American activists in the Bayou City did not retreat in the face of the Cold War. Rather, they responded to repression by redirecting their efforts. Although the space for radical protest may have been somewhat curtailed, they continued to join unions, combat segregation on the job, and to come together in their neighborhoods and civic clubs. Above all, they worked to organize and then wield their newfound power at the ballot box.

As Moses LeRoy later observed, the Progressive Party movement of 1948 failed to elect candidates in Houston, but the contentious campaign that year did alert local officials and Democratic Party leaders that black voters had arrived. Still, the city's numerous, diverse African Americans represented anything but a single bloc vote. Black leaders of all political and economic persuasions understood this and came together to found the Harris County Council of Organizations (HCCO) in 1949. The cross-class, *mono*racial coalition quickly grew to include over sixty separate black political and civic groups, giving it a size and diversity that soon allowed it to eclipse the NAACP as the hub of black political life in Houston.[20]

The LeRoys and other black union activists seamlessly transitioned their efforts to the council, where they advanced not only the quest for black electoral power but also broader struggles for civil rights and economic justice. They served as diplomats, connecting the black masses to their social betters and helping the professionals mobilize a potentially massive group of voters that the council would otherwise be unlikely to reach. Collectively, Houston's black labor leaders already had years if not decades of experience organizing in both the labor and civil rights movements, and they were now able to bring their expertise to bear on the larger cross-class coalition. More important, each union leader quite literally represented hundreds if not thousands of ordinary black workers—large, relatively stable memberships that filled the union coffers with far greater financial resources than the average black civic club. LeRoy and other black unionists could communicate with, round up, and turn out black workers not simply by canvassing their homes but also by talking to them on the job. And they had deep relationships of trust forged over years of worksite battles.

It is little wonder, then, that three of the four HCCO founders had close ties to organized labor, and many more union men appeared among the council's "charter members." LeRoy became a key organizer and officer of the new coalition despite having been "branded a red [herring]" for his support of fair employment and the Progressive Party during and after World War II. He had remained a close friend and loyal ally of Lulu White's even after she resigned from office in the local branch at the height of the Red Scare. He, Mrs. LeRoy, and White all "ended up on a list of suspected 'reds'" assembled by vigilante white "Minute Women" in Houston in partnership with the House Un-American Activities Committee (HUAC). Likewise, Moses LeRoy had previously enjoyed a close relationship with editor Carter Wesley, and the pair had traveled together to a national black media convention in Washington, D.C. Still, as Wesley's campaign against White intensified in the late 1940s, the journalist "splattered red paint" on LeRoy as well, charging the union leader with Communist sympathies and seeking to distance himself and the NAACP from LeRoy's leftist influence.[21]

Despite McCarthyism, LeRoy remained sufficiently influential at the railroad yards and in the community, and he was invited to that first meeting of the HCCO at First Shiloh Baptist Church. Council founders George Nelson, Sid Hilliard, and F. T. Henry all had ties to the labor movement, and they had been in the trenches of the NAACP with LeRoy since the middle of the war.[22] LeRoy and Henry also worked together in the Greater Fifth Ward Citizens League. LeRoy had also proven his worth on the ground by mobilizing his neighbors behind the Progressive Party. He received an invitation to the council's first assembly and signed up to become a charter member of the HCCO, along with the president of his union and Julius White, Lulu's wheeler-dealer husband. He soon became a formal leader of the council, serving as its parliamentarian and in other top posts for years to come.[23]

The council also attracted the leaders of the city's all-black unions. Freeman Everett's two massive waterfront unions, the Longshoremen's (ILA) Local 872 and the Hod Carriers and Common Laborers (HCCL) Local 18. Together they represented a bastion of power for the black labor and civil rights movements, and, by extension, for all of black Houston. As Everett traveled across the state on his organizing expeditions, new leaders took charge of local affairs and gained control of the unions when he retired in the mid-1950s. J. E. "Jimmie" Middleton became president of Laborers Local 18, while ILA Local 872 elected a new militant president, Raymond Duncan, in 1955. Duncan quickly increased the role of the local in community and political affairs as well as its physical presence—a new, shiny union hall soon towered above the docks, symbolizing in brick and mortar the power of the massive all-black union. Leaders of the National Alliance of Postal Employees (NAPE), Heman Sweatt's union, likely joined the HCCO as well, as did black union activists in the CIO steel and autoworkers unions.[24]

Although civil rights unionists filled the ranks of the HCCO, the council focused its efforts on electoral politics. LeRoy and other black labor activists in the HCCO represented working people and sought to embed economic issues into the larger council's agenda, but their membership in a cross-class, diverse coalition required that they also work with African American elites: businessmen, ministers, doctors, lawyers, and university administrators. Indeed, many of the erstwhile union organizers doubled as small businessmen, and many hoped that political action would open the door to more upward mobility. Each of these varied participants brought their own agendas, ideologies, and priorities to the HCCO, but through careful negotiation, HCCO members elected a representative group of officers that could, in turn, connect with a wide range of voters in each of the city's several black neighborhoods and worksites. Throughout the early 1950s, the HCCO continued to organize, working largely under the radar but also endorsing and turning out voters for white candidates in several key local races.

The HCCO was not without conflict. Council leaders and even the smaller subset of labor delegates frequently disagreed about how best to utilize their growing bloc vote. One faction, which included Middleton of the Laborers Local 18, formed alliances with white contractors associations. These relationships bore fruit on the shop floor as well as in politics. The union grew rapidly, as did the quantity of union construction work. By the end of the decade and into the 1960s, Local 18 forged a tight relationship with County Judge Bill Elliott, a politically moderate chief administrator of Harris County. Their support for his campaigns resulted in various forms of patronage, including the awarding of local contracts to builders who hired members of Middleton's fast-growing union. At the same time, other members of the HCCO, led by LeRoy, worked to mobilize the council behind a wide range of labor organizing and civil rights causes—which, at times, put the HCCO at odds with the same local authorities whom other council members had just helped to elect.[25]

In other words, disagreements over political strategy and tactics raged within the so-called black community of Houston, as well as among the leaders of the city's black unions. The HCCO's diverse leadership did its best to contain such internal differences and to direct community organizers toward the realm of electoral politics, but they were only partially successful in both objectives. Generally, the patronage politics of Middleton and most African American professionals managed to coexist with the community activism of LeRoy, Nelson, and other militants. Black businessmen often responded positively to the unionists' calls to contribute to the development of black community institutions and to aid civil rights causes. The council's activist wing then reciprocated by holding their noses and campaigning for the best available compromise candidate endorsed by the entire HCCO.

The cross-class and at times compromise-centric council did not, however, shy away from taking public stands in support of civil rights. In 1953, Hilliard spoke for the HCCO when he denounced the conditions in the city's "horrible" segregated black schools. He cited "improper heating, inconvenient restrooms, improper drainage, and unsanitary cafeterias" as the group's major concerns—all within the confines of "separate but equal." In 1955, HCCO cofounder and small businessman M. L. Ward, who served as the council's first president, wrote to the U.S. attorney general to request an investigation into the White Citizens Council, a group formed to wage "massive resistance" against school integration in the wake of the landmark *Brown v. Board* decision.[26] Two years later, in 1958, the HCCO "launched a boycott move" against the Houston school board after the body planned to require special summer instruction for black teachers. While district administrators claimed that the program would close an "academic gap" between white and black teachers, the HCCO responded that their plan was an "insult" and recommended that African American teachers and principals stay home in protest. Moreover, the remedial training would be spread out over three years, a period that council members believed was "motivated solely by the desire . . . to indefinitely delay desegregation in Houston's public schools." The council planned to mobilize "a large Negro delegation" to show up at the next school board meeting.[27]

Perhaps as an outgrowth of this activity, the HCCO achieved a major breakthrough in 1958 when it helped elect Mrs. Charles E. White to the local school board. Mrs. White (Hattie Mae was her given name, though she never used it publicly) became the city's first black elected official since Reconstruction. White's election from a heavily black but not majority-black district "shocked the conservative political establishment" and drew the ire of local white supremacist vigilantes. One retrospective on her life adds that her "car windshield was splintered by air rifle pellets and a gasoline-soaked cross was set ablaze in her yard after the election." The white supremacists' fears were somewhat confirmed soon after Mrs. White took office, when she publicly withdrew her support for a tax hike and bond issue at the request of the HCCO.

The council argued that both proposals represented "another attempt of the school board to maintain segregation" and promised an "active campaign" in opposition to the measures.[28]

The HCCO adopted an even more militant stance in 1959 when it staged a campaign to protest police brutality. Pulling no punches, new council president Aloysius Wickliff sent a complaint letter to the police chief and mayor charging Houston police with making "mass arrests" of African Americans "without just cause." Claiming that it had signed affidavits documenting numerous cases of abuse, the HCCO complained that police officers routinely picked up black residents, falsely charging them with drunkenness. The HCCO further charged that the police at times planned "preconceived" sweeps conducted solely to boost the police department's number of arrests. Wickliff added that black prisoners were frequently crammed into paddy wagons or jail cells and then sometimes "abused" or "intimidated"—and some even died "under peculiar circumstances" while in custody. The department's top "brass" also harassed the few black officers on the force, dispatchers used the word "nigger" on the radio, and some white officers demanded that their black counterparts remove their hats in their presence.[29]

The issue was promptly swept under the rug by the mayor, where it might have remained if not for an extraordinary case of police brutality that surfaced less than two weeks later. Eldrewey Stearns, a twenty-six-year-old graduate student at Houston's all-black Texas Southern University, claimed that he was beaten and "degraded to the level of a dog" after being stopped and arrested on traffic charges. "I was dragged behind a closed door in the jail and held by one officer while two others beat me," Stearns told the city's lead daily newspaper, the *Houston Chronicle*. News of Stearns's arrest and beating led the council to renew their calls for a wholesale investigation of routine police brutality. Stearns testified before the city council and identified the badge numbers of the two jailers who beat him. (The following year, Stearns would emerge as the leader of the student sit-in movement.)[30]

The close ties of some HCCO members to Houston's white elites did not, then, prohibit the organization from taking militant action in support of black civil rights. Rather, like the NAACP before it, the council put forth a surprisingly broad agenda for building black political power and first-class citizenship. Despite the obstacles presented by at-large voting, place elections, and the poll tax, the HCCO successfully organized and wielded a black bloc vote. It endorsed and elected the best available white candidates and at times ran its own African American candidates against nearly impossible odds, if only to register a protest. This was hardly a politics of making backroom deals or peddling influence. Rather, the HCCO built its power by prioritizing black working-class issues like police brutality and appealing specifically to black working-class voters. In September 1959, for example, as city leaders ignored the council's petition regarding the Stearns case, HCCO leaders announced that it would support Rev. Edward V. Hill, a black Baptist minister, for a seat on the City Council. In answering the call, Hill became the first black candidate for this at-large position since 1946. Hill promised to serve "all the people," but he underscored his race and working-class background: "I believe my ability to serve the city will be aided by my having come up through the lower income bracket and by being a member of a minority group," he said.[31]

Civil rights and working-class issues remained on the front burner throughout the decade, even if the mass marches and militant actions of the 1940s were no longer a feature of Houston's civic life. Complaints against police brutality, the fight to desegregate schools, and the quest for autonomous political power all dovetailed in the diverse HCCO. Civil rights unionists like Moses LeRoy brought their experiences to bear in the broader coalition and helped to advance the movement's larger agenda. At the same time, throughout the decade, LeRoy used the HCCO to extend his influence among workers at the Southern Pacific Railroad and continue his struggle for promotions and opportunity on the shop floor and in his union.

LeRoy grew more active than ever in both electoral politics and in his union auxiliary at the precise moment that his still-segregated Freight Handlers Local 6051 gained increased autonomy from its white counterpart. In 1951, an amendment to the Railway Labor Act prohibited racially exclusive union auxiliaries. LeRoy's unit finally became an equal affiliate of the Brotherhood of Steamship and Railway Clerks (BSRC), a change that afforded him and his colleagues all the rights and privileges of full membership in the union. They could finally vote in state and regional union elections, and they received improved if not fair representation on the shop floor. The new law did not, however, abolish the segregation of local unions. LeRoy's union became BSRC Local 1534, but it remained all black and was still forced to depend upon the white local for collective bargaining. Nonetheless, in the context of the Jim Crow South, even this partial victory represented a giant leap forward, especially at the height of the Cold War.

At the worksite, at the union hall, and in the community, LeRoy continued to lead the fight for equal access to skilled jobs. He had already served as his union's legislative representative and secretary, and in 1955 he became president of the newly formed Local 1534. That year he traveled to Boston to represent his union at the Brotherhood's international convention, where he introduced a floor resolution that "exposed the bias in the two lines of progression, showing that Negroes were prohibited from promotions." As white delegates from Texas and the South sneered and "white-washed" the situation, union members from California and the Northeast cheered LeRoy's courage.

They even picked him up and carried him around the convention hall and then bought him drinks afterward at a nearby bar.[32]

What one black worker called LeRoy's "gallant fight" did not produce immediate and sweeping change in the Brotherhood, but it did result in at least one promotion back home at the Southern Pacific yards in Houston. M. J. Richmond, a former president of the black union auxiliary who had worked there since the 1930s, became an "apprentice section stockman" in a move that the *Informer* claimed would "shatter a tradition of job discrimination in the company." The unnamed author, perhaps editor Carter Wesley, added that "Labor circles in Houston hailed the announcement as the biggest news in Southern labor relations and as a broad step toward wiping out job bias because of color. . . . The promotion was a death blow to the old practice of two lines of progression." LeRoy cautioned that much work remained to be done, but he still noted the historic nature of—and future possibilities presented by—Richmond's promotion. It was "a great achievement in labor relations in the South," he told the *Informer*. "It proves that we can work together in harmony without friction in this democratic process. We are part and parcel of the labor movement and I don't see why we should not be integrated in it. We are going to carry on until we reach our full objective of complete integration."[33]

Nothing less than complete integration was both a long-term goal and also a short-term imperative. LeRoy carried the demand with him into every meeting he held as the union's president and as chairman of its Protective Committee, which was responsible for processing shop-floor grievances. Even within the confines of the still separate and unequal Brotherhood, LeRoy battled against segregation in all of its forms. Since 1910 the Southern Pacific had run a local hospital for its twenty-three thousand Texas and Louisiana employees who either fell ill or were injured on the job, as well as for their families and the occasional infirm passenger passing through. Funded by worker payroll deductions, the so-called Sunset Hospital provided at least 129 beds, of which no more than twenty-two were "assigned to Negroes and a like amount to Mexicans." The hospital boasted "above average care and maintenance," but LeRoy recalled that it relegated black workers to a small single room on the third floor of "one little wing." Black orderlies, nursing aides, and presumably maids and porters helped run and maintain the entire hospital. LeRoy attempted to win equal access for black patients, but no change was forthcoming in company policy. Defeated but undaunted, LeRoy instead organized the maids and orderlies to join his union, along with the hospital's white workers. As chair of the union's Protective Committee, he would receive a call whenever one of the new union members in the segregated hospital had a grievance. He would leave his post and march confidently to the convalescent grounds, while the railroad's management watched with baited breath. "They hated to see him coming to the hospital because they knew something was going to happen," Mrs. LeRoy later recalled. "You could see them out their peepholes," Moses agreed. He thus began a long tenure as a staunch advocate for the hospital's workers, both black and white, a task he continued until the late 1960s, when the company closed down the hospital rather than integrate it.[34]

Bread-and-butter economic issues remained at the core of LeRoy's union activism. The railroad operated a federally insured credit union for its employees, a fringe benefit that, like the hospital, excluded black workers. "Negroes couldn't borrow any money or put any money in," LeRoy recalled. "We tried on several occasions to become members." Rebuffed, the black workers formed their own credit union before the company finally capitulated. "So that all fell, too," he added.[35] Even more glaring than the segregated credit union was the ongoing exclusion of black workers from promotions to skilled positions and the accompanying higher pay. Stuck in Group Three, LeRoy eventually moved into a white-collar post in which he worked pushing paper in an office. Still, his work remained unrecognized and undercompensated. Like many workers of color across the country, he endured the added humiliation of training the employees who passed over him. "I broke in many whites in top clerical positions, but I was never classified as a clerk," he recalled.[36]

Fighting and winning within his union and on the job in the 1940s allowed LeRoy to build a base of followers that he carried into the struggle for civil rights in the community in the 1950s—and then back to the worksite as well. During World War II, organizing black workers had meant building a vibrant civil rights unionist movement in collaboration with Lulu White and the local NAACP. A decade later, LeRoy continued to combine the struggle for economic parity with the larger black freedom struggle, but he now did so under the radar by influencing the most viable and militant local organization around, the HCCO.

For her part, Erma LeRoy carried on in her role as a "helpmate" to her husband as well as a leading community activist in her own right. Although men dominated the leadership positions of the HCCO, LeRoy and other women performed much of the on-the-ground work of registering and turning out new voters. She also remained close to Lulu White, even after her forced resignation from the NAACP in 1949. That same year, just two months after her unsuccessful bid for the legislature, LeRoy served on the local branch's Education Committee and joined White in organizing a new women's study group, the Chat-An-Hour Social and Cultural Club. Ten black women attended the first meeting in White's parlor, and over the next two decades the ladies would meet frequently to discuss sundry books on "Negro life" and works written by African American authors. Excluded from many of the smoke-filled back rooms in which the HCCO men made decisions, the women of the movement carved their own space for discussing the pressing issues of the day. LeRoy also continued to assist White in her new capacity as director of branches for the Texas State Conference of the NAACP, a post that White held until her death in 1957. LeRoy traveled with White across the state, slowly and invisibly doing the "spadework" of organizing new branches even as the association endured the state attorney general's legal witch hunt. Back in Houston, where White retreated from many community groups after her removal from the branch, LeRoy emerged as a leader in numerous black women's groups. By the end of the decade, she landed a position on the board of the all-black "Blue Triangle" branch of the YWCA, a key institution that provided services for poor women and organized teas and a wide range of social and cultural events for African Americans. If Moses served as a diplomat between the black workingmen and entrepreneurs of the city, Mrs. LeRoy (nobody but Moses ever called her "Erma") performed the same tasks for Houston's black women, connecting the working poor to black high society and the institutions of the women's club movement.[37]

The two LeRoys were truly a team. Following Lulu White's death, Moses again ran for and won a leadership position in the local NAACP, becoming its treasurer and helping to end the factional struggle that had long plagued the branch. He and Mrs. LeRoy resumed working closely with Christia Adair, White's replacement, collaborating in the NAACP as well as HCCO business and political affairs. Mrs. LeRoy became an officer in the branch by the early 1960s. The couple bought and moved into a small bungalow at 3322 Drew Street in the Third Ward, the city's most respectable black neighborhood and home to Moses's mother and daughter as well as the NAACP's Adair.

Segregation and oppression remained, but tireless community, labor, and political activism had landed the LeRoys in a better position than the one they had occupied when they married two decades earlier. More important than material comfort was the fact that the duo remained key civic organizers and even occupied new leadership positions just a few years after appearing on the list of "suspected reds." Far from being discredited, the LeRoys thrived. Their decades of advocacy and diplomacy had positioned them at the center of the battle against Jim Crow in Houston right on the eve of the student sit-in movement.[38]

In fact, their influence extended beyond Houston, as the LeRoys joined a revived effort to build a statewide organization to mobilize the black vote. Like the HCCO, the Texas Council of Voters (TCV) had its origins in the battle to defeat the white primary and the chaotic efforts to turn out and unify African American voters in its wake. Back in 1936, A. Maceo Smith and other African Americans in Dallas had organized another group, the Progressive Voters League (PVL), which had succeeded in organizing the city's African Americans to pay their poll taxes and vote, especially in the nonpartisan municipal election of 1937. The PVL's leaders quickly expanded the league statewide and even nationally, but the increase in voter registration did not translate to victories at the polls. They remained excluded from partisan races by the white primary, and at-large elections diluted their power at the local level. The Supreme Court's ruling in *Smith* in 1944 offered a new opportunity but also a strident internal conflict over strategy: should the PVL remain nonpartisan or cast its lot with the white supremacist Democratic Party?

W. J. Durham, the general counsel of the NAACP and a leader in the Dallas branch since relocating there in 1943, advocated for the latter route and split from the PVL, founding the Texas Club of Democratic Voters in August 1944. As one chronicler put it, Durham promised to "gain control in every precinct where black voters were in evidence" and, more important, to "assure black people living in small towns that they need not be afraid to vote." A bitter fight ensued in which both the PVL and the future TCV tried to outmaneuver the other. The league won the first battles, defeating TCV in a series of elections for Democratic Party precinct chairs in Dallas in 1946, but Durham's group won the war, as the attorney negotiated a series of agreements with white liberals that eventually positioned him as their go-to man to organize the black vote. The PVL split again in 1948 when its president joined the Progressive Party movement. The remaining leaders formalized the league's affiliation with the Democratic Party that same year, but by then the damage had been done. Branches of the PVL continued functioning into the 1960s, and the league survives in Dallas into the twenty-first century. Still, as historian W. Marvin Dulaney concludes, it "never regained the unity and political strength it enjoyed" before *Smith*. Durham's TCV, in contrast, rapidly organized new chapters across the state and became the leading black political network in Texas by the mid-1950s. The LeRoys served as the on-the-ground organizers of the TCV in Houston, and Moses would eventually become the statewide council's first vice president and Durham's top lieutenant.[39]

Civil rights unionism looked different after the chill of the Cold War, but it continued unabated, as the LeRoys' experiences make plain. Even white liberals and labor leaders continued to recognize its potential, while the LeRoys actively sought alliances across the color line. Of course, the duo had joined with white radicals in the labor movement and Progressive Party of the 1940s, but the Red Scare cut such partnerships short. By the late 1950s, word of the LeRoys' prominence in the NAACP, the Railroad Brotherhood, the HCCO, and the TCV had made its way into white labor circles once again. State and national staffers of the newly merged Texas AFL-CIO hired first Moses and then Erma to conduct voter-registration drives on behalf of its Committee on Political Education (COPE). Evidence of their work for the committee in this period remains fragmentary, but it is clear that they traveled together and separately across East Texas to spread the message that African Americans could win civil rights by exercising the vote. Such experiences also drew them into new conversations with the white leaders of the local labor council, the Harris County AFL-CIO, as well as with the city's white liberals. Soon, the LeRoys, along with the NAACP's Adair, would return to the HCCO and encourage the all-black coalition to experiment in forging new interracial alliances. Both locally and statewide, their own bloc vote could only go so far, the LeRoys determined. They needed to reach out to others who could assist them in the fight against Jim Crow. As luck would have it, their soon-to-be allies had recently arrived at a strikingly similar conclusion.[40]

The Rise of the "Liberal Movement"

In 1952 the Texas state Democratic Party experienced its third split in as many presidential election cycles. Eight years earlier, in 1944, the Texas "Regulars" attempted to withhold the state's support for Roosevelt, and, four years after that, Texas Dixiecrats joined the movement against the inclusion of a civil rights plank in the platform of Harry Truman's reelection campaign. Then, in 1952, with Governor Shivers indicating that he might again oppose the eventual Democratic nominee, a group of mostly white liberals led by Maury Maverick walked out from the party's state convention in San Antonio. Carrying cardboard cutouts of donkeys, the Democratic symbol, they marched through the rain and held a rump gathering at La Villita, the plaza Maverick had built with New Deal funds during his term as mayor. Their bolters' suspicions were confirmed a month later when the national party nominated Adlai Stevenson, whom conservative Texans perceived as a northern liberal who would support labor, civil rights, and ongoing federal control of the oil-rich Tidelands, a hot-button issue of the day. Governor Shivers responded by leading the rest of the Texas Democratic delegation in endorsing the Republican nominee, General Dwight D. Eisenhower, who then carried the state for the GOP for just the second time in history. The two parties nominated the same two presidential candidates four years later in 1956, and Shivers again denounced the Democratic nominee and then led the state into the GOP column in November. In each case, after being shouted or voted down at a state convention, a group of liberals assembled and staged their own counterprotests, forming an ad hoc caucus of self-proclaimed "loyal Democrats."[41]

As the decade wore on, these quadrennial rituals slowly produced a permanent organization of mostly white liberals that used these convention conflicts to secure a lasting foothold in state and national politics. The group began humbly, when a handful of Houston plaintiffs' lawyers gathered together in

1953 to lick their wounds from the battles fought and lost the previous year. They stormed the temple of the county and the statewide Democratic Party apparatuses by 1956, formed a parallel statewide organization, and scored a major victory at the polls the following year. Along the way, the battle-hardened white activists laid the groundwork for the expansion of their "liberal movement" into the state's nonwhite communities.

At the center of the struggle was a Greek American labor lawyer with the decidedly nonethnic name of Christian Dixie. Born in Memphis in 1914, Dixie shared the story of many children of recent immigrants to the United States. His father lacked a trade, so he opened a restaurant serving the cuisine of his homeland, purchasing an older establishment called the Dixie Café. The family name had been Giannacopoulos, the Greek version of "Johnson," but customers preferred to call the restaurateur "Dixie," and he soon changed it to better match his brand. The new name did not provide enough good advertising to keep the business afloat, so he moved it to Little Rock. When he continued to struggle in the new locale, he moved on to Dallas by the late 1920s. The younger Dixie spoke Greek as a first language but learned English as well, and he became "Chris" to his friends. He later recalled that, despite the fact that his immigrant father had little interest in American politics, the elder Dixie often counseled Chris "that there were only two great men in the world, Jesus Christ and Franklin D. Roosevelt." The family stayed put long enough for Chris to finish high school in Dallas in 1931, when he enrolled in the private Southern Methodist University before transferring to the University of Texas the next year.[42]

Dixie's time at the university in Austin proved formative. He was particularly influenced by Professor Bob Montgomery, an economist who supported the pragmatic experimentation of the New Deal and advocated idealistic solutions to the woes facing Texas agriculture and industry. Montgomery "pulled things together for me, as he did for many others," Dixie later recalled. He and his classmates debated the causes of the Depression, began to think about the many possibilities of bold public policy, and Dixie became "a semi-political animal." He and a few other students organized the first Young Democrats club on the campus and then formed a breakaway group of Progressive Democrats, as the intraparty squabbling of their elders made its way into the student chapter. The latter group, founded in 1935, included many future leaders of the liberal movement, but for the moment they contented themselves with playing politics, renting a house, setting up an office, and offering liberal resolutions up the party's chain of command.

Dixie remained in Austin until 1936, when he graduated from law school. After a brief stint back in Dallas, where he lost a race for a seat in the legislature, he moved to Houston in February 1938. Arthur Combs, a labor lawyer and

Labor lawyer and liberal political leader Chris Dixie addresses the Texas Democratic Convention in Austin in 1964. Dixie, an organizer of the Harris County Democrats, Democrats of Texas, and later the Texas Organization of Liberal Democrats, pioneered a block-walking program in Houston in the 1950s that would become a model for liberals of all colors across the state. Courtesy *Austin American-Statesman* Photographic Morgue (AR.2014.039), Austin History Center, Austin Public Library, Texas, Image AS-64-45972-03a.

partner of the leftist Arthur Mandell, had written to Professor Montgomery in search of a new associate who would be politically "compatible" with the radical firm. The economist recommended Dixie, even though the young, "semi-political" lawyer had no training whatsoever in labor law.[43]

Dixie quickly established himself in the firm by winning a series of key cases for the city's rapidly expanding unions. In his first case, he represented a massive local of the Oil Workers International Union (OWIU-CIO) at the Shell refinery just outside town. The company refused to respond to the workers' petition, so Dixie filed litigation with the National Labor Relations Board and through the courts, resulting in the legal recognition of the union's right to represent the workers as well as securing its first collective-bargaining agreement. Dixie also helped get locals started at the Gulf and Texaco refineries in Port Arthur, ninety miles up the coast, and he represented the Teamsters union as they organized over-the-road truck drivers. Although the OWIU and other contemporary unions did little to combat racial discrimination on the shop floor, the unions' impact on the status of both black and white workers could hardly be overstated. Imperfect as they were, the unions replaced systems of favoritism and patronage with industrial jurisprudence and empowered workers to participate in a sort of shop-floor democracy. Workers of all colors gained stable employment, rising wages, and protection against arbitrary dismissal. On a larger scale, the labor movement in Houston's refineries, steel mills, and factories had pried open a serious chink in the state's conservative political armor. Dixie observed that once the unions had become organized and improved the bread-and-butter issues of wages and working conditions, their leaders built their treasuries and turned their attention toward improving the general welfare of all working people through electoral politics.[44]

Dixie likewise transitioned from establishing himself to engaging in larger political causes. After serving in World War II, he returned to Houston and dove into Democratic Party politics. He and his wife Katie joined the gubernatorial campaign of liberal professor Homer Rainey in 1946 and attempted to bring black voters into the county party that year, the first election year after *Smith*. The Red Scare split the liberal movement asunder as his senior partner Mandell was branded a Communist along with Herman Wright, a fellow young associate at the firm who had cofounded the Progressive Democrats with Dixie at the University of Texas. Both supported the NAACP as well as the Progressive Party campaign in 1948, but Dixie had remained a stalwart, if stunned, liberal Democrat. He recalled that many of his compatriots "were terribly fearful that Joe McCarthy and others didn't know the difference between a Communist and a liberal and they pulled in their horns." For the next six years, he added, "liberal activity in this county was pretty well suppressed through intimidation."[45]

The reorganization of white liberals began in earnest during the 1952 primary campaign, when former state district judge Ralph W. Yarborough, an East Texas native living in Austin, decided to run for governor. A rather ambivalent gubernatorial candidate, Yarborough had once stood unsuccessfully for attorney general, and he threw his hat in the ring in 1952 only after being slighted by the incumbent governor Shivers, who urged him not to run again for that lesser post. Once on the campaign trail, Yarborough found active supporters among former student activists from the University of Texas and labor lawyers from the state's leading firms in Houston and Dallas—men like Chris Dixie and his partners at the firm he now ran. Creekmore Fath, another Progressive Democrat alongside Dixie at the university who had also lent a hand in the 1938 pecan sheller strike in San Antonio, ran the campaign from Austin. With Fath at the helm, Yarborough campaigned as a vague populist who believed in standing up for the little people. His message connected with urban industrial and craft workers as well as tenant and small farmers in his home region of the state, including, to Yarborough's surprise, a large number of African Americans.[46]

The ragtag campaign had little chance of success. Robert E. "Bob" Hall, a student at the University of Texas law school originally from the Rio Grande Valley, became Yarborough's traveling advance man at the age of twenty-one. Hall traveled one or two days ahead of the candidate's caravan and finalized the logistical arrangements for Yarborough's varied appearances. It was not glamorous work. In most cases Hall would arrive at a courthouse square in a small Texas county seat and begin by asking nearby merchants for two things: a place to park a pickup truck that could double as a stage and bandstand, and an electrical hookup so they could plug in the campaign's public address system. At every meeting, large and small, and at every courthouse square, he worked to collect information from likely voters and slowly built the campaign's low-tech mailing list and database. Dozens to hundreds of nearby farmers—almost all white—assembled at each rural rally in order to hear Yarborough's fiery rhetoric. Hall worked the crowds with index cards, collecting names and addresses and then sending them back to the campaign's headquarters in Austin, where Fath or another staffer added the information to the campaign's low-tech database, a series of three-ring binders. As soon as the speech concluded, Hall sped off to the next town, where he would again find a merchant with an outlet and a parking spot and repeat the process. Organizing in urban areas was not substantially different: Hall arrived early, attended meetings at union halls, churches, and civic clubs, frantically collected index cards, and sped off to the next locale.[47]

As Hall's story suggests, Yarborough lacked the organizational apparatus to mount a serious challenge to the incumbent governor. The liberal wing of the Democratic Party of the 1930s and 1940s had succumbed to the Cold War, and no liberal movement had yet emerged in its place. Yarborough declared his candidacy just two days before conservative Shivercrats swept the precinct conventions, and the two months between Maverick's convention walkout in San Antonio and the primary gave him little time to combat the governor's well-built machine. Money was also tight: campaign checks often bounced, and the traveling caravan depended upon contributions on the road to make it to the next stop. Yarborough got clobbered. Shivers won the nomination easily, 61 percent to 36 percent. Still, Yarborough garnered nearly half a million votes and carried twenty-one counties, mostly in his home region of East Texas.[48]

Dixie and other Houston liberals supported Yarborough even though he was not yet particularly liberal. He represented an alternative to Shivers and the Red Scare, and he showed concern for the common folk. Still, it wasn't until after the primary that the candidate embedded himself among the Houston liberals. Dixie recalled that Yarborough recognized the need to build a base in Harris County, so "he came here and literally attended precinct meetings with small groups of people and talked about his plans for the state government of

Texas and what was wrong with Allan Shivers." Yarborough helped to gather together a nucleus of activists who would carry the banner for liberalism in the city for decades to come. The group brought together labor and plaintiff-side lawyers like Dixie and J. Edwin Smith as well as white labor leaders such as Eddie Ball of the Steelworkers and John Crossland of the Oil Workers. Ball was a native of the Rio Grande Valley who had worked his way through law school before becoming a union staffer. Crossland was a veteran of the bitterly fought organizing drive at Shell and a leading anti-Communist in the local CIO, but as president of his union he had made the transition to focusing on political education and remained a committed liberal. Each of their wives joined them, with Katie Dixie and Virginia Smith gaining particular distinction in the day-to-day organizing. Countless wives of ordinary white union men and a smattering of white union women rounded out the core group.[49]

When Shivers succeeded in handing the state to Eisenhower in November, Dixie remembered, "we had to start on this long hard road to make the [state] party loyal to the national Democratic Party." The cadre turned their ad hoc committee into a formal organization, the Harris County Democrats (HCD). They held their first membership meeting on Texas Independence Day, March 2, 1953, adopting a constitution and electing attorney Ed Smith as the club's first chairman. An official history holds that "this organization was integrated from the beginning" and "had an open-door policy from inception," even though only a handful of African Americans or Mexicans Americans were intimately involved in its first decade. Moses and Erma LeRoy likely participated from near its inception, as did Houston NAACP executive director Christia Adair.[50] In general, wealthy and middle-class white liberals, labor lawyers and other plaintiff-side attorneys and their wives, and a few white union families filled the HCD's ranks.

The group got a major boost in early 1954, when Mrs. R. D. (Frankie Carter) Randolph joined the HCD and quickly became its chief benefactor and lead organizer. Born in 1894, she came from a wealthy East Texas lumber-producing family and in 1918 married a naval corps pilot who later became a prominent Houston banker. Still, her Bourbon origins and bourgeois lifestyle eventually succumbed to her lived experience, as she got involved in a variety of volunteer social programs during the Great Depression. She became a supporter of President Roosevelt, joined the League of Women Voters, and advocated for public housing and flood control projects in poor areas.[51] In 1954, she joined the HCD and provided money, as Dixie put it, "to accelerate the organization and make it amount to something." The group had previously hired a single part-time staff person, and Dixie and other leaders each contributed ten dollars a month, a not unsubstantial sum, to finance its operations. Now, with Randolph's backing, the HCD added several full-time organizers to the payroll and expanded its presence on the ground. Randolph provided many thousands of dollars of her own money and took advantage of her position in high society to raise additional funds from her wealthy friends. Yet she also did much of the dirty work, spearheading the organization of precinct and area clubs across Houston, which in turn recruited dozens and then hundreds of new activists into the HCD.[52]

Randolph, Dixie, and other HCD leaders rallied behind Yarborough's second gubernatorial campaign in 1954 and used it to build up their local organization. Democratic Party rules mandated a labyrinthine system in which voters chose the party's leaders and nominees through the "Texas two-step," a combination system of caucuses and conventions in addition to a direct primary election and, in most cases, a primary runoff. In presidential election years prior to 1960, another set of conventions preceded the state-level contests. Such layers meant that any political organization's success depended upon building a street-level organization, precinct by precinct. HCD leaders, like their counterparts in the HCCO and their predecessors in the 1930s and 1940s, began each biennial election cycle by identifying areas with a high number of sympathetic voters and then finding candidates to run for judge or captain in each favorable precinct. Harris County included more than two hundred party precincts, so just this first step represented no easy task. The selected precinct captains then attended HCD Area Council meetings where they learned how to conduct door-to-door outreach to voters in advance of the two-step primary and caucus. On Election Day, HCD's recruits first mobilized their rank-and-file supporters to go to the polls and vote during the day and then dragged them to the precinct convention at a local school, church, or civic hall that night. Turnout and prior organization then determined whether each captain could win his or her evening caucus and get elected as the party's official precinct chair, a post that also included serving as a delegate to the county convention and as a member of the county party's Executive Committee. If a HCD captain could pull enough voters to both the polls and the caucus, he or she could carry the precinct for Yarborough and other liberal candidates in the daytime and build power for the liberal HCD at night. For the latter, HCD understood that by controlling the precincts, they could capture control of the county party and then send a delegation to the state convention that would oppose Shivers and support the national Democratic ticket. The goal was to regain the White House from Republican control, but it all started by winning the precincts.

For the still brand-new HCD, 1954 proved to be a banner year. The liberal group won enough precinct conventions that it took control of the county executive committee "for the first time." Yarborough carried Harris County, previously the "bellwether" for the conservatives, by twenty-five thousand votes. Statewide, his total jumped nearly 160,000 votes above his showing in

1952, and he garnered 47.8 percent of the vote. Most important, Yarborough denied Shivers an outright majority, as the governor tallied only 49.5 percent of the total and fell 6,464 votes short of victory. Against all odds, the increasingly liberal Yarborough had forced the right-wing incumbent into a runoff. He trailed Shivers by only twenty-three thousand votes, or just 1.7 percent of the total cast. To say that Dixie and company were elated would be an understatement.[53]

The relationship of the HCD and Houston's liberal movement to Yarborough and vice-versa was cemented in the 1954 runoff campaign. Dixie recalled that "Shivers let out a scream that 'The trouble is in Harris County where there's a bunch of radicals down there.'" Indeed, there was no denying that the HCD had denied the governor his majority. Yarborough's work there had paid off, as had Dixie and company's organizing and Mrs. Randolph's generous contributions. Shivers denounced Yarborough as a "minion" of the subversive HCD, a tool of the CIO, and an ally of the NAACP and Americans for Democratic Action (ADA), the national liberal club founded by Eleanor Roosevelt. Shivers blasted labor, civil rights, and liberal organizations in the same breath, and, in the process, pushed them together. As Dixie put it, "He created, in some part, the liberal coalition by forcing us together in self-defense." Although that alliance would not truly reach fruition for years to come, the battle lines were clearly drawn as early as the summer of 1954. In the short term, HCD activists feverishly prepared to mobilize their constituents again to vote for Yarborough in the runoff. Huge numbers of African Americans and many Mexican Americans also supported the challenger, as did poor whites—especially in rural areas.[54]

For his part, the governor claimed that Yarborough supported integration and was in bed with the Communists and labor goons. In the final days of the campaign, Shivers declared an all-out war on the CIO, using a small strike of retail clerks in Port Arthur as a launching pad for a broad attack on nearly all of Yarborough's key supporters. A twelve-minute advertisement, "The Port Arthur Story," displayed footage of the small city sitting empty, devoid of foot traffic. A voiceover charged that the union had brought Communists into the strike, crippling the town's economy, but it failed to note that the vacant streets seen were recorded just after dawn, not at midday as the narration implied.

Such deceptions aside, Yarborough simply couldn't keep pace with the incumbent's fund-raising, bully pulpit, and well-established precinct organization. Shivers easily defeated Yarborough by more than 90,000 votes, 53 percent to 47 percent. The incumbent secured the Democratic nomination and with it an unprecedented third term in the governor's mansion and ongoing control of the Texas Democratic Party.[55] Soon after, at the state convention, Shivers repaid his many campaign debts, which included launching a frontal attack on the HCD. The governor "isolated and insulted" HCD delegates, and the liberals failed to influence the state platform or leadership.[56]

Yarborough's quixotic campaign inspired the HCD activists to continue fighting. The next two years were periods of "intensified organization" in which the HCD built upon their initial local success to lay a foundation for long-term coalition building and power at the statewide level. In 1955, the group's Steering Committee grew to "more than 500 policy makers." The HCD sharply criticized the closed-door cliques that dominated conservative political organizations, contending that the people could be better represented through transparent debate than by the special interests, led by developer Herman Brown, who assembled in Suite 3F of the Baker Hotel downtown. "Always opponents of the 'smoke-filled room,'" the HCD's historian later wrote, the "Harris County Democrats had to start using an auditorium for its meetings."

In May 1956, one of these open, integrated meetings became the site for an early attempt to build a multiracial liberal alliance. As it was later described: "The first candidates interviewing committee was formed with members from the Harris County Democrats, AFL-CIO, and [the Harris County] Council of Organizations. (This later became the coalition.)" In addition to endorsing liberal candidates at the local and state levels, the outreach effort helped the HCD again carry enough precincts that it could control the county convention. At the first state convention in June of that year, the group managed to elect its executive secretary, Mrs. Randolph, to the post of Democratic National Committeewoman. For the first time since the Depression, liberal Texans gained a seat at the state party's table and also had a voice in national politics.[57]

Still, the HCD and liberal Democrats across Texas remained marginalized in the state Democratic Party. Building upon the HCD's success as well as his base in East Texas, Yarborough again ran for governor and made a solid showing in both the primary and the runoff, narrowly losing to sitting U.S. senator Price Daniel by just 3,171 votes out of nearly 1.4 million cast. Yarborough again carried Harris County by a wide margin, but he failed to penetrate the conservative strongholds of Dallas and South Texas. Like Shivers, Daniel engaged in race baiting on the campaign trail, though the attacks were, according to one historian, "not as vitriolic" as they had been in 1954. Many liberals claimed that Yarborough would have won a fair and free election, but Shivers still controlled the state's electoral machinery, and he gladly handed the statehouse over to his chosen successor. Daniel and Shivers further encouraged a conservative victory by mobilizing the political bosses of the Rio Grande Valley, home to a storied tradition of infamous acts of mass voter fraud. Conservatives may have stuffed many urban boxes as well.[58]

To make matters worse for the HCD, at the second state convention in Fort Worth in September 1956, the conservative wing of the party again outmaneuvered and isolated the liberals. In fact, both factions had become the political footballs of Senator Lyndon B. Johnson, who had announced his intention to seek the presidency that year. At the first state convention, the moderate Johnson made a series of deals to form an ideologically diverse delegation to the national conference that pledged its support for Johnson's campaign. Hoping to position himself to appeal to northern liberals, Johnson also tolerated the HCD's Randolph in her bid for a seat on the Democratic National Committee. By the time of the second "governor's" convention, a ritual held only in presidential election years, Johnson had failed to secure the presidential nomination and now joined Governor Daniel in kicking out the liberals in order to take full control of the state party apparatus. Although he leaned conservative and was close with the Suite 3F crowd, Johnson above all wished to create a party in which every official at every level was primarily loyal to him. With Johnson's stamp of approval, the Shivers-Daniel leadership flatly refused to seat the HCD members, opting instead for a conservative challenge delegation. Doing so allowed the party's right wing to dominate the proceedings and adopt a platform that opposed civil rights and ignored the national party's dictates. Shivers again led a delegation to the national convention that refused to support the party's presidential nominee, Adlai Stevenson, and the former governor again carried Texas for Eisenhower that fall. Four years had passed, but the powers-that-be remained the same.

The decision to ignore the liberals' credentials violated the party's by-laws, and the liberals refused to retreat until physically threatened. "WORST OF ALL," the group's official history reads, "Mrs. Randolph and hundreds of other loyal Harris County Democrats, after being chosen delegates by a virtual landslide," were forced to deliberate in a rump convention in a "cow-barn" outside the official hall. "Convention management, backed up by armed possemen [sic], unseated the legal, loyal delegation and gave our seats to conservatives." Liberals and labor delegates from San Antonio and Dallas—including George and Latane Lambert—joined the HCD in walking out of the convention in protest.[59]

Several months after the convention, in December, the liberals formalized their rump caucus into a statewide permanent organization, the Democrats of Texas (DOT).[60] Led by Mrs. Randolph, the DOT essentially expanded the HCD into a statewide group. Throughout the late 1950s and into 1960, it would provide the glue that tied Democratic activists together between conventions and campaigns. Like the HCD, it remained a predominately white group, led by labor lawyers like Chris Dixie and a few wealthy "independent" liberals like Mrs. Randolph. Yet it also included numerous labor activists like the Lamberts and a handful of African American and Mexican American activists—many of whom were unionists like Moses and Erma LeRoy. Paired with the founding,

Mrs. R. D. (Frankie Carter) Randolph speaks to the Democrats of Texas in convention, Austin, Texas, May 1958. Photograph by Russell Lee. Courtesy Texas AFL-CIO Collection, Special Collections, The University of Texas at Arlington Library, Arlington, Texas, AR110-29-21 [#58109-A].

in 1954, of the *Texas Observer*, a liberal weekly newspaper that Mrs. Randolph also endowed, the DOT represented an institutional home in which liberal Democrats could continue to organize, maintain cohesion between elections, and continue forming deeper interracial ties.

White liberal Democrats in Texas had found a standard-bearer for their cause in Ralph Yarborough and had developed a way to stay organized in between election years. Yet two problems remained. First, though Yarborough's electoral defeats were becoming increasingly narrow, he had still failed to win an election. Second, and much more pressing, was the fact that Yarborough struggled to define his positions on civil rights, and, as a result, he had not yet managed to attract substantial numbers of African American and Mexican American voters.

Campaign advance man Bob Hall recalled that Yarborough's staffers initially had no idea how to approach African Americans as potential supporters. Politics in the candidate's hometown in East Texas remained a largely all-white affair, as it had been since the repression of the People's Party (or Populists) near the turn of the twentieth century. The poll tax reigned supreme, making it exceedingly difficult to register and mobilize poor white voters, let alone blacks. The white primary had formally excluded African Americans from state and local partisan politics until 1944. Less than a decade passed between the *Smith* ruling that year and Yarborough's first campaign, and by the 1950s even the most liberal candidates still remained focused on turning out the poor white vote. Jim Crow prohibited social interaction between blacks and whites, so political contacts were few and far between. Outside of San Antonio, many

Mexican Americans in South Texas continued to face repression at the hand of Anglo ranchers, and political bosses still dominated local politics. Even Bexar County remained lukewarm toward Yarborough.

According to Hall, Yarborough's campaigns typically acquired African American supporters by accident, not as part of an intentional outreach effort. In the cities, the advance team contacted African American activists whom they knew about through the labor movement and its law firms. Some of these contacts dated back to the Progressive Party of 1948 or even the pecan sheller movement a decade earlier, while others remained less well known. Moses and Erma LeRoy served as Yarborough's surrogates in black Houston, where the couple arranged countless events for the candidate throughout the 1950s. The Lamberts had relocated to Dallas, so each time Yarborough visited North Texas, their phone would ring, and through the Lamberts the campaign would reach the local branch of the NAACP. In San Antonio, Maury Maverick and then his son helped Yarborough find platforms on the West and East Sides, though the liberals there did not always succeed in delivering the endorsements from across the tracks. Hall later observed that the African American and Mexican American activists the Yarborough campaign depended upon were not always the right leaders; that is, they were not necessarily the people who had the most influence in the black and brown communities. But they were the people that the white liberals knew, and that was a start.[61]

While countless poor whites and a growing number of blacks rallied around Yarborough, the candidate's own record on race and civil rights at times created suspicion among African Americans. He tried to walk a tightrope that allowed him to maintain black and liberal support but did not offend the racist sensibilities of some of his white farmer and labor backers. He also grappled with his own East Texas roots and unconsciously white supremacist sentiments. Following the *Brown* decision of 1954, he maintained that he opposed "the forced co-mingling of the races" in schools but believed in equal schools for "Negro citizens" and the voluntary reconciliation of the races. He further hid behind the slogan of "states' rights" but added that the Supreme Court decision deserved further study. On occasion he slipped into his East Texas vernacular, an idiom that blamed African Americans for the region's economic woes. Hall recalls one rally on the North Side of Houston in 1956 at which Yarborough became especially passionate while rhetorically laying into the banks, insurance companies, and oil giants who enriched themselves at the expense of ordinary working Texans. While a mixed-race crowd of union members and liberals looked on, Yarborough screamed at the elites who lied to and stole from the poor, finally exclaiming, "But you and I know that there must have been a nigger in the woodpile somewhere!" Hall remembers being immediately crushed on a deeply personal as well as professional level. All of the campaign's work to cross the tracks and the color line hung in the balance with every one of the candidate's public pronouncements, and statements like this one set that part of the campaign back months, if not years. The relationship between the campaign and black activists was fundamentally "dishonest" and "hypocritical," Hall later recalled. The candidate and staffers talked out of both sides of their mouths, while many African American activists lacked the influence they claimed to possess, or they intentionally double-crossed Yarborough on Election Day.⁶²

For their part, black activists remained divided in their response to Yarborough, the HCD and DOT, and the larger "liberal movement." In 1954, R. R. Grovey, the former plaintiff in an early white primary case, wrote a letter to the editor in which he listed six reasons that African Americans should vote for the conservative incumbent Shivers. His arguments boiled down to a mix of skepticism about Yarborough and the liberals and pragmatism in regard to joining the winning team. Shivers had "made the state a good governor," Grovey began. On the key question of segregation, he told black voters, the two candidates were so similar that "you have little to choose between." He obliquely criticized Yarborough's "approach to the Negro vote," registering a complaint not unlike the claim of dishonesty that Bob Hall observed from within the campaign. More important for Grovey, however, were the practical politics. Putting himself at odds with the mission of the HCCO, he flatly stated that "it is a mistake for Negroes to attempt to bloc their votes in any election." Moreover, the black vote had been misdirected. "For the last four elections, since the Negroes have been voting, they have joined whole-heartedly with a group of so-called Liberals and cast their majority with a group of people who had no chance to be elected." This was a losing strategy, he added, citing the maxim that " 'To the victor belongs the spoils.' " Finally, Grovey criticized the white liberals in HCD who reached out to African Americans, charging that the former "made fools" of the black leaders who collaborated with them. "The so-called Loyal Democrats are aiding and abetting the establishment of two or three Negroes as political dictators in Harris County," he fumed. Prominent African Americans had given "large contributions" to the loyal liberals and had been appointed leaders as a result, a combination that would make black citizens "of all men [the] most miserable."⁶³

While Grovey criticized the liberal movement, its candidate, and its black sympathizers, many among the leadership of the HCCO, clearly adopted a different tack. In citing large donors as the new kingmakers in black politics, Grovey may have been referring to Hobart Taylor Sr., owner of a taxicab company and real estate magnate who had long supported the local NAACP and had emerged as a leader in the HCCO. Taylor at times cozied up to conservative politicians, but he also remained a behind-the-scenes supporter of liberals as well as the struggle for civil rights. Back in the 1940s, Taylor, in exchange for his opposition to a city plan to take over the local private bus company, received the company owner's agreement to remove the screens that segregated black passengers and to hire black drivers. This represented the definition of the smoke-filled, backroom deal, but it got the job done. In 1957, with Yarborough on the rise, Taylor sat down with the HCD's Mrs. Randolph and Christia Adair of the NAACP and offered to subsidize Adair's salary if Randolph put her to work in the Democratic Party headquarters. The HCD seized on the chance to extend its reach into black neighborhoods. Randolph fired off a letter to liberal party activists in the area, urging them to assist Adair in organizing clubs that would bring together members from several adjacent precincts. Moses and Erma LeRoy also remained steadfast supporters of Yarborough and the liberal movement in Houston. Like Taylor, they used their position in the HCCO to steer the broader organization toward an alliance with the predominately white HCD.

Their efforts paid off. In the late 1950s, the HCD extended its material support for and collaboration with the HCCO all the way down to the precinct level. As it had previously done in white neighborhoods, the HCD assisted the HCCO in identifying local leaders, winning precinct conventions, and turning out voters for liberal candidates. The expertise and resources of the HCD allowed the all-black HCCO to greatly expand its influence on the ground and in the county Democratic Party. Grovey may have been correct in observing that the loyal liberals were conspiring with a handful of black leaders to create an African American bloc vote, but by the end of the decade his concern was not shared by most of his contemporaries. Most black leaders instead joined Taylor, Adair, and the LeRoys in the joint HCD-HCCO organizing campaign. Moses LeRoy became chairman of the HCCO's Candidates and Issues Committee and thereby gained entrée to the HCD's inner circles. While the latter group imagined itself as an alternative to the smoke-filled rooms of their conservative counterparts, its early efforts to build coalitions with African Americans often took place behind closed doors, where LeRoy and other HCCO officers met privately with Randolph, Dixie, and the rest of the HCD's top brass.[64]

While some black leaders like Grovey criticized the sincerity of the white liberals' efforts to organize black voters, many HCD activists likewise remained suspicious of their counterparts in the HCCO. Yarborough staffer Bob Hall contended that many ministers and self-appointed black political leaders cared more about their own positions and power than the struggle for civil rights or liberal public policy. They served as diplomats, and they depended upon segregation and poverty to maintain their status as intermediaries between blacks and whites. Curiously, he included the LeRoys in this category, although he was unaware of their history in radical politics as well as their roles as liberal voices in the internal political debates within the HCCO and Houston's black communities. Chris Dixie similarly held that ordinary black voters often proved more liberal than their official leaders, a dualism that forced the HCD to adopt a strategy of "going under and around the organizations and getting to the rank and file." Dixie also maintained that Mrs. Randolph had in fact organized the HCCO, a patently false statement given that the council predated Randolph's arrival on the scene by a half-decade. Dixie maintained that white liberals had given the vote to African Americans, perhaps reflecting an unconscious assumption that black people could not win and wield it for themselves. Surprisingly, NAACP leader Adair told a similar story, suggesting that although Randolph's role in the HCCO was not foundational, the white liberal matron and the HCD did have a substantial impact on the council, providing it with resources and training to expand its influence and purview.[65]

Such was the nature of the very tentative coalition between white liberals and black community organizers in the final years of the decade: a mixture of mutual admiration and need along with persistent distrust and suspicion. African American liberals used the white liberals to gain the upper hand in the ideologically diverse, all-black HCCO. White liberals struggled to identify the black leaders who were on their side and to distinguish them from those that only paid them lip service. It was a volatile concoction, as are all coalitions between leaders from such distinct home bases. More often than not, it held together and succeeded in electing countless liberal precinct judges of both races and electing a number of other officials. Still, the fact that these new representatives remained all white would become a constant source of tension.

The persistence of such disagreements did not prevent the liberal movement from scoring a pair of major victories at the polls. First, in 1957, Yarborough finally won an election. Price Daniel's victory over the perennial liberal candidate for governor in 1956 forced Daniel to vacate his U.S. Senate seat, and Shivers appointed as replacement a conservative businessman with no plans to hold the position over the long term. The state constitution required a speedy special election that would not require either a simple majority or a runoff to fill the vacated seat. Lyndon Johnson, the other U.S. senator from Texas, led an effort in the state legislature to change the election code in order to prevent the liberal Yarborough from slipping into office, but his maneuver failed. The lack of a powerful incumbent created a wide-open statewide race. Yarborough, in the words of his biographer, "was in the fifth year of nearly nonstop statewide campaign, so the people of Texas knew him well." Anti-Communist archconservative Martin Dies emerged as his main opposition, but he was too reactionary to win the support of Johnson, Daniel, or even Shivers. So Yarborough's well-tested campaign staffers whipped out their well-worn three-ring binders and began contacting their tens, if not hundreds, of thousands of supporters. Finally, after a massive liberal get-out-the-vote mobilization, Yarborough carried a plurality of 38 percent, defeating Dies by a wide margin and ascending to the U.S. Senate with only 364,605 votes. A year later, as an incumbent, he easily won reelection to a full six-year term.[66]

The liberal standard-bearer finally had an office from which he could operate and repay his longtime supporters. He became "the People's Senator," opening his office to liberal, labor, and civil rights activists and serving as a dignitary and speaker at countless community-organizing events. He served as a resource for organizers of all colors and as an advocate for their associations. His victory did not bring immediate liberal change to Texas, but it did provide longtime activists with some degree of hope.

At the local level, the HCD seized the momentum it had helped to create. In 1957, a local lawyer named Bob Eckhardt took over as chairman of the HCD and set out to take the liberal group to the next level. Another round of precinct organizing and the coalition with the HCCO allowed the liberals to help elect and reelect Yarborough, who carried Harris County by twenty thousand votes in 1958. That year, the HCD also backed eight victorious candidates for the state legislature and finally elected the county chairman of the entire Harris County Democratic Party apparatus. This last, seemingly inconsequential, victory held tremendous importance. Despite its dominance in the precincts and conventions and its success in electing Mrs. Randolph to the Democratic National Committee, the HCD had failed to elect the county chairman of the entire party, leaving it in the hands of hostile conservatives who manipulated the electoral machinery and convention rules to their own advantage. By seizing the official party's top post, the HCD could now control the elections themselves. For Chris Dixie, Mrs. Randolph, and other veteran activists, nothing could be more significant. As the decade came to a close, Houston's liberal movement had triumphed locally, cobbling together a ragtag bunch of lawyers, union activists, and black leaders into a force that took on and vanquished the politicians of the oil companies, the Suite 3F crowd, and the larger conservative Establishment. Charging forward with heads of steam, the liberal activists were now poised to take their fight for the soul of the Democratic Party to the statewide level. It was again time to find more allies for the struggle ahead.[67]

John J. Herrera and Politics in "La Colonia"

Houston's black and white activists found willing partners in an unlikely place: the city's Mexican American *colonia* (settlement). Led by attorney John J. Herrera, a faction of *mexicano* leaders pushed their historically stolid civic organizations to launch a series of active civil rights campaigns, including efforts to address both racial and economic discrimination. These initiatives, in turn, led these liberal LULACers (members of the League of United Latin American Citizens) and members of the American G.I. Forum (AGIF) into political action and eventually into coalitions with like-minded African American and white activists from the HCCO and HCD. Although little evidence survives that documents the political life of Mexican Americans in 1950s Houston, it is clear that a group of residents in *la colonia* joined the statewide upsurge of Mexican American activism and built a powerful new electoral force in their neighborhoods—and they did so in intimate conversation with like-minded white and black organizers.

Mexicanos made up only 5.8 percent of the population of Houston in 1950 and a similar proportion in 1960, as both the *mexicano* numbers and the entire city population nearly doubled in size. Unskilled laborers predominated, and the Mexican American *colonia* in the city was in fact an amalgamation of geographically distant neighborhoods scattered from Magnolia Park (east of downtown) to *el Segundo Barrio* along the Houston Ship Channel and isolated pockets within the Fourth, Fifth, and Sixth Wards. Since the first large wave of Mexican immigrants arrived in Houston after the 1910 Revolution, many efforts to organize the city's *mexicanos* were confined to only one or two of these small enclaves, while a select few organizations transcended neighborhood boundaries and brought in Mexican American residents from throughout the city. At the dawn of the 1950s, Council 60 of the League of United Latin American Citizens (LULAC) remained the oldest, largest, and most important citywide civic organization. It traced its origins to the early 1930s and was composed primarily of "blue-collar workers," but its demographics, location, and political stances were constantly disputed throughout its long history, continuing into the 1970s. At times relatively conservative Mexican American businessmen dominated its leadership and membership rolls, while relatively liberal activists took control in other periods.[68]

Across Texas and in many places throughout the Southwest, LULAC quickly became the dominant advocacy organization among Mexican Americans following its inception in 1929. Led by members of the growing Mexican American middle class, it aimed to combat the many forms of Juan Crow. LULAC took aim at bossism and other means of political disfranchisement, school segregation (ostensibly based on language), exclusion from juries, and all other slights or discrimination based on ethnicity, including segregation at work, in housing, and in public accommodations. Despite this ambitious civil rights agenda, historians have long characterized LULAC as assimilationist, conservative, and elitist in its orientation. The group prohibited women and noncitizens of the United States from membership, its male leaders tended to be professionals, and it often shied away from or outright opposed labor conflicts such as the pecan sheller strike. LULAC even fought against the classification of Mexicans as a separate racial group in the census and other government documents, maintaining that they were instead white ethnics not unlike Jews or Italians. This dedication to whiteness, some scholars have argued, cut them off from the black civil rights movement and even, at times, helped to reinforce Jim Crow. Yet in truth there was tremendous variation within LULAC on the ground. Some ladies' auxiliaries engaged in outreach to immigrant women, while some local councils dove headfirst into working-class struggles. The political inclinations of its leaders remained incredibly diverse, as were the strategies and tactics they employed to achieve their goals. Although a handful of its leaders may have internalized a self-image of being white, many more understood themselves in hybrid terms, as both Mexican-origin and patriotic Americans. John J. Herrera and the members of LULAC Council 60 in Houston tended to be liberal in their politics, syncretic in their national identity, and, in most cases, from humble socioeconomic origins.

Herrera was also a veteran and a member of the American G.I. Forum (AGIF). Founded in 1948 by a group of Mexican American veterans led by Dr. Hector P. Garcia of Corpus Christi, the AGIF first rallied to help *mexicanos* who had served during the war gain access to the many benefits of the Servicemen's Readjustment Act of 1944, popularly known as the G.I. Bill. The forum made great advances in this area, but its major leap forward came in 1949, when a funeral home in Three Rivers, Texas, refused to accept the remains of Private Felix Longoria, a native son who had been killed while serving in the Philippines. Garcia rallied his legions behind the clear case of ethnic discrimination and disrespect to an American hero, and the case gained national attention. Garcia negotiated with the recently elected U.S. senator Lyndon B. Johnson and secured an agreement in which Longoria was honored and buried in Arlington National Cemetery. The AGIF had proven it would act, and also that it could win. Mexican American veterans across the country flocked into the organization, establishing countless local chapters from California to Washington, D.C. Garcia would remain its national president, chief organizer, and key decision maker for decades to come, establishing Corpus Christi as one of the main hubs of the postwar Mexican American civil rights struggle. Still, like LULAC, the AGIF has often been dismissed by historians and scholars of Chicano/a studies, for many of the same reasons. The forum has been depicted as malecentric, obsessed with whiteness and patriotism, and fundamentally conservative. Although this portrait of the AGIF contains more than a kernel of truth, the aggressive activism of Herrera and other like-minded Mexican American veterans belies such simplistic readings of what was in fact a large, diverse, and, at times, militant and effective organization.[69]

Herrera and other liberal Mexican American leaders in Houston advocated full civil rights for all *mexicanos*, beginning with working people and including both U.S. and Mexican citizens. LULAC and AGIF served as vehicles for these leaders' activism, but so too did other parts of their professional lives. As an attorney, Herrera dedicated much of his law practice to the fight for civil rights. Born in 1910 in Louisiana, Herrera joined LULAC in 1933, a year before he graduated from high school in Houston. He worked as a shoeshine boy, busboy, waiter, and finally a union cab driver as he attended South Texas School of Law, an avocation that soon landed him in the middle of the struggle for fair employment practices. "From 1939 to 1943," he later wrote, "acting on protest from Latin-Americans and negroes [*sic*], that the Houston Shipbuilding Corporation and Brown Shipbuilding Corporation were discriminating in employment matters, I gradually worked out an upgrading . . . so that by 1943 they were working in ALL CRAFTS and GRADES and one-third (1/3) of the personnel of the shipyards were of Mexican-Americans and one-third (1/3) were Negroes." He was admitted to the bar in 1943 and immediately filed the state's first formal Fair Employment Practices Committee (FEPC) complaint, a claim against Shell Oil Refinery "alleging discrimination against Negroes and Mexican-Americans" by both the company and the union. The fair employment campaigns helped revive Council 60, which had gone into decline during the Great Depression. After the war, Herrera aided FEPC investigator Carlos Castañeda in petitioning Congress and the Truman administration to extend the committee's mandate after it expired in 1946. He later joined the legal team led by San Antonio attorney Gus C. Garcia that represented LULAC and won two landmark civil rights cases concerning Mexican Americans—*Delgado v. Bastrop* (1948) and *Hernandez v. Texas* (1954). In between, Herrera served as the national president of LULAC for 1952–53, a period in which he traveled around the state and successfully organized some fifty new local councils. A leading Mexican American politician of the 1960s wrote that Herrera "was a lonely voice" in the late 1940s and early 1950s, organizing LULAC, dabbling in politics, and "in the courtroom representing clients who spoke no English and knew not their rights under the law."[70]

In fact, Herrera did more than dabble in politics; rather, he represented the leading edge of the liberal faction of Mexican American civil rights activists entering the political arena. In the late 1940s, Herrera worked for the unsuccessful U.S. Senate campaign of liberal ex-governor Jimmy Allred and then the successful bid to the same office of Lyndon B. Johnson in 1948. Throughout the 1950s, he traveled to the Rio Grande Valley of South Texas with attorney Garcia, U.S. senator Dennis Chavez of New Mexico, and Dr. Hector P. Garcia of the AGIF. They sought to "stimulate voter interest and participation among Mexican-Americans" in the region, persuading them to "continue their loyalty to the Democratic Party" and to help "heretofore non-voters to become franchised citizens." They gathered information for their civil rights cases and conducted voter-registration drives simultaneously. Forum leader Garcia later remarked that only Herrera had the "guts" to go to the South Texas town of Edna to "face the gun happy police in order to get the information we needed." For fourteen years Herrera broadcasted a weekly Spanish-language program on Houston radio station KLVL in which he "discuss[ed] current LULAC programs" before an audience of 300,000 Spanish-speaking listeners on the Texas Gulf Coast. Herrera also used the show to urge Mexican Americans to pay their poll taxes and vote.[71]

In 1954, 1956, and 1958, Herrera ran unsuccessfully for a seat in the state legislature, campaigning with the backing of a coalition of labor, liberal, *mexicano*, and African American groups. Evidence remains thin on these races, but documents from Herrera's personal collection suggest that he decided to run at the urging of "a group of businessmen, including Jewish and Negro leaders," a likely reference to activists in the HCD and the HCCO. He ran "as a Liberal" with significant support from local African Americans, who did not run their own candidate for the same place in the legislature. His backing among Mexican Americans was even stronger. When he launched his bid in May 1954, Herrera was just days removed from his landmark victory in the *Hernandez* Supreme Court case, positioning him to capitalize on his years of service in LULAC (of which he had been the national president two years earlier) and many other Mexican American civil rights and community organizations. Herrera remained popular among rank-and-file LULACers, who hoped to return him to its presidency, but Herrera declined to seek that office in order to pursue a seat at the table of state politics.[72]

On the campaign trail, Herrera took public stands in support of black civil rights and organized labor and actively wooed those constituencies. He did not shy from controversy but made his politics plain at the front and center of his campaign announcement and platform. "I will vigorously oppose any action by the Legislature to circumvent the Supreme Court's decision desegregating our schools," read the first plank. "In view of the increasingly serious economic situation and the unemployment problem," he wrote in his second point, "I am in favor of a public works program financed by the Federal and State Governments." While the suburbs may have boomed in the 1950s, Herrera believed that many hard-working people were falling behind. Part of the problem was the conservative turn in labor law beginning with Taft-Hartley. "As a member of organized labor and an organizer among the low income groups of both the AFL and CIO Unions," Herrera added, "I will endorse any labor bill calculated to help organized labor and give management a fair hearing in connection with any bills affecting the working man in Texas." In short, racial and economic justice represented the core issues of his candidacy. He also was opposed to the sales tax, and endorsed jury service for women, higher teacher salaries, tighter regulation of the insurance industry, and the legalization of liquor by the drink.

In his third race in 1958, Herrera approached Election Day confident that he would finally win—despite the continuation of the poll tax and at-large elections that stacked the odds against him. He had garnered more than thirty thousand votes in his previous effort, and he believed that his commonsense approach to legislating and a "person to person hand-shaking campaign" would convince voters of his "record as the champion of the underdog." He planned a "final big push" with volunteer "telephone workers, 'card pushers' at the precincts, automobiles and drivers" to turn out all of his potential supporters on the critical day. His liberal platform and supporters in "a strong LABOR-NEGRO-LATIN coalition," he hoped, would finally push him over the top.[73]

Yet Herrera's optimism proved misguided, as he lost again in 1958—even as Yarborough and the HCD celebrated their triumphs that year. Significantly, no reference to his three bids for the legislature was recorded in any of the leading sources on either the HCD or the HCCO. Both black and white activists supported his campaigns but still perceived the city's *mexicano* population as too small and disorganized to prove consequential to their own future plans. Instead, black and white activists remained focused on working with each other. Still, Herrera's early career as a civil rights, political, and labor activist suggests that a liberal faction of Mexican American activists were actively developing an expansive agenda for racial and economic justice during this period—and they did so in the electoral arena in concert with the city's leading black and white activists.

Although scholars have claimed that Mexican American activists in the period organized around claiming their whiteness, Herrera's work in LULAC, in the courtroom, and in politics instead combated discrimination against *mexicanos* by asserting their place as an ethnic minority and by working alongside African Americans, organized labor, and white liberals. He and his supporters did not, as one historian has put it, make a "Faustian pact with whiteness" in which they claimed a white racial identity in order to distance themselves from blacks, thereby contributing to the maintenance of Jim Crow. Rather, Herrera portrayed himself as a "champion of the underdog" who fiercely opposed racial segregation, demanded labor rights, and sought independent political power for *mexicanos* as a distinct group.[74]

To be sure, another faction of conservative LULACers led by Houston restaurateur Felix Tijerina advocated an entirely different vision of Mexican American advancement and utilized a divergent set of tactics to achieve its goals. Tijerina vehemently defended segregation and personally enforced it at the restaurant he owned. He became a local LULAC officer and then the organization's national president from 1956 to 1960, the longest tenure in the group's history. But his politics could not have been more different from those of Herrera. In 1952 and again in 1956, Tijerina and his allies joined Governor Allan Shivers and the rest of the state's former Dixiecrats in endorsing Republican Dwight Eisenhower in the presidential election. He defended Eisenhower's vice president, Richard Nixon, against criticism from LULACers across the country, including those in Nixon's home state of California. (Herrera and other Mexican American liberals in Houston joined black and white activists in endorsing Democrat Adlai Stevenson.)[75]

The multiple fault lines of class, ideology, strategy, and tactics that divided the Herreras and Tijerinas and their respective supporters in Houston—and indeed their counterparts across the state and nation—proved clearer to contemporaries than to present-day historians. While a small, conservative faction of activists that aligned with Tijerina has dominated the scholarship on the subject, Herrera's life suggests that there existed another contingent of Mexican American civil rights advocates who maintained close ties to working people and to organized labor as well as a far more liberal political sensibility. That ideology and the realities of on-the-ground politics encouraged Mexican Americans like Herrera to engage in coalition building with not only whites but also African Americans. In many ways, Herrera had much more in common with the city's white labor lawyers such as Dixie and black labor activists like the LeRoys than he did with his co-ethnic Tijerina.[76] And he wasn't alone—across the state, and especially in San Antonio, a liberal wing of the LULAC- and AGIF-led Mexican American civil rights movement would increasingly separate itself from the organizations' conservative moorings and launch a new, more aggressive phase of the struggle in the years to come.

More immediately, Herrera's campaigns and then a long-shot gubernatorial bid by Henry B. Gonzalez of San Antonio galvanized many Mexican American activists in Houston to form a new political alliance by the end of the 1950s. Like the HCCO, the new Civic Action Committee (CAC) brought together a diverse range of businessmen, union members, and professionals who sought to unify and mobilize the city's growing Mexican American vote. Founded in 1958, the group leaned liberal but remained nonpartisan and did not immediately ally itself with the HCD. One evening in the summer of 1958, CAC hosted a barbecue in the backyard of Mr. and Mrs. E. P. Leal to raise funds for the Gonzalez race. "An important thing happened during that campaign," a successor group's official history reads. "Mexican Americans for the first time organized to help a politician." Tickets to the event cost ten dollars each, an astronomical sum, and "skeptics said it couldn't be done." Still, at the end of the night, CAC leaders crowded around an outdoor picnic table "jubilantly piling a mountain of dollar bills" in front of the smiling candidate. Gonzalez's stoic campaign manager, "who smiles but rarely," also rejoiced, as the total added up to $1,000. The account concludes, simply, "Political history was made that night." Herrera had laid the groundwork, and he soon became active in CAC as well. Mexican Americans in Houston had finally developed their own autonomous political institution and had begun to experiment in bloc voting as well as interracial coalition building. From this humble beginning, the city's political life would eventually be transformed.[77]

The dawn of the Cold War wreaked havoc on the labor and civil rights movements that had flowered during the Great Depression and World War II. Undeterred but not unfazed, many activists responded by redirecting their energies into new channels, often cross-class, monoracial coalitions that sought to organize and turn out their members for political action. For Moses and Erma LeRoy, the struggle for political representation through the new HCCO continued to dovetail with the fight for civil rights in the community and upward mobility without racial discrimination on the job. For labor attorney Chris Dixie, society lady Mrs. Randolph, and the leaders of the new steel and oil workers unions, the creation of a new liberal-labor organization of "loyal" or "national" Democrats represented the best path forward for achieving economic prosperity and political democracy for all peoples. The local HCD became the bedrock of a larger "liberal movement" that succeeded in seizing control of the county's official Democratic Party and spun off a statewide organization, the DOT. Through great trials and tribulations, it even won some elections, elevating several liberals to the state legislature and landing Ralph Yarborough in the U.S. Senate. The white liberals did so, in part, by forging new interracial alliances with the city's and the state's African American and Mexican American activists. The latter group, though numerically small in Houston, still managed to carve out a place in the city's political landscape, as liberal organizers led by Herrera broke away from the rigidity of LULAC to form CAC, a full-fledged, autonomous association that would remain the center of local Mexican American politics for decades to come. Just as the HCD and the HCCO sought to build upon their local efforts to develop statewide organizations, the CAC would soon become one branch of a larger effort to extend the influence of the growing Mexican American vote across Texas.

All of these groups worked first and foremost to organize their respective bases of support. They did so separately but simultaneously, and they all had similar needs if not the same goals and priorities. Class and ideology divided each ethnic group, compelling the most aggressive black, brown, and white activists to attempt to cross the color line in search of mutual support. The predominately white HCD needed the LeRoys and Herrera in order to extend their own outreach across the tracks into the city's African American and Mexican American neighborhoods. Both the intraracial divides and the interracial coalitions would emerge in much sharper relief in the 1960s, but their origins lay in this previous decade. The seeds of a coalition had been sowed.

The deepening of ties between black and brown activists and the predominately white labor movement and white liberal Democrats would represent the final step in building a multiracial electoral and civil rights alliance in Houston and across the state. All that they needed was a model for how to truly cross the many axes of difference that separated them, for how to transcend the misunderstandings and even, at times, mutual suspicion that so often remained in these first interracial experiments. They would soon find a blueprint in San Antonio.

Chapter 4

Minorities Combine

G. J. Sutton, Albert Peña, and the Democrats of Texas

"Negro Wins Jr. College Race," blared the banner headline of the April 4, 1948, edition of the *San Antonio Light*. G. J. Sutton, the undertaker who had organized African Americans in support of the pecan shellers and Maury Maverick in the late 1930s, had won a seat on the city's Union Junior College Board. He became the first black elected official in South Texas since Reconstruction, a feat that surprised most contemporary observers. If that weren't enough to scare the city's white elites, the title of an accompanying side article said even more: "Minorities Combine, Win," it read. Sutton had formed a coalition with Gustavo C. "Gus" Garcia, a militant Mexican American attorney, who in turn gained a place on the board of the San Antonio Independent School District. A stunned columnist opined, "A potent combination of San Antonio minorities Saturday made political history that amazed the nation."[1]

Ten years later, another Mexican American community leader from San Antonio toured Texas as part of a long-shot campaign to become the state's next governor. The fact that he did so at all proved remarkable—most *mexicanos* in the state remained disenfranchised, and conservative white elites dominated politics at all levels. Yet ordinary Mexican Americans flocked to his campaign events, celebrating the unprecedented rise of one of their own. Even more extraordinarily, the campaign also enjoyed the support of countless African Americans.

Long forgotten and still scarcely understood, these fleeting moments of black-brown collaboration serve as bookends to a decade of intense but separate community organizing among both the city's and the state's most militant African American and Mexican American civil rights activists. Each group individually engaged in the gradual, painstaking process of developing their own distinct bases of power. Yet they did so while keeping one eye on coalition building across the color line.

Behind the scenes and largely beyond the gaze of the city's leading businessmen and politicians, San Antonio became the incubator of the state's first enduring multiracial civil rights coalition. This coalition had its origins in part in the massive influx of migrants and capital during the military buildup of World War II, a trend that continued as the city's military bases remained open into the Cold War. Veterans among the new arrivals mixed with hometown descendants of the old Maverick campaigns to launch a new wave of organizing efforts. On the city's East Side, African American activists put forward an expansive vision for an all-out assault on Jim Crow, staging a broad campaign for both racial and economic justice. These organically radical activists encountered opposition from their own so-called race leaders, but they also found new ways to publicize their activities and communicate with residents in their community as well as possible allies across the city. At the same time, a growing civil rights movement and liberal political mobilization among Mexican Americans on the West and South Sides likewise challenged the intermediaries that had long run the city's barrios.

Intermittent partnerships between like-minded black and brown activists slowly and unsteadily progressed toward lasting relationships of mutual need, support, and finally trust. Differences did not disappear, and a full-fledged, permanent coalition would not emerge until at least 1960. Yet the experiments in San Antonio in the fifteen years after World War II laid the foundation for future collaboration across the color line. Black, brown, and even white activists searched for and discovered ways to work together that added up to a model for future cooperative efforts at both the local and statewide levels. A new age in Texas politics was dawning.

Action and Reaction

Sutton and Garcia's quiet alliance began earlier that year, when the two activists agreed to support one another's electoral aspirations. Sutton sought a position on the San Antonio Union Junior College Board, the body responsible for administering the city's two segregated public schools of higher education. The black school, St. Philip's College, had long been the pride of the East Side, and Sutton's father had long served as its principal. But after World War II, when many African American veterans in San Antonio and across the nation brought home heightened expectations of greater racial equality, it was clear that St. Philip's would continue to be separate and unequal as compared to the all-white San Antonio College. Like its primary- and secondary-school counterparts in the age of Jim Crow, St. Philip's received less public funding per pupil, lower salaries for its faculty and staff, and used textbooks and instructional tools only after they had been discarded from the white junior college. Sutton's candidacy called for equality in fact as well as under the law and, even more radically, it asked for a voice at the governing table. In the era before *Brown v. Board* (1954), such demands did not call for integration but were still so outlandish that they were summarily dismissed by white observers without much need for comment.[2]

For his part, Garcia sought a seat on the board of the San Antonio Independent School District. An unpredictable but brilliant lawyer, Garcia ran for office on behalf of La Liga Pro Defensor Escolar (the School Improvement League), a group founded by local LULACer (member of the League of United Latin American Citizens) and businessman Eleuterio Escobar. According to historian Mario T. Garcia, the league simultaneously aimed to improve the city's "Mexican schools" and to desegregate its Anglo institutions. It had tried every weapon in its arsenal, but the school board's continued inaction convinced the group that it needed to field its own candidate.[3] Gus Garcia had previously led the legal effort to close down a segregated "Mexican school" in nearby Cuero, and he was now preparing a broader constitutional challenge of the entire practice of segregating Mexican American and "Anglo" children. Tall, light-skinned, with movie star looks and a silver tongue, Garcia had emerged as the lead attorney for both LULAC and the brand-new American G.I. Forum (AGIF). He was the obvious choice to serve as the struggle's public face.[4]

Little evidence survives of how exactly Sutton and Garcia came together. The first daily newspaper report on Sutton's candidacy suggested that he had formed an alliance not with Garcia but with Cline Thomas, an African American candidate for the school board. When that unsubstantiated rumor was laid to rest, the fact of a real black-brown coalition between Sutton and Garcia was so unnatural and unexpected that it warranted special comment. "Some strange alliances have sprung up," wrote the *San Antonio Light*'s pseudonymous columnist Don Politico, "thereby adding credence to the ancient saw about politics and strange bedfellows. An interesting trade between G. J. Sutton, negro undertaker . . . and the Latin American groups backing Gus Garcia's candidacy . . . has been arranged." Escobar's School Improvement League promised to get out the vote for both candidates in exchange for support from Sutton's bloc as well as that of Valmo Bellinger, the son of the former black political boss who inherited the East Side wing of the city machine. Bellinger endorsed the biracial duo but left Thomas, the other black school board candidate, out in the cold. Anglo opponents from the affluent North Side who ran on a "Better Schools Ticket" couldn't quite figure out which of the black men was the true threat but nonetheless circulated literature that "talked darkly of an east-westside combination." Indeed, race remained a central issue throughout the campaign. Sutton and Garcia's ethnic backgrounds were noted every time their names appeared in the paper, which also reminded voters of the unprecedented fact that two "Negroes" appeared on the same ballot. Adopting a conciliatory tone, Garcia alluded to the racial nature of his opposition immediately after his victory: "I feel no rancor toward anyone in spite of

"G. J. Sutton Congratulations Pour In: Negro undertaker swamped with phone calls after victory," read the caption beside a photograph from this series that appeared on the front page of the *San Antonio Light* on Monday, April 5, 1948—two days after the historic election of the first African American official in the region since Reconstruction. Courtesy *San Antonio Light* Photograph Collection, UTSA-ITC, Image L-3992-B, San Antonio Express/ZUMAPRESS.com.

the attempt on the part of a few selfish people to inject an issue of hatred and prejudice into the campaign," he said.[5]

The two candidates' victories may have caught many white observers unaware, but the central importance of their coalition strategy and its potential long-term impact were immediately apparent to contemporary journalists. A record twenty-one thousand people voted in the standalone school elections in which no higher-level races were contested. Garcia won a plurality of nearly eight thousand votes, finishing first overall and securing one of three places in a field of seven on the school district board. Sutton pulled just over seven thousand votes, winning a seat on the junior college board by finishing second overall, just seventy-nine votes ahead of the defeated incumbent (a margin that would be further reduced after a recount).

The coalition strategy had proven decisive in Sutton's race and added to Garcia's sizable victory. Don Politico noted that the duo made history by staging the year's most sophisticated campaigns on the ground. Garcia's staff and volunteers represented "the only group functioning in an organized manner at all the polls." The attorney "went into the race to win" and "built up organization in every precinct. It was Latins for a Latin." For his part, "Sutton made a phenomenal race" in which he "ran well" in the urban areas "but was hard pressed" in the affluent white suburbs. The impact of the new elected officials would be palpable, the columnist speculated. Both the West and East Sides were mobilized as never before. Garcia's rise promised to bring the usually secretive school board meetings "into the light of day. . . . and citizens groups, even from the west side, will be heard." Sutton commented that his election confirmed that "all racial and religious groups should be represented in a democracy."[6]

Indeed, the swearing in of both officials signaled the beginning of a new era for San Antonio politics as well as the city's nascent black and brown civil rights movements. Garcia brought the most militant Mexican American activists into the halls of power for the first time and used his post as a launching pad for new campaigns. Soon after the election, Garcia filed and successfully argued the case that made the segregation of Mexican Americans in schools illegal in Texas, *Delgado v. Bastrop ISD* (the case did not address the segregation of African Americans). Two years later, in 1950, Garcia joined local School Improvement League and NAACP leaders in demanding that a planned $9.3 million school bond referendum include an earmark provision that would guarantee roughly one-third of the funds for black and West Side (Mexican American) schools. The provision never made it onto the ballot, but the bond passed, and Garcia successfully directed the funding toward the city's black and brown neighborhoods.[7]

As the first black elected official in South Texas since Reconstruction, Sutton likewise used his newfound notoriety to extend his influence in East Side and city politics. In 1949, he sought to mobilize his supporters again on behalf of an antimachine Anglo candidate for mayor, A. C. "Jack" White. In so doing, he shattered his brief partnership with black boss Bellinger and directly challenged the supremacy of the longtime East Side race leader. In what Don Politico called "one of the most intensive political battles of all time" on the East Side, Sutton turned outside the neighborhood, to a multiracial group of antimachine political activists who had come together in the Organized Voters League (OVL). With these new allies, Sutton aimed to use the mayoral race to gain the upper hand in the internal political struggle of the city's African Americans. The plan worked. On May 31, 1949, White defeated the machine's incumbent. Reports credited Sutton and the diverse OVL with carrying White into office and noted that the new mayor had promised to repay his supporters with appointments to local boards and commissions. Sutton was particularly interested in gaining a voice on the governing body of the city's public hospital, but White never came through on his campaign promise. Still, the election helped Sutton pull the East Side further away from Bellinger and into his own hands.[8]

Sutton also used his position as a bully pulpit to attack segregation in public facilities as well as inequality in the local schools and junior colleges. He did so in a surprisingly militant manner. In 1949, Sutton went to bat for the local chapter of the National Alliance of Postal Employees (NAPE), Heman Sweatt's all-black union. The Alliance, which counted ninety-five members in San Antonio, requested the use of Comanche Park for its annual picnic, an event that attracted one thousand guests. County commissioner A. J. Ploch refused to grant the union permission to use the park but offered to personally pay for the rental of an alternative venue.

Sensing he had the moral and practical high ground, Sutton led a delegation of union leaders who confronted Ploch in "a stormy session" recorded by a daily newspaper reporter. "Why won't you let us use Comanche park?" Sutton asked, feigning ignorance. The commissioner replied obliquely, "It would save confusion, that's all." Sutton continued the act and pressed him. "What confusion do you anticipate?" Ploch then explained that he had been inundated with calls from irate white citizens after considering a similar request the previous year, and he did not want to endure such a reprisal again. "You're discriminating against the Negro, aren't you?" Sutton boomed. "You were elected by the people and you have a negro electorate. Isn't that right?" Ploch responded candidly, "That's right—if you put it that way. But the negro people haven't ever used it before." Sutton escalated again. "You're setting yourself up as a dictator. . . . You are guilty of inciting confusion when you make such a statement." Ploch had reached his limit, and he fired back angrily, "I've done more for you people than any damn commissioner before." Then one of the union leaders pointed out that this time, it was different: "We didn't have the ballot in the old days," he said. Ploch finally capitulated and opened the park to the union, handing Sutton another highly visible victory for both the race and his own controversial alternative to the patronage politics of the machine.[9]

As this episode suggests, Sutton did not shy away from using confrontational tactics to fight Jim Crow. A year after opening the park, in 1950, Sutton appeared before the school board as part of a group of NAACP leaders who were demanding equal funding for the city's black schools as well as the desegregation of a local stadium. When the board president refused to discuss the board's decision to shutter and replace one black elementary school, Sutton attacked his tone and again called a leading white official a "dictator." Speaking from the visitor's podium, Sutton turned to another member of the board and began questioning him directly. The latter replied by calling for "somebody to throw him [Sutton] out." The room descended into chaos, and the board president screamed at the city's first black elected official in decades: "You can't come down here and tell this board what to do just because you are a smart nigger." The newspaper reported that Sutton then "thrust his face close to [the president's] and angrily exclaimed, 'Don't ever call me that.'" Sutton's ally Gus Garcia leapt to his feet and separated the two men before taking control of the meeting and promptly adjourning it. Through such bold rhetoric, strident altercations, and steadfast advocacy as a political insider, Sutton constantly challenged the city's established white leadership and demanded that it either integrate or live up to the dictate of "separate but equal."[10]

The 1948 election and its aftermath signaled the return of independent African American and Mexican American voters and community activism on the San Antonio political scene. It marked the re-creation of a multiracial alliance, and it allowed the most militant black and brown activists to gain leverage in their battles with their more conservative race leaders. While the war was far from over, the 1948 coalition gave Sutton and Garcia and their militant colleagues unprecedented room to maneuver. It also alerted white elites to the possibility of a sustained multiracial assault on Jim Crow and Juan Crow.

San Antonio's conservative city fathers responded to the election and the renewal of militant community activism by reorganizing their system of governance in order to ensure the ongoing exclusion of black, brown, and white liberals. Like their counterparts across the Southwest, white businessmen in San Antonio launched a campaign for municipal "reform." They lambasted bossism and ward politics, both of which they had championed for decades. With the machine now under fire at the polls and discredited in the business community, they turned to advocating efficient, corporate-style government. District elections would be entirely supplanted by at-large elections, which they argued would guarantee that politicians put the interest of the city as a whole ahead of any parochial neighborhood concerns. Of course, the practical consequence of this structural change was to guarantee that only white candidates could win election. The elections would remain nonpartisan, a holdover from the earlier system that effectively kept precinct organizations out of city politics. A new system of management and governance would accompany the new electoral procedures. Reformers promised the installation of a city manager system in which elected members of the city council were to be removed from daily supervision of municipal affairs. The mayor would henceforth serve as a figurehead and chairman of the council, but the city manager would hire department heads who in turn would professionalize the entire civil service. All of the changes would promote economic development and geographical expansion of the city's boundaries. The rising tide of growth, they promised, would lift all boats.

The reformers triumphed, changing the city charter to create the new system in the municipal elections of 1951. The new city charter had experienced some growing pains as the first weak mayor battled the city manager for control, so members of the Chamber of Commerce sought to solidify their grasp.

In 1954, sixty chamber members assembled to form the Good Government League (GGL), a nonpartisan group that would preempt such bickering by selecting a slate of prescreened candidates for all future municipal elections. The GGL grew to three thousand members by the time of the 1955 city elections, thereby incorporating all potential enemies and guaranteeing that debate would take place only behind closed doors prior to the nomination of reform-friendly, consensus candidates.[11]

For the next decade, the GGL was unbeatable at the polls, tallying an unblemished 53–0 record. Activists like Sutton and Garcia had limited power in such settings, and they probably would not have attended the meetings of the GGL even if they had been invited. Black boss Bellinger gained entrée to the GGL but had few spoils to show for his support. Likewise, a group of elite Mexican Americans formed a "Westside GGL" and actively supported the white elites' efforts. They were rewarded with a few council positions as long as they continued to subordinate their demands to the elites' vision of economic growth and political domination. Although Sutton and Garcia remained in office into the 1950s, their protests and petitions increasingly fell on deaf ears. The elites had reestablished control.[12]

The East Side Trio

African American activists on the East Side continued to organize even as the political winds shifted against them. While Sutton kept one foot in the public arena, he also renewed his efforts to build lasting community institutions that could support the broader black freedom struggle. He soon found allies in a pair of kindred spirits, the Reverend Claude W. Black Jr. and photographer and publisher Eugene Coleman. Together, the trio would put forward an expansive vision of civil rights that challenged the political and economic foundations of Jim Crow. As Bellinger and other African American community leaders returned to the patronage politics of old, Sutton and the more militant activists demanded full integration, independent political power, economic opportunities, and community development. Their expansive vision harkened back to the prior coalitions and laid the groundwork for new, unprecedentedly powerful interracial alliances by the end of the new decade.

Rev. Black was a San Antonio native, born in 1916 and raised in the family home on the East Side. His father worked the Pullman lines and joined A. Philip Randolph's Brotherhood of Sleeping Car Porters back when doing so could result in termination of employment or physical violence if discovered by the company. Claude W. Black Sr. served as a shop steward and steadily climbed the ranks of the union, eventually becoming a local vice president. His salary was small, but he made more in tips than most black workers could

An undated portrait of a young Rev. Claude W. Black Jr., without his trademark black-rim glasses. Courtesy Claude and ZerNona Black Papers, Trinity University Special Collections and Archives, San Antonio, Texas.

ever hope to see at once. Riding the rails was a good job that helped the family buy a small house, but it also kept the elder Black away from his home and family for long stretches of time. The younger Black slept on a covered back porch and worked for his uncle's ice company as his mother pinched pennies and took in boarders to maintain the household. Somehow the parents still squirreled away enough money to create a small college fund for the son.[13]

Black Jr.'s political education began when he was a child. Randolph visited the family when he passed through San Antonio, and years later the reverend still recalled his father and the union president talking about race relations and civil rights late into the night. "I remember being drawn into those discussions like a moth to a flame," he later remembered. "I would not say anything, because they were adult conversations. Nevertheless, I was amazed that these men had the guts to stand up for their rights."[14] Randolph, he recalled, perhaps hyperbolically, was his "mentor and idol."[15] Like others before him, Black Jr. joined the youth chapter of the NAACP led by Euretta Fairchild. Their campaigns centered on basic community improvements, beginning with a demand that the city install fire hydrants on the East Side. "Even though our homes were burning down, it would take us many years of protesting and petitioning to finally receive them," Black remembered.[16]

Black Sr.'s tips eventually allowed the junior Black to seek higher education, a privilege that eluded the vast majority of African Americans. Still, his options were limited. He briefly attended St. Philip's College on the East Side before transferring to Samuel Huston College, an all-black private school in Austin.

He pledged Omega Psi Phi and became "an Omega man," but he found the academic rigor of the former freedmen's institute lacking. Black transferred again in 1935, this time to Morehouse in Atlanta, one of America's best black colleges. Morehouse men took great pride in their schooling, he later recalled, and they competed with one another as each sought "to make a name for himself in the world." Of course, they did so in a rigidly segregated world, a place in which Jim Crow was even stronger than it was in Texas.[17]

Several years later the future Reverend Black discovered his calling. While traveling door to door selling life insurance to sharecroppers and tenant farmers in East Texas, Black marveled that many of his customers were happy despite their poverty. Their worldly salvation—and his—was found in the church. Black enrolled at Andover Newton Theological Seminary in Massachusetts, where he earned a master's degree and became an ordained Baptist minister. He returned home to San Antonio in 1943 with a new sense of purpose, and he began preaching in a "soul saving ministry" at the East Side's Cameo Theatre. He hoped to "reach the unapproachable," mostly poor folks who did not attend church regularly.[18] Soon after, he also helped a group of church women form the San Antonio Mother's Service Organization.[19]

In 1946 Black moved to Corpus Christi to pastor St. Matthew's Baptist Church, where he developed his ministerial strategy of connecting the church to social and political action in the community. Black circulated petitions and gathered signatures for a campaign to replace an old, unsafe bridge near the church—a key infrastructure improvement that was often denied to black communities along the Gulf Coast. It took time, but the city eventually made the repairs. On another occasion, Black's father helped him secure A. Philip Randolph as the church's annual Men's Day speaker. At the time, Black later recalled, the union leader was "advocating that African Americans boycott joining the military until the president [Truman] agreed to integrate it." The local papers reported on the church's sponsorship of such an incendiary speaker, but no reprisals against Black or the church were forthcoming.[20]

In 1949 Rev. Black again returned home, this time permanently. He became the minister of what was then known simply as First Baptist Church, a massive fifteen-hundred-member congregation in the heart of San Antonio's East Side. Social action remained central to his work, and the reverend soon started service programs that connected the church to the everyday needs of community residents. The crown jewel was an innovative daycare program. Black later remembered that it solved two problems: it provided working mothers with much-needed child care during the day while simultaneously offering preschool education to kids who otherwise would have started kindergarten at a disadvantage. Black appointed a board of directors led by lay officials from his church, and after several years of work the daycare opened its doors in 1957.[21]

Rev. Black's wife, the former Miss ZerNona Stewart, also connected the family to a wide range of service programs in the larger East Side community. The couple met during World War II, when ZerNona, a native of Oklahoma, came to San Antonio to direct the Colored USO housed at the Sycamore Street YWCA. A graduate of Emerson College in Boston, and a decade older than Black, ZerNona had been married twice before, and had a teenage son who lived with his grandmother while ZerNona traveled to support the family. She was not the typical debutante of the 1940s East Side, but Black remembered that no other ladies "displayed the class that ZerNona did." More important, ZerNona tested him both privately and publicly, calling upon him to speak at community events and demanding that he too commit himself to service. "I'd never had that happen to me before," he recalled. "Imagine, a woman challenging what a man had to say in those days?" After a long courtship, the couple married in 1946. ZerNona had already quit her position at the USO, and she later taught part time at St. Philip's College while taking on a wide range of community projects.[22]

The wartime boom had transformed nearly all aspects of San Antonio, and one consequence was an extreme housing shortage on the East Side. Prior to their marriage, ZerNona had rented a large house from the founder of St. Philip's College, and Rev. Black moved in right after their wedding. They sublet half of the building to Mr. and Mrs. Eugene Coleman.[23] It may or may not have been the coincidence of landlord and tenant that first brought the Blacks and Colemans together, but in any case their relationship endured. For the next three decades, the two families joined the Suttons in a protracted effort to improve daily life and win independent political representation for the East Side.

Born in 1921 and raised thirty-five miles southeast of Dallas, Eugene Coleman attended Houston College for Negroes (now TSU) before being drafted into the U.S. Army Air Force in 1944. The service sent him to San Antonio, where he was stationed at Brooks Field. There, he later recalled, he "had problems." Coleman was a noncommissioned officer, but base supervisors asked him to perform menial tasks simply because he was black. When he refused, as he often did, he gained a reputation as a troublemaker. After numerous disputes, Coleman ended up assigned to the base's newspaper, the *Brooks Field Observer*. He had "a little schooling" in photography, and he was now allowed to use his training to take pictures of base training activities and social events. But he still chafed at his supervisor, a black officer who Coleman believed was too passive in accepting discrimination at the base. Seeking a way out, he took the admissions test to go to Tuskegee to become a pilot, but his high marks weren't enough to overcome his alleged bad attitude. Finally, he was transferred across town to Randolph Air Force Base, where he remained until his discharge in 1947.[24]

Despite his experiences of racial discrimination, Coleman decided to remain in San Antonio. He married, moved in with the Blacks, and opened his own photography business. While still in the service, Coleman had developed a new process that allowed him to develop film and make prints in about a half-hour, and he put this faster method to use as part of his business. Rather than wait for customers to come to him, he attended dances and social events at various nightclubs, took snapshots of revelers, and developed pictures of them immediately, fulfilling his "while you wait" slogan. At the same time, he built a portrait studio at St. Paul Square on the edge of the East Side, where he soon attracted a loyal following among San Antonio's African American residents.[25]

Much to his surprise, the photography trade also brought Coleman into the civil rights movement. Coleman later remembered that

> G. J. [Sutton] and Claude Black were trying to get this integration deal started. They started through the housing situation. We understood that there was some money available for housing for minorities, and all we had to do was apply for it. Now, the City would not apply for it because we had contractors here that had been tied up with slum housing for poor people and building houses any kind of way they wanted to build them, and wherever they wanted to build them. And they [poor people] would have to go and live in them and have to pay for them, no matter what it costs.

Substandard dwellings dovetailed with the East Side's inventory shortage to create a housing crisis for African Americans in Jim Crow San Antonio. While the federal government offered some hope to activists Sutton and Black, local government stood in their way. According to Coleman, city leaders deferred to the interests of developers and builders and prevented the formation of a local housing authority that would be eligible to apply for federal grants under the Housing Act of 1949. "So G. J. and Claude came to the studio" with a request, Coleman recalled. "'I tell you what I need you to do for me,'" Sutton told him, rather than asking. "'We need to do some pictures of these slum areas and show them the need for housing for blacks, and we need to close up these slums and get these slumlords out of the way and stop these folks from building the houses out here that aren't up to standard.'"[26]

Sutton and Black had settled on a public relations strategy centered on exposing the terrible conditions in the city's slum housing, and Coleman, the East Side's eminent photographer and by then a personal friend of the reverend's, was the man for the job. The trio visited Ellis Alley, one of the city's most dilapidated areas. Coleman recalled that "everyone was afraid to go in there and take pictures because it was dangerous—the landlords would eradicate you." But Coleman had a friend from the service who lived there and agreed to let the activists photograph his house. The activists took the developed prints to the mainstream daily press, but they wouldn't print the images nor run their story. Neither would the black press, the *San Antonio Register*, take up their cause. Coleman recalled that the latter was "tied up with advertising," but it is also likely that the paper's publisher, black political boss Bellinger, would not have wanted to publicly challenge the city fathers. "So we decided, let's just put out our own paper and we'll get this message out," Coleman remembered. "We'll just call it SNAP, because it will be snapshots to show people what we were doing."[27]

"It was supposed to be a temporary thing," he continued, designed initially to assist only the housing campaign.[28] But *SNAP News* instead became an institution in its own right, an independent, underground black newspaper that was willing to challenge both City Hall and its allies on the East Side. It began as a booklet of photographs of the slums, but it soon added images of African American social events, clubs, and community life. Eventually, short news stories began appearing next to the images. And, increasingly, *SNAP* served as a forum for Coleman's incisive political commentary, with fierce editorials produced in collaboration with Sutton and Black and carried into the community by all three men and the dozens of activists with whom they worked. The SNAP House, where the newspaper was printed, became one of the group's organizing headquarters. And Coleman helped recruit countless supporters to the cause, especially among the many young veterans who had served their country during the war and refused to accept Jim Crow in its aftermath.

Sutton's election to the junior college board, the return of Rev. Black, the development of his social gospel, and the publication of the first *SNAP* in 1949 together created a turning point in East Side politics. In all likelihood, nobody appreciated it more than Sutton, who had worked to outflank the city machine's black wing as far back as the 1930s. Now, after a decade in the trenches, he had found a pair of dedicated organizers to join him, a place to gather and develop strategy, and above all an efficient way to spread their message to the masses.

Albert Peña's Neighborhood

Across town on the West Side, a similar process of quiet organizing and base building was likewise underway. Gus Garcia had broken open the electoral arena, but he and other Mexican American activists encountered fierce opposition within their own ethnic group. In what one scholar has dubbed "the illusion of inclusion," the rising GGL from its inception offered spots on its biennial electoral slates to a small number of hand-picked Mexican Americans, often leading businessmen who eschewed ethnic politics but were willing to

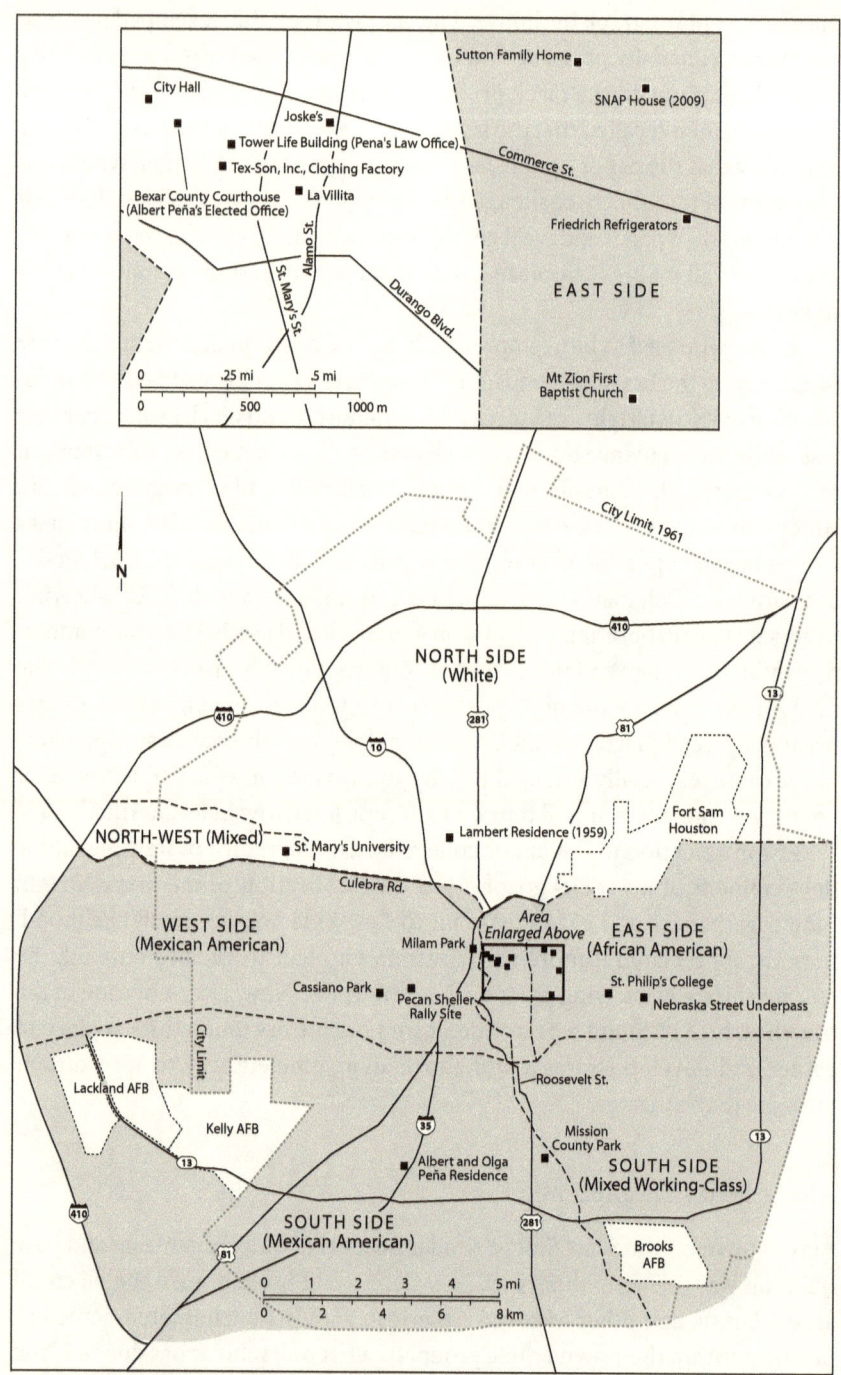

San Antonio neighborhoods and landmarks

serve as the West Side's official spokesmen. The arrangement gave the favored politicians seats on the city council and other governing bodies as well as entrée to the backroom meetings where the real decisions were made. Like Bellinger on the East Side, this "conservative sector" of the city's Mexican Americans prioritized access to power and patronage, and they gained both, in increasing amounts, throughout the 1950s and 1960s.

On the other hand, activists in the "liberal sector" of Mexican Americans advocated independent organization and autonomous political power. For them, the spoils of victory were not enough. As long as the GGL could choose their leaders, they contended, the poor *mexicano* residents of the city's barrios could not speak for themselves and would therefore never determine their own futures. Liberal activists remembered that the city fathers had fiercely resisted both the pecan sheller movement and Gus Garcia's school campaigns, and they maintained that the GGL's current offerings amounted to only token representation. The barrios remained malnourished, underdeveloped, and powerless, and only a new, independent movement could change that. As political scientist Rodolfo Rosales puts it, "the approach to political inclusion was the most visible demarcating line" among Mexican Americans in postwar San Antonio, with the two different philosophies "creating an intense internal conflict." Sharp disagreements split the conservative and liberal sectors, even as individual activists would switch sides from time to time or even form temporary partnerships on specific campaigns.[29]

Over the course of the 1950s, the "liberal sector" on the West Side picked up steam and eventually gained the upper hand, transforming San Antonio's larger political scene in the process. The shift began with the arrival of attorney and community organizer Albert A. Peña Jr. Born in 1917 on the West Side of San Antonio, Peña served in the navy during World War II and attended St. Mary's University in San Antonio on the G.I. Bill. He went to the South Texas School of Law in Houston, graduating and passing the bar in 1950.[30]

It is unclear exactly how he developed a passion for politics, but he credits a group of "liberal-minded" white labor activists with educating him on party and precinct politics while he was in law school in Houston. In 1948, steelworker Eddie Ball brought Peña into Truman's presidential campaign, and the duo sat in the black section at a local speech by Congressman Sam Rayburn in protest of the ongoing segregation of the Democratic Party.[31] Upon his return to San Antonio, Peña went to work as an attorney, joining his father and brother at the law firm of Peña, Peña, and Peña. He had little interest in traditional legal work, however, and his wife Olga urged him to get more involved in his community. He joined the American G.I. Forum (AGIF) and soon found himself at the center of the Mexican American struggle for civil rights. In 1951 forum leader Hector P. Garcia asked Peña to investigate some school discrimination complaints that the group had received from *mexicano* residents of the small town of Hondo, forty miles west of the West Side. Peña traveled to the hamlet, where he learned that the district maintained two schools: one for Anglos, one for *mexicanos*. The local district declared that it separated students based on language proficiency, rather than ethnicity—in other words, they couldn't attend the main Anglo school because they couldn't read in English. The school board disingenuously claimed that this was constitutional, and Peña appealed the case to the Texas State Board of Education.[32]

What happened next transformed Peña from a novice civil rights attorney into a community organizer and political activist. The state school board refused to issue a ruling on whether or not the policy was constitutional. Peña later recalled, "We couldn't get any decision from them and the people in Hondo . . . were getting pissed off at me because I was like the rest of them [civil rights lawyers]; I wasn't doing anything." The school year was just about to begin, and the families were growing desperate. Back in Hondo, Peña called a special meeting of all the *mexicano* families at the Guadalupe Church. "I am not the best lawyer in the country," he told them, "but we are going to integrate these schools."

Peña urged the parents to attempt to register their children in the "Main Plant," or the Anglo school. "And we are going to stay there if it takes all day or it takes a week or it takes a month," he added. "We are going to stay there until they enroll our children in the school. And that is what we did."[33] *Mexicano* parents approached the Anglo school, got in the registration line, and then tried to enroll their kids when it was their turn. When the registrar rejected them, they moved to the back of the line and repeated the process. "We stayed there all day and we were singing," Peña later recalled. They sang and tried to have fun as they registered and were rejected, over and over again, from the early morning to the early afternoon. In the interim, a newspaper picked up the story, and the state school board in Austin frantically called a special meeting to deal with the crisis. Around 1:00 P.M., four or five hours into the demonstration, the board sent the district a telegram instructing it to integrate. It was the direct action protest rather than the lawsuit that scared them. Peña later recalled, "They were told by their lawyers the best thing to do is integrate, because they are going stay there, because this Albert Peña, he is a radical, and I don't know what else they called me. But he is going to stay there until you integrate them, so that is what they did was that they integrated both schools."[34]

A second school case centered in Lytle, Texas, completed Peña's baptism into politics. This complaint came from parents via the League of Latin American Citizens (LULAC), the oldest Mexican American civil rights organization in the United States, founded in Texas in the 1920s. Several lawyers had already investigated the issue and had come back with nothing, so LULAC leaders asked Peña for help. Representing LULAC Council 2 but working pro bono, Peña traveled to Lytle, a small town twenty-five miles southwest of San Antonio, and discovered a remarkably similar example of segregated schooling. He again appeared at a hearing of the school board, where one minister in attendance called him a Communist. Nevertheless, the school board relented and integrated the schools. Peña had now developed a formula that worked both for the *mexicano* residents of small towns like Hondo and Lytle and for Peña himself: "I got calls from all over South Texas and I would either go down there, I would talk to the school board and the superintendent, and I didn't have to go to court anymore. I didn't have to get any more hearings. They would integrate the school districts," he later remembered. As a result, Peña adds, he also became "well known in South Texas and in Bexar County," which in turn "started my political career."[35]

Peña and other San Antonio activists sought to harness this groundswell of energy in the political arena. Gus Garcia's 1948 campaign had shown that independent *mexicanos* could win, but the rise of Anglo reformers and their conservative Mexican American allies threatened to turn back the clock. For his part, Garcia encountered stiff resistance on the school board and was consumed with litigating a series of civil rights cases outside the city on behalf of the AGIF and LULAC. He traveled far and wide, eventually arguing one of those suits, *Hernandez v. Texas*, before the U.S. Supreme Court in early 1954. More important, his campaign machinery had evaporated. Although it had won increased funding for West Side institutions, the School Improvement League no longer mobilized the barrios as effectively as it had. Reflecting these shifts in power and priorities, Garcia resigned from the school board in August 1952 and relocated to McAllen in the Valley soon thereafter.[36]

By 1952, Peña also recognized the need to develop new, independent institutions, innovative strategies, and above all, far-reaching coalitions. He later recalled that, on the one hand, "they had a liberal group in San Antonio, but they had no Mexicanos." On the other hand, "the only Mexicano groups we had on the West Side, they were either controlled by some politician in the courthouse or some *vendido* [sell out]." Peña paired up with Willie Maldonado, the head of the all-*mexicano* laborers union, and a handful of other activists to organize the Loyal American Democrats (LAD). Despite its universal name, it organized only Mexican Americans, was explicitly "liberal-minded," and did not accept as members any politicians or paid political staffers. Peña looked for activists who "didn't belong to any of the factions over there on the West Side" and were thus "strictly independent" of the neighborhood's "*vendidos*."

The group's patriotic title also masked its heterodox agenda. Organizing at the height of the Korean War, Peña and company constantly had to guard against anti-Communist accusations. "Loyal" and "American" both reflect the activists' conscious effort to guard against such threats. They needed this cover because of their simple but, for the time, outlandish goal: to independently organize Mexican American residents of San Antonio into an explicitly partisan club that could, in turn, support liberal politicians. By positioning the group to avoid the existing factions and race leaders who collaborated with the GGL, Peña created an unprecedented, autonomous institution through which the "liberal sector" could begin mass organizing among *mexicano* Democrats. It also positioned the group to work alongside the local loyalist faction of white Democrats, who were reorganizing under the direction of the old liberal ex-congressman and former mayor Maury Maverick in protest of Governor Shivers's deepening rift with the national party.[37]

The at-large municipal elections installed by the "reformers" made city council races all but impossible to win, so Peña and the LAD had to develop a new strategy. Together, they narrowed the group's focus to precinct-level organizing with the ultimate goals of electing liberals to the state legislature and taking over the Bexar County Democratic Party. Peña later recalled, "What happened was that we learned how to organize by becoming very active in the precinct conventions, and we learned how to carry our conventions. We had our delegates. . . . We would have poll tax drives and it was very difficult because you had to pay, it was $1.75 and $1.75 was a lot of money. . . . We talked about Mexicano power and [told citizens that] the only way we are going to have a voice is by voting." They believed that they should share in the promise and responsibilities of postwar liberalism. "'We the People,' that's us," as Peña put it. "If we gripe about government, we are griping about ourselves because we are government and we are not going to change it unless we organize."[38] On a more concrete level, LAD deepened its involvement with the Democratic Party and began to seek out supporters in each of the precincts. Trial and error taught them "organization" and "how to take over conventions."[39] Olga Peña created a card file that listed the group's precinct leaders and helped them turn out voters and bodies.[40] West Side printer and liberal activist Ruben Munguia similarly honed new skills by participating in local party gatherings. He recalled that Maury Maverick "recruited me to participate in precinct convention politics. . . . I told him I didn't know what to do. . . . He said he just wanted me to participate so as to learn how they work."[41]

LAD activists gradually taught themselves how to win at the polls and in party politics. In the spring of 1952, Peña, Maverick, and Munguia staged a rump caucus during the Democratic Party's county convention in hopes of electing a liberal to serve as county chairman. The San Antonio Labor Council of the AFL opposed their selection, but the liberals remained recalcitrant and forced the conference to hold several rounds of voting, delaying the selection of the chairman late into the opening evening. Their education continued.[42]

In late May, Peña joined the rump convention at the Democratic Party's state convention, which was held in San Antonio. As many as two thousand mostly white liberals, including the nucleus of the incipient Harris County Democrats (HCD) in Houston, bolted from the official meeting after Governor Shivers denied the party's support for presidential candidate Adlai Stevenson as well as the national platform. They staged their own convention under the canvas tents of La Villita, a historic Spanish colonial district restored by Maverick during his term as mayor. Peña jockeyed for position alongside white liberal members of the Organized Voters League as well as G. J. Sutton and local labor leader H. S. "Hank" Brown. The Bexar County caucus ultimately elected Peña as an alternate-at-large in a statewide delegation that would attempt to get credentials for the upcoming Democratic National Convention in Chicago. The multiracial group assembled at the rump convention proved fleeting in the short term, but Peña would collaborate with many of its members in the years to come.[43]

The pair of conventions showed Peña and LAD that the group still needed to prove its mettle. In October 1952, it did just that, taking to the streets to sponsor a rally in support of Adlai Stevenson. Munguia, Peña, and a close ally of Sutton's were among eight local liberals who were named to the statewide campaign committee, but party conservatives opposed the event and did everything they could to stop it. LAD asserted its own power by threatening, in Munguia's words, to "send telegrams to every Mexican community between here and California, telling them of what you have done and what Adlai Stevenson will do always, and we'll make them all Republicans."[44] A loose coalition cohered around the presidential campaign. Kathleen Voigt led efforts to build enthusiasm among middle-class white women, Hank S. Brown organized unions, Munguia and Peña distributed Spanish-language literature in the barrios, and Sutton coordinated "back yard meetings" on the East Side.[45]

Stevenson arrived in the city by rail and caravanned to Milam Square on the near West Side, where more than five thousand *mexicanos* cheered the national Democrat. Hector P. Garcia of the AGIF and attorney Gus Garcia gave preliminary speeches that whipped the crowd into a frenzy. Amid cries of "Olé Adlai," "Viva Steven-sohn," and "Viva Adelaido," the candidate took his turn, acknowledging and pandering to his ethnic hosts while butchering their language. Stevenson "took off in Spanish with a bit of Italian and French flavor attached," according to one newspaper report, and "he declared in very good tourist-Spanish: '*Teyngo goosto dey ver cuandos Democratas hie, y el cuadro de Nouviember veyremos cuandos votos hie parra el partiddo Democrats*'" (I am glad to see so many Democrats here . . . and on November 4, we will see how many voters there are for the Democratic Party). Switching back to English, Stevenson praised the patriotic contributions of "Spanish-Americans" in Texas before acknowledging the discrimination they continued to face and offering liberal solutions to their plight. "You have not always found the welcome you deserve," he said. "Your lot has often been harder than it should have been. And so you have special interest in the programs . . . of our Democratic administration." He laid out his understanding of the Mexican American agenda, one that promised economic advancement that would cross racial lines. "We have labored hard to replace slums with decent housing, to wipe out unemployment, to guarantee fair wages, to provide security for our older people," he said. "And with every gain in living standards we have gained something even more important—an increasing self-respect and dignity for all Americans in every walk of life."[46]

The rally was the first visit to San Antonio's barrios by any presidential candidate and thus represented the greatest achievement yet for Peña and other liberal *mexicano* activists. It announced LAD as a new force in city and state politics, and it confirmed the group's belief that liberal Democrats from Washington to Bexar County could appreciate and empathize with their situation and serve as allies in the struggles ahead. Following the rally, thousands of *mexicanos* followed the candidate to the Alamo, where he addressed twenty thousand mostly white listeners. They hadn't yet achieved parity with the local white Democrats, but LAD activists did win recognition and demonstrate their power to mobilize huge crowds. In another sign of the group's growing influence, on the day before the election, Olga Peña served as the assistant hostess of the campaign's last coffee gathering for women precinct workers. Conservative Democrats led by Governor Shivers ended up carrying the state for the Republican nominee, Dwight Eisenhower. Nonetheless, LAD activists knew that their commitment to organizing in the trenches of precinct politics had paid off.[47] Indeed, Peña and other liberals continued to work door to door, street by street, and block after block. The factional dispute in West Side politics continued, and the conservative group continued to hold the upper hand, but the tide had turned.

Albert P., Henry B., and the East Side

Through LAD and countless precinct committees and local civil rights organizations, Peña and his allies slowly built a powerful, independent political apparatus. They did so not simply by organizing *mexicanos* but also by building coalitions with like-minded activists across the color line. Peña in particular forged new ground, deepening his partnerships with Sutton, Maverick, and other black and white labor and liberal activists while simultaneously strengthening his own base. His decision to forge new interracial alliances both stemmed from and shaped the interior politics of San Antonio's Mexican American communities, propelling Peña and some of his comrades into elected office and permanently altering the balance of power within the local and state Democratic parties. Over time, multiracial collaboration would prove to be more than a sideshow or afterthought to the process of ethnic mobilization. Rather, coalition building would emerge as the key method through which the "liberal sector" of activists would finally (albeit partially) vanquish its conservative foes.[48]

Peña began making overtures to black and white activists around town in the early 1950s. From the early days of LAD forward, Peña later recalled, "we started working with the Blacks, [a] very small group of Blacks" led by Sutton.[49] Little evidence survives to document the early relationship between the two cadres of activists, but it's clear that a common political philosophy helped bring them together. Both groups trended toward the liberal end of the spectrum, and both participated in the 1952 walkout from the state Democratic convention led by Maury Maverick. Both men demanded independent representation and autonomy from the elites that filled City Hall and the Chamber of Commerce. Both sought civil rights, taking to the streets to engage in direct action when necessary, and both had ties to the labor movement. Most important, both approached electoral politics as a means to winning power for their communities, rather than as an end in itself. Inclusion on boards and commissions meant little for Peña and Sutton if they did not also have the freedom to vote how they wished. Tokenism would be inadequate, and only community organizing could produce an autonomous force capable of demanding significant social change.

The "very small group of Blacks" and the "liberal sector" of Mexican Americans also shared an affinity for a charismatic, truly independent politician named Henry Barbosa Gonzalez. Born in 1916, "Henry B.," as he was affectionately known, grew up in a relatively prosperous household on San Antonio's West Side. He attended predominately Anglo schools, receiving a classical education at Jefferson High, San Antonio College, and the University of Texas at Austin. One biographer writes, "The story goes that he used to practice English and oratory in front of a mirror at home, and was reading Descartes and Carlyle by age sixteen." After a stint in the service during World War II, Gonzalez got a job at the local courthouse and eventually rose to the rank of chief probation officer. He helped his father run a translation service and became an officer and staffer of an elite hemispheric voluntary association, the Pan American Progressive Association (PAPA).

Gonzalez's connections to leading Mexican American and Latin American businessmen did not, however, give him automatic entrée to the San Antonio political elite. In 1950, he ran on a liberal ticket for the state legislature and made a surprisingly strong showing, advancing to the runoff. Although Gonzalez's candidacy failed, Maury Maverick Jr., the son of the former mayor and congressman, attributed his own narrow victory in securing another place in the legislature to the West Side's all-out vote for Gonzalez. In 1953, Gonzalez won a seat on the city council as part of the "San Antonians" ticket, a new group of municipal reformers who had grown disenchanted with the previous wave of reform led by Mayor White. His rare victory over the "silk-stocking" Citizens Committee came at a unique moment of disorder and discord within the Chamber of Commerce crowd and contributed to the formalization of the GGL over the next election cycle. Yet it also pulled *mexicanos* further away from the old West Side machine and created an opening for new forays into independent electoral organizing. For his part, once in office, Gonzalez proved himself a skilled negotiator among members of both tickets, and he briefly served as mayor pro tempore. Both the new GGL and the People's ticket offered him a spot on their slates for the 1955 elections. He declined both offers and was reelected as an independent after the GGL decided not to oppose him. He even carried a few North Side boxes.[50]

Gonzalez remained fiercely independent, refusing to subsume his political career to the broader organizing projects of LAD and other Mexican American activists in the "liberal sector." Gonzalez labored to find a middle ground that allowed him to draw support from conservative Mexican Americans as well. White liberals flocked to his camp, as did African Americans—including Sutton and his colleagues. By practicing what later became known as "triangulating," Gonzalez established his own base of power independent of both the GGL and Peña's "liberal sector" of Mexicans Americans.

Still, Gonzalez and Peña frequently collaborated, especially in these early days of heightened Mexican American political activism—and they did so in close contact with both black and white collaborators. Peña and other LAD activists used Olga's card file and the two Peñas' positions in the leadership of the local AGIF and LULAC chapters to mobilize voters to elect Gonzalez to the city council in 1953. In October of that year, Peña signed on as one of a half-dozen attorneys who filed a suit on behalf of the local NAACP that challenged the state's ban on interracial boxing matches (they won the case a year later). Sutton was an honored member of the San Antonio unit, which also hosted the annual convention of the State Conference of Branches. Albert Peña and labor and political activist George Lambert, now living in Dallas, were among the speakers at the gathering's workshops. Several months later, in the spring of 1954, Peña enjoyed both the new councilman Gonzalez's support and that of many black leaders as he launched a campaign for state representative. By then the president of the AGIF, Peña ran at the urging of a ticket of Anglo liberals that included incumbent Maury Maverick Jr. With the election coming just months after Maverick Sr. passed away from a heart attack, the prodigal son sailed to victory, but Peña and his slate partner in the runoff went down to defeat. Political scientist Rosales concludes that both the 1950 and 1954 legislative elections established a new trend: "Although the Chicano precincts generally supported the liberal ticket as a whole, Anglo-dominated precincts did not support the Chicanos on the tickets." First Gonzalez helped to elect Maverick, and, four years later, Peña helped the liberal get reelected. The Anglo candidates on the ticket did their part and steadfastly stumped for Peña, but their constituents simply would not pull the lever for the *mexicano*. Still, Peña made history as the first independent Mexican American to seek that post, and he came surprisingly close to winning the countywide contest.[51]

Over the next two years, Peña and his allies moved to consolidate and extend their base for both community action and electoral politics, again in intimate conversation with the city's Anglo liberals and black activists. Olga Peña continued to build the grassroots organization, launching a poll tax drive via the AGIF and deepening her involvement in the local club of Democratic Women—and adding each new name of a potential supporter to the group's card file. In 1955, Albert Peña narrowly won election to the presidency of LULAC Council 2, the venerable civil rights organization's oldest and only active local unit in San Antonio. Rosales writes that Peña's slim margin "was indicative of the conflict over goals" within the organization and the *mexicano* community at large, but the victory still marked a significant achievement for the liberal faction. Peña, who had previously served as the political action committee chair of the historically apolitical group, quickly ratcheted up the council's work in the electoral arena. Using LULAC's substantial financial resources to toil in the trenches, Peña helped reelect Gonzales that year and then appointed Munguia to implement a poll tax drive in anticipation of the 1956 elections.[52]

It would turn out to be a banner year for the city's Mexican American liberals. Peña and Gonzalez agreed to appear together on a liberal Democratic slate, along with a third Mexican American activist who ran for justice of the peace. LULAC's poll tax and block-walking campaigns represented the organizational core of the effort, but Gonzalez, as an outspoken city councilman, lent the effort some much-needed star power. A close examination of the returns from Peña's previous campaign for state representative had shown that fully two-thirds of his vote had come from a concentrated section of the city on the *mexicano* West Side and the racially mixed, working-class South Side. His strongest boxes formed the heart of the first precinct of the Bexar County Commissioners Court. While at-large elections and the GGL nominating process made municipal positions impossible and state legislative races just beyond reach, the county commission included four members from separate, geographically defined districts known as precincts (along with the presiding

Newly minted County Commissioner Albert A. Peña Jr.'s organization had grown so strong by the 1956 general election campaign that he warranted a visit from U.S. senator John F. Kennedy during the Massachusetts liberal's visit to San Antonio. The "Ole! Adlai" Stevenson sign anticipated the "Viva Kennedy" slogan and campaign that would engage Mexican American voters four years later. Courtesy *San Antonio Light* Photograph Collection, UTSA-ITC, Image L-4880-M, San Antonio Express / ZUMAPRESS.com.

officer, the "County Judge," who was elected at-large). Thwarted in city and state politics, Peña tossed his hat in the ring for the county's Precinct 1. He was a virtual shoe-in, though the city's Anglo papers overlooked the reality on the ground and discounted his effort. The justice of the peace race was also an easy one, with a *mexicano* candidate virtually guaranteed the victory. But Gonzalez had set his sights even higher, contesting a countywide election in hopes of becoming the first Mexican American state senator in more than a century. Many observers thought that he was committing political suicide. His at-large run for the legislature in 1950 had failed, as had Peña's in 1954. Anglos had shown that they wouldn't support *mexicano* candidates when it mattered.

But two years later, all three candidates triumphed on Election Day. Gonzalez beat the odds and won without a runoff. In addition to maintaining his broad support on the West Side, he attracted both major factions on the African American East Side and enjoyed strong backing among white liberals, who turned out in large numbers for Ralph Yarborough's third gubernatorial race. San Antonio would never be the same.[53]

Gonzalez and Peña both recognized that African American voters generally and Sutton in particular had contributed significantly to their success. Both the *SNAP* trio and Bellinger's *Register* offered vociferous support for the two politicians, and the black leaders walked their talk by turning out their respective followers on Election Day.[54] The *mexicano* elected officials, in turn, repaid their debts by making themselves visible on the East Side and standing up for black civil rights once in office. It was a reciprocal relationship in which the African American activists used the *mexicano* politicians as much as the reverse. Sutton and other East Side leaders escalated the grassroots campaign for civil rights at the very same moment that they worked to win elections, and both Gonzalez and Peña delivered on their promises and proved themselves steadfast supporters of the black freedom struggles.

The fruitful exchange began immediately. In his first term in 1954, Gonzalez nominated both Sutton and Bellinger to fill vacant positions on the city council. Neither was selected by the larger body, but the attempt alone proved deeply symbolic.[55] Then, as Sutton, Black, and *SNAP* publisher Coleman began approaching the council to demand inclusion for African Americans, Gonzalez emerged as their most reliable ally.[56] After a racial incident at a public pool in April 1954, the city passed an ordinance over Gonzalez's protests that desegregated its parks and tennis courts but codified the existing segregation of city pools. The local NAACP filed a federal suit early in 1955.[57] Rev. Black later recalled that the issue became a crisis that summer when the director of an African American vacation Bible school ignored segregation and called to reserve a West Side pool designated for whites (in this case, including *mexicanos*). The pool's manager didn't realize that the caller and thus the children who would be attending the school were black, and he made the reservation. As the children "began jumping out of the bus and running to the pool," the manager realized his mistake and "demanded they get out at once. The children were so disappointed and the adults were humiliated," Black added. "Rumors of the incident spread, and later that same day, the city council called a special meeting to address the issue." The city's African American activists responded by calling on the city to pass a new ordinance that would guarantee their inclusion.[58]

Councilman Gonzalez sponsored a law to this effect, which the council passed on June 19, the anniversary of Emancipation in Texas. The ordinance immediately came under fire from a number of directions. *SNAP* reported that "members of the City Council in San Antonio began a serious study of the swimming pool situation," including possibly rescinding the ordinance itself "in view of recent trends."[59] Nevertheless, the law stood. Gathering momentum, and enjoying the support of the rowdy East Side trio, Gonzalez introduced a series of new measures that desegregated all city facilities. The council passed these as well, making San Antonio one of the first cities in the South to integrate its public buildings and services.[60] Struggles in the private sector would continue for another decade, but these victories in the public arena represented a significant accomplishment that also underscored the tremendous power of electoral politics in the black freedom struggle. The activists learned that it was in the city council, not the courtroom, where progress could be achieved—often very quickly.

Peña and Gonzalez treated their black constituents much as they approached their *mexicano* ones, attending community events, assisting organizing efforts, and politicking on the East Side. For example, in 1957, Gonzalez came to the neighborhood to participate in dedication ceremonies for a new educational annex at the predominately black Antioch Baptist Church.[61] That same year, Albert Fuentes, who served as Peña's chief of staff and proxy after the election, joined Sutton and Black on the directorate of a new African American "Political Action Group." Fuentes became its second vice chairman.[62] Similarly, at Black's "Bible Study Week" at Mt. Zion First Baptist Church in January 1958, Peña attended one session and "spoke on the organizational features of the . . . Democrats of Texas," the emerging statewide liberal political organization that grew out of the HCD in Houston.[63]

Both Peña and Gonzalez took stands against segregation in their official capacities as well. In 1957, along with state senator Abraham Kazen, recently promoted Senator Gonzalez filibustered for thirty-six hours in protest of ten new segregation laws proposed by conservative Democrats in the wake of the *Brown* decision. The filibuster killed eight of the ten bills. East Side residents responded via the NAACP, which showered awards on Gonzalez at both local and statewide functions over the next several months.[64] Perhaps more significant in concrete terms, in the spring of 1959 Commissioner Peña moved a resolution that ended discrimination in the awarding of county contracts for construction projects. The measure required "all future contracts for county construction clauses forbidding the contractor from discriminating against any employe [*sic*] or applicant because of race, religion, color, or national origin." The motion passed and became law, giving Sutton and other East Side activists a signal victory in their decadelong battle against segregation by the county government. *SNAP* effusively praised Peña's leadership, and the bond between the black activists and the *mexicano* politician grew even tighter.[65]

Indeed, the lines dividing them had already begun to blur. In December 1957, Peña was elected to the board of the local NAACP branch, and the next spring he became the chair of its education committee. Soon after, he attempted to appoint Black to a position on the county's hospital board but was blocked by his colleagues on the commissioners court. A year later, Peña backed a multiracial group led by Sutton that approached the city council and demanded a municipal fair employment ordinance. "Minority groups consider it to be a RIGHT rather than a privilege to earn a living," Sutton told the city fathers. "Discrimination can be found in every phase of business, INCLUDING government." Peña felt much the same way. He hired brown and black employees to work for him at the county, forced the commissioners court to adopt ordinances that created equal economic opportunities, and worked side by side with the NAACP as it continued to agitate against segregation in all walks of life, including at work. Peña's support for the black freedom struggle cemented his partnership with Sutton and other militant activists on the East Side.[66]

The African American organizers, in turn, rallied behind Peña and Gonzalez and made the two politicos their own champions. Sutton, Black, Coleman, and the other black activists that surrounded *SNAP* understood their freedom struggle in broad terms, encompassing not only the integration of schools, swimming pools, and other public accommodations, but also equal opportunities in employment and myriad economic concerns. They recognized that winning on the civil rights front meant fighting for independent political representation, and they tackled both tasks with gusto. They adapted readily to changing circumstances and made their mark at every turn. Although they often clashed with the *Register*'s Bellinger, a stalwart ally of City Hall, they nonetheless tried to win his support for their causes and found ways to work with him when they could. In fact, the editorials penned by *SNAP* activists treated Bellinger much like they did any other politician, lauding him when he did what the more militant civil rights activists wanted and viciously assailing him when he didn't. More generally, Sutton and company were flexible and pragmatic, utilizing an approach that gave them few permanent allies and even fewer enduring enemies. They looked everywhere for support of their organizing, and they found it in unexpected places. While they at times clashed and at other times collaborated with Bellinger's apparatus, their secret and most lasting weapon turned out to be interracial coalition building. By forging intimate ties to like-minded Mexican Americans as well as white labor, civil rights, and liberal political activists, Sutton and the *SNAP* activists managed to outflank the more conservative black leaders. For their part, *mexicano* militants like Peña and the independent Gonzalez likewise overcame their own conservative coethnics and reactionary Anglos by depending upon the support of the outspoken Sutton and even, at times, the more staid Bellinger.[67]

Born in the quotidian electoral and civil rights battles of the Jim Crow 1950s, the city's flowering if still tentative black-brown alliance achieved unprecedented success at the local level, opening the city, county, and state governments to independent political representation for the first time. It had changed local laws and even paralyzed the state's segregationist legislature. This alliance would soon make an even bigger splash in Texas politics, but whether the city's and the state's white liberals and labor leaders would be ready for it remained to be seen.

Henry B. Governor and the DOT

At the beginning of 1958, two years after the liberal slate led by Peña and Gonzalez carried both men into office, the statewide "liberal movement" arrived at a crossroads. Two years earlier it had succeeded in electing Mrs. Randolph of Houston to the Democratic National Committee, but the liberals remained excluded from the state party and were forced to stage a rump convention in a Fort Worth "cow barn." The liberals licked their wounds and formed the Democrats of Texas (DOT), a new statewide body that could coordinate their activities moving forward. The next year, the liberal faction's standard-bearer, Ralph Yarborough, finally won an election and became the state's junior U.S. senator. Now, in 1958, just one year removed from that, Yarborough already faced a tough reelection challenge. To make matters worse, the senator had served as the movement's gubernatorial candidate in the past three elections, and there was simply nobody who could fill his shoes and mount a credible campaign for statewide office. Finally, the liberal movement remained predominately white, and the degree to which the grassroots black and brown activists would embrace any DOT initiative remained an open, thorny question.

Mrs. Randolph and other DOT leaders surveyed the landscape and considered Gonzalez. His filibuster against segregation the previous legislative session had propelled him to statewide prominence, making his name one of a few that would be recognized by voters across Texas. For his stand, Gonzalez had won the state NAACP's "Citizenship Award" and was named "Latin American Citizen of the Year" by the Alba Club at the University of Texas, among other honors. As one of his future staffers put it, Gonzalez began accepting "speaking engagements all over the state and became the acknowledged 'symbolic' leader of Texas' 'combined Latin and Negro minorities of two and a half million.' Newspapers throughout the state referred to him as 'liberal Senator Gonzalez.'"[68]

The fiercely independent Gonzalez was beloved among the state's "combined minorities," though he was chagrined to be known as either a "race leader" or a "liberal." Most observers believed it inconceivable that any challenger could defeat the incumbent segregationist Price Daniel, and a "Meskin" stood an even slimmer chance. DOT leaders concluded that he had potential but was not yet ready for the big time. Rumors began to circulate that the liberal movement wanted Gonzalez to run for lieutenant governor, a post that included presiding over the senate and rivaled if not exceeded the top job in terms of actual legislative power. For the liberals, Gonzalez represented the perfect sidekick, a charismatic campaigner with a passionate base who could bring votes from the state's black and brown citizens to a still unnamed white savior atop the ticket. Gonzalez and Peña had each helped to elect Maverick Jr. in San Antonio, so the strategy at least had a chance of paying off statewide. For his part, Gonzalez was a masterful legislator and probably would have excelled in the position, but he had no interest in playing second fiddle. Avoiding the issue and perhaps poking fun at the limitations presented by his ethnicity, he announced that he would not seek the number two post because the lieutenant governor's mansion was "not big enough for his family of eight children."

The white liberals continued to search for a gubernatorial candidate but found none. The populist former governor and U.S. senator W. Lee "Pappy" O'Daniel soon threw his hat into the ring. O'Daniel remained staunchly anti-labor and passionately committed to segregation, both conservative stands that promised to siphon some votes away from the incumbent Price Daniel. At the same time, Pappy hosted a popular folksy radio show that lampooned the state's business and political elites, making him wildly popular with Yarborough's base of white yeoman farmers. Gonzalez saw through the histrionics of "Pass the Biscuits" Pappy's populist sheen and remarked that the choice facing voters was no more than one between "tweedle-dum" and "O'tweedle-dum." As liberal and labor leaders desperately searched for a strategy to combat the two-headed monster, Gonzalez's name again emerged, this time as a candidate for governor.[69]

Gonzalez read the tea leaves and announced that he would seek the Democratic Party nomination. He did not ask the liberals' permission to run but maintained his independence throughout. He understood that his campaign would have little chance of success—he was "a Latin" and a Catholic and had been branded a "liberal." He also faced a powerful incumbent governor that controlled the state's electoral machinery and the party at every level. Gonzalez had no network or organization that spanned the state and little money to spend. Still, he had little to lose. His position in the state senate was secure for two more years, and more statewide publicity couldn't hurt. More important, he believed that voters should be presented with an alternative to Daniel and O'Daniel and that the two conservative candidates should be forced take public stands on the issues.

Gonzalez's decision to launch a quixotic statewide campaign put the white liberals and labor leaders of Texas in a bind. Both groups prioritized the reelection of Ralph Yarborough, and they believed that their approach to the governor's race would impact the senator's chances. Endorsing the "Latin," Catholic, filibustering Gonzalez would limit their ability to turn out the rural white "brass collar" Democrats who had formed the backbone of Yarborough's many campaigns, they maintained, and the liberals could count on the support of the blacks and Mexicans no matter what. As Gonzalez's future aide would put it, both the newly merged Texas AFL-CIO and the DOT "reasoned that discretion was the better part of valor and their weak position in state politics would be weakened even more if they supported Gonzalez." DOT and labor leaders were furious with Gonzalez for forcing their hand, but they had not yet found another liberal candidate who was ready to mount such a long-shot effort.[70] And the liberal movement's position in the party and Texas civic life was indeed precarious: as the DOT made gains throughout 1957 and prepared for the 1958 precinct conventions, the official State Democratic Executive Committee (SDEC), led by Governor Daniel, declared war against the DOT. Party leaders branded the DOT a "splinter group," and the governor proposed eliminating the precinct conventions entirely in order to avoid a liberal challenge. When the Harris County Democrats won control of the party's county executive committee in May 1958, the SDEC's chief organizer vowed to cripple the DOT statewide in the upcoming primary. Many DOT leaders felt that their embattled caucus could hardly take a chance on the upstart Gonzalez.[71]

Yet the real elephant in the room remained the group's internal racial politics. Since its founding in the winter of 1956–57, the DOT remained all but lilywhite. For its first six months, none of the organization's temporary governing or work committees included a single African American or Mexican American member. The problem was corrected by the time of the DOT's first full executive board meetings in the summer of 1957, but only token representation replaced complete exclusion. DOT leaders appointed R. P. "Bob" Sanchez of the AGIF and attorney W. J. Durham of the NAACP and the Texas Council of Voters as at-large members of the board. Still, Durham did not attend the meetings, perhaps because they were held in the segregated Stephen F. Austin Hotel near the capital (he did send telegrams with regrets, and he was once represented by a local proxy). No other black activist appears in the organization's early history. Among Mexican Americans, only Albert Peña and another other forum member from the Rio Grande Valley served as elected representatives from their respective state senate districts. Gonzalez addressed a meeting of the DOT's steering committee, an even larger governing body, but he did so only to discuss his cosponsorship of a bill that would have created partisan voter registration. Discussions of integration or any other issue regarding race remained absent from the board's meeting minutes until late November, when a "Committee on Principles" that included Peña and Sanchez (but no African Americans) reported out a laundry list of general subjects of interest. "Civil Rights" appeared alongside and equal to agriculture, education, financial policy, and a handful of other general concerns. The struggle against the caste system wasn't a priority for the DOT, as it was for black and brown activists across the state. The DOT may have been integrated on paper, but it could not have been more different in its daily operations from the flourishing reciprocal alliance in San Antonio, in which black and brown activists exchanged favors, and full civil rights and independent political power were the main objectives.[72]

The Gonzalez campaign meant that the DOT would be forced to confront or dodge the racial issue—or maybe both—at its second annual mass convention in late May 1958. Before the gathering, newspapers across the state were filled with contradictory reports on the organization's likely stance toward the candidate. One commentator remarked that the DOT "wound up without a gubernatorial candidate on which it can make a statewide appeal in the boondocks. (Henry Gonzalez is poison at the East Texas box office and viewed with something less than warmth in many other areas, if indeed he is viewed at all)."[73] A few days after Gonzalez formally launched his campaign, another observer stated that Gonzalez had a chance to win the group's blessing even though the Texas AFL-CIO and the Young Democrats had "skirted approval or disapproval" of Gonzalez at their own recent gatherings. Meanwhile, the leading local affiliate of the DOT, the Harris County Democrats, had endorsed Yarborough but took no stand on the gubernatorial race, and many expected DOT to follow suit. Still another vocal faction of DOT leaders had come out against Gonzalez, but the issue remained up in the air.[74]

The most impactful report added detailed information on the DOT's internal structure, but it moved beyond reporting the facts in an apparently intentional smearing of the liberal movement. Authored by the husband of an SDEC committeewoman, the front-page piece in Austin's newspaper of record warned that "A political alliance of four minorities marshaled under the unified command of 'Democrats of Texas'—DOT—is massed for an all-out effort to capture Texas politically." The group's allies included the Texas AFL-CIO, the NAACP, "a strong ultra-liberal segment of Latin-American voters," and the Texas Farmers' Union. Mrs. Randolph served as its "front"—a term that evoked McCarthyite witch hunts—while Senator Yarborough remained the group's "kingpin." For his part, Gonzalez, the "filibustering liberal integration leader in the legislature, who had the most favorable labor 'score board' rating" in the last session of that body, was but a pawn in the larger scheme, a "last minute draftee" tapped by Randolph "to cinch a segment of the Latin-American group." References to the "NAACP" appeared repeatedly throughout the text, as did an ominous photograph of W. J. Durham, the sole black board member, albeit an absentee one. The author also reminded readers of the presence of the other at-large board members: Sanchez, a Mexican American agitator; several leaders of organized labor (read in the 1950s subtext as labor racketeers); and a pair of former white liberal leaders of the Democratic Women (whose nontraditional activities threatened both patriarchy and white supremacy). The same group had long been a minority in Democratic Party circles, the piece added. "For the first time, however, it presents the real threat of a combination of minorities." It was time for true Texas Democrats to read between the lines and take their stand, the piece suggested. Race remained the core issue. "Politically DOT has isolated the loyal Democrats of East Texas through its NAACP affiliation. Labor, too, has isolated some of its own membership in the industrial areas of Texas wherever integration is an issue." It was only natural that white workers, small farmers, and country merchants should defect from the DOT, the piece concluded, since the group remained committed above all else to civil and women's rights.[75]

Reeling from such attacks, at its convention the DOT focused on the issues—except civil rights—and Gonzalez was nowhere to be found. None of the convention speeches made explicit references to integration, though some promised to uplift the conditions of *all* the people. "You are the shock troops of Texas democracy," keynote speaker Walter Hall, a small-town banker from Dickinson to the southeast of Houston, triumphantly declared. He lauded the audience for their tenacity in the face of many defeats and for their commitment to building a party with integrity in which the will of the voters was respected. He made no mention of civil rights. In his report, DOT secretary-treasurer Creekmore Fath, a former Yarborough campaign manager and leading Austin liberal, added that "The DEMOCRATS OF TEXAS are here to stay." He talked about the board's ongoing negotiations with SDEC toward a Code of Ethics and some degree of power sharing, and he declared that Governor Daniel "must be forced to keep his 'cotton-pickin' hands off the party machinery." He too didn't say a word about civil rights, and neither did Mrs. Randolph nor Senator Yarborough nor any of the other featured speakers.[76]

In a less triumphant and ultimately less flattering moment, Fath focused squarely on the group's internal racial politics. After blasting the governor, Fath changed the subject abruptly. "At this time I would like to commend the members of the Executive Board and Steering Committee who have given so generously of their time and money to our common effort," he said. "In passing, however, I would like to point out one thing—one member-at-large of the Executive Board elected last May 18 [1957]—was not present at that organization meeting, nor has he ever attended a single meeting or participated in any of the work of the organization. That board member is W. J. Durham of Dallas. This year I urge you to select officers from those Democrats present here today who will agree to give of their time in working for the organization." A moment later, Fath seemingly switched subjects, offering a response to the news articles that had smeared the DOT in the days prior to the convention. Yet the new topic turned out to be closely related, and it too had everything to do with race. The group had decided at its previous convention to "confine its resolutions and public stands to matters relating to Democratic Party Structure and organization—such things as party registration and the like," Fath noted. "To attempt to attribute to this organization any position on any other matters using the Communistic technique of 'guilt by association' is fraudulent, false, malicious and un-Texan." The subtext was just as clear as it was in the yellow journalist pieces he was denouncing: to tie the DOT to the NAACP and then portray it as a civil rights organization amounted to libel. For Fath, the DOT was nothing more than a liberal political organization committed to good governance. Its attempts to build a coalition by including at-large board members had distracted from this purpose, and removing Durham from office now would limit the group's liability. It was time to completely sever the group's tenuous ties with the civil rights movement.[77]

White DOT leaders thus insisted that the group represented *all* of the people even as they systematically excluded black participation and issues. This proved just as true for Chris Dixie and Mrs. Randolph of Houston as it did for Fath, and the same could be said for most if not all of the group's state and local officers. Although the group was formally integrated, its leaders held meetings in segregated spaces, refused to talk about race, postured defensively against "fraudulent" claims to the contrary, and ultimately purged a longtime political and civil rights activist for not working hard enough for the cause. They claimed they did so to avoid upsetting the prejudices of their East Texas brethren, but in fact most white liberals believed that integration remained a distant pipe dream, that African Americans would have to wait patiently for change, and that white liberals alone knew what was best for the state's poor, regardless of color. They celebrated the battles fought and lost in the long struggle for democracy, but they continued to understand that political goal in white supremacist terms. Their desire to speak for all Texans foundered on the shoals of their own unconscious racism.[78]

Mexican Americans like Peña gained entrée for two reasons: they remained legally classified as "white" in both the U.S. Census and within Texas officialdom and, more important, they represented the majority of the population in every county south and west of San Antonio. Peña was the most outspokenly liberal elected official in that entire region, and he used his local interracial alliances to win election as the DOT board member from Bexar County. The

DOT could hardly exclude him or his fellow AGIF leaders in Corpus Christi and the Valley, but that didn't mean that DOT leaders prioritized their issues either. For Mexican Americans, as for African Americans, the struggle for rights and recognition remained paramount. Gonzalez's gubernatorial campaign promised to put their people and issues on the radar in Austin and even in Washington. Nothing mattered more, yet the DOT wavered.[79]

For his part, gubernatorial candidate Gonzalez did not appear on the lists of featured speakers included in invitations to the gathering, and his convention address remained unsanctioned and unconfirmed until moments before it began. After a full day of deliberation, the meeting was set to adjourn, when Paul Montemayor, the Mexican American leader of the steelworkers union in Corpus Christi who had just been elected to the DOT steering committee, announced that Henry B. Gonzalez had arrived and would give a speech. His appearance was "not certain until he walked in the door," according to one report. Two DOT representatives from San Antonio then hoisted Gonzalez onto their shoulders and paraded him into the hall along with nearly one hundred other delegates—including virtually all of the *mexicanos* in attendance. Montemayor led the procession across the floor as both cheers and boos rained down from the various local units seated above. Although there was "some apparent displeasure at the late appearance," one report noted, the crowd of fifteen hundred warmed up once Gonzalez began speaking and then showered him with applause, and "he was pulling yells of approval before ending his speech." Gonzalez reassured the ideologically diverse, largely white audience by emphasizing his independence. Calling himself a " 'no-handle' Democrat," Gonzalez in typical fashion refused the labels assigned to him and refused to take sides in the factional disputes riddling both the Democratic Party and the DOT. He told the delegates that he had asked the steering committee to withhold a formal endorsement, thereby sidestepping that controversy. He highlighted his prolabor record and promised more aid to working people, and he leveled fierce attacks at Governor Daniel. He boasted that he had traveled six thousand miles on "scouting expeditions" before officially launching his campaign and added that he was "just warming up." The crowd was "steamed up over his campaign" before DOT leaders cut him off after twenty minutes to adjourn the meeting. Still, he nearly stole the show, according to one reporter, and he might have displaced Yarborough from atop the "DOT pedestal" had the convention lasted longer. The convention ended on a high note and with a final prayer. In what was likely a compromise among its many factions, it did not officially endorse any candidates but served as a platform for both of the liberal leaders. Still, Gonzalez remained marginal, his name added to the final program but the text of his speech missing from the final printed proceedings.[80]

Although they remained unable to prevent the upsurge of reaction in the liberal movement in 1958, Peña and other black and brown activists continued to advocate for civil rights in the DOT. In the wake of an apparent controversy over the issue, the paragraph of Fath's report in which he called out W. J. Durham was omitted from the convention's printed proceedings. Before the meeting adjourned, Sutton was quietly elected to replace him as the sole black board member-at-large. Both small but significant changes had Peña's fingerprints all over them, yet neither Peña nor Sutton would accept tokenism for long.[81]

More immediately, while the DOT equivocated on the Gonzalez campaign and ultimately dodged the race issue in the service of all-white realpolitik, the emerging black and brown civil rights movements rallied around Gonzalez's candidacy and used it to advance their own causes. For the African Americans of SNAP House, the decision to endorse Gonzalez was obvious. He had proven himself a solid defender of civil rights on the city council and in the state senate, and the East Side activists had supported him in each of his campaigns. Moreover, the gubernatorial effort dovetailed with the group's local political goals. In an editorial denouncing the reelection bid of county commissioner A. J. Ploch, *SNAP* made a special note of the incumbent's heavy-handed opposition to Gonzalez's campaign for governor: "How could you be so cold blooded as to forbid the Mexicans, who give so much of their sweat and blood, to work for Mr. Henry Gonzales [*sic*]?" the columnist asked. "You have threatened them with loss of their jobs if they are found working for Gonzalez. . . . Mr. Ploch, if you fight Gonzalez, you are fighting every Negro and Mexican in our County. You are also fighting anyone who stands for right and justice."[82] A full-page advertisement for Gonzalez appears in the same issue, and op-eds backing him appeared in *SNAP* throughout the campaign.[83] Boss Bellinger likewise backed Gonzalez, underscoring the latter's remarkable ability to unify warring factions.[84] African Americans across Texas likewise turned out en masse for Gonzalez, rewarding him for his municipal integration ordinances and his courageous filibuster in the legislature.

Mexican Americans flocked to his campaign, even as Gonzalez worked to transform his image from that of an ethnic politician to a candidate with cross-cultural appeal. Although most *mexicanos* statewide remained unregistered, the registration drives of the two recent Yarborough campaigns and of the AGIF had added more Spanish surnames to the rolls than ever before. In Houston, activists including John J. Herrera formed the Civic Action Committee and gained new momentum from Gonzalez's visit to the Segundo Barrio (Second Ward).

In San Antonio, Albert and Olga Peña and the activists from LAD had worked closely with Gonzalez since his first election to the city council in

1953, and they again mobilized the West and South Sides five years later. In the interim, the Peñas had built an extensive card file and potent grassroots precinct organization that succeeded in delivering the barrio votes to Gonzalez in 1955 and to both Gonzalez and Peña in 1956. But soon after their joint victory that year, the two politicos began to drift apart. Lalo Solis, a longtime member of both LAD and Gonzalez's old PAPA society, left the Peña organization to work full time for Gonzalez. Now a state senator, Gonzalez no longer invited the firebrand county commissioner to accompany him to meetings, opting instead to build bridges with black supporters, labor leaders, and wealthy liberal whites. Publicly, Gonzalez ceased appealing to ethnic solidarity among *mexicanos* except in the Spanish-language media. While Peña focused on solidifying his position as a leader of an ethnic voting bloc in the city's West and South Sides, Gonzalez sought to maintain his independence from any one group and to cross over into mainstream white politics. Finally, Gonzalez's statewide "kamikaze" campaign drained resources from Bexar County liberals and the local DOT unit that otherwise could have supported Peña's group. The split was neither complete nor immediate, nor was it initially acrimonious, but it was palpable on the ground. Gonzalez staffer Solis began building a parallel political organization and assembling his own card file of supporters, and Gonzalez increasingly attended gatherings across town and around the state without his former collaborator and lead grassroots strategist. Nonetheless, despite the gradual falling apart, both Albert and Olga Peña joined the legions of Mexican Americans statewide who organized on behalf of the Gonzalez campaign. They also used the race as an opportunity to strengthen their own local organizations and to reach new *mexicano* voters.[85]

For his part, Gonzalez hit the campaign trail, driving around the state in his station wagon and speaking before a wide variety of Mexican American and African American groups as well as many white liberal and labor organizations. Many white working-class and liberal activists in the state's urban areas gave him their votes and volunteered in his campaign, but they did so without the official sanction and, critically, the vast financial resources of the larger labor and liberal movements. The campaign reached countless thousands of people, and it brought great energy to all of the local organizations it touched along the way. Still, it was a ragtag operation at best. Gonzalez lacked a statewide voter turnout apparatus and did not even establish a true campaign headquarters. The candidate remained so independent that he did nearly everything himself, not trusting others to campaign for him. Campaign finances were also tight. Gonzalez raised and spent only $17,000 on the race, less than a fifth of Price Daniel's $91,000 budget. It was classic Henry B., a man crisscrossing the state by himself, beholden to nobody, and determined to make a point.

Gonzalez's massive appeal made up for his lack of resources, but it wasn't enough to win the election. He emerged as a leading candidate and made a powerful showing, pulling nearly 250,000 votes to finish second in the race. He surpassed the total of right-wing populist "Pappy" O'Daniel by more than seven thousand votes, yet the incumbent Daniel garnered nearly 800,000 votes and won the primary without a runoff, 61 percent to Gonzalez's 19 percent, with Pappy just behind. Gonzalez enjoyed broad support in urban areas and carried eleven counties in South Texas. This last fact proved the most significant. Gonzalez won along the border without the endorsements of the region's powerful political machines. The bosses did not oppose him either, but the fact that so many *mexicanos* in the Valley had registered and voted on their own led "some observers to conclude that Latin-American voters were entering a new political phase." Indeed, their influence would continue to grow in the coming years.[86]

For Mexican American activists statewide, the fact that Gonzalez got second place on a shoestring represented a major victory. Moreover, as the only liberal in the race, Gonzalez carved out new space for *mexicanos* in statewide politics and brought together white liberals, labor activists, African Americans, and others in support of a common cause. His example would remain on the minds of community organizers of all stripes and colors in the years ahead. They had no way of knowing that Gonzalez's "kamikaze" campaign would not be easily replicated. His unique crossover appeal had won him nearly a quarter-million votes, but that number would remain the highest total for a Mexican American candidate in a statewide race for the next forty-four years. And in the short term, it was little more than a glorious defeat. Gonzalez returned to San Antonio and to the state senate, where he looked toward the future and eagerly built his newly invigorated organization. As always, he remained independent of the new multiracial coalitions that would soon pop up all around him—with Peña and Sutton at the helm.

From 1948 to 1958, San Antonio's African American and Mexican American activists waged a continuous war with the city's conservative elites. Both the black East Side and the brown West Side remained internally divided, as many self-appointed race leaders formed alliances with the Chamber of Commerce crowd downtown. The more militant community organizers responded by looking across the color line for support. Remarkably, they found plenty of such assistance readily forthcoming.

The story of the Sutton-Garcia alliance rarely makes its way into history books, and the patient base building and interracial experimentation of the long 1950s have all but been lost from the state and the nation's collective memory. At the time, however, the idea of forging a black-brown coalition was anything but abstract. East Side activists desperately battled against Jim Crow in all of its forms. First they demanded the equalization of segregated services, and then they pushed for complete integration. Their demands extended beyond the sharing of space to include economic issues such as equal access to jobs and real political power.

Those battles were not sideshows to the main civil rights struggle but rather central components of the movement. Sutton and company learned experientially that power at the polls meant something tangible in the fight for access, civil rights, and equal opportunity. Their political activism did not represent a watering down of the movement but a means to an end, a principal strategy in the larger campaign for freedom.

Mexican American activists likewise engaged in a struggle for independent political power, not simply for its own sake but as a tool in their own broader movement for civil rights. The most militant among them sympathized with the black freedom struggle and also recognized that both groups needed allies. Garcia, Peña, and Gonzalez did not support black civil rights simply because it was the right thing to do, though that moral compass certainly guided them. Rather, they all recognized that they needed black support in order to achieve their own objectives. Peña especially came to this conclusion after diving into the intricate internal politics of the Texas Democratic Party. From the first rump convention in 1952 forward, he began searching for ways to use his base among *mexicanos* in San Antonio to steer the Democratic Party and the DOT toward supporting the black and brown civil rights struggles. In the next two years, the formerly distant objective of creating a multiracial alliance that could take control of the party and use it to extend liberalism's promise to all citizens would begin to look like an attainable goal. The key, it turned out, would be organized labor.

Chapter 5

Unions Are Needed So Desperately Here

The Rebirth of the Labor Movement and the Seeds of the Bexar Coalition

On March 14, 1959, "More than 1000 marchers, representing 60 union locals" from across San Antonio staged a parade that began at the Labor Temple and ended in a rally in front of the Alamo. Speakers encouraged a group of striking *mexicana* garment workers and highlighted their struggle's larger implications. The national AFL-CIO's assistant organizing director, Franz Daniel, told the crowd that workers must at times strike for their own "self-respect." In the process, he added, they could be personally transformed: "You will discover capabilities that you never thought you had.... It will change your entire way of life.... Let no man, no kind of propaganda make you waver one bit." Father Sherrill Smith, assistant pastor of Mission Espada and a community liaison for the Catholic Archdiocese in San Antonio, added that workers had a "moral right" to strike.

In characteristic fashion, Albert Peña set the marchers' sights squarely on San Antonio's business elites and the larger stakes of political power and economic opportunity in the city and state. "I do not agree with the Chamber of Commerce philosophy that the way to attract industry to San Antonio is to make it a low wage town," Peña told the one thousand assembled union members and supporters. "I will fight any effort, any movement to keep San Antonio a cheap labor town." He added, as one daily newspaper writer paraphrased him, that "union members were witnessing a rebirth of the labor movement in San Antonio." The liberal weekly *Texas Observer* agreed: "The labor movement of San Antonio came alive in a way it has not demonstrated for at least twenty years."[1]

The reciprocal relationship between the black East Side activists and Peña's "liberal sector" on the West Side had grown into a long-term partnership. G. J. Sutton and others in the barrios and ghettos had been organizing since the pecan sheller strike of 1938, and they had carried forward the idea and at times the practice of cooperation between African American and Mexican American activists. So too had white liberals like Maury Maverick Sr., along with his son and other protégés. Episodes of sporadic collaboration between blacks, browns, and whites had given way to more intimate ties by the close of the 1950s. Peña's newfound status as an elected official had given him the clout necessary to cooperate on more equal terms with white liberals and organized labor. He had proven that he could mobilize the barrios, wedged his way into the Democrats of Texas (DOT), and become a major player in the local Democratic Party. Episodes of sporadic collaboration between blacks, browns, and whites gradually gave way to more intimate ties by the close of the 1950s.

Yet in San Antonio and across the state, the predominately white labor movement remained the missing piece of the puzzle. Reliably liberal on economic issues, the Texas AFL-CIO and its local units, the Central Labor Councils, remained tepid at best on civil rights. A labor endorsement had the potential to give liberal Democratic candidates of any color a fighting chance. But if labor balked at backing a liberal in the all-important party primary, as it did when it refrained from endorsing Henry B. Gonzalez in 1958, the candidate's defeat was all but assured. Since the DOT had proven to be an unreliable ally, only organized labor could offer the resources to mobilize large numbers of white voters, especially among the vast working class. At the local level, the *SNAP* activists and Peña's Loyal American Democrats group had learned how to walk precincts and go door to door to get out the vote with meager funding. But even then, they needed allies both on the campaign trail and in office. Organized labor represented the sole group that could afford to buy endless campaign workers, turn out voters, and tip the balance of power in local and state government. The Texas AFL-CIO's lobby even had access to the halls of power in Austin, an asset that few African American and Mexican American groups could boast. For Peña and Sutton, labor represented a golden goose, potentially more important than white elites in helping them to win civil rights, economic opportunities, and real political power for their communities. Labor could give them the edge in their ongoing battle against their own coethnics, helping them work around their less aggressive race leaders.

But in San Antonio, labor remained relatively small, and it was dominated by the conservative building trades, the leaders of which often had close ties to the contractors who ran City Hall. And, of course, labor was white. A few *mexicanos* and even fewer blacks had penetrated the ranks, but the union leadership of the city and state remained the province of Anglos. Many unions continued to discriminate against nonwhite members, and very few white labor leaders in Texas cared at all about civil rights. Unions were often obstacles to fair employment rather than advocates for workplace equality, though they did advocate for full employment and other economic policies that would help the state's nonwhite poor. Despite their differences, the civil rights activists and union leaders agreed that the election of liberal politicians represented a key means to their separate ends. They looked for ways to come together even as they recognized their divergent if overlapping self-interests. Throughout the previous decade, they had just as easily coalesced around particular candidates as they had split apart in regard to others.

Yet in the late 1950s, a trio of local labor struggles would bring the black, brown, and white labor and civil rights activists together in new, surprising ways. Two union campaigns would force the San Antonio labor movement to reconnect to the masses of *mexicano* (and to a lesser extent black) workers in the city. In so doing, the unions would also be compelled to confront and better understand the growing black and brown civil rights movements. A third union effort would rally white male craftsmen around a liberal leader who had come to believe that organizing black and brown workers was the key to the labor movement's success at both the worksite and in electoral politics. Taken together, the labor struggles of the late 1950s in San Antonio would result in the "rebirth" of organized labor, not in the same stolid mold of the previous decades, but in a new dynamic form reminiscent of the 1930s. The battles would forge new bonds between activists across the color line, laying the groundwork for labor's addition to the black-brown coalition in the city and eventually statewide.

A New Foothold at Friedrich

The first of the new union struggles took place in 1957 at Friedrich Refrigerator, a sizable factory with about a thousand employees in the heart of the East Side. Despite the plant's location, the shop floor was dominated by German American skilled craftsmen. Yet several other ethnic groups joined them, albeit lower on the occupational hierarchy. The next group on the totem pole consisted of Polish-descended workers, many of whom were unskilled migrant laborers from nearby farms, some of whom shared cultural ties to the Germans. Mexican Americans and African Americans occupied the bottom rung, laboring more or less side by side at unskilled manufacturing tasks. About half the workers plantwide were Mexican American women (*mexicanas*).[2]

In 1957, the International Union of Electrical, Machine, and Radio Workers (IUE) arrived in San Antonio and began to organize the Friedrich workers. The national union had its origins in the second Red Scare, when the CIO chartered it in order to raid the membership of the Communist-led United Electrical Workers (UE). The newer IUE remained staunchly anti-Communist, but its success on the shop floor depended upon emulating its rival's progressive politics. Its tactics mirrored those of the Red UE—both unions encouraged militant, rank-and-file-led industrial unionism. And both unions fostered interracial and interethnic collaboration similar to that of the Fort Worth packinghouse workers. In short, thanks to this unusual history, black and brown workers had a chance of inclusion in the new IUE.

The key rank-and-file organizer at Friedrich turned out to be a Polish farmer-turned-worker named Paul Javior. Like many small farmers in South Texas, Javior had learned to speak Spanish at a young age—despite the American conquest, Spanish remained the language of commerce among local ranchers, farm workers, farmers, tenants, and merchants alike. Javior's native tongue was Polish, but he picked up English in school. His older brother, a driver for a nearby brewery, introduced him to both German culture and trade unionism in San Antonio. Javior began to work part time at the brewery, earning more in a few weeks on the job than his family cleared in an entire harvest. He finally left home to get a full-time job at Friedrich Refrigerator, a nonunion but stable employer with wages that still impressed the young farmer. Inside the plant, Javior's trilingual abilities and experience at the brewery allowed him to forge friendships across ethnic lines. At the same time, his rural upbringing and exclusion from old-stock Anglo and German cliques predisposed Javior to align himself with African American workers as well. When the IUE showed up at the plant gate, Javior was the right man to connect them to countless working people throughout the plant.

He began by recruiting Ruth Harris, a "Mexican woman with an Anglo husband" (as he later put it) who was already a recognized leader among the factory's vast group of *mexicana* workers. As the campaign grew to include a majority of the Friedrich employees, IUE organizers and rank-and-file leaders decided to "button up"—that is, to ask their supporters to announce the union's presence by wearing IUE buttons on the shop floor. Many workers feared reprisals for displaying their sympathies, but Harris stood up at a union meeting and declared that she was ready to confront the boss. Hundreds of women followed her lead, while the men, led by Javior, accompanied them as they marched into the plant. The display of broad support for the union made it obvious that it could win a National Labor Relations Board (NLRB)-supervised representation election. In an unusual move, Friedrich management accepted the union as the workers' bargaining agent and negotiated a first contract without delay. Soon after, the members elected Harris to the post of chief steward, and Javior became an officer of the newly formed IUE Local 780. Both joined the union staff by the early 1960s.[3]

The IUE's victory at Friedrich represented a landmark triumph for industrial union organizing in San Antonio. A few garment shops had operated on and off under union contracts, but these were typically small, fly-by-night concerns that closed soon after the union arrived. Most relied entirely upon Mexican American women for workers. The arrival of the IUE marked the first time that a multiracial industrial union had secured a permanent foothold in the city. For the next several decades, the union hall on East Commerce Street across from the factory would serve as a gathering place for union members, a launching pad for countless new organizing efforts, and a site for coalition building with both black and brown civil rights and political activists.

The hall also represented a potential new base for aspiring liberal politicians. Like most contemporary unions, the IUE asked its members to contribute to its electoral program through voluntary extra dues earmarked for politics. But the IUE was unusual among unions in the period in that it continued to enjoy broad rank-and-file participation in all of its activities, even after the original organizing and contract campaigns had concluded. Local 780 provided dollars, bodies, and, above all, block walkers for the San Antonio AFL-CIO. And perhaps most important, its leaders brought the relatively radical vision of interracial cooperation forged on the shop floor to the labor movement as a whole. In the years to come it would provide consistent votes for the growing multiracial coalition spearheaded by Sutton, Peña, and various white labor and liberal activists.

The Lamberts and the Great Tex-Son Strike

The second major union campaign that contributed to the rise of a multiracial liberal coalition occurred at Tex-Son, a garment factory of three to four hundred workers located just north of downtown San Antonio. The mostly *mexicana* workers there had enjoyed representation by the International Ladies' Garment Workers' Union (ILGWU) for two decades before they went on strike in 1959. Earlier that year, the shop's owners, Harold and Emanuel Franzel, hired Theo Weiss, who was an attorney, president of the San Antonio Chamber of Commerce, and a well-known union buster. When the union's contract expired, Weiss took charge of the company's negotiations team and flatly refused to bargain.

Union members walked off the job in February 1959. The company responded by hiring a group of strikebreakers that didn't shy away from attacking the strikers on the picket line. Images of bloodied *mexicana* unionists and scabs soon filled the pages of the city's newspapers, leading to calls for order and eventually the arrest and harassment of countless strikers by local police—just as the city had responded to the pecan sheller uprising two decades earlier. The union responded to the beatings with outrage, parading the local's rank-and-file leaders in a public relations campaign that portrayed them as helpless Cold War–era mothers under physical assault by unscrupulous bosses who colluded with corrupt law enforcement agencies. The ILGWU also launched a nationwide boycott of Tex-Son products, circulating literature that emphasized the strikers' matronly, ladylike, and fashionable qualities.

Scholarly accounts of the conflict disagree on the causes and meanings of the union's maternalist portrayal of the strikers. Historian Irene Ledesma argues that the predominately male ILGWU leadership misrepresented and essentialized these working women by insisting upon an image of motherhood that precluded the recognition of the women's own agency. The *mexicana* workers' full potential remained underutilized, she concludes, crippling the strike from the start.[4] In contrast, historian Lori Flores contends that the strikers themselves adopted the maternalist image as a strategic response to negative press coverage and a concerted appeal to Cold War ideals of domesticity. In this version, the *mexicanas* played a critical role in determining the strike's message, and they earned and enjoyed the support of the few Anglo women workers at the plant, ILGWU organizers, male trade unionists, and local Mexican American politicians. Although the union could have done more to support the strike, Flores contends, the real obstacles in its path remained the company's successful outsourcing of union work, hiring of scabs, and the general antiunion, right-to-work climate of 1950s Texas.[5]

While both renderings of the Tex-Son strike illuminate the importance of gender in shaping the union's strategy, the links tying the conflict to the city's developing liberal electoral and civil rights coalition remain unexamined. A closer look reveals that the Tex-Son strike drew strength from and contributed to the development of the statewide struggle for democracy in several significant ways. The Texas director of the ILGWU at the time of the conflict was none other than George Lambert, the longtime labor, civil rights, and political organizer who had participated in virtually every major campaign in Texas since the Ford beatings of 1937 and the pecan sheller uprising of 1938. With Lambert at the helm, the union launched the massive boycott of Tex-Son products that, in turn, brought unprecedented exposure to the travails of the Mexican American working people at the bottom of the state's economy—however flawed its message may have been in regard to gender. Both George Lambert and his wife Latane were intimately involved in the flowering multiracial electoral coalition, laboring in positions that helped the strikers win especially strong and public support from the predominately white San Antonio AFL-CIO Council and from recently elected county commissioner Albert Peña. It is only through this wider lens that the full picture becomes clear: the Tex-Son strike grew into a cause célèbre not simply because of the courage and tenacity of the *mexicana* workers in the face of violent and prolonged opposition. It did so due to its particular timing, location, staffing, and, above all, its close relationship to the rapidly expanding coalition-building efforts that surrounded it.

The presence of the Lamberts in San Antonio during the Tex-Son strike was more than a coincidence. Both had worked with various garment and clothing worker unions since they met in North Carolina in 1937, and they brought their decades of combined experience in the trenches of stolidly antiunion Texas to bear during the Tex-Son struggle. The duo had left town soon after the pecan sheller strike and had traveled around the state and region, with George working for the Amalgamated Clothing Workers of America (ACWA, or "the Amalgamated") and Latane joining him on and off. George became the Amalgamated's state director in February 1939, and Latane soon set out on her own for Commonwealth College, a "resident labor school" in the Ouachita Mountains of Arkansas. There she met other wayward southern leftists like herself, including school director Claude Williams and singer-songwriter Lee Hays, the college's music director, who is best known for singing bass in a pair of folk supergroups, the Almanac Singers and, later, the Weavers. Reuniting whenever possible, the Lamberts continued to bounce around Texas until the birth of their first child, David Lee, in San Antonio in July 1939—just a month before the riots against the Communist Party meeting at the Municipal Auditorium. They made their way north soon after his birth, ultimately settling into a home in East Dallas. Along the way, the new mother renounced the party in protest of the signing of the nonaggression pact between Hitler and Stalin, a tactical alliance that many of the Old Left found unconscionable. She wedged her membership card behind the sign posted on the rear of a cheap motel room door in Waco, and she never looked back.[6]

Both Lamberts continued to organize for the ACWA, other CIO unions, and various political causes. In 1941, when George joined the army, Latane took over many of his duties in the labor movement. By 1946, despite having a small child, Latane had "helped in almost every CIO effort in the state," and she held the post of regional director for the ACWA. On May 6 of that year, Latane attended the Southwestern CIO Education Conference in Fort Worth, where she joined a group of four women activists as "union songbirds" who entertained the other attendees. The following week, Latane traveled to Atlantic City, New Jersey, to attend the international convention of the ACWA. She was one of several "rank and filers, Amalgamated organizers, who have worked in the South" who "took over" a session debating the union's future participation in Operation Dixie. A white woman from Tennessee, a black man from New Orleans, and Lambert and another white woman union president from Dallas were all featured in a union publication after the gathering. While the others spoke with optimism about the prospects of the southern organizing campaign, the article reports that Lambert, "a distinctly good-looking person who has organized clothing and garment workers and nut pickers all through Texas . . . warned that 'Operation Dixie' isn't going to be a 'cozy little affair.' Mrs. Lambert added, with a charming grin, 'and while we are organizing, we will also do something definite about political reaction in Texas.'"[7] In short, Latane continued to be a highly respected activist in her own right, not merely filling in for George but offering her own ideas to help shape the future of labor and political organizing in Texas and across the South.

George returned from the war in 1946, resuming his duties at the Amalgamated. Latane soon went on the road again to work as a union organizer, this time for the United Hatters, Cap, and Millinery Workers, AFL. In 1949 and into 1950, Latane worked to train a new field representative, Cora Valentine, while supporting organizing campaigns in El Paso and Corsicana, Texas, as well as Greenville, Alabama. Throughout the 1950s, Lambert joined a group of women organizers in various garment and clothing workers unions who traveled together around North Texas in order to bring more and more women into the house of labor.

In 1951, George resigned his post with the Amalgamated to become a "full time political organizer" in and around Dallas. There, in the 1950s, writes the labor-published *Dallas Craftsman*, "he and his wife organized [a] 'Get-out the vote' campaign for the NAACP which became a national model for effective voter participation in the Democratic Party."[8] As this quotation suggests, labor, civil rights, and political action blended seamlessly in the daily organizing of both George and Latane Lambert. For the next six years, until they moved back to San Antonio in 1957, the couple operated a mom-and-pop political consulting firm, working as freelance organizers for a wide variety of liberal electoral causes and cobbling together a living from a series of temporary jobs. They simultaneously continued to volunteer as leaders of numerous civic groups. The historical record rarely specifies whether or not they were paid for a particular task. But it does clearly show a tremendous range and successful record of protracted, diverse activism. In conservative Dallas at the height of the Cold War, George and Latane Lambert continued to carry forward the expansive vision forged in the trenches of the labor movement of the 1930s and 1940s.

George bounced back and forth between Washington, D.C., Detroit, and Dallas. He served as a local leader of Americans for Democratic Action (ADA), the national membership organization of liberals founded in 1947 by anti-Communist liberal Democrats, including Eleanor Roosevelt and the UAW's Walter Reuther. He also chaired the Dallas-area branch of the Texas Social and Legislative Conference, the first statewide liberal political coalition founded by the Texas State CIO Council during the war.[9] At the same time, Lambert collaborated with the NAACP and other civil rights organizations in Dallas and across Texas. In 1953, for example, he partnered with the local and regional offices of the NAACP to combat a proposed hike of local transit fares. He conducted a ridership study and presented it to the Dallas city council, which uncharacteristically rejected the private contractor's planned increase.[10] Later that year, Lambert joined the Dallas delegation to the NAACP state convention in San Antonio, where he spoke on "Techniques for Improving Inter-Group Relations in Texas." He also helped his local chapter host the next national convention in Dallas in 1954.[11] Latane likewise served on committees in the branch, and the couple worked with W. J. Durham and other local and national NAACP leaders to plan a "Bill of Rights Day" rally in Dallas in January 1956.[12]

By that time, both George and Latane Lambert had become the primary liaisons between Dallas's black and white activist communities. As leaders of the local NAACP, the couple tied the association to white liberals in the ADA, organized labor, and other liberal Democrats—as well as the reverse. When white liberal groups sought electoral alliances with African Americans, the Lamberts served as their point of entrée. With the Lamberts as the bridge, a tentative interracial alliance called the Dallas County Democratic Organizing Committee developed in the state's most conservative major city. In late 1954, George conducted a study of the recent runoff election and selected "priority precincts" in which to focus their voter registration and poll tax collection efforts in January 1955. Lambert was charged with contacting the NAACP and coordinating the drive in four key black districts, out of a total of fifteen "priority precincts" that his study identified. The larger coalition's registration effort thus depended heavily upon the NAACP and black precincts, and Lambert bore the responsibility of crossing the color line to deliver these critical voters. W. J. Durham served as a key leader among the coalition's African American wing.[13] Latane Lambert participated in this drive as well, and she also tied the coalition to several Democratic women's clubs in Dallas, of which she was a frequent officer.[14] The Lamberts' method of gathering and interpreting voter data and then putting it to work in new, precinct- and block-level mobilization efforts became the template for labor's nationwide Committee on Political Education and similar initiatives across Texas and the nation.[15]

By the time of Tex-Son strike, George and Latane Lambert had spent the last two decades making slow but steady progress in the struggle for democracy, chalking up a series of small victories along the way. Drawing upon their experience in the pecan shellers' strike and the clothing workers unions, they developed a pragmatic but radically interracial approach to politics in a staunchly conservative locale at the height of the Cold War. They made a series of minor contributions at the local level, but the more enduring legacy was the bond they developed with the city's and the state's African American civil rights activists. Such ties became the foundation of experiments in interracial electoral alliances that, in turn, would develop more fully in the 1960s.

The couple returned to San Antonio in October 1957, when George became the staffer for the joint council of the city's ILGWU locals.[16] In this capacity, Lambert led the internal organizing efforts that preceded the public act of striking Tex-Son, and he then coordinated the behind-the-scenes campaign to gain support for the workers and win the protracted conflict. Most critically, Lambert managed the "Don't Buy Tex-Son" boycott that lay at the heart of the union's public appeals for solidarity as well as its long-term strategy for winning the strike.

Thanks to their long-term activism, both Lamberts were keenly aware of the stakes of the Tex-Son fight. They would have agreed with brewery worker George Eichler, the head of the San Antonio AFL-CIO Council, who aptly summarized the historic nature of the conflict one year into the strike: "it has become a key struggle in the battle of vicious anti-labor forces in this community to further weaken the Labor Movement in Texas."[17] At the local level, the Lamberts knew that while they were in Dallas, San Antonio Chamber of Commerce president Theo Weiss had been hard at work waging war against the ILGWU. Weiss had destroyed four other locals since 1953. One small union local at the Bernhard Altmann Company had won a short strike in 1957, but it too was on Weiss's hit list. Tex-Son remained as the lone sizable union holdout in the city and one of the few in the entire South. And Weiss had now convinced its owners to dig in their heels—even as they began "farm[ing] out" work to nonunion factories in Mississippi. Both the future of labor in Texas and the garment union's survival were very much up in the air.[18]

The gravity of the situation compelled George to develop a new strategy. Harkening back to the pecan sheller movement of 1938, Lambert devised an approach that centered on rank-and-file participation and leadership.[19] As early as the fall of 1958, he began assembling a negotiating committee composed of and led by *mexicana* workers in the plant. The committee, in turn, recruited new members to the union and mobilized them for a unanimous strike vote, and the committee quickly took charge when the walkout began the following February. In May 1959, as the conflict continued, Lambert worked with the local president and strike committee head, Gregoria Montalbo, to form a delegation of workers to give a presentation on their struggle to the international convention of the ILGWU in Miami. He also helped her prepare her speech to the convention.[20]

Rank-and-file union leadership rarely springs forth spontaneously, and it is frequently repressed or overshadowed by high-level union bureaucrats when it does. Yet Lambert remained committed to fostering ordinary workers' activism up until the strike's bitter end. Rather than stealing the spotlight from Montalbo at the Miami convention, Lambert organized a delegation of rank-and-file workers to represent themselves. He confined his own activities to behind-the-scenes work, producing a rough-cut, silent version of the short film that would later circulate in union halls across the country: *Mother Is On Strike*.[21]

At the same time, Lambert also understood the importance of winning outside support for the strike, and he drew upon his personal relationships with local labor and political leaders to win unprecedented public endorsements and financial assistance for the union. The city's labor and liberal movements, in turn, were revitalized by the garment workers' struggle. George Eichler's Brewery Workers union and the San Antonio AFL-CIO Council both became key supporters of the strikers, as did many of the council's member unions. So too did Commissioner Albert Peña. Optimism abounded from all corners after the March 14, 1959, march on the Alamo. Still, the strike dragged on with no end in sight.

The broader labor movement's support for the garment workers remained significant as the weeks of picketing turned into months and then years. In August 1959, six months into the strike, Eichler jumped at the opportunity to use the international convention of the Brewery Workers union being held in San Antonio to stage another demonstration of solidarity. State and local laws, enforced by police harassment and upheld in local courts, had temporarily restricted the picketing activities of the Tex-Son strikers. The Brewery Workers responded by leaving their convention site and picketing the factory on the strikers' behalf. One paper reported that "A jeering, singing mob of 350 International Union of Brewery Workers convention delegates" attempted to keep scabs out of the plant. City police again cracked down on the pickets, this time arresting the president of a Philadelphia local and the international union's general counsel. Both were "released without charges, and received official apologies the next day"—actions that indicate the relative power and respect given to white, skilled, male craft workers by local authorities and underscoring the significance of this group's support for unskilled *mexicana* industrial workers.[22] In another example of solidarity, the Nuevo Laredo, Mexico, local unit of the Confederación de Trabajadores Mexicanos (CTM), the Mexican counterpart to the AFL-CIO, hung a banner over the international port of entry, urging Mexican citizens to avoid scabbing at Tex-Son or purchasing the struck company's products while visiting the United States. One Nuevo Laredo newspaper responded to the violence by headlining a story, "Salvajismo Contra Mujeres" (Savagery against Women).[23]

As labor unions in two countries rallied behind them, Lambert and the strike committee coordinated rank-and-file participation on the picket line and launched an unprecedented boycott. Throughout the summer and fall, Tex-Son workers descended on area department stores in order to ask retailers to stop selling the company's products. When businesses refused, they launched informational pickets outside the stores, distributing handbills that informed consumers of the strike and asked them to refrain from buying Tex-Son clothes. Their tactics worked. By September, nine months into the strike, boycott campaign chairman Rinaldo Panetta reported that nearly two hundred stores, including more than eighty in Texas, had removed Tex-Son products from their shelves. Some two hundred more stores had agreed to refrain from reordering Tex-Son clothes until the strike was settled. Panetta appealed to union members nationwide to meet again with local retailers in their cities to deliver the union's message ahead of the annual visits by Tex-Son's traveling salesmen. He also appealed directly to the retailers.[24]

Workers alternated between picketing the factory and distributing leaflets downtown, constantly reinventing their tactics as Tex-Son and the company's business and law enforcement allies sought to contain the conflict. Efforts to stage informational pickets at Joske's, a high-end department store in San Antonio, represent a case in point. In July 1959, city police arrested Lambert and twenty-one strikers as they distributed handbills outside the store. With television and radio reporters looking on, the union took advantage of an opportunity for free public relations. Police claimed that the hand billing violated both the federal Landrum-Griffin Act that restricted secondary boycotts as well as the state O'Daniel law that prohibited mass picketing. Lambert consulted with the unions' attorneys and lobbied the international union for permission to continue "mass hand billing" despite the arrests. Several months later, Tex-Son workers returned to Joske's, this time carrying helium balloons with the slogan "Don't Buy Tex-Son" printed on them. Strikers handed the balloons to children as they entered the store with their parents. Once inside, the kids released them and let them float to the ceiling, allowing the union to spread its message not only in front of but also inside the department store. The workers also solicited nearly five hundred letters from Joske's customers asking the company to remove the Tex-Son line.[25]

Strikers carried the boycott to other cities in Texas and beyond, where they experienced a mixture of resistance (including police harassment and arrest) and cooperation from retailers. Foley's department store in Houston filed unfair labor practice charges against the union after a group of "union seamen, electricians, and garments workers" staged an informational picket in front of the business. Countless other retailers used every tool available to scare the pickets away. Others readily cooperated, including those that depended upon union members. An ILGWU staffer reported that Best Taylor's in Houston was one such case: the retailer "Says, get me off your list in a hurry. . . . His business is near the NMU hall and does business for the Seamen." The strikers also visited stores in San Antonio and beyond, checked their inventories for Tex-Son attire, and reported their findings back to Lambert. As the company increasingly outsourced more and more work to low-wage subcontractors in Mississippi and throughout the South, members of Lambert's staff and striking workers followed the money. They set up boycotts and solidarity

A cluster of balloons that union activists handed out to kids outside Joske's department store in San Antonio, winter of 1959–60. The messages printed on them included "Don't Buy Tex-Son Clothes" and "Tex-Son Factory on Strike, ILGWU and AFL-CIO." Courtesy International Ladies' Garment Workers' Union, Local 180, San Antonio, Texas, Special Collections, The University of Texas at Arlington Library, Arlington, Texas, AR30-1-3.

pickets in front of the factories doing Tex-Son work, even in the most remote places where organized labor scarcely had a presence at all. Members of the ILGWU in faraway states staged pickets of their own to compel local retailers and branches of chains to drop Tex-Son products.[26]

While the boycott sought to financially strain the company, Lambert and the strikers faced fiscal problems of their own as the strike wore on. In response, they reached out to and received support from a wide variety of sources, including many of the key players in the city's and the state's liberal political coalitions. As secretary of the San Antonio AFL-CIO Council, George Eichler represented one of the strikers' most influential and deep-pocketed supporters. In addition to orchestrating the massive March 1959 parade and the Brewery Workers' action in August of that year, Eichler made repeated calls for local unions to support the boycott and also to send financial contributions to the strikers. Even after the ILGWU international union pulled its support for the strike in late November 1960, Eichler asked each of the local labor council's member unions to adopt one of the eighty remaining strikers who "have carried on a magnificent battle for more than 19 months against one of the most rabidly anti-union employers in San Antonio" and still remained

Unions Are Needed So Desperately Here   183

on the picket line even without strike pay.²⁷ Three months later, in February 1961, local union and strike committee president Gregoria Montalbo credited Eichler's council and the Texas State AFL-CIO with providing the critical financial support needed to continue the strike.²⁸ And as Christmas approached in 1962—some two years after strike benefits had ceased—the San Antonio council again voted to donate an additional fifty dollars to the thirteen Tex-Son strikers who remained on the picket line, blacklisted from local employment and still determined to win.²⁹

Of course, the fact that local unions contributed financially to the Tex-Son strike is not unique in the annals of labor history. Union members frequently donated to other locals' strike funds and were often asked to respect picket lines and to boycott products of unfair employers. Yet the conflict at Tex-Son remains unusual: it was an atypically long struggle, it was waged and led by Mexican American women workers, and it happened in a place that had grown unaccustomed to militant labor conflicts. It represented the first time that local AFL unions had supported *mexicana* strikers (the AFL had opposed the CIO-led struggles of the 1930s), and it was the first example in which the local labor movement continued to support local workers years after their own international union had abandoned them.

In short, the Tex-Son strike had fulfilled Albert Peña's prediction that it would reenergize the city's labor movement, even as it failed to protect the union members who walked off the job. In so doing, the struggle also deepened the ties between organized labor and the city's leading liberal political leaders and civil rights activists. Of course, Peña was involved in the strike from the beginning. He connected the union to his brother and law partner Richard Peña, who served as the union's primary lawyer for the first ten months of the strike. The practicing attorney's tasks included countless court appearances and paying bond fees for arrested workers—including on at least one occasion twenty women arrested on a single day for mass picketing.³⁰

When the international union cut off strike benefits in November 1960, local committee leader Montalbo asked Commissioner Peña to visit the union hall to meet with the *mexicana* workers who wished to continue the fight. George Lambert also attended the meeting, though he reported that his presence was "completely accidental." In a letter to his superior, Lambert noted that the committee members "were determined to keep the strike going and asked his [Peña's] help in interceding with the ILGWU and with other unions in getting them some financial support." The fact that the strikers appealed to Peña is itself telling—the civil rights lawyer turned politician had become a passionate supporter of labor rights and likely represented many of the women workers on the county commission. He represented a dependable ally capable of advocating for their interests even as the union bureaucracy seemingly turned its back on them. Still, Peña deferred to Lambert's expertise at the meeting. The union organizer reported that he "told him and the Committee that I could see no hope that the strike could be won, that the International had decided it was a lost strike and had for that reason withdrawn financial support and that I could see no purpose in making any effort to continue it." The firebrand county commissioner did not agree, Lambert added. "Peña said that to the contrary he felt that the loss of the Tex-Son strike would be a serious blow to the entire labor movement here and particularly to the chances of Latin-American workers organizing and improving their living standards. He told the Committee that he would do everything he could, including getting them out of jail at no charge if need be, to help them as long as they wanted to keep the strike going."[31] Despite Lambert's opposition, Montalbo and the committee asked Peña to write a letter to appeal to ILGWU president David Dubinsky.[32]

Peña did so the following week. His letter was reprinted in the San Antonio *AFL-CIO Weekly Dispatch*, the labor newspaper, along with a sympathetic preface. Peña's words underscored his commitment to the strike and to labor and working-class struggles generally. "I met with the ladies of the Tex-Son strike committee last week," he began. "Faced with a bleak and cold Christmas, hardship, abuse, jail, the committee agreed to continue the picket line. I have known many men with less courage and few men with more courage. If the Tex-Son strike dies, it will die hard—to the last agonizing breath. And if the Tex-Son strike dies, every man and woman in the labor movement in San Antonio will die a little, too." His entreaty to Dubinsky was direct and highlighted not only the conflict at hand but the future implications of defeat. A lost strike at Tex-Son stood to undermine his own daily organizing work and the future of the emerging multiracial coalition. "I appeal to you in behalf of working people in general in the city of San Antonio who are paid the lowest wage scale of any large city in the United States," Peña writes. "I appeal to you because if this strike fails people like me will have a very difficult time selling the union movement to the vast majority of people in our town. And Unions are needed so desperately here."[33]

It remains unclear whether Dubinsky replied to Peña's appeal. In any event, the international union did not reverse its decision, and strike benefits did not resume. For the next two years, first one hundred, then eighty, and finally thirteen women remained on the picket line on their own dimes until the factory closed its doors for good. Weiss had busted the union, but the union's tenacious members and innovative boycott had forced the company to leave town.

Still, all was not lost in the arena of local politics. Eichler and Peña's unflinching support tightened the bonds between organized labor and the "liberal sector" of *mexicanos*. Likewise, the Lamberts' ongoing activism linked the strike to the rising liberal political coalition in San Antonio. Although only fragmentary evidence is available, it is clear that Latane in particular focused on precinct-level organizing and countywide relationship building, moving beyond the worksite to the conflict's larger electoral implications. Soon after their return to the city, she became the corresponding secretary of the Bexar County Democrats, a liberal group chaired by Peña that also included liberal Anglo judge Charlie Grace and several local labor leaders. In May of 1960, Latane, Peña, and G. J. Sutton helped coordinate the group's takeover of the Democratic Party's county convention. Latane and George Lambert both served as block walkers and on-the-ground coordinators for Henry B. Gonzalez's campaigns as he was reelected to the State Senate in 1960 and then to the U.S. Congress in a special election in 1961, when Latane also helped run the Democratic Party headquarters. Gonzalez reciprocated by actively supporting the garment workers' union. By February of 1962, Latane had become the secretary of a new alliance, the Bexar County Democratic Coalition, as well as the coordinator of the organization's all-important poll tax and get-out-the-vote committees.[34]

George and Latane Lambert's involvement in the Tex-Son strike and boycott, and the political action that followed, proved anything but tangential to the real story. The longtime activists connected the Tex-Son struggle to the blossoming local labor-liberal coalition and local civil rights organizations, the leaders of which sustained the strikers in unprecedented ways. For the first time, white male craft workers led by Eichler supported a strike of Mexican American workers—women, no less. They made common cause with the daughters of the pecan shellers and with firebrand civil rights activists Peña and Sutton. They were unlikely bedfellows, but they were now all in bed together nonetheless.

Even in defeat, the Tex-Son strike revitalized a moribund local labor movement and cemented the pieces of the city's multiracial coalition. By focusing narrowly on the strikers themselves, including the gendered representations of the women workers, historians have inadvertently overlooked the larger transformations taking place around them—changes in which they played a critical role. The three-year Tex-Son strike and boycott should be remembered not simply as a heroic act of courageous but marginal workers, nor simply as a transitional moment in the long Chicano/a movement or the development of Chicana activism. Clearly it was all of those things. But it was also a watershed in the development of a unitary movement for democracy in San Antonio and across Texas, a moment when a small local conflict helped engender a permanent coalition that would, in turn, transform the state's political and economic history.

H. S. (Hank) Brown of the United Association of Plumbers and Pipefitters Local 142, San Antonio, speaking at the Texas State AFL-CIO Convention, August 1960. Courtesy Texas AFL-CIO Papers, Special Collections, The University of Texas at Arlington Library, Arlington, Texas, AR110-29-4-9 [#60127-d].

H. S. "Hank" Brown and the Building Trades Strike

The Tex-Son strike also coincided with another massive strike, one that is completely absent from mono-ethnic histories of Chicano/a labor and politics in San Antonio. While historians have focused exclusively on the *mexicana* garment workers, contemporary observers presented the two conflicts in tandem. In fact, the liberal *Texas Observer* ran a front-page story on the other battle, a strike by the city's white male building trades unions, directly beside a piece on Tex-Son. Inside, the paper ran a pair of biographical sketches on the principal organizers of the two strikes, profiling George Lambert of the garment workers union right next to the leader of the craftsmen, a plumber named H. S. "Hank" Brown.[35]

Like Lambert, Brown was a foreigner by Texas standards, having been born and raised in the Ohio River Valley. His father was a shop floor leader in the Amalgamated Tin, Iron, and Steel Workers, the old-stock all-white craft union that had infamously fallen victim to Carnegie Steel's Pinkerton squads in the Homestead Strike of 1892. Born in 1920 and a child during the Depression, Brown grew up in a union milieu. He accompanied his dad on summer trips to West Virginia, where they lived in miners' camps as they began organizing industrial unions even before the formation of the CIO. In 1936, Brown left home and began to roam, riding trains and living in "hobo jungles" as far away as Florida before returning to Appalachia to join John L. Lewis's United Mine Workers. The militant union president who spearheaded the "real movement" in the mountains served as Brown's role model, a man whom he later recalled did more for the people of that region than anyone before or since.[36]

Brown continued to wander before arriving in San Antonio in 1939. He got a job as a laborer at a nonunion plumbing shop and soon became a helper. Yet his growing skills (and white skin) still did not gain him entrée to the exclusive Plumbers and Steam Fitters' Union, which controlled access to the top of the trade. A tight-knit "old German clan" controlled the local unit and passed down the craft from generation to generation. Probably coincidentally, Brown courted and married Sophie Weigman, the daughter and sister of two German union plumbers. He later recalled that marrying into the clan still did not make him a son. He worked on a temporary permit until 1943, when a wartime labor shortage and new local leadership finally allowed him to become a full member of the union. He was then drafted into the army.[37]

When he returned to San Antonio in 1945, Brown quickly rose through the union ranks, becoming the plumbers' business agent in 1946 and, soon thereafter, a delegate to the local Building Trades Council and the Texas State Federation of Labor (TSFL). All three posts taught him new lessons. Still just twenty-six years old, Brown learned experientially about bread-and-butter labor issues, parliamentary procedure, and electoral politics. Sometime in the 1940s, he later remembered, the plumbers picketed a builder named H. B. Zachary, who was putting up housing projects. When a group of carpenters crossed the picket line and continued to work, several plumbers, including Brown, stormed in on their meeting and "went down there and stomped the hell out of a bunch of them, and set an example that it wasn't healthy to be contributing to scabbing on us when we were fighting for what we believed was righteousness and justice." Brown recalled that the issue was resolved quickly, in contrast to later disputes that were resolved over months or years through the grievance procedure or in the courts.[38]

Around the same time, Brown also cut his teeth in the Democratic Party. He served as the county manager for liberal professor Homer Rainey's 1946 gubernatorial campaign and worked for Truman in 1948. By the early 1950s, Brown found even more time to commit to electoral politics, serving as chair of the Labor League for Political Education and working in collaboration with local and statewide groups of white liberals prior to the formation of the DOT.[39] He recalled, "It was a good time, there was a lot of work, so you didn't have a lot of unemployed people breathing down your collar, so you could spend an hour or two here and there working in politics. And it all related back, of course, to your members because if you don't have a friendly city council and a friendly county council or commissioners court . . . it shows up on the workers." For Brown, the mandate was simple. "So it's important that we be involved all the way to the precinct all the way to the white house," he added. "I've believed that ever since I was involved back with John L. Lewis and my dad."[40] In this period Brown also "began to work with some of the Mexican-American leaders, [and] some of the Negro leaders, and that was my first involvement with a kind of coalition."[41] In 1952, he joined Maury Maverick (Sr.), Peña, and Sutton in walking out from the state Democratic Convention, but he then clashed with Sutton over the election of delegates on the rump slate for the national gathering. The exchange was acrimonious but not consequential, as Sutton's candidate carried the day. Brown then led one wing of the local Stevenson presidential campaign that helped launch Peña's political career.[42]

Brown did right by his members in the plumbers union as well as the growing liberal wing of the Democratic Party, which he helped connect to the city's black and brown activists. But he left town just as their joint efforts began to bear fruit. In 1952, as a young district vice president of the TSFL, Brown ran for the federation's presidency but narrowly lost. A year later, the state body's executive secretary, Jerry Holleman, hired Brown as his assistant. Brown recalled that he later got a "fancy title as Education Director" but "actually, I was a cook and bottle-washer and did whatever had to be done." That year he served as the TSFL's "leg man" in the state legislature, leading labor's lobbying effort in the capital.[43]

Still, the "education" part of his title was far from empty. Brown toured the state offering seminars to local labor councils. The workshops taught both union and political skills, offering training that was especially needed in the "boondocks" of East Texas, the Rio Grande Valley, and the faraway Panhandle. By visiting two labor councils per month, Brown canvassed all of the far-flung locales over the course of a year. He spread news of the latest legislative developments, shared stories of his experiences in the electoral field in San Antonio and Austin, and asked each delegate to add extra political contributions on top of their dues. He continued his own experiential education while also getting his name and face in front of countless union members across the state.[44]

Brown's star was rising in union circles, but a twist of fate sent him back to San Antonio and directed his energies back into Bexar County. Following the merger of the TSFL and the Texas State CIO Council in 1957, Secretary Holleman slashed Brown's education program budget, and Brown feuded with another federation officer as well. He returned to the Alamo City to discover that his old local's business agent had become an ineffectual drunk. The union's membership, which had tripled during his own tenure at the helm, had contracted under his successor. Brown assembled a team of officers, stood for election, and returned to the local's leadership in 1959. Brown remembered that the union's relations to local contractors had also deteriorated and that, combined with the "Eisenhower economy," had brought wages to a recent low. The union's members voted overwhelmingly to go on strike.

Over four hundred of them walked off the job on August 3, 1959. The sheet-metal workers union joined them. The employers responded by shutting down their operations across the city, effectively locking out the workers in hopes of ending the strike. By early September, Brown estimated that the strike had already cost $125,000 in lost wages, $250,000 in lost revenue for the employers, and $500,000 to the public in construction delays. The union itself lost $4,000 per month in dues while doubling its expenses. The *Observer* reported that the strike brought the city's building industry to "a virtual standstill," a condition that only got worse when five additional trades joined the walkout in early October.[45]

Like the leaders and supporters of the Tex-Son union, Brown believed that labor was at a crossroads during the tumultuous strikes of 1959.[46] Although wages and slack time were the immediate causes of the craftsmen's strike, the conflict also raised larger questions surrounding the city's method of economic development and distribution of political power. Echoing Albert Peña's speech at the Alamo, Brown told the *Observer* that three factors combined to keep San Antonio a "low-wage town": the presence of large federal employers that prohibited collective bargaining (until the 1960s), the lack of heavy industry or large manufacturing concerns, and "the overabundance of cheap labor that normally is available—Latin-American, primarily."[47]

As a member of an exclusive craft union, Brown could have responded to these challenges by circling the wagons, protecting his all-white membership, and blaming the low-wage *mexicano* workers for the city's economic woes. Yet Brown took the opposite approach. "Everybody has a right to make a decent living," he told the *Observer*. "The solution to all of this is the organization of the Latin-American people, of this unskilled labor pool" of day laborers, janitors, maids, elevator operators, department and grocery store clerks—"all those dollar-an-hour-and-less jobs," Brown said. And "unless this job is done by the trade union movement," he added, "this town will always be a low-wage town."[48]

Brown's expansive understanding of the labor movement's challenges and future responses might initially appear marginal to his time and place, yet Brown kept getting elected to run his union's affairs. As other trades joined the strike, he became their spokesman too. He quite literally represented San Antonio's union craftsmen—an all-white, all-male constituency of so-called labor aristocrats. In the fall of 1959, they lined up behind Brown and hit the streets to demand a fair share of the "Eisenhower economy" while simultaneously marching in lockstep with low-wage, unskilled, nonwhite, and even female industrial workers. "It's a rough fight. A good fight," Brown concluded one month into the strike. "We'll win it, but it's gonna take a while."[49]

Eve of a New Coalition

In November 1959, members of the Texas AFL-CIO from across the state converged on San Antonio for their annual convention. Father Sherrill Smith, who had joined the Tex-Son march at the Alamo, offered the invocation.[50] As the dual strikes of the building trades and garment workers raged on, Albert Peña welcomed the delegates with a rousing speech that looked to both the past and future of the labor movement in San Antonio. "I am proud to be called a friend of Labor," he began. "I am proud to be a part in joining with you in a movement that is not only concerned with the welfare of the working man of Texas but the public welfare of Texas in general." Peña next drew a line in the sand, defining a vast and diverse House of Labor and then separating it from its enemies in the Chamber of Commerce. "I also think of organized labor in terms of a plumber who lives across the street whose daughter goes to school with my daughter; the carpenter who lives on the corner who is active in my church and civic affairs and who attends all precinct conventions and is dedicated to integrity and liberalism in the Democratic party," Peña said. "I also think of the hod carrier who lives around the block and is struggling to get his oldest boy through law school. I also think of that demure young lady who works for the telephone company who lives next door to me. These are the people who symbolize the labor movement here in Bexar County and in the State of Texas." The plumber and the carpenter, his audience knew, were white union craftsmen—the traditional face of organized labor. Peña recognized their efforts, at work and in electoral politics, but he also called attention to labor's new faces. "Hod carrier" meant unskilled and nonwhite, and the allusion to law school suggested that Peña's own *mexicano* neighbors and friends worry about the same things that Anglo workers did. The "young lady" from the phone company was also welcome in this new, revived, diverse labor movement, though she still remained "demure" or deferential to the union men. In short, Peña defined the "we"—that is, who labor should include, and what it should fight for. And he noted that all of them were united in attending precinct conventions and fighting for a liberal, honest Democratic Party—the exact goals of the DOT.[51]

On the other side of the fence Peña situated his favorite enemy, the Chamber of Commerce. He noted that the city's boosters celebrated its missions and tourist destinations, but they "cannot brag about the fact that San Antonio is a cheap labor town." One in three workers earned less than $1,000 annually, he said, far below the national average of more than $4,000 per year. This discrepancy was no accident, he added. Rather, "there is a combination of powerful forces organized to keep it that way." He turned to history and the current strikes to hammer home his point. "And this is the way it has been since the pecan shellers strike . . . this attitude has persisted for a long time— yes, my friends for too long. And this is the attitude that our trade unions and Garment Workers here on strike have to combat. And it is a hard fight. We need your help. . . . As a matter of fact, these forces are dedicated to bust the union movement here in San Antonio, don't you forget that!"

Peña closed with a call to action. He noted that poll tax sales were lagging, and that Texas labor should be able to mobilize at least 400,000 voters to join with other liberal groups "for a better Texas tomorrow." He asked delegates to visit the DOT booth in the lobby to "join our movement." He concluded by laying out a formula for moving forward: "This is your movement," he said. "This is the coalition of Organized Labor, the so-called minority groups, the farmer, the little business man, this is the natural coalition that Maury Maverick said in 1950 will 'some day elect a liberal governor of the State of Texas' and I really believe that. But we must work together with a mutual understanding of our many problems in this coalition."[52]

Indeed, Maury Maverick's old alliance of two decades earlier had been reborn, with many of the same pieces and even some of the same leaders. On the East Side, G. J. Sutton and the *SNAP* activists were on the march, while Peña's West and South Sides continued to organize. Both civil rights struggles put forth expansive visions of the future and were moving toward gaining independent political power. In the last few years of the 1950s, they found new organizational homes and allies in a suddenly vibrant, growing, and increasingly diverse labor movement led by individuals with similarly broad outlooks as well as the resources to launch unprecedentedly large new organizing initiatives. In fact, Hank Brown gave the next welcome address to the convention, echoing many of Peña's points, and showing the delegates from across the state what a multiracial liberal coalition could look like.[53]

"Giant Union Drive Planned for S.A.," blared the front-page headline of the daily *San Antonio Express* the day after their speeches. "Local union leaders aim to use the big state AFL-CIO convention as the springboard for 'rebirth' of a massive new organized labor movement in San Antonio," the story began, marking "the beginning of a new era" for labor.[54] Still, the paper missed Peña's larger point: that "labor" now meant a diverse movement committed to profound political and economic change.

After thirteen weeks, the contractors caved to Brown's demands and agreed to a wage hike, the establishment of an apprenticeship program, and a new pension fund. His own union's conditions met, Brown still kept the plumbers home until the builders' associations also settled with the remaining, less-powerful trades, including the unskilled, nonwhite and Common Laborers Hod Carriers union. The entire struggle lasted four months and eighteen days.[55] Solidarity across trades and a desire to organize the unorganized low-wage labor pool underlay its success. Asked about his philosophy in a 1971 oral history interview, Brown recalled, "I guess I have always been a blend of an industrial union guy with a childhood background of a steelworker—coal mining—who just accidentally got into the plumbing business and became a union craftsman."[56]

With his own house back in order, Brown returned his attention to electoral politics, a task that centered upon building relationships with the growing liberal factions in the city's Mexican American, African American, and white communities. To be sure, organizing efforts on Sutton's East Side and Peña's West Side had continued unabated during Brown's long absence from the Alamo City, and it was their work that opened the door to sweeping change. Still, it was the renewal of a small but militant labor movement that represented the final breakthrough. The union's victory at Friedrich Refrigerator in 1957 and the two strikes that began in 1959 together connected the residents and leaders of those predominately nonwhite neighborhoods with the unions of white, male, skilled craftsmen—for the first time in the city's history. Although the workers at Tex-Son lost their immediate battle on the employment front, the ways in which Lambert and Brown rallied the labor movement around them created new relationships of trust, solidarity, and mutual need among activists of all colors on the ground. For Brown, it drove home the need to deepen his ties to Peña and the growing black and brown freedom struggles. For Peña, the loss at Tex-Son represented a setback for his constituents, but it also signaled an opportunity. Tightening bonds with labor leaders and white rank-and-file members meant that Peña, Sutton, and other veteran civil rights activists could now extend and advance their partnership in the electoral arena and in the larger black and brown liberation struggles. They would reach more voters than ever before and even attract white workers like the IUE's Javior to their causes.

The union had been busted, but the nascent multiracial alliance snatched a victory from the jaws of defeat. Brown, Peña, and the Lamberts forged an alliance in the streets and on the picket line. Sutton was not far behind. By the end of the decade, they had developed a working model for multiracial cooperation that would soon become the blueprint for the statewide coalition—a formidable alliance that no journalist or elected official could overlook.

Chapter 6

We Shall Be Heard

Civil Rights in Black and Brown from the Sit-ins to Viva Kennedy

On Friday night, June 2, 1961, members of the Progressive Youth Association (PYA) held a fund-raiser at the headquarters of the all-black Longshoremen's Local 872 beside the Houston Ship Channel. For the previous fifteen months, the PYA had staged sit-ins to desegregate local department store lunch counters, movie theaters, interstate bus stations, and even city and county government buildings. Many facilities had opened their doors to black customers as a result, but real integration and equality remained a long way off. The PYA planned to present a commemorative plaque to local union president Raymond Duncan and to thank the union men for supporting their direct action movement, hoping that doing so would spark a new round of contributions from rank-and-file workers. The youth leaders rented a pickup truck and began playing music in front of the International Longshoremen's Association building at Seventy-Fifth and Memphis Streets, right next to the docks. Suddenly, Houston police officers burst onto the scene and shut down the party, claiming that the organizers had not pulled a permit for the PA system. The officers brandished tear-gas guns and hurled "abusive language toward" the eight hundred longshoremen who milled about, watching the action. A handful of workers ran to their cars to retrieve their shotguns while union officials pleaded for calm. The "badly outnumbered" police briefly detained the union's chaplain, then arrested four PYA members and four union men and fled. As one PYA leader put it, "They hauled ass—fast!" Duncan moved the party inside and turned on the jukebox, the union members got out their wallets, and "it rained money."[1]

A few days later, on June 7, "more than 500 Negro longshoremen and their wives marched in an angry mass" to City Hall, along with hundreds more PYA members and supporters, students and adults alike. Inside, according to newspaper reports, "the group crowded the corridors of City Hall and overflowed the City Council chamber." Union president Duncan addressed the council and said that the union-PYA meeting had been peaceful until the police "busted in and tried to incite trouble," nearly causing a riot. Mayor Lewis Cutrer tried to cut off his testimony, but Councilman Louie Welch continued to question the longshoremen's leader. Duncan pulled no punches as he linked the raid on the party to a pattern in which police routinely abused black workers, including shaking them down on paydays.²

The union's show of force as well as Duncan's stinging testimony convinced city authorities to drop the charges against the eight people who had been arrested. The march on City Hall represented the largest single demonstration in the PYA's existence, as union members swelled its ranks and dwarfed the size of the usual student-led protests. It demonstrated in stark terms the power that organized black workers could wield in the larger civil rights movement. And it underscored just how much had already changed. Throughout the 1950s, the Harris County Council of Organizations (HCCO) and other black organizations had struggled to make their voices heard. Although local electoral and civil rights coalitions were beginning to flourish, and labor was again on the march, white supremacy continued to dominate the state, from the capitol to the county courthouses and city halls and throughout the Democratic Party.

Now, the sit-ins were changing all that, forcing city councilmen to sit and listen as African Americans aired their complaints and compelling even the most intransigent elected officials to respect their rights. In the spring of 1960, black college students began occupying segregated downtown lunch counters and other public accommodations across the state, demanding service as equals. The sit-ins heralded a critical tactical innovation that would attract a new set of youthful activists to the long civil rights movement, even as the fresh troops would continue to depend on the support and experience of older veterans of earlier struggles.³ It proved to be a reciprocal exchange: the courage and tenacity of the students spurred the wizened, longtime labor, civil rights, and political activists of previous decades to join the youth in the streets. The presence of the elders, in turn, helped to transform the sit-ins into a broader movement that addressed not only integration but also many of the decades-old, expansive goals of civil rights unionists like Moses LeRoy and black community organizers like G. J. Sutton. In less than three years after the first sit-ins, the revived African American civil rights movement would succeed in desegregating public accommodations in urban areas throughout Texas and the South, scoring a major victory on the road to their larger goals of equal treatment, improved economic opportunities, and real political power.

At the same time, many of these activists would continue to organize in the electoral arena. Direct action demonstrations would fuel the flames of the multiracial political alliances, especially in San Antonio. Mexican American students would join the sit-in movement there, and momentum in the streets would open up new opportunities at the ballot box and in the all-important Democratic Party conventions. Together, the black-brown alliance would reach new heights of power in the party, mobilize a statewide Mexican American vote with unprecedented punch, and provide the margin of victory in the

1960 presidential election. That triumph, in turn, would slowly give rise to a new political logic and ultimately a statewide liberal coalition.

Moses LeRoy and the Houston Movement

On February 1, 1960, four students at North Carolina A&T College staged sit-ins at a Woolworth's lunch counter in Greensboro, triggering a wave of copycat demonstrations across the South. Scarcely organized or coordinated, these protests reached Houston on March 4, when Eldrewey Stearns, a twenty-six-year-old law student at the newly renamed Texas Southern University (TSU) in Houston's Third Ward, led a group of black students in staging the city's first sit-in demonstrations at a Weingarten's grocery near campus. The protests soon spread to numerous lunch counters throughout the neighborhood and finally downtown.

The students' tactics were new, but the civil rights movement was not. Veteran civil rights unionists like Moses and Erma LeRoy and the black union leaders along the waterfront swung into action and provided critical aid to the student-led demonstrations. In so doing, they helped the younger activists connect the fight for equal access to the expansive freedom agenda of the past. In fact, the older activists' longtime struggles against employment discrimination and for independent political power soon became key demands of the student movement, linking this new phase of the movement to the longer, broader, multiracial quest for democracy.

A native of Galveston, Stearns had "been disrespectful of racial bars most of his life," according to Saul Friedman of the *Houston Chronicle*. "When he was in the service in Oklahoma he applied, without publicity, to become a student at a white college in Lawton, where he was accepted." Once there, he refused to go to the back of the bus and went wherever he wanted in the segregated Sooner state, always carrying a copy of the Constitution in his back pocket. Stearns told Friedman, "I was what some white folks in the South call a 'smart nigger'. . . . And I paid for it plenty." He left the region and went to Michigan State University in order to "get an American education and not just [a] Southern education." He returned to Houston after graduation and worked as a janitor and waiter while beginning his graduate studies at TSU. In August 1959, Stearns "blew up" when a police officer called him "boy," and his reaction landed in him in jail, where two officers beat him. Stearns registered his complaint with the HCCO, which in turn used his case to renew its demand that the city investigate systemic police brutality against African Americans.[4]

When TSU students launched their own sit-ins, Stearns emerged as the group's leader. Their protests followed the national pattern: the operators of the stores shut down the lunch counters, allowed the black students to sit without providing them service, and finally ushered them out at the end of the day. The protests gradually swelled, as did white resistance. Three days after the first protest, on March 7, two masked white men kidnapped and brutally beat a young black man who was unaffiliated with the movement, carving the letters "KKK" into his abdomen before leaving him hanging by his feet from a tree. The Houston police increased their presence at the demonstrations and managed to prevent future violence while also refraining from arresting the protestors. The mayor appointed a biracial committee and charged it with coming up with a plan for facilitating voluntary integration by the targeted merchants. The students agreed to halt their demonstrations while the negotiations took place, but after dragging its feet for months, the committee dissolved without taking action. Undaunted, the retailers continued to refuse service to blacks.[5]

Stearns attended the early April 1960 founding meeting of the Student Nonviolent Coordinating Committee (SNCC) in Raleigh, North Carolina, and returned to Houston reenergized. On April 25, 1960, he led a small group of largely demoralized students in renewing the protests. They requested service at the Greyhound bus station café, and, to their great surprise, they were served without incident. This unexpected victory reinvigorated the movement, which was reorganized that night into a formal group called the Progressive Youth Association (PYA). In early May, Stearns and the PYA extended their targets downtown and launched a boycott and mass picketing of the intransigent retailers. The public relations director of the Foley's department store chain responded to the pickets by organizing a complete media boycott of the demonstrations. TSU administrators, black businessmen, and even the black weekly papers all collaborated with the white elites in an attempt to discourage the student protestors. Meanwhile, the white businessmen agreed behind closed doors to participate in a coordinated, gradual desegregation plan, which they quietly implemented by September. The PYA ended up achieving the integration of the city's lunch counters and large retail establishments, even as a coordinated media blackout sapped the group's momentum.[6]

While local businessmen and the mayor and police chief congratulated themselves for their enlightened leadership and their avoidance of the unrest that ravaged other southern cities, black civil rights activists remained far from content. Both the PYA members and longtime activists in the HCCO and local NAACP knew that Jim Crow continued to dominate the lives of African Americans in Houston. Employment discrimination remained nearly ubiquitous, and public buildings were still sharply segregated, as were countless cafés and other public accommodations. Whites retained disproportionate political power and virtually every elected office, and many of the city's black and brown residents lived in slums and struggled to get by.

Prompted by the December 1960 U.S. Supreme Court ruling that prohibited segregation in waiting rooms and restaurants involved in interstate travel, Stearns and the PYA came up with a new strategy. Long before the first freedom riders set out to "test" the court-mandated integration of interstate bus service in the South, PYA members in Houston began sitting in at the city's Union Station train terminal. After several months of ignoring the protestors and closing down intermittently, the station café operator grew exasperated and called the police in late February 1961. The subsequent arrest of fourteen PYA demonstrators energized both the students and the city's older, longtime civil rights activists. In the next four months, PYA protestors added new targets to their list, staging sit-ins at a Loew's and other movie theaters, the City Hall and county courthouse cafeterias, and other locales. Police responded with mass arrests that netted nearly two hundred charges.[7]

The demonstrations of 1960 and 1961 brought the PYA an outpouring of support from older activists who were veterans of the civil rights and labor movements as far back as the 1920s. As the protests intensified, Moses LeRoy emerged as the key diplomat who built support for student activists among the community's diverse elder leadership. Both Moses and Erma LeRoy served on the PYA's Advisory Board, with Moses's name appearing near the top of the youth group's letterhead. Both also remained activists in the local NAACP, which was slowly rebuilding from its near destruction by the State of Texas Attorney General's Office. (Mrs. Leroy became president of the reorganized branch by 1965.)

Moses continued to serve as the parliamentarian of the HCCO, a position that made him an officer and gave him a voice in the council's exclusive executive committee. In March 1960, with LeRoy as an officer and key activist, the HCCO met and endorsed the first student sit-ins, pledging "its full 'support and efforts'" to the protests. In May, the council's president denounced the mayor's biracial committee, on which he served, when it failed to take "immediate action on open lunch counters." The council also cosponsored a local referendum on school desegregation.[8] A year later, in May 1961, the HCCO demanded yet another investigation of police practices, this time to probe the arrest of the Loew's theater demonstrators. Moses LeRoy—now almost sixty-three—personally took to the streets alongside the students. Many photographs of the youth-led demonstrations of that era feature a lone older figure marching and singing in their ranks, a gray man frequently unidentified but who is almost always the aging civil rights unionist.[9]

LeRoy also helped lead the effort to raise money from black businesses, unions, and elites to pay for the students' bail and other legal expenses. He did so primarily among other members of the HCCO, aided by his friend and ally

Quentin Mease, the head of the city's all-black South Central YMCA. Mease was accustomed to securing donations for the Y from black businessmen and clergy, so immediately after the arrests at Union Station, he activated these networks and won a resolution of support from the city's association of black doctors. He also brought in a series of large contributions from African American professionals.[10] In 1962, Mease and LeRoy helped the HCCO raise $8,000 to free the student protestors who were jailed again after failing to pay their fines for the Union Station sit-ins the previous year.[11]

LeRoy was just one of several black unionists who added fuel to the student-led fire. Howard Middleton Jr., an officer of Hod Carriers and Common Laborers Local 18, worked in construction in the daytime and attended classes at TSU in the evenings. Like LeRoy, Middleton was a member of the PYA's Advisory Board, and he probably served as an officer of the PYA as a student. Middleton helped coordinate the direct action campaign and personally participated in lunch counter sit-ins and marches downtown. He later recalled that a white man with a "country" appearance entered a restaurant in which he sat-in, threatening the demonstrators with a loaded gun before leaving the scene without incident. Middleton walked side by side with other students, but as a slightly older workingman, he also brought his young daughter with him to the demonstrations. He was surprised to discover that his daughter's presence helped him avoid being arrested, so he remained on the streets while the other students went to jail. Left outside, Middleton and his brother Jimmy, the president of Local 18 and also a PYA Advisory Board member, appealed to the union's nearly five thousand members to raise money for the civil rights cause, passing the hat at union meetings and on the job and funneling the cash to the students and their lawyers.[12]

Stearns and the PYA received substantial financial assistance from black rank-and-file members, collecting small and large contributions at countless meetings of the all-black Railroad, Longshoremen, and Hod Carriers locals. Most of them proceeded without incident, unlike the June 1961 gathering at the Local 872 hall that nearly turned into a police riot. Still, even that incident cemented the bonds between the youthful PYA members and ordinary black workers, and it led to the largest demonstration of Houston's sit-in movement.

For its part, the student-led PYA also contributed to the broader economic justice struggles of civil rights unionists. In January 1961, for example, they conducted sit-ins at City Hall that opened the cafeteria to the city's few black police officers.[13] More generally, their demands almost always included requests that retailers hire or promote black workers, and the PYA's own accounts of the group's accomplishments often centered on jobs. A June 1961 letter from a PYA member to the *Houston Chronicle* listed its "achievements." Just below the phrase "Lunch Counters" (presumably to note their integration) is an accounting of the number of black employees hired by nine different local retailers. Ralston Drug led the way by adding sixteen black cashiers, while Weingarten's hired fourteen more. Weiner's was listed as hiring four new black "salesladies," and U-Tote-Em hired four black "managers." PYA also boasted the integration of Jeppesen Stadium, two parks, and the local bus stations—all listed simply as "Open." Yet the desegregation of these public sites occupied a subordinate position when compared to the detailed reporting on which retailers hired how many black workers and in what capacities.[14] By October 1961, Stearns boasted that eighty-six lunch counters and public places had been desegregated since the launch of the student protest movement. In an interview with Stearns, the *Houston Chronicle* reported that "Negroes have gotten better, higher paying jobs in many places. 'More than $1 million has been added to the paychecks of Negroes who have gotten better jobs,' Stearns said."[15]

Like the PYA and the black unionists who supported it, the HCCO and NAACP continued to agitate for economic justice throughout the early 1960s. The leadership of the HCCO and NAACP overlapped, with both including Moses LeRoy. In February 1961, as the PYA launched its sit-ins at Union Station and local bus companies, the HCCO launched its own battle for public ownership of the city bus system. Longtime activist and barber George T. Nelson collected over four thousand signatures that eventually forced the city to renegotiate its contract with a private operator, keeping fares low while improving service for black workers.[16]

The organization also advocated for black working people in debates about municipal financing, employment, and governance. In January 1962, a spokesman for the HCCO, which the city's leading newspaper called "the city's most powerful Negro organization," threatened to oppose a $40.5 million bond issue "unless the city requires contractors to open hiring to all races." The HCCO representative noted that black workers faced widespread discrimination "on all work involving artisans or craftsmen." If the federal government required fair employment practices among its suppliers, he added, the city should adopt a similar ordinance "requiring contracts on city jobs to have nondiscriminatory clauses." Mayor Lewis Cutrer quickly came out in opposition to a fair employment ordinance, charging that it infringed upon the free market, employers, and craft unions. At the next city council meeting, just three days prior to the bond referendum, another attorney and HCCO member named Francis Williams pressed Cutrer on the issue, and the mayor claimed that the issue had been referred to the public works and legal departments for consideration. Williams replied that the HCCO would not wait, and it withheld its endorsement on the bond issue.[17] Eleven months later (December 1962), in response to a similar proposal, the HCCO announced that it would join the local AFL-CIO and sixteen other organizations in supporting a $9.6 million bond issue to build a new domed stadium that would become the landmark Houston Astrodome. The HCCO's president explained that stadium construction "will provide employment for all people," including jobs for African Americans. Apparently the council's flexing of its muscles had produced some promises of change on the job front, even though a city ordinance remained elusive.[18]

When the NAACP recommitted itself to the struggle for equal employment opportunities around the same time, Moses LeRoy was again at the forefront. In September 1962, the association's general counsel Robert Carter and labor secretary Herbert Hill visited Houston to launch a national initiative against "racial discrimination in industrial employment," with the Bayou City as its "starting place." They hoped to develop a "body of law" to use in court, collecting on-the-ground data as they had during the build up to *Brown v. Board*. Hill told the newspaper that both unions and industry would be targets, since both were "preventing Negroes from developing the skills that are required by automation and other industrial advancements," producing a "labor crisis" for African Americans. "So, we are giving priority to such problems as the elimination of racial lines in the determination of job seniority," Hill added. At the local level, the report added, "Negro labor leaders agree that job discrimination in local industry and in unions is a serious problem. Moses Leroy [sic], . . . active in the affairs of the Brotherhood of Railway Clerks and delegate to the recent state A.F.L.-C.I.O. convention in San Antonio, commented, 'Our experience certainly bears out the analysis of conditions in labor made by the N.A.A.C.P.'" A month later, the *Houston Chronicle* reported that the association was making good on its word, representing "an all-Negro union local" in a hearing on a racial discrimination charge. A trial examiner for the National Labor Relations Board was set to hear the complaint of Ivory M. Davis, a worker at the Hughes Tool Company and member of a segregated company union. Davis charged that the all-white company union refused to process his grievance because he was black and not a member of the white local.[19]

Throughout the early 1960s, then, black students, unionists, and professionals collaborated in the struggle to desegregate public accommodations and improve access to better employment opportunities. These two seemingly divergent goals actually dovetailed, with much overlap in personnel, tactics, and philosophy. Moses LeRoy remained a common thread weaving together these diverse groups of African American activists. From his vantage point, the student-led protest movement represented just the latest phase of a much longer freedom struggle. It was the culmination of decades of street-level community organizing in the Fifth and Third Wards, networking and organizing with other black unionists, and careful negotiation with black elites. If the Cold War had all but destroyed the NAACP, and the HCCO had largely replaced it as the new coordinating body of Houston's black political life, the PYA provided the shot in the arm that reenergized and renewed the long civil rights movement. Civil rights unionists like the LeRoys and the workers along the waterfront injected all three organizations with a broad vision of economic justice and helped connect this expansive agenda to a new generation of activists.

Diverse groups of African Americans in Houston came together, albeit briefly, in a broad-based struggle for both freedom and jobs. For a moment, from the first demonstration until late 1961, the protests in the streets activated intergenerational and cross-class networks that tied the civil rights unionism of the 1930s and the political activism of the 1950s to the newest struggles for spatial integration. The energy of the sit-ins would also underpin the movement's next phases, as both veteran and newly inspired activists continued to work for equal economic opportunity and independent political power.

In the short term, the sit-ins provided leverage for black elites to broker deals with their white counterparts, resulting, against all odds, in the desegregation of public accommodations. Yet such negotiations would never have taken place had it not been for the pressure applied by Stearns, the PYA, and veteran activists like Moses LeRoy. Moreover, the backroom dealings helped the city save face, but they did not produce substantial material improvements nor lead to autonomy in the electoral sphere.

Stearns himself would ultimately chafe at the desire of elites to direct the struggle out of the streets and into the boardroom. The PYA's goals were always "bigger than a hamburger," to use legendary organizer Ella Baker's phrase for the movement's broader objectives. By the fall of 1961, Houston's black elites seized control of the movement by wielding the power of the pocketbook. Major donors decided that their financial contributions to the struggle should result in control, and a group of students who also shied away from further protests collaborated with them and took over the PYA. All future direct actions (and financial transactions) would be approved by the Houston Sit-in Foundation. Stearns soon suffered the first of many mental breakdowns and temporarily disappeared from the scene, returning just long enough to complete the fight for integrated public accommodations in the spring of 1963. Once again, his threats of renewed demonstrations would open space for the elites to broker the final changes.[20]

Desegregation had been accomplished, but justice and power both remained distant goals. Some of the students, aided by unionists like the LeRoys and Middletons, would find new paths to carry the struggle forward, pairing their direct action protests with sophisticated political organizing in the years ahead.

The Multiracial Movement in San Antonio

Like the struggle in Houston, the direct action movement in San Antonio represented a continuation of previous activism rather than a sharp departure from it. In fact, longtime adult activists in the local NAACP staged the first sit-in protests, with area college students and youth joining the protests once they were underway. The sit-ins extended the longer freedom struggle by introducing new tactics and increasing its visibility, but the goals, players, and pitfalls remained largely the same. Community organizers like G. J. Sutton, Rev. Claude Black, and publisher Eugene Coleman all participated in and mentored the new crop of younger activists, sharing their battle-honed vision for a movement that included economic justice and real political power in addition to civil rights. And when the direct action phase of the struggle encountered roadblocks and began to sputter, the veterans helped the youth redirect their energies into new, more rewarding arenas—particularly electoral politics.

San Antonio's movement was also unique in that it had a multiracial component. From its inception, the black student activists mobilized by the NAACP paired up with Mexican American and white students from other area colleges. At St. Mary's University on the West Side, Mexican Americans led the Students for Civil Liberties (SCL), an interracial group that spearheaded many of the city's direct action demonstrations. While the group's goals focused squarely upon ending formal segregation against African Americans, its diverse membership also helped it connect to the growing Mexican American civil rights struggle.

The idea of launching a direct action campaign against segregation in San Antonio restaurants actually predated both the formation of the SCL and the famous sit-ins in Greensboro, North Carolina. In December 1959, the local branch of the NAACP announced plans for a campaign, and on January 17, 1960, the association "launched a program against discrimination in downtown eating facilities." Writing a guest column in *SNAP News* in late 1960, branch president Joseph Luter noted that the program included "plans for an extensive membership drive and a drive against discrimination in Employment Practices." As student sit-ins shook Houston and other cities across Texas and the South in early March, a youth leader of the local NAACP sent a letter to San Antonio's downtown retailers demanding integration. When the business owners failed to respond, Rev. Black and NAACP state youth director Harry Burns, also of San Antonio, organized a mass meeting of 1,500 local African Americans. The activists signed up at least five hundred attendees who pledged to stage sit-ins if the merchants did not meet their demand. Faced with this very real threat, the retailers capitulated, and six chains opened their lunch counters to black patrons on March 16, 1960.[21]

As in Houston, city officials and black and white business leaders celebrated their enlightened response to the threatened protests, yet the conflict was only beginning. The city's leading downtown department store, Joske's, continued to treat African Americans as second-class customers, restricting them to shopping and eating in the store's basement and steadfastly refusing them service at its elite, second-floor Camellia Room restaurant. On April 23, 1960, the NAACP launched sit-in demonstrations inside the store. In response, Joske's temporarily closed the lunch counters, then erected rope barriers manned by store security guards to keep black patrons away from the store's restaurants. The association picketed on the street outside, its protestors entreating would-be customers to boycott the business and at times physically blocking their paths into the store. The city sent hundreds of police officers to push the pickets away from Joske's front entrance. Rev. Black, as an officer in the local NAACP branch and the head of the city's black Baptist Ministers Union, helped lead the demonstrations. He later recalled that "one of the officers walked up to one of the preachers that was blocking the restaurant entrance and slapped him. The preacher just looked at him and walked off." A few moments later, it got personal. Black remembered, "The same officer started to threaten and curse me out. He said, 'You better shut up or I'm going to take you down nigger!' The officer did not mean to the police station. He meant that he would beat me. So I just turned around and continued to march with the others."[22]

Joske's management closed the restaurant following the incident, but the pickets and boycott continued. The *Texas Observer* reported in early May that "groups of students from San Antonio College, St. Phillips Junior College, Trinity University, and Our Lady of the Lake" joined Black, the ministers, Sutton, and the other NAACP activists, adding that "they would continue appearing indefinitely at the store's two eating places." The brothers of the white Rho Beta Gamma fraternity at St. Mary's added to the pressure, presenting a petition to Joske's management and demanding a meeting. "Meanwhile, store employees acknowledged that business was suffering," the *Observer* reported. "An NAACP spokesman said 20,000 'I Have Quit Joske's' tags have been printed and more ordered." The standoff continued until late summer, when the store finally caved and integrated all of its restaurants.[23]

The NAACP had also demanded that Joske's hire African Americans as cashiers and representatives on the department store's main sales floor. The tail end of the integration fight downtown coincided with the beginning of a broader fight for fair employment practices. In July 1960, the Labor & Industry Committee of the branch asked its youth advisor, Miss Beverly Johnson, to organize a group to spearhead the effort. Johnson organized a new Youth Council that then elected as its president William "Bill" Donahue, a student at the all-black St. Philip's College. The group conducted a survey of white-

Rev. Claude W. Black Jr. (fourth from left) and other African American community leaders confer with police officers after praying and picketing outside a Handy Andy grocery store in San Antonio, August 8, 1960. The store was one of many targets of local civil rights activists, who demanded not only the integration of public accommodations but also equal employment opportunities. Courtesy *San Antonio Express* Photograph Collection, UTSA-ITC, Image E-0006-102, San Antonio Express/ZUMAPRESS.com.

owned businesses in the East Side in early August, and they found that most stores employed African American "checkers." One chain of grocery stores, Handy Andy, conspicuously did not. The chain's several East Side locations had few or no black employees and no black workers in higher-level or managerial positions. After the youth subcommittee had "many conferences" with Handy Andy management that were unsuccessful, the full NAACP board sent a letter to the company demanding action and then followed up by picketing the chain's East Side stores.

Led by Johnson and Donahue, the association's youth wing took the lead in the picketing, a fact that irked some NAACP members. Yet, as Luter explained, it was the young members' future at stake, and adults should support their goals. "Youth know they must meet the challenge," Luter wrote in *SNAP*. They were adapting to the fast pace of technological and social change in the late twentieth century, he continued. "They know that they will have to compete, and they want an equal chance at every phase. We must help them and give them an opportunity to destroy those impediments that will hinder them. To hold them down would retard them and make them unfit to meet the challenges of such a fast, progressive, existence as we are experiencing." The end of summer and the return of the school year required that adults now step up and take the youth's position picketing the several Handy Andy stores. "We will need people to carry pickets," Luter wrote, urging readers to contact Miss Johnson "and schedule the time you can give in this effort. We can use the services of every able-bodied person in San Antonio in this program. Remember this is your fight! Our youth by their own will and initiative want jobs when they finish school."[24]

Many older activists responded to Luter's call and showed up for picket duty. Sutton served as a spokesman for the protestors. Rev. Black recalled that the branch used the same tactics that they had tested at Joske's—standing in doorways, turning back customers and urging them to boycott, and refusing to back down amid threats of violence. Charles Hudspeth, a longtime leader of the branch who was close to Black, had a gun pulled on him by a white man. "The man began pointing his gun and yelling obscenities at Hudspeth," Black remembered. "Without flinching, Hudspeth calmly turned around and kept on picketing. That was a scary moment for us all. We just knew that he would be shot." Black adds that he and other NAACP activists forever teased Hudspeth about the incident, joking that he "came this close to being a hero!"[25]

The standoff continued. In mid-December, the Labor & Employment Committee commended "the citizens of San Antonio for your cooperation of selective buying" and noted that picketing would continue at one location "during most evenings after 5:00 P.M." The committee again asked supporters "to withhold patronage from all Handy Andy stores, pending a favorable reply to our request for the hiring of cashier-checkers, and other levels of better positions."[26] At some point the following spring or summer, the NAACP and Handy Andy reached a settlement. In July 1961, Bill Donahue reported that the chain had not yet integrated "in true proportion," but the protests did result in blacks "being employed in equal status in stores all over the eastern section of the city and part of the west side." A month later, he added that the "placard carrying protest" had been discontinued after the protestors achieved their "desired end," but he also reminded *SNAP* readers that the selective buying campaign would soon resume if necessary. The struggle continued, but NAACP leaders could at least take credit for the hiring of some African American checkers at Handy Andy.[27]

The activities of Donahue's NAACP Youth Council began to overlap with those of the SCL, which was based at St. Mary's University on the West Side. On Lincoln Day, February 12, 1961—while the boycott of Handy Andy was still underway—students from all six of the local colleges staged a stand-in at the Majestic Theater. Led by Leonel J. Castillo and Perfecto Villareal, two *mexi-*

cano students at St. Mary's, SCL members approached the box office window in integrated pairs. One black youth joined either a white or a "brown," as each of twenty-five duos attempted to purchase tickets. As each set of partners was rebuffed, they returned to the end of the line and continued cycling through, thereby preventing the theater from making sales to other customers for three hours. Similar actions took place simultaneously in Austin, Dallas, Houston, and elsewhere, most likely coordinated through the NAACP or student government associations.[28]

In San Antonio, SCL members would repeat the stand-ins five times over the next five months. Their addition to the desegregation campaign brought much-needed support and legitimacy to the cause. Castillo, who chaired the group, also served as the president of the student government at St. Mary's as well as assistant editor of the *Rattler*, the campus newspaper. As such, he could explain the protestors' tactics to new audiences and urge more students to participate. In one *Rattler* article, Castillo detailed the preparations for and execution of the stand-ins. The process began at campus SCL meetings, which were "marked by an intenseness that is seldom found in college groups. Discussions are quiet and marked by a sense of urgency. . . . The participants are not, by any means, the ordinary apathetic type." Three student council presidents from area universities had attended the gatherings, he wrote, as had many campus leaders from across San Antonio. All conversations centered on the next action, and there was "little doubt in anyone's mind that this is the only way left to influence the policymakers of the theaters." The group's officers set the dates and times for each protest, secured legal advice, and led a training session prior to the demonstrations in which new recruits would learn the rules of nonviolent civil disobedience. They instructed the students to prepare for incidents, to direct questions to their elected leaders, and to take frequent but short breaks to maintain their stamina. On the big day, "the standers-in are greeted at the theater by television cameras, theater managers, policemen and curious onlookers," Castillo noted. "Some passers-by voice their approval; very few voice their disapproval. A larger number simply stare at the line." The mostly white and *mexicano* group attracted attention but no violence or arrests, as had their black counterparts at Joske's and in Houston. The police kept the sidewalk clear for them, and management remained cordial. A few spectators even joined in.[29]

The stand-ins did not immediately result in the desegregation of the Majestic Theater, but they did bring black and brown youth together in an unprecedented fashion. Sutton, Peña, and other activists had all experimented in black-brown alliances as well as partnerships with white liberals, but the uniting of the NAACP Youth Council and the SCL represented the first joint effort and the first protracted contact among student activists of the different racial groups. In fact, the membership of the groups ended up blending, leading to Donahue and the SCL's Villareal coauthoring a piece in *SNAP* that described the unique campaign. The duo characterized the group simply as "a multi-ethnic group whose members are dedicated to the fight for full and just acceptance of Negroes in San Antonio and elsewhere." The increasingly mixed-race group proved so effective and militant that Donahue eventually resigned his post in the NAACP Youth Council so he could focus his energies on the more diverse SCL.[30]

The multiracial demonstrations also offer some insight into the larger meanings of civil rights and direct action demonstrations among young Mexican Americans of the period. "What is a stand-in?" Castillo asked in a *Rattler* editorial. "It is the direct application of ethical principles to a specific situation. Its aim is the acceleration of the desegregation process. Its means are peaceful and just." He blasted students who remained indifferent, especially those that believed that "the Negro is satisfied and happy." But those who believed in integration needed to take action and "temper all movements with as much charity as possible." Citing Gandhi, Castillo added that "bigotry in reverse" should not occur and that "great care must be taken that the segregationists are not hated. Only the injustice itself deserves the righteous wrath of the just." The campaign must be "based in trust" so the "good sense and better qualities of the segregationists be [made] more apparent." Castillo's philosophical embrace of Gandhian nonviolence may not have been universally accepted among all *mexicano* youth in the city or state in that era, but it was popular enough that he was elected to positions of authority at what was still then a predominately Anglo campus. The available evidence suggests that many Mexican American students supported his efforts, as did Albert Peña and other *mexicano* adult activists. For Castillo, it was a simple question of human rights, along with the ethical imperative of empathy. "Let us imagine ourselves in the position of the Negro college student," he wrote. "How long could you take it?"[31]

Whatever their motivations, the student activists in SCL continued their campaign into the summer. Castillo graduated with honors and left town to join the first class of Peace Corps volunteers, but SCL nonetheless escalated the protests at the Majestic Theater under the leadership of Villareal. They staged stand-ins "Sunday after Sunday" at the Majestic and declared August 23–31 as "Theatre Integration Week" in San Antonio. "The group 'hit' theatres that they had not filed a complaint with in the past," Donahue reported in *SNAP*, and it conducted a survey of one thousand theater customers. SCL found that 89 percent of regular patrons said that they would continue attending if integrated, while only 2 percent said no. The study "disproved the old 'common consent' theory," according to Donahue, leaving only bigotry to explain the Majestic's intransigence.[32]

After another entire school year of activity, the campaign finally paid off by the summer of 1962. SCL had continued protesting while also engaging in "intense negotiations" behind the scenes. Donahue reported that youth activists traveled to Dallas and Austin "to confer with company officials" and met with "top level executives of the Interstate Theatre chain," which owned the Majestic, when these executives came to San Antonio "to settle the persevering demands for complete integration." The group also conducted outreach with consumers as "other SCL members went to the people and told the story." Finally, "after fifteen packed months of active negotiation and public relations," the theater desegregated its operations. Working with local leaders, the San Antonio Interracial Committee, and the Catholic Interracial Councils, SCL chairman Villareal also secured a commitment from "other local businesses [to] consider such a policy" of nondiscrimination. Donahue optimistically concluded, "racial equality in San Antonio . . . is a going reality that is achieving larger proportions everyday. . . . Racial discrimination . . . will become a thing of the past."[33]

Although the Majestic Theater integrated its seating, true "racial equality" would prove much more difficult. As Donahue knew, the protests at Joske's, Handy Andy, the Majestic, and other stores merely opened the door for progress. Employment opportunities remained restricted, while the East Side's infrastructure and housing were still substandard. Just as they had in the 1950s, Sutton, Black, and now Donahue continued to organize for fair employment, neighborhood improvements, and independent political power.

The concern with employment affected nearly everyone and ran particularly deep in the East Side's associational and political life. The local, state, and regional units of the NAACP remained committed to the fight for equal employment, and not only in conjunction with the sit-ins. In 1962, the San Antonio NAACP adopted job opportunities as an area of "major emphasis." Late that year, the local unit hosted the meeting of the Texas State Conference of Branches, including a workshop on employment issues moderated by Harry Burns, of the branch, and labor leader Hank Brown.[34] The local NAACP launched a campaign at Southwestern Bell called "Operation Telephone Company," which would be "the beginning of a concentrated move toward integration of employment in local municipal utilities," according to a report in *SNAP News*. Burns reported that he had sent letters asking businesses to pledge to "hire regardless of race, color, or creed, when there is an opening." When the telephone company agreed to do so, the branch organized a group of "highly qualified" applicants to go to its employment office and seek work. The applicants, all black women, "ranged from teachers through stenographers," and some were "over-qualified" like one who was multilingual and had worked as an operator in New York. The applicants were interviewed and reported being "graciously treated." Burns considered it a "favorable first step," though no one was immediately hired.[35]

The link between the direct action protests and the fight for employment rights came full circle in the summer of 1962, when the East Side activists received news that reignited the fight against Joske's. Teamsters Local 968 in Houston sent notice that the company had fired a black truck driver there named Arthur Parker for organizing his fellow drivers to join the union. Teamsters staffer Ray Schafer added that it was "invariably" the "Negro or Latin American" who got fired under such conditions, and that "The Houston truck drivers are on strike to help Parker get his job back." *SNAP* added a threat and call for support to the bulletin: "Joske's should remember that it was only a short time ago that they ran into a picket battle with NAACP for refusing to serve Negroes at their lunch counters. We feel sure Joske's does not want this repeated. Please give the union your full support in helping Parker regain his job."[36]

On June 15, *SNAP* ran a front-page feature on the situation, adding more details and featuring a photo of one of the Houston strikers. Parker "personally signed up most of his fellow employees for the Union," which won an NLRB-supervised election 18 to 7. Joske's then laid him off, claiming that there was a lack of work. It also refused to negotiate with the union. The NLRB held a hearing and determined that Parker was in fact dismissed for union activities, and it ordered Joske's to reinstate him. The company then attempted to buy him out, but he refused, fearing that other companies would also blacklist him for being a union activist. When Joske's listed a vacancy in the trucking department but transferred someone else instead of rehiring the laid-off Parker, his "fellow employees voted unanimously to strike for the purpose of getting Parker's job back." The union began picketing Joske's Houston warehouse, two Houston stores, the site of the protests in downtown San Antonio, and another store in suburban San Antonio. The Teamsters business agent reported that customers were respecting the picket line and refusing to shop at Joske's four department stores in the two cities.[37]

Two weeks later, *SNAP* reported that the union had won. "Please Trade at Joske's," blared a large headline on the conflict. Teamsters' Local 968 "says thanks" to "the many individuals who helped the strike at Joske's of Texas in San Antonio. Joske's agreed to reinstate the employee, and to sit down and negotiate . . . for a contract." Union head Schafer stated that he felt "that *SNAP News* was very instrumental to bringing about a successful conclusion to this strike."[38] Meanwhile, a front-page blurb in the same issue noted that Teamsters Local 657 in San Antonio had also won a grievance. Hollis Hilton, a black worker, had been fired but was "recently restored to his employment through negotiations of the Teamsters Union." Hilton, a member of the union, received pay for his lost time. He commented, "It is wonderful to belong to a Labor organization where there is no racial discrimination." He may have overstated the state of racial harmony inside the Teamsters, but clearly the union had upset the old Jim Crow arrangement in which white bosses could fire black workers arbitrarily.[39]

The Teamsters' strike against Joske's brought *SNAP* activists and San Antonio's black civil rights movement together with organized labor in unprecedented ways. Most unions did practice racial discrimination, even if they at times stood up for wrongfully terminated workers like Hollis Hilton. Collaboration between the longtime East Side activists and the unions wasn't entirely new, but the relationship often had been fraught with friction. Now the ties between civil rights and labor activists were growing more intimate. About a month after the dual Teamsters' victories, the East Side paper ran another, self-reflexive report. "SNAP Goes Union," the headline declared, accompanied by a large union label bug and a photograph of Coleman with his hand raised as he took the oath of membership of the Amalgamated Lithographers of America Local 83. "Now a Union Shop," the article concluded, "SNAP and C. & S. Printers are prepared to bring to you the latest methods in the field of printing." It was a symbolic gesture, but one that carried great weight among labor leaders and the many white rank-and-file workers who measured their allies by their willingness to "Buy Union."[40]

Veteran civil rights activists and their youthful protégés extended their economic justice work into struggles over the built environment, continuing a decades-long quest to improve the infrastructure and housing stock on the East Side. As early as 1958, *SNAP* had editorialized about the "Nebraska Street Death Trap," a dangerous railroad underpass on a main thoroughfare. The narrow tunnel under the tracks flooded frequently, and even in the best of times it was not wide enough for two lanes of traffic and pedestrians traveling in both directions. In the early summer of 1961, Sutton, Black, and Donahue all collaborated to organize "a protest movement" to demand that the city replace the tunnel. With television and other news media on hand, "Long lines of cars were detoured from passage through the 'exterminator.'" The city council had allocated $180,000 to remove and replace the underpass, but "not even a pebble" had been moved, even after the protests. "This is the only such construction in San Antonio," Donahue reported in *SNAP*, adding, why should it be here, in our neighborhood? He continued: "A Mass March to City Hall to inform these well meaning city fathers that their eastside peers are fed up and want this exterminator removed is [seemingly] the only answer. I'm ready to go HOW ABOUT YOU?"[41]

The campaign picked up steam in January 1962, when a black airman stationed at a local base died in a traffic accident in the underpass. *SNAP* published a photograph of a bus approaching the "death trap" and pledged to run it on the front page with the caption "How Long?" until the city made the necessary repairs.[42] Donahue asked readers who wished to join the effort to contact him or Robert Gomez, another SCL activist and *SNAP* contributor, who also made a pitch for support in his column.[43] On February 7, Sutton, Black, publisher Coleman, "and many other citizens and civic leaders" went to the city council to make their case but found the chambers "deserted at 9:30 A.M." Meetings normally ran into the afternoons, leading Coleman to conclude that the council had learned of their plans and had "ducked" them to avoid the issue. *SNAP* retorted: "WE SHALL NOT STOP. We shall not be deferred, nor shall we be put off and pushed around. We shall MARCH ON CITY HALL, we shall sit-in at city hall, and we shall be heard, FOR WE SHALL SPEAK."[44] They returned the next week and found the city council in session. A representative of the railroad was also in attendance, and the city fathers passed a resolution to construct a "new, wider underpass" by September. The protests and editorials had worked. *SNAP* continued to run photographs of the construction project until it was completed on schedule (and it added a new weekly picture until the sidewalks were finished several months later). Decades later, the site—once the subject of great controversy—now appears as an otherwise unremarkable four-lane road passing beneath a railroad bridge, but a small blue road sign on the rusted trellis designates it the "Coleman Underpass."[45]

The black civil rights movement in San Antonio, like its counterpart in Houston, connected new youth-led organizations with longtime activists in a broad struggle, one that demanded not only integration but also employment opportunities and other forms of social and economic justice. Through the NAACP, the SCL, and *SNAP News*, San Antonio's most militant African American organizers staged a series of sit-ins, stand-ins, marches, and other direct action demonstrations that combined to transform their city. Lunch counters, restaurants, movie theaters, and grocers all opened their doors to black patrons, and, more important, many of them hired African American workers for the first time. Coordinated—and at times multiracial—campaigns resulted in substantial progress in making jobs available at area defense contractors, municipal utilities like the phone company, and countless private employers. Civil rights activists even found common ground with trade unions, which took up the fight for civil rights on the shop floor. The activists also applied significant pressure to city officials and raised their voices at City Hall, continuing their long struggle for influence in the political arena.

Despite this long list of accomplishments, both contemporary journalists and latter-day historians have downplayed the role of protest and community activism in the transformation of San Antonio's racial politics. In May 1960, the liberal *Texas Observer* reported that the city was "almost completely integrated" and that change had been accomplished "without strife or bitterness and with little fanfare." The paper credited the "quality, the courage, and the foresight of its leadership—religious, political, business, and civic—which has faced, in interracial harmony and cooperation, the great challenge of integration." While elites among both races "quietly conferred," white department store and restaurant managers eschewed "Southern social customs with ease and grace."[46] In other words, desegregation was a quickly and easily awarded gift from enlightened leaders, black and white, not the product of a protracted, intentional fight by determined civil rights organizers. Historians have reached similar conclusions.[47] Yet the reality is that desegregation in San Antonio was not a product of bargaining between black and white elites; rather, the negotiations themselves were the results of direct action protests.

Likewise, there is much evidence of "strife and bitterness" toward civil rights demonstrators and little proof of "interracial harmony and cooperation" beyond the social relations of the protestors themselves. Police officers slapping religious leaders, guns being pulled on protestors, city business and political leaders dragging their feet for months if not years—all of these are signs that San Antonio looked more like Birmingham than a racial paradise on what one scholar calls the "Southern periphery." At the same time, the expansive vision of San Antonio's civil rights leaders, the relatively slow pace of progress in the always-present field of employment, and the major significance to activists of seemingly innocuous issues like the Nebraska Street "Death Trap" all point to the need to reevaluate the true meaning of integration. Perhaps elites should receive some credit for the desegregation of public accommodations, but the bulk of the evidence indicates that activists such as Sutton, Black, Coleman, Donahue, and even Castillo led the push for the full integration of those businesses, for the opening of economic opportunities for the city's black residents, and for altering irreversibly the distribution of power in San Antonio. As in Houston, they did so while working around their city's traditional black leadership, who maintained their role as diplomats to the white elites by trying to mute and contain the movement. The movement produced sweeping, unprecedented change and awakened the city's black and brown youth, whetting their appetites for more formal power. The longtime East Side activists had undoubtedly made themselves heard. And they were just getting started.

"You Can't Call This Undemocratic"—The Triumph of the Bexar Coalition and the Collapse of the DOT

In the streets and at the ballot box, the pace of change quickened in the early 1960s. Across the state, the sit-ins gave the liberal wings of the black and brown communities an edge over their conservative coethnics. Militant leadership and tactics had proven effective, and the success of direct action had changed the terms of the debate, moving activists to turn from the gradual winning of rights to demands for complete, immediate integration. Economic opportunity and real political power were no longer distant goals but loomed on the horizon, just waiting to be secured.

When the direct action phase of the black civil rights movement opened a door for democracy in Texas, veteran activists of all colors plunged through it, particularly in the electoral arena. To be sure, civil rights agitation and political activism were never separate, and the fight for political recognition and power often went hand in hand with quests for integration and equal opportunity.

Activities in one field often reinforced work in the other, so the seismic shifts in the national and state political landscape beginning in 1960 created new possibilities for both civil rights struggles and electoral activism on the ground. The changing context energized new groups of community organizers and created or revived alliances among longtime agitators. The pressures, opportunities, and implications of the long presidential election cycle created newly powerful electoral constituencies composed of liberal Mexican Americans and African Americans. These new blocs, in turn, raised the profile of veteran black and brown civil rights activists and helped them become full partners in the state's nascent "liberal movement." The sit-ins meant that they would no longer take a back seat in the state's multiracial alliances and that civil rights would move toward the center of their coalitions' agendas. Activists like Sutton and LeRoy had shown their power in the streets, and now they meant to exercise it in party politics.

Even before the sit-ins, Albert Peña had suggested a new path forward for the state's liberals. At a speech to the Harris County Democrats (HCD) in the summer of 1959, while labor conflicts engulfed his hometown, Peña told the mostly white professionals and union men in the audience that they must become even more liberal if they hoped to advance their cause. "Freedom is liberation from everything undemocratic," he began. Pointing to Roosevelt's four freedoms, a framework with which the delegates were all familiar, Peña extended the concept of "freedom from want" to include "a positive affirmation of equal rights in education, hospital, and medical care. Freedom for all working men to organize into labor unions for better working conditions and decent wages ... [and] Freedom from discrimination and segregation in all public and quasi-public facilities."

Labor and civil rights struggles were not tangential to embracing liberalism, he suggested, and the vehicle for achieving true freedom was an unwaveringly liberal Democratic Party. Peña put the battle for the soul of the party bluntly. "You are either liberal or conservative," he said. "There cannot be a moderate view on the rights of labor because we might lose some of our business contacts. There cannot be a middle of the road on civil rights for fear we may lose some of our friends in East Texas." Self-styled "moderates" advocated gradualism or delay or "anything but the right view," he declared. After chiding the group for failing to endorse Gonzalez the previous year, Peña told them that real change will come to Texas "only after liberalism is clearly defined by liberals without equivocation, evasion, or fear of controversy." Doing so will bring together "the natural liberal coalition: organized labor, the Negro, and the Latin American, the farmer, the small businessman and the independent liberal." This may be a difficult route to victory, he concluded, but it's "the only way I want to win."[48]

The delegates roared their approval. Peña had given a similar speech at the Democrats of Texas (DOT's) third state convention in Austin a few weeks earlier, and it was sufficiently rousing that Chris Dixie and other HCD leaders invited him to do it again in front of their full membership. Six months later, state DOT leader Mrs. Frankie Carter Randolph tapped Peña to chair the organization's Committee on Issues, and, in February 1960, he reported to the fourth annual convention an ambitious agenda for the group that included, prominently, the struggle for civil rights. In many ways, he had unwittingly primed the white audience for the sit-in movement ahead. With Sutton and Hank Brown waiting in the wings in San Antonio, Peña promised to transform the formerly elite, all-white statewide DOT into a truly grassroots, multiracial organization. The rising militancy of the black civil rights movement further strengthened his hand, reaffirming the importance of his broad vision of freedom in liberal electoral politics.[49]

Yet both Peña's ambitious agenda and the DOT's own prospects ran headfirst into a wall by the name of Lyndon B. Johnson (LBJ). Now the majority leader of the U.S. Senate, Johnson had begun positioning himself for a run at the presidency as far back as 1956. That year he and Sam Rayburn, the Texan Speaker of the U.S. House of Representatives, had cut a deal in which both wings of the state party had agreed to support Johnson's "favorite son" candidacy for the nation's top office. The campaign was ceremonial: Governor Allan Shivers and Governor-Elect Price Daniel agreed that the Texas delegation would put Johnson's name into nomination at the national party gathering and that they would vote for him on the first round of balloting, but they would remain free to abandon him after the honorary ritual was complete (which is exactly what they did). The liberals got a seat for Mrs. Randolph on the Democratic National Committee and were promised much more. Yet in the end, Mrs. Randolph and the liberals walked out in protest and then organized the DOT, while Shivers led a defection of conservatives to Eisenhower and again carried the state for the Republican in November.

As the 1960 convention cycle approached, Johnson's ambitions were well known: he wanted to move beyond a ceremonial "favorite son" vote and instead bring an obedient delegation to the Democratic National Convention in Los Angeles that would go "All the way with LBJ." Yet doing so would require him to regain control of the Texas Democratic Party, which by then was composed of not two but three competing factions.

On the left, white liberals in the DOT mistrusted Johnson because of his ties to the Establishment and his willingness to sacrifice party democracy when it suited him. They believed that he had sold them out in 1956 and had undermined their struggle for "party integrity" at nearly every turn since his ascent to the Senate in 1948. Many liberals and labor leaders viewed LBJ as nothing more than a tool of the Suite 3F crowd in Houston. He did the bidding of the state's biggest businessmen and had no special concern for ordinary folks, and now he hoped to do the same thing in the Oval Office. In their eyes, LBJ was nothing like the liberal icon he would become after his presidency.[50]

Likewise, black and brown civil rights activists remained skeptical of Johnson's commitment to their causes. In 1956, LBJ as Senate majority leader had avoided signing the Southern Manifesto against integration. The next year, he passed the nation's first Civil Rights Act since Reconstruction, overcoming multiple southern filibusters to broker a compromise that ultimately left everyone unhappy. Most observers believed that "the master of the Senate" had gutted the bill's substance to appeal to his southern colleagues while still passing it to improve his credibility among black and white northern Democrats—with an eye toward winning their support in 1960. Within Texas, Johnson had done nothing special to endear himself to the state's African Americans. Instead he had maintained close alliances with segregationist local officials and the captains of industries that discriminated against black workers. He appeared all too happy to ignore the racial status quo, even if he didn't stand on a soapbox defending it.[51]

Johnson's relationship with Mexican American activists was also strained. Latter-day biographers would attribute Johnson's interest in human rights to his days as a teacher at a "Mexican school" in the South Texas town of Cotulla in 1928. There, the story goes, he saw firsthand the suffering of poor *mexicanos*, and he resolved to do something about it. This conviction led him to become an egalitarian administrator of the National Youth Administration in Texas, a New Dealer in Congress, a moderate southerner in the segregationist Senate, and eventually the creator of the War on Poverty and the Great Society. Whatever his internal motivations, the record is clear that as a freshman senator in 1949 (after winning his seat with boss-delivered Mexican votes the year before), Johnson responded to Dr. Hector P. Garcia's pleas to bury the slain soldier Felix Longoria, an act of compassion that endeared him for decades to many members of the American G.I. Forum (AGIF) and the League of United Latin American Citizens (LULAC). Yet as historian Julie Leininger Pycior has shown, Johnson's relationship with the Mexican American civil rights movement remained contradictory. LBJ advanced the activists' interests when it was advantageous for his own political career, and yet he simultaneously undermined their organizing efforts. He often allied with their antagonists even while dispensing favors to them, typically through Garcia, his closest *mexicano* client. For most Mexican American leaders in 1960, however, Johnson had yet to prove that he was much better than other segregationist Texas officials. Like most politicians, he could not be trusted to stand up for them when it counted. At best, the jury was still out.[52]

Ironically, the far right wing of die-hard Dixiecrats in Washington and at home had also turned against Johnson. Outraged by his moderation on civil rights and skeptical of his entreaties to northerners, former Shivercrat and O'Daniel activists in the Texas Democratic Party fought for representation in the local and state parties while continuing to flirt with Republicans in national politics. They organized into a John Birch Society–style shadow group called Freedom in Action (FIA), which, under the leadership of businessmen Jack Cox, had secretly begun fielding candidates in nonpartisan municipal elections as part of a longer-term strategy to reclaim the Harris County party apparatus.

Attacked on both sides, Johnson depended upon the party's vast center, an amalgamation of Establishment conservatives and former Shivercrats whom the native son had actively courted since 1956. Led by Governor Daniel, most party and elected officials now pledged to support LBJ in 1960, and the senator's men quickly got to work browbeating the rest into submission. Members of every county Democratic club and party caucus felt the weight of the senator's patented "Lyndon lean." As became his trademark, Johnson offered to reward his friends with posts in the party and appointed positions in government, and he threatened to punish his enemies using every force he could muster. Having seen to it that there would be no clear-cut liberal candidates for statewide office, Johnson's backers maneuvered to subsume the party's divisions to the unifying force of his presidential campaign.

White liberals were paralyzed by the onslaught. They carried out their biennial routine of selling poll taxes in December and January and focusing on get-out-the-vote efforts in advance of the May primaries and county conventions. In late February, the DOT held their fourth convention and passed a wide range of liberal "issue" resolutions but ultimately failed to take a stand on Johnson's campaign. Dallas labor lawyer and local coalition leader Otto Mullinax pushed a measure intended to call out and embarrass LBJ, but he later withdrew it when it drew opposition from organized labor and national committeewoman Mrs. Randolph. The convention also rejected another proposition, pushed by a Johnson supporter, that would have commended the senator for his stands in support of civil rights. The usually sympathetic *Texas Observer* called the DOT gathering a "puzzled posture" and added that liberals were "fighting for footing in the tide of a Johnson year."[53]

The liberals' confusion remained evident in May and June 1960, as various local units adopted divergent strategies regarding Johnson and the upcoming state convention. Houston liberals were trounced at the polls and at precinct conventions on May 7, losing three incumbent state representatives to conservative challengers in the first primary and two more in the runoff. As the *Observer* put it, "Forces friendly to Freedom in Action" came out en masse to support Jack Cox, their former leader who had resigned his post to run against Daniel in the Democratic gubernatorial primary. Daniel clobbered Cox, but the right-wing FIA turnout had allowed the "middle of the road" conservatives to easily win their precinct conventions, which in turn allowed them to dominate the Harris County party convention. There the Johnson conservatives voted down the perennially proposed loyalty pledge, which would have required all national delegates and electors to support the Democratic nominees (Shivercrat conservatives had defeated this liberal measure in 1952 and 1956 as well). In response, Mrs. Randolph and members of the HCD repeated their traditional ritual of staging a walkout from the county convention. They held a rump meeting and promised to send a challenge delegation to the state gathering and, if necessary, to the national convention in Los Angeles. FIA members and sympathizers, meanwhile, held their own caucus that declined to endorse Johnson and appointed still a third delegation of their members to go to Austin. Although the FIA forces were strongest in Houston, the conventions played out similarly in Dallas, Austin, and El Paso, where liberals in all cases bolted their gatherings and hoped to take their cases to the credentials committee at the state convention.[54]

In contrast, in San Antonio, the new coalition of civil rights and labor activists decided to cut a deal with Johnson's supporters. As a result, they gained control of the county convention, passed a series of unprecedentedly liberal resolutions, and finally appointed themselves as delegates to the state gathering in Austin. The key differences were the power of San Antonio's multiracial liberal alliance and the pragmatism of its leaders. A liberal ticket led by Franklin Spears, a white freshman incumbent, and attorney and West Side activist John Alaniz, a Peña acolyte, swept the city's legislative races. Their presence on the ballot helped give the multiracial group of civil rights and labor activists an edge at the precinct- and county-level conventions. Local party chairman Jimmie Knight had campaigned hard for Johnson, but he lacked a clear majority at the Bexar County gathering because a right-wing conservative group refused to support LBJ. As the next biggest bloc, what the *Observer* called the "labor-Latin-Negro group led by Albert Peña" wielded tremendous power and received partnership offers from all of the other factions. Kathleen Voigt, head of a small "independent" white liberal faction, tried to convince Peña's group to join hers in backing Adlai Stevenson. The anti-Johnson conservatives offered to join them in sending an uninstructed delegation to Austin, a move that would have represented a clear slap in the face to LBJ.

Peña, along with labor leader Hank Brown and the East Side's G. J. Sutton, instead dealt with the Johnson forces in exchange for a seat at the table. Knight instructed his precinct leaders to elect Peña as chairman of the convention, and the Bexar County Democratic Coalition was born. Peña carried the highly symbolic chairman election 549¼ to 397½, defeating archconservative attorney Hubert Green, who, ironically, would represent Handy Andy when it responded to civil rights protests the following year. The formula for victory was clear: the *Observer* reported that "The Knight coalition included Johnson people, labor, East Side Democrats (Negroes), and West Side Democrats (Latin-Americans)." The latter three groups agreed to support Johnson at the state convention, while the Johnson backers signed off on a wide range of liberal resolutions, including the DOT's loyalty pledge, support for Mrs. Randolph's reelection as national committeewoman, and an endorsement of the "students participating in the 'sit-ins.'" Members of the Johnson-Daniel faction also joined the convention majority in going on record in favor of school integration, the repeal of the right-to-work law, the creation of teacher tenure, recognition of teachers' unions, and support for old-age medical insurance and "other welfare measures"—all longtime liberal demands. It even passed one measure that "called for equal rights for women."

The "labor-Latin-Negro" alliance in San Antonio, tentatively forged in the late 1950s, had achieved a new level of power. Unlike previous experiments, this victory was not a flash in the pan but the first signal of a permanent realignment of Bexar County politics. Jimmie Knight got Johnson his convention votes, Peña was elected chairman, Sutton chaired the resolutions committee, and Brown chaired the delegates committee (which also included Rev. Black). The coalition forwarded the most radical set of resolutions ever passed by a Democratic county convention in Texas, if not the South as a whole, along with the state's most diverse delegation to the convention in Austin.

Mrs. Voigt, the leader of the "independent liberals located in the upper-income north side precincts," attacked Peña, a longtime Stevenson supporter and leader of the local DOT club, for abandoning the liberal cause by "making a deal" with Knight. Scoffing at the posturing of Voigt's group of "swimming pool liberals," Brown offered the coalition leaders' response. "Sure we made a deal. It's done every day in politics," he said. "A better word is compromise, which is a cardinal principle of the Democratic Party. Check the delegation list, and you will find the delegates are from every walk of life. There are labor union members, sure, but you will also find a corporation president and many businessmen on that list, along with many Latin-American and Negro citizens. You can't call this undemocratic." Longtime labor activists George and Latane Lambert, who had participated in a similar coalition over twenty years earlier, rounded out the Bexar County delegation.[55]

The effectiveness of the San Antonio model, the absolute failure of the "independent" white liberals, and the successful horse trading with the Johnson forces were all repeated at the state convention on June 11. Once again, Peña and the "labor-Latin-Negro group" became a hot commodity, using their presence as a key swing vote among the party's factions to transform their own status from marginal to powerful. By playing their cards right, they again parlayed that liminal position into more power, recognition, and support for their own causes.

For their part, the white liberals sought to hold the DOT line. "The issue of the convention . . . was party loyalty," said Alex Dickie of Denton, the head of the Texas Farmers Union and vice president of the DOT. He demanded a roll-call vote on the loyalty pledge—the perennial liberal demand that the party's delegates pledge themselves to the national ticket. But Johnson's forces had already "psychologically cut the ground out from under" it, the *Observer* reported, by adopting an alternate loyalty resolution with softer language. The substitute measure stated that it was "understood" by candidates for elected offices, party leaders, and delegates to the national convention that acceptance of their positions meant that they would support the national ticket "in good faith." This alternate pledge aimed to prevent the threatened liberal walkout by putting the nominees on record while also assuaging the members of conservative county delegations who remained leery of northern Democrats.[56]

Johnson's backers believed their candidate needed the appearance of a unified bloc from his home state as he prepared for the main event in Los Angeles. Governor Daniel held a series of meetings at the mansion in the days before the state gathering, and politicking continued late into the night at the convention hotel. The leaders of the Texas AFL-CIO, who had promised to participate in a walkout if the DOT pledge did not pass, met first with Daniel and then with Johnson and Rayburn the evening before the opening gavel. The next morning they backtracked, instructing the caucus of labor delegates from various counties to soften their stance on the loyalty issue and refrain from bolting, no matter what. The incensed union members rejected their leaders' pleas and opted instead for an "every man on his own" policy toward the walkout. DOT leaders Mrs. Randolph and Creekmore Fath continued to push the loyalty-or-else position, hoping to keep in line the few liberals who were actually seated as delegates. The group had a sound truck and grandstand set up a few blocks away at Barton Springs Park, sitting ready and waiting to hold the rump convention. The San Antonio group was the only large liberal-led delegation that had won its county convention and could count on being seated, but its chairman, Albert Peña, was nowhere to be found.[57]

As it turned out, he had been up working before dawn. Around four in the morning he had received a phone call from one Johnson operative inviting him to breakfast with the Senate majority leader. Peña recalled, "So I got up, and when I got there, he had already talked to the other members of the coalition and the only thing he wanted was a promise that we wouldn't walk out. Because it would embarrass him . . . for the people in Texas to walk out on the convention." Johnson told Peña that he had spoken with the labor delegates from Bexar County and had promised them help in Washington. He had also met with Sutton and had guaranteed that the convention would elect him as "the first Black delegate from Bexar County" to the national gathering. "So I said, 'these guys have already made a deal, come on, I want to go along with them,'" Peña remembered. "We weren't going to walk out, but nobody said that. He [Johnson] said, 'Now what do you want?'" With the state's most powerful politician staring him down across the table, Peña did not hesitate. "I said, 'I want two things,'" he recalled. "'I want *Mexicano* representation to the national convention and I want you to place someone on the platform committee . . . from Bexar County that will vote for the majority civil rights plank that is going to be presented.'" Johnson agreed to both conditions. Peña, Sutton, and labor leader Jack Martin were all elected as delegates. And "the coalition was represented for the first time in the national convention," Peña added.[58]

Peña and company had managed the preconvention politicking perfectly. The liberal, militant leaders of the East and West Sides would have unprecedented representation, and the coalition would stand and be counted in support of a strong national civil rights plank. Still, the veteran organizers took out an insurance policy, using the floor debate over Dickie's loyalty motion to demand publicly that the party leaders help the county coalition's slate of candidates for the state legislature, including the reelection bid of state senator Henry B. Gonzalez. As the *Observer* put it, the white liberals were blindsided as the deal was announced. In exchange for the coalition's agreement to refrain from bolting from the convention hall, Johnson and Daniel pledged to help elect the liberal Democratic legislative candidates from San Antonio over their Republican opponents in November. Then, "in a dramatic, on-the-floor convention caucus" of the Bexar County delegation, Peña and Sutton vouched for the agreement with the party chieftains. Maury Maverick Jr. put forward the loyalty pledge nonetheless, but the "labor-Latin-Negro" alliance defeated it by a 3-to-1 margin. "The decision of the Bexar caucus broke the back of the bolt from inside," the *Observer* concluded.

In the end, only five or six delegates from Bexar went through with the walkout. Maverick, a longtime supporter of Peña and the coalition, stayed inside, as did George and Latane Lambert, Brown, and all of San Antonio's labor caucus. Dickie cast the tie-breaking vote in his own county caucus—against his own original loyalty pledge. Led by Peña, Bexar County cast its 315 votes against the motion. Several labor activists voted to hold the line, but another, a rumper from Dallas, conceded that the walkout was "shot to hell." In the end, about two hundred DOT members assembled in the heat on a hilltop overlooking Barton Springs, but only fifteen of them wore official delegate badges. Mrs. Randolph conceded complete defeat, which was also accompanied on a personal level by her removal as a national committeewoman. The Godmother of white Texas liberalism had lost her seat and foundered on the shoals of a multiracial civil rights coalition that had overtaken her vision and eclipsed her leadership.

The favorite son Johnson easily won the state convention's endorsement, 2,252 to 40. The dissenters were likely the FIA group from Mrs. Randolph's home of Harris County, a group that assembled in a corner of the convention hall in Austin under a massive Confederate flag. Meanwhile, Fath, the DOT secretary-treasurer, criticized labor and Peña for cutting deals and abandoning the walkout. Yet it had been a failed plan from the outset. The liberals' losses in the Harris, Travis, Dallas, and El Paso county conventions meant that the dissenting delegates would all need to win challenges before the credentials committee before their votes would be counted. Even if all of them had been seated, they would not have had a clear majority of the convention and might have lost on the loyalty pledge anyway. As it was, each of their delegations was refused, with only Latane Lambert dissenting in each vote on the credentials committee. Bexar County's delegation ended up representing nearly all of the liberals who had been seated and who could therefore properly walk out as recognized delegates to the state convention. The other challenge delegations were never seated and were merely ignored by party leaders, as were the handful of dissidents in the park. As the *Observer* noted, Johnson "shelled, isolated, and slaughtered" the liberals and moved on. The DOT soon gave up on its plan to contest the official delegation to the national convention, and it ceased holding regular meetings thereafter.[59]

For his part, Peña defended his stance. He had never committed himself to the pledge-or-walkout binary, he contended. He was reportedly "dubious" when only a third of a preconvention meeting of would-be rumpers signaled that they could expect to be seated at the convention. Peña openly discussed the terms of the deal, telling the *Observer* that he, Sutton, and Martin traded votes and "Johnson is to send money into the campaigns for [Bexar County] Democratic nominees for the [state] House and Senate [and] Daniel is to campaign on the spot, physically, for the legislative nominees . . . including Sen. Henry Gonzalez." Peña added that he "had four groups he was trying to keep together for the November election," and that mattered more than the ideological crusade of the DOT's white liberals. In other words, maintaining the coalition of liberal Mexican Americans, African Americans, labor, and the Johnson Democrats was the most important goal. Keeping that group together was paramount to winning the legislative races that fall and furthering his own long-term goals. Sutton agreed and voted against the loyalty pledge and the walkout in order to gain representation at both the national convention and in local politics.[60]

The Texas State AFL-CIO's weekly newspaper also defended its leaders' apparent about-face, drawing comparisons to the great mythic battles of the Texas Revolution. "The liberal movement in Texas has been disposed for too many years to seek out a succession of Goliads and Alamos in which it could fight to its mortal end," its editor opined. "This is a fine endeavor for liberals who carry only responsibility for their personal conduct and not the additional responsibility of what happens to the farmers . . . or the working men and women . . . when they guess wrong. . . . As for labor, if we could have changed the results we would have. Since we couldn't we will busy ourselves getting ready for San Jacinto."[61] Like Peña and Sutton, labor won a seat at the table and lived on to fight another day.

The Bexar County Democratic Coalition had scored another victory. A decade earlier, a sitting elected official had called Sutton a "nigger" in the middle of a public meeting, while Peña had traveled the dusty roads of South Texas organizing demonstrations to open Anglo schools to *mexicano* children. The Loyal American Democrats had been forced to battle just to get Adlai Stevenson to step foot in the barrio, and *SNAP* had gone to the mat to integrate the city's swimming pools and lunch counters. The summer of 1960 was indeed a far cry from the bad old days. Sutton and Peña would now go to Los Angeles as the official delegates representing their corner of Texas. And they did it by working together.

¡Viva Kennedy! (In Black and Brown)

Johnson would fail to secure the Democratic nomination for president. When John F. Kennedy ended up securing the nomination, the Texas delegation was shell-shocked, with Governor Daniel indicating that he would not campaign for the liberal senator from Massachusetts. But Kennedy's "surprise" choice of

LBJ as his running mate reenergized Johnson's supporters in Texas and across the South. The latter's "presence on the ticket assuages Southern resentment of the strongest civil rights plank in the party's history," the *Observer* reported. "But it also threatens to alienate some Negro and labor voters."[62]

As delicate a balancing act as it might have been for Kennedy, the combined ticket provided new opportunities for black and brown civil rights organizers in Texas. Thanks to their support of Johnson at the state convention, Sutton and Peña gained entrée into the highest circles of the Democratic Party at the national convention in Los Angeles, where they could hold their leaders' feet to the fire and make them keep their promises. When Texas's representative on the platform committee agreed to vote against the strong civil rights plank, Peña objected. He went to Governor Daniel, the delegation's elected leader, and explained that Johnson had promised him a yes vote on the issue. Daniel was incredulous, but at that moment, Sam Rayburn walked into the room. Rayburn affirmed that Peña was correct and instructed the delegate to vote in favor of the civil rights resolution. At another juncture during the gathering, Peña and Sutton attended a secret meeting in which the two candidates stood before black delegates from across the country in order to reassure them regarding Johnson's record on race. The duo looked on as LBJ duly promised to follow Kennedy's lead and support the party platform, including its stand on civil rights. They must have struggled to avoid smiling. The Bexar County coalition's stand had paid off.[63]

It paid off again soon after the convention, when Kennedy campaign staffer Carlos McCormick came to San Antonio to meet with Peña. McCormick "said that he had contacted people throughout South Texas" in search of a chairman for the campaign's "Latin American division" in Texas, Peña recalled. In fact, Peña himself had been queried by a party organizer, and he had recommended Dr. Hector P. Garcia and several other leaders of the AGIF. Peña also suggested that Sutton chair the "Negro division" of the campaign, adding in his letter that he was "sure many recognized Mr. Sutton's leadership abilities as a delegate from Texas" in Los Angeles. Unsurprisingly, Jerry Holleman, the head of the Texas State AFL-CIO, had been chosen to head up the labor wing of the campaign, but rumors swirled concerning the Latin American nominee. When he came to San Antonio, McCormick told Peña that "the majority" wanted him to take the job.[64]

Peña's response reflected his decade of participation in the Mexican American civil rights movement and would also set that struggle's agenda for years to come. He said he would take the job if the campaign met two conditions. "Number one," he told McCormick, "that we will be recognized as a political . . . force in Texas . . . and we will only work directly with the Kennedy's and not . . . with the state Democratic party, because they have sold us out too many times." Peña also asked for "some top level appointments" in the new administration. McCormick agreed, but Peña was not satisfied and wanted a guarantee. They picked up the phone on Peña's desk and called Robert Kennedy, the candidate's brother and campaign manager, and McCormick repeated Peña's demands. Bobby agreed.[65] Nobody paused to consider the fact that Peña's two goals—autonomy and incorporation—were somewhat contradictory, as he, like other *mexicano* activists, wanted both to shape their community's own destiny and to be accepted by the current powers that be. Such incongruities were not yet apparent, but they would prove critical in the coming years.

For the moment, however, Mexican American civil rights leaders simply celebrated the federal intervention into Texas affairs and hastily organized the Viva Kennedy clubs. Gonzalez and Garcia became the division's honorary cochairs, while Peña did the nitty-gritty work. Peña immediately hit the road, crisscrossing South Texas to organize clubs in each county. He met up with longtime labor activists and leaders of LULAC and the AGIF, many of whom had already begun forming clubs on their own. AGIF executive director Ed Idar wrote to Peña just before McCormick's visit, informing him that he had formed a group in Hidalgo County in the Lower Rio Grande Valley. "This Club is supposed to work hand in hand with the county organization on behalf of the ticket down here," Idar told him, "while at the same time giving the liberal faction among the Latinos an opportunity to work within their own organization to see if we can get a maximum vote out in November."[66]

The same philosophy undergirded the formation of Viva Kennedy clubs across the state. Peña contacted veteran Mexican American activists in each town. He later recalled that "we decided that we were not going to accept any money from anybody. We were going to do it on our own. We sold one dollar memberships.... If you didn't have a dollar, you became a member anyway." County by county across the Valley, and from one big city to the next, "we organized, we organized," Peña said. In Houston, Peña contacted John J. Herrera of LULAC Council 60 and Roy Elizondo, a local leader in Gonzalez's 1958 gubernatorial campaign who had since organized the growing Civic Action Committee. In Dallas, he contacted United Auto Workers activists Francisco F. "Pancho" Medrano and Franklin Garcia, both of whom became officers in the local Viva Kennedy club. In Fort Worth, AGIF state officer Gilbert Garcia helped launch the local club, where he was joined by members of the radical United Packinghouse Workers of America. Back home in Bexar County, Peña's assistant, Albert Fuentes, shared organizing duties with Gonzalez's right-hand man, Lalo Solis.[67]

One report from the Valley indicates both the intensity of the campaign and the fervor that surrounded it. Led by Idar and his law partner and fellow activist R. P. "Bob" Sanchez, the Hidalgo County Viva Kennedy club had grown to be the largest along the border, and organizers held formal biweekly meetings and countless activities "down to the community level." Sanchez reported that a string of appearances by dignitaries including Peña, U.S. senator Ralph Yarborough, and Gonzalez helped the cause, as did the fact that "all the generals got off their tails and on their feet to work right along with the privates." As he toured precincts in one last-minute round of door-to-door canvassing, Sanchez recalled, "Groups of little Mexican boys gathered at corner grocery stores would see me walking down and then would holler, 'Viva Kennedy.' "[68]

While countless *mexicano* labor, civil rights, and political activists organized the "Latin-American division" of the Kennedy campaign, African American organizers across the state likewise rallied around the Democratic ticket. In early October, more than two hundred black activists representing local political clubs in forty-six counties across the state assembled in Austin to reorganize the Texas Council of Voters (TCV), the group originally founded by NAACP attorney W. J. Durham of Dallas after the fall of the white primary in 1944. The council's reformation stemmed directly from the exigencies of the Kennedy-Johnson campaign: its members gathered after the Progressive Voters League (PVL) had grown ineffective at the statewide level, leaving the state's quarter-million registered black voters without coordinated leadership. With attorney Durham again serving as chairman, and civil rights unionist Moses LeRoy of Houston as vice chair, the members of the reincarnated TCV voted five to one to support the Democratic ticket.[69]

At the local level, a few weeks later in Houston, the HCCO brought together its sixty member organizations to discuss the presidential race. The *Chronicle* reported that their endorsement might affect the decisions of some forty-five thousand likely African American voters in Harris County. "The council's endorsed candidates in the past four or five years have won the Negro vote," the paper continued. "After strong pro-Republican opposition led by George T. Nelson, long advocate of civil rights for Negroes," the HCCO endorsed Kennedy and Johnson. Nelson, a onetime supporter of segregationist governor Allan Shivers, likely calculated a Republican victory and hoped that an endorsement of Nixon would result in patronage. Moses and Erma LeRoy joined the majority in supporting the Democrats, with the council's other black unionists likely joining them. Following the endorsement, the HCCO began "working feverously" to coordinate the campaign with leaders of precinct organizations, fraternal lodges, and civic associations, the paper added. Over seventy thousand black voters were registered in the county, making the estimate of forty-five thousand HCCO votes both attainable and potentially decisive.[70]

Both the local and statewide efforts depended upon the on-the-ground organizing of Mrs. LeRoy. As early as the winter of 1959–60, she and Moses worked on special assignments for the Texas AFL-CIO, travelling across Texas

Texas AFL-CIO president Jerry R. Holleman (left) with Moses and Erma LeRoy, identified by *Texas AFL-CIO News* staff as representatives of the "Brotherhood of Railway Clerks [who] assist[ed] with poll tax drives," February 2, 1960. Naming them as simple trade unionists downplayed both their decades of civil rights activism and the unprecedented support that organized labor had contributed toward mobilizing the black vote. Courtesy Texas AFL-CIO Collection, Special Collections, The University of Texas at Arlington Library, Arlington, Texas, AR110-29-2-57 [#60006-a].

to organize African Americans for the liberal cause. Her initial reports on the state's black vote were bleak, as both internal factionalism among African Americans and voter suppression by white authorities stymied mobilization efforts. In the black neighborhoods of Dallas, three separate factions and thirteen elected precinct chairmen had attempted to steer the city's black voters. Yet after countless meetings and "buttonholing of individual key people," LeRoy reported to Texas AFL-CIO headquarters, "we were finally successful in bringing them together into a coalition to wage a mammoth all out poll tax campaign." In Waco, the county tax assessor-collector flatly refused to appoint more than two African Americans deputy voter registrars, which meant that they were the only black citizens who could legally register voters.[71] Many African Americans in the rural areas of East Texas faced terror and intimidation when they tried to organize their fellow black citizens. Some did so clandestinely, as was the case in a "whispering campaign" in Rusk and an "undercover . . . Progressive

Association" that led political activities in Bryan, LeRoy reported. It was both rare and notable when she discovered local leaders who risked taking public stands, at times at great costs. "I found a lady heading the leadership in Jacksonville," she wrote by way of example. "Some time ago a cross had been set on her lawn because of some militant stand she had taken but she is still fearlessly carrying the ball." In response to LeRoy's visit, the local leader again "rallied her forces . . . [and] they voted to set the machinery in motion immediately."[72]

LeRoy discovered that the race problem extended even to sympathetic whites, especially in East Texas. "As I moved from area to area, I observed some frustration due to the lack of communication between liberal Whites and Negroes," she wrote during her travels in the 1960 primary campaign. Many ordinary African Americans simply lacked information and were thus placed "at a disadvantage when it comes to making decisions, with regards to candidates." LeRoy felt her presence there on the ground had produced real progress. While local labor and DOT leaders had previously chosen black diplomats who lacked real followings in the community, she was now identifying the right leaders and connecting them with "strong union men." The Texas AFL-CIO had "made friends" among the state's black voters, she added, thanks to "my being sent to sit down and discuss candidates and issues with them, plus supplying them know how in the way to organize to get the vote out . . . [and] making voting records available where they can analyze the factual information for themselves."[73]

In the fall of 1960, when Mrs. LeRoy spent the final six weeks before the election campaigning on behalf of the labor federation, the energy of the Kennedy campaign had transformed the situation on the ground. Travelling to more than thirty cities in Central and East Texas, "I was fully occupied both night and day with conferences, public meetings, and individual canvassing" in black neighborhoods, she reported. She discussed with local residents the issues that "were of concern to the Negro masses and labor," which included improvements in the minimum wage, job security, health benefits, social security, and "the various facets of Civil Rights, such as, equal protection under the law, equal educational opportunities, equal job opportunities, equal accommodations in public facilities, world peace, etc." Mrs. LeRoy's audiences understood "the role played by the Republican-Dixiecrat coalition" that had blocked progress in Texas and Washington for the past decade, she added, and "they seem to be fully aware that the enemies of Labor are also the enemies of Civil Rights." In the areas she visited, black voters were "leaning heavily toward the Democratic ticket," she added, noting that they favored national Democrats and particularly Kennedy's record and "straight forward approach."

In addition to helping the immediate campaign, Mrs. LeRoy contended that her canvassing would lead to long-term gains for the state's labor, civil rights, and political activists. "The reaction to the Negro-Labor Coalition was very favorable," she reported. "My visit to these areas served as a stimulus. . . . They were doing nothing to get out the vote [before my arrival. In] Areas where work had been done earlier this year, people were more easily mobilized. The lines of communication between liberal Whites and Negroes have grown stronger." African Americans were joining the white-led DOT clubs and Democratic Party organizations in several smaller towns, including places where they were a numerical minority or in which they had long been excluded from party functions. In Lufkin in East Texas, a local leader of the all-black PVL had improved his organizing methods after he attended one of labor's area Committee on Political Education (COPE) conferences, another venue that would have been lily white in the recent past. "As I moved about, Negroes were exceedingly glad to hear that Texas State AFL-CIO and the Texas Council [of Voters] had joined ranks to get out the vote," Mrs. LeRoy concluded. She advised that the groups should maintain their relationship, invite more black leaders to attend COPE meetings, and return to the same local groups regularly in the years ahead.[74]

While Peña led the Viva Kennedy drive and Mrs. LeRoy spread the gospel of the Kennedy campaign across black Texas, Sutton mobilized the East Side and all of San Antonio. He had returned home from Los Angeles convinced that Johnson was "committed to the platform," and he quickly mobilized his friends at the SNAP House behind the effort. "There is only one way to Vote Nov. 8," *SNAP News* proclaimed four days before the election, "the Democratic Ticket." Coleman wrote that the editors "could go on and on relating hundreds of reasons why," but two main reasons stuck out. The first was local: "The Democratic Party is one big happy Family, and we are a part of the family. We have been included in everything democratic in Bexar County. G. J. Sutton was elected as a delegate to the National Convention." Second, the Democratic nominee was a proven supporter of black civil rights. "When Rev. Martin Luther King was recently jailed, it was the Kennedy Camp [that came] to Rev. King's aid." *SNAP* concluded that readers should vote the entire Democratic ticket, including Henry B. Gonzalez for state senate and the Franklin Spears–led liberal-Latin coalition slate for the state house of representatives.[75]

In the final days and weeks of the campaign, the East Side activists held a series of events and rallies in support of the ticket in collaboration with liberal whites and *mexicanos*. On October 25, the Bexar County Democratic Women held a reception to honor several national women dignitaries of the party, including in attendance "Mrs. Lyndon Johnson, Mrs. Robert Kennedy . . . and Mrs. Jean Kennedy Smith, sister-in-law of Sen. Kennedy." Between 3,100 and 3,500 people attended the gathering, which was cohosted by Mrs. Maury Maverick Sr., the late former mayor and congressman's wife. Lou Nelle Sutton, G. J.'s wife, also "served as one of the hostesses," assisted by club officers

Latane Lambert and Olga Peña. On Sunday, October 30, Mr. and Mrs. Sutton hosted a morning coffee honoring the Democratic candidates. A multiracial group of approximately 150 people, which included Henry B. Gonzalez and legislative candidate John Alaniz, attended the gathering at the Suttons' home on the East Side. Vice presidential nominee Johnson and Governor Daniel followed through on their promises to campaign for the liberal legislative candidates who were endorsed by the Bexar County Democratic Coalition. In addition to providing funding throughout and touring the city with Kennedy in September, Johnson came to San Antonio for his last speech prior to the election. Sutton, Peña, Alaniz, and former school board member Gus Garcia greeted LBJ at the airport, joining the rally at "the end of the trail."[76]

On November 8, Kennedy and Johnson narrowly prevailed in Texas and nationwide. They carried the Lone Star State by less than fifty thousand votes out of over 2 million cast, with Nixon's campaign charging voter fraud and initially refusing to accept the results. "Landslide Lyndon" had almost certainly drawn on South Texas bosses when he won the 1948 Senate race by eighty-seven votes, so it was by no means out of the question that some chicanery continued in 1960.[77]

Yet the candidates and most observers attributed their victory in Texas to the dramatic increase in African American and Mexican American voters. Two days after the election, Kennedy fired off a series of telegrams to Peña, Idar, and a number of other leaders from the campaign's "Latin-American" division. "Congratulations on the magnificent job turned in by the Viva Kennedy Clubs in Texas," Kennedy wrote. "The margin of victory in Bexar, Nueces, and El Paso counties and the Rio Grande Valley was a prominent significance in carrying Texas." Peña later added that the 1960 turnout was the highest percentage ever of Mexican American voter participation, and that their support for the ticket was "instrumental" in putting Texas back in the Democratic column. The West Side of San Antonio gave Kennedy-Johnson a victory of seventeen thousand to three thousand for Nixon (nearly 6–1). Reports from the trenches reached a similar conclusion. "The jubilation down here is tremendous," Bob Sanchez exclaimed days after the election. "My fat head is so full of beams [sic] yet and my imagination so overwhelmed that I cannot sit here and give you every detail of the campaign but I can tell you at this time that unquestionably the thing that carried it was the unification and organization of the Latin people throughout this area."[78]

Meanwhile, the African American vote in Texas followed the national pattern, going overwhelmingly for Kennedy. Some "dominantly Negro" precincts in Texas went as much as 10–1 for the Democrats, while Kennedy carried the entire East Side of San Antonio by a 3-to-1 margin. (Valmo Bellinger and other conservative blacks had aligned themselves with the Good Government League and the GOP.) Statewide, the black vote stopped the

Democrats' bleeding in Harris, Dallas, and Tarrant (Fort Worth) counties, while the "Latin-Americans" carried the next three largest urban counties: Bexar (with Sutton's help), El Paso, and Nueces (Corpus Christi). Mrs. LeRoy had helped African Americans in East Texas mobilize in unprecedented numbers, while labor and white liberal Democrats could celebrate the simple fact that the state's archconservatives had failed to keep it in the Republican column. Liberalism, they claimed, was alive and well in Texas.

At the very least, the Bexar County Democratic Coalition and its constituent parts had again asserted their collective importance in state politics, providing the critical organization and votes to deliver Texas's electors to Kennedy and Johnson. In so doing, it laid a foundation for increased activity within the Democratic Party and proved again that it deserved a seat at the table. Peña and the Viva Kennedy clubs brought diverse elements of the Mexican American civil rights struggle together into a coordinated statewide campaign, while African American voting power delivered the punch promised by the sit-ins.[79]

More generally, three watershed developments occurred in rapid succession in 1960. First, inspired by a new generation of activists and led by veteran organizers, African Americans asserted their independence and rejected the old ways of negotiating gradual change. Savvy organizers like Sutton and Mrs. LeRoy translated the gains in the streets into real electoral power, bringing civil rights into the corridors of high politics and fulfilling the dream of wielding the black vote that had dated back to the fall of the white primary in 1944. Next, the "labor-Latin-Negro" alliance supplanted the white, elite Democrats of Texas as the unquestioned leaders of the liberal movement, bringing a new kind of liberalism along with them. The activists replaced southern gradualism and racial paternalism with a multiracial coalition that aimed to extend the New Deal to all Americans by prioritizing the struggle for civil rights. Finally, the "unification and organization of the Latin people" was simply unprecedented. What present-day observers call "the Latino vote" was born among Mexican Americans in the fiery Viva Kennedy campaign spanning from Bexar County to the furthest reaches of Texas and the Southwest.

The Lone Star State was a very different place than it had been just a year earlier, peopled with highly visible, newly aggressive political actors that didn't look like the palefaces of time immemorial. Yet whether each of the ascendant groups could build on their momentum and collect the spoils of victory remained an open question, and translating the brief moments of victory in a single election year into a permanent reconfiguration of power and resources would prove easier to imagine than to execute.

Chapter 7

Trying to Reach Substantially Unanimous Agreement
The "Latin Vote" and the First Democratic Coalition

In the winter of 1961, Henry B. Gonzalez and Maury Maverick Jr., the two liberal legislators and frequent allies from San Antonio, each declared their candidacies for the U.S. Senate seat vacated by Lyndon B. Johnson. Each of the two politicians believed that he was the true champion of the ideological left, the "unreconstructed fighting American liberal of the old school," as Gonzalez would put it. Each served as de facto representatives of larger blocs within Texas society and political life. As any casual observer could have guessed, Gonzalez would attract the state's newly organized "Latin Vote," while Maverick depended upon the white "swimming pool" liberals scattered across San Antonio's North Side, the city's plaintiffs lawyers and few liberal white merchants, and both group's counterparts in the Democrats of Texas (DOT). Both candidates had proven that they had substantial appeal among members of labor unions and rank-and-file white working people, and both had built coalitions with African American civil rights activists over the years. A tentative tactical coalition among all of these groups had formed during the Kennedy-Johnson campaign the previous summer and fall. Now, just a few months later, the question of which man would attract the larger multiracial flock threatened to tear it all apart. It would take two years of experimenting in coming together, hashing things out, falling apart, and reuniting before the answer would become clear to all.

Across the board, efforts to build on the momentum of the Kennedy-Johnson election proceeded in fits and starts. Each constituent part of that campaign believed that it was responsible for the margin of victory and had consequently earned unprecedented political capital. Each group moved quickly to collect the spoils, yet harnessing the energy of a single election into lasting influence proved easier said than done. Mexican American activists returned to work quickly, transforming the Viva Kennedy clubs into a permanent organization and a force in Texas politics. Their new group, the Political Association of Spanish-Speaking Organizations (PASO), would bring together a diverse collection of *mexicano* labor, civil rights, and political activists that—despite their common cultural heritage—would fiercely debate the organization's program and methods throughout its formative years. The victors of those internal battles would ultimately rededicate the group to multiracial coalition-building and militant organizing tactics, but the often belligerent process would prove gut-wrenching for all involved. Organized labor likewise sought to extend its influence, while white "independent" liberals hoped to find new ways to reorganize after their crushing defeat at the 1960 state Democratic convention. Meanwhile, even as they carried forward the struggle for jobs and freedom, African Americans continued to search for footing in the political arena. At every stage, they too would disagree internally over the best path forward, with some activists working to extend the successful pragmatic pact with LBJ and others recommitting to the idealistic cause of liberalism for all. Direct action demonstrations continued, but veteran activists focused their efforts on translating the progress in integrating public accommodations into improved economic opportunities and real political power.

Each group would experiment separately with new tactics and alliances, with one wing of leaders from each bloc trying to overcome the Gonzalez-Maverick split by finding new ways to collaborate across the color line. The result would be a draft version of the Democratic Coalition, the first truly multiracial statewide alliance in Texas history. Although its founding would signal a turning point, all would not go according to plan. Each group's separate desire for power led to interracial fissures that would divide the coalition's members until the gubernatorial runoff election of 1962. That campaign, in turn, would produce new evidence of just how much power they could collectively wield—if they could extend their cautious joint forays into a more robust alliance.

Hank Brown and the New Texas AFL-CIO

While the presidential election of 1960 raised the profile of African American and Mexican American civil rights and political activists in Texas, it had unforeseen consequences for the state's labor movement. Kennedy and Johnson wasted little time after the election in selecting the president of the Texas AFL-CIO, Jerry Holleman, to serve as one of the three assistant secretaries of the U.S. Department of Labor. Holleman, who left Texas to go to Washington in early January 1961, would work on national labor policy and oversee the President's Committee on Equal Employment Opportunity. Speculation abounded that the patronage placement resulted from labor's support for LBJ in the nomination process. Whatever its cause, Holleman's departure left a vacancy in Texas, and into the void jumped the plumber from San Antonio, H. S. "Hank" Brown.[1]

Brown brought a vast knowledge of the state's labor movement, his own experiences in the Bexar County Democratic Coalition, and a militant brand of trade unionism to the presidency of the Texas State AFL-CIO. He had served for six years as the state federation's education director, had led and won the longest strike in the history of the San Antonio's building trade unions, and had been elected executive secretary of the statewide Building and Construction Trades Council. He had also allied himself with the growing, predominately Mexican American industrial union movement in San Antonio and had joined with Peña and Sutton in a powerful, multiracial electoral coalition.[2]

Brown thus had impeccable credentials in labor circles as well as the unusual practical experience of having participated in multiracial political partnerships. The former fact got him elected president; the latter provided his vision, bringing San Antonio–style labor, civil rights, and electoral strategies to bear in state politics. The transformation was not immediate, but by the time he was through with it, Brown would transform the Texas AFL-CIO into a civil rights organization and the driving force behind a rising statewide multiracial alliance.

To be sure, the Texas AFL-CIO had already begun to embrace the growing black and brown civil rights movements, beginning with the passage of a compromise civil rights resolution at its founding convention in 1957. Even earlier, the old Texas State Federation of Labor (TSFL) under Holleman's leadership had hired a part-time advisor on "Latin-American Affairs," a resident of the Rio Grande Valley whose primary responsibility was to maintain a relationship with the official Mexican labor movement, the Confederación de Trabajadores Mexicanos (CTM). Yet the advisor, Andrew C. McLellan, was also active in Mexican American political and civil rights circles in South Texas, so his job for the TSFL included doing "anything we could to assist our own [Texas] citizens of Latin-American descent." McLellan developed a close friendship and rapport with Holleman, sending the state president regular reports on his activities. In 1953, McLellan and American G.I. Forum (AGIF) leader Ed Idar coauthored the report "What Price Wetbacks?," a detailed study of the use of undocumented Mexican workers and the negative effects it had on U.S. citizens of Mexican descent as well as the Texas economy. In 1954, in addition to supporting the roundup of undocumented workers in "Operation Wetback," McLellan, Idar, and other Mexican American activists used labor money to organize around the gubernatorial candidacy of Ralph Yarborough. A year later, in 1955, both the TSFL and the Texas State CIO Council sponsored the Mexican American activists' efforts to organize a training conference for other liberal, labor, and civil rights–oriented Democrats across the Rio Grande Valley.[3]

In short, the state labor movement, based in Austin and led by white union activists, worked through McLellan, a Mexican American with an Anglo name, to develop ties to *mexicano* political clubs and civil rights groups in South Texas that included the G.I. Forum and local chapters of the League of United Latin American Citizens (LULAC). McLellan's work gave the labor movement credibility among Mexican American activists and laid the foundation for future collaboration in the region. More important, he also contributed to the causes of the civil rights activists: fighting the "wetback problem" and the continuation of the bracero program as well as organizing for better political representation. (The bracero program brought Mexican nationals to work in the United States during the emergency labor shortage created by World War II, but agricultural and railroad interests had succeeded in having it extended for nearly two decades into the postwar period.) These had long been the G.I. Forum's top priorities, and McLellan brought the activists both outside interest and much-needed financial resources from organized labor. McLellan left the position in 1955 to work for ORIT, the Organización Regional Interamericana de Trabajadores (Inter-American Regional Workers' Organization), the following year.[4]

Prior to the 1957 merger convention of the Texas AFL-CIO, Holleman and other officers worked to revive the temporary Latin American Affairs convention committee and began making new contacts in the Valley to replace McLellan. Robert P. "Bob" Sanchez, a G.I. Forum officer who would soon become law partners with Ed Idar in McAllen, ended up being their main contact. In January 1957, Sanchez worked with the state federation in developing a Spanish-language pamphlet for use in that year's poll tax drive, gathering statements from a wide range of "eminent" Mexican American civil rights activists. George I. Sánchez (no relation), an outspoken education professor and New Deal activist at the University of Texas, urged readers, "For your children's children, for your town, for your country—pay your poll tax." The pamphlet concluded, "*Sea ciudadano de primera categoria*—Be a first class citizen."[5] In contrast, Dr. Hector P. Garcia of Corpus Christi, the president of the G.I. Forum, refused to contribute a quotation for fear that his name would be associated with organized labor. Through Bob Sanchez, the Texas State AFL-CIO assured him that the pamphlet would not have the name of state federation, the Forum, or any other organization. Garcia still declined, though he did request copies of the pamphlet for distribution. Despite its efforts, labor remained toxic in South Texas in 1957, though some common ground could be found when it came to politics.[6]

For the next several years, with Bob Sanchez serving as its liaison, the state federation gradually gained a more complete understanding of the struggles of ordinary *mexicanos* in South Texas. At labor's merger convention in 1957, the Latin American Affairs Convention Committee adopted a set of resolutions that focused on the U.S.-Mexico border and relations between the two countries' national and state labor movements. It recommended that "every effort should be made to organize groups on both sides of the border for . . . mutual benefits," and then it added a single paragraph on improving the livelihood of "tax-paying United States citizens" in the Lower Rio Grande Valley who were forced to work as migrant farm laborers due to job competition from "alien workers."[7]

But the next year, Sanchez, who began sending monthly reports to the state AFL-CIO officers in January 1958, pushed the committee and the state leadership toward an increased focus on the issues facing Mexican Americans within Texas.[8] Jack Martin of San Antonio chaired the convention committee, which briefly reiterated the need for binational labor cooperation before focusing most of its report on domestic issues. "It was noted that the influx of braceros forces resident workers to migrate away from their homes . . . depressing their entire economic standard" and causing "social and economic chaos" in both the United States and in Mexico. "The committee feels, therefore, that [by] continuing the program we are doing no service to our brothers in Mexico." It finally called on the state federation to "do everything within its power to bring about the abolition of the bracero program." The committee also brought up — for the first time — ongoing issues of discrimination against "Americans of Latin American descent" by scattered local unions. It did not identify discrimination within labor as a systemic problem, since the situation varied depending on geography.[9] Finally, the committee brought up another longtime grievance of Mexican American activists in the region: the issue of cross-border "commuters." Unlike braceros, who worked on temporary visas while living in the United States, these Mexican workers obtained permanent visas to work in Texas but did so while continuing to live across the Rio Grande in Mexico. They commuted back and forth across the border daily, working for wages that were considered substandard in Texas while benefiting from the lower cost of living in Mexico. Sanchez and the committee argued that the practice lowered wages and caused unemployment among U.S. citizens, including Mexican Americans.[10]

Bob Sanchez played a critical role in the Latin American Affairs Committee's transition from international to local affairs. After the 1958 convention, he wrote to President Holleman with his opinion of the proceedings. He noted that he and other committee members had needed to fight hard through a long, fiery debate in order to pass the resolution to abolish the bracero program. Sanchez also reported that the committee had discussed the "border commuter problem." He closed with a long, passionate plea for an increased focus on the problems of Mexicans Americans in the United States. "We don't have to reach down to Latin America to find constructive issues to solve regarding Latin American problems; we have them right here in Texas," he wrote. "Work should be done . . . to sell the political philosophy of organized labor to the Latin people of the state." He called on Holleman to print and distribute more Spanish-language literature on unions and in organizing campaigns. "And by all means," he added, "organized labor should put more emphasis on poll tax programs affecting Latins in the state."[11]

Sanchez's opinion became the policy of the state labor movement. The next year, the Latin American Affairs convention committee reaffirmed the previous resolutions and added the need to fight for improved working conditions and wages for agricultural laborers in the state. It called for a new minimum wage law for farm workers and the extension of "all the benefits guaranteed to the bracero" to "domestic migrant workers." The committee also recommended a new drive to organize unorganized workers, especially along the Texas-Mexico border. Finally, it demanded a congressional investigation into the "alien labor commuters."[12] Sanchez praised Holleman for his support of the committee and its Mexican American leadership. "I have often argued in various circles that there are no better experts on Latin American Affairs than we damn Mexicans," he exclaimed. He added that he was pleased to see more *mexicanos* at the convention than ever before, a fact that would prove significant because "the Latin population of the State is growing by leaps and bounds, [and] it is important to see that this segment of the population is instructed in the cause of labor and in overall democratic phylosophy [*sic*]."[13]

Organized labor and the Mexican American civil rights struggle were becoming more and more intertwined. The bracero, commuter, and agricultural labor "problems" were longstanding grievances of Mexican American civil rights activists that simultaneously undercut labor's efforts to organize unions in the region. This common ground brought the two very separate struggles together, as did their mutual need for one another in the arena of electoral politics.

It was not always an easy relationship. In fact, Sanchez at times struggled to make ends meet while carrying out labor's program in the Valley. In early 1960, Sanchez billed the state federation for his services, asking for "lawyer rates" of $50 per day. Holleman countered that he was not hiring a lawyer and could only afford to pay "worker rates." Labor does not need an attorney, Holleman wrote. "It does require a person whose heart and sympathies are with the Latin people . . . [and] who is effective . . . in the Latin community." Holleman acknowledged that being aligned with labor could cost Sanchez in terms of customers at his law practice and in terms of prestige in the community. But the job did not call for "a person who feels any compulsion for respectability." Rather, Holleman added, "It must always be remembered that anyone [who] succeeds in improving the social, economic, and political lot of the Latin community . . . *will automatically become controversial.*" As for the financial implications of their arrangement, "There is inevitably a period of struggle." Just as workers who go on strike face reprisals and economic hardships, so too do community organizers and political activists experience personal and professional difficulties. "You are going through your most difficult period," Holleman told Sanchez in April 1960, because "You are so near success, politically, that you are at your most controversial period." Sanchez could choose to retreat amidst the turmoil, Holleman added, or he could "give that extra surge or push that is needed to elect your friends and thereby become more respectable."[14]

Sanchez decided to stick it out, and the result was an unprecedented victory for the Latin-labor coalition in South Texas in the Viva Kennedy campaign of 1960. Having already sold poll taxes in all the barrios along the border, Sanchez joined his law partner and fellow Forum leader Ed Idar in founding and directing the massive Viva Kennedy club in Hidalgo County. The duo directed countless meetings and returned to the area's poor neighborhoods to turn out unlikely *mexicano* voters. Organized labor provided much-needed funding for their get-out-the-vote effort, which succeeded in carrying the Valley for Kennedy and Johnson. Their efforts were triumphant even in nearby Willacy County, a more rural area that the Democrats carried despite "plenty of gloom." Sanchez reported that the victory was "a complete restoration of faith and undoubtedly we can keep going forward."[15]

Though inspiring, the national victory did not immediately translate into significant gains at the local level. South Texas remained a bastion of low-wage, unorganized labor heavily controlled by a handful of economic elites and political bosses. Yet with Bob Sanchez's help, organized labor had made significant progress toward establishing ties with Mexican American civil rights and political activists in the Valley, and Kennedy's victory brought considerable hope to veteran organizers in the struggle. The "extra surge" was still forthcoming, but labor and Latins alike gained some psychological reinforcement that their strategy was working. Sanchez would continue to advise labor's Latin American Affairs Committee for years to come.

While labor began to commit itself to the domestic affairs of the state's *mexicanos*, it also made headway in relation to liberal politics and black civil rights. At the state Democratic convention in 1960, labor leaders asserted their independence from the broader "liberal movement" by scuttling the walkout and supporting LBJ. That same year, delegates to the Texas AFL-CIO convention passed the body's strongest ever set of resolutions in support of civil rights, including measures that explicitly supported the sit-ins, fair employment, welfare spending, and a minimum wage for agricultural workers.[16]

The pace of change within the Texas State AFL-CIO further accelerated with Hank Brown's arrival at its helm. After Holleman went to Washington, the body's executive board appointed Brown to the federation's presidency on an interim basis. He soon discovered that he could not work with his second-in-command, Secretary-Treasurer Fred Schmidt. Once Brown took office,

Schmidt, an oil worker, commenced his own campaign for the presidency, organizing resentful members of the old CIO industrial unions and forming a splinter caucus to air their grievances. The oil and telephone workers rallied other unions behind Schmidt, but Brown found strong support among steel- and autoworkers. With solid support from the craft unions, Brown survived Schmidt's challenge and won what newspapers called "labor's civil war" by a 2-to-1 margin at the federation's convention in Galveston in late July 1961. Brown was reelected to a full term, and Roy R. Evans, a leader of the United Auto Workers' massive aircraft Local 893 in Grand Prairie (near Dallas), became the body's secretary-treasurer.[17]

Brown won by stressing the need for "rallying the troops to the battles of picket-lines and elections." He wanted to "aggressively" expand the membership of organized labor through conventional unionization campaigns and to win in the political arena by bringing the San Antonio coalition model to statewide races.[18] Drawing on his South Texas origins, Brown aimed to reverse the perception of organized labor in that area's local affairs. Not only did he not seek "respectability," as his predecessor had cautioned against, but rather he believed that union organizers should be "looked upon as downright dangerous if not subversive." The area that needed this most was the Rio Grande Valley, Brown believed. There, as the *Observer* paraphrased his sentiments, "workers suspected of having union sympathies 'unaccountably' discover one day that a sudden economy move at the cannery has lopped off their jobs, that no other employer in the region needs them, that their landlords absolutely have to have their home back, and that their credit is no longer good at the stores where they have been shopping for years." Most of these workers, Brown knew, were Mexican Americans, and they absolutely had to be organized for labor to succeed at a statewide level. He also "relishe[d]" the idea of organizing the region's farm workers, but upon taking office "admitt[ed] it is a long way off."[19] By winning "labor's civil war," Hank Brown brought a radical vision of new organizing and multiracial coalition politics to the state federation and, by extension, to Texas state politics. He built upon the groundwork laid by Bob Sanchez and others over the previous several years and would soon find another willing collaborator in a new statewide organization led by his friend from back home, Albert Peña.

"Only the Mexicanos Can Speak for the Mexicanos"

At the same time that Hank Brown was reforming the Texas AFL-CIO, Mexican American activists came together with another, more inward-looking purpose: to transform their newfound sense of unity and electoral success into a permanent political force. On November 26, 1960, less than three weeks after the presidential election, members of the "Viva Kennedy-Johnson Clubs" from across the state came together in San Antonio to discuss their plans for the future. Peña chaired the meeting, opening with his assessment of their improved status. "We have achieved one great goal . . . 'RECOGNITION,'" he announced at the outset. Now, Mexican Americans could reasonably expect patronage appointments in the new administration. In his speech to the group, Henry B. Gonzalez offered a similar assessment and urged those in attendance to begin collecting poll taxes for 1961. Educator and activist George I. Sánchez addressed the gathering and succinctly laid out its mission: "We have long been represented by people that truly know very little of our people," he said. "We want to be represented by one of our many qualified people." The group formed three committees: one to craft a "Statement of Particulars" (chaired by Sánchez), one to focus on selling poll taxes, and a third to formalize the organization. Those in attendance drafted a telegram to send to the president-elect and designated a delegation to attend the inauguration in Washington in January.[20]

As the members paused to celebrate Kennedy's taking office, Sánchez began drafting the new organization's mission statement. The product of his labors, "The American of Mexican Descent: A Statement of Principle," became the defining credo of Mexican American political activists in Texas in the 1960s. While "recognition" and upward mobility remained significant, most of the agenda Sánchez developed centered on labor issues and uplifting the poor. The statement, signed only by the "Viva Kennedy Texas Organization," noted that Mexican Americans were "the forgotten people," barely noticed by policy makers and "almost completely and systematically excluded" from public service in Austin and Washington. For several pages, Sánchez laid out the oppressed status of his group, detailing their poverty, lack of access to education, and substandard employment. He noted that they were often undercut by "commuters," "wetbacks," and "braceros." Yet no Myrdal Report, government commissions, or even works of fiction brought their plight into public debate— they were simply forgotten. The statement concluded with nine principles "for a brighter tomorrow." The federal government should improve education, guarantee basic health and welfare needs, and better regulate the border with Mexico, he wrote. Most important, Mexican Americans should be utilized to fix the wide range of problems, Sánchez pleaded, asking that the government take advantage of the talents of the few *Mexicanos* who had gotten ahead in order to help the poor masses.

Finally, Sánchez turned his focus inward, expanding his views on the need for better, more accountable leadership. The "Mexican-American of the Southwest" has had spokesmen who have not been good advocates, he wrote, men who were poorly qualified to make far-reaching judgments on his needs. These included "non-Latin officials whom he helped to elect and some of his own people who are, at best, only incidentally concerned over the crises faced by his fellows." Current local and state officials had failed to connect with the common man, he wrote, including the handful of Mexican Americans who had improved their own status while neglecting their people. Well-intentioned liberals of all races had also failed the Mexican American, mostly because they made decisions that affect *mexicanos* without going to the grassroots for advice. The solution, the statement of principles concluded, was self-determination: "It is our purpose here . . . to underline the fact that only the *mexicanos* can speak for the *mexicanos*—and that it would be well to assess very carefully the claims of any individual, *mexicano* or otherwise, who would speak for us." The objectives were thus the eradication of poverty and discrimination and the fostering of economic opportunity; autonomous, democratic organizing for independent political representation represented the means.[21]

In early February 1961, the group of Viva Kennedy leaders from around Texas assembled again in Victoria, on the gulf southwest of Houston, where they formally founded their new organization. Peña again chaired the gathering, which he said he hoped would result in the "historic" formation of a "strictly political organization among Mexican-American people." It was born out of a "practical political necessity . . . because the only thing politicians respect is votes." By organizing, Peña added, *mexicanos* could "make their voice heard and their vote counted." It was now time to expand on the foundation provided by LULAC and the G.I. Forum and focus squarely on the quest for independent representation and real political power.

The activists debated and passed a constitution and by-laws, christening their group the Mexican-American Political Association (MAPA). Garcia of the AGIF declined to serve as the state leader because he wanted to focus on building MAPA at the national level. Peña was then nominated and elected by acclamation, making the San Antonio barrio leader *the* statewide spokesman for *mexicanos* in the political sphere. Bob Sanchez, the advisor to the Texas AFL-CIO, was elected regional vice-chairman for South Texas. Ed Idar Jr., Sanchez's law partner and a longtime G.I. Forum staffer, became the group's acting secretary, while a representative from Houston's Civic Action Committee was named regional vice-chairman for East Texas.[22]

Several labor activists joined Bob Sanchez in launching MAPA, and labor issues were never far removed from the activists' discussion of electoral organizing. In fact, the meeting of the new, ostensibly "strictly political" organization concluded with a presentation by Garcia and Idar on the "commuter problem along the Mexican border." Idar presented a resolution on the issue that had recently been approved by the Laredo branch of the G.I. Forum. It was moved and unanimously approved that MAPA prepare a similar resolution and send it out to all interested parties. Although the presence of trade unions would be the source of controversy in the organization in later years, the concerns surrounding labor issues and the *mexicano* working class were present from the start.[23]

A new political force was thus founded in Texas, bringing together diverse civil rights, political, and labor activists under the fiery leadership of Albert Peña. In early May it changed its name to the Political Association of Spanish-Speaking Organizations (PASO), following the lead of a national meeting organized by Garcia.[24] By any name, the new organization's creation itself represented a declaration of independence by Mexican American political activists in Texas, a polyglot group who pledged to use the vote to uplift their *raza* (race or people). Along with its counterparts in California and across the Southwest, PASO would become the bedrock of what pundits in the present-day call the "Latino vote." In the short term, however, it remained unclear how the new voice of the state's *mexicanos* would make itself heard.

Gonzalez v. Maverick and the Special Senate Election

The incipient organization would face its first test even before its founding was complete. In early December 1960, Henry B. Gonzalez, who had just been reelected to the state senate, announced his candidacy for LBJ's vacated seat in the U.S. Senate. The race was already shaping up to be a dandy. Governor Daniel had appointed as interim senator Democrat William Blakley, a former Shivercrat archconservative from Dallas who had held the post briefly in 1957 and now wished to occupy it full time. In 1957 Blakley didn't want the job, and a single round of balloting among all candidates allowed the populist Ralph Yarborough to become a U.S. senator with just a plurality of the vote. In response, conservatives in the legislature added a runoff round to the procedure for special elections. In order to pave the way for Johnson's run in 1960, legislative leaders changed the state law again, this time to allow LBJ to appear on the ballot as a candidate for both the presidency and the Senate. The law still applied in November when he appeared as his party's nominee for both vice president and senator but did not campaign actively for the latter job. Johnson's election opened up his Senate seat, and now Blakley, as interim senator, had a head start going into the two rounds of special election balloting that would take place in early 1961.

The state's political observers salivated at the wide-open field. Gonzalez's entry into the race raised the question of how high the Kennedy tide would crest, but within a few weeks Maury Maverick Jr. also threw his hat in the ring, adding a second bona fide liberal to the crowded field. The two San Antonio legislators and frequent allies each called on the other to withdraw from the race, but neither did so. On the right, in addition to Blakley, stood John Tower, a Republican from Wichita Falls who had run against Johnson in absentia the previous November and received 40 percent of the vote. His high total was at least partially a fluke caused by Johnson's dual positions on the ballot, and, in any event, it seemed unlikely that any Republican could defeat a Democrat in the runoff. In the center were two well-financed moderates, U.S. congressman Jim Wright of Fort Worth, who enjoyed the support of that city's labor movement as well as the backing of the state's business establishment, and Attorney General Will Wilson, a career politician who was preparing to run for governor and was considered a "moderate" on race. Ultimately, twenty-two candidates filed for the position.[25]

The special election threatened to split asunder the tentative coalition that had been formed in the conventions and campaigns of the previous year. Throughout the winter of 1960–61, labor and DOT leaders, including Albert Peña, Hank Brown, Mrs. Randolph, and Chris Dixie of Houston, tried to bring together diverse activists from across the state to coordinate first a poll tax drive and then to seek common ground on a candidate in the special Senate election. On February 8, 1961, they met together in Austin for the first time as the "Democratic Coalition," but the otherwise momentous gathering was marred by the fact that they failed to reach agreement on the current campaign.[26] The Texas MAPA, *SNAP News*, and most Mexican American and African American organizations across the state all rushed to endorse Gonzalez. Three days after the Democratic Coalition meeting collapsed, labor's Committee on Political Education (COPE) endorsed Maverick in a vote that Gonzalez called "rigged." Although the DOT was no longer organized enough to hold a formal endorsement meeting, most white "independent" liberals fell into line behind Maverick, who had long been associated with the "liberal movement."[27]

The coalition thus split along racial lines, with predictable results. Although he was disappointed that his white friends had again slighted him, Gonzalez barnstormed the state in his station wagon and again built a vibrant campaign on a shoestring budget. He was "impatient with the delay in leveling out the racial upheaval[s]" in Texas and antsy about his position in state politics, according to one report. Now was the time for change. Logging forty-five thousand miles in the month of March, and spending less than $15,000—a tenth of his most well-financed opponent—Gonzalez again held court with local Viva Kennedy groups and countless Mexican American and African American political and social clubs. While the state senator claimed that he "made no special appeal to Negroes" and that they didn't "owe [him] anything special," he remained a favorite of black activists thanks to his 1957 filibuster against segregationist legislation and his ongoing, unflinching support for integration. In Beaumont, one report noted, Gonzalez cancelled a reservation for a hotel banquet hall because the establishment would not assure him that his black supporters would be admitted. At each tour stop he also appeared alongside African American candidates, including G. J. Sutton, who was running for a seat on the San Antonio City Council.[28] Although most black groups supported Gonzalez, in some cases African Americans adopted a strategy in which they endorsed one of the centrists that they believed had a realistic chance of winning the race. The Harris County Council of Organizations (HCCO), for example, made no endorsement after its members split their votes between Attorney General Wilson, a racial "moderate," and the ultraliberal Gonzalez. The lack of a two-thirds majority by either candidate "killed endorsement," Mrs. Erma LeRoy reported from inside the meeting, leaving the member organizations of the council "free to endorse anyone they choose." (Evidence of the statewide Texas Council of Voters' (TCV) position on the race remains elusive, suggesting that it also refrained from endorsing either candidate.)[29]

While Gonzalez campaigned on pocket change, Maverick's effort drew upon the vast resources of labor and the old DOT's "independent" liberals to send countless workers into the field. White union members flocked to his campaign events, while brass-collar Democrats at the country crossroads turned out rural audiences and sent him large donation checks. Among African Americans, Mrs. LeRoy again hit the road on labor's dime, this time to campaign for Maverick. Her decision to do so was pragmatic: after the HCCO failed to back Gonzalez, she considered Maverick "the most electable liberal" and argued that casting a ballot for anyone else amounted to "a vote for a conservative, who will vote against everything Kennedy is advocating." Still, disagreement among black voters in Houston and Dallas was so great that she decided it would be wasteful to spend money turning out the vote in those big urban areas. Instead, LeRoy traveled to sixteen different small- and medium-sized towns in three weeks, returning to many of the same rural locales and chatting with the same "individuals, labor groups, ministerial unions, heads of federated clubs, civic groups," and "key workers" with whom she had visited the previous year. At many stops along the way, "it was apparent that people were waiting for someone whom they had confidence in to steer them in the right direction . . . before making a decision, or a commitment," she wrote. Most of the people she encountered wanted to support Gonzalez, and a Wilson representative had also preceded her at many stops. "I joined in mutual admiration" of Gonzalez, she wrote. Yet when her audiences "came around to seeing his chances in the run-off are practically nil, they joined in support of Maverick."[30]

The election campaign resembled a train wreck in slow motion—all observers knew disaster was coming, but they could not stop it nor tear away their gazes. While grassroots organizers chose their sides and hit the campaign trail, activists on all sides understood that the zero-sum election endangered the larger effort to build a multiracial coalition. Days after the COPE endorsement meeting, state federation president Hank Brown wrote to consultant Bob Sanchez that he was aware that "Labor's action in support of Maury Maverick, Jr. for the U.S. Senate has of course caused us great consternation" among the other coalition partners. "We realize that we have in some places and in some regard caused us a setback in our relationship with the Latin American and the Negro groups in Texas," he added. Brown praised Gonzalez effusively but added that there were "many considerations in such a situation." Sanchez replied that he understood that Maverick had long been a close friend to labor and might even be more electable than Gonzalez in the runoff. He added that he had a "rather heated argument with Henry himself on this very question." But for the newly emboldened Mexican American activists no nuance was needed. Sanchez wrote: "Latin leaders like myself, with Henry in the race, have nowhere else to go but with Henry unless we want to commit political suicide and be ineffective in politics for years to come." *Mexicanos* were no longer willing to defer to Anglo leadership. The question was what the "Latins" would do in the runoff, Sanchez noted. At that point, he concluded, "your task and mine is to see that the old coalition in this State of labor, Negroes, and Latins is once again together so that we may swing it." Brown agreed and suggested that the duo should gather a diverse group soon after the early April election to "discuss the feasibility of a joint cooperative effort in the run-off."[31]

In the end, neither Gonzalez nor Maverick advanced to the runoff. Brown had hoped that labor's Maverick would make it to the next round, or at least that a moderate such as Wilson or Congressman Wright might continue forward. Instead, Republican darling John Tower led the field, with 31 percent of the vote, followed by the conservative Democratic incumbent William Blakley, with 18 percent. Each had laid claim to "true conservatism." The two moderates finished third and fourth but still would have finished behind Tower had their totals been combined. The sum of votes for the two liberals, who finished fifth and sixth, would have exceeded Blakley's tally by a percentage point. Maverick narrowly defeated Gonzalez, but the *Observer* noted that the more important takeaway was that "the solid liberal vote in Texas is not sturdy enough to support two candidates."[32]

If only there had been one liberal instead. As the Senate seat slipped away, black, brown, and white activists were all forced to regroup. Mrs. Randolph of the DOT advised her friends and fellow activists to simply "go fishing" on the day of the runoff in early June. Upset about the Gonzalez defeat and the slow pace of patronage coming from Washington, PASO refused to endorse Blakley. "In order to prove our worth and our 'guts,'" national organizer Hector P. Garcia wrote after the election, "the Texas 'PASO' organization decided that they would not help 'Democratic' Senator William Blakley. We had to prove to the Democratic machinery that they could not win without our work and help." Black activists surrounding *SNAP News* in San Antonio likewise blasted Blakley as a continuation of the Shivers-Daniel segregationist wing of the party, noting that he had led the interrogation of Robert Weaver, a high-level African American Kennedy appointee. The paper urged readers to vote for a "thinking man's candidate . . . John Tower." In Houston, the HCCO endorsed Blakley, but it did so only after President Kennedy reluctantly did the same.[33]

Tower carried the state by ten thousand votes, becoming the first Republican senator in Texas history and the first from his party in the South since Reconstruction. Liberal and moderate Democrats had indeed stayed home as Blakley gained only half of the almost half million combined votes cast for Wright, Wilson, Maverick, and Gonzalez in the first round. Black voters all but abandoned the election: in eighteen heavily black precincts in Dallas with over nineteen thousand poll tax holders, less than three thousand voted in the runoff. Garcia reported that Mexican Americans followed PASO's lead and withheld their support from Blakley, giving the organizing new "recognition and prestige."[34]

Yet withholding an endorsement with the result being the election of a conservative Republican hardly counted as a victory for many *mexicanos*, including the liberal Albert Peña. San Antonio's East Side activists could rejoice in having vanquished one bigoted Democrat, but doing so bolstered the strength of their longtime opponents in the local Good Government League. And the election was nothing less than disastrous for the Texas AFL-CIO, which watched as two legislators with perfect prolabor records cut into each other's vote totals in the first round and then sat out the main event. Independent white liberals returned from their fishing trips and looked for a new way forward. Brown and Peña would soon offer a promising path.

The Coalition Takes Shape

On July 7, 1961, within a month of Tower's victory, a diverse group of "some 75 people from over the State of Texas" assembled in Austin in the ballroom of a downtown hotel. Many of the attendees were veteran white activists from labor or the old DOT clubs, though Albert Peña, Erma LeRoy, and other black and brown organizers joined them. They discussed the recent "political developments that brought us to our present position," and Peña and Maury Maverick Jr. opened the meeting with remarks of "good will . . . concerning the recent senatorial campaign." Everyone there knew it had been a disaster. Looking ahead to the elections of 1962, they assembled again as the Democratic Coalition. Hoping to avoid a repeat of their collective failure in the special Senate election, they sought to reach agreement on which liberal candidates would enter the various statewide and congressional races in the coming year. But as their conversations continued throughout the summer and fall of 1961, other goals and questions popped up. Who would lead the new Democratic Coalition? How would it relate to other liberal forces in the state, to the Kennedy administration, or to African American and Mexican American organizations? Could they really reach a consensus on which candidates to field and endorse? How else might they advance toward their respective objectives? For the next several months, the leaders of the state's embattled multiracial alliance would convene in regular sessions to hammer out the details of their partnership. Their process would reveal both the necessity of their coming together and the many pitfalls that constantly tore them apart.

Having mended fences after the strident Senate campaign, the participants in the revived coalition began their July gathering by floating a wide range of ideas for how to best combine their resources and avoid splitting their votes in future campaigns. Don Ellinger of the AFL-CIO's COPE department suggested that they create a formal coalition, which "would consist of people who would meet together because they were recognized by the other people as possessing judgment and political influence within different segments of the political community called Texas, meeting for the limited objective of trying to reach substantially unanimous agreement on limited political targets." Another activist proposed a "Forum" that would foster discussion among diverse liberals but would not participate in lobbying or political action. Finally, a leader of the DOT argued that the liberal caucus should take the lead and that the group should focus on taking over the formal Democratic Party apparatus. The delegates agreed that each of the three concepts could serve as a "rallying point around which all liberals could coalesce," but they didn't immediately decide on any one route. Yet when Brown, Peña, and Houston attorney and Harris County Democrats leader Chris Dixie all cast their lots with the coalition approach, a loose version of it quickly became the dominant statewide organization among Texas liberals of all colors. The old DOT survived, but it had been replaced in effect by the new coalition.[35]

Still, the new body remained diffuse and ill defined. It lacked a constitution and bylaws and did not aspire to create them. Modeled on the Bexar County Democratic Coalition, the statewide body included representatives from all constituent groups and featured a chairmanship that rotated between meetings. Brown, Peña, and Dixie did most of the work behind the scenes, while fifteen veteran activists set the agenda for the statewide body and sent out calls for larger mass meetings. Peña served as chair of the steering committee, which also included labor leaders Brown and Ellinger, white liberals Maverick and Mrs. Randolph, and TCV leaders Moses and Erma LeRoy as well as Dr. Marion J. Brooks. The attendees of the larger gatherings clashed time and again over whether the coalition needed governing rules and what those regulations might look like, but in the end three loose principles emerged in lieu of a formal structure. Dixie suggested that the coalition's "'direction and objectives' should include the right of any participating group to disagree, that [the] coalition should be 'open ended' so that any group with similar objectives might take part, and that specific objectives include the impending elections and poll tax campaign." Hank Brown summarized the group's stable structurelessness in similar fashion following a gathering of 150 to 200 coalition members in September. He told a reporter, "The main purpose of this meeting was to try to find ways to get the thinking of these various groups going down the road together," Brown said. "I believe it was the consensus that the groups should retain their own identity in their respective areas but should come together whenever they consider it important enough to reach agreement on objectives. There was discussion but no agreement on the various forms of organization this could take."[36] Perhaps a little skeptical of this approach, the *Observer* added that the coalition sought a "*modus vivendi* . . . between a tightly-organized DOT-type organization and complete, though cordial, anarchy."[37]

A series of coalition meetings revealed that the need for a renewed poll tax campaign represented one area of clear agreement among all its constituents. Although voter registration might seem routine, the coalition's plan for a new drive represented an ambitious, even revolutionary proposal. The program called for a broad-based, statewide registration drive for 1962—a "full-scale, as never before" seen "sweeping" effort to recruit "unprecedented numbers" of liberal Democrats, as the *Observer* put it.[38] The coalition planned to hire a multiracial group of coordinators for the ambitious campaign, including at least one "Negro" and at least one "Latin-American" for three months each. The drive also called for a project that would target the wives of male union members "who often do not vote" and another drive that would focus on registering federal employees who until recently had been rendered inert by the McCarthy-era Hatch Act prohibitions on their political activities. The coalition set a hefty budget of $8,750 for these areas of special emphasis and appointed Dixie to lead the alliance's fund-raising efforts. Labor added its "regular county level" poll tax campaign that would include in-plant organizing drives and tabling at shopping centers "in friendly areas." Local liberal-labor coalitions were tasked with creating "Full Citizenship Committees" that would hire full-time coordinators, one for each of the largest twenty-two counties. Each group within the alliance would be responsible for recruiting one deputy registrar per one hundred members. Spanning the entire state, from El Paso to the Valley to the Panhandle, and from country crossroads to the barrios and ghettos and union halls of the big cities, the plan sought to transform the state by drastically expanding the franchise. No voter-registration drive on this scale had ever been attempted. In a word, it promised democracy.[39]

Journalists speculated about the viability of both the poll tax campaign and the coalition itself, even as they lacked a clear idea of what was happening inside the group's meetings. The leaders of the multiracial group's gatherings had barred reporters, and many coalition participants had given only surface answers in response to the reporters' persistent questioning. More important, the media's framing of the alliance remained clouded by the ongoing salience of white supremacy in Jim Crow Texas: contemporary journalists worked with the unconscious assumption that whites would take the lead in any political alliance and that nonwhites would remain in subordinate positions. One report in the *Houston Chronicle* detailed the plans of the "liberal Democrats" assembling in Austin without so much as mentioning the presence of African Americans or Mexican Americans. Other articles praised the coalition and noted the fundamental roles played by Hank Brown and Chris Dixie in organizing it, but their authors neglected the contributions of Albert Peña or Moses and Erma LeRoy. Even the reporters who appreciated the novelty of the partnership's diversity often lacked understanding of the origins of black and brown political formations. Although they reached positive conclusions about the alliance's amorphous shape and future plans, they overlooked the connections between politics and civil rights and instead cast African Americans and Mexican Americans as mere "liberals" of color with no separate agendas or special circumstances. In other words, they were seen as not speaking for themselves but rather as mere clients of their white labor and liberal patrons.[40]

In contrast, the most prescient reporting on the alliance came in an *Observer* editorial that argued that the meetings were notable in their own right. Editor Willie Morris held that one could not understate "the necessity of the *coalition* itself—a complex of groupings that includes the Latins and labor, the Negroes and independent liberals, and the Democrat brasscollars at the forks and beside the creeks." The amalgamation of these diverse groups meant that "Texas liberalism stands a superb chance of coming into its own statewide in '62," Morris added, if the activists could solve the "crucial questions" that threatened to divide them. Taking seriously the divergent needs of the different constituencies, the editor concluded that "Only through a mutual respect and an understanding of one another's occasionally differing ambitions and hopes can Texas liberalism . . . bring squarely into the active political arena those values we hold in common."[41] The issue was not whether a mostly unitary group of liberals could agree, he suggested. It was whether the races, each with a different agenda, could do so.

In fact, as the coalition leadership—if not all of its participants—knew, race was *the* question that the alliance needed to address if it wanted to move forward. Of course, other internal divisions also threatened to tear apart the group: the liberals' distrust for organized labor after the botched 1960 walkout remained so great that Hank Brown's welcome speech at an early meeting was removed from the gathering's official minutes. For the same reason, Dixie and Peña rather than Brown often introduced new ideas to the group and served as the coalition's principal spokesmen to the press.

Still, race was paramount. Despite Peña's prominent role in the coalition's mass meetings and his chairmanship of its steering committee, the group's leadership remained far from egalitarian. Coalition members had ignored COPE organizer Ellinger's urging that they create a formal structure in which African American and Mexican American activists would together comprise half the leadership. Instead, they decided to keep the coalition structureless, precluding such guarantees of representation and internal democracy. Black and brown activists comprised nearly half of the members of the group's first ad hoc governing body, but only LeRoy and Peña represented those constituencies on the all-important, eight-member Candidate Screening Committee. The rest were white liberals and labor leaders. It may have been a multiracial alliance, but the coalition was not yet representative of the people for whom it spoke.

Moreover, during the first several months of the coalition's existence, the priorities of its black and brown members often diverged from those of their white counterparts. While white activists in the former DOT and labor focused squarely on the upcoming elections, Peña's PASO and LeRoy's TCV were equally concerned with the status of patronage appointments in the new federal administration. When Senator Yarborough addressed a diverse meeting of the steering committee to discuss Kennedy's legislative program, the conversation digressed when black and brown leaders "expressed anxiety over the [lack of] Federal appointments" for their constituents. Eighteen months earlier, George I. Sánchez, in his founding statement for PASO had captured the desperate desire of many Mexican American professionals who wanted to lend their hands in helping the national government end poverty and discrimination. Now they felt as though they had been personally left out, their community's needs ignored. Similarly, black activists hailed the appointment of several African Americans to prominent positions in the new administration but maintained that some posts should also be distributed among their own ranks here in Texas. To be sure, some individual activists in both groups sought lucrative federal jobs solely for their own personal self-interests. Yet the salience of the patronage issue suggests that something more was at stake. Black and brown activists felt responsible for carrying the Democratic ticket to victory in Texas, and now they expected some of the spoils, not just for themselves but for their larger communities. They wanted liberalism to be more than a great idea: they wanted to play a part in implementing and expanding its promise as government officers.

Whatever their motivations, by the middle of 1961 they looked around and saw that they were not getting their pieces of the pie. They attributed their exclusion to race, but that was only one cause out of many. In fact, many white liberals also felt snubbed. With the exception of labor's Holleman, no members of the coalition's constituent groups had found their way to a patronage job in Washington or a federal post at home. White delegates joined the black and brown activists in lambasting the administration, and the group blamed Senator Johnson for blocking the many nominees whom they had put forward. They called on Yarborough to advocate much more fiercely for their cause, but many black and brown activists did not believe that the liberal senator would do so fairly. The strident conversation ended with a resolution to send a "representative group" of coalition leaders to personally present the issue to President Kennedy. For many activists, patronage had become a zero-sum game; for black and brown activists, it was also a test of the sincerity of the white liberals in both Texas and Washington.[42]

Race mattered in every small act of the coalition, in every conversation and every public and private statement. Yet, paradoxically, the demands of the black and brown civil rights movements remained on the back burner of the alliance.[43] The coalition's mission explicitly focused on political activities, and, for many white liberals, that meant that the group should steer clear of divisive social issues and instead focus solely on elections. Of course, for many African American and Mexican American activists, the battle for political power was part and parcel of their larger liberation struggles. The white view carried the day. Discussions of civil rights were completely absent from the group's official minutes throughout this period. Coalition spokesmen highlighted the fact that black and brown activists were part of the alliance, but they refrained from commenting on integration, equal employment opportunity, or the extreme poverty of the ghettos, barrios, or the poor rural areas of South and East Texas. Although the sit-ins had produced new alliances on the ground in San Antonio and Houston, the statewide coalition's evasion of the race issue reaffirmed the fact that state politics and congressional races remained the province of color-blind liberalism. The alliance claimed to speak and seek uplift for *all* the people, but it did not address the special needs of its most oppressed members.

Despite such public positioning, the hidden interior discussions of coalition members turned out to be much more candid. At the group's second mass meeting in September 1961, one labor staffer took handwritten notes that recorded a series of revealing exchanges, all of which were later omitted from the formal typed version of the body's official minutes. In an open discussion of the registration campaign a couple of hours into the gathering, Moses LeRoy raised his voice from the floor, becoming the first black speaker to address the polyglot group that day. He asked his colleagues how the coalition would sell poll taxes in the rural areas where African Americans had not been deputized by the local white authorities. The simple question addressed the topic at hand but profoundly challenged the color-blind logic of the campaign. It suggested that the coalition's goal of registering liberal voters could not be achieved without paying special attention to African American civil rights. The problem was unique to black Texans, but unlike school desegregation or employment discrimination, it fell squarely within the confines of the coalition's narrow focus on electoral politics. It was a clever intervention in a conversation that otherwise erased the black freedom struggle. Still, LeRoy's comment was ignored, and the conversation soon shifted to other subjects, including the never-ending debate about the many layers of liberal coalitions and forums and the old DOT.

A few moments later, G. J. Sutton again raised the issue of civil rights. He posed LeRoy's question again: What should the coalition do in places where we are not allowed to buy poll taxes? Doubtlessly indignant at having been ignored, and showcasing his trademark flamboyant style, Sutton reminded them of the contradiction plaguing the coalition's work. The alliance claimed that it wanted to sell poll taxes to "East Texas Negroes," but it was doing nothing to address the fact that black Texans were being denied their right to register to vote. LeRoy then jumped in again, recalling his experiences traveling with Erma in the 1959–60 poll tax drive when they found "constant fear in East Texas." Labor chief Brown replied that a "national committee"—probably the AFL-CIO's civil rights group—was calling upon the government to ensure the right to vote. Such a reassurance probably did little to assuage the black activists' concern, and it clearly did not solve the immediate problem. A Dallas attorney suggested that the coalition print "Buy Poll Tax Here" signs that could be displayed on houses to make it easier for people to find the deputies, and Mrs. LeRoy seconded his idea, indicating that it could help African Americans as well. In the end, the multifaceted proposed poll tax program passed with three amendments: that it would be accompanied by a long-term campaign for the tax's abolition, that the campaign would print the large placards as suggested, and, most importantly, that the coalition would conduct investigations when poll tax purchases were denied. J. E. Middleton of the Houston Hod Carriers Local 18 moved the adoption of the report as amended, and the coalition passed it, taking its first major unified action. The civil rights activists thus carved out some space for their demands in the larger coalition program, even if the group had ignored their special needs previously and then erased them from the official record after the fact.

A second exchange in the handwritten notes for that same afternoon is likewise revealing. After the group took a lunch break, the notes read, "Chairman Peña apologize[d] to Negro friends for segregated facilities and recommended use of other meeting place in the future." There was no discussion. Instead, Hank Brown began reciting the voting records of the various incumbents who would face reelection in 1962.[44] Still, the announcement must have carried great weight for the coalition's black members. LeRoy and Sutton had each spent the past year and a half battling for the integration of public spaces and the past two and a half decades fighting for political power, economic opportunity, and basic human dignity and respect. The use of a segregated hotel or restaurant at a coalition meeting that claimed to be inclusive would have represented more than a slap in the face. Sensing this, Peña made a public statement and took responsibility for the group's shortcoming. Still, it is no wonder that African American activists remained skeptical of the white liberals' professed good intentions. Even labor leader Brown, who had worked with Sutton in politics and with black unionists in union halls across Texas for years, simply did not notice that the coalition had planned the gathering in a segregated space. The unrecognized racial privilege of the white delegates could not have been displayed more clearly.

Yet Peña himself did not suffer exclusion from the luncheon, and no mention was made of Mexican Americans being refused service at the hotel. Rather, as this episode suggests, the positions of Mexican Americans and African Americans in the coalition remained distinct. Throughout Jim Crow Texas, *mexicanos* faced discrimination in all walks of life, but they remained legally classified as white. Class and status often determined whether individual *mexicanos* could access particular public spaces, as did phenotype or skin color. In much of South Texas, *mexicanos* comprised the majority of the population, and Mexican American professionals had little trouble navigating Anglo society (even if they remained excluded from its most elite circles). In Austin, as in faraway Dallas and East Texas, Mexican Americans wearing suits could expect access to the most exclusive all-white restaurants and hotels. Poor *mexicanos* were not so fortunate. Still, the fluidity of their situation as a group contrasted sharply with the absolute segregation that restricted virtually all of the state's African Americans, including well-dressed professionals like Sutton. State law mandated segregation in public facilities, schools, and many other situations, and local laws often added more constraints. A few light-skinned African Americans managed to pass in white society, but as soon as one drop of black blood was revealed in their ancestry, they would revert to being "Colored."[45]

Coalition members of all races were aware of this elaborate system of social control, and they understood the subtle differences between Jim Crow and Juan Crow. The divergent realities of segregation necessarily shaped their planning for the poll tax drive, which in turn gently steered the white delegates toward recognizing and subverting the customs of caste. The campaign proposal called for a "Special Program for Negro Texans" in which a full-time organizer would focus on rural counties in which African Americans represented more than 20 percent of the population. The staffer would be expected to create Full Citizenship Committees in each county and to deputize poll tax agents. The unstated assumption was that these committees would exist for black citizens and would function independently of any white Democratic organizations in their vicinity. Meanwhile, in the major cities, "the coalition should encourage a special sub-committee to work with Negro organizations, churches, and leadership to recruit deputies or agents, and to develop a January drive in organizations and neighborhoods. This sub-committee should work as part of the Full Citizenship Committee." In other words, the white leadership of the urban coalitions needed to take special steps to assist the separate black organizing drives happening across town, but black activists would be incorporated as junior partners in local, white-led alliances.

The "Special Program for Latin-American Texans" was substantively the same, but the context of Juan Crow remained disparate and allowed for more racial mixing. A full-time organizer would canvass rural areas and set up Full Citizenship Committees in the all-*mexicano* counties of West and South Texas. In the urban areas, the proposal added, a special subcommittee "should be assigned the duty of making certain that the Latin areas and voters are covered by the general program." Unlike the black ghettos, the "Latin areas" and *mexicano* voters were not wholly separate from their white counterparts and could even be covered by the "general" (read: white) campaign. The poll tax plan for the barrios did not mention churches or newspapers as it had for black neighborhoods, nor did it expect the organizer to contact the *mutualistas* (mutual aid societies) that formed the bedrock of many *mexicano* communities (as it had demanded of African American churches). Rather, the expectation was that Mexican Americans had their own "organizations and leaders," just like their white counterparts. In the white liberal imagination, then, African Americans were separate and distinct, wedded to churches and newspapers, while Mexican Americans were akin to white folks, warranting no special sensitivity or outreach.

The poll tax proposal's provisions for a special project for "union wives" further illuminated the salience of both race and gender. It called for the coalition to send special resolutions to union locals as well as the Women's Activities Department (WAD) Committees in each local labor council or COPE unit. A special letter would be mailed out to union women "urging the two vote per family theme" and giving information about how to pay poll taxes. "The WAD should plan to have every union wife telephoned," the proposal continued, utilizing phone banks at union halls where possible. No full-time organizer was needed—the Texas AFL-CIO already had one on staff. More important, the (white) union wives were already legible to the white male activists. They made sense. They could be counted and defined and contacted through their union men husbands, and they could be expected to double his vote faithfully. They also had resources: a department in the bureaucracies of every local union, labor council, and COPE committee; volunteers ready to work the phones; phone numbers to call and addresses where they could receive mail. In contrast, the state's black and brown voters—union and nonunion, male and female—lacked these assets and specificity. They existed as abstractions, located in distant corners of the state or in dangerous neighborhoods across town. They had no phones, no last known residences. And this was true despite the fact that Erma LeRoy and Bob Sanchez had already worked on special assignments in which they had assembled lists with names and contact information for key local leaders and then mailed them back to Texas AFL-CIO headquarters. The black and brown votes remained terra incognita.[46]

The unspoken assumptions built into all three special projects underscored both the novelty of the 1961–62 poll tax campaign and the effort's staggering cultural incompetency. The drive was unprecedented in its scope and ambition and even bolder in its belief that it could overcome the enormous barriers created by the state's long tradition of white supremacy. It was an undoubtedly flawed and yet profoundly beautiful vision: simply put, it aimed to democratize the state by working together. Whatever its drawbacks, it proved sufficiently powerful that Moses and Erma LeRoy, Albert Peña, Hank Brown, and countless other veteran activists embraced its promise. The campaign would reach to new corners of the state and across cultural lines as never before. At the very least, it would put boots on the ground.

Although rancorous debates over structure and race dominated the coalition's meetings, the end product proved greater than its parts. Following the September meeting, Texas AFL-CIO press secretary Lyman Jones wrote a memo to Brown in which he laid out his candid impressions of the gathering. The discussions were "slow-moving and argumentative," he wrote, but they led to "several positive accomplishments." The coalition had appointed a Candidates Screening Committee "with all participating groups represented." This amounted to a small but important step, he added, especially in light of the liberal groups' failure to coordinate a single entry into the Senate race the previous spring. It was far better to talk about these issues now than a week after the filing deadline, Jones quipped. The coalition had also named a Patronage Committee that now planned to go to Washington, a fact that might seem unimportant to labor but carried great weight among black and brown activists. The committee "took a good deal of the heat out of the situation—so far as elements within the coalition are concerned," Jones wrote. "That is, Latins and Negroes, who have been inclined until now to lump all Anglos together somewhat as opposed—or anyway not too friendly—to their patronage views, now know we are beginning to work together." Jones also noted that the strident, plodding conversation had its own hidden benefits: "The tedious pace and the long-winded talking of this meeting means that at the next meeting we can move faster and with less talk," he concluded. "I know of no human activity which requires the exercise of more patience, the absolutely [sic] necessity of letting everybody get his views and gripes aired, than the political coalition of this kind. Later, I think, this will be seen as a good step forward." Jones recognized that the work was just starting, that whatever progress they had made remained tentative. Still, his tone was optimistic, suggesting (as had myriad reporters) that the coalition would continue toward becoming a robust, multiracial liberal alliance.[47]

A few weeks after the coalition's pivotal September meeting, PASO members assembled in Laredo for that group's largest gathering yet. The delegates again celebrated their newfound unity, and they relished in the fact that they had helped to defeat the conservative Democratic senator Blakley. Yet there were also signs of internal strife. PASO sought to unite all Mexican American organizations for political activity, but distinctions of class, ideology, and tactics all threatened to divide its members. Such differences would not disrupt the Laredo gathering, but they remained present just below the surface. For example, J. O. "Pepper" Garcia of Dallas reported that he and other working-class activists, including his brother Franklin Garcia and Francisco F. "Pancho" Medrano, had decided to organize a new PASO chapter in the city after the old leadership of the Viva Kennedy clubs refused to get active. A lone member of the original group protested that the labor activists had splintered away, and Albert Peña, as state chairman, agreed to meet with both parties immediately after the gathering and then visit the city to try to bring the two factions together. In the end, the two groups would remain separate, with the more conservative, middle-class branch withering away and the "Dallas Labor-PASO" becoming the dominant chapter in the city.

The assembled PASO members also debated the organization's position in regard to participation in the Democratic Coalition. The discussion revealed that PASO consisted of a diverse group of activists whose political agendas diverged as often as they overlapped. Peña, Pepper Garcia, Bob Sanchez, and other labor and liberal activists present believed that PASO should endorse full participation in the coalition, especially after Peña explained that doing so did not commit PASO or individual members of PASO to endorsing or voting for particular candidates or taking stands on any specific issues. The meeting minutes recorded that Peña "explained that it operates somewhat on the same lines as a coalition . . . in Bexar County . . . [where] people and organizations are invited to participate . . . but that everybody understands clearly that there is no commitment involved if a person goes to a particular meeting." Peña added that "everybody realizes that in matters of this sort the majority doesn't necessarily decide an issue" and that all it requires is "that everyone get together and discuss an idea or an issue or a candidate . . . to see if agreement can be reached." The idea electrified Pepper Garcia, who asked if PASO chapters should join local coalitions as well, but a member of Dallas's old Viva Kennedy club suggested caution. County Judge Roberto Benavides of Laredo, an elected official with ties to conservative white Democrats, added that he "failed to see what the object was of trying to get PASO groups to participate in coalitions," when its main and original purpose was "to stimulate Latin American political participation." Attorney and veteran activist Ed Idar of McAllen argued that "we should strive to think PASO, to talk PASO, and act PASO and only PASO and leave out all references to other groups." He maintained that the *mexicano* group should remain "completely non-partisan" and that the DOT and other Democratic groups have often "refused to pay any attention to the problems of the Latin American population." He said it "would not hurt" if PASO chapters had "an observer or two" at local and state coalitions, but they must "simply" observe and remind all involved that "PASO would act independently on its own." Peña agreed that previous liberal groups had at times sold Latin-Americans "down the river," but he added that he personally had "enough experience" in coalitions to participate in this one and "yet not be sold a bill of goods." After hours of conversation, the gathering agreed to participate in the coalition's poll tax campaign, but many if not most of the participants remained deeply skeptical of the larger goal of building a multiracial liberal alliance. Similar cleavages would be repeated at virtually every PASO gathering in the next two years.[48]

As PASO debated the idea of a coalition at its state meeting, the Bexar County Democratic Coalition continued its work at the local level, this time with national implications. In July, within weeks of the statewide coalition's first meeting, Henry B. Gonzalez announced that he would seek the congressional seat vacated by Paul Kilday, an archconservative who had been appointed to a post in the Kennedy administration. Kilday had held the seat since 1938, when he had defeated Maury Maverick Sr. in the wake of the pecan sheller uprising. Maverick Jr. had long hoped to reclaim his father's post, and he had defeated Gonzalez in the statewide special U.S. Senate election in April. But in Bexar County, Gonzalez had clobbered the junior Maverick, beating him twenty-six thousand votes to nine thousand. Gonzalez "proved once and for all that he was still king of Bexar County liberal politicos," the *Observer* reported, and Maverick bowed out to endorse his former opponent and friend.

In August, Maverick hosted a dinner ostensibly in honor of Peña, but its real purpose was to continue the "healing of wounds between myself and Gonzalez, etc., plus other political factors," Maverick wrote.[49]

With Maverick having stepped down, the grassroots of the local coalition swung into action behind Gonzalez's campaign. Peña convinced Lyndon Johnson to support Gonzalez's bid, and the vice president visited the city to campaign for Gonzalez in person. Peña also continued to chair the Poll Tax Committee of LULAC Council 2, which joined the Bexar County Democratic Coalition and did its part in turning out voters. Union organizer Franklin Garcia took leave from his job with the Amalgamated Meat Cutters to campaign for Gonzalez, while George Lambert and the embattled ILGWU organized both union members and nonunion *mexicanos* to get out the vote. Latane Lambert ran the coalition headquarters out of the couple's home and worked all hours of the night coordinating the campaign. On the East Side, Sutton and other coalition members again went all out for Gonzalez, and *SNAP* ran numerous ads and editorials in support of the state senator.

The results were astonishing. In November, Gonzalez carried 55 percent of the votes cast and defeated his Republican challenger by more than ten thousand ballots. Some 95 percent of the registered voters on the West Side turned out on Election Day, with 93 percent of them casting their vote for Gonzalez. One box went 688–7 in his favor. Gonzalez also carried the black East Side by an 11-to-1 margin and carried 70 percent of the racially and economically mixed South Side. A white coalition candidate for state representative appeared on the same ballot and rode Gonzalez's coattails to victory, despite the GOP's strategy of fielding a conservative Mexican American against him. The latter pulled only 22 percent of the West Side vote, confirming that politics, ideology, and class could all trump ethnic allegiances alone.[50]

Gonzalez would soon become the state's first Mexican American congressman. And since he had won by a substantial margin in an off-year election characterized by record turnout, his position appeared secure. Gonzalez's triumph also leant legitimacy to the Bexar County Democratic Coalition and, in turn, to the statewide effort that had been modeled on it. Soon after the election, when Chris Dixie called the members of the statewide alliance to another gathering in Austin, he declared that Gonzalez's "sweeping victory . . . is proof that we can win—if (1.) Poll taxes are paid [and] (2.) Poll tax holders are 'gotten to the polls.'"[51]

With Gonzalez's victory in hand, PASO's tentative endorsement, and another stamp of approval from the TCV, the revived Democratic Coalition could now move forward. Its leaders must have paused to enjoy a few moments of deep satisfaction. The fissures of the Senate campaign had given way to a new and exciting, if still flawed, statewide partnership. Of course, the alliance was not entirely novel: efforts to build similar bodies went back as far as the CIO-led Texas Social & Legislative Conference of the 1940s and early 1950s. Yet those earlier attempts were largely unidirectional entreaties by organized labor to seek allies in their own fight for the general welfare of working people.

Now a multiracial democracy appeared on the horizon. The rise of the black civil rights movement, the increasing electoral prowess of African American activists in Houston and San Antonio, the re-organization of the TCV, the growing presence of African Americans and Mexicans Americans within the labor movement, the rise of the Bexar County Democratic Coalition, the success of Viva Kennedy, and the birth of PASO—all these had combined to transform the political landscape. Black and brown civil rights and labor activists had gained more clout and independence in the electoral arena, and they had won a degree of the "recognition" they had long sought. It was becoming clear to activists of all colors that no Democrat could win without their support, and the leaders of organized labor and white liberals were forced to make room at their tables. They did so clumsily and not without considerable arm-twisting and pushing back from the black and brown activists. Yet the fact that the new Democratic Coalition had supplanted the old DOT and that activists such as Brown, Peña, and Dixie were now steering the ship offered all parties hope that they could continue to work together for mutual benefit. They knew that there would be growing pains, but they still believed that over time they could build a truly egalitarian, multiracial statewide alliance. Voter registration would prove to be the critical leap forward.

"If You Haven't Paid Your Poll Tax You Can't Lead"

According to Texas election laws, citizens who wished to participate in the democratic process were required to register and pay a poll tax prior to January 31 of each year. Prior to 1962, a series of court decisions had led to a few changes in the law, so by then anyone who was twenty-one years of age or a senior over sixty could register for free by obtaining an "exemption certificate" rather than a poll tax receipt. Regardless of how voters enrolled, elections could be won and lost during the registration period, especially for liberals and civil rights activists who depended upon signing up and turning out sporadic voters. For the coalition, nothing was more important than using the brief months prior to the annual deadline to dramatically expand the franchise.

The Democratic Coalition launched its registration campaign in December 1961, as all Texas political groups turned their attention to the next year's primaries. Although PASO remained lukewarm to the coalition as a whole, it readily embraced the poll tax drive and requested that the alliance hire one of its members as the "Latin-American" coordinator of the joint campaign.

Gilbert Garcia of Fort Worth, a PASO founder and officer with roots in the AGIF, got the nod. For the allied project among African Americans, the coalition returned to its longtime "bridge leader," Mrs. Erma LeRoy.[52]

Both activists hit the road, "traveling throughout the State helping people in local communities set up their individual poll tax drives."[53] LeRoy reported after her first week that she had set up shop in Lufkin in East Texas and had already recruited thirty "block workers." She had plans to visit twelve of the thirteen counties within the Seventh Congressional District, where the coalition hoped to oust a segregationist ten-year incumbent. Along the way, LeRoy learned from local people that the incumbent had been visiting his black constituents for the first time in his tenure, underscoring the increased importance of the black vote after 1960. In each county, LeRoy recruited "a respected and civic minded citizen who has worked with me before" to serve as coordinator for the coalition push, and each of them, in turn, "has promised to work up a county wide mass meeting to whip up the enthusiasm of the citizens." All of the local rallies would build up to a districtwide mass meeting in January, she added. Most important, she used the campaign to develop the leadership capacity of local activists. "I am not taking an active part in these mass meetings," she wrote back to Hank Brown at the Texas AFL-CIO. "I am encouraging them to do it on their own."[54]

LeRoy drew upon the courageous people and myriad contacts she had met and cultivated in her tours of East Texas dating back to 1959, if not earlier, but she enjoyed few other resources that could be mobilized for the campaign. Ordinary African American residents distrusted local white Democratic leaders and, at times, their allies in the black community. In Grimes County, the Ministerial Alliance "is backing a forceful young minister to do a county wide job for the first time," she reported, and young leadership was being developed to replace the old guard. More often, she noted that local people remained immobilized until she arrived. "I am encouraging them to harness every available organization, fraternal, civic, social, ministerial groups, beauticians, barbers, boy scouts, and any other group or individual they can get without any ill effects, to do a door to door, block by block, section by section campaign," she wrote. "They seem to look on the scheme with favor, and have agreed to take the responsibility and put it into action. I have asked them to build card files for future use."[55] In many cases, the self-appointed black leadership simply refused to take public stands in the campaign. She wrote an open letter to race leaders across the district, calling on them to support the youth who had propelled the fight for freedom through direct action demonstrations. Citing a saying attributed to an eighty-three-year-old woman in Alabama who had just registered for the first time after a lifetime of waiting, LeRoy signed off simply, "If you haven't paid your poll tax you can't lead."[56]

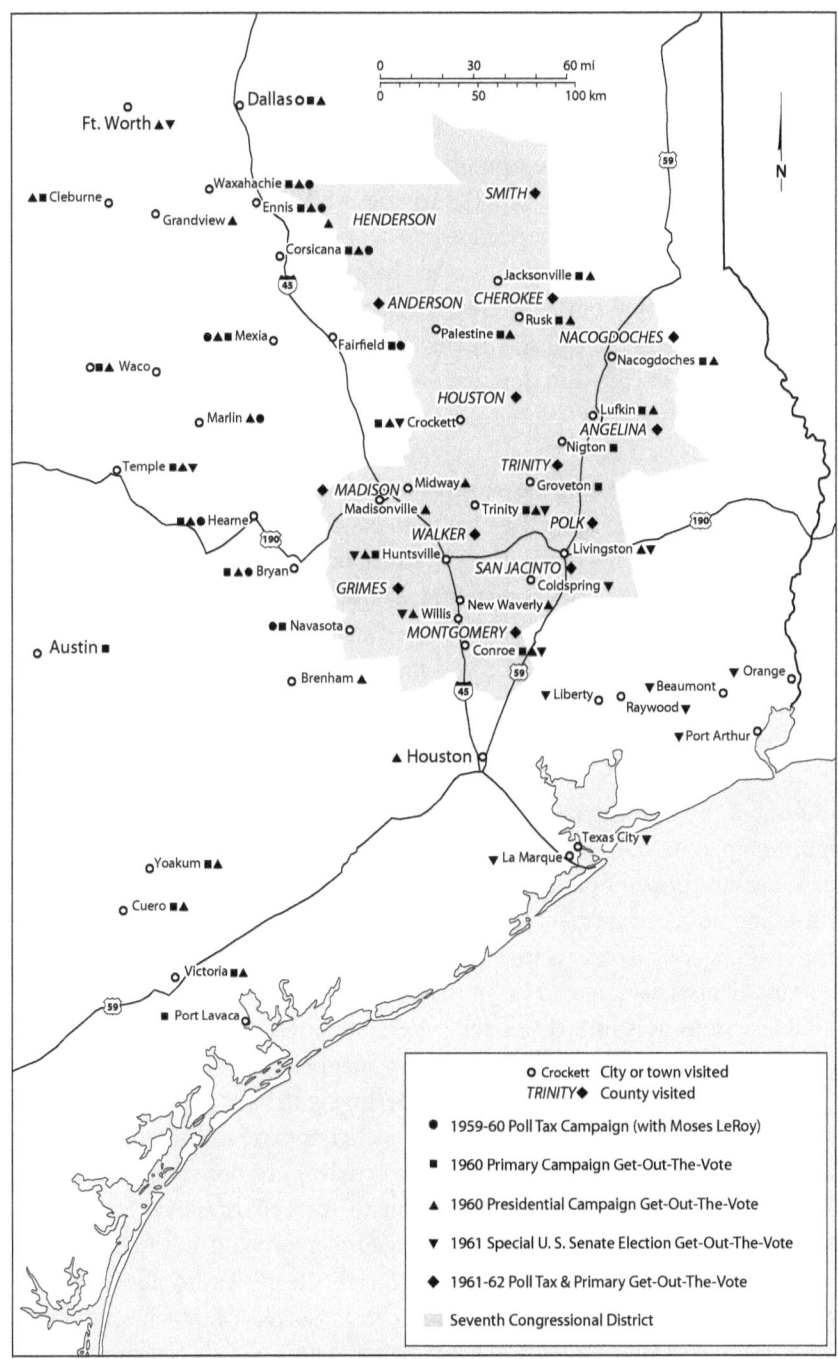

Communities visited by Mrs. Erma D. LeRoy, 1959–62

LeRoy also reported that voter suppression remained an issue in rural East Texas, making the coalition's work there more important than ever. In Coldspring in San Jacinto County, all voters were required to register in person at the county courthouse—nobody else could be deputized, and the "agency forms" that allowed people to register by proxy were simply refused. Polk County lacked a single black deputy registrar, while Cherokee County counted only two. Anderson County remained the worst: there, a successful grassroots campaign among African Americans had helped elect a friendly county sheriff, but "Whites learned of their efforts and organized too." The hostile whites had then defeated the sheriff's reelection bid, and the new county leadership had since declined to deputize black registrars. LeRoy noted that the loss of a friendly sheriff "caused general suppression where the leadership is concerned."[57]

Garcia began pounding the pavement a few days after LeRoy but also made quick progress in bringing the coalition campaign to the far reaches of the state. Leaving from his home in Fort Worth, he first met with Albert Peña to work out a schedule for meeting with local PASO chapters and other groups. Then he returned to North Texas, fanned out across the Panhandle, and finally worked his way down to Laredo and then to the Valley. He loaded up his car with coalition propaganda and then asked a labor staffer to mail him an additional one thousand bumper stickers and posters, figuring that he would exhaust his supplies by the time he reached McAllen. Working his way from one small town to the next, he met with crowds ranging from four to one hundred people and helped anywhere from one to five of them at each stop become authorized poll tax deputies. "Two to four hours were spent with these people in each respective city or town, teaching them how to fill out and use poll tax books, etc.," Garcia reported. Almost everywhere he went, "the county officials have agreed to cooperate with us in this project," he added.[58] One exception was in Sweetwater, where, he noted, the "County does not permit deputies—to Latins, anyway." Many people in the small towns of West Texas informed him that they were still dealing with basic problems of school segregation and discrimination in public accommodations—in 1962! His work in West Texas was not unlike Mrs. LeRoy's to the East; both encountered the still-too-strong hand of Jim Crow and Juan Crow. Yet as Garcia moved into South Texas, the political landscape changed. Garcia could now make contact with established Mexican American civil rights leaders who possessed significant political capital and other resources. In Corpus Christi, he connected with Hector P. Garcia, in McAllen he worked with Bob Sanchez and Ed Idar, and in Laredo and environs he could count on the support of the all-powerful county judge Benavides.[59]

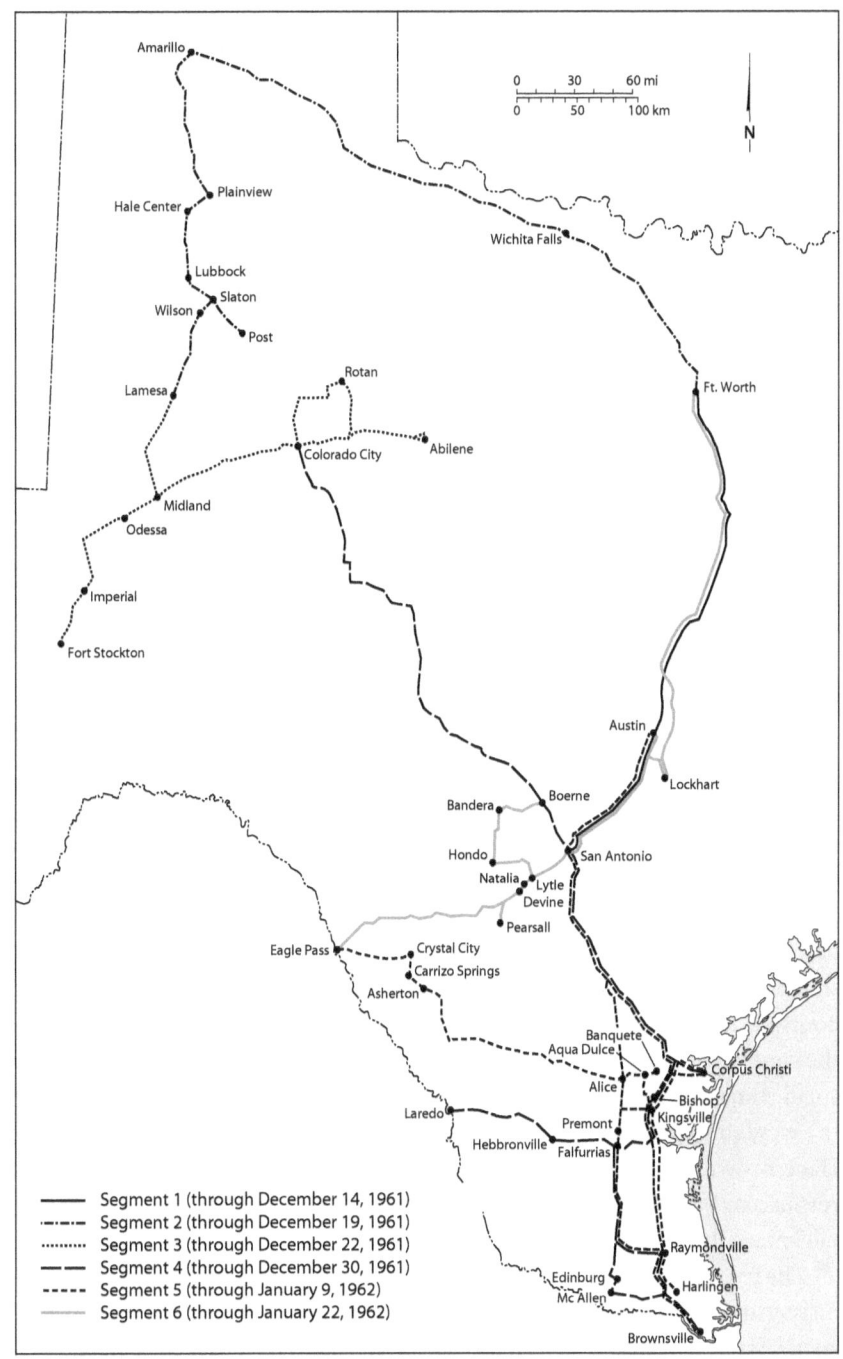

Approximate route of Gilbert Garcia, December 1961 to January 1962

Garcia could also draw on the grassroots network of PASO, which was far more extensive than that of the TCV. He attended a Valley area meeting of some eight hundred PASO leaders in Laredo on December 27, boasting that he had logged over ten thousand miles in two weeks of crisscrossing West Texas (the actual number might have been half that). He told the delegates that his goal was "to organize where organization is needed" and that future campaigns in that part of the state could potentially register 100,000 new voters. After praising the poll tax campaign, PASO state chairman Albert Peña advised members to focus on organizing "in our local areas" and added that chapters "should not, under any circumstances, commit ourselves in state-wide political races." The Tower victory and the growing viability of the Republican Party in Texas meant that the Anglo Democrats must accept them in their "community" in order to win PASO's support, Peña argued. African Americans still faced near-complete exclusion in the countryside, while *mexicanos* could demand and expect recognition as an autonomous political force. The PASO delegates appointed a committee to screen candidates for office and another to plan the organization's first statewide membership and endorsement convention, which would be held in San Antonio in February 1962.[60]

Both Garcia and LeRoy traveled on a shoestring. The coalition's initial budget for the specialized black and brown registration campaigns allocated $2,500 to each effort, a sum that was intended to cover both salary and travel costs for the organizers. In the end, Garcia and LeRoy received $200 per week, including both wages and expenses, and ended up working less than two months. Garcia reported that he stayed in the homes of friends in many towns and that he was often treated to free meals, but he still cleared only around $200 for three seven-day work weeks. His financial situation got worse in early January, when a thief with unknown motivations broke into his car, shattering a window and stealing many of his possessions, including his lists of contacts. A mechanical failure then added another $124 in expenses. To keep the campaign going, Garcia appealed to labor leaders for more aid and raised small sums from local chapters of PASO, the AGIF, and other groups along the way, a tactic that ultimately collected $280 from the grassroots activists. Hank Brown reimbursed the repairs to the car with labor funds, but coalition resources dwindled to the point that some of Garcia's later invoices might never have been paid.[61]

The two organizers earned only modest wages and not much glory from the nitty-gritty work of trudging past dusty West Texas tumbleweeds or through sticky East Texas swamps. Still, their travels brought the coalition's message to more territory than ever before, and resulted in more black and brown deputies and registered voters than in any previous gubernatorial election year.

Their reports also provide a window to the conditions faced and aspirations held by African American and Mexican American activists in the early 1960s. While white coalition leaders focused narrowly on winning the next election, black and brown civil rights and political organizers still battled rampant discrimination, voter suppression, extreme poverty, lack of effective leadership, and even paralyzing fear among the state's nonwhite poor. Their work underscores both the great promise and opportunities presented by the coalition and also the persistent unique needs and ambitions of the two civil rights movements. Whether the coalition could bridge those gaps and effectively mobilize the thousands of new registrants would be tested in the year ahead.

A Mess of Pottage and a Near Miss

The registration period ended on January 31, 1962. Within two weeks, a series of meetings of the coalition and its constituent parts would determine the course of the year's elections. All eyes turned to the gubernatorial primary, as six Democrats filed for the office, with three standing above the rest. On the right stood the incumbent Price Daniel, a former Shivercrat states-rights segregationist and ex-senator who now sought an unprecedented fourth two-year term as a no-longer-extremist governor. On the center-right, John Connally, an LBJ protégé and longtime staffer, had resigned his post as secretary of the navy to seek the nomination back home in Texas. He was conservative in all senses but not a demagogue when it came to race, and he enjoyed the support of Johnson, the vice president's vast campaign apparatus, and virtually all of the state's business leaders. In terms of ideology, little separated Daniel and Connally, and their constituencies often overlapped on the ground. On the left was Don Yarborough, a Houston attorney with a recognizable name but no relation to the U.S. senator. "Don," as liberals called him to avoid confusion, had made a very good showing when he ran for lieutenant governor in 1960. A youthful admirer of Kennedy, he positioned himself as the only dependable liberal candidate in the race, and he even pledged his support for the president when it came to civil rights. No candidate for statewide office had ever run as an integrationist, and Don didn't always do so loudly in 1962, but neither did he shy away from the issue.[62]

Coalition leaders assembled in Austin on February 8 to assess the poll tax drive and determine whether they could work together in the primary. The hot-button issue of patronage had died down some in the fall when the administration agreed to split the available positions between conservatives and liberals. A coalition "Potomac Committee" that included Albert Peña, Erma LeRoy, and Mrs. Randolph had traveled to Washington to explain its stand on the issue, and despite the fact that few *mexicano* and black Texans secured appointments, the matter was now on the back burner.[63] Instead of debating it further, the members of the coalition turned to more pressing concerns. Erma LeRoy and Gilbert Garcia reported on their work in the field, and coalition leaders debated how they would pay off the debt incurred during the poll tax campaign. The Candidates Screening Committee presented its report, indicating strong but far-from-unanimous support for the liberal Don Yarborough.[64]

Here's where the rubber hit the road: since the coalition had an amorphous structure, and its informal operating procedures did not bind any member to the group's actions, the multiracial group could not endorse candidates in any way that had meaning. Many of its leaders would be bound by the dictates of their home organizations. While "independent" white liberals could freely give their approval and urged the coalition to unite behind Don, PASO, the Texas AFL-CIO, and the TCV all had internal procedures that required them to hold separate endorsement conventions. For its part, PASO had authorized its representatives to participate in coalition proceedings solely as "observers" and had resolved that no other group would preempt the newly emboldened group from making its own decision for how to best steer the "Latin vote."[65]

Moreover, each constituent group of the coalition advanced different priorities and remained more than leery of their partners' intentions. While Don represented the obvious choice for the white liberals, a rumor surfaced in mid-January that Peña had secretly committed to Connally. Yarborough jumped on a plane and visited Peña's office in the International Building in downtown San Antonio. "Observers noted voices rose to near shouts at times," wrote columnist Don Politico in the *Light*, but Peña insisted he was waiting for the PASO meeting to steer him.[66] An invisible campaign in which the candidates surreptitiously visited the key kingmakers of each faction was gathering steam across the state. By the time that Peña arrived at the Democratic Coalition meeting on February 8, both he and Hank Brown had resolved that the alliance could not endorse anybody at that time. They limited the agenda to reports on the poll tax campaign and a cursory discussion of the candidates and held their breath for the future. They planned to call a second coalition gathering after their respective groups' meetings in hopes that some agreement might be reached to move forward together.[67]

Instead, the separate conventions proved disastrous. Even before the PASO delegates assembled on February 10, signs of a split within the group had emerged. In late January, George I. Sánchez, who had written the organization's founding statement, and PASO secretary and veteran G.I. Forum leader Ed Idar exchanged a series of passionate, at times acrimonious, letters on the upcoming endorsement conference. Ironically, it began when Idar asked Sánchez for hundreds of copies of his recent article in the *Chicago*

Jewish Forum, a piece that restated and expanded upon the original "American of Mexican Descent" treatise. Sánchez made arrangements for sending the reprints and added a quick aside that he preferred one of the two liberal candidates for governor. A skeptical Idar replied, "We can not get anything done by continuing to support 'protest' candidates just because they speak a good line." Senator Ralph Yarborough had failed to deliver for Mexican Americans when it counted, Idar added. He had a near-perfect record on labor issues, but he had voted to continue the bracero program, the key workplace concern that mattered most to *mexicanos*. Idar suggested that all candidates should be considered, including the incumbent Daniel. Rather than endorse the most liberal candidate, Idar argued that PASO should support those that would truly deliver patronage and real inclusion. Sánchez responded that Don Yarborough had visited his home and convinced him that the liberal attorney was an "out-and-out integrationist" with genuine concern for the *mexicano* people. In contrast, LBJ and party conservatives had consistently "cut our throats," and Connally and Daniel would likely do the same. "Are we going to be mad at a minor demon and hug to our bosom Satan himself?" Sánchez asked.[68] Significantly, Idar agreed with Sánchez on the subject of black civil rights, stating that he could not support the Republican Jack Cox because of his extreme segregationist history. Neither side of the dispute appealed to whiteness, nor did they define their own struggle in opposition to African Americans. Their concern was with the Democratic Party and all of its separate factions.

Neither of the *mexicano* activists registered their concern about the fate of the coalition, as had Peña, yet outside commentators fretted out loud about the larger implications of PASO's upcoming endorsement. While Sánchez and Idar understood that PASO was at a crossroads and worried a great deal about the future of Mexican American political organizing, they both hoped that unity could be maintained among *mexicanos* after the endorsement convention. Both also agreed that PASO had to decide what was best for Mexican Americans instead of responding to the dictates of white liberals or anyone else. In contrast, white liberals believed that Don was the best candidate and did not understand or appreciate PASO's quest for self-determination. Writing in the *Observer*, editor Ronnie Dugger argued that the greatest threat to the liberal cause was that PASO or another single group in the coalition would abandon it for "a mess of pottage." An outraged Idar replied to Dugger by again listing the many ways that liberalism had failed *mexicanos*, adding that he was aware "of the steps the new Democratic Coalition is taking to reunify the liberal movement." Moreover, Idar noted, he was "sympathetic to it. But it is going to take time to re-establish the confidence that has been lost." He concluded that PASO's main function was to provide a united voice for Mexican Americans, and as Sánchez had written, only *mexicanos* should speak for *mexicanos*.

Sánchez congratulated Idar for the fine missive and wrote that he hoped that the *Observer* would print it. The two Mexican American activists made up, at least momentarily.[69]

And yet, their philosophical differences continued, mirroring the organization's internal differences writ large. Idar demanded spoils and recognition and was concerned with choosing a candidate that would win the election. Sánchez wanted the candidate whose views most closely resembled the group's "Statement of Principles" and did not believe that real gains could be made by supporting a more viable, less ideologically committed candidate.

The convention unfolded just as Idar's and Sánchez's letters had anticipated. Peña noted that the gathering was "historic" for "Mexican-Americans in Texas" since it was the first time that their collective "vote [was] no longer 'for sale' to the highest bidder." Thanks to PASO, "leaders who act in private to 'feather their own nests' will not be tolerated by the people they are supposed to represent," he added. The gathering would be "an experiment in democracy" that "could change the complexion of politics in Texas."[70] The group's Candidate Screening Committee spent the entire opening Friday of the convention interviewing candidates, and all day on Saturday the candidates made speeches on the floor. Governor Daniel emerged as the favored candidate after promising several top patronage appointments, inclusion in his campaign, and one hundred jobs for Mexican Americans on the state highway patrol. When questioned about his attendance at the PASO meeting, Daniel told reporters that he had just become aware of the fact that *mexicanos* faced discrimination—after six years as governor and a previous stint in the U.S. Senate. However dubious his claim, Daniel's promises tickled the toes of many longtime activists like Idar. The recognition, the jobs, the prestige—he promised all of it, and he was the front-runner who was best positioned to deliver on his promises. Even Daniel's detractors agreed that the fact that Daniel, Connally, and other candidates had attended the PASO meeting at all demonstrated just how much the terrain of Texas politics had shifted. After decades in which Democrats of all stripes had all but ignored *mexicanos*, they now came in droves, hats in hand, pandering and begging for the same group's stamp of approval. The *Observer* later commented that the convention had showed that PASO "flexed its muscles on the state level" for first time. One candidate for a lessor office called it simply the beginning of "a new political era in Texas."

On Sunday morning, Peña called the convention to order, urging unity and reminding the delegates that they all must pledge to support the nominees of the majority. He offered them an opportunity to leave at that moment if they were not in agreement with the pledge. After leading the push to secure the group's endorsement for Yarborough, steel workers union leader Paul Montemayor of Corpus Christi left, noting that he was bound to follow the endorsement of labor's upcoming COPE convention. George I. Sánchez rose to speak on the organization's founding principles and concluded that they contradicted a possible endorsement of Price Daniel. Labor liaison Bob Sanchez also stumped for Yarborough, while Idar and poll tax organizer Gilbert Garcia spoke in support of Daniel. Connally had been considered the most likely candidate to receive the group's endorsement prior to the convention, but his bid went up in flames as he could not complete with Daniel's prestige but matched the incumbent ideologically. G.I. Forum leader Hector P. Garcia soon joined the ranks of Daniel partisans. After much discussion, and over many objections, Hank Brown was allowed to address the convention. Contrary to rumors that suggested otherwise, the minutes recorded, Brown "stated that organized labor had made no decision concerning any race and that the decisions would be made at the labor convention next week."

Peña called the question on the gubernatorial race. The delegates had nominated only Daniel and Yarborough, Connally's support having collapsed entirely. The organization's die-hard liberals voted for Yarborough, while its more conservative members supported the incumbent and his promises of jobs and recognition. Daniel received a narrow majority, and a motion that he be "elected unanimously" then passed. Ignoring the pledge to support the victors, George Sánchez walked out in protest. The "mediocrity and indifference of the past five years do not permit me to go along with this frankly expedient endorsement," he told reporters after the convention. "Principles rather than petty patronage must dictate our political choices." Launched with so much optimism, the momentous PASO gathering disintegrated into confusion. It ended on a somber note but still completed the ritual election of officers. Peña was returned as chairman, Idar promoted to executive secretary, and labor activist Franklin Garcia became the state organizer.[71]

Although all sides promised unity after the vote, the disagreement between the two factions of PASO leaders split the organization apart at the grassroots. Governor Daniel immediately hired six PASO members to join his campaign staff, demonstrating that he would follow through on his promise of future patronage appointments. Idar went to Austin to work in the campaign's state headquarters, yet the glory of recognition was marred by the rift surrounding the endorsement itself. By the end of March, Idar was forced to defend himself against charges that he had cut a deal with the governor prior to the convention. He pleaded with the rank and file to follow the party line, arguing that "a vote for Daniel is a vote for PASO," but the rift continued to widen.[72] The massive Hidalgo County chapter voted nearly 3–1 to repudiate the state convention's action and opted for no endorsement instead.[73] Meanwhile, Sánchez and many liberal Mexican Americans publicly opposed Idar and campaigned feverishly for Yarborough.[74] Paul Montemayor and most *mexicano* unionists did so

Liberal Democratic gubernatorial candidate Don Yarborough arrives at Mueller Airport in Austin and addresses an adoring crowd from atop the wing of his campaign's barnstorming Cessna jet on May 16, 1962. A "Viva Don" sign in the background attempts to link the candidate to Kennedy's successful efforts to mobilize Mexican American voters two years earlier, but, statewide, PASO remained divided internally and did not deliver a bloc vote to either candidate in the primary runoff. Courtesy *Austin American-Statesman* Photographic Morgue (AR.2014.039), Austin History Center, Austin Public Library, Texas, Image AS-62-36092-01a.

as well, following the dictates of labor's COPE, which had "recommended" Don the week after the PASO meeting. The Bexar County Democratic Coalition also endorsed the liberal, leaving Peña in the unenviable position of chairing two organizations that had backed warring candidates. In a personal compromise, he withdrew from the local contest but also promised that his troops would not obstruct coalition activists on the West Side. He maintained his support for Daniel but refrained from campaigning at home or among the divided legions of PASO members across the state.[75]

For his part, newly elected Congressman Henry B. Gonzalez sat the whole thing out, remaining independent as ever. Increasingly estranged from Peña and his own sometimes deputy, Lalo Solis, the "no-handle" Democrat Gonzalez refused to align with any larger organization. He remained aloof to both the Democratic Coalition and PASO and did not attend the PASO endorsement convention, claiming he was too busy in Washington. He offered no official endorsement in the governor's race, but Eddie Montez, his top staffer at home in San Antonio, led the Connally campaign on the West Side in an "unofficial" capacity. The *Observer* concluded that Gonzalez understandably needed to repay his debt to LBJ, who had stumped for the *mexicano* during his congressional campaign just a few months earlier. Then, on Election Day, the West Side was inundated with a campaign palm card displaying a photograph in which Connally appears, whispering into the ear of President Kennedy, who is listening intently. Above the picture, the text reads, "Vote for Connally." But underneath the image, the caption reads simply, "Henry B. Gonzalez." One veteran campaign staffer in Bexar County told the *Observer* that it was the "cleverest thing I ever saw." The simple advertisement, not much larger than a business card, effectively linked Connally to the liberal president and suggested that Gonzalez had signed it at the bottom. Gonzalez was running unopposed for reelection, but his name was still on the ballot. The card told voters to go out and vote for their local champion, the beloved Kennedy, and the untested Connally in tandem. And yet it said nothing that would discredit Connally among conservatives, and Gonzalez maintained plausible deniability. The congressman neither endorsed nor refuted the cards and instead continued his detached silence.[76]

The other parts of the coalition were likewise divided internally. Although most black and white unionists joined their *mexicano* counterparts in campaigning for the liberal Yarborough, the all-white building trades and Fort Worth aerospace workers favored Connally. As direct action demonstrations continued to convulse and destabilize their cities, African Americans again disagreed in the political arena. The TCV held a state convention in which it decided to refrain from endorsing any candidate, its members having split between Yarborough and Attorney General Will Wilson, the racial moderate who had run well in the special Senate race the year before. The HCCO in Houston gave Don a narrow majority but was unable to muster the two-thirds majority that the council required for an official endorsement.[77] In San Antonio, while Sutton had joined in the Bexar Coalition's endorsement of Yarborough, *SNAP News* also ran numerous paid ads for Connally, including photographs of the former navy secretary alongside John Kennedy and slogans that the former would serve as a governor "for all the people." Another ad prominently featured Lieutenant Commander Samuel L. Gravely, the nation's first African American commander of a warship, noting that he had been appointed by Connally. An occasional article in *SNAP* mentioned that one or another local organization was supporting Connally, but Claude Black and Sutton were conspicuously absent from this coverage. The available evidence indicates that they worked for Yarborough as part of the coalition but did not fully commit to his campaign. Meanwhile, many of their more conservative coethnics took public stands in support of Connally. Ruth Bellinger led Connally's effort in San Antonio. Rev. H. Rhett James of Dallas, who had led the sit-ins there, also worked for Connally, as did black businessman Hobart Taylor of Houston. For her part, civil rights unionist Erma LeRoy again hit the campaign trail with support from the Texas AFL-CIO, stumping for Yarborough and a liberal candidate for U.S. House in the Seventh Congressional District.[78]

On Election Day, May 5, Connally led the field with 30 percent of the votes, followed by Yarborough, who garnered 22 percent. Don narrowly edged out Governor Daniel, the incumbent and onetime front-runner. Connally's superior resources, charisma, backing from big business, and access to what one observer called "Johnson's unique man-in-every-county 'organization' of political debtors" helped him carry the day. So too did PASO's defection prove decisive. With the group's endorsement of Daniel splitting PASO asunder and rendering Peña ineffective in San Antonio, Gonzalez's man on the West Side, Eddie Montez, pulled off a political miracle. Precincts that reliably voted 15–1 for liberal candidates turned over to the conservative Connally. Across the state, Connally made huge inroads in black and brown boxes. Yarborough carried his base of Harris County and the industrial counties of the Upper Gulf Coast, the heart of the state's labor movement, but he lost by wide margins in the other three big cities (Dallas, Fort Worth, and San Antonio).[79]

Yarborough's labor and liberal supporters moved quickly to shore up their support among African Americans and Mexican Americans, but PASO remained sharply divided. George Sánchez and other liberals appealed to the organization's officers, asking them to endorse Yarborough in the runoff. But conservative County Judge Benavides of Laredo maintained that the organization's officers did not have the authority to change the convention endorsement. Peña and the other officers decided to follow his lead, not wanting to make the division in the organization's ranks worse. "Peña reiterated that PASO must continue as a force in Texas," read the minutes of the board's meeting. The officers offered no endorsement and allowed local PASO chapters to make their own decisions as appropriate to their local conditions.[80]

In Houston, Dallas, and San Antonio, local PASO chapters all endorsed Yarborough for the June runoff, all in conjunction with local multiracial, liberal-labor coalitions. The HCCO endorsed him, as did *SNAP News* and a suddenly very visible Sutton. The Bexar County Democratic Coalition regrouped around Yarborough, but more conservative African Americans in

San Antonio and across the state continued to campaign for Connally. White liberals and labor activists remained with Yarborough.[81]

In the end, it was too little too late for the state's nascent Democratic Coalition. Connally narrowly won the nomination, defeating his liberal foe by just 26,000 votes out of more than 1.1 million cast, a 51 percent to 49 percent victory. The LBJ protégé's appeal to black and brown voters again proved decisive. The defection of the former group, attributed to Connally's service as navy secretary and his claims of close ties to the Kennedy administration, had a "telling effect." The West Side and all of Bexar County again went for Connally by a 2-to-1 margin. A daylong rain slowed turnout in the labor strongholds of Harris County and the Upper Gulf Coast, sealing Don's fate.[82]

No group felt the sting more than PASO and especially its liberal wing, led by Peña. PASO's deal with Price Daniel failed to win them more than temporary recognition in the campaign, and it did not result in jobs, patronage, or lasting political power, as the group's leaders had hoped. Peña remarked after the election that Connally "rode two horses at the same time—successfully. He solicited support of the anti-Kennedy people by repudiating [his] program; and he solicited support of people friendly to Kennedy by using the prestige" of his cabinet appointment. Connally enjoyed countless other advantages, yet he just barely won. Still, the "run-off primary proved that overwhelming newspaper support, unlimited finances, and promiscuous labeling doesn't insure [*sic*] victory for a candidate," Peña added.[83]

The down-ballot results proved equally revealing. In the race for lieutenant governor, labor had gone all-out for state house speaker James Turman, a fierce supporter of liberal legislation in the recent session. In contrast, PASO, the TCV, and local black and brown organizations all opposed Turman due to his past support for segregationist measures and his failure to speak out on the issue since. They lined up instead behind a state senator from Central Texas whom, they recalled, had backed Gonzalez's famous filibuster against Jim Crow in 1957. In contrast to the governor's race, in this case each ethnic group was united internally, but the coalition remained totally fragmented. Turman advanced but then lost in the runoff to a conservative, proving that the labor-liberal alliance could not win without African American and Mexican American support.[84] Meanwhile, in the Seventh Congressional District, the liberal backed by Mrs. LeRoy, the Texas AFL-CIO, and most African American groups lost by only forty-one votes. There, it seemed clear, the coalition's poll tax and get-out-the-vote campaigns were working, even as they had fallen short.[85] In San Antonio, where Connally's campaign, led by Ruth Bellinger, defeated Sutton's half-hearted Yarborough effort by one thousand votes on the East Side, the *SNAP* activists' white candidate for district attorney carried the same precincts by over five thousand votes. This divergence indicated that a coordinated, yearlong effort by the militant black activists and the coalition could have produced better results for Yarborough as well.[86]

The Democratic Coalition had failed to prevent the split of its membership, and each of its constituent parts remained fragmented internally. Still, Yarborough had come astonishingly close to victory. He had proven that he was electable, yet he remained unable to win the runoff with the coalition's various elements still scrambling to overcome the chaos of the primary. Yarborough increased his vote total between the two rounds by a staggering 221,000 votes, while Connally added only 134,000. The campaign was working, the coalition was gelling, but it had simply run out of time. Had scarcely more than thirteen thousand voters switched sides, Yarborough would have carried the day. It was the closest margin of defeat for a liberal gubernatorial candidate since Ralph Yarborough lost to Shivers in 1954.[87] The confusing, heartbreaking campaign had given black, brown, and white activists some reasons for hope.

By the summer of 1962, Texas had made major strides toward becoming more democratic, and many activists looked to the future with optimism. After the sit-in movement and the Viva Kennedy clubs had changed the terms of debate, organized labor deepened its commitment to "Latin-American Affairs" and the Mexican American civil rights struggle within Texas. Local organizing by Mexican Americans grew into a permanent, if fractured, political force, while a series of elections proved both the potency and the fragility of the "Latin vote."

Black, brown, and white activists experimented in building the statewide Democratic Coalition, a body that boosted voter registration and turnout to unprecedented levels but ultimately failed to unify its members behind consensus candidates. Still, the cause of liberalism, which had appeared dead after Johnson crushed the DOT at the state convention in 1960, had been resurrected. Labor had taken control, its idealistic leader, Hank Brown, convinced that he could rally the scattered and poorly-organized white liberals while also working in collaboration with Peña and black civil rights activists. Although PASO had miscalculated and the coalition had proven unable to unite its diverse constituents when it mattered, the simple fact that all parties were now assembling in the same room represented a remarkable foundation for the future. And despite the fact that Connally had nabbed the nomination, his direct appeals to black and brown voters further underscored their growing power—no Texas conservative had ever campaigned so actively for their support. If labor and the liberal factions in each racial group could harness that energy, there was no telling how much they could accomplish.

Nonetheless, each group understood that they had come painfully close to electing a liberal, avowedly integrationist Democrat in the 1962 cycle, and they all tried to learn from their mistakes. Albert Peña wrote in *SNAP* that PASO should continue "not as a pressure group but as a right and a sincere desire to participate in government." It was important to address the particular needs "of our ethnic group," he added, but only by practicing democracy. It remained paramount that *mexicanos* join with other "groups who have been friends in the past," namely, "organized Labor . . . Negro[es] . . . and independent liberals." Each of these groups must work together "through mutual respect for each other's problems," and there was simply "no other way" to move forward.

Peña argued that the coalition and its members failed when they stopped short of their principles. Rather than throw around labels, it was now time to restate the coalition's core beliefs. "I believe that every man has a right to a job, decent wages and hours, adequate education, the best of medical care and a decent place to live. I believe that every man should have an equal opportunity to get these things," Peña wrote. "And when the Liberal coalition has failed to advocate any one of these basic beliefs, either individually or collectively, we have failed as a liberal idea." PASO needed to admit that its endorsement of Daniel had hindered the larger cause. Speaking as "a friend of labor," Peña added that COPE members had failed at their last convention "when they didn't ask the candidates who addressed them to take a strong position on 'Right to Work' Laws—which, after all, are the 'Guts' of the Labor movement."

"Our future is to play the role of the conscience of the Liberal movement," Peña concluded, "and address ourselves to the task of eliminating the evils of discrimination [and] segregation in job opportunities, education and housing. We must fight for federal aid to education, medical care for the aged, and the elimination of unfair labor laws. It is in your hands to change the political complexion of the State of Texas."[88] As it turned out, a series of *intra*racial conflicts would soon set the stage for a new wave of *inter*racial collaboration.

Chapter 8

Separating the Wheat from the Chaff

Intra*racial Divides Give Way to* Inter*racial Unity*

In the fall of 1962, Albert Peña found himself in a pickle. As the state's politicos switched their focus to the general election in November, Peña and other liberal activists worked to hold Democratic gubernatorial nominee John Connally's feet to the fire. The firebrand commissioner and Texas Political Association of Spanish-Speaking Organizations (PASO) chairman called on Connally to "take the lead" in abolishing the poll tax "and in setting up a Fair Employment Practices code in State Government."[1] Still licking their wounds from their acrimonious endorsement convention and defeats in the primaries, PASO members had gathered again and reluctantly endorsed Connally for the November election, "with the qualifications that the state Democratic platform would be in keeping with the national Democratic platform." But at the Texas Democratic Party convention in September, Connally flatly refused to consider PASO's recommendations. After all of his parliamentary maneuvers failed, Peña ended up as one of just three dissenters who voted against the nominee's state party platform, a document that ignored civil rights and took no stand on the much-despised poll tax, right-to-work law, and bracero program.[2]

Peña's ongoing defiance of Connally earned him strident criticism from all quarters. Hostile newspaper columns laid into him: "May we suggest . . . that he should see his eye doctor," wrote the editorial board of the *San Antonio Evening News*. "Peña's vision is blurred terribly. He can't even see a bandwagon." Connally was steamrolling toward victory, the paper added, and everyone else in Texas politics had fallen into line. Organized labor had reluctantly endorsed the likely next governor, and he had campaigned hard for black and brown votes and managed to win over many of them in the primaries. Peña alone had failed to get the message. PASO "obviously doesn't speak for very many Spanish-speaking people," the editorial concluded, adding that Peña's claim that he would now appoint a committee "to study the platform" and reconsider the organization's endorsement appeared more than ridiculous. "In what telephone booth will you meet, Mr. Commissioner?"[3]

His back against the wall, Peña sensed an opportunity. Five days later, he wrote to PASO members across Texas and urged them to come to a full-scale convention in lieu of a small committee meeting. The state chairman issued a challenge to PASO members: the group is either "a moving, vital force in Texas politics, or it isn't," Peña wrote. It is either "independent thinking . . . or it isn't." It is either "the conscience of the aims and aspirations of the Mexican-American and all well-meaning Texans, or it isn't." Peña included a copy of the editorial in his letter. He noted that he was not upset by the "personal vituperation." Rather, "What does aggravate me is the insinuation that PASO is nonexistent, that PASO is a figment of my imagination." Such charges were not new, he added, as similar claims had been made about the Viva Kennedy clubs in 1960. But now, "The time has come, that if PASO exists, a public display of our representation across the state is vital, if only to prove its existence. . . . We must decide the future role of PASO. Is PASO dead?"[4]

Five hundred delegates representing twenty-one counties answered with their feet, descending on San Antonio just ten days after Peña mailed his letter. Two hundred of them assembled beside a telephone booth on the corner of Houston Street and Soledad and rallied before marching to the Gunter Hotel. Preceded by his legions, Peña entered the hotel ballroom to a standing ovation. Then, after more than three hours of debate, the convention voted to withdraw its endorsement of the Democratic nominee. Dr. Hector P. Garcia, the founder of the American G.I. Forum (AGIF) and renowned Mexican American activist, said that PASO's telephone booth demonstration and endorsement retraction proved that "people with names like Gonzalez, Fuentes, [and] Peña can do as good a job in American political life as a man named Jones or Smith."[5]

Peña's bold response under fire did more than save PASO from fizzling away into insignificance. It highlighted a growing dynamism among Mexican American activists and heralded the growing power of the liberal faction within PASO. In February, when George I. Sánchez had staged a one-man walkout to protest the group's endorsement of Price Daniel, fewer than one hundred delegates representing just over 1,300 paid members had debated PASO's future. In October, despite a pair of crushing defeats at the polls, Peña challenged the body to rally for its existence, and five hundred of the group's active members answered his call. In fact, the organization was growing in both size and militancy. Peña and the liberal wing of PASO had gained the upper hand within the group and were poised to seize full control of it. Over the next sixth months, PASO would transition from being a timid association of *mexicanos* seeking patronage to an aggressive civil rights movement working in a tight alliance with organized labor, African Americans, and the liberal Democratic Coalition.[6]

At the same time, the rally at the phone booth represented just the most dramatic expression of the growing polarization occurring across racial lines in Texas politics. African Americans split between those who had backed Connally in the primaries and those who remained ambivalent or lukewarm toward his entreaties. Organized labor reconsidered its endorsement of Connally at a COPE (Committee on Political Education) convention but narrowly voted to stay with the nominee, whom delegates considered "the lesser of two evils." On the other side, a growing Republican Party attacked Connally from the right.[7]

In short order, African American and Mexican American activists would both take to the streets, reenergizing their respective civil rights movements with new campaigns for complete integration, real political power, and equal economic opportunity. In San Antonio, the activists of the SNAP House would launch a new wave of protest and a potent electoral challenge. In a South Texas hamlet, PASO would join forces with new allies to overthrow the Anglo good ol' boys who had long dominated the town's *mexicanos*, staring down terror and intimidation from law enforcement and sending shockwaves across the nation. The rising pressures unleashed by such militant organizing would drive a wedge into the centers of the black and brown political communities of Texas, thwarting their leaders' time-worn appeals for *intra*racial unity. Soon the most aggressive black and brown activists across the state would render that idea untenable and would replace it instead with something new: a full commitment to *inter*racial partnerships.

Observers on all sides believed that Texas was on the precipice of becoming a two-party state, but the future of the liberal left wing of the Democratic Party remained uncertain. The shifting terrain and growing acrimony would soon lead union leaders and white liberal activists to separate themselves further from the party's conservatives. Responding to the changing times, the multiracial Democratic Coalition would develop a bold new strategy and structure and would insert itself into both civil rights movements, ultimately bringing them together as one.

New Shapes in Texas Politics

In November 1962, the Democratic nominee Connally defeated his Republican rival Jack Cox by a sizable margin. Cox garnered 660,000 votes in the "most impressive" showing by a GOP gubernatorial candidate since 1869. However, Connally exceeded that total by 100,000, thanks to a record turnout of 1.5 million voters. The returns revealed that conservatives had abandoned the Democratic Party en masse for the GOP, but such defections "were more than offset by the adhesion of liberal, labor, Negro, and Latin precincts to the Connally banner." Despite PASO's withdrawn endorsement, Peña had campaigned hard for the entire Democratic ticket, primarily to support local legislative candidates as well as Gonzalez's bid for a first full term in Congress.[8] Having registered its protests, the party's left wing held its nose and pulled the big lever on Election Day, carrying Connally to victory. They did not elect their preferred candidate, but they had demonstrated their power. Even conservative Democrats like Connally and his predecessor, Price Daniel, could no longer run as ardent segregationists. In fact, Connally only won by making special appeals to African American and Mexican American voters.[9]

In the days following the election, liberal Democratic strategists began crunching the numbers. African Americans, Mexican Americans, urbanites, and Republicans had all voted in record numbers, creating a viable two-party system in the state and indelibly shifting the political terrain. Most conservatives had flocked to the GOP, which meant that those that clung to the reins of power in the Democratic Party were rapidly losing their base. The state appeared likely to follow the example set by Bexar County in the previous six years: there, black, brown, and white liberals, labor leaders, and small farmers proved that they could constitute a majority if they stuck together. Conservative Democrats, in turn, would likely continue Connally's pattern of staying viable by building alliances with conservative black and brown leaders. And the GOP would continue to grow by cutting into the right wing of the Democratic Party, a process that would accelerate once "pragmatist" Republicans supplanted the Birchers and other right-wing extremists who had long carried the party's banner in Texas.

"For liberals as for the G.O.P.," longtime liberal activist Larry Goodwyn wrote in the *Observer*, "1963 can be a year of consolidation or—if they are diverted—a year in which that consolidation is postponed." The conservatives in the middle would attempt to maintain their "coalition of big business interests with minority voters," a fact that threatened to pull away votes from the left to account for losses on the right. In order to succeed, then, liberal candidates "must be more liberal, more explicitly integrationist," and more committed to holding the coalition together. White liberals could position themselves as better alternatives to Connally-style conservatives only by taking clear, unequivocal stands on civil rights. Yet "this is easier said than done," Goodwyn cautioned, "because the pace of change, in racial attitudes and in racial expectations, is far swifter than most liberal politicians realize."[10]

In fact, "the pace of change" would turn out to be even faster than he had anticipated. Veteran activist George Sánchez replied to the postmortem election coverage in the *Observer*, commenting in a letter to the editor that the paper had erred "in assessing the political temper of the minority groups; that is, in underestimating their potential, a potential that can become reality with devastating suddenness." The rise of Henry B. Gonzalez and other liberal *mexicanos* "symbolized . . . the revolt against the old guard," Sánchez added. That said, now both the *Observer* and white liberals in general must be careful not to "throw the Negroes and the *mexicanos* . . . into the old guard camp" by downplaying their real, immediate need to end discrimination. In fact, the *Observer* "through inadvertence, has been guilty of alienating some of the *mexicanos* who fundamentally are liberals," he noted, while organized labor had done the same through "its treatment of the 'minority' groups" on the shop floor.

Sánchez concluded by defending his statement "that only *mexicanos* can speak for the *mexicanos*," and he extended on it as well. "I will reiterate that seeming chauvinism by saying that only the Negro can speak for the Negro," he added. If organized labor and "the self-anointed liberals" want to wield the several hundred thousand votes of these groups, "they had better seek counsel from those Negroes and *mexicanos* who really know their people." Coalition organizers needed to ask why and how black voters helped to defeat Yarborough, and to look more closely at where the *mexicano* vote went following PASO's failed endorsements. "If the liberals have the gift of leadership," Sánchez concluded, "they had better begin using it now and not play the last-minute game of 'after all, under the skin, we are all brothers.' Hell!"[11]

For the next half-decade, black, brown, and white activists would all work together to answer Sánchez's call for leadership. The process began with the revival of the Democratic Coalition. Just days after the general election in November 1962, a multiracial group of about forty "Democratic 'Warhorses'" from the previous year's coalition assembled in Austin and began talking about the future. Called together by the Texas AFL-CIO's Hank Brown, the leaders discussed the chaos of the campaigns of 1962 and the failures by various coalition partners to hold true to the robust liberalism that Albert Peña had long championed. Like the previous incarnation of the coalition, this new group decided "against a formal constitution, by-laws, or officers," but it did appoint a full-time "researcher-writer . . . to put out the newsletter, carry out the 1963 poll tax program . . . and perform other research duties as the need arises." To fill this post, they selected Larry Goodwyn, a former associate editor of the *Observer* and "press aide" in the Don Yarborough campaign. The multiracial group of activists began sketching plans for the coming two years, outlined a fund-raising plan, and named a temporary steering committee that included Peña, Brown, Bob Sanchez, and Latane Lambert, who had just coordinated the Bexar County Democratic Coalition's successful campaigns in 1962.[12]

The reorganization of the coalition proceeded from idea toward reality in January 1963, when about one hundred members of the former coalition again assembled at a downtown hotel in Austin. Labor lawyer Chris Dixie of Houston reported that a diverse committee of coalition members had met with Senator Ralph Yarborough to confront him about his general failure to respond to the liberals' needs and especially his poor responsiveness to Mexican American and African American organizations. In his remarks, Texas AFL-CIO president Hank Brown reminded the multiracial group that no single leg of the coalition alone could serve as the "custodian of the public welfare" or the spokesman for real liberalism. Rather, he agreed with George Sánchez that only *mexicanos* should speak for *mexicanos*, only blacks for blacks, and only organized labor for labor. Brown called on the independent liberals to "put your money where your mouth is or quit," and he pledged to raise $100 each from one hundred different labor leaders in order to donate a sum of $10,000 to the coalition's operating expenses. The other delegates passed the hat and raised $1,500 in cash and pledged $3,500 more. Countless attendees called for unity and better organizing to coordinate their efforts in 1963. Coalition staffer Larry Goodwyn presented thirteen graphs and charts that had undergirded his postmortem electoral analysis in the *Observer*, and he called on coalition members to do more to win the black and brown votes. "If we're gonna get those votes, we're gonna earn them," he said. "These are our folks," Goodwyn noted, but "They ain't votin' for us because we ain't doin' right by them."[13]

Meanwhile, he added in a subsequent newsletter, the "new facts of life in Texas politics have clearly not been lost on the new legislature," which was quickly becoming more tolerant when it came to race. Just six years earlier, the house had passed a bevy of new segregation acts with as few as five dissenting votes among 150 members, while only three dissenters, led by Henry B. Gonzalez, filibustered against the laws in the senate. Now, a bill repealing one of the 1957 laws had attracted thirty cosponsors in just two days. A more radical option from a member of the Bexar County Coalition proposed to overturn all of the segregationist laws passed six years earlier and to create a new Division of Civil Rights in the state attorney general's office. These previously outlandish suggestions fell just three votes short of a majority. Goodwyn quipped that many of the conservative legislators who had long opposed civil rights and labor legislation were "rapidly undergoing a change of heart."[14]

Throughout the spring of 1963, Goodwyn and other coalition leaders took to the road to share their analysis of the "New Shapes in Texas Politics." He and Brown made the pitch to labor's COPE, urging the white union leaders to recognize civil rights as falling within their own self-interest. Albert Peña brought the analysis to PASO and the Bexar County Democratic Coalition. Most important, Goodwyn paired up with Arthur DeWitty, an African American journalist and leader of the Texas Council of Voters (TCV) and NAACP in Austin. Together, the biracial duo crisscrossed the state, speaking to local coalitions and separate black, brown, and white audiences in Dallas, Fort Worth, Austin, San Antonio, Houston, and several smaller towns along the Gulf Coast.

By late March, Goodwyn drew on these experiences to propose a formal program for the statewide coalition. The coalition was working, he contended, and now it needed an extra push to reach the next level. More than 4,300 activists had joined the mailing list to receive the coalition's *Democratic Newsletter*, and he was hopeful that circulation would grow to twenty-five thousand by the end of the year. Its leaders had agreed to launch yet another voter registration effort for 1964, but this one would be the largest ever, aiming to add 200,000 new voters to the rolls. The key to expanding its outreach would be the development of a new project that built upon the traveling presentations of Goodwyn and DeWitty over the previous six weeks. Reflecting on that experience, Goodwyn wrote that the project so far had been "unquestionably effective." The duo had added three thousand African American names to the mailing list, an unprecedented quantity that would give the white liberals unparalleled ability to conduct direct outreach to these previously illegible, off-the-radar, unlikely voters. Moreover, they had raised $200 in small contributions from black citizens "who have heretofore not been active in politics above the local level." This money would be earmarked to fund travel for African Americans to attend regional and statewide coalition meetings, addressing another age-old structural failing of previous alliances—the inability of black delegates to speak for themselves at coalition gatherings due to a lack of financial resources. With no shortage of self-congratulation, Goodwyn concluded that he and DeWitty had served as "a sort of living example of the kind of society the average Negro is trying to achieve." They modeled interracial partnership through their actions, with DeWitty serving the added purpose of reassuring black and brown audiences that the white coalition leaders were finally sincere this time around. At each stop, their presentations had "stirred activity at the local level in a manner not achieved in the past in Texas," and now the coalition needed to develop a long-term program to ensure that the newly motivated masses remained active.

The linchpin of the effort would be the creation of the coalition's "Team Program," a grassroots organizing apparatus based on the Goodwyn-DeWitty pairing. A first draft of the proposal suggested that the coalition should form six interracial teams across the state, each with a black staffer paid by the alliance and a white partner serving as an unpaid volunteer. Together, each pair would cover one or more congressional districts, traveling from county to county recruiting and training twenty-five additional biracial teams of grassroots activists. The salaried African American organizers would take the lead and shoulder most of the burden, holding responsibility for recruiting precinct workers and sending their names back to state headquarters, organizing new local chapters of "Negro Voters Leagues" where needed, and assisting "in the amalgamation" of new and existing black organizations into their respective local liberal coalitions. The white staffers would be recruited from existing liberal organizations across the state, would make speeches, and would return home, charging the coalition only for their expenses. The proposal also called for the hiring of three statewide coordinators, one black, one "Latin American," and one white liberal. Their duties would include, respectively, organizing an African American voters league in every black community, a PASO chapter in every town in South Texas, and the creation of a functioning local coalition in every county. All together, the six black regional leaders and three state coordinators, only one of them white, would recruit and train enough local activists to provide the backbone for a mass voter registration campaign.

It represented a bold proposal, but not one without its flaws. It encouraged the coalition to make an investment in organizing black and brown voters unlike any ever attempted. Two years earlier, in 1961–62, the alliance had spent less than $4,000 to hire Mrs. Erma LeRoy and Gilbert Garcia for two months of work in the poll tax campaign. Two solitary organizers had covered vast swaths of territory, each encompassing dozens of rural counties as well as all of the urban neighborhoods populated by their ethnic groups. Now, the "Team Program" promised to hire nine organizers, eight of them nonwhite, with a total budget of $40,000. The money would have to come from outside the state, from private foundations and labor organizations committed to expanding the franchise. (The state coalition's headquarters, salaries for Goodwyn and a secretary, and the newsletter would continue with funding furnished "by Texas liberals of all races and by Texas labor.")

Yet there were serious conceptual and practical limitations to the plan. First, all six teams would be led by African American organizers, leaving Mexican Americans to continue with a single statewide coordinator. Worse, the sole white staffer would be charged with coordinating the activities of the other eight by spearheading the efforts to organize local coalitions. The unspoken assumptions between the lines of the document remained numerous and potentially devastating. Whites were already organized enough that they could be easily located from among the ranks of existing liberal groups, and they had sufficient individual resources that they need not receive salaries to serve on the teams. In contrast, black and brown activists were asked to create new chapters and then to subsume those new bodies to local coalitions led by whites. Black and brown voters had failed to support liberal candidates due to problems of communication and outreach, the plan suggested, neglecting the many ways in which white liberals had fallen short in the eyes of African American and Mexican American leaders. And the white state coordinator was naturally the leader of the local coalitions, the sole person who could bring the black and brown groups into the fold—without needing to pause to examine why they were not already there. A pernicious, unconscious white supremacy dripped from the proposal's pages, perhaps nowhere more than in the statement that the interracial teams themselves represented the society to which African Americans aspired. Black Texans wanted integration, the proposal assumed, and now whites were going to give it to them.[15]

Warts and all, the Democratic Coalition of 1963 was beginning to take shape. It promised to reach deeper into the state's black and brown communities than ever before, but it had not yet developed a plan that could counter both the intense inequality and urgency of the moment and the persistent white supremacist culture that permeated its work. It would take several additional months of meetings and rancorous debate before a final course of action would take shape. Still, a foundation was now in place. Meanwhile, as the white labor and liberal leaders pondered the coalition's future, black and brown organizers would launch a new wave of demonstrations and political engagement. And their militant advocacy would, in turn, force all members of the coalition to recognize the centrality of the fight for civil rights.

The Black Civil Rights Movement at a Crossroads

"Texas Is Integrating," read the headline of a special report in the *Texas Observer* in late June 1963. The lengthy article detailed the advances and limitations of desegregation in the Lone Star State, noting that "Integration has become respectable," even as economic issues continued to constrain African Americans' aspirations. "With alacrity that would be easy to exaggerate but is nevertheless slightly dizzying, public officials and private businessmen in the state have been opening white-only facilities and schools to Negroes." Only East Texas, "the left anchor of the deep South," and the "rurally-dominated Texas legislature" remained as holdouts.

Yet the remainder of the article continued to outline all of the areas in which black Texans remained far from equal—particularly in employment. The federal government had begun to reverse this trend with compensatory action in favor of African Americans in a few well-publicized cases, including at the Dallas Post Office and several large government contractors. Nearly all of organized labor had begun integrating, and its leadership was "firmly in favor of equal treatment and integration of Negroes into all Texas unions." Yet craft union leaders continued to drag their feet on admitting black members, and the legislature had balked at the Texas AFL-CIO's efforts to pass new state laws that would have prohibited all employment discrimination, by union and company alike.

Meanwhile, outside of East Texas, most restaurants and theaters had quietly integrated, but few African Americans could afford to patronize them anyway. Schools had begun integrating, but only slowly and under court orders did districts concede even token inclusion. The Democratic Coalition had integrated some black voters into the party's liberal wing, and conservative Democrats and even Republicans had begun to embrace African Americans, yet the state's elected officialdom remained nearly lily-white. "Integration thus makes much news in Texas," the piece concluded, "but continued segregation seldom does."[16]

The black civil rights movement, which had burst onto the scene with the sit-ins of 1960, had seemingly retreated from view in the face of continued progress. Still, most ordinary African Americans remained far from content.[17] Economic opportunities were inaccessible and political power elusive. Beneath the veneer of civility and peaceful advancement, liberal and working-class black activists were continuing to organize. They were forced to maneuver around the new political realities within their communities: namely, the facts that the novelty of integration had expired, that some of their erstwhile allies had been incorporated into the white-led power structure, and that so much still remained to be done. At both the local level and statewide, African American activists would respond to these challenges by returning to the streets, launching new local political campaigns, and deepening their connections across racial lines.

African American activists in San Antonio continued to set the standard for militancy in Texas. As they had for more than a decade, G. J. Sutton, Rev. Claude W. Black, and Eugene Coleman kept up the fight for complete integration, economic opportunity, and independent political power. They had made significant progress toward their long-term goals, yet the Good Government League (GGL) and the Chamber of Commerce still dominated local civic and economic life. Restaurants and theaters had "voluntarily" desegregated their accommodations and staffs, the elites claimed, and African Americans should be grateful for the gifts they had received. The militant black activists who frequented the SNAP House were not. They wanted justice to be guaranteed, not as a gift, but "as a right," in words of Rev. Black. They demanded that "voluntary" commitments must be replaced by an ordinance—there must be integration by law. Above all, there must be democracy; the activists continued to demand and work for an independent voice in the city's and the state's governance.

As always, electoral politics and civil rights organizing dovetailed. Sutton first ran for the San Antonio City Council in the spring of 1961, around the same time that local activists were fighting for jobs at Handy Andy and launching the first demonstrations to integrate movie theaters. Sutton's campaign sheds light on the dynamics at play in the city's politics throughout the early 1960s. He met fierce opposition from the business-friendly GGL, and that, combined with the poll tax and the at-large electoral system, all but ensured his defeat. Still, "Sutton did himself and the city of San Antonio proud. He drew representative votes from all sections of the city," wrote student activist Bill

Rev. Claude Black and G. J. Sutton demanded a local ordinance to guarantee their civil rights and picketed City Hall as representatives of the local NAACP chapter, June 12, 1963. They are conferring with Roy Barrera Sr., a Mexican American attorney whom Governor John Connally would appoint as Texas secretary of state in 1968. Courtesy *San Antonio Light* Photograph Collection, UTSA-ITC, Image L-6175-A-3, San Antonio Express/ZUMAPRESS.com.

Donahue in *SNAP*. Sutton's campaign needed a 90 percent turnout from the East Side's African American precincts to offset the conservative North Side. He didn't get it, as more than one in ten black voters voted against Sutton. Donahue remarked that this was America and anyone was free to do as he pleased, and to support candidates of one's own choosing. But, he added, "I find it impossible to comprehend the reason a person . . . would go cavorting around a Negro, or a white precinct for that matter, attempting to persuade persons to vote for a white man who had done nothing and hasn't promised to do anything for the Negro, and in so doing [commit] the JUDAS act of stabbing a fellow Negro in the back."[18]

Sutton ran again in 1962, only to be stymied once again by opposition from the GGL and conservative African Americans.[19] Still, independent candidates continued to run in order to protest the domination of the GGL, add their strength to local coalition tickets, and build political support for the future. For example, on April 9, 1962, just a month before the first primary that year, Sutton, Black, and the head of the local Pullman porters union sponsored a series of seminars at Black's Mt. Zion First Baptist Church on three consecutive weekday evenings. A white liberal government professor from St. Mary's University was the keynote speaker at the "School for Community Political Participation," while "other local dignitaries" joined various panels. The school also displayed demonstration voting machines so "the public" could come and acquaint themselves with how to actually pull the lever on election day.[20]

Political activities continued to contribute to civil rights organizing and vice versa. In the fall of 1962, local NAACP president Harry V. Burns sent a letter to Mayor W. W. McAllister in which he criticized the city for failing to end racial discrimination. The city's inaction, Burns wrote, "is not only retarding moral progress, but is also retarding economic progress." For evidence he pointed to a group of 750 black civilian air force workers who had refused to move to San Antonio's Randolph Field in protest of the city's persistent segregation. Burns added that the housing available to African Americans also remained substandard "because of the racial pattern." The mayor replied without irony that San Antonio "certainly has no integration problems at all" and "segregation is virtually nonexistent."[21]

The mayor's intransigence and willful ignorance touched off a new wave of protest activities in the local NAACP, led by Burns and Black. On October 23, 1962, as described by historian Robert Goldberg, Burns again wrote to McAllister asking that the city council "pass an ordinance outlawing discrimination in public accommodations." The mayor refused to hold public hearings or put the item on the council agenda, and he replied that "the majority opinion" among council members "was that we were stepping out of bounds as a government agency to direct the policy of private business." McAllister reiterated the city's preference that private businesses integrate in a voluntary manner. On February 13, 1963, Burns, Black, and two of their coalition friends (a white and a *mexicano*) visited the council chambers to deliver their own proposed ordinance that would levy a fine on any merchant who discriminated based on race, religion, or color. The council took it under advisement before rejecting it two weeks later, refusing "coercion of white businessmen as the means to integration," as Goldberg put it. "City officials counseled patience and favored continuing the voluntary approach," but they also agreed to appoint a biracial committee to further "study" the NAACP's proposal. Although the formation of the commission seemed like progress, civil rights activists remained dubious. They had seen this tactic used against them before: a blue-ribbon task force, even an interracial one, would likely produce only symbolic recommendations with no real enforcement power. At the very least, the deliberations of the committee would delay the coming of more substantive change. Only an immediate change in the law would satisfy them.[22]

The political motivations of the GGL-dominated city council and GGL mayor were never far from the surface. The activists' push for an integration ordinance coincided with municipal elections, and that year the NAACP and the SNAP House crowd again fielded an independent candidate for the city council. This time it was Rev. Black. Sutton and Coleman swung into action behind his campaign, and this time they managed to recruit Valmo Bellinger to join the effort. A few conservative African Americans opposed the reverend's bid, but most fell into line, recognizing the need for a single black representative on the council. Black represented a consensus candidate, and the East Side united as never before. Still, the activists knew that black support would not be enough; the fact that council members were elected at-large meant that Black needed to attract support from across the city. Serving as the chairman of the campaign, Sutton called on the other members of the Bexar County Democratic Coalition to endorse the effort. He stated that the city's forty thousand African Americans had given their votes to many white and Mexican American officials—liberal and moderate—and they now expected that loyalty to be reciprocated.

In the middle of March, Sutton and Bellinger organized a tea party on the East Side and invited all of the city's elected officials to attend. The event soon became a "roll call" in which candidates were asked to publicly pledge themselves to the campaign. Both the liberals and the moderates appeared suspect, and Bellinger said that each official was "either with us or against us." Albert Peña led the charge, swearing his loyalty and adding that "Every candidate who has received the support of the Bexar County Coalition should publicly announce for the Rev. Claude Black as I am doing here tonight." The rest of the city's Anglo and *mexicano* liberals followed suit, as did the coalition and the local chapter of the Young Democrats. This alone represented a major achievement: Sutton had sought the endorsement of the multiracial alliance in his previous bids but had been disappointed each time. Now, the coalition and even some moderates backed Black's campaign. One politico remained conspicuously absent: Congressman Henry B. Gonzalez maintained that he did not want to involve himself in local races, though one paper noted that he had no problem endorsing a mayoral candidate in New York City. In any event, the roll call had worked, showing the activists exactly which elected officials would come to their aid.

The campaign had great symbolic value beyond the immediate election. Black told the tea party that at the heart of the campaign was the GGL's failure "to meet its obligations to the needs of minorities." He offered sharp, personal criticisms of Mayor McAllister, noting that he had scuttled plans for a local variation on the Peace Corps as well as the proposed integration ordinance. In fact, McAllister was an old enemy of the activists dating back to the late 1940s, when his policies as head of the San Antonio Junior College Board proved so disagreeable that they spurred Sutton to run for and win a seat on that body in 1948. Fifteen years later, McAllister claimed that the current city council represented all of the city's citizens and that they did so through consensus among its members. He charged that the firebrand Black threatened to disrupt the general harmony that had brought prosperity to the city. "Sure they say this is unity," the pastor said, "but we standing on the outside say this is not unity, but control." The election was not about strong personalities or individuals as much as the larger importance of seeking independent representation, of giving the East Side an opportunity to speak for itself. Although many observers suggested that the campaign was destined to wither under the juggernaut of the GGL, Black saw it in different terms. "We can't lose in this race, because we're not seeking an office," he said. "We're seeking a cause. . . . If we don't knock the door down this time it will be so loose on its hinges it won't take much strength to knock it down next time."[23]

On election day, April 2, Black polled more than fifteen thousand votes, demonstrating strong support from a diverse range of the city's residents in "all sections of town." Still he trailed his opponent by eighteen hundred votes and went down to defeat. *SNAP News* looked on the bright side, declaring that his broad backing showed that "we live in a community that can look beyond the color of a man's skin and vote for a man that is qualified." In the event of a future vacancy on the council, "a cross section of the community should be consulted," the paper added, and Black would be a logical choice to represent all San Antonians. In his "County Comment" column in *SNAP*, Albert Peña added that Black had "won the respect of the community. No political campaign is entirely lost if issues and principles are discussed. And Rev. Black raised and forcefully articulated the primary issue in the Campaign: the need for the minority voice on the Council, to stand-up and speak-up and explain minority problems." Minorities, Peña explained, included not just African Americans and Mexican Americans but also organized labor and other "social, economic, and educational minorities." Black would speak for them all. He "lost the first skirmish, but he will eventually win the battle," Peña added.

"And San Antonio will be a better town as a result." *SNAP News* concluded that the election had also helped the activists prepare for the future. "It separated the wheat from the chaff," Coleman wrote, making plain "whose side who is on." In other words, Black's campaign had revealed which of their allies could be counted upon to stand for justice and which would remain aloof when it really mattered.[24]

Having defeated the electoral threat, GGL leaders continued to stonewall progress on civil rights. At the end of May, the council-appointed committee reported back and encouraged an "accelerated voluntary desegregation program conducted under city government auspices," as historian Goldberg put it. A city-sponsored "Committee on Desegregation" headed by a white GGL member would canvass private businesses, asking their owners to sign pledge cards indicating their willingness to desegregate by the Fourth of July. Valmo Bellinger, Rev. Samuel H. James, educator Joseph Scott, and other "traditional" black leaders supported the new plan, but it was not good enough for the more militant East Side activists organized in the NAACP and *SNAP*. "They were giving the privilege," Black later recalled. "We didn't want a privilege, we wanted a right. They were holding the power in their own hands." Integration was not a gift to be bestowed, he contended. It needed to be the law of the land. Just before his death, the ninety-one-year-old Black nearly jumped out of his wheelchair when recalling the moment, raising his voice yet again: "I WANTED IT AS A RIGHT!"[25] At the same time, the more aggressive organizers rightfully claimed credit for ratcheting up the heat that made the city budge at all. Their incessant demonstrations "provided the lever that moved the powerful conservative community off dead center—even if only an inch or two," they boasted. "While the newspapers criticize the NAACP for picketing, it is obvious that those few sign carriers marching around City Hall was the element that forced the city of San Antonio to take its first major step insuring [*sic*] basic human rights for all its citizens."[26]

Although the San Antonio City Council continued to drag its feet on an ordinance, raising the demand in council chambers, mobilizing independent black voters for Black's campaign, and picketing City Hall to win a "voluntary" desegregation plan all represented significant steps forward for black activists. As always, action in the electoral field and civil rights organizing on the ground contributed toward their long-term goals of achieving independent political power and equal economic opportunities. Sutton, Black, and Burns would soon escalate their combined struggle for integration "as a right" into a statewide fight.

Meanwhile, as the black civil rights movement in San Antonio reached for new heights, Houston in 1963 remained what one journalist termed "a Backwater of the Revolt." There the sit-ins had served to strengthen the hands of black businessmen, who contributed financially to the cause while working behind closed doors to undermine ongoing militant protests. Following their effective takeover of the Progressive Youth Association (PYA) in the fall of 1961, black elites in Houston had worked to contain future demonstrations while improving their relationship with the city's white political and economic leaders. They continued to participate in the Harris County Council of Organizations (HCCO), but increasingly they focused on their own, upper-class organizations. And they were wildly successful in terms of gaining recognition and patronage from white elites, in large part because they promised and effectively delivered a significant portion of the city's vast black electorate.[27]

Working-class African Americans and the city's more militant activists disagreed internally over the best way to respond. The LeRoys and other liberals continued to seek independent political power and deepened their partnerships with like-minded Mexicans Americans and whites in PASO and the Harris County Democrats (HCD). Others, including the Middletons of the Laborers Local 18, joined the elites in demanding jobs and patronage from "moderate" whites. Howard Middleton, the former night student demonstrator and officer of the union, dabbled in the liberal coalition that included the HCD but remained a steadfast supporter of county judge Bill Elliott, a moderate Democrat. In his view, the liberals simply could not match Elliott's offer of jobs. And such loyalty paid dividends. Under the leadership of the Middleton brothers, the all-black Local 18 grew from a few hundred to over five thousand members, wages jumped exponentially, and the quantity of work grew to make the job steadier than ever before. Howard became the union's training director and worked to elevate some union members to semiskilled positions (though African Americans were still excluded from the craft unions). His brother Jimmie's voice became one of the most important within the HCCO, where he brokered deals that succeeded in channeling many black voters into Judge Elliott's fold, at least at the local level.[28]

In all likelihood, Moses and Erma LeRoy privately scoffed at the Middletons' arrangement, noting the a priori limitations of power obtained through patronage. Yet publicly, the veteran civil rights unionists continued to walk a fine line between their history of radical convictions, their ties to labor and desire to build broad multiracial alliances, and their still paramount need to cultivate support within the HCCO. They were able to do so thanks to their continued support among black unionists and neighbors in the Third Ward. By effectively organizing his precinct, Moses remained an officer of the HCCO, and the couple maintained a degree of influence even as the organization became more conservative.[29]

Yet this strategy was only partially successful. While LeRoy and other liberal activists had for a period successfully mediated between the black elites and the student demonstrators, and they had continued the fight through the NAACP and HCCO, they struggled to keep their footing by the dawn of 1963. Direct action demonstrations and militant civil rights organizing on the order of San Antonio had all but disappeared.

As in other parts of the state, civil rights and political organizing remained inseparable, but in Houston that meant that many of the city's erstwhile leaders of the direct action struggle now stumped for conservative candidates in order to win patronage. Their vehicle was the United Political Organization (UPO), a statewide body based in Austin but harboring close ties to black elites across the state. A group of black leaders who had been early backers of John Connally's gubernatorial bid came up with the idea for creating the UPO while attending the governor's inaugural festivities in January 1963. None of the black labor or liberal Yarborough supporters had received invitations to the celebration, which was the first of its kind to be integrated. As they basked in their newfound access and power, these economically elite but politically conservative race leaders decided that they needed a way to share information, coordinate patronage appointments, and organize against the rabble-rousers in their communities. Their informal conversations soon gave rise to the UPO. Rev. H. Rhett James, who had led the sit-ins in Dallas earlier in the decade, served as the group's executive secretary. Hamah King, an attorney who led the efforts to bail out and represent student PYA demonstrators in Houston, served as its state vice president, while George Washington Jr., another key attorney from the Houston sit-in movement, rode the UPO to a high-level appointment in the state government. Educator Joe Scott of San Antonio was honored at the UPO's early July 1963 convention, and he used the occasion to attack black activists who partnered with organized labor. "I say to devil with national, state and local coalitions," Scott thundered. For all their rhetoric, many craft unions still refused to admit African Americans, he charged. If African Americans can serve at the top levels of the state government, Scott added, surely they have the capacity to work as pipefitters and carpenters. Scott then offered his own call to action, one that flew in the face of the liberal Democratic Coalition: "Unified we can be our own power and we can outvote organized labor."[30]

The UPO "is at present a conservative Negro organization," the *Observer* concluded. "Its leaders do not renounce militance for civil rights; they simply do not practice it, and they support politicians who view it askance. The main thing U.P.O. wants from these politicians is appointments and jobs." Ronnie Dugger, the *Observer*'s editor, was willing to give it the benefit of the doubt, adding that "Negroes can not be blamed any more than anyone else for giving in to the benefits men in power hand out to those who support them politically," and it was indeed possible that the UPO would remain distant from some of Connally's big business bedfellows. Still, Dugger added, as long as M. J. Anderson of Austin, "the leading pro-Connally Negro politician in Texas" continued to steer the group, the UPO "has no chance of being regarded as an independent, democratic organization."[31]

The black civil rights movement in Texas thus found itself at a crossroads in the spring and summer of 1963. In the "backwater" of Houston, a group of conservative elites had seized control of the direct action struggle and effectively removed it from the scene. Statewide, led by the UPO, a group of "conservative" African Americans sought to direct the energies of the movement into political action for candidates who promised patronage but not democracy. On the other hand, in San Antonio, civil rights organizers continued to demonstrate in the streets while also working to wed the struggle to liberal candidates and multiracial coalitions for independent political power. Sutton and company had gained the upper hand in the intraracial battle in San Antonio, dragging most of the traditionally reserved race leaders along with them. Veteran activists in the left wing of Houston's HCCO sought to emulate them and regain control from their own conservative counterparts, but for the moment, the UPO faction maintained the advantage. Across the state, it was not yet clear which tendency would prevail, but a parallel movement among Mexican Americans and a growing understanding of civil rights among white labor and liberal leaders would soon tip the balance in favor of the militant black organizers. And unbeknownst to all, within months, a solitary activist in Austin would provide lightning in a bottle, spurring a mass mobilization that would bring the entire Democratic Coalition into the center of the civil rights storm. Among all groups, *intra*racial conflicts would soon give way to *inter*racial collaboration.

The Crystal City "Pilot Project"

On April 2, 1963—the same day that Rev. Black took his stand against the GGL—a coalition of organized labor, PASO activists, high school students, and ordinary *mexicanos* celebrated a hard-fought victory in the municipal elections of Crystal City, a small agricultural hamlet 120 miles southwest of San Antonio. For the first time since the advent of Juan Crow in the region fifty years earlier, the majority group of *mexicano* working people had discarded the Anglo and Mexican American elites who had long monopolized local politics, replacing the old *patrones* with a group of independent, liberal, ordinary folks. *Los cinco candidatos*, as the five independent candidates came to be known, were drawn from the ranks of the working class, since none of the town's small-time *mexicano* professionals were willing to risk their status by joining an electoral revolt against the city's Anglo leaders. Instead, Juan Cornejo, the business agent of the local Teamsters union and an employee at the city's spinach packinghouse, headed the ticket and soon became the mayor.

Historians have hailed the "Crystal experiment" as the opening salvo in the Chicano movement. It was the first "revolt" against Anglo domination in the area, and it laid the groundwork for the more colorful, student-led movement that emerged near the end of the 1960s.[32] This characterization is accurate, but scholars have not explored the revolt's relationship to the state's evolving multiracial liberal coalition. The election did, in fact, mark an unprecedented uprising, a challenge to South Texas whites so powerful that the state called out the Texas Rangers to contain it. Yet the revolt was not a sharp break from the past, and it was more closely connected to the contemporaneous Democratic Coalition than to the future Chicano movement. Crystal City would mark a turning point in Texas politics, but not just for *mexicanos*. It would fundamentally reorient the emerging liberal alliance toward direct action, confrontational tactics, and unapologetic support for civil rights. In so doing, it would also open up more space for the black freedom struggle and liberal politicians of all colors.[33]

The Crystal City uprising had its origins in the fall of 1962, when Albert Peña returned from the state Democratic convention in El Paso determined to demonstrate the independent voting power of PASO and the state's "Latin vote." The group's withdrawal of its endorsement of Connally and the rally at the phone booth set PASO back on track for the future. Yet PASO leaders needed to find a way to go on the offensive after having had little success in three years of endorsing candidates for statewide office. "It was the wrong way—the ineffective way," an anonymous Peña aide told Carlos Conde of the *Dallas Morning News*. "We decided to work from the bottom up—organize the rank and file and concentrate on a mayor's race, or city council or even county sheriff." Conde added that "Pena and his PASO group wanted to show everyone what the 'sleeping giant,' as they like to call the Latin American voters, could do when aroused from its traditional doldrums." The group soon began looking for a "pilot project" that would be "ripe enough for the spectacular political splash that it wanted to make."[34]

It found a perfect case in Crystal City. There, in the self-proclaimed "spinach capital of the world," Teamster Juan Cornejo and Andrew Dickens, an Anglo retired oil field worker, had already launched a poll tax drive among local *mexicanos*. Dickens was furious with the county attorney over a soured land deal, so he joined forces with Cornejo, the local "Teamster-PASO man," whom he judged to be another likely dissident. The duo began registering voters on their own and only later went to Teamsters' regional director Ray Schafer and the statewide PASO's Peña for help. Cornejo's local Teamsters union represented about three hundred workers, all *mexicanos*, so the drive began there. Next the duo hired unemployed *mexicanos* to serve as their canvassers. These campaign workers, according to Conde, "knocked on doors at nights, stopped Latins on the street, in taverns, and even visited the crews out in the fields on pay day." By the time the campaign had concluded, with little outside assistance, Dickens and Cornejo had netted 1,129 Spanish-surnamed voters on the local registration rolls. Most were working-class Mexican Americans for whom the $1.75 poll tax "came hard," requiring the organizers to collect nickels and dimes from many individuals who were "on the installment plan." At the same time, only 542 Anglos paid their poll taxes, creating a 2-to-1 margin in favor of the *mexicanos*. The total number of political participants was abysmal but not atypical. Less than seventeen hundred of Crystal City's population of ten thousand registered to vote. Still, the fact that eight thousand of the town's residents were "stoop labor" who were "hopping mad" at the Anglos gave the *mexicano* organizers hope that they would receive broad-based support moving forward.[35]

With the voter rolls now closed for the year and the numbers on their side, PASO and the regional Teamsters arrived in full force, convinced that a local victory was possible. Money for manpower came from the Teamsters and the Texas AFL-CIO, while PASO and the union both supplied skilled, experienced political organizers. The first to arrive was Martin Garcia, a PASO district director from Kingsville and a part-time law student at St. Mary's University on the West Side of San Antonio. The Teamsters hired him, offering a salary of tuition, books, and expenses for his next semester. "His assignment was to plan the campaign, provide a list of candidates and then serve as over-all campaign manager," wrote Conde.[36]

The next organizer to arrive in Crystal City was Henry Muñoz Jr., known to many by his nickname, "The Fox." Born in Laredo in 1920, Muñoz served in World War II and mustered out to San Antonio, where he became a union printer. A decade later, after serving as a paid union staffer, he left the trade to attend St. Mary's University, graduating in 1960.[37] He took a job with the Bishop's Committee for the Spanish Speaking, a clerical advocacy organization that he helped to connect to both ordinary *mexicanos* and various labor and civil rights groups nationwide. He lent support to a lawsuit filed by the Texas AFL-CIO to force the federal government to end the border "commuter problem," making common cause with labor's Latin American Affairs Committee, the AGIF, and other Mexican American organizations. At home in San Antonio he launched a program to train *mexicanos* for jobs as tractor-trailer drivers in partnership with the local Teamsters union.[38]

In early 1962, Muñoz hoped to expand on this partnership, so he invited Teamsters' president Jimmy Hoffa to come to San Antonio to consider organizing migrant farmworkers. The union had intermittently approached agricultural laborers in California and elsewhere, so bringing the campaign to Texas was not totally out of the blue. Several *mexicano* farmworkers joined Muñoz in greeting Hoffa's plane at the airport, carrying signs reading "Help us, Jimmy." Muñoz asked for $350,000 to launch a three-year "pre-organizational program of teaching the migrants to the thought of union efforts, and conditioning the state legislature to the thought of easing up some of the anti-labor restrictions now on the books." Hoffa did not flinch at the price tag, and he soon sent three staffers to San Antonio to continue researching the proposed program. Meanwhile, Hoffa's visit "prompted bitter comments from church and business leaders" in the city who complained about Muñoz's affiliation with a labor "racketeer." "I wasn't aware of Hoffa's ever being convicted of racketeering," Muñoz later recalled. "It's like these migrants are drowning and Hoffa comes along and throws them a tube, and you tell them don't take that tube because it comes from Hoffa. Does that make sense?"[39] Hoffa's field agents decided against a grand campaign to organize farmworkers, but the union brass was sufficiently impressed that it hired Muñoz in January 1963 to "study the Latin American migrant force in the United States for the Teamsters."[40]

Muñoz's personal history and previous contact with national Teamsters' leaders helps to explain how and why the union committed itself so fully to the Crystal City revolt, adding a key coalition partner for local organizers and state PASO leaders alike. The Teamsters' arrival cannot be attributed simply to the fact that Cornejo was a member or because the union represented the small California Packing plant there (it was owned by Del Monte). Those conditions existed in countless hamlets throughout the country. Rather, the Teamsters were specifically looking to make inroads in Texas—including among Mexican American agricultural and packinghouse workers. Once international union officials learned that a poll tax drive was underway, they realized it was their opportunity to make an entrance. They hired the man they knew, Henry "The Fox" Muñoz, and quickly dispatched him to Crystal City.

Muñoz joined PASO's Martin Garcia and the local organizers just as the poll tax drive was ending. Teamsters' regional director Ray Shafer of San Antonio, an influential member of the Bexar County Democratic Coalition, deployed Carlos Moore of Fort Worth to join them. Muñoz recalled that the three staffers were welcomed to the town by the Texas Rangers. The trio went "down there on the main drive, and we were flagged down and harassed by Captain [A. Y.] Allee. This was January 31 of 1963," the last day of the poll tax campaign, and the town's Anglo leaders had just realized that *mexicanos* had more than doubled the Anglos' numbers on the registration rolls. "From then on, Allee would come in at all hours of the night and take me out into the woods and threaten to shoot me—take me out every night," Muñoz added. "I could almost set my watch by what time he'd come in.... I [knew that] at 12:15 at night he'd be there and take me out forty or fifty miles in the woods and give me all kinds of hell."[41]

With the poll tax drive complete, the three organizers and local union leader Cornejo began formulating their strategy. Muñoz recalled that they "went to the mayor of Crystal City . . . and all that we asked was one representative—one Mexicano—on the City Council. 'No,' he said, 'Hell, no. That's out of the question.' Then we decided to fill the ticket." Garcia called local PASO activists and poll tax drive participants together for a meeting on February 8. The twenty-three *mexicanos* who showed up named their group the Citizens Committee for Better Government (CCBG), and seventeen of them agreed to stand for local office. The list was then trimmed to thirteen, then seven, and finally the group chose the *cinco candidatos*. As anticipated, Mexican American businessmen and professionals wanted nothing to do with the campaign. *Los cinco* were workers, like the "lower socio-economic Latin American community" that they sought to organize. "The candidates represented the plight of their group," Conde wrote in the *Dallas Morning News*. "Their average education was about the seventh grade. They dressed in workmen's clothes. They had little knowledge of city economics and government. They deeply resented the Anglos." They were not the "best qualified" Mexican American candidates by traditional standards, but, as Cornejo pointed out, "We are educated in the way of our people." Muñoz recalled the criticism levied at their slate, but he said the decision was simple. "You didn't have many Ph.D.'s and masters' degrees walking down the street in Crystal City when people [were] starving," he said. "But we did find cinco candidatos that had the guts and fortitude to run." Martin Garcia took on what journalist Conde called the "monumental task of shaping up five unpolished hopefuls into presentable candidates, keeping them in line and writing their speeches."[42]

Los cinco candidatos and the three organizers began preparing for the April 2 election, while Peña and Shafer monitored the situation from San Antonio. Albert Fuentes ran back and forth between the two cities and kept them up to date on the campaign's developments. Garcia took the five candidates to city hall to file for office, but "the clerk said there were no application blanks," according to Conde. "They didn't argue. They had obtained a Thermo-fax copy earlier and Garcia typed out five applications. They turned these in and demanded a receipt." They ordered ten thousand campaign posters—one for every resident of the town; five for every registered voter—and developed a message centered on "anti-Anglo" sentiments "based largely on racial, economic and social inequalities." They began holding "official" meetings every Sunday and "unofficial" gatherings almost every day. "The crowds kept getting larger," Conde reported. The organizers began identifying and "cultivating" local leaders to organize, manage, and address the growing rallies. Rank-and-file activists plastered the city with campaign posters, only to have them torn down each night. They posted new ones the following days and collected the torn-down posters, displaying the latter at the weekly meetings. "Sure the 'gringo' says he loves you," activists told the crowds. "But he loves you in your place—below him where he can control you." The torn-down posters were vivid examples of what gringos thought of *mexicanos*, organizers said. But "This is a democracy, and in a democracy, majority rules. We are the majority."[43]

Even more telling signs of Anglo resistance were the growing number of economic reprisals and the increasing visibility of the Texas Rangers. Muñoz recalled that the "cinco candidatos became prime targets of the city administration and Captain Allee and his Texas Rangers.... One of them used to own a small photo shop, and the first thing the city officials did, they declared that he had to put in new wiring and this and that, so actually, they closed him down. The other one was working in a gas station as an attendant, and they fired him." The Rangers, who were sent by Governor Connally to "keep the peace," took over the local law enforcement agencies and imposed an informal curfew that applied only to the town's *mexicanos*. Captain Allee shut down bars and clubs frequented by *mexicanos* and proved true to his reputation of terrorizing and beating *mexicanos* who stepped out of line. The rallies continued, but activists faced frequent physical assaults and threats at the hands of the Rangers. Economic reprisals continued against many campaign supporters, and Cal-Pack, the spinach-packing plant, soon joined in by firing three Mexican American workers for wearing campaign "tags" to work.[44]

This last instance of retaliation proved to be a critical turning point. A "PASO-Teamster man" told Conde that the campaign was "gaining ground daily but the people still showed a weakness.... The Latins were afraid that the Anglos would start getting rough with them and that we would not protect them." But after the firing at Cal-Pack in mid-March, the Teamsters swung into action. The union contract protected employees from such reprisals, and organizers "moved in swiftly and had [the fired workers] reinstated." The union members, at least, were convinced. Anglo managers now had to bow down to the pressure from out-of-town Teamsters' officials. The electoral revolution promised to complete this transformation in daily power relations, extending it beyond the work site to City Hall. The spirits of the rank and file were further bolstered on March 24, when three state representatives from Bexar County, including two Mexican Americans, came to Crystal City to speak at a mass rally, as did "PASO and Teamster brass," probably Albert Peña and Ray Shafer.[45]

Around the same time, the rest of the Democratic Coalition became aware of the campaign and rallied behind it. Albert Fuentes attended the statewide coalition meetings, where he reported on the Crystal City campaign and passed the hat for contributions. Hank Brown overlooked the fact that the Teamsters often competed with the state AFL-CIO and dispatched desperately needed, generous funds to the Crystal City organizers for the last stretch of the campaign. Jim Phelps of Houston, an "independent" liberal who chaired the January 1963 meeting in which the coalition was reborn, sent $100 to PASO for the campaign of *los cinco*, matching the single largest individual contribution to the effort. Moses LeRoy, the longtime African American civil rights unionist from Houston and a member of the Democratic Coalition's new Steering Committee, added five dollars to the pot, and professor George Sánchez gave ten dollars more. The statewide PASO also sent out an appeal for contributions from its members and local chapters, raffling off a TV at the rate of five chances per dollar.[46]

In the final weeks of the campaign, thanks to the critical financial support from across the state, the Teamster-PASO organizers ramped up their voter-education efforts in Crystal City. "For those that could not read, the campaign leaders worked out a numerical system for the voter to memorize," Conde reported. The organizers prepared "sneak cards," small versions of a filled-out sample ballot that voters could carry (illegally) into the voting booths. Carlos Moore trained the candidates on the election code and other legal matters, leading local people to call him a "big city lawyer" even though he was not an attorney. And one lawyer who was a member of the San Antonio PASO chapter trained election supervisors to work at the polling places.[47]

The night before the election, the candidates staged a final mass rally to prepare the voters for the final push. As wind ripped through outdoor Juarez Plaza, and as dusk turned to night, Martin Garcia kicked off the addresses, speaking in Spanish. "We're here tonight because deep in our hearts, we're all Mexicans, and tomorrow we're going to vote for our people," he said. PASO's Albert Fuentes welcomed the gathering corps of out-of-town reporters by saying, in English, that they were witnessing "a people setting themselves free through the ballot box." Then he turned to the crowd, reassuring them in their native tongue. "Do not be afraid," he said. "The victory we win tomorrow is here tonight. The Anglos know this now. More important, we know it too." José Ángel Gutiérrez, the leader of a group of local high school students and recent graduates who had served as some of the organizers' most reliable local activists, also addressed the throng. He sharply refuted the incumbents' claims that discrimination did not exist in the city: "we have only to look around us to know the truth," he said. "We look at the schools . . . the houses we live in . . . the few opportunities . . . the dirt in the streets . . . and we know."[48]

On Election Day, April 2, 1963, the Anglos made one last-ditch effort to win the race by suppressing the *mexicano* vote. Muñoz recalled that "Cal-Pack put up a notice that this particular time on election day, they were going to work overtime—start working at five o'clock in the morning and work until nine o'clock at night." Once again, the union contract came in handy, protecting the several hundred *mexicano* workers at the plant who had paid their poll taxes. A clause in the contract required the company to give workers time off to go and vote. Shafer had instructed Muñoz to "read the riot act to the Cal-Pack officials," which Muñoz did, and each worker ended up getting two hours off to head to the polls. Meanwhile, local "growers told migrant workers that instead of paying them fifty cents per hour to pick carrots, they were going to pay them a dollar, if they stayed in the fields until way past 8:00 P.M." But the organizers had prepared the *mexicano* crew leaders for this tactic, instructing them to begin their shifts in the early morning so they could get the full day's pay and still make it to the polls. "At four o'clock [in the afternoon] everybody was going to get in the truck and not go home, but [go] straight to city hall and vote. And, that's exactly what happened. All the crew leaders got the people to City Hall before the closing of the polls, and they won."[49]

When the votes were finally counted, all five *mexicano* candidates for city council had narrowly prevailed. Elated local residents paraded down the streets, hoisting organizers Garcia and Fuentes and all of *los cinco* onto their shoulders while screaming, as one report put it, "a couple of *mexicano* versions of the rebel yell." Once in office, the new officials elected Cornejo as mayor, completing his transformation from humble union representative to the town's chief executive. The victory could not have been more complete. Garcia remarked that "fear and tradition have been conquered. There is a new respect. Self-respect. They have won."[50]

The support of the Democratic Coalition had proven critical in helping the movement get over the top. In addition to the many small contributions and the resources and networks of PASO and the Teamsters, coalition staffer Larry Goodwyn had slipped into town the previous afternoon, bringing another last-minute infusion of cash to assist the get-out-the-vote effort. On behalf of the statewide alliance, Goodwyn quietly provided aid for all of the unanticipated costs of the final push. Such expenses would have included the standard costs of electioneering in the era: refreshments for the evening rally; the last-minute printing of flyers and placards; stipends for poll watchers, block walkers, drivers, and crew leaders; and many other small but critical charges. The nearly $400 he spent in two days dwarfed the sum of the previous contributions and provided the campaign with a much-needed final burst of energy. Goodwyn also sensed the public relations potential of the moment and recorded it for a piece in the next *Texas Observer*—in which he omitted his own and the coalition's roles in the otherwise painstakingly detailed cover article. Instead, he highlighted the role of local people. "In South Texas," he

A GIANT AWAKENING
(NO LONGER THE SLEEPING GIANT)

PASO split in half during the 1962 gubernatorial primary and again following the Crystal City revolt the next year. Hailing from the prolabor/liberal wing of the association, this June 1963 cartoon shows PASO freeing "Mexican American Voting Power" from the bonds of "Apathy." Note that "labor" is providing critical assistance in helping PASO cut the ties—which have already been severed in Peña's San Antonio and Crystal City. Courtesy Dr. Hector P. Garcia Papers, Mary and Jeff Bell Library, Texas A&M University—Corpus Christi, Folder 233.14.

wrote simply, "the vanguard of a million *mexicanos* have begun to make their voices heard."[51]

Yet the victory on April 2 was just the beginning of the struggle, and the harassment and intimidation of the town's *mexicanos* continued after the election and even after *los cinco* took office. "Naturally, the establishment didn't like it," Muñoz recalled. "They said, 'Oh, this is bloc voting.' It was all right when they work it, but not the poor Mexicanos. Oh, no. They're ignorant, and all that kind of stuff." One of the triumphant candidates, who had skipped work to campaign on election day, was fired from his job at the Economart. Another new councilman who worked as a truck driver had his salary cut in half. The Texas Rangers stayed in town long after any threat of a disturbance had subsided. In fact, the cowboy gunslingers continued to attack supporters of *los cinco*, including Mayor Cornejo, whom Captain Allee personally assaulted. The leader of the Rangers shadowed the councilmen, and Governor Connally ignored Cornejo's complaints and appeals to remove the Rangers. It took an appeal from Senator Yarborough to U.S. attorney general Robert F. Kennedy and the arrival of the FBI before Connally finally withdrew his troops.[52]

Cornejo and company soon discovered that governing was wholly different from campaigning, and ongoing Anglo opposition continued to thwart the new council's ambitions. Two years after the successful uprising, in 1965, Anglos and elite Mexican Americans would organize a biracial rival slate and defeat Cornejo's ticket of working-class *mexicanos*. The white conservatives had warmed up to an alliance with elite Mexican Americans and ultimately conceded some tangible improvements to win over the town's barrios.[53]

Although the independent revolt of *mexicano* workers would eventually be defeated, the final reversal should not detract from the movement's earth-shattering short-term impact. For the first time since the advent of Juan Crow in South Texas, ordinary Mexican Americans—aided by PASO, the Teamsters, and the Democratic Coalition—had organized and overcome their local Anglo overlords. Just as important, they had also discarded the "Uncle Toms" or *Tío Tomáses* of their own ethnic group. An editorial in the *Corpus Christi Caller-Times* a month after the election aptly summed up its broader meaning: while the old *patron* system had largely died after World War II, it had been replaced by "a distinctive middle class" that "identified itself with the Anglo population rather than the Latin." If they participated in politics at all, "they tended to side with candidates and slates chosen by Anglos." In contrast, the Crystal City "revolt" marked a new "benchmark in the political history of Texas," a rebellion not only against Anglos but the *mexicanos*' own self-appointed race leaders. The *cinco candidatos* won with the help of the Teamsters and PASO, and they "represent workers, not the Latin middle class," the editorial concluded. The election signaled the renewed strength of PASO and its improved ability to build "a coherent political organization" for both working-class and professional *mexicanos*. Although the future remained unclear, it appeared that, through PASO, Mexican Americans would soon join "with Anglo liberals and labor to control the [Democratic] party at most levels. This apparent minority eventually might become a majority and assume control of Texas politics."[54]

"PASO Doble"

The Crystal City election clearly represented a declaration of independence for Mexican American working people and liberal activists like Peña. Yet the editors' hope that the Mexican American middle class would rally around it proved unfounded. In fact, the Crystal City revolt would lead directly to another split within PASO as well as criticism of the Democratic Coalition's role from "independent" white liberals.

Surprisingly, these fractures would end up helping Peña and the coalition. The controversies surrounding Crystal City would compel the remaining moderates and conservatives within PASO to withdraw permanently from the organization, leaving it securely in the hands of Peña, Fuentes, George Sánchez, Bob Sanchez, and other liberal and labor leaders across the state. Far better equipped than their more conservative counterparts to participate in the growing Democratic Coalition, the liberal-labor activists would emerge unencumbered by the presence of the less-militant middle-class members in the same organization. Meanwhile, the Crystal City victory would reaffirm for labor leaders Hank Brown and the Teamsters' Ray Shafer why their organizations mattered in the broader civil rights and electoral struggles, leading their organizations to adopt more radical positions and extend their participation on the ground beyond their substantial financial contributions. This, in turn, would help them convince white "independent" liberals to follow their example.

Yet in the immediate aftermath of the Crystal City revolt, many of the members of the Democratic Coalition were alarmed rather than encouraged by the successful campaign. Goodwyn's lengthy feature in the *Observer* brought the story of *los cinco* to audiences across the state and triggered a debate among white liberals over the role of anti-Anglo prejudice in the political mobilization of ethnic minorities. Editor Ronnie Dugger criticized the Teamster-PASO campaign rhetoric and charged discrimination "in reverse," while contributor Hart Stilwell and other white liberals attacked *los cinco* for not including a single Anglo on their slate. Cornejo maintained that no Anglos were willing to join them, despite repeated entreaties, but the criticisms continued. Professor George I. Sánchez responded by blasting Dugger, reminding him that he had "been fighting racism since you were wearing three cornered pants." Sánchez reiterated that those who wanted to represent "mexicanos" must understand their circumstance, "identify with it, and dedicate yourself to the reforms indicated by that circumstance. If that's racism, make the most of it." If Anglos wanted to avoid future uprisings, they needed to end discrimination—it was as simple as that. "Let Crystal City be a lesson to other communities in Texas," Sánchez concluded. "These people, Negroes or mexicanos, are not cattle but citizens of the United States; with, as the saying goes, 'all of the rights and privileges thereunto appertaining.' . . . How my heart bleeds for the Crystal City 'Anglo' politicians!"[55] Immediately after the victory, Henry Muñoz opined that the only issues were "hunger, and exploitation, and a tradition of poverty to overcome." Martin Garcia agreed, but he added that saying so in that manner "does not make it any easier for us to make ourselves understandable to our liberal friends."[56]

As it turned out, PASO would have just as much trouble explaining the campaign to moderate and conservative Mexican Americans. The developing split within PASO centered on one issue: control by the Teamsters. Journalist Carlos Conde reported that the two organizations had agreed to use one another in Crystal City. The campaign was "Teamster-manned," he added, but "fronted by PASO."[57] Yet this pragmatic, mutually exploitative and mutually beneficial relationship proved hard to swallow for many PASO activists, including national president and cofounder Dr. Hector P. Garcia. The Teamsters' alleged connections to organized crime on the East Coast marked the union as un-American, and the longtime leader of the AGIF refused to share his bed with Jimmy Hoffa, regardless of the short-term benefits. Organized labor of any persuasion remained anathema to many conservative PASO members, leaders like Laredo's Judge Benavides or the Bonillas of Corpus Christi, who had long argued that participating in coalitions with labor or accepting labor's money amounted to accepting external control of PASO. The confrontational nature of the Crystal City campaign also irked many moderates, who balked at the organizers' "anti-Anglo" rhetoric and their electoral strategy "based largely on racial, economic and social inequalities."

In contrast, liberal PASO leaders defended the coalition effort and Peña's leadership of PASO. In McAllen, labor advisor Bob Sanchez and liberal county commissioner Leo J. Leo explained to critics that the organization was not creating a "race problem" between Anglos and *mexicanos* but was responding to fifty years of discrimination. Until Mexican Americans are proportionately represented in government, they argued, future Crystal City–style campaigns would be necessary. The coalition with Teamsters was appropriate and effective in this local effort, but such collaboration did not require a future commitment to continuing the partnership elsewhere. Sanchez added, "Certainly PASO shall look to the possibility of forming a coalition with any other organization or individual in a locality wherever we shall find it convenient but we shall certainly always retain our individuality and shall never become either subservient or controlled." Sanchez and Leo concluded that they looked forward to a day without distinctions based on ethnic origins, a moment in which they could "disband PASO and quietly go home."[58]

For his part, Peña faced harsh personal criticism for the part he played in the Crystal City revolt. In early May, just one month after *los cinco* triumphed, the other four members of the Bexar County Commissioners Court censured Peña for a letter he wrote in support of the insurgent candidates, charging the PASO leader with "injecting racism into the election." Peña had written that he had "all the faith in the world that our people in Crystal City are proud and conscientious, and that you will unite and elect the only true Mexicanos in the race." The Commissioners Court's resolution accused Peña of practicing discrimination and using Bexar County letterhead to address the people of Crystal City, giving the "false impression that Bexar County itself was supporting the vile and vicious attempt to set citizen against citizen." Peña fiercely protested, claiming that their real objection to Crystal City was the fact that 95 percent of the people voted. The censure passed with his sole dissenting vote.[59]

Such was the atmosphere that prevailed as PASO prepared to hold its second annual state convention in early June 1963. Albert Fuentes had planned to run for the state chairmanship, but his personal role as "one of the key strategists" of the Crystal City campaign had eroded his support. Fuentes then launched a "draft Peña" movement to convince the organization's only chairman (and his boss) to stand for another term. Martin Garcia added that "The theme of the convention will be 'Remember Crystal City. . . . We are going to push the idea that the organization must be aggressive and find allies wherever it can in order to be successful." Garcia chaired the district that included the dissidents from Nueces County, but he was confident that the Peña-Fuentes faction of which he was part would prevail. "The convention will develop into a fight between liberals and ultra-liberals," he said, "those who want to follow the path of Crystal City and those who want to sit and wish the problem away." In contrast, the leader of the more conservative faction, attorney William Bonilla, "said he believes PASO should concentrate on political education of Latin American citizens," limiting its activities to voter registration, discussion of issues, and nonpartisan candidate forums. The contrast between the two philosophies could hardly have been clearer.[60]

The convention itself unfolded as predicted, with Peña's "ultra-liberal" faction prevailing by a wide margin. The anti-Teamster group knew that they had lost soon after they arrived, but they still attempted a wide range of parliamentary tactics in order to boost their vote totals. National chairman Hector P. Garcia blasted Peña and gave a speech "implying [that] PASO [was] run by Teamsters," according to the official minutes. When the final vote for chair was taken, Peña defeated Willie Bonilla by a vote of 41–20, and Dr. Garcia walked out of the hall in disgust.[61] Garcia then met with reporters outside, casting the issue in individual terms: he complained that the PASO delegates had chosen Ray Shafer of the Teamsters over him, the longtime leader of the AGIF, and by extension, he felt, they had chosen Anglo allies over the Mexican American civil rights struggle. Ramiro Casso and Leo J. Leo, both "ultra-liberals" from the Valley, replied that Garcia's "insinuations" of Teamster control were "just bunk," adding that Garcia had planned to walk out no matter what and that his real dispute with Peña was purely personal.[62]

In fact, the dissenters' campaign against the Crystal City cohort both preceded the convention and became a permanent split in its wake. Prior to the gathering, Garcia had organized a rival PASO chapter in San Antonio, a group led by Henry B. Gonzalez's aide Lalo Solis. Days after the convention, Garcia fired off a series of angry letters to his allies in the Kennedy-Johnson administration, charging that the Teamsters had taken over the organization and that Peña and Fuentes now planned to use PASO to mount challenges to both Governor Connally and Congressman Gonzalez in 1964. A month later, the Nueces County chapter led by Garcia formally withdrew from the state organization, but a local liberal organized a rival club and sought recognition from Peña. Both groups operated under the same name, leading reporter David T. Lopez to conclude that the county was stuck with a "confusing '*PASO doble*'" (literally, "double PASO"; it also references the Latin American ballroom dance).[63]

Across the state, bitter and disenchanted members of the anti-Teamster faction withdrew en masse from the organization, and some even flirted with reviving the Viva Kennedy clubs, creating a "Political Union," or some other "*PASO doble*" that could outflank Peña's group. Gilbert Garcia, the AGIF leader who had served as PASO's organizer for the Democratic Coalition poll tax drive in early 1962, fired off a pair of angry letters to Ed Idar, who had skipped the convention after resigning from PASO and "all political activities" the previous summer. Garcia claimed that the convention outcome was apparent as soon as he arrived. "The labor people had its big guns, Don Yarborough people had its goons, Teamsters were heavy, and the liberals from Houston combined with Austin were ready [*sic*]. There wasn't a Chinaman's chance much less a Mexican chance." The AGIF people were largely missing, and several "sincere and honest" chapters were conspicuously absent. Several "paper" groups led by labor activists carried most of the convention weight, he added.

Yet his own list of paid-up PASO members by county suggested that the question was not sincerity but level of organization. The liberal faction included several of the largest chapters in the organization. In Dallas, Franklin Garcia of the meat cutters union had organized a sizable club of laborers, as had Martin Garcia in his hometown of Kingsville. Zavala County, home of Crystal City, boasted a large chapter of over one hundred members fresh off of their victory, while the liberal PASO groups in Harris and Bexar counties had years of experience working in coalitions. On the other hand, Gilbert Garcia's Tarrant County club counted only twenty-five members, and his "sincere and honest" allies simply did not show up.[64]

When the dust settled, Texas State PASO and most of its local affiliates were firmly in the hands of Albert Peña and his liberal-labor faction. Albert Fuentes was reappointed as state executive secretary, its top administrative post. More important, the dead weight of the more conservative members was gone. PASO was free to pursue future Crystal Cities at the local and statewide levels, and the firebrand Peña remained the group's spokesman. The convention concluded with a series of routine resolutions addressing the bracero program, the "commuter problem," and the poll tax, as well as a series of new initiatives. The group reaffirmed its commitment to nonpartisanship, but it also sent congratulations and thanks to Senator Yarborough for his stance against the Texas Rangers in Crystal City. PASO also reaffirmed its independence from external control and its policy that all members must respect the majority's decisions. Finally, the delegates pledged to act in "solidarity with other minority groups."[65]

All of this added up to a new direction for the future, one centered on militant, confrontational organizing, support for independent candidates, and a general willingness to engage in coalitions with labor, liberals, and African Americans. Peña explained his position regarding the controversy and the future in his remarks to the convention. "I have no apologies to make," he said. "Contrary to some reports" that the people there were "agents of a mysterious and dangerous PASO conspiracy led by Albert A. Peña, Jr.," the truth is that "the sleeping giant simply woke up. . . . So the Mexican-American voters organized politically and made the necessary changes—not by bullets, by ballots." PASO served as a guide, but the revolt was led by the people of Crystal City. PASO would play a "major role" in state politics in the coming years, he added, and it would do so as part of a multiracial liberal alliance. "And the number one issue, the number one problem, is the issue of civil rights for everyone, and what is more important, equal opportunities to obtain these rights." Peña closed by acknowledging that he had made mistakes and that the group had experienced several "differences of opinions, and at times heated debates. But," he added, "this is the way it is in a democracy."[66]

Often depicted as the tragic collapse of the nationalist project of fostering *intra*racial unity, the deep cleavage in PASO and the mass defections of the anti-Teamster faction had in fact opened up new space for its liberal wing to engage in *inter*racial collaborations. With Peña and the liberals and labor activists in control of all facets of the organization, PASO could now engage in the local and statewide coalitions with neither hesitation nor remorse. A triumphant Peña spent little time lamenting the group's transition and instead looked ahead to the fast-approaching election year. He knew that their work was just beginning, and that the coalition would prove key to getting the job done.

Social Learning

The new party alignment after the 1962 elections, the reorganization of the Democratic Coalition, the early experiments and draft proposal for the "Team Program," the growing civil rights movement in San Antonio, the rise of the UPO, the successful "Chicano revolt" in Crystal City, and the liberal victory in the PASO convention—all of these would lead black, brown, and white liberal and labor activists to recommit themselves to grassroots political action and militant demonstrations in the coming years.

The state Democratic Coalition would become their common vehicle. The rapid pace of change and the local struggles erupting across the state had convinced all of the organizers of their need to work together. Most critically, in a matter of months, the burgeoning liberation struggles had forced the thinking of the white activists to evolve. White labor and liberal leaders had learned experientially that they would need to defer to the black and brown civil rights activists in order to move forward. Finally they, like the coalition's black and brown members, had come to accept George Sánchez's idiom that each group needed to speak for itself.[67]

The shift began back in April, when the draft proposal for the "Team Program" had provoked a heated but productive controversy among coalition leaders. Although the debate itself has not survived the test of time, the available sources make it clear that the proposal led to the creation of a radically new leadership structure for the coalition. Since 1961, the coalition had engendered noncommittal and haphazard meetings of top leaders of labor, PASO, African American groups, and white liberal Democrats, but in the end each partner was left free to go its own way, and there was little cohesion among the larger group. Gathering together in April 1963—within weeks of the thrilling municipal elections—the multiracial group determined that the coalition must henceforth be more deliberately democratic, that it must guarantee equal representation for black and brown participants in order to encourage transparency and unified action.

The traditional structurelessness was no longer viable. Although they still refrained from creating a constitution and by-laws, coalition leaders recognized the need to appoint officers and develop a formal power-sharing arrangement. The old, broadly representative but informal agenda and Steering Committee of about ten members gave way to an official "Policy Committee" of sixteen leaders, intentionally organized to include four members from each "leg" of the coalition: Mexican Americans, African Americans, organized labor, and "independent" white liberals (mostly former members of the DOT). The new Policy Committee turned the years of experimentation in multiracial coalition building into a more intimate partnership in which each group was guaranteed equal representation. Among the members of the committee were a wide range of familiar veteran activists, including Albert Peña of PASO, W. J. Durham of the TCV, Francis Williams of the HCCO, Texas AFL-CIO president Hank Brown, and Houston labor lawyer and HCD leader Chris Dixie.[68]

It bears repeating: this latest version of the Democratic Coalition was unprecedentedly, and intentionally, representative. The continuing black and brown civil rights movements, the multiple declarations of independence by PASO and African American leaders in the many elections of the early 1960s, and competition from conservative whites all encouraged liberal whites to do more to include other coalition members as full rather than junior partners. For their part, black and brown activists across the state would no longer accept a back seat. Although many of the members were holdovers from earlier collaborative efforts, this newest incarnation of the coalition constituted a significant departure from the past. It formally recognized—for the first time— the independence and agency of its nonwhite participants.

The new, deliberately democratic structure allowed for dialogue to take place in the open and on equal terms. On June 1, 1963, a week before the strident PASO convention, the sixteen-member Policy Committee met in San Antonio to discuss the coming year's work. Each of the four-man caucuses had worked autonomously to recommend twenty-one additional people who would represent each leg on the coalition's Steering Committee, a body with one hundred members that would draw equally from each group. The smaller Policy Committee had no power to approve these recommendations, as the Coalition considered each group's decision final, but the leaders of the whole body rubber-stamped the four lists and ratified the expanded leadership structure. The intricate process—and the fact that it appeared prominently in coalition reports as well as in the *Observer*—revealed just how obsessed coalition leaders had become with developing rigidly democratic internal practices, further separating this latest incarnation of the group from the ad hoc coalitions of years and decades past.[69]

The new governance system in place, the Policy Committee continued revising its plan for action. A new version of the "Team Program" revealed both the growing power of the black and brown legs of the coalition and the white liberals' increased acceptance of nonwhite leadership. Although Larry Goodwyn likely authored both drafts of the Team Program, and both documents followed the same basic format, they could not have been more different. Many of the subtle vestiges of white supremacy in the original proposal had been altered or removed. In its evaluation of the project so far, for example, the revised text made no claims about "the society the average Negro is trying to achieve." Instead, it argued that the "team is a living example of intergroup action," a less flowery, less paternalistic, and more humble turn of phrase that underscored the simultaneous education of both black *and* white participants. The goal of the Team Program had likewise transformed. It now centered on "reaching what might be called the 'natural grass-roots leadership' of the Negro and Latin-American masses," not finding and educating the otherwise inert nonwhite poor. The duties of the six field directors and three state coordinators had also changed dramatically. The old language calling for the black team members to aid "in the amalgamation" of existing Voters Leagues into the local branches of the coalition was wholly omitted from the amended document. In fact, the structure and functions of the local coalitions had themselves been reformulated.

The greatest, most revolutionary alterations to the proposal concerned the role of white liberals. The sole white state coordinator would no longer direct the larger effort, nor would he (the plan used only "he") steer the local coalitions. The coordinator would likewise not be expected to commandeer local black and brown organizations nor subsume them to the more familiar groups of white liberals. Rather, the revised proposal stated, the white coordinator would be asked "to prod existing local [white] liberal organizations into incorporating the Negro and Latin-American organizations in the local Democratic Coalition, *with the minority group leaders in policy-making positions in the Coalition's leadership*." The local alliances needed to follow the example of the statewide body, the new document added. "Unless white liberal Texans, at the local level, abandon the old practice of meeting alone, adopting their own program, and then going out to 'sell' the finished product to their political allies among minority groups—unless this folk custom ends, any success attained by a mass voter registration drive will be illusory and the political 'coalition' that is projected will be a soap bubble."

In this new reimagining of the Team Program, the fundamental problem to be solved was not how to convince black organizations to heed the white liberals' message but rather how to correct the existing white groups' failure to substantively include African Americans and Mexican Americans. The proposal drove home this point time and again, feverishly trying to convince the former DOT leaders at the grassroots that they themselves had contributed to the fragmenting along racial lines of the liberal movement. The white liberals, who had long protested the reactionary politics of the Shivers-Daniel wing of the party, had inadvertently practiced exclusion as well, the new draft noted. Still, it gave them the benefit of the doubt as it called them to action. "Most white liberals in Texas now realize—for reasons of internal Texas politics—the need for a rapid revamping of the old power relationships among reform-minded persons in all races," the proposal read. "The makeup of the Steering Committee of the Statewide Coalition is proof enough of the new awareness." Yet the recent electoral trends meant that white liberals needed to move beyond acceptance toward active inclusion, the proposal added. The danger was not demagoguery but the inertia of indifference. "Habit, left to itself, dies hard," the document noted. "At this stage of the development of Texas liberalism, segregation, as an idea, is dead, but the *political habits* of segregation tend to pop up from time to time in such matters as the internal structure of the local liberal political organization—unless there is some countervailing pressure to remind everyone that they are about to do something that they have all agreed went out of style some time ago." It was up to the white liberals to abandon the folk customs of white supremacy and actively combat it. An egalitarian leadership structure at the local level would represent the key to moving forward in unison.[70]

The new plan contained one final striking change: the all-black regional staff had been replaced by a mixed group in which half of the paid organizers would be Mexican Americans. The three African American field directors would cover Dallas, Houston, and Austin, as well as their surrounding areas, while the *mexicanos* would direct projects in San Antonio, the Rio Grande Valley, and El Paso. Each would extend outward into nearby congressional districts that had large nonwhite populations and in which liberals stood a good chance of defeating incumbent Dixiecrats or Republicans. There is no smoking gun in the historical record of how or why this shift in the program took place. Still, one can infer that Albert Peña and other leaders of the Mexican American wing of the coalition would have immediately recognized the lack of attention to their group in the original proposal and would have demanded a share of the staff equal to African Americans. *Mexicano* activists frequently contrasted the lack of national attention to their plight to the overwhelming interest of eastern liberals in the black freedom struggle, and they carried this chip on their shoulder to every mixed gathering they attended. On a smaller scale, conflicts over the distribution of resources among the black and brown legs dominated coalition meetings, with Mexican Americans demanding parity at every turn and typically winning it. Indeed, Goodwyn later recalled that "there was never a meeting of the coalition" that was not dominated by disputes between black and brown leaders over equality in power-sharing, representation, and expenditures. Such deep-seated fissures underscore the unprecedented and organically radical nature of the entire coalition enterprise.[71]

The revised "Team Program" reflected the social learning that had occurred among activists of all colors over the previous several months. The flowering black and brown civil rights movements—in which formal electoral politics always represented a critical arena—had forced the Democratic Coalition's white activists to reassess their future role in building the multiracial alliance. Black and brown civil rights activists had separated themselves from their more conservative coethnics while confronting the whites and each other about the inequities and paternalism contained within the proposal's original draft. The program's likely author, staffer Larry Goodwyn, had spent another two months traveling the state with DeWitty and other coalition leaders, and he had witnessed firsthand the mass movements in San Antonio and Crystal City. The duo had also been exposed to the high-and-mighty condescension of many white liberal leaders at the local level, longtime activists who still claimed to speak for all the people even though no black or brown people came to their meetings. Clearly the revised document responded to all of these experiences on the ground.

Before concluding its June meeting, the Democratic Coalition's Policy Committee again broke with tradition by adopting a written statement of principles. The coalition had three purposes, they agreed: to extend multiracial communication and collaboration from the domain of the leadership to each group's rank and file, to develop "programs beneficial to the cause of progressive democracy," and to build precinct organizations that would strengthen the grassroots support for the new projects. Organizing the rank and file would produce increased numbers of registered voters, which would then lead to the electing of good liberal public officials. This conception of purpose no longer centered on loosely coordinating separate campaigns. Rather, the coalitions now sought to actually organize together, and the "Team Program" (or something like it) would represent the first step. The statement of principles also included the group's consensus regarding the key issues facing the coalition in the coming year. It listed eight areas of mutual interest and concern, including the repeal of the poll tax, voter registration, fundraising for precinct organizing, and encouraging candidates to announce their bids as early as possible. The statement detailed how the coalition would work together in the political arena. "Individual participants in the coalition are, of course, free to support candidates of their own choosing," it read. "However, the coalition will seek to promote maximum consultation among its members on the selection of candidates so as to encourage the kind of general agreement that will result in coordinated political effort." No single person would be bound, but all four legs would coordinate their endorsements. Or, as Ronnie Dugger of the *Observer* would put it, "they will not, as a coalition, support any candidate who is opposed by a majority of any one of their four constituent groups. . . . If any one of the coalition's four 'legs' refuses to flex, the coalition stumbles."

Most important, the statement defined the coalition's single most important issue: civil rights. Equality under the law was "essential to the building of a more just society and, as such, deserves the energetic support of all," the statement read. Moreover, "The working out of a joint effort whereby genuine progress can be achieved in the emotional and politically volatile area of civil rights will be one of the chief objectives of the coalition, as it functions on a day to day basis throughout 1963–64." The statement added that most African Americans and Mexican Americans were also poor, and that meant that the legal plight of working people affected them as well as white workers and union members. Perhaps throwing a bone to the labor leg of the coalition, the statement added, "state laws restricting employee rights . . . [are], with the broad area of civil rights, of central concern in building a more progressive Texas."

The group's unprecedented commitment to an expansive vision of civil rights was highly symbolic. As the *Observer*'s Dugger noted, "For many years Texas liberals treaded softly . . . on civil rights, evolving integrated practices in their meetings, but generally emphasizing advanced policy positions in other areas." In contrast, the coalition's new leadership structure and its prioritizing of racial equality marked a radical new departure for Texas liberalism, one that made it possible to envision it becoming a truly multiracial movement.[72]

Just as remarkably, the egalitarian system of governance, heightened theoretical prowess, and bold priorities were accompanied by a plan of action, a way to implement the coalition's program at the precinct level, from the major inner cities to the furthest reaches of the state. The Policy Committee approved the "Team Program" with minor modifications, adopting its premise that a mass voter registration drive and educational project at the grassroots level represented the key tool in the larger, critical fight for freedom. The project "is an attempt to forge a political weapon against segregation—to complement legal and mass action weapons," the revised proposal concluded. Only a robust, democratic multiracial alliance was capable of making it work. Yet it would not be enough to activate black and brown voters, the proposal cautioned, "unless they are immediately incorporated into full-fledged members of local Democratic Coalitions, speaking for the party as a whole. Unless this is done, the 'coalition' will fragment and the political assault on segregation will be blunted."[73]

The Democratic Coalition's multipronged war on Jim Crow and Juan Crow would soon capture the attention of the state and, indeed, the nation. More immediately, staffer Goodwyn again hit the road, driving to New York City, Washington, D.C., and Atlanta to raise the external funding that would undergird the joint organizing project. Brown, Peña, Durham, Dixie, and the rest of the coalition's leadership began preparing for the first meeting of its new one-hundred-member Steering Committee and then a statewide convention and press conference at which they would announce their plans. Their radical experiment in multiracial democracy was finally underway.

The first half of 1963 had seen a flurry of activity. New electoral patterns encouraged white liberals and labor leaders to deepen their commitment to civil rights, and the renewed militancy of the black and brown liberation struggles pushed the issue of racial equality to center stage. African Americans demanded complete, immediate integration, and they wanted it not as a handout but as a fundamental right. Mexican Americans stared down the Texas Rangers, the Anglo establishment, and dissenting voices in their own organizations—and won. Each group fractured internally as a result, with white liberal Democrats pulling further away from the party's conservatives, black activists dividing over the question of seeking patronage or independent political power, and Mexican Americans in PASO splitting again in response to the Crystal City uprising and the questions it raised about coalition building with labor.

Within each ethnic group and across the color line, the most militant activists "separated the wheat from the chaff," as *SNAP* had put it, distinguishing their *intra*racial antagonists and solidifying their *inter*racial collaborators. At the same time, the on-the-ground organizing of the black and brown civil rights movements extended the promise of postwar liberalism, making the movements' calls for equal treatment and representation the litmus test for multiracial cooperation. Haltingly at first, then more confidently, the state's black, brown, and white activists came together and revived the Democratic Coalition. They rededicated it to bringing the franchise to heretofore off-limits barrios and ghettos of the state's major cities and even to the remote corners of Texas. After battling through their own differences and educating the leading white activists experientially, they dedicated themselves to a new wave of concerted action and hatched a plan that would reach thousands of new rank-and-file recruits. The coalition would again launch a voter registration drive, but this time the mobilization would seek to transform society rather than simply elect a few good officials. Civil rights had become the ends, electoral politics solely the means. The Mexican American "forgotten people" had cast their lot with the black freedom struggle and the white-led labor movement, and together they were fast becoming the state's leading political actors. And just as George Sánchez had predicted, now that the possibility for sweeping change appeared imminent, it would arrive "with devastating suddenness."

Chapter 9

They'll Never Separate Us Again

The Multiracial Democratic Coalition on the March

"About 300 veteran Democrats and liberals turned up" for the Democratic Coalition's first statewide general assembly in Dallas in mid-July 1963, wrote Ronnie Dugger of the *Texas Observer*. "The four-way division of leadership was symbolized at the front table during the main session," Dugger added, graphically demonstrating the new group's structure and priorities. Political Association of Spanish-Speaking Organizations (PASO) chairman Albert Peña presided over the meeting from center stage, flanked to his right by Texas AFL-CIO president Hank Brown and Texas Council of Voters (TCV) leader W. J. Durham and to his left by liberal leader Chris Dixie and staffer Larry Goodwyn, among others. The polyglot cast of characters at the head table hailed from across the state, as did the hundreds of activists of all colors in the ballroom audience. "Members of the Negro minority were well represented, as they have not been at equivalent conferences in recent years," Dugger noted.[1] Instead of a sea of white faces with a smattering of black and brown ones, this meeting was evenly split between African American and Mexican American civil rights and community leaders and white labor leaders and liberal political activists. Based just on appearance, the current coalition was something altogether different in Texas politics.

More substantively, the coalition's revamped leadership structure and explicit commitment to civil rights promised to transform a loose alliance of mutually suspicious parts into a diverse, formidable whole capable of expanding the franchise by putting unprecedented numbers of boots on the ground. Bringing together record numbers of black, brown, and white activists from all over Texas under a single roof alone signaled a monumental accomplishment, the product of years of experimentation, of successes and failures, of working in concert and then falling apart in trial and error. Now the multifarious labor, civil rights, and community organizers had finally assembled to hash out their plans to hit the pavement together, planning to work side by side to elect liberal politicians who would prioritize the black and brown liberation struggles. And if that failed, they agreed, they would be prepared to demonstrate in the streets together as well. Texas had never seen anything like it.

Despite such novelty and promise, each partner still harbored some reservations. The night before the main gathering, forty-five African American activists gathered in a private session at the Moorland YMCA in the black section of downtown Dallas. Led by attorney Durham, G. J. Sutton, Arthur DeWitty of Austin, and civil rights unionists Moses and Erma LeRoy, the group reviewed their "grievances against past liberal coalitions in Texas" before discussing the challenges presented by the rise of the United Political Organization (UPO), a new organization composed of conservative black leaders. Next, and most crucially, the liberal African Americans in the coalition prepared their own set of demands, a list of five additions to the body's statement of principles that would codify and extend the practice of equal representation and power for all participants. The black activists insisted that the coalition go on record that it would only endorse politicians "who will work for the enactment of legislation, local, state, and national, which will afford equal opportunities and equal protection of all citizens without reference to race and color in every facet of American life." Most important, the caucus clarified that doing so meant that "the coalition will support no candidate or issue that will place the Negro in the untenable position of accepting or defending tokenism or gradualism as symbolized by the so-called 'voluntary approach' to civil rights."

After Dr. Marion "Jack" Brooks of Fort Worth presented the group's stipulations on the floor of the full coalition gathering the next day, Durham, the renowned NAACP attorney and head of the TCV, rose to address the crowd. He first indicated his allegiance to the liberal cause before shifting gears to endorse the caucus's ultimatum. Durham "delivered a free-swinging attack on . . . the U.P.O. . . . joshing Connally for introducing to Texas a new phenomenon, the conservative Negro," the *Observer*'s Dugger noted. Then he added that he had "been coalitioning a long time, and had had to leave a coalition after its failure to endorse Henry Gonzalez for governor" in 1958. That year, a top officer in the predominately white Democrats of Texas (DOT) had assailed Durham personally, and the timid but proud liberal organization had refused to cast its lot with the black and brown civil rights movements. Such disappointments aside, Durham added, he was now "back coalitioning again," ready to move forward with his formerly unreliable allies. The many former members of the old DOT in the room winced at his criticism but remained silent, having recognized in the intervening half-decade that they could only move forward in the fight for democracy if they truly included the black activists, critiques and all.[2]

Previous alliances might have faltered when confronted with the caucus's demands, either because there would not have been sufficient space for the black activists to present their demands or because the white activists would have shied away from candid reminders about their past shortcomings or acrimonious discussions about the future. Instead, as Dugger put it, the debate on the black caucus's proposed principles "epitomized the willingness of the . . .

conference to face the civil rights issue without flinching." First, a white liberal district attorney defensively objected that "any implication that any candidate is best qualified" because of his or her race "would be untenable." The black caucus had not demanded the right to endorse only black politicians but rather the right to veto candidates of all colors who were not committed to complete, immediate integration. Still, the white liberal's fear of not-yet-proposed race-based slates suggested that he, like many whites, remained at least unconsciously uncomfortable with the caucus's underlying goal of black self-determination. In any event, moments after this exchange, labor's Brown offered what he believed to be a friendly amendment in which each reference to "Negro" be accompanied by a list of the other three coalition groups. G. J. Sutton, his longtime partner in the Bexar County alliance, protested that doing so would water down the black activists' statement, which he thought should be "preserved as a justified set of grievances." Friendly motivations aside, Sutton told Brown that "he couldn't twist this around," that the white members of the coalition needed to take a stand for the black civil rights movement on its own. Dugger observed that "Brown retorted that he might have been guilty of manipulations in the past, as had Brother Sutton, but that at the outset of the coalition, there should not even be a suspicion of anything devious, and that if his amendment was not acceptable, they should sit down and make it acceptable."

The meeting had become borderline explosive; one more match might set it—and the revived Democratic Coalition—alight. Instead, cooler heads prevailed. Peña, serving as the presiding chairman, paused the proceedings and instructed each of the four legs of the coalition to caucus in each of the four corners of the ballroom—African Americans in one corner, Mexican Americans in another, labor in a third, and finally the white "independent" liberals in another. As each group held their separate meetings, Sutton and Brown approached one another and reached an agreement: that the coalition would adopt the black caucus's new principles as originally written but that another motion would clarify that the entire statement would apply to all four elements, as Brown had proposed. Yet as they hammered out their deal, the meeting of the African American corner adjourned, its participants returning to the convention floor to inform the other partners that they had accepted the Brown amendment. The "independent" white liberals also accepted the compromise. More important, the African Americans' grievances had been explicitly aired, and the remedy debated in the open among all parties. In the end, initial enmity and distrust gave way to mutual agreement and a willingness of all parties to adopt the other's view in order to work together. The coalition adopted Brown's language and moved forward, the black activists finally convinced that their white and Mexican American counterparts were sincere. Disagreements did not disappear but were put on the table and addressed by all.³

The coalition's "fundamental preliminaries accomplished," the delegates at the July convention proceeded with their business. Randolph Blackwell, field director for the Voter Education Project of the Southern Regional Council in Atlanta, addressed the multiracial gathering and urged them to stick together. "You must not fail," he said. Then, turning to Brown, he added that had such a coalition existed, it would have defeated the Taft-Hartley Act, so "Let's roll the union on." The message was clear: just as white liberals needed African Americans, the coalition needed labor, and labor needed it. The delegates again caucused in their four respective corners and elected the four cochairs of the Democratic Coalition: Peña, Durham, Brown, and longtime political activist Franklin Jones of Marshall (for the "independent" liberals).⁴

The final, and most important, piece of business centered on creating a plan for voter registration and mobilization. The group set their first goals: support for a November 9, 1963, referendum to amend the state constitution by abolishing the poll tax, followed by a mass registration drive for the 1964 elections. Then the coalition members came up with a method for how to get there. It formed a group "devoted wholly" to the campaign and soon chartered it as a nonprofit organization, Voters of Texas Enlist (VOTE). Delegates "then agreed to form local coalitions on the same basis of leadership equality in numbers; to work through the women's activities division of the state labor organization and the Texas state Democratic women's committees" in order to prepare block-walking kits using the county voter registration lists; and "to drum up poll tax [campaign] workers" from white liberal groups, PASO, the TCV, and "Negro and white college students."⁵

Following the meeting, the four cochairs of the new statewide, multiracial, and egalitarian Democratic Coalition announced itself to the Texas press and political establishment. It declared its goal of expanding the franchise and began preparing to do it. Civil rights would come to the Lone Star State, they declared, and it would happen at the ballot box that fall. A new, deliberate foray into democratic organizing had begun.

Perhaps to ensure that the larger Democratic Coalition actually took up the fight for civil rights, the leaders of the black caucus also fired off a telegram to Governor Connally, asking him to "speedup desegregation in Texas." The statement, signed on behalf of the executive committee of the TCV, called on Connally to follow the examples of Governor Bert Combs of Kentucky and North Carolina's Governor Terry Sanford by issuing an executive order that would end segregation immediately. The telegram specified that he had the power to do so not only in publicly owned facilities, parks, and hospitals as well as public employment but also in the private sector, in "all businesses operated in the state requiring a state license." The leaders added that "every means available to our elected officials should be used." Coalition cochair and TCV president W. J. Durham signed the letter, as did the LeRoys, Rev. Claude Black and G. J. Sutton of San Antonio, Harris County Council of Organizations (HCCO) leader Frances Williams and precinct leader Barbara Jordan of Houston, and the rest of the coalition's black leaders. The process of "coalitioning," it seemed, had also renewed the bonds within this group of militant black activists, laying the groundwork for the first-ever coordinated, statewide civil rights campaign.[6]

The Democratic Coalition was finally ready for action. What one newspaper called the "marriage" between "the three ethnic groups" would enjoy a "honeymoon period" in which all of the pieces of the puzzle briefly came together in a coordinated drive for not just political power but also labor and civil rights. Before it was extinguished, the coalition would reach deeper into the state's black and brown neighborhoods than ever before, reactivating old networks of veteran activists and recruiting and training tens of thousands of new grassroots organizers. It would create additional space for PASO and labor to extend their joint organizing efforts and would help the Texas AFL-CIO become a civil rights organization in its own right. And it would support the arrival of the black civil rights movement on a statewide level, resulting in a new wave of direct action protests and culminating in the state's largest demonstration to date.[7] At nearly every turn the liberal activists would be confronted by conservatives of all colors in both political parties. Yet the process of coalition building would eventually succeed in harnessing the vast "potential" of the state's African American and Mexican American residents, forever transforming Texas politics. And, just as important, it would consolidate and expand the power of local coalitions, setting the stage for another wave of upheaval in the state's urban areas.

Texas Labor and Black Civil Rights

On June 11, a month and two days before the Democratic Coalition's coming-out party, another southern governor, George Wallace, had fulfilled his pledge to stand in the "schoolhouse door" to prevent the integration of the University of Alabama. His theatrical performance may have made him look good in front of his constituents, but it failed to forestall the admission of the institution's first black students, and it ended up incurring the full wrath of the federal government. That evening, an exasperated President Kennedy, already pushed to the brink by the violent police attacks on protestors in Birmingham, took to the airwaves to announce his plans to introduce in Congress a new package of federal civil rights bills. He argued that the new law should not only prohibit state-sponsored segregation but should also curb discrimination in privately owned public accommodations—the lunch counters, movie theaters, department stores, and other retailers and conveyances that had been the targets of demonstrations in Texas and across the South since 1960. A few hours later, Medgar Evers, the head of the NAACP in Mississippi, was gunned down in his driveway by a white supremacist sniper. The busy day signaled to America that the Second Reconstruction was coming, that the federal government would finally intervene to end Jim Crow in the South. It also indicated that the intrusion would be expansive in scope, that the South would not go down without a fight, and that some civil rights activists would be forced to pay the ultimate price for liberation.

Kennedy's speech emboldened the black freedom struggle's organizers and antagonists and ratcheted up the already tense atmosphere in Dixie to a fever pitch. In Texas, the president's call provided legitimacy and support for African American civil rights activists who had long been fighting for complete integration by law, equal employment and other economic opportunities, and real political power. At the same time, it forced the state's and the nation's labor movements to reexamine the racial practices of their member unions, creating new opportunities for reformer Hank Brown to wed his struggle to the burgeoning civil rights movement.

Just three days after Kennedy's address, Brown joined three hundred state and local labor leaders from across the country in traveling to Washington to join the president for a "special White House Conference on Civil Rights and Equal Employment Opportunity." Brown reported that, following the conference, the national AFL-CIO approved "and adopted for our guidance" a five-step proposal for organized labor to take action in the "increasingly urgent and ever more critical civil rights crisis confronting our country." State labor federations were urged to create "a working committee to cooperate with the federal government in ending job discrimination," to rally support for the administration's economic and social legislation, to participate actively in local "multi-racial committees" or create them if needed, to encourage the advancement of "minority-group union members to positions of leadership and responsibility" within the labor movement, and to step up "voter registration drives."[8]

Experience had taught Brown two truths about the Texas labor movement: that he could expect stiff resistance from among the ranks and that national AFL-CIO dictates could provide the necessary cover to sell an aggressive civil rights program to the federation's often reluctant affiliates. At the Texas AFL-CIO's founding convention in 1957, an ad hoc Civil Rights Committee had reported out a list of militant resolutions. The group praised the "more than 100 local school districts that are now in their third year of compliance" with the

Brown v. Board decision and attacked the "recent rise of so-called 'Citizens Councils' and other Ku Klux Klan type organizations in the state of Texas," adding that "We recognize them for what they are." Other recommended measures called on member unions to "take steps to provide equal job opportunities" for all and suggested that the state body "use every means available to insure no discrimination within the locals themselves." Finally, the committee called on the federation to go on record in support of "an effective and enforceable fair employment practices act" and to urge the legislature to adopt it. African American members of the Hod Carriers Local 18 of Houston, *mexicano* steelworker and PASO activist Paul Montemayor, and white women from the telephone company all gave passionate speeches in support of the committee's report, but in the end the federation fell victim to the timidity and fear of the convention's white delegates.

A long, cantankerous floor debate ended when one white delegate suggested that the federation replace the package of resolutions produced by the state committee with a list of bland recommendations from the national AFL-CIO. Although the text of the federal measure may have been even stronger than the Texas committee's version, it was also more remote and therefore less meaningful. Rather than having to justify their vote for or against school integration and fair employment at home in Texas, white union leaders could merely inform their memberships that they agreed to go along with national AFL-CIO policy, blaming federal intrusion for forcing them to change under duress. They did not have to stand up and be counted as for or against the civil rights movement. The unsurprising result of the rhetorical timidity was predictable inaction at the local level. Employment discrimination remained rampant, and most unions did little to aid the black freedom struggles in their surrounding communities. And the issue disappeared from the deliberations of the statewide labor movement: each year thereafter, the convention of the Texas AFL-CIO reaffirmed its compliance with the national federation's civil rights policy while continuing to do nothing meaningful on the ground.[9]

The timid, do-nothing stance of the state labor federation's convention delegates persisted as late as August 1962, drawing sharp criticism from African American activists and white liberals. That year, the annual convention committee on civil rights reported out a series of strong resolutions designed to finally end all forms of racial discrimination within organized labor. In addition to six key new paragraphs that attacked "continued anti-Negro practices in plants and craft unions," the committee proposed to create "'permanent machinery' to investigate and rebuke Texas unions that discriminate against Negroes," according to a report in the *Observer*. The convention committee, which included Houston's Moses LeRoy, would have become permanent and gained a degree of enforcement power, but "moderate integrationists in league with segregationists from locals that still follow Jim Crow practices" defeated the committee's majority report. Delegates approved a dissenting minority report that reaffirmed the previous platform that had been in place since 1957 and added a few new points hailing "'better' social and economic equality," the removal of race-baiting from statewide political campaigns, and the successful integration of all convention facilities "for the first time" in the merged federation's history. The minority report also called for "more detailed information," including "continued compliance with the practice of the [Texas AFL-CIO] Vice-Presidents being required to make written reports of civil rights progress in their area."[10]

NAACP regional secretary Clarence Laws of Dallas "criticized the Texas AFL-CIO for not adopting" the stronger original resolution proposed by the committee, according to a newspaper report, and for failing "to set up a board to study racial discrimination." Laws told the paper that labor's continued inaction was "most lamentable" and wrote a letter to Hank Brown calling on labor to do more to support black civil rights. An obviously frustrated Brown replied by noting the state leadership's various efforts to improve the situation, but Laws maintained that their "commendable efforts" were still not enough. Brown attended the NAACP state convention in San Antonio later that year, joining a panel on "Expanding Job Opportunities for Minority Groups." Yet the official policy of organized labor remained gradualist at best at the end of 1962.[11]

What a difference a year made. The new national guidelines passed down by the AFL-CIO in the wake of Birmingham and Evers and Kennedy's speech in June 1963 shattered the tradition of inaction within the Texas labor movement and opened the door for sweeping change. Brown and state secretary-treasurer Roy Evans had long been supporters of integration, but now they had more room to maneuver, allowing them to become full-time activists in the struggle who could push the federation's members further and faster than ever before. Brown's call to local labor leaders to join the new permanent "working committee" on civil rights reflected both his stillborn efforts to date and the new leverage offered by the moment. "We are already involved, of course, in many of these proposals—but in an informal and uncoordinated way," Brown wrote. All that had changed was that the national AFL-CIO had suggested that the state organization better plan and coordinate its activities in a "swift and meaningful" manner. "Of course, there will be thorny problems to solve," Brown added. "But solve them we must—for the good not only of the state and the nation, but for the future of the labor movement as well."[12]

Brown called together approximately thirty-five union representatives from across the state for the committee's organizational meeting on July 17, 1963, in Austin—three days after the conclusion of the Democratic Coalition convention in Dallas. Reporters from the *Houston Chronicle* and *Post*, the *Dallas News*, the *San Antonio Express*, AP and UPI wire services, KTBC in Austin, and CBS News looked on, forming a group that would have constituted an unusually large press corps for an annual statewide convention let alone a single committee meeting.[13]

The committee included a diverse range of participants, from longtime civil rights unionists to the most conservative members of all-white craft unions. The liberals dominated the meeting, thanks to the interventions of Brown, Evans, and the national AFL-CIO. Frank Wallace of the Fort Worth Packinghouse Workers, J. E. "Jimmy" Middleton of the Houston Laborers Local 18, and veteran organizer George Lambert of the ILGWU were among those that advocated for aggressive action in support of civil rights. Representatives of the steelworkers and communications workers joined them, while leaders of the UAW and the oil workers probably joined the representatives of the building trades in advocating gradualism and moderation in labor's formal public statements on the issue.

Such gradualism on the part of many white unionists can be attributed both to the southern racial attitudes that dominated the period and to the leaders' pragmatic calculations that taking a moderate stance would help them avoid a backlash among their members. For example, the head of the Dallas AFL-CIO Council accepted Brown's appointment to serve on the committee, but he did so only "after thinking the thing over." It was "something of a hot potato, here at least," he wrote to Brown. The local umbrella organization had met to consider the issue but decided "that we would be better off at this time without any public statements." The Dallas group did agree to assist a federal agency working to ensure equal employment opportunity in the defense industry, but it would only do so "without publicity." Private advocacy was all that Dallas labor leaders thought they could manage without causing a revolt in their ranks.[14] An anonymous member of the oil workers along the Gulf Coast likewise wrote to Brown, arguing that aggressive support for civil rights would cause a backlash. After boasting that their local unions had long been integrated and did not practice or condone discrimination, he noted that "recent efforts of the various Negro organizations, using political and pressure tactics, have created a new resentment among the whites unequaled since reconstruction days." When labor leaders take public positions in support of civil rights, "we suffer a loss of strength sorely needed for collective bargaining and political action . . . [and] we jeopardize our security and growth by a too aggressive pursuance of our Civil Rights policy." Too much advocacy for civil rights would "make organizing in the South practically impossible," he concluded, "so must we now stop wasting our . . . strength on this one single issue."[15]

Such evidence of white resistance underscored the fact that despite Hank Brown's liberal leadership, the outcome of the Civil Rights Committee's founding meeting on July 17 remained a far from foregone conclusion. Still, for civil rights unionists like Middleton and Lambert, this was the debate they had been waiting for, and they were determined to seize the moment. Rodger Coyne of the U.S. Department of Labor set the tone for the gathering in his opening address, one geared primarily toward the representatives from the craft unions. "The Negro suffers," he said, "because of his skin. But he also suffers because often he is an unskilled worker in a society that has not found the way to full employment." It was not enough to wait for black workers "to come knock on the door and ask to be let in," he added. Instead, "You must go out and find them and bring them into the apprenticeship program. . . . We have to . . . go to the minorities with open arms and tell them we're here to help." H. A. Moon of the UAW, an industrial union, replied that the companies his union represented simply refused to hire black workers "in the skills." He added, "Make the companies hire 'em, and we'll take 'em in." George Lambert agreed that employers were often to blame for discrimination in hiring. He asked that more be done to create equal employment opportunities in the private sector, including among firms that do not contract with the federal government. Lambert, the longtime organizer for the garment workers, knew all too well that his own union's members were all women and often women of color, but that management remained the domain of white men.[16]

Brown presented the national AFL-CIO's proposed program to the committee, and, despite some members' objections, the more militant civil rights activists in the group carried the day. In the end, the committee unanimously passed a "Statement of Policy" that included a long list of demands—a set of resolutions for immediate integration that far exceeded anything the Texas labor movement had ever considered. They endorsed the Kennedy administration's civil rights program, but most of the document centered on internal union affairs and state politics. They called upon all affiliated unions to accept all members without discrimination, to remove racial identifiers from lists in hiring halls, to make all referral services colorblind, to end discrimination in apprenticeship programs, and to "make certain that the seniority clauses of their agreements are not discriminatory . . . [nor] applied in a discriminatory manner." Perhaps responding to Moon and Lambert, they added a note that employers should likewise urge their associations to ban employment discrimination based on race or national origin.

The committee's statement then took a radical turn, demanding "the State of Texas to act officially in the total civil rights field." Racial discrimination was "but one of the discrimination evils present in Texas society," the statement continued. Discrimination based on age, sex, and union membership also prevailed. The final list of demands was startlingly comprehensive, calling on the state to pass laws guaranteeing equal pay for women, equal employment opportunity for racial minorities in the public sector, and collective bargaining rights for all. It also asked the state to join the Texas AFL-CIO's lawsuit against the "border commuter" problem and pass a minimum wage law of $1.25 per hour "so that economic bondage ceases to keep 1,500,000 Texans in serfdom." The committee saved the best for last: after noting that the federation had already written to John Connally to urge the creation of a state "multi-racial committee" that would work to abolish racial discrimination, it added that the issue had since become so urgent that the governor should instead call a special session of the legislature to specifically address "the total civil rights field."[17]

The state's labor movement, which had adopted a do-nothing policy less than a year earlier, had affected a complete about-face. Instead of rhetorical squishiness and practical inaction, the Texas AFL-CIO had set a bold course, organizing a new permanent statewide Committee on Civil Rights and Equal Employment and publicly assailing the governor for his refusal to support the movement. Going out on a precarious limb as far as rank-and-file union members were concerned, Hank Brown and Roy Evans led labor into the coalition on one hand and into a battle with the governor on the other. Within months, the labor bosses would soon double down, transforming the Texas AFL-CIO into a civil rights organization in its own right.

Labor's bold demands made headlines across the state, but Connally's office initially had no comment. Instead, in the coming days, the standoff between labor and the governor would take a curious turn. The governor had already planned to address civil rights at his regularly scheduled press conference on the afternoon of Thursday, July 18—the day after labor's Civil Rights Committee meeting in Austin. His staff indicated that he would also reply to labor at that time.[18] But instead of responding to the call for a special session, Connally highlighted and took out of context a single statement made by secretary-treasurer Roy Evans during the Civil Rights Committee meeting. The statement had been so insignificant that it did not appear in the meeting minutes, nor did it merit headlines in initial newspaper reports on the gathering. During a discussion of the "commuter" system and what he termed the "deplorable" wages and working conditions along the border, Evans told the committee that "there may be a need for demonstrations down there." A small, four-paragraph United Press International wire report buried deep inside one newspaper carried Evans's comments, while two short paragraphs in a much-larger, page-five story on the committee meeting appeared in another publication. Evans added that he had met with Fidel Velasquez of Nuevo Laredo, the head of the Mexican labor movement across the border, and that Velasquez had agreed to cooperate in the demonstrations. Evans believed the protests would also improve relationships with Mexican workers on the other side of Rio Grande. The "commuter" and border issues were included in the "Statement of Policy" that came out of the committee meeting, but the oblique call for "demonstrations" and binational labor collaboration both remained absent.[19]

Still, Connally jumped on Evans's comments to launch a counteroffensive against labor from his bully pulpit. At his weekly Thursday afternoon press conference, the governor first laid into Evans and the state's labor leadership, accusing them of "trying to inflame racial issues in Texas," in the words of one newspaper report. The governor praised the business elites of Texas who, he believed, had "made remarkable progress in civil rights . . . without coercion or compulsion." Attempting to separate union members from their unscrupulous leaders, the governor added that Evans and Brown were nothing but "propagandists [who] have now chosen to attempt to inflame this issue for purely personal selfish gain." Connally concluded by pandering to white Texans' fear of disorder and loss of status amid the swelling civil rights movement. "Should any racial unrest or crisis now develop in Texas," he warned, "the officials of the state AFL-CIO must take full credit."[20] The issue was not the persistence or injustices of Jim Crow, he implied, but the white agitators who sought to foment discord. Certainly ordinary white union members and the general public would disagree with such radical tactics. Connally promised to share his own vision for change—without demonstrations or violence—in a prime-time televised speech the following evening.

In just a few words, the governor had succeeded in shifting the media focus from labor's call for a special session on civil rights to the "irresponsible" leadership of the Texas AFL-CIO and the threat of an uprising among Mexican Americans along the border. Forced to play defense, Evans replied that the governor was "misinformed as to exactly what I said." During the committee's discussion of issues on the border, Evans maintained, he had proposed that they first hold a conference of "responsible representatives" of the U.S. and Mexican labor movements, "business interests and government agencies to try to resolve the miserable situation that exists along the border." If the conference failed, then "it might be that a series of demonstrations would be productive." Queried a few days later about the exact tactics that he was advocating, Evans noted that he intended "peaceful and non-violent" action, he said—"such things like the Boston Tea Party, strikes and sit-ins."[21] Still, the damage had been done, and the ball was now in the governor's court.

That Friday, July 19, at 9:30 P.M., Connally delivered his televised address on civil rights. He did so, he had said, because it was "a serious problem" that required leadership from his office, and because the people were "entitled" to learn his views prior to his participation in the upcoming National Governors' Conference. In his speech, Connally urged patience and voluntary progress, calling for "persuasion and cooperation, not passion or compulsion." He said he opposed the president and attorney general's bill that mandated integration as it applied to private businesses and associations, arguing that it infringed upon the property rights of individuals. He added that discrimination should be ended in all public, state-owned establishments, and that he would do "everything within my power" to ensure equal treatment for African Americans, including access to voting rights, quality public education, and equal economic opportunity. One report noted that "initial response to the speech," presumably among whites, "was encouraging."[22]

Other members of the Democratic Coalition rallied to Evans's defense and assailed the governor's position. The day before the speech, Albert Peña, acting as PASO's state chairman, joined labor's call for a special session on civil rights. He called on the legislature to "end all segregation in public places" and asked the governor to follow "the positive leadership of President John F. Kennedy." Peña sent a telegram to Connally's office that he then presented to the newspapers. It included a demand for "fair employment legislation to insure [sic] equal job opportunities for Latin Americans and Negroes. . . . I sincerely believe such action by you would prove to the world that Texas is ready to step into the 20th Century," Peña concluded. A day after the speech, Clarence Laws of the NAACP also blasted Connally's stance on the issue. He said that the governor's position was "no more palatable" than those of the archsegregationist leaders of Mississippi and Alabama. "Connally's pious, sugar-coated platitudes" were simply unacceptable, Laws added. "He would leave [integration] up to the pleasures of those who have a long history of exploitation of minorities." Perhaps reacting to Connally's fearmongering in regard to South Texas, Laws cautiously noted that the group preferred to gain civil rights without demonstrations, but direct action might be necessary. "If we think demonstrations will help. . . . Then we'll demonstrate," Laws concluded.[23]

In contrast, the UPO, the conservative African American group, praised Connally's speech and sought to defend the governor. The address represented "the most significant and positive statement on civil rights by a public official in the history of the state," the group declared. It called on the state's two U.S. senators to make their views known, particularly hoping to "smoke out" Ralph Yarborough, who had remained relatively quiet on the subject. Still, even the UPO disagreed with the governor with regard to privately owned public accommodations. As one reporter put it, opposing any part of Kennedy's program was tantamount to political suicide for any "Negro who aspires to racial leadership . . . in these stormy times."[24]

Connally's speech dominated the headlines for several days, but the Texas AFL-CIO and the Democratic Coalition soon countered with their own public relations campaign. They took to the airwaves, creating a thirty-minute television program, "Civil Rights in Texas," and setting up screenings on local networks across the state. In the half-hour paid spot, the state labor federation's media chief moderated a panel discussion featuring Arthur DeWitty, the Austin TCV leader and coordinator of the coalition's "Team Program," alongside professor and PASO activist George I. Sánchez and labor's Evans. The Texas AFL-CIO made the film available on tape and set up more than a dozen showings, including two dates in Austin, and one each in Beaumont, El Paso, Fort Worth, Houston, San Antonio, Laredo, and Weslaco (in the Lower Rio Grande Valley)—all in July and early August 1963.[25] The federation's selection of this trio and the program's timing and distribution reflected organized labor's understanding of what "Civil Rights in Texas" meant. It was a multiracial issue that included both the black and brown struggles and in which organized labor could play a key role. It encompassed the cities as well as rural areas and stretched from the border to the panhandle. In order to reach its members and allies across the state, labor literally took its show on the road. Though crude by present-day standards, at the time the program represented a significant commitment of financial and human resources, demonstrating that the leaders of the Texas AFL-CIO were no longer content with rhetorical posturing and instead wanted an on-the-ground presence in the multiracial civil rights struggle. And they created this presence—critically—by drawing on the coalition they had been building for years, if not decades.

"Battle Lines Drawn for Civil Rights Showdown in Texas," read the headline of a July 21 article in the *Brownsville Herald*. Labor, Peña, PASO, the NAACP, the TCV, and the Democratic Coalition all stood on one side, while the governor, the UPO, and the state's conservative political and economic elites stood on the other. The Texas AFL-CIO had created a permanent Civil Rights Committee and adopted positions that were unimaginable less than a year earlier. The other coalition members had joined labor in demanding concrete action, while the governor had deflected their entreaties through a combination of "pious platitudes" and a creative counteroffensive designed to discredit labor's leaders in the eyes of their own members and the general public. Connally took a position that "certainly would have been considered liberal by the standards of a few months ago, if not today," according to one journalist. Yet the governor's own allies struggled to defend him as the state's increasingly militant African Americans, Mexican Americans, and white liberals and labor leaders all called for immediate change.[26]

The Texas AFL-CIO had committed itself to the black and brown liberation struggles, and in so doing, it had become the governor's leading antagonist. With a backlash growing among its largely white membership, labor still had time to retreat from the fight. But instead, it would continue to deepen its ties to the most militant black and brown activists and would soon join the Democratic Coalition in launching an unprecedented drive for democracy in the Lone Star State.

A Lone Wolf Howls

Sitting in was not part of their plan. As "Civil Rights in Texas" aired across the state, and labor began planning a confrontation on the border, a self-styled "lone wolf" decided that he had waited long enough for his freedom. Booker T. Bonner, or "B. T.," as he was known, was already one of the state's most recognizable civil rights activists by the summer of 1963, but he had taken an unusual path to prominence. Born in rural Wallis to the southwest of Houston in 1927, Bonner was not from a leading family, like G. J. Sutton, nor was he a union leader like Houston's Moses LeRoy. He was not a minister or a lawyer or an undertaker. He was the son of a sharecropper and seamstress who took in boarders to make ends meet. Still, as B. T. later recalled, he "had a photostatic mind where I could read and remember" everything. However helpful, native intelligence did not result in upward mobility for African Americans in rural East Texas in the 1930s and 1940s. Bonner's mother sent him away for school, and he graduated from high school in Houston in 1944 before joining the service at the tail end of World War II. Bonner mustered out and began attending Texas Southern University using veterans' benefits, but he dropped out when his mother died without warning in 1950. Her passing drove him crazy: for the next two years he struggled with alcoholism until finally he lay down in the center of a highway one night and was hit by a car. Against all odds, Bonner survived being run over, recuperated in a Veterans Administration hospital, and made his way to Austin, where he planned to enroll at the all-black Huston-Tillotson College. He ended up going to the barely integrated University of Texas instead—because a summer session class there cost only eight dollars. B. T. got himself one of the few jobs available to black men in Austin—as a cook—and began working his way through school. He majored in history and government and hoped to become a teacher.[27]

In 1960, a friend of Bonner's invited him to a "stand-in" at a movie theater on the university's drag. As in San Antonio, the protestors' strategy called for demonstrators to go to the ticket window, ask if the employees would sell tickets to members of all races, and when they said no, go to the back of the line and do it again. In Austin, a group called Students for Direct Action (SDA) coordinated the demonstrations. Bonner recalled that whites were "running it" and about seventy of the eighty protestors were white. The strategy "didn't make sense to me," Bonner said. So the second time that he approached the box office, he asked to talk to the manager instead of politely returning to the line as instructed. His move scared the SDA leaders, who quickly intervened and then moved him away from the window. "Here's this new one who isn't following the rules," Bonner remembered. "I didn't want to waste my time." On the third pass through, Bonner again asked to talk to the manager and then stayed at the window until he was able to do so. Again, the SDA leaders removed him, and then took him out for a beer to explain the strategy to him. But Bonner would not be convinced. "I disagreed with the format," he added.[28]

Bonner made a name for himself outside activist circles in March 1961, when he decided to chart his own course for the ongoing desegregation struggle. He staged a one-man hunger strike in front of the Texas Theater, a "hungry vigil" that lasted over sixty hours. "Last November it was, I was walking a picket line up and down here," he explained to the *Texas Observer*, "and it dawned on me that I was angry, that the situation was wrong and [I asked myself] what could I do to impress people how serious this was." Bonner maintained that he was not a member of SDA, who had continued to hold periodic demonstrations at this theater and another down the street. In fact, B. T. had brought the idea to an SDA meeting but then balked when a white member called for a vote. The self-identified "lone wolf" instead sat on a stool by himself near a lamppost in front of the box office, where he refused to eat and drank only four glasses of water throughout the duration of his protest—two and a half days. About ten supporters, mostly white students, kept him company at different times. "The intention . . . was to bring attention to what was happening here and to try to prevail upon a person's mind," Bonner added. Passers-by shouted various epithets at him, and on two different occasions, mobs of whites rushed him, but ultimately let him be. The bold, individual action in the capital city captured the attention of the news media, and "from that point on I was considered one of the most radical blacks in the state," he later recalled.[29]

In 1962, Bonner, like activists around Texas, supplemented his civil rights activities by venturing into electoral politics. He got involved with Don Yarborough's gubernatorial campaign, but once again, he "disagreed with the format." The white liberal staffers went to Austin's black ministers in order to gain support for the effort, but Bonner believed they were barking up the wrong tree. "I've always had a problem with them thinking that preachers led the black community. Most blacks don't go to church, just like most whites don't," Bonner recalled. "I tried to explain to Don that he wasn't going about getting the black vote right, but they . . . didn't have time. I said that John Connally was going to beat them 2-to-1 in our neighborhood" of East Austin. Campaign staffers were incredulous, stating that they had just been there. "I said that he had been meeting with the political and religious types; I had just been at the barbershops. They had all gone to a state convention [of barbers], where they saw a speaker named John Connally." Disgusted, Bonner refused to work for the campaign in the runoff. But he continued to work on his own, in order to prove a point. "I'm going to show you what could have happened," he recalled saying. "I'm going to work two of those 2-to-1 precincts" where Yarborough had lost badly and reverse the outcome for the runoff. "And I turned them around, along with a third nearby," Bonner added. "So we became a little more compatible, started talking again after the election."[30]

B. T. Bonner had proven himself a wildcard, totally brilliant and maddeningly iconoclastic. He chafed at white students, at white liberal organizers, at black ministers and traditional elites, and he claimed that he had a better formula for organizing African Americans for civil rights and political action. He would soon have an opportunity to prove his points.

As the Democratic Coalition resumed its activities in the winter of 1962–63, Bonner attended the meetings and offered his views. He joined DeWitty, Durham, Sutton, and LeRoy in the leadership of the TCV and became part of the coalition's thirty-two-person executive committee. He joined the other TCV leaders in demanding that Governor Connally issue executive orders to speed up desegregation in Texas, and like them, he was livid when the governor's July 19 speech indicated he would stop far short of that.

Ten days later the iconoclastic activist returned to his earlier form and again took matters into his own hands. Around 10:30 in the morning on July 29, Bonner entered the reception area of the governor's office inside the capitol. He asked for a meeting with Connally but was informed that the chief executive was in Houston for the day. He asked for an appointment and was refused. Then he sat down in a chair in the lobby and declared that he would wait until Connally returned. That evening, he took a break from his one-man sit-in to join a group of "more than 50 white and Negro pickets" for a march outside the governor's mansion. The pickets, which Bonner himself had organized, included twenty students from the predominately white University of Texas and protested Connally's "moderate position" on integration, in words of one newspaper report. The group circled the mansion and then made their way to a rally on the steps of the capitol. Bonner led the parade and carried a sign reading "Freedom, All Here, Now." Other protestors distributed handbills that labeled Connally a segregationist, charging that "Texas now has a Jim Crow governor of the worst kind." After the march, Bonner reentered the capitol and resumed his solo sit-in in the foyer of the governor's office.

Around 11:00 P.M., the capitol guards closed the lobby and moved Bonner downstairs into the main rotunda. They stowed away the benches and other furniture, but Bonner remained, catching a few hours of sleep on the terrazzo tile floor. The next morning he went back upstairs and again parked himself in a soft chair outside Connally's office, where he struggled to stay awake as he continued waiting. One observer told a reporter that Bonner had not eaten since he arrived. Finally, that afternoon, after twenty-seven hours, he was given an audience to see the governor a week later. He left the capitol triumphantly, smiling for the newspaper cameras while flashing a large piece of paper confirming his appointment. Still, Bonner promised to continue the

Iconoclastic activist Booker T. Bonner shows off a slip confirming his appointment with Governor John Connally, July 30, 1963. More than two years after his one-man hunger strike first landed him in the newspaper, the sit-in at the capitol made Bonner the face of the state's civil rights movement and put him at the center of the newly aggressive Democratic Coalition. Courtesy *Austin American-Statesman* Photographic Morgue (AR.2014.039), Austin History Center, Austin Public Library, Texas, Image AS-63-41693-01a.

demonstrations, and a small group picketed the mansion again that evening. Bonner added that he had an eight-point set of civil rights proposals to present to the governor, but he would not reveal the specifics to the press.[31]

With this simple act, B. T. Bonner reignited the black civil rights movement in Texas. He also brought tremendous pressure upon Connally, whose speech ten days earlier had temporarily quieted if not silenced his critics. Bonner's rogue sit-in had immediate political implications, especially in regard to the ongoing debate between the more militant and conservative factions of African American leaders. Journalists were preoccupied with Bonner's ambiguous class status, self-styled radicalism, and criticism of traditional black leaders. A "college-educated Negro waiter," in the words of several reports, Bonner was "tied by the bonds of race and circumstance to the table waiter's trade" but was nonetheless "urbane and intelligent" and "highly-articulate." He declared that he represented no organization, considered himself well to the left of the NAACP, and had nothing but disdain for the UPO.

"Putting the heat on Connally [was] incidental to both" of his "two primary objectives," wrote columnist Jon Ford of the *San Antonio Express*. First, he hoped to rally his "ultra liberal group" to show that Texas supported the federal civil rights legislation, and second, he was "aflame with the idea of breaking up existing political power centers among members of his own race." Bonner, who had unsuccessfully sought a seat on the city council a few months earlier, attacked the conservative black leaders of Austin, led by the UPO's statewide president, M. J. Anderson. "They use ruthless methods to try and kill off ambition," Bonner said. "Everything they advocate is a form of gradualism that has failed in the past. They favor negotiations and compromise. . . . When the meetings are over, the white man turns into the private club and the Negro heads for the elevator. I'm not interested in negotiating privately until they are ready to drink with me in public."

Traditional leaders replied by criticizing Bonner. "This is one of the best cities I have seen for fine feeling between the races," said J. J. Seabrook, president of Huston-Tillotson College. "This fellow Bonner is looking for sensation and publicity. . . . If this keeps up, he could get out of town people in here and whip this thing into a frenzy," he warned. White journalist Jon Ford summarized the conflict: "The hassle began to resemble a kind of political tong war in which an emergent liberal group seeks to wrestle power from the hands of moderates."[32]

At the same time, the white business establishment in Austin wasted no time in flexing its muscles. On July 31, the day after the conclusion of his sit-in, Bonner's employer, the "swank" Club Caravan at the Villa Capri motel in Austin, weighed in by firing him, though a manager claimed that the discharge had "nothing to do with Bonner's integration activities." Apparently the club was not yet ready to have the "Negro waiter" sit down and drink with its elite white patrons. Like many civil rights activists across the South, Bonner still had his life, but he had lost his livelihood in the cause of freedom.[33]

Although Bonner's sit-in began as the work of a "lone wolf," it immediately came to symbolize something much, much larger. His ties to the TCV and the Democratic Coalition meant that the sit-in was never only about integration but also had broad political ramifications. Although Bonner had not waited for the endorsement of any group to bring his "ultra liberal" group of college students and Austin activists to the capitol, his actions certainly advanced the multiracial liberal civil rights agenda. It reflected and exacerbated the deep-seated and growing tension between African American liberals and the conservative black elites of the UPO. It showed that direct action demonstrations were not the product of a sinister plot of white labor leaders but an organic protest originating in the state's marginalized black communities. It drove home the point that gradualism and patience would no longer suffice—that only "Freedom, All Here, Now" would satisfy the reignited civil rights movement. And it showed the swiftness and power of white conservatives' reaction and resistance to real change.

In short, Bonner's protest had called all of the state's political actors to task: it embarrassed the governor and his allies in the UPO, and it forced Bonner's own bedfellows in the TCV and the Democratic Coalition to take a stand. Each group would be forced to defend its respective position in the month ahead. More immediately, within days of the sit-in, Bonner made plans to have several other TCV officers from around the state attend his parlay with the governor. The group also began preparing for a mass demonstration that would take place in Austin on August 28—the same day as the March on Washington.

The Border Wage and Job Conference

While Bonner fanned the embers of the black civil rights movement into a raging fire, organized labor responded to the governor's attacks by launching an all-out campaign to improve working conditions along the U.S.-Mexico border. It remains unclear precisely why labor leaders chose to emphasize this particular point from their long list of civil rights issues, though it likely began with not wanting to back down in the face of Connally's attacks. Labor certainly saw the border region as an area for potential membership growth, though leaders also recognized that it could take years to overcome the extreme hostility toward unionism among the area's political and economic elites—and the resulting fear among unorganized workers. Still, the Teamsters had been flirting with organizing farmworkers in the Rio Grande Valley, and at least one AFL-CIO affiliate union had made some headway among the area's industrial workers. Also, Hank Brown was a native of San Antonio and had long relished the idea of organizing along the border.

Perhaps most important, South Texas had long been critical to the labor movement's political goals of building a liberal Democratic majority in the state, and labor had recently developed key political allies there through the Democratic Coalition and PASO—which itself had become a sort of labor organization. Certainly there were more community activists with which to partner along the border as compared to rural East Texas, where the black civil rights movement remained all but stillborn. And there were not many white union members in South Texas, so they could not attack labor's civil rights initiatives from within, as some white unionists were already doing in the state's major cities. Labor also had a loose organizational infrastructure in the region, thanks to the Latin American Affairs Committee, which began with a lone advisor in the late 1940s, was carried forward by Bob Sanchez in the 1950s, and became permanent in 1961, when the state federation filed its federal lawsuit against the green card "commuter problem."[34]

For all of these reasons, then, the Texas AFL-CIO took its stand not in East Texas or in one of the metropolitan areas, but in Laredo. In an ironic twist, just as the black civil rights movement was descending upon Austin, Brown and Evans went to the border. The state labor leaders continued to offer vociferous support to the black civil rights movement, but their most ambitious activism and most direct involvement lay elsewhere. The sensation they created in Laredo would reinforce and justify their decision.

On Saturday, August 3, over three hundred union members, PASO activists, and residents of Laredo gathered in that city's Jarvis Plaza in the midafternoon, braving 103-degree heat to hear the reports from the Texas AFL-CIO's Border Wage and Job Conference. The previous day, members of the state federation's permanent Committee on Latin American Affairs had come together in a nearby hotel to discuss the "deplorable" wages and working conditions of the mostly *mexicano* labor force along the Rio Grande. On Saturday morning, PASO leaders from across South Texas joined them, as did representatives of state and federal government agencies as well as a handful of local merchants and several officials of the Confederación de Trabajadores Mexicanos, Mexico's official labor movement. Dan Rather and a national crew from CBS News, along with other reporters, looked on as the main session of the conference got underway in a downtown auditorium. And then in the afternoon, outside in the square named for a Confederate hero, Congressman Henry B. Gonzalez gave an hourlong speech attacking the region's growers and industrialists and highlighting the plight of the poor. Several other political and labor leaders also addressed the crowd, which, despite the heat and the sun beating down, frequently interrupted the speakers with raucous applause.[35]

The organizers of this event were labor leaders Roy Evans and Hank Brown, who had decided to transform what had previously been a regular meeting of the Latin American Affairs Committee into the opening salvo of their campaign to organize along the border. Mindful of the need to respond to Governor Connally's personal attacks in front of the state's media, they had called a conference of all parties who contributed to or were affected by the region's low wage scale to address the issue, in their words, "by cooperation and common sense, and if this does not work, by demonstrations." The latter method had been the subject of the governor's ire, who had told the state that blood would be on labor's hands if the protests were to turn violent. The Border Wage and Job Conference was their antidote—a creative combination of the negotiations and civility that Connally advocated along with a set-piece rally that would showcase labor's power to mobilize in the streets while stopping short of the kind of unruly "demonstration" that the governor feared. And it would all take place in front of a salivating press corps.[36]

Predictably, the leading business interests in the region attacked the conference in the press before it even got underway. One report noted that "labor union officials from both sides of the Rio Grande sit down . . . to air the dirty linen of Texas employers along the Texas-Mexico border." A few small farmers and merchants had agreed to participate, the report added, but representatives of "large organizations of businessmen and growers" had remained silent on whether they would attend. One spokesman for a local chamber of commerce went on record to say that Evans was "just trying to stir up something," and that labor leaders were "making a mountain out of a molehill." Another business interest, an attorney for "several of the Valley's largest employers," added that "they just don't know what the situation is here."[37]

Evans shrugged off such comments. "We hope that everyone will agree on the nature of the [wage] problem and reach areas of agreement," he told a reporter. But "if the meeting is boycotted by businessmen, we will present an alternate plan for mass demonstrations." The day before the full conference began, he addressed a gathering of the Webb County Central Labor Council in Laredo, and that evening he went on television there to state his case for the conference. Evans "sharply criticized 90 per cent of Texas management, Gov. Connally, and U.S. Rep. Joe Kilgore who represents the [Lower Valley]," wrote one reporter. Addressing his union brothers, he responded to criticism that labor merely wanted conflict. "They say we are trying to inflame the people," he said. "You're damn right. We're trying to inflame the people—against injustice. We think this is the time for demonstrations in spite of what the governor says." That evening on television, Evans noted that Laredo was "the poorest city in the United States," with abnormally high unemployment and more than half of its residents living in poverty. But a "political revolution is coming" along the border, he said. "Things are happening in this area" as "the new, young leadership" of labor and PASO were demanding accountability from the region's elected officials.[38]

The day before the event, on Friday, August 2, the Latin American Affairs Committee convened in Laredo's Plaza Hotel. As in the past, much of the discussion centered on the ongoing "commuter problem," but such conversation was now accompanied by a new sense of urgency and militancy. Hank Brown reported that the federal suit was dismissed but was now on appeal and would be taken to the Supreme Court if necessary. At the same time, he added that the federation was asking the Kennedy administration to establish a $1.25 per hour minimum wage for commuters by executive order. While Mexican union leaders from south of the river looked on, Brown explained that the new wage, which far exceeded the prevailing rate on the Texas side of the border, would force employers to hire domestic laborers instead.[39]

Yet, for the first time, the committee moved toward a plan for direct action protest and increased on-the-ground organizing. Franklin Garcia, who had been stationed on the border as an organizer for the meat cutters since 1961, said that he was unhappy with the "progress made by the union," the committee, and "the President's civil rights program," according to a report. "I want more and I want to move faster," Garcia said. "I want to eliminate the word mañana." The committee's cochairman, steelworkers' representative Paul Montemayor of Corpus Christi, agreed: "I hope we have demonstrations.... The Lord knows they are long overdue," he said. A national AFL-CIO official claimed that the economic situation along the border was worse than it had been twenty years earlier, and Hank Brown noted that "the only way workers in this area are going to have economic justice is to be like hornets—get in a nest and organize." J. H. "Henry" Villareal, the secretary of the Lower Rio Grande Valley Central Labor Council, announced that he had recently been hired by the state federation to do public relations in his area, with the aim of educating citizens on the idea of unionism and independent political action. Brown added that the trial project's goal was not to "organize the workers overnight" but to invest long-term in improving the condition of ordinary people in the area. "If the job can be done without labor organizing we certainly will support it," he said. "Our immediate objective is not to organize, but to educate."[40]

The public phase of the conference took place on Saturday, August 3. As expected, the region's leading businessmen boycotted the parlay, but a few merchants and small farmers did join the approximately one hundred union and PASO members who gathered to discuss the region's low wages and poor working conditions. At least a half-dozen media outlets, including CBS News and the UPI, looked on, as did veteran activists George and Latane Lambert, who had made the trip from Dallas solely to observe the momentous event. J. Ed Lyles of the Texas Employment Commission, whose reappointment the Texas AFL-CIO had vehemently opposed, surprised observers when he endorsed their call for a $1.25 state minimum wage law—making him the highest ranking official in Texas government to do so. Even so, the conference remained one-sided, as not a single business leader participated in the Saturday morning panel discussion.[41]

Albert Peña closed the morning session with a characteristically electrifying speech in which he linked the border organizing campaign to the broader multiracial struggles for civil rights and independent political power. He again claimed that civil rights were the most important issue facing the state and nation, "especially in the field of fair employment practices and wages and hours." Peña added that it was not just a "moral problem" but also a "meat and potatoes" issue, and only strong legislation could fix the problem. He attacked the governor's program directly: "I cannot buy the sugar-coated, so-called moderate approach to civil rights," he said. Such sentiments were segregation in disguise and emphasized "order" over "justice." If Connally truly believed in voluntary integration, Peña added, he should immediately issue executive orders that would end all discrimination related to the state. There was only one solution, Peña concluded: "We have to join, if we haven't already, the old-fashioned political revolt developing all over the state of Texas . . . [which was] started by independent-thinking Mexican-Americans who insist that they be recognized as an integral part of the political community." And the way to do it was to join the Democratic Coalition in registering 200,000 more Mexican Americans to vote in 1964.[42]

Finally, on Saturday afternoon, Henry B. Gonzalez and Hank Brown led the list of speakers at the rally at Jarvis Plaza. Prior to the conference, the Webb County Central Labor Council had worked to invite ordinary Laredo citizens to attend the rally, promising that it would be a "large public meeting" in which the "results" of the multipartite conference would be announced. Circulating an "invitation to the public" written in Spanish, local organizers highlighted the presence of Gonzalez, "a true friend of all of the citizens of our town" and an honorable representative in Washington. "Citizens, don't miss" it, the flyer concluded. But once again, the political elites of far South Texas foiled the labor leaders' plans. Roy Evans claimed that "the local political machine" and area businessmen had put pressure on local citizens (or employees) to keep them away from the public rally. "We have the facts and they don't want to face up to them," Evans added, referring to the region's business leaders.[43]

Some three hundred people, mostly rank-and-file union members, ended up attending the rally. Since businessmen had boycotted the meeting, Brown laid out the program approved by labor's Latin American Affairs Committee the previous day. Most significantly, it called for a new annual appropriation of $30,000 to hire a full-time public relations officer in each of three border cities in order to begin to crack the wall of opposition to unionism and independent political action that dominated the region. Gonzalez, who had helped kill the renewal of the bracero program in Congress a few months earlier, still railed against the system of "slave labor" that depressed wages in the area. He also hit the "commuter" program and paused to thank organized labor for taking an interest in the area's plight. He was "highly complimentary" of the Texas AFL-CIO, according to one report. "He asked if the AFL-CIO wasn't speaking up for the poor, who would?"[44]

The Border Wage and Job Conference thus ended much as it had begun: as a gathering of allies coming together to take on an impossible task in the face of intransigent opposition. It did not result in new jobs, nor even new dialogue with South Texas elites. However, it did shine new light on what had previously been an unspoken and unacknowledged truth in Texas political life. It was a "demonstration" of another type: one that showcased the extreme poverty of the border region, the area's intractable local machine, and the full meaning of "civil rights" as it applied to Mexican Americans.

Organizer Franklin Garcia of the meat cutters had introduced a resolution Saturday morning that called for state and federal action "to prohibit employers from intimidating, coercing, discriminating against, or firing, employes [sic] for political activities." The attendees approved the measure, which got to the root of the problem. If the conference and rally were any indication, labor had underestimated just how fiercely employers were going to fight to prevent change from sweeping the region. The fact that "big labor" could only hire "public relations" officers and that their first assignment was "not to organize, but to educate," underscored just how much work remained to be done.[45]

But the arrival of labor along the border meant that someone cared, that the statewide coalition's most powerful leg had committed itself to joining the "old-fashioned political revolt" led by "independent-minded" Mexican Americans. Brown maintained that they would be there for the long haul: "We are prepared to work so long as there is any hope for a better tomorrow for these people."[46] Labor had thus committed itself to the *mexicano* civil rights movement even more completely than it had joined the black freedom struggle. In both cases, their efforts would bear fruit not only in terms of flashy direct action demonstrations but also, they hoped, in the strengthening of the Democratic Coalition at the polls.

The March on Austin

Back in Austin, other members of the Democratic Coalition continued to step up the pressure on the governor. B. T. Bonner and his small group of Austin "ultra liberals" led the charge, but he was also joined by a number of coalition activists, first from San Antonio and then from Dallas and Houston. Thanks to his sit-in, Bonner had won an appointment with Connally, but the wars of words and political maneuvering would continue, leading to the chief executive's rejection of the activists and culminating in the state's largest civil rights demonstration to date. Critically, both the massive March on Austin and the organizing along the way depended upon the ongoing vibrancy and salience of multiracial collaboration.

The political stakes of the black civil rights movement became clear on August 1, when three distinct groups each shared their stances on integration at separate events in Austin. Bonner, who had been fired from his job the previous day, led a group of seven pickets—five white, two black—who again assembled outside the governor's mansion. Meanwhile, a "segregationist group of 10 white youths," led by a member of the White Citizens' Council, also marched outside the stately colonial building. The two marches "crossed" but "there were no incidents," according to a report. While both groups engaged in direct action for their respective causes, members of the UPO also assembled in the capital city, where they agreed to send telegrams to U.S. senators Tower and Yarborough, asking them to end their "silence" and speak out on the issue of civil rights. The conservative African American club reiterated that it supported the president's push for "enforceable legislation," and it pledged to lobby the state's congressional delegation "by direct contact." The group quickly added that it continued to support the governor despite the fact that they disagreed about privately owned public accommodations. One report added that the UPO considered Connally's position "the most positive stand of any state official in Texas history."[47]

The conservative governor, his black allies, and the far right of explicit white supremacists all loomed as potential roadblocks as Bonner prepared for his August 6 audience with Connally. Although he had staged the sit-in alone, Bonner knew he needed help from the coalition. He had previously written a letter to the governor's office requesting a group meeting, and he felt he had been assured as much when he scheduled the appointment. He invited other members of the liberal TCV from San Antonio and Dallas, and a mixed-race group of activists made their way to Austin for the big day. The TCV activists included G. J. Sutton, Rev. Claude Black, and Dr. Ruth Bellinger McCoy of San Antonio's East Side, along with E. Brice Cunningham of Dallas, the council's executive secretary, and Bonner. The two liberal leaders of San Antonio's Mexican American West Side were also represented: Albert Peña sent Henry Muñoz, who had quit the Teamsters to work full time for the commissioner, and Henry B. Gonzalez sent his aide, Lalo Solis, identified in reports as a simple "restaurant owner." A student at the University of Texas who took part in Bonner's local group rounded out the delegation.[48]

The mixed group approached Connally's office, ready to present its demands, but the activists were refused entry by the governor's assistant, who stated that only Bonner would be permitted to see the governor. Connally may have refused the group because of the demonstration the night before, when Bonner staged his sixth protest at the governor's mansion, accompanied by approximately sixty other pickets. The group chanted "Freedom, yes; Connally, no," and again marched across the street to the capitol. In any event, when the governor's aide refused to admit the entire delegation, Bonner flatly refused to go it alone. "I'm not making this fight for Booker T. Bonner," he told reporters afterward, "and I cannot speak for one million Negroes [in Texas]." That evening, Bonner and a group of about forty supporters again picketed the governor's mansion, carrying signs reading "He wouldn't see us." A segregationist group of hecklers followed them to the capitol, chanting "Bonner, you ran away today" (and other, more "obscene" comments).[49]

The delegation had planned to present the governor with a petition for an eight-point civil rights program. After refusing to meet Connally by himself, Bonner gave the petition to the press but said that he did not plan "to submit it through the back door"—gesturing to the Jim Crow practice in which African Americans were expected to seek service or enter buildings through rear entrances. The program itself reflected the long-time aspirations of the militant group of liberal and working-class civil rights activists. They demanded that the governor issue an executive order ending "racial discrimination" in all state-owned facilities, parks, and hospitals as well as a state ordinance prohibiting segregation in privately owned public accommodations. They also asked for immediate integration of every school district and the state's higher education system. Most important, they demanded that the governor issue orders that would immediately integrate state jobs, remove racial references from all applications for state employment, and withhold state funds from contractors who practiced discrimination. They also called for repeal of the 1957 school segregation laws (which Henry B. Gonzalez had filibustered) and "a minimum wage of not less than $1.25 per hour."[50]

G. J. Sutton criticized Connally for refusing to meet with the group, drawing attention to the governor's preferential treatment of other visitors while feigning political naiveté. "We just don't understand what reasoning the governor has," he said. "Seemingly, it's the policy of the governor to see Negroes one at a time. It would take a long time to get our problems over to the governor individually." Sutton gestured toward the cozy relationship between Connally and the UPO while attacking his failure to keep the door open for groups of liberal African Americans. Privately, Sutton returned home to San Antonio and began making plans for the August 28 march.[51]

While Sutton assailed the governor's hypocritical actions, Bonner soon found his own character under attack. A reporter from the *Fort Worth Star-Telegram* dug up an old file in a Houston courthouse that showed that Bonner had been convicted of "mail theft" in 1945, when he was seventeen years old. Bonner initially refused to respond, declaring that his past was off limits to reporters, but within twenty-four hours he admitted to being convicted on a charge of federal "embezzlement." He had been sentenced to three years in prison, but the sentence was suspended on condition of good behavior. He was soon drafted into the army, and the suspension was excused early as he was sent to Korea. "I am a little disturbed about spending all that time over there for nothing and coming back and finding out that I am not so good," Bonner explained to the *Dallas Morning News*. He added that he had "been a pretty angry person all my life but not a bad person."[52]

The revelation of his criminal past called into question his claim of employment discrimination based on race, but Bonner maintained that race, not his conviction, was the reason that he could not get good jobs. He stressed that the civil rights campaign would continue. "We've given up on the governor," he said, adding that various groups were now making plans for the August 28 march on the state capitol. The "self-styled leader of the effort," in the words of one journalist, also acknowledged that he was no longer at its helm. "This isn't mine now," Bonner told him. "It belongs to several groups of people."[53] Despite such pronouncements, Bonner was again at the head of a protest at the governor's mansion just two days later, on August 9. A group of forty people joined him in picketing, and Bonner told reporters that the group would demonstrate every Friday in support of Kennedy's civil rights bill.[54]

Behind the scenes, Bonner, Sutton, and African American organizers across the state began preparing to march on Washington and Austin on August 28. San Antonio activists added a sit-in at City Hall to their agenda, while activists from Houston, Dallas, and Fort Worth all prepared to join the state and national protests instead. Harry Burns, the head of the San Antonio NAACP, explained that the sit-in "would be for civil rights and job opportunities."[55] He continued to attack the so-called moderate alternative. "The voluntary desegregation program . . . has proven very unsatisfactory," Burns said. "Not one week has passed since July 4 that we have not received some reports of discrimination against Negroes. Any further delay is further inference to businessmen that they can continue to practice segregation." Burns also reported that fifteen San Antonians had already left for Washington while a "large delegation" would caravan to Austin in "10 to 20" carloads on the morning of August 28. Eugene Coleman, publisher of *SNAP News*, was appointed to act as parade marshal from San Antonio.[56] The president of Houston's NAACP chapter likewise indicated that one busload of protestors would travel from his city to Washington and another would participate in the Austin rally.[57]

Albert Peña also organized on behalf of the predominately black civil rights march, spreading news of the planned action and building support for it among local PASO chapters. On August 22, Bexar County PASO passed a resolution going on record in favor of the demonstrations planned for Austin and Washington and "urging Governor John Connally to meet his responsibility as the Chief Executive of this state and as head of the Democratic Party in Texas, by meeting with the Demonstrators in Austin and using his influence and prestige to redress these wrongs." On August 25, Peña brought this resolution to a regional PASO meeting in Houston, where he also gave a passionate speech endorsing the march. "It is my sincere hope that the freedom or so-called protest march . . . will awaken the conscience of all Americans," he began. The "much-debated public accommodations section" was particularly important, he added. "The affronts and denials that this section, if enacted, would correct are intensely human and personal. Very often they harm the physical body, but always they strike at the root of the human spirit. From the time Negroes leave home in the morning en route to school or work, to shopping or to visiting, until they return home at night, humiliation stalks them." Despite the fact that slavery was abolished one hundred years earlier, "the Negro remains in bondage to the color of his skin," Peña concluded.[58]

Throughout all these preparations, Bonner remained the undisputed leader of the March on Austin. He formed the Freedom Now Committee, and it was

The "Freedom Now" March proceeds from Rosewood Park in the all-black East Austin neighborhood westward down East Twelfth Street toward the state capitol, escorted by police. The Democratic Coalition unequivocally endorsed the demonstration, which occurred on the same day as the March on Washington, August 28, 1963. Courtesy *Austin American-Statesman* Photographic Morgue (AR.2014.039), Austin History Center, Austin Public Library, Texas, Image AS-63-42093-10a.

this group that obtained a permit for the two-mile parade route, from Rosewood Park in all-black East Austin, past the capitol grounds, and culminating in a rally at the nearby Wooldridge Park downtown. He said he didn't know if twenty-five or ten thousand marchers would attend the event, but no matter what, they would raise their voices in protest. A white segregationist claimed he expected three thousand counterdemonstrators from around the state, despite the fact that Governor Connally urged them to stay home to avoid an "incident."[59]

When the big day finally arrived, around one thousand demonstrators joined the civil rights march as it wound its way across Austin in 102-degree heat. Perhaps a fifth of the marchers were white, and a handful of Mexican Americans also participated. Several hundred Austin teenagers organized by Bonner joined the veteran activists from across the state. "Freedom Now" was the march's main theme, but demonstrators also carried countless homemade signs. Some compared Connally to George Wallace of Alabama or Orville Faubus of Arkansas, while others carried creative slogans linking labor and civil rights: "No more 50¢ per hour" and "Segregation is a new form of slavery." One read "Kennedy *sí*, Connally no." The marchers sang movement songs attacking the governor: "Tell John Connally, we shall not be moved."[60]

The march made its way past the capitol without stopping—organizers claimed that the police had turned on the lawn sprinklers to keep them off the grounds, while the governor continued conducting "regular business" inside. Only eleven segregationists heckled the group until they were removed by police. Having "given up" on Connally, who made it clear he would not receive them, the leaders had canceled earlier plans to again present him with their eight-point petition. Rev. Black of San Antonio later noted the contrast between Connally, who flatly refused to meet with them, and President Kennedy, who had met with civil rights leaders earlier that morning, prior to the March on Washington.[61]

Instead, the marchers in Austin kept walking to a nearby park, where they assembled to hear a range of speakers "roast" the governor. "The rally appeared to be as much an anti-Connally political affair as a demonstration for racial equality," the *Dallas Morning News* reported derisively. The *Observer* stated that "the rally linked themes of racial justice and opposition to Connally." Both its sympathizers and detractors agreed that the march's implications extended beyond the immediate push for the federal civil rights bill to include a broader push for political power. The speakers also left no doubt in the crowd's mind: Dr. Brooks of the Fort Worth NAACP and TCV called on the protestors to come together "to sweep the statehouse clean."

Rev. Black put it in Manichean terms that highlighted the legacies of slavery and the persistence of low-wage labor and political powerlessness. The rally represented an historic moment, the pastor began, reaffirming the Declaration of Independence and the revolutionary movements of Nat Turner and John Brown and continuing the tradition of the Israelites' Exodus from Egypt, which "occurred when Moses became chairman of the committee for freedom march," Black said. More important was the fact that ordinary people had come to understand the causes of their oppression. "The little people of our state have located the center of authority," he boomed, pointing past the crowd toward the capitol. "The men who lay the lashes on our backs, who cause us to work for less than we're worth, are located in the center of that granite building over there. We have discovered the center of authority and therefore we

A large crowd assembled at Woolridge Square Park after the march to hear speeches by Rev. Claude Black, Moses LeRoy, W. J. Durham, and Henry Muñoz, among others. Each orator pointed to the multiracial protest as evidence of the moment's unprecedented unity across the color line as well as the Democratic Coalition's conflict with the UPO, the group of conservative African American professionals allied with Governor Connally. Courtesy *Austin American-Statesman* Photographic Morgue (AR.2014.039), Austin History Center, Austin Public Library, Texas, Image AS-63-42087-06a.

have marched." The building was built by black convict laborers, he added, but it "now houses those who determine the bread on our table, the clothes on our backs, and the shelter over our heads." Knowing this, Black added, "It's not strange that this Governor that talked well during his campaign and yet now has sold out to those who would restrict and limit us is not here to greet us." Such tactics would no longer be tolerated, the reverend declared. Politicians could not use "the Negro as a whipping boy" and hope to get elected, nor could they only bestow "partial freedoms" on African Americans. "We have come to warn Gov. Connally and all the other segregationists that their days are numbered," Black thundered, making no distinction between the Texas governor's gradualism and the massive resistance of his more outspoken counterparts across Dixie. And the rally that day represented "just the beginning of the march," he concluded. "For we shall march into every polling place in our state ... under the banner of civil rights [and] justice for all men.... Tell Governor Connally that we are on the march!"[62]

The crowd roared its approval. After Bonner offered a few words, Moses LeRoy took the stage and addressed the throng, giving a brief speech that connected the rally to his decades of activism in the trenches. "Fellow Americans, this is one of the happiest moments of my life," LeRoy began. "We have come out here because we agree to raise, to pick [up] the conscience of America and to let the world know that we are tired of second class citizenship." He told the crowd that he had "been in this fight a long time" and had that he had shared these experiences with a group of younger black activists at a meeting on the evening before the rally. "I have helped carry the ball to the two-yard line," LeRoy said he had told the youth. "And now it's dependent upon you now, you youngsters, and I'm looking into your faces, and I don't want you to give up the faith, but to carry the ball on to victory. I'm in your corner."[63]

The lineup of speakers and diverse participants at the rally reflected the vibrancy of the statewide Democratic Coalition and its local affiliates. Francis Williams of the HCCO emceed the event, and Ruth Bellinger McCoy spoke for the Bexar County Coalition. Sutton was among those in the crowd, as was Martin Garcia, the lead Teamsters-PASO organizer of the Crystal City uprising. Mrs. Erma LeRoy attended the event and shouted to one reporter: "The governor is politically dead!" Larry Goodwyn walked alongside Sutton for parts of the march and told the *Observer* in no uncertain terms that the Democratic Coalition "endorses peaceful demonstrations for civil rights." The leaders of the Texas AFL-CIO could not attend the march: they were holding their annual convention in Houston at that exact moment. Hank Brown sent a letter of encouragement instead, and a black unionist from Houston served as labor's official representative and read Brown's speech. Peña was a featured speaker at the labor convention and was also absent from the march, but Henry Muñoz represented him and PASO and read a speech on Peña's behalf.[64]

Still, the strongest statements linking the civil rights struggle to the larger political sphere came from W. J. Durham, president of the TCV and Democratic Coalition cochair. The March on Austin represented the TCV's "first answer to the pro-Connally United Political Organization (UPO)," wrote Ronnie Dugger of the *Observer*. For his part, Durham made their opposition clear: "I think UPO stands for 'Under political orders,'" he said. It "is made up of bought conservative Negroes who have their hands out for money and who jump on all other Negroes."[65] Noting that the group had recently singled out and criticized the TCV's alliance with organized labor, Durham retorted that "The Negro today needs all the help he can get, he needs all the friends he can get, he can't turn a single friend away.... When our sons and daughters and husbands and wives are in jail in South Carolina, in Mississippi, in Alabama, who was it that wrote a check for $160,000 for bonds for those children? It was labor," he shouted as the crowd's roar drowned him out. "Those are the kind of men that my governor wants you to fight," Durham added.

Durham and other speakers drove home the importance of the Democratic Coalition and liberal politics to the future of the black civil rights movement. "There are 874,000 potential Negro votes in Texas now, there are more than 800,000 Latin Americans, and a huge labor vote, and there's a whole heck of a lot of independent white citizens with their honest convictions," Durham added. "Tell them that on Election Day, when it next comes around, each of us will remember him." He then singled out each of Connally's fallacious arguments. While the governor claimed that the Civil Rights Act would restrict private property without precedent, the lawyer Durham countered that the state had intervened to create Jim Crow on private railroad cars a century earlier. Connally had told the protestors to stay home from Austin and Washington, but Durham replied that no change would have been made had the movement not taken its cause to the centers of power in the *Smith* and *Sweatt* cases after World War II. "If I hadn't gone to Washington, I wouldn't have been voting today," he said, and "we would not have our children graduating from the leading colleges and universities in this state."[66] Finally, Durham concluded, again taking aim at the UPO:

> The day is over when he [the Governor] can separate Negroes, except those few who are conservative and have gotten super rich. They'll never separate the Latin-American and Negroes again in politics. They'll never separate the independent white man and the Negro again. They'll never separate labor and the Negro again. We're going to march on the street, pray on the streets, sit in the streets, walk on the streets. We're going to fight at the ballot box and in the courts. I believe that's the last message I've got for my governor.

Other speakers echoed this refrain. Bonner noted that "Negroes, Latin Americans and labor union members will be 'registered to vote in unprecedented numbers,'" while Brooks said that African Americans would "stick together with their liberal, labor, and Latin-American allies."[67]

Meanwhile, the leaders of the UPO were fully aware of the march's frontal assault on their organization. Rev. H. Rhett James of Dallas, the organization's executive secretary, told reporters that "he did not attend the march because of the 'planned political overtones.'" The TCV and the Democratic Coalition, he charged, were "using the race issue" to promote Don Yarborough's as yet unannounced campaign against Connally in the 1964 Democratic primary. James said the UPO did not oppose demonstrations but wanted them "pitched on issues and not personalities." James added that Durham's statements were just "sour grapes."[68]

Such criticisms intentionally obscured what Dugger of the *Observer* called the "linked themes of racial injustice and opposition to Connally" by attempting to downplay the formal political power wielded by elected officials who largely determined the status of civil rights on the ground. For organizers such as Bonner, Sutton, Durham, and the LeRoys, however, these issues were inextricably intertwined. Just as Peña had criticized PASO and labor for making politically expedient alliances, the activists of the TCV believed that the UPO could not demand freedom while subordinating it to the governor's program of moderation. Only independent political action could result in self-determination, in the ability to choose one's own representatives and create public policies that reflected the longtime aspirations of their community. While the leaders of the UPO had "their hands out for money" and were getting "super rich," the liberal African American activists demanded nothing less than complete autonomy, immediate integration, and equal opportunity.

They did so by seeking multiracial alliances with like-minded Mexican American and white activists. While *intra*racial conflict raged, *inter*racial cooperation offered these activists opportunities to outflank their opposition as they continued their decades-long quest for political and economic democracy.

Mexicans Americans and the white-led labor movement did much the same thing, advancing their own protracted struggles for democracy by seeking (and finding) alliances with one another and with African Americans. Each group depended on the other, and the Democratic Coalition was their hope for the future. After three decades of experimenting in "coalitioning," as W. J. Durham called the agonizing up-and-down, back-and-forth process, veteran activists were now deliberately attempting their boldest coordinated action yet. They did not always agree with one another, but the multiracial partnership was anything but expedient. The next year would test whether it would meet their extremely lofty expectations.

Columnist Jon Ford of the *San Antonio Express-News* commented a few days after the march that the Democratic Coalition had "rattled enough swords" in recent weeks to make "even the most complacent conservative Democrats" recognize its presence. While speakers at the civil rights march lashed out at the governor, the Texas AFL-CIO in convention in Houston simultaneously endorsed the demonstrations in Austin and Washington, "passed strong integration resolutions," and reiterated its call for Connally to call a special session on civil rights. The labor gathering itself served as a sort of parallel rally for the coalition. Albert Peña was a featured speaker, and he didn't change his tune for the audience of union men. Instead, he reiterated his belief that civil rights represented the most important issue facing liberals of all colors and drove home the point that voluntary integration and gradual change were not enough. "I will not buy the sugar-coated, moderate approach of Gov. Connally," Peña said. The labor delegates also decided to withhold support from any candidate who refused to advocate the repeal of the right to work law, which the governor had failed to do in 1962. For his part, Connally had openly snubbed both the civil rights demonstrators and organized labor. Durham also addressed an earlier session of the labor gathering, leading a slate of Democratic Coalition speakers who all promised to deliver change at the ballot box.[69]

Yet journalist Ford also cautioned that "estimates of the potential united strength of the coalition vary widely." The alliance's path to victory would not be easy, despite predictions that conservatives would defect to the GOP, Ford noted. Still the multiracial "liberal movement" was far more than "sour grapes," as UPO leader Rhett James had claimed. The Democratic Coalition "may not accomplish anything spectacular in 1964," Ford concluded, "but spectacular results are not outside the realm of possibility." And no matter what, it was clear that the coalition represented "a figure and force to cause politicians intent on self preservation to sit up and take notice."[70]

Voters of Texas Enlist

While the wars of words between the multiracial group of civil rights activists and Governor Connally and his supporters made most of the headlines, behind the scenes the quotidian organizing work of the Democratic Coalition quietly got underway. The poll tax that had defined their work for decades suddenly appeared to be on its last legs. Across the South, the Kennedy administration had responded to the civil rights movement by attempting to channel its energy into voter registration, but the poll tax and other methods of voter suppression had blunted its success. In September 1962, Congress had proposed to the states the Twenty-Fourth Amendment, which outlawed the poll tax as a prerequisite for voting in federal elections. The bill was weak in that it did not ban the system outright, yet it avoided a filibuster and even attracted some support from southerners because it did not address state and local contests. Members of the Democratic Coalition in Texas viewed the proposed amendment as good news. When a joint House-Senate committee of the legislature scheduled preliminary hearings on a new voter registration law for December 1962, the Democratic Coalition's newsletter opined that the state appeared likely to ratify the amendment and repeal the state poll tax as well. Members of the coalition's temporary steering committee testified before the committee, urging a system that included permanent, partisan registration without tax or literacy requirements in an enrollment period that would extend up to thirty days prior to each election.[71]

But as the 1963 legislative session got underway and the bill wound its way through the legislature's committees, all of these proposals fell by the wayside. Instead, over the protests of Texas AFL-CIO officials, Governor Connally allied with conservative leaders in the Texas State House and Senate to write a registration bill that actually made it harder to vote. With the Twenty-Fourth Amendment and the end of the federal poll tax now most of the way toward ratification, the state legislature sidestepped the national issue and focused instead on the state law. The final bill maintained annual registration and the January 31 deadline and scheduled a special referendum election on the repeal of the state poll tax for November 9, 1963. While members of the Democratic Coalition favored any move toward abolishing the tax, they testified before the senate that holding the election in an odd-numbered off year would dramatically reduce turnout and make the chances of repeal less likely. The problem, they knew, would be especially acute among the "unlikely" voters that the coalition hoped to mobilize, and, in any event, the registration window for the year had already ended. The referendum did not even promise full repeal: the legislature had inserted a provision that would create a twenty-five-cent registration fee if repeal were to pass, giving the voters the choice between the existing $1.75 tax and a "two-bit" alternative.

To add insult to injury, the legislature also banned the "agency form" that volunteer deputy registrars had used to sell poll taxes door-to-door or at community or union meetings. The form had been the "mainstay of political organizational drives to get people qualified," the *Observer* noted, and now poll tax canvassers would be able to do little more than bring would-be voters to officially sanctioned poll tax payment substations. The cumulative effect of these laws in restricting the franchise was intentional. As one state legislator defended it, democracy is not the distribution of "equal political rights" but the exercise of the vote by an educated electorate. "People who take the most interest in government are the ones that are leading the community," he maintained. "There is no need to get voters by the truckload coming to register. The mere argument that you want to get more voters to the polls has never appealed to me."[72]

As the rhetoric at the March on Austin and the labor convention in Houston suggested, the Democratic Coalition had high hopes for 1964. The key to victory would be the mass registration of African American and Mexican American voters. Passage of the November 9 referendum repealing the poll tax would greatly simplify their task. But even if the referendum failed, building an organization now would pay off when the annual poll tax season began immediately after the special election.

Soon after its mid-July meetings, the coalition formed a new nonprofit organization called Voters of Texas Enlist (VOTE) to coordinate the upcoming campaign to repeal the poll tax. Project VOTE would work "to extend the coalition to the grass roots with maximum speed" by developing an army of "blockworkers" in heavily African American and Mexican American precincts across the state. Preliminary plans called for full-time paid "project officers" to fan out across the state, select volunteer "precinct captains" for each polling place, and for those activists to recruit one blockworker for each group of twenty voters in their target area. The plan called for reaching 240,000 black and brown voters through 12,000 blockworkers. Doing so would dramatically boost turnout in black and brown neighborhoods and rural districts from historically low figures that hovered around 10 percent in off-year elections to three or even five times that percentage. If they could "get-out-the-vote" on that scale, coalition activists believed they could not only tip the scales in the repeal referendum but also set the stage for a massive voter registration effort immediately afterward and a liberal victory in 1964.

Born as it was from the Democratic Coalition, VOTE from the start incorporated a diverse group of veteran African American, Mexican American, and white activists. If "only the mexicano can speak for the mexicano," as George Sanchez had long asserted, then only *mexicano* project officers could recruit *mexicano* precinct captains, who could in turn find *mexicano* blockworkers who would then successfully turn out twenty *mexicano* voters each. The same held true for African Americans and white labor union members, though the latter remained the province of the AFL-CIO's COPE, while VOTE focused on black and brown voters. Consequently, dozens of longtime labor, civil rights, and political activists—who had fought countless local battles over the decades and more recently built the Democratic Coalition and the civil rights campaigns of the summer—quickly transitioned into the on-the-ground leadership of Project VOTE.

Project VOTE got underway in earnest soon after the March on Austin in late August. At the center of the project would be "a blockworker program that reaches into the precincts on a house-by-house, street-by-street basis." Preliminary arrangements had already been laid, the plan said, by developing "a working relationship . . . between labor and the rank-and-file leadership" of black and brown activist groups. "The task now is to put this working relationship to use . . . to cash in on the cooperation between labor and the minorities that has already been accomplished by the Coalition."[73]

The process was relatively simple in theory, but it would require "one hell of a lot of grubby, detailed work." First, "poll tax lists and criss-cross directories must be broken down into block lists" of twenty voters, groups that would be passed along to the individual blockworkers. The separate county lists and directories were later "put through IBM machines, to re-shuffle them by street address and produce 'walk lists'" for each blockworker. The second step was to recruit the rank and file and sell them on the program. The plan cautioned that "nothing is more useless than a list of 20 people, however well organized it may be by blocks, if there is no blockworker to contact them." To avoid this, it proposed that local African American and PASO organizations stage "a huge mass meeting in [each of] the 15 priority cities." At each of these gatherings, representatives from the coalition's Team Program led by Arthur DeWitty of the Austin TCV and Martin Garcia of PASO would lead pep rallies in support of political action. This motivational-speaker arm of the coalition had been "thoroughly tested" and proven to be effective, coalition leaders claimed. The final step of the plan was to get the lists of twenty voters into the hands of the blockworkers "in such a way that they know (1) what to do (2) when to do it (3) that a check will be made on them." VOTE headquarters would secure tens of thousands of fliers and put them into packets of twenty along with instruction sheets for the individual blockworkers. It would also set up a "telephone boiler operation that contacts the blockworkers and checks on them." Finally, the local project officers, a group composed of one full-time "minority group person in each city," were charged with updating card files, sending names of each new blockworker recruit back to headquarters, helping "ram-rod recruiting of blockworkers," and "co-ordinat[ing] with Negro organizations and with PASO."[74]

Coalition members contributed funds and personnel to Project VOTE as it got underway in August and September. The budget, which rapidly ballooned, depended heavily on donations from "independent" liberals and labor. An initial budget projection for the repeal campaign get-out-the-vote effort asked for only $17,000, of which $7,000 had already been raised. The budget called for an addition $5,000 each from the "independent" liberals and the Texas AFL-CIO. Labor, of course, also allocated money for COPE—for which it had appropriated a whopping $300,000 for the entire 1964 election cycle (the late August convention increased the total from $180,000 in 1962). VOTE, which targeted black and brown voters, most of whom were not union members, initially appeared to be a drop in the bucket. But costs quickly jumped skyward: by October 6, the Democratic Coalition and VOTE had already spent a combined $21,500, and staffers asked for an additional $24,000 for the last month of the campaign. The final cost ended up approaching $70,000.[75]

While the budget reflected a sizable financial contribution from two legs of the coalition, the staff depended heavily upon members of the other two—as well as black and brown labor people. In fact, VOTE brought together a diverse group of many of the coalition's most battle-tested activists. Larry Goodwyn remained the executive director; Albert Fuentes, the longtime PASO leader, directed activities among Mexican Americans; and Erma LeRoy coordinated the project's African American "leg." Both Fuentes and Mrs. LeRoy also served as "co-directors" of the entire campaign, while Latane Lambert conducted labor outreach and helped Goodwyn run the state office. Barbara Jordan, an African American attorney and activist in the Harris County Democrats who had run unsuccessfully for the legislature in 1962, coordinated Houston activities, where she was joined by two other paid project officers. B. T. Bonner was the "project officer" for black voters in Austin. Other veteran Mexican American and African American project officers rounded out the campaign staff, along with Team Program coordinators DeWitty and Garcia.[76] Taken together, the twenty "project directors in the field" in sixteen different cities were almost all black or brown, while the nine-member state staff reflected the egalitarian leadership structure of the four-legged Democratic Coalition. Labor donated a full-time coordinator and much-needed dollars and conducted its own outreach effort to its predominately white membership. Project VOTE did the rest.[77]

In the seven weeks prior to the November 9 vote, the project officers frantically contacted friendly precinct captains, found new precinct leaders where none existed, and worked to make sure that each area would have one blockworker for every twenty voters by election day. The officers met frequently with their volunteers to check on their progress and then called or mailed headquarters with contact information for each new blockworker. They knocked on doors, house-by-house, street-by-street, and attended countless meetings of local civil rights, fraternal, and social organizations in their assigned communities.

In some cases, they organized various clubs as they worked. Albert Fuentes of PASO, assigned to coordinate *mexicano* participation in the effort, simultaneously used his post to make contact with and revivify established PASO chapters while also organizing new ones. His one surviving report provides a snapshot of the day-to-day activities of a VOTE organizer. On September 25, Fuentes informed coalition headquarters that blockworker programs had already been established in "Mexican-American precincts" in El Paso, San Antonio, Corpus Christi, Austin, Dallas, Fort Worth, Houston, and Hidalgo and Cameron Counties in the Lower Rio Grande Valley. Fuentes had "personally contacted the PASO groups in each of these areas . . . conferring with them about the blockworker program and urging them to fully co-operate." Fuentes also reported that PASO chapters existed in fifteen additional counties from Orange in Southeast Texas to Webb County out west (Laredo). Again, he had been in touch with each group in order to explain the "Coalition and VOTE program, and the need for the immediate campaign to repeal the poll tax. The groups have also been advised and urged to obtain the poll lists and maps of each Mexican-American precinct in their county [sic], and to use these materials in a person-to-person canvass." Fuentes also had plans to attend meetings of PASO chapters in six different locales in the coming month, including one in San Antonio that would feature "free beer and tamales."[78]

Few staffers barnstormed the entire state in this manner, but Fuentes's report still indicates the systematic, comprehensive, and high-paced nature of the campaign. Lambert, Mrs. LeRoy, and Goodwyn all crisscrossed Texas to attend various meetings, as did Team Program coordinators DeWitty and Garcia, who held mass meetings in each of the sixteen different project cities. On a smaller scale, each of the twenty project officers routinely visited each of their target precincts, reported on the status of each one, held countless community meetings, recruited leaders, and returned again and again until each one was organized. And they also attended statewide meetings to report on their progress.[79]

While VOTE staffers worked to spread the coalition to the grassroots, the group's detractors also made their voices heard. Governor Connally remained the coalition's critic-in-chief, and Albert Peña bore the brunt of the criticism. Back in May, the Bexar County Commissioners Court censured Peña for his role in the Crystal City uprising. Peña and the local PASO chapter rebutted the charges, but it was clear that his fellow representatives had turned against him. On September 1, the San Antonio columnist writing under the pseudonym Don Politico commented that Peña had become two men with wildly different fortunes. "The political star of PASO Chairman Pena is twinkling high and merrily in the Texas skies," he wrote. "But that of Commissioner Pena has dipped into near permanent eclipse." While Peña had spent much of the previous week out of town attacking Governor Connally before the Houston PASO and the state AFL-CIO convention, he remained under fire whenever he came back to San Antonio, the columnist noted. On seven different occasions the other commissioners had thwarted him, including in appointments to local boards and one case in which they denied Henry Muñoz a job on the county's payroll.[80]

Still, the loudest criticism came from the governor himself. At a League of Women Voters summit called to promote the repeal campaign, Connally surprised observers when he used his keynote speech to attack the commissioner, calling him "Boss Peña" and charging him with trying to amass bloc votes "to take over the state" through PASO "with the help of the AFL-CIO unions and Negro groups." Addressing the largely blue-haired "non-partisan" group, Connally claimed that Peña and the Democratic Coalition were attempting to capture the nonpartisan poll tax initiative that the league had long advocated. Organizers from the sponsoring group and the audience afterward questioned whether the governor's statements helped or hurt the repeal effort, according to newspaper reports. "Roy Evans, state AFL-CIO treasurer who often spars politically with Connally, expressed puzzlement as to 'why he did it. Is he really for repeal?'" Evans asked. The labor leader also defended the Democratic Coalition's cochairman. "Denying that Pena is a 'boss,' Evans said the San Antonio politico is 'an influential individual,' but he is the antithesis of the old 'patron.' 'Why is it wrong for Latin Americans and labor and Negroes to encourage citizenship, but never wrong for big business to do the same?' Evans asked." The labor leader stated the coalition's case ably, but Peña needed little help. The PASO chairman laid into Connally days later, noting that the governor was a beneficiary of the Viva Kennedy movement and the integrationist administration that he now opposed. "I will never understand why the governor would deliberately alienate minority voters to satisfy personal whims of segregationists. I will never understand why the governor would make a whipping boy out of organized labor." The only way for the Democratic Party to continue to win "is to register more Mexican-American and Negro voters," Peña added.[81] The *Texas Observer* joined in the chorus in attacking Connally's speech, arguing that it distracted from the repeal effort and could only be attributed to a change in strategy in which the governor was counting on a white backlash against civil rights to keep him in office.[82]

Despite the governor's hostility, VOTE's coordinators and project officers continued their work. As the end of their seven-week campaign on the ground neared, they were approaching their goal of recruiting 12,000 volunteer blockworkers who would in turn reach 240,000 African American and Mexican American voters on Election Day. They lagged behind, but not by much. Nearly 9,000 blockworkers had signed and returned "Freedom Pledge Cards," and just under 8,000 "actually received blockworker kits" with walk lists prior to November 9.[83]

As the campaign entered its final week, Goodwyn and the statewide coordinators fired off a pair of newsletters tailored to "Official Block Captains" in which they urged the local volunteers to make the final push. The texts reflected a clear shift in rhetoric: instead of invoking the importance of democracy, or liberalism, or progress, the messages emphasized liberation. "The job you will be doing this week is the most important political work you have ever done in your life," read the first, sent in the first week of November. "You are helping us all take a big step toward freedom." The nomenclature of everything in the campaign had likewise been transformed. Instead of asking the captains to pick up their blockworker or Democratic Coalition packets, VOTE staffers asked them to come to local headquarters to help pack "freedom kits" for other volunteers. The upbeat memos praised the accomplishments of regional coalitions in Fort Worth, Waco, Galveston, Beaumont, and Port Arthur—all of which had reached their recruitment quotas and were now seeking alternates in key precincts. "Everyone knows now that the blockworker program is the biggest thing ever to happen in Texas elections," one message boasted. Over 7,500 captains were already working, each charged with mobilizing twenty of their neighbors. In Houston, the HCCO, "the largest Negro political organization anywhere in the South" was doing a "tremendous job" under the direction of Barbara Jordan. Statewide, the project represented "the biggest army for freedom ever raised in Texas!" Winning the referendum would add "thousands of new voters in this fight for freedom." The newsletters reminded the block captains to visit personally with each of their twenty voters, canvassing and recanvassing until every last voter had been contacted and directed to the polls. Each of the volunteers could also expect phone calls from local headquarters in which the coordinators would check on their work. Finally, the staffers invited the volunteers to join them at local listening parties to hear the results come in, with "the ticket for admission [being] your Freedom Kit." The coalition had indeed come a long way from the color blindness of the old DOT.[84]

Still, such optimism and lofty rhetoric did not produce a victory at the polls. The repeal referendum failed by a margin of 56 percent to 44 percent, or 72,000 votes of almost 525,000 cast. Writing in the *Washington Post*, the *Observer*'s Ronnie Dugger attributed the measure's defeat to a rising "white backlash" against civil rights militancy. The repeal became a "liberal cause," and "the prospect of Texas Negroes and Latin-Americans voting in proportion to their numbers alarmed segregationist whites." Yet the backlash was not limited to the eleven rednecks who staged the white supremacist counterdemonstration on August 28. Rather, "The prospect of poorer voters menacing business control of the Statehouse neutralized what had started out to be support for repeal from . . . the conservative establishment," especially in the last few weeks prior to the election when what Ralph Yarborough called "corporate interests" launched an intensive media blitz. Dugger also commented that Connally's speech blasting Peña for attempting "bloc voting" had awoken fears among the white electorate and "hurt the cause of repeal."[85]

The election marked "the first test" of the Democratic Coalition's blockworker program, Dugger added. While VOTE leaders conceded that they did not, in two months, reach their goal of 240,000 contacts, they believed that the method had worked as planned, boosting African American turnout *above* the rate of white voters. Dugger wrote: "Liberal leaders appear to be convinced that the block workers approach, persisted in, will yield better dividends in 1964. Many Negro volunteer workers and Latin-Americans became involved in precinct activity for the first time." A key tool, Dugger added, was an open letter from Martin Luther King Jr. that appeared in the blockworker kits for black districts. "In the Delta of Mississippi, in Alabama, in southwest Georgia, in so many places we cannot vote," King wrote. "I call upon you to vote for repeal of the poll tax . . . and unleash a flood-tide of new voters to help us secure our full rights as Americans."[86]

Indeed, the numbers were both encouraging and disturbing. According to a "Statistical Resume" compiled by VOTE project officers, "Latin turnout in blockworker precincts, statewide, was approximately 25%" as compared to 11 percent in *mexicano* precincts that were not part of the project. Turnout in African American precincts worked by the project reached 36 percent, far exceeding the rate of 13 percent in precincts beyond the project's scope. Anglo turnout averaged 26 percent in all precincts. Clearly, the get-out-the-vote effort had a measurable effect, more than doubling black and brown turnout. Moreover, at the local level, it provided the margin of victory in Houston and San Antonio. In the former city, 55.2 percent of whites voted against repeal, while 87.1 percent of blacks voted for it, amidst a record black turnout of 30.5 percent in forty-two key precincts. Only 24 percent of eligible whites voted. The repeal measure passed with 53.6 percent of the votes, a margin of six thousand ballots. In blockworker precincts in San Antonio, where VOTE had both African American and Mexican American projects, 83 percent of blacks and 76.2 percent of browns voted for repeal. It passed overall, with almost 54 percent of the vote. Project VOTE also boosted African American turnout in both Dallas and Fort Worth, where roughly 80–90 percent of blacks voted for repeal. Fort Worth blacks made up one-sixth of the total local electorate, tripling their influence year-over-year from 1962. In the small town of Weslaco, in Hidalgo County in the Lower Valley, Mexican American turnout jumped 15 points, from 25.3 percent to 40 percent. The county as a whole enjoyed turnout in project areas of 31.5 percent—the best statewide performance of any "Latin" area. In short, the coalition's blockworkers had boosted black and brown voting to unprecedented levels.

Yet the growing backlash was also statistically apparent. In Dallas and Fort Worth, white voters in the 1962 Democratic primary had approved a nonbinding referendum on the same question. In conservative Dallas, the margin was scant, but in Fort Worth, more than 60 percent of whites had voted for repeal in 1962. In 1963, turnout fell precipitously in both cities, and those whites that showed up did so to vote against repeal. Over 60 percent of whites in each city voted against the measure.[87] White resistance was strongest in sixty-five "relatively small 'confederate' counties" in East Texas, which together contributed half of the statewide margin against repeal, according to another coalition report.[88]

While repeal failed, Project VOTE had worked, and the effort fulfilled the coalition's larger goal of laying the groundwork for the 1964 primaries. Goodwyn summarized the staff's evaluation of the blockworker program: "For the first time in Texas history, Negroes voted more heavily in an off-year special election than in the preceding Democratic primary," he wrote. "That the special election concerned an issue, rather than political candidates, underscores the effectiveness of the blockworker get-out-the-vote drive." Given a little more time, or a little more money, the campaign would have recruited all twelve thousand blockworkers "with a corresponding increase in the turnout." More important, "the massive organizational effort . . . has produced a trained precinct army of eight thousand blockworkers to pour into the poll tax campaign. The state of readiness . . . is thus greater than at any time in the history of poll tax drives in Texas." It was now time to "tighten the existing blockworker organization" and launch a new wave of workshops to train the "combat team" for the next round. As Dugger also noted, many of these rank-and-file volunteer activists had engaged in precinct-level political action for the first time. It would not be their last.[89]

The Democratic Coalition had finally come into its own. In the days following the election, Goodwyn penned a postmortem report outlining the successes and failures of Project VOTE in the repeal campaign. Optimism abounded. Despite the fact that they were forced to contest an off-year election with confusing ballot language and lacking any candidates, issues, or TV advertising, the coalition had made significant progress. In the context of a white backlash and a dramatic decrease in white turnout, black and brown voting had increased substantially, a fact that was "almost entirely attributable to organization," Goodwyn wrote. Moreover, "The precinct army developed in this election is now known, identified, and reachable" and could be counted upon again in the future. A mailing list "on stencils" could now reach five thousand blockworkers, and nearly four thousand more had signed "Freedom Pledge" cards. "We are staying in contact with people and they will not only be the shock troops of V.O.T.E.'s poll tax effort, they will be the coalition's precinct brigade in next year's Democratic primaries," he added. Across the state, the blockworker program had broken the back of old machines centered on patronage and paid canvassers. In Corpus Christi and other areas, the coalition's effort represented the first precinct-level mobilization campaign among local *mexicanos*. In Houston and Galveston, the bastions of organized labor, most white unionists voted for repeal even as other whites turned against it. Goodwyn added that such data led to another "not-so-tangential conclusion: the coalition concept will win in the Deep South when Southern labor is organized, when southern labor leaders work actively within a coalition to educate their rank-and-file on civil rights." Most important, the campaign had "validate[d] the person-to-person concept" of the precinct-level program, proving that it worked. Liberal leaders of all colors could look forward to more progress and real change in the near future. The Democratic Coalition had emerged from defeat with "the first statewide volunteer political army among the minorities of any Southern state," Goodwyn concluded. "They can't take those 6,000 blockworkers away from us and they can't take away the vision of a new South. The Coalition is as inevitable as the tide. It is the only way for the South to come out, the only way."[90]

Indeed, the statewide multiracial alliance had come a long way from its origins in the disastrous 1961 Senate campaign and even from its stormy internal deliberations in the spring and summer of 1963. Against all odds, diverse labor, civil rights, and community activists from across the state had come together, hashed out a plan of action, and then executed it on the ground. Organized labor had rededicated itself to the cause of integration, and B. T. Bonner had ignited a wildfire in the streets. The Democratic Coalition had survived frontal attacks on its key leaders, and their increasingly fanatical enemy, Governor Connally, now appeared to be on the ropes. With another year of fund-raising, planning, and organizing, the coalition could reasonably assume that the sky would be the limit. Indeed, journalists agreed that the liberals appeared likely to go all out for Don Yarborough in a rematch with Connally in just a few months, and the activists' prospects were rapidly improving. Events seemed to be proceeding according to plan until late November 1963, when John F. Kennedy made his way to the Lone Star State to try to heal the growing gulf in the always acrimonious Texas Democratic Party. The president would not survive the voyage, and Texas liberalism would never recover.

Chapter 10

New Power for Texas Minorities

Winning the Battles, Losing the War

"What Now?" asked C. L. Mangus, a leader of the International Brotherhood of Electrical Workers Local 60 in San Antonio, one week after the assassination of President Kennedy in Dallas. Writing in *SNAP News*, the white union craftsman captured the sentiment of the nation and especially the legions of veteran labor and civil rights activists who stood on the precipice of victory. "President Kennedy has left clear guidelines for us to follow," Mangus noted, and "myriads of HIS people" would continue his work, including Ralph Yarborough, Henry B. Gonzalez, and Albert Peña. But those that fought and opposed the president would also continue their work, Mangus added. So "let us each and every one go out and get a POLL TAX and USE IT on every possible occasion.... Let us keep the plans of President Kennedy alive.... [and] Let us be sure that HIS PEOPLE are kept in a position to carry on the work he began."[1]

Sitting next to the president and Mrs. Kennedy in the motorcade that day in Dallas was another couple, Governor and Mrs. John Connally. While the nation's chief executive recoiled from shots to the head, Connally grimaced as bullets wounded his back, wrist, and thigh. In a surprising twist of fate, the governor, who campaigned by both attacking the president and basking in his glory, who drew the ire of Kennedy's fiercest supporters for opposing the Civil Rights Act, who vehemently attacked the "bloc voting" that put the president in office—would now forever be linked to the martyred leader.

Unlike Kennedy, however, Connally survived, and his popularity soared. Conservative Texans who despised the president's policies in life patriotically flocked to him in death, defending the Massachusetts liberal in the face of the right-wing extremism that killed him. Connally, the rational, relatively moderate friend of new President Lyndon B. Johnson, emerged as the man to lead them through the turmoil of demonstrations, civil unrest, political violence—and just below the surface—a shifting political landscape that threatened all the privileges, passed down from generation to generation, of white supremacy. It was a world turned upside down, and Connally appeared to be the only one who could turn it back to the way it was.

Johnson quickly announced that he would carry forward Kennedy's policies, including the controversial public accommodations section of the civil rights package, but he also supported the political resurgence of his more conservative protégé, Connally. In fact, the reunification of the state's fractured Democratic Party had helped motivate the Kennedy-Johnson tour of Texas. Johnson feared that the liberal and Republican assaults on Connally would hurt the national ticket's ability to carry his home state, and he hoped to end the party's internal divisions before they got any worse. Still, even with the unifying force of the assassination, the tour did not succeed in closing the deep, ideologically driven rift between the state's multiracial liberal Democratic Coalition and the old-line conservatives that still dominated the party.

Yet the assassination did give Connally an air of personal invincibility, and it permanently crippled his opposition. Labor leader Hank Brown later remembered the "terrible, tragic assassination that changed the history of the whole world. It's changed politics in Texas. I think Texas was moving fast, more and more to the liberal viewpoint, when—Boom!" Although Brown exaggerated the immediate impact of the attack, he accurately reflected the changing terrain on which the coalition would be forced to operate henceforth. The multiracial group of liberals had already decided to continue Project VOTE to register black and brown voters en masse for 1964, and the campaign would proceed as scheduled. Coalition leaders asked "What Now?" and arrived at the same answer that Mangus advocated in the pages of *SNAP*: buy poll taxes and use them.

But for whom? Liberals of all colors knew that Connally would be difficult if not impossible to defeat. They also believed that they must work to reelect Johnson to the presidency and Yarborough to the Senate and help a wide range of prolabor and pro-civil rights candidates gain seats in the state legislature. Yarborough, in particular, was expected to face strong conservative opposition in the Democratic primary, as the assassination did nothing to bolster his popularity with the party's right wing. And the Republican Party now posed a legitimate threat to both the senator and the president. Whether or not the governor's mansion proved to be off-limits, coalition leaders would reason, the process of democratizing the state must continue. And the mass registration drive led by Project VOTE and its "army" of eight thousand volunteers represented a way—the only way—to keep fighting.

Veteran black, brown, and white labor and civil rights activists would also look beyond the next election and continue organizing in their long-term struggles for liberation. Although they recognized that some progress had been made by 1963, the diverse organizers also knew that they must continue the broad fight for independent political power in local and state politics, improved economic opportunities, and an end to all forms of racial discrimination. For its part, the Texas AFL-CIO would continue to lay the groundwork for unionization along the border and in the barrios of the major cities, an effort that dovetailed with the Democratic Coalition's ongoing quest to foster robust, local coalitions as part of Project VOTE. The statewide multiracial alliance would also lend its support to a sit-in movement in Huntsville—a small town in East Texas that refused to integrate through 1965, a full year after the Civil Rights Act. Ironically, that campaign would prove successful in its immediate objectives but would also contribute to the dissolution of the Democratic Coalition. Disagreements within the multiracial alliance over goals and strategy and the pressure of its participants' ongoing, unconscious white supremacy would produce interracial acrimony and suspicion that gradually displaced the hard-won mutual trust of the previous years and decades. Still, despite its gradual coming apart, the Democratic Coalition and its members would win their fight to a remarkable degree. Their massive voter registration campaign in 1964 would break down the doors of the Democratic Party and would forever transform Texas politics. At the same time, the erstwhile coalition activists would also lose, as statewide power, and genuine small-d democracy, remained elusive.

Operation Bootstrap

As the Democratic Coalition prepared to transition Project VOTE from the repeal election to the 1964 poll tax campaign, the Texas AFL-CIO also expanded its own organizing project among Mexican Americans. The program—now dubbed "Operation Bootstrap"—sought to foster unionism and political activity among Mexican Americans, growing from the one-man trial project announced in July 1963 to include five "public information officers" (PIOs) by the end of the year. Three were assigned along the border and one each went to San Antonio and North Texas (including both Dallas and Fort Worth). As the poll tax campaign began in earnest in December, Operation Bootstrap overlapped with Project VOTE on the ground, especially in Dallas and San Antonio, where labor-funded PIOs collaborated with VOTE's "project officers" to build local coalitions to register black and brown voters. In effect, the Operation Bootstrap PIOs served as de facto staffers of the Democratic Coalition.[2]

Following the recommendations of labor's Latin American Affairs Committee meeting in Laredo, the delegates to the Texas AFL-CIO annual convention in Houston in August 1963 approved an annual budget of $30,000 for Operation Bootstrap. The program, recalled activist Henry Muñoz, "was that the labor movement of Texas was going to go out into the field [below] what we call affectionately the 'Mexican-Dixon Line'—that's San Antonio to El Paso and south—and preach unionism and preach to organize politically." The first PIO remained on the payroll in Brownsville, and he was joined soon after the convention by organizers in Laredo and El Paso. In mid-December, Muñoz left his job with Albert Peña to serve as the PIO for San Antonio (he had also been slated to work as Project VOTE's coordinator for the West Side).[3]

The fifth and final PIO, Francisco F. "Pancho" Medrano, operated north of the "Mexican-Dixon" line in Dallas, where he had long been active in the United Auto Workers (UAW), local labor and political organizing, and the rising black and brown civil rights movements. A union member since 1941, he fought against discrimination on the job and became a shop steward and later a local officer. He served also as a chapter officer of the American G.I. Forum (AGIF), became active in the local Viva Kennedy club, and then became an officer in the Dallas "Labor PASO" led by J. O. "Pepper" and Franklin Garcia. The chapter built an informal local coalition that crossed racial lines, while Medrano personally joined the NAACP, aided the sit-in demonstrations of black students at downtown department stores, and collected poll taxes for the all-black Progressive Voters League. He also attended the March on Washington on August 28 as part of the UAW's delegation.[4] In March 1963, on a temporary assignment from UAW headquarters in Detroit, Medrano traveled to Crystal City to aid the campaign of the *cinco candidatos*. Teamster organizer Carlos Moore invited Medrano to stay and join the unprecedented effort. Medrano brought not only his organizing skills but much-needed money from the UAW, funds that allowed the town's *mexicano* working people to face down economic reprisals and intimidation by the Texas Rangers and successfully get out the vote.[5]

In short, by hiring Medrano, the Texas AFL-CIO tapped into his deep reservoir of experience and an extensive local and statewide network. Medrano was not a speechmaker but was extremely charismatic in meetings. He was equally at ease when talking to migrant farmworkers or in the presence of President Johnson, whom he met in 1964.[6] Most important, he showed up at a wide range of community gatherings, a key quotidian task that proved essential to building the Democratic Coalition on the ground. In the second half of December alone, Medrano met with leaders of the machinists union, his UAW local, and the Dallas AFL-CIO Council. He also trained poll tax deputies at Lott's Funeral Home (a black-owned business), attended a NAACP meeting sponsored by a local reverend, participated in a Political Association of Spanish-Speaking Organizations (PASO) meeting at the county courthouse, held a gathering of liberal members of the League of United Latin American Citizens (LULAC) at campaign headquarters, and joined white liberals for a get-together at a Tex-Mex restaurant. He also contacted a representative of the Texas Employment Commission, a pair of black ministers, two Mexican American "community leaders," students at the historically black Bishop College, and the president of the all-black Tarrant County Precinct Workers' Council in Fort Worth. Medrano held a poll tax meeting at his house near the

Francisco F. "Pancho" Medrano (center) posing with African American political activists at the Moorland Branch of the YMCA in Dallas during the campaign to repeal the poll tax, October 6, 1963. The photograph appeared on the front page of the next *Dallas Express*, the city's leading black newspaper, helping to cement the coalition on the ground. From the Marion Butts Collection of the Texas/Dallas History and Archives Division, Dallas Public Library, PA2005-4/7.

barrio of Little Mexico in Dallas and planned a gathering of Texas Council of Voters (TCV) and PASO activists in Fort Worth. He also attended a meeting of a new local coalition in Dallas organized by Latane Lambert, a group with which he hoped to further extend his outreach.[7] Showing films on labor and civil rights became one of his favorite tactics, his "specialty," as he later put it. In early January 1964, Medrano screened a film produced by the UAW that featured Dr. Martin Luther King Jr. at a meeting of the local coalition in Fort Worth. With the help of Lenora Rolla, a local African American leader, he then took the show on the road, displaying it four additional times in four separate black Fort Worth precincts by the end of the month.[8]

On at least one occasion, Medrano's organizing activities spilled over into a direct action protest. At some point during the campaign, Medrano, J. O. "Pepper" Garcia, VOTE project officer and journalist Julia Scott Reed, and other staffers and volunteers were sitting in their downtown campaign office trying to decide what to eat for lunch. Pancho suggested that they should go to El Fenix, the city's first Tex-Mex restaurant, located just a few blocks away. The others probably laughed; Medrano was certainly joking when he said it. They all knew that El Fenix remained a segregated holdout despite the fact that virtually all of the city's lunch counters and restaurants had already integrated their seating. They also knew that the restaurant was the economic foundation of the conservative Martinez family, a wealthy and influential group of Mexican Americans who curried favor with the city's white elites by opposing civil rights militancy and supporting conservative politicians. Much like the "West Side GGL" or the remnants of the black machine on the East Side of San Antonio, the Martinezes practiced diplomacy and stood in the way of efforts to achieve independent political power. And the food was terrible to boot.

When the activists stopped laughing at Medrano's suggestion, Pepper Garcia suggested that they go for it; after all, El Fenix represented the perfect target. The multiracial group of a dozen or so local coalition activists—black, brown, and white; labor, civil rights, and political organizers—left their campaign headquarters, walked the few blocks to the restaurant, and opened the door. They quietly took a seat at a large table toward the rear of the restaurant, not far from the hallway where the kitchen sometimes served poor *mexicanos* (blacks were refused service entirely). The manager, a member of the Martinez family, followed the lead of the segregationists of 1960: he asked them to leave and promptly closed down for the day. The restaurant did not integrate until well after the Civil Rights Act of 1964.[9]

In Dallas, then, as in San Antonio, Houston, and statewide, the multiracial liberal and labor coalition continued to separate itself from the white conservatives and their Mexican American and African American allies. At the same time, Medrano's frenzied activities over less than two months both depended upon and deepened the intimate ties that flourished between the Democratic Coalition's black, brown, and white activists on the ground. While the public pronouncements of Brown, Peña, and Durham garnered the newspaper headlines, the hidden, daily activities of rank-and-file organizers suggest that people like Medrano, Pepper Garcia, Julia Scott, Lenora Rolla, and Latane Lambert represented the key intermediate leadership that carried the coalition and Operation Bootstrap from an Austin hotel or convention floor to the level of the grassroots. "House-by-house, street-by-street," as Project VOTE's architects had put it, they successfully organized local branches of the Democratic Coalition that brought the statewide effort to countless ordinary black, brown, and white working people across Texas.

Medrano may at first appear an extraordinary figure, but he was not exceptional. In San Antonio, where Henry "the Fox" Muñoz served as an Operation Bootstrap PIO at the same time, the Bexar County Democratic Coalition was also rolling—as it had been for more than a half-decade. Muñoz also engaged a wide range of coalition partners and covered a tremendous amount of ground in very little time. In his first two weeks on the job, he met with the Democratic Coalition's leading East Side activists: G. J. Sutton, Rev. Claude Black, Dr. Ruth Bellinger McCoy, and *SNAP*'s Eugene Coleman. Within a month he had made "personal contact with every [union] Business Agent, President and Secretary-Treasurer of all Locals in San Antonio." Like Medrano, Muñoz spent much of his time pushing the poll tax campaign and working with Peña and other local elected officials, church leaders, and numerous fraternal, social, and "patriotic" associations. As the PIO for not just San Antonio but all of "South-Central Texas," Muñoz also traveled to Austin, New Braunfels, and other nearby towns. He attended Bexar County Democratic Party Executive Committee meetings and local coalition gatherings—all while advancing the poll tax campaign of Project VOTE. Muñoz also helped a group of migrant farmworkers in the sugar beet industry testify before a hearing of the U.S. Department of Labor. By the end of January, he reported that he had personally sold 1,460 poll taxes and 237 exemption certificates.[10]

As in Dallas, the ties between labor, civil rights, and political organizing in San Antonio remained tight. In fact, in February, the Texas AFL-CIO agreed to loan Muñoz to Albert Peña "for a week for the purpose of raising money for his filing fee and campaign" for reelection. (The fact that the commissioner needed such assistance is itself revealing; the firebrand politico who served as cochair of the statewide Democratic Coalition operated on a shoestring and lacked the personal wealth to even enter the race without raising money in the West Side community.)[11]

Muñoz was also exploring new ways to extend the role of the Texas AFL-CIO and the Democratic Coalition beyond protests and political action. Even before he joined Operation Bootstrap, Muñoz wrote a proposal for the Bexar County coalition to secure funding under the Manpower Development and Training Act (MDTA) of 1962. He did so in the summer of 1963, while he served as Peña's private employee. The proposal was sponsored by the Manpower Committee of LULAC Council 2 (of which Peña was a leader), a local liberal group called the Manpower Development Council, and the "City-Wide Citizens Committee for Job Opportunities" led by Black, Sutton, and Coleman. In March 1964, Muñoz wrote to labor leader Roy Evans, urging the Texas AFL-CIO to incorporate antipoverty efforts into Operation Bootstrap. "I sincerely believe we should push real hard to start the End of 'Poverty' War in our border areas, the Valley and certainly amongst migrant farm workers and their families," Muñoz wrote. "This poverty war will be a key issue in the presidential election, and we should capitalize on it. The MDTA proposals I drew for LULAC and Negro groups are pretty well becoming a reality."[12]

Muñoz's final statements proved overly optimistic—a later report indicated that the Good Government League–led City Council had appointed an intermediary commission that had then stalled the proposal—but it's clear that the organizer's pleas were received favorably among labor leaders in Austin. In the summer of 1964, Muñoz sent Evans plans to expand Operation Bootstrap in collaboration with LULAC and the AGIF to include more PIOs who would serve "as a guiding light to making many things available under the War on Poverty Program." He advocated partnering with all willing community organizations and seeking funding from a wide range of government agencies. "We must help every segment of the Spanish-Speaking and Negro communities with all available means in [the] War on Poverty . . . [including] unionization where possible," he wrote. By working with a broad range of groups, the program could "rely on the neighborhood grassroots leaders" so that "so-called leaders do not get their capricious and unreasonable ways." Instead, "we go to the people themselves with our record of the common good."[13]

Medrano, Muñoz, and the other three PIOs all brought the Democratic Coalition to the grassroots, contributing to Project VOTE, "preaching" unionism and political education, and building or extending local civil rights coalitions. Their assignments went far beyond bread-and-butter unionism. Still, union dues paid their bills. Consequently, Brown, Evans, and the Latin American Affairs Committee had to constantly engage in "selling" Operation Bootstrap, the commuter lawsuit, and other committee expenditures to the full membership of the Texas AFL-CIO. Success in electoral politics was one way to show their value to the larger mission of labor, as was tangible progress in terms of organizing the unorganized into unions and bringing them under collective bargaining agreements. All of the PIOs contributed to these efforts. Muñoz joined the Valley operatives stationed along the border in supporting liberal candidates for Congress in a pair of Democratic primary races in 1964, and, in the Lower Valley, another PIO spent much of his time alongside organizer Franklin Garcia of the Amalgamated Meat Cutters, waging the project's most successful union organizing drive.[14]

The PIOs' efforts on the ground and the public relations campaign within the ranks of organized labor paid off. Led by steelworker staffer and longtime PASO activist Paul Montemayor of Corpus Christi, the committee designed a glossy pamphlet showcasing the work of Operation Bootstrap, highlighting the fact that new organizing and thus new members were making it increasingly self-sufficient. They circulated the flyer prior to and at their August 1964 annual convention, which was held in Brownsville in order to bring white labor leaders from across the state to see the poverty of the border region firsthand. Delegates approved a $20,000 increase in the program's yearly budget, bringing it to a total of $50,000. The Texas AFL-CIO soon hired Muñoz to serve as the first director of its new Department of Equal Opportunity, and the program eventually grew to include, in Hank Brown's recollection, "damn near a dozen PIOs."[15]

Through Operation Bootstrap, then, as through Project VOTE, organized labor extended its commitment to the Democratic Coalition by providing it with on-the-ground organizers and much-needed financial resources. These experienced union men also engaged in civil rights, political, and even anti-poverty activities—melding the labor movement to the longtime aspirations of the state's largely unorganized African American and Mexican American working people. With Hank Brown and Roy Evans at its helm, the Texas AFL-CIO had all but completed its transition from being a powerful supporter of the multiracial struggle for democracy to becoming a civil rights organization in its own right.[16]

"Time for the Harvest"

Like the PIOs of Operation Bootstrap, the leaders of the state Democratic Coalition dove headlong into the poll tax campaign in December 1963. The failure of the repeal referendum on November 9 meant that, once again, the alliance would need to sell poll taxes in preparation for the 1964 elections. Just before the assassination, coalition staffer Larry Goodwyn had proposed a new poll tax program to get underway immediately and continue until the registration deadline of January 31. He suggested that all project officers be put back on the payroll by November 25 and recommended that VOTE be expanded from sixteen cities to twenty-two urban areas, along with two "less intensive" rural programs covering nearly eighty heavily black and brown counties. The plan called for renewing the registrations of roughly 300,000 African Americans and Mexican Americans in the targeted areas and adding 325,000 new registrants. Goodwyn requested a budget of $98,000 for the entire campaign but suggested that only half of that amount would be allocated from Texas—the "rest will come, if it comes at all, from out-of-state" foundations. "Organizationally, we are in the best shape ever," he concluded, "we have trained a vast army . . . we have sold the coalition at the grass roots . . . and history is on our side."[17]

The death of the president and the hospitalization of the governor slowed down the launch of the new program but did not alter its goals. On December 7, 1963—a little more than two weeks after the assassination—the Executive Committee of the Democratic Coalition assembled in Austin to take stock of the new situation. There were no fireworks at the meeting, only solemn dedication. The coalition sent a resolution of sympathy to Mrs. Kennedy, adding that the alliance "joins the whole nation in its sense of bereavement at the loss of one of the greatest exponents of liberalism in our generation." The liberal leaders applauded President Johnson for his pledge to carry forward the liberal agenda of "our fallen chief" and praised Senator Ralph Yarborough for endorsing the civil rights bill. The coalition also fired off another message in which they wished Governor Connally a speedy recovery. Now was not the time for factionalism, they sensed, but rather the moment to rally behind LBJ and Yarborough as they faced reelection in the coming year. No mention was made of Connally's political future. Still, "This committee dedicates the Democratic Coalition to the achievement of these goals within a harmonious Texas Democratic Party," the meeting concluded. It urged all Democrats to support the civil rights legislation and sent letters to that effect to all members of the Texas congressional delegation, asking them to help the bill get out of committee. Unity mattered, their actions suggested in sum, but there was still work to be done.[18]

The plan for the poll tax drive largely paralleled that of the repeal election, but with a few new additions. African American and Mexican American project officers would again be hired on a full-time basis in each of the targeted cities. These local coordinators would again work with precinct leaders to supervise the "army" of volunteer blockworkers, and the Team Program motivational seminars would again take place in each city. Yet this year the coalition would add a few new wrinkles: it would devote renewed attention to strengthening alliances at the local level, it would make a concerted effort in selected "low-income Anglo" precincts, and it would support a special project among black college students. "For some time, spontaneous and uncoordinated efforts by local college groups have demonstrated the energy, dedication, and overall potential for constructive activity by these young people," one status report explained. With support from the Democratic Coalition's state office, two African American students at Prairie View A&M College traveled to eight black colleges across the state, contacting leaders of each school's student government. The duo gave the campus leaders some five thousand poll tax forms and instructed each to register their fellow students and to bring the forms home over Christmas break. Each student leader was also asked to assess the status of the on-the-ground organizing efforts in their home communities and report back to coalition headquarters in January. This new initiative would allow the coalition to better target the most active of the rural black communities previously canvassed by Mrs. Erma LeRoy and to develop new grassroots leaders among the youth. These new leaders would join project officers and precinct captains in the final days of the registration period in late January, when "*every* grocery store in *every* Democratic precinct is to be manned all day on an organized basis by voluntary poll tax deputies."[19]

Finally, and most important, while the Democratic Coalition would continue to recruit deputy registrars to bring voters to pay their poll taxes in person, the agency forms that had previously represented their main tool had been outlawed by the new registration law passed the previous summer. To work around this prohibition, Project VOTE created "registration-by-mail" blanks that would allow voters to send their poll taxes directly to the offices of the county tax assessor-collectors. Better yet, any blockworker could distribute these forms and help voters submit them; becoming a certified deputy registrar was no longer a requirement. The coalition planned to print one million of these forms as the centerpiece of its goal of registering some 625,000 black and brown voters in the project's target areas.[20]

As the campaign got underway, VOTE leaders again appealed directly to the grass roots, sending its "Message for Official Block Captains" to the thousands of volunteers in its database. Like previous versions of this mass newsletter, this issue tied the registration campaign to the struggle for civil rights and helped to connect readers to a larger movement for democracy in Texas. "Are you ready to help out in the fight for freedom?" the headline asked. Huge advances could be made right now, "if you do your part," it added. Together, the campaign could achieve its immediate goal of "an all-time record in new poll taxes" in order to reach a total peak of 100,000 African American voters in Houston and 300,000 statewide. Activity at the grass roots was producing change at the top, the newsletter noted. The director of the blockworker program in Waco was now seeking a seat on the county commission, a feat that would make him the first black commissioner in the state. In Houston, VOTE leader Barbara Jordan was preparing another run for the state legislature, and she now stood "an excellent chance to become Texas' first Negro state representative." A Mexican American coalition leader in the Rio Grande Valley was "favored to win" his race for sheriff in Hidalgo County. The new office seekers both reflected the changes wrought by the Democratic Coalition and promised to extend its influence. "Everyone realizes these important new opportunities are opening up only because of the growth of poll tax sales in our precincts," the treatise concluded, and now more help was needed to get them over the top. "Every single person who really cares about freedom must pitch in and help out by becoming a POLL TAX BLOCKWORKER."[21]

The blockworker plan proceeded as planned, but its initial results were mixed. "Poll tax payments are disappointing to the liberal Democrats so far," reported the *Texas Observer* on January 24, with just one week of registrations remaining. One cause, it speculated, was the assassination, which set back the coalition's campaign by nearly a month and also made Don Yarborough's candidacy seem unfeasible. Another was that Senator Ralph Yarborough had not yet drawn a serious conservative primary challenger. Lyman Jones of the

Texas AFL-CIO told the paper "that last fall the liberal-labor coalition extended itself educating people *against* the poll tax, and now, in a vague sense that has real meaning at the grass roots, have to switch course and educate them *for* it (i.e., to pay it)" [*sic*].[22]

The promise of free voter registration for federal elections as the Twenty-Fourth Amendment neared ratification also hurt the number of state-level poll tax receipts. Congress had proposed the measure back in 1962, and it was finally ratified by the requisite thirty-eighth state on January 24, 1964. When the amendment entered into force, it outlawed the poll tax as a requirement for *federal* elections, but state and local races remained untouched. Texas had decreed that it would respond to ratification by creating a new window for "free Federal registration" after the end of the state poll tax period, a schedule that would force registration campaigns to run wholly separate drives. More important, would-be registrants now faced a dizzying, shifting legal landscape, and many surely skipped the state-level registration in favor of the free federal ballot. The latter would aid the candidacies of Johnson and Ralph Yarborough, coalition leaders knew, but it would not help Don Yarborough in a hypothetical rematch with Governor Connally. With such confusing change on the horizon, the coalition continued to sell poll taxes as usual until the January 31 deadline and then renewed its efforts with another, smaller register-by-mail drive during the free federal window.

The overall result was staggering. In combination with Operation Bootstrap, labor's normal Committee on Political Education (COPE) program for (predominately white) union members, and other efforts across the political spectrum, the Democratic Coalition helped bring total voter registrations in Texas to their highest levels ever. Although precise figures are unavailable for Project VOTE's effect in its targeted areas and demographics, it is safe to say that the final tallies fell short of the lofty goals originally set by coalition leaders, but only slightly. By the end of the full registration cycle, some 300,000 African Americans, as many as 400,000 Mexican Americans, 300,000 mostly white "union people, and indeterminate numbers of liberals . . . registered to vote." The ballpark total of 700,000 nonwhite voters included free federal registrations and doubtlessly encompassed countless voters untouched by Project VOTE. Yet it was an impressive sum nonetheless. The eighteen months of coalition organizing and six months of sustained VOTE efforts doubtlessly accounted for the bulk of the huge jump. In the ten "major population areas of Texas," all of which were targeted by VOTE projects, the total voter registration reached 1.6 million, more than half of the statewide total. "These same ten areas have been the target areas for every Coalition campaign in 1963–64 . . . the 1963 poll tax repeal election, the 1964 poll tax drive, and the 1964 free voter registration drive," reported the coalition's *Democratic Newsletter*. In fact, the "only significant" use of the free federal registrations occurred in precincts worked by the coalition, adding to the rolls between 64,000 and 91,500 voters at a cost to VOTE of only $8,500. Labor lawyer and Democratic Coalition leader Chris Dixie observed that Project VOTE achieved its voter registration goals using only $60,000, a pittance when compared to the "several millions" spent by "Northern liberals . . . in the old South."[23]

"It is now time for the harvest," the *Democratic Newsletter* concluded. "All of us must immediately contact the headquarters and organizations in our county and pledge to do the necessary telephone canvassing and blockwork. If the voters turn out, the real Democrats win . . . It is simple as that." Yet the prospect of harvesting the high registration numbers did not produce a clear path of action for the primaries. As early as December, the *Texas Observer* noted that "Most everyone was speculating . . . that Don Yarborough could not feasibly oppose Gov. John Connally in 1964."[24] As the February 3 filing deadline for candidates neared, the four Democratic Coalition cochairmen called a meeting of its thirty-two-man executive committee and the four codirectors of Project VOTE. Since some of the positions overlapped, this group of roughly thirty-eight people would come together to shape the coalition's future. All of the familiar faces would be there—Albert Peña and the veterans of PASO's now-dominant labor-liberal faction; plaintiffs' attorney Chris Dixie and his band of Harris County Democrats (HCD) activists and independent white liberals from across the state; W. J. Durham, G. J. Sutton, Moses LeRoy, and other longtime civil rights activists from the TCV; and labor officials led by Hank Brown and Roy Evans.[25]

All four legs of the alliance were preparing to hold their own respective endorsement conventions within the next month, so the February 8 coalition meeting represented the decisive moment in which the diverse activists would seek consensus on the upcoming candidacies for state and federal office. Don Yarborough had formally tossed his hat in the ring to oppose Governor Connally, but the filing deadline came and went without a serious candidate emerging to oppose Senator Ralph Yarborough. Only an independently wealthy conservative businessman filed to oppose the senator, and he did so without the support of either the Johnson-Connally wing of the party or the Shivers-led far right. Meanwhile, Albert Fuentes, the longtime PASO and coalition activist, announced his own candidacy for lieutenant governor without seeking permission from anyone. His mentor, Albert Peña, faced a stiff primary fight from multiple GGL candidates in his own bid for reelection. In Austin, civil rights gadfly and coalition officer Booker T. Bonner ran for the Travis County Commissioners Court, while the coalition's Houston director and HCD activist Barbara Jordan had officially announced her bid for a seat in the state legislature.

It quickly became clear that the Democratic Coalition could not agree on a course of action in the statewide races and would endorse only the reelection bid of Ralph Yarborough. Many observers held that the national leaders of the UAW and the United Steelworkers had made a deal in January with the White House that Johnson would work to prevent a credible conservative Democratic challenge to Senator Yarborough if the labor leaders worked to keep the Texas AFL-CIO from endorsing Don Yarborough in the gubernatorial primary. Helping to reelect Ralph Yarborough would help the president to win friends among northern liberals whom he was courting for his own reelection campaign that year. For its part, the Texas AFL-CIO remained eager to keep a prolabor senator in Washington, where he could help overturn the Taft-Hartley Act's right-to-work provisions, and labor doubtlessly heeded the conventional wisdom that Connally could not be defeated anyway. Clandestinely and reluctantly, it seems, Brown and Evans agreed to the deal.[26]

Two years had elapsed since the Democratic Coalition had failed to endorse Don Yarborough until it was too late, and despite all of the progress and social learning throughout the intervening period, the alliance again splintered over the gubernatorial race in 1964. As expected, days after the coalition meeting, labor's COPE refrained from endorsing candidates in state-level races, sidestepping not only Don Yarborough's campaign for governor but also Fuentes's bid for lieutenant governor. Within weeks, PASO, the TCV, and the new Texas Organization of Liberal Democrats (TOLD; composed of white "independent" liberals) all endorsed Don, and first PASO and then the others also lined up behind Fuentes. Individual union members who wanted to work for statewide candidates "who are friendly to organized labor are encouraged to do so," a Texas AFL-CIO newsletter noted, but the labor movement's institutional resources would not be available to the liberal candidates. It was a heavy price to pay for Ralph Yarborough's reelection and the abstract notion of party unity.

The indignant memories of Connally's stand on civil rights remained too raw for the coalition's black and brown legs. W. J. Durham, who stood alongside Bonner and the San Antonio activists when they were rebuffed from the governor's office said, in Dugger's words, that "he wants a governor who will see him just as he would any other visitor." Peña recalled that Connally attacked him as "Boss Peña . . . because I believe in the dignity of all men" and in their rights to "have a decent job at an adequate wage, to eat at the places they want to eat at, and go to the shows they want to see." TOLD chairman Franklin Jones of Marshall joined Durham and Peña in denouncing Connally, leaving organized labor on its own in a détente with the governor.[27]

Still, all hope for concerted action was not lost. One feature article in the left-leaning *Vanguard* magazine argued that labor's nonendorsement of Don Yarborough "has caused no apparent strain on the Coalition," despite the fact that the other legs had all endorsed the liberal. Labor had defended its realpolitik, and the unprecedented registration numbers among black and brown voters helped to smooth over the conflict. A March meeting of the coalition had reaffirmed the alliance's commitment to the civil rights movement even as the activists failed to reach an agreement in the electoral sphere. Likewise, in a speech at the TCV convention, Hank Brown "reaffirmed his confidence in the Democratic Coalition," reported the *Observer*'s Ronnie Dugger. In the coalition, Brown said, "they had been able to disagree but continue meeting and working together." Brown told the TCV delegates, "I know we disappointed you at [the COPE convention in] Arlington.... I might say I myself have moments of disappointment.... But in the making of the Coalition we have the foundation" for the future. Brown added that the state federation had recently hired an African American PIO in East Texas and was about to hire another. He added that the rights to have a union and decent wages and working conditions also represented civil rights, and he defended labor's decision to prioritize the Senate race as part of its effort to win better federal labor policies for all.[28]

The Senate race proved much simpler. Whereas many African Americans and Mexican Americans had quibbled with Ralph Yarborough in previous years, the senator's explicit support for the Crystal City uprising and tacit endorsement of the August 1963 marches on Austin and Washington had eased their concerns. At the same TCV endorsement convention in March 1964, Yarborough made his first public address before a black political convention, a speech in which he "made his support of civil rights legislation abundantly clear." He read a passionate, integrationist letter from one his white constituents that also, in the words of an unnamed *Observer* reporter, "embodied the evolution of this East Texas native from a segregationist in the ways of his home people into a representative of the present times." Yarborough noted that he had voted in the commerce committee to advance the public accommodations portion of the civil rights package and in the labor committee in favor of a fair employment practices act. TCV delegates, including Moses and Erma Leroy, Claude Black, G. J. Sutton, and Dallas's Juanita Craft (and probably B. T. Bonner), voted to endorse Senator Yarborough, becoming the fourth and final coalition leg to do so.[29]

The Democratic Coalition thus rallied around getting out the vote for Ralph and for local liberals in the primary election. Coalition leaders also revived the age-old liberal dream of taking over the state party machinery. They published a new handbook for grassroots activists instructing them on how to take over their precinct conventions. Victories there would allow the growing local coalitions to dominate the county gatherings and then exert influence at the state Democratic convention and maybe even write the Texas party's platform. It would also ensure that the Texas delegation to the Democratic National Convention would endorse not only Johnson but Johnson's *program*—and therefore Kennedy's as well, including the Civil Rights Act that throughout the spring remained tied up by a southern filibuster.

More generally, the Democratic Coalition in Texas moved away from confrontation and toward incorporation. While Project VOTE had appealed to "freedom" to motivate volunteer blockworkers during the registration campaign, explicit references to the struggle for civil rights all but disappeared from the alliance's *Newsletter* and other outreach during the primary campaign. The fractured gubernatorial race meant that the coalition could not weigh in on this formerly paramount issue; only Ralph Yarborough and the convention campaign appeared as topics in the group's mass appeals. VOTE ceased to operate as an independent unit, but VOTE codirector Latane Lambert of Dallas, project officer Lenora Rolla from the TCV in Fort Worth, and Gus Gonzalez from PASO all joined Senator Yarborough's campaign staff for the primary election. All members of the coalition rallied behind Ralph's campaign, but the coordinated effort no longer represented a crusade for civil rights.[30]

In the end, the fates of the two Yarboroughs and other liberal candidates mirrored their expectations. The senator cruised to victory. Don Yarborough lost to Connally by a 3-to-1 margin, carrying only 5 out of 254 counties. Without the backing of VOTE or an official labor endorsement, PASO, the TCV, and other black and brown groups lacked the ability to run a statewide campaign against the wildly popular governor. Fuentes also went down to a lopsided defeat. At the local level, Peña held his seat, as did Bexar County's liberal legislative delegation. Other liberal legislative candidates in Houston and Dallas suffered heavy losses, while VOTE's Barbara Jordan made "a strong showing" even in defeat. B. T. Bonner lost his bid for county commissioner, as did the coalition's African American leader in Waco.[31]

To add insult to injury, at the state Democratic convention on June 16, Governor Connally again gutted the urban liberals, denying them a seat at the party's governing table despite their clear victories in the precinct- and county-level gatherings. President Johnson allowed Connally to have his way, and the governor wanted nothing more than to exact revenge on Albert Peña, who led the legal Bexar delegation and had represented a thorn in Connally's side for years. Spurned and refused seats by the credentials committee, liberal leaders of all colors from San Antonio, Dallas, and Houston led a walkout of some 1,300 liberal precinct leaders from across the state. It was the largest bolt in years, and the most diverse ever. It simultaneously showed just how much and how little had changed since the days when the Shivercrats had forced out the nucleus of the all-white Democrats of Texas in 1956. The liberal wing of the party had become multiracial, but it remained marginal in state politics. The conservative delegates finally agreed to the liberals' age-old loyalty pledge and accepted a resolution endorsing the "aims and goals" of President Johnson. Still, the liberals remained on the outside looking in, while Governor Connally continued his opposition to the public accommodations section of the civil rights bill.[32]

As summer turned to fall, the strategy of cooperation with national leaders appeared to be working. The Senate, led by majority whip Hubert H. Humphrey, finally broke the Dixiecrat filibuster and passed the Civil Rights Act, and LBJ signed it into law on July 2. The prohibition against discrimination in public accommodations became Title II; employment discrimination was banned by Title VII. At the same time, Humphrey became the party's vice-presidential nominee after engineering the crushing defeat of the Mississippi Freedom Democratic Party, a biracial challenge delegation led by grassroots movement activists, at the party's national convention in Atlantic City. For the nation, the summer took a huge step forward in the legislative arena, but several steps backward when it came to recognizing the need for black self-determination.[33]

Back in Texas, only one option remained. All four legs of the Democratic Coalition agreed to support "LBJ—HHH—RWY . . . the Straight Democratic Ticket." Latane Lambert moved from Yarborough to Johnson headquarters while simultaneously coordinating the coalition's newest get-out-the-vote drive. Renato Cuellar of the Lower Valley PASO, who had run unsuccessfully for sheriff in Hidalgo County, served "as the Mexican-American staff man on the Coalition program." Rolla, an African American, and Martin Wiginton, a white liberal who had replaced Goodwyn as the coalition's executive director in late June, rounded out the on-the-ground leadership.[34] Coalition cochairs Brown, Durham, and Peña made peace, ending any animosity left over from the primary campaign as they plowed forward together toward the November general election. Still, Franklin Jones of TOLD, the coalition's white liberal cochair, became despondent, lamenting the fact that the liberal movement had become so thoroughly dominated by its longtime nemesis, LBJ.[35]

Such misgivings aside, the coalition revived its campaign at the block level and swung into action behind the straight ticket. Polls showed the Democratic candidates leading their Republican opponents by margins of approximately 60 to 40 percent, as the extremism of GOP presidential nominee Barry Goldwater and the familiarity of Johnson seemed to guarantee that the president would carry the state. Yet coalition leaders urged their supporters not to grow complacent. "A tragic defeat is ahead if Texans let the political polls put them to sleep. Remember . . . polls only show how voters would vote if they all go to the trouble of voting . . . polls do not show how many voters will turn out on election day." Ralph Yarborough appeared especially vulnerable. After sleepwalking through his primary campaign against a political unknown, he now faced a fierce challenge from George H. Bush, a Houston oilman who promised to make the formerly extremist Texas GOP into a respectable electoral force.[36]

The four get-out-the-vote coordinators possessed far fewer resources and even less time than VOTE had at its disposal in the repeal election a year before. The Democratic Coalition, which had always operated on a tight budget, was close to broke once again by July. Wiginton promised to raise funds for the project and prepared a new pamphlet that outlined the coalition's history and future projects. He sent it out along with an appeal for donations, but it remains unclear whether it garnered much of a response. More significantly, few of the local project officers from the poll tax campaigns stayed on as local coordinators of the effort by October, though many veteran activists continued to serve in that capacity. Presumably, some of the new names were former precinct leaders who had been promoted. Yet in some cases the project officers were recognizable veteran white liberals, a stark contrast to the virtually all-black or brown local leaders who coordinated the 1963 repeal referendum (additionally, some African Americans and Mexican Americans may have joined the local staffs of the official campaigns). In any event, with just weeks to go before the election, the number of volunteer blockworkers had stalled at nine thousand, and another five thousand were still needed to reach their goal of turning out the occupants of 350,000 households (at the rate of twenty-five homes for each worker, to contact 500,000 voters overall). "We may lose without more volunteers," the coalition's *Newsletter* cautioned. It called for each reader to recruit two new blockworkers: "You should contact every possible friend, relative and neighbor and ask them to volunteer."[37]

Coalition activists continued to get out the vote until the polls closed, but their last-minute efforts probably were not necessary. Johnson carried Texas in a landslide, with Senator Yarborough not far behind. "New Power for the Texas Minorities," read a page three headline in the *Texas Observer* immediately after the election. "Aroused probably in large part by the racial demonstrations of the last three years and afforded clearly outlined friends and enemies by the stands public figures took on the civil rights law, more Negroes registered, and then those who were registered voted in higher proportions than they did in 1960," the article surmised. "*This* was a backlash," declared white liberal leader Franklin Jones of TOLD. While Kennedy had carried about three-fourths of the votes among the state's "two big minorities," Johnson and Yarborough won 95 percent of their votes. "In dense racial ghettos in the big cities," the numbers were 98 percent and 99 percent, respectively. Yet the coalition and federal candidates' combined "straight ticket" strategy—designed to speed up the lines at the polls—also carried conservative Democrats to victory. Connally won by a margin of 1.2 million votes, while Johnson led Goldwater by 700,000 and Yarborough defeated Bush by 330,000.

The Democratic Coalition's influence and reach were most apparent in precinct-level returns from the Senate race. "The minorities were a decisive factor in Sen. Yarborough's victory," the *Observer* concluded. In Dallas County, "minority precincts" in which the coalition's blockworker program was active voted for Johnson 24–1, and Yarborough's edge was nearly that high (22–1), giving each candidate margins of over twenty thousand votes. The difference was a spike in turnout among African Americans: thirty-two thousand voted in 1964, up from eleven thousand in 1962 (an off year). In Bexar County, "in the 43 Latin-American precincts" worked by Peña and the coalition on the West Side, Yarborough won by twenty-four thousand votes. In the "14 Negro precincts" on the East Side, G. J. Sutton's coalition-affiliated apparatus delivered a margin of ten thousand votes to the senator. Yarborough carried the county by only twenty-nine thousand votes. In Houston, the Harris County Democrats, the coalition's local wing, increased African American turnout in thirty-seven precincts from forty thousand in 1960 to fifty-three thousand in 1964. Yarborough won several key urban areas—and the election—thanks to the black and brown votes organized by the coalition. The harvest had come in even better than expected.[38]

In the end, Kennedy's assassination did not derail the ultimate goal of many Democratic Coalition leaders who sought to build independent political power for the state's African American and Mexican American residents. Nor did it deal a fatal blow to the cohesion of the statewide coalition. Yarborough's victory was a significant triumph that reelected the longtime standard-bearer of the liberal movement in Texas. The senator would remain a powerful ally for liberals for the next six years. President Johnson was likewise reelected, and his policies had moved to the left. He passed the Civil Rights Act, ending segregation in public accommodations and outlawing employment discrimination—two longtime goals of African American activists like Sutton and the LeRoys. Liberals of all colors had high hopes for the Great Society, and labor leaders believed they were finally going to win reforms to federal labor law.

Yet the tragedy in Dallas did derail the Democratic Coalition's two-year-long goal of landing one of its candidates in the governor's mansion. The United Political Organization (UPO) was in retreat, but the conservative blacks (and browns) who supported Connally remained a threat to liberal activists who sought to extend their own influence. In fact, Connally had outpolled both Senator Yarborough and President Johnson, ensuring that his brand of "moderation" and his personal charisma and quasi-martyr status would continue to thrive in Texas for years to come. Moreover, Yarborough's and Johnson's victories were not accompanied by significant gains for black and brown candidates in local and state legislative offices, and liberals remained excluded from intraparty politics.

Still, the black, brown, and white activists in the coalition had stuck together when it mattered, demanding and earning a place in Texas politics. While the assassination pulled the rug out from under their most ambitious dreams, the multiracial liberal coalition still managed to assert its power and win a statewide race. It was a far cry from the near-complete disfranchisement of the 1920s. More important, participation in the Democratic Coalition, Operation Bootstrap, and other local civil rights efforts across the state transformed the activists themselves. Project VOTE's unprecedented "blockworker" program altered the political landscape of Texas by finding thousands of local volunteers and transforming them into effective political organizers. The activists who recruited them also learned how to build local coalitions along the way. For the statewide Democratic Coalition, then, the 1964 elections represented both a great accomplishment and a mere interlude in the political warfare that had dominated Texas for decades. Thwarted in state politics, the activists would assess their progress, plot their next steps, and eventually propose some radical changes to the coalition's structure. Their trials by fire would continue to serve them in the years ahead.

"A Reevaluation of the Coalition Concept"

In the winter and spring of 1965, the Steering Committee of the Democratic Coalition convened to take stock of the political landscape and make plans for the upcoming year. All was not well. "There are reports circulating of post-election differences within the Democratic Coalition," began another short note in the *Observer* in late December of 1964. Dallas attorney W. J. Durham, the president of the TCV and chair of the coalition's black leg, wrote a letter to members of his organization's Executive Committee in which he raised the possibility of leaving the four-legged coalition and instead joining with Mexican Americans to form "a coalition of the two minorities only." A TCV leader from Fort Worth quickly responded in the negative and strongly rebuked Durham for even asking. But the persistent tensions between the black leg and the rest of the coalition remained clear. "Basically Negroes are just as impressed as everyone else who understands Texas politics with their political power," the piece continued, "and they want no back seats." In the 1964 general election, nearly 70 percent of the 350,000 registered black voters in Texas came to the polls, and virtually all of them voted for Johnson and Yarborough. Together, black and brown voters had given each of the candidates approximately 450,000 votes, nearly 30 percent of their statewide totals. With many local labor leaders also questioning the value of the Democratic Coalition and opposing the federation leadership's stands on civil rights, Durham's was a fair question to pose. The attorney also brought up the group's other longtime objective beyond civil rights and political action: the gaining of patronage appointments for qualified black professionals. At the local level in Dallas, Durham, veteran activist Julia Scott, and other liberal African Americans had just formed the Dallas County Council of Organizations for Political Action, making peace with a group of pro-Connally blacks led by the UPO's Rev. H. Rhett James. An old question resurfaced: would the alliance with labor and liberal whites produce more dividends for the race than other possibilities?[39]

The Democratic Coalition responded by citing its effectiveness in registering and turning out voters in the blockworker precincts of Project VOTE and by recommitting itself to the ongoing fight for civil rights. The most tangible program to emerge from the four-legged discussions was an ambitious plan to sponsor a series of summer leadership institutes in Austin that aimed to train a new generation of civil rights, labor, and precinct activists. The original proposal called for five two-week sessions of three hundred students each, allowing the coalition to train fifteen hundred new organizers in just a ten-week period. The students were to be "drawn more or less equally" from among the coalition's four legs, and the institute would give each youth an opportunity to leave his or her hometown, meet and interact with other student leaders from throughout the state and across the color line, and learn the skills needed for effective political and direct action. The coalition would then help students return home to formulate and execute plans of action to fit their local areas' needs. The elaborate and lofty program never came to fruition, as various objections and logistical concerns scuttled it early in 1965. The plan languished until later that spring, when the Texas AFL-CIO decided to go it alone, rolling out a similar program in which seventy-five youth from across the state came to St. Edward's University in Austin for a two-week conference in June.[40]

While the Texas AFL-CIO pulled off the slimmed-down summer institute, the structure of the statewide Democratic Coalition continued to come under fire, this time from the white liberals. After labor's deal with Lyndon Johnson in which the unions pledged not to oppose Connally in exchange for the president's support for Senator Ralph Yarborough, the leaders of the white liberal "leg" of the coalition came together to form their own organization and independently endorse liberal Don Yarborough. The liberals created TOLD, quipping at their first press conference that the name was apt, since they had told other people the right path for years. But the group's chairman, attorney Franklin Jones of Marshall, resigned his post within weeks of the general election as liberals struggled for traction and the coalition grew increasingly strident internally. Veteran activists Latane Lambert and Chris Dixie worked to revive TOLD in Jones's absence, but the interrelated questions of power sharing and structure in the coalition would not go away.[41]

In April, *Observer* editor Ronnie Dugger proposed a novel solution: discard TOLD and form a new organization, "this time as undifferentiated liberal Democrats—not as labor, not as Negroes, not as Mexicans, not as 'independents,' but as whoever they are, in whatever personal reality they live: as persons." Dugger added that "The coalition certainly can be continued under that name if its members so desire. . . . Let whatever strengths the Democratic Coalition has had be brought forward into this new group; let the coalition's structural and conceptual weaknesses pass away. Let then, the Texas liberals come into organized concert simply as persons, no matter their color, their walk of life."[42] Dugger later reiterated his point in stronger words: "I have watched the Democratic Coalition long enough to have become convinced that, while it is a worthy organization and has done good work, it is not a democratic organization. Its very zeal for civil rights has trapped it into the structural segregation of Negroes, Latin-Americans, labor, and 'independent liberals,' four separate categories. The truth is that it is a front for organized labor."[43]

While Dugger proposed throwing out the baby with the bathwater, other voices offered continued support for the coalition, both on the local level and statewide. Senator Yarborough himself wrote to former TOLD leader Jones, informing the latter "that he had heard some 'rumblings of rivalry, of defeatism, or quislingism for a few bones—bones with less meat on them than cabrito barbecue' in the Democratic Coalition." The senator added that all of the work put in to "building this effective political instrument" may be for naught if its leaders don't pay attention and strengthen the coalition. "It is imperative that the leaders and the various organizations dedicated to the welfare of the people stay in close and continuous communication," Yarborough wrote. "The immediate future for the progressive forces of democracy in Texas is bright—if the wreckers and dividers are thwarted in their efforts to spread pessimism, distrust, defeatism, and disunion among our ranks." Yarborough added that the liberals should not allow the "corporate power structure" to divide them. "Those who exploit the people . . . realize the dangers of their impending political defeat better than do many of our friends." he concluded. "That's why they are working so hard to bury the Democratic Coalition."[44]

Former coalition staffer and *Observer* contributor Larry Goodwyn similarly defended the need for ongoing collaboration across racial lines, even as he accepted the need for structural changes. Referring to TOLD as "a participating unit" of the still extant statewide Democratic Coalition, Goodwyn reported that a diverse Steering Committee planned to issue a call for a new organizational meeting led by "a cross-section of leading Texas liberals, [including] members of Negro and Mexican-American minorities as well as the 'Anglo independents'." In addition to creating a new statewide body, Goodwyn noted, the new group's informal Steering Committee had also embraced a shift toward independent local action. Although the proposed group's unitary structure "implies a reevaluation of the coalition concept as a statewide political instrument, there was no dissent, even from those liberals most closely identified with the coalition movement." Goodwyn concluded, "The prevailing view was that coalitions, in their various forms, must stand or fall as viable political institutions on their development at the local level."[45]

While African Americans and white liberals separately questioned the value of the Democratic Coalition, labor's relationship to the coalition and to the Mexican American PASO also grew tense. Dugger and TOLD acting chairman Dixie argued that the latest proposed organization should be fiercely independent of organized labor, a group that the liberals felt was too susceptible to outside political and economic pressures. Internally, conservative labor leaders led by H. A. Moon of the Dallas UAW attacked the coalition for being too focused on integration, while Nate Slough of the Texas State Industrial Union Council added to the chorus of those who felt that the coalition had fallen short of its goals. "While the coalition concept is valid, the Coalition as an organization was foredoomed to failure," he wrote. "Mechanically and structurally, it was completely inadequate and unworkable." The *Observer* also speculated that the liberal leaders of the Texas AFL-CIO may have lost enthusiasm for the coalition after PASO elected Albert Fuentes as its new chairman. Fuentes, who had been a protégé of Albert Peña, broke away from the coalition in 1964 when he launched his quixotic campaign for lieutenant governor without consulting any of the body's four legs. By 1965, Fuentes was beginning to flirt with the Republican Party, including an alliance with U.S. senator John Tower, who would face reelection the following year. Longtime PASO leader Peña resigned his post as state chairman in order to refocus his efforts in San Antonio, but he argued in his farewell speech that the organization should never endorse any candidate that voted against the Civil Rights Act of 1964, as Tower had. Still, as the commissioner turned his attention to the local front, the statewide direction of the group he had helped found and guided for half a decade remained uncertain.[46]

The coalition as a body was thus falling apart, with each of its constituent elements searching for traction in the altered postassassination political environment. The white liberals hoped to subsume cultural differences by emphasizing ostensibly race-neutral open debate and ideological unity among like-minded individuals. Still, the larger multiracial liberal movement in Texas lacked a clear sense of direction. In fact, the confusion was so great and the liberal movement in such shambles that rumors emerged that none other than Texas AFL-CIO president Hank Brown might run for governor in 1966. A few months later, Ronnie Dugger of the *Observer* briefly campaigned for U.S.

Senate as an independent.[47] For now, however, the white liberals as well as a handful of African American and Mexican American leaders of the fading coalition all hoped that a new organizational structure might revive their combined struggle for democracy in Texas.

"This Has Turned Everything Upside Down"

Then came the Huntsville movement. On one level, it was unremarkable—just one of many struggles across the Deep South aimed at enforcing the Civil Rights Act on the ground. A group of otherwise unknown local students tested the law by staging direct action demonstrations and protests downtown, and the local power structure conceded eventually to some of the activists' demands. But on another level, the Huntsville movement represented a key turning point, a synergy of previous work and a new departure in the multiracial history of civil rights and liberalism in Texas. The local protests grew out of the Democratic Coalition's previous organizing; inspired a new wave of interracial solidarity; bolstered a younger, more aggressive group of indigenous local leadership; and attracted the attention of national civil rights organizations. Yet in doing so, the movement also made clear that the search for traction among activists of all colors had become more slippery than ever.

It began at the Texas AFL-CIO's summer leadership institute in Austin in June of 1965. For two weeks, the students learned and debated, discussing the past and the future of the combined labor and civil rights movements. Four African American youth from Huntsville were in attendance, including the son of the president of the town's NAACP chapter and two children of Kermit Davison, a local black labor leader. They and other attendees left the conference with a new sense of urgency and the need to do something to continue the fight. Perhaps more important, they had gotten to know one another and in some cases became friends.[48] The conference ended with a brief foray into what has later become known as experiential learning. The *Observer*'s Larry Goodwyn reported that "a group of interested [white] liberals took up funds to send the most highly motivated of the young people at the conference to Mississippi." The tour lasted only a week, but the students gained firsthand experience in the trenches of the Student Nonviolent Coordinating Committee's (SNCC) effort to register voters and continue the momentum of the previous year's Freedom Summer.

They returned home to Texas ready for a fight, and their mentors who had been active in the Democratic Coalition searched for an outlet for the youth's enthusiasm. Huntsville appeared ripe for the picking. Segregation there continued, the coalition had long had a presence there, and the town "was alive with Negro disillusionment about the slow pace of change." Finally, coalition leaders were equally unhappy about their lack of success in registering and turning out voters in East Texas. A groundswell of civil rights activity there would help them build a base for both local and statewide liberal integrationist candidates. With these talking points in hand, Rev. William Oliver, a white minister of a black church in Beaumont who had spoken at the summer institute, approached a group of Houston white liberals and raised enough money to send a small group of students to Huntsville for a month.[49]

In short, the Huntsville movement was from its inception a product of the Democratic Coalition and its relatively long history of local networking, voter registration, and support for civil rights demonstrations. Labor trained the multiracial cadre of students, and white liberals sent them first to Mississippi and then to Deep East Texas. Interracial connections forged between black and white labor and liberal leaders provided the infrastructure for the youth-led movement.

The spark quickly arrived at the tinderbox, and events unfolded in rapid succession. Two students, one an African American who had just graduated from Lamar State College and the other a white Harvard student from Dallas, arrived in Huntsville on July 15. They looked up their friends from the labor conference and Mississippi trip, starting with seventeen-year-old Gerald Davison, son of the labor staffer. The white student and Davison accompanied a friend and the friend's father on a routine trip to an auto mechanic in nearby Trinity County. The scene of a young white man that nobody recognized driving across the county and through the seat's downtown along with three local black men did not go unnoticed by local police, the chief of which followed the mixed group to the garage and promptly arrested the white student on suspicion of burglary. On the way to jail, the police chief told the white student from Dallas that he shouldn't be there, considering "'the nigger situation being what it is'" in East Texas. The Harvard student was released two hours later, but his arrest "seemed to galvanize some of the Negro students in Huntsville."[50]

The younger Davison and the other Huntsville students who had attended the labor workshop began organizing, rallying their friends around the cause, founding a new civil rights group, and launching demonstrations, all within seventy-two hours. They opened an office in a building owned by the senior Davison and organized an evening meeting of adult activists from the local Voters League. The next day, some forty students convened and founded Huntsville Action for Youth (HA-YOU), which they referred to using the shorthand "Hey you." They drew up plans to stage direct action protests at two leading institutions of the still-segregated downtown: the Life Theater and the Texan Café.

The confrontation began in the afternoon on Sunday, July 18. Stand-ins desegregated the theater within two hours. The student demonstrators, now with heads of steam, continued down the street to stage sit-ins at the Texan and also at the nearby Raven Café. The operators of the Texan agreed to serve a few of the students at a time, a gesture that failed to satisfy the group. The protestors began singing freedom songs, and those that were served paid their bills and emerged onto the courthouse square. There they faced down crowds of white hecklers before assembling and marching triumphantly in formation back to HA-YOU headquarters.[51]

Demonstrations resumed the following afternoon and continued, steadily escalating over the next week. Gerald Davison and five other students were briefly arrested, then released, and a photographer from a Houston daily newspaper was beaten, though not "brutally." HA-YOU fired off a telegram to Governor Connally asking him to send in state troops to monitor local law enforcement, but no such aid was forthcoming (though the Federal Bureau of Investigation dispatched agents who helped to protect the demonstrators). On the third day of protests, July 20, the students distributed flyers in the community and held a mass meeting of 250 supporters on the lawn outside a local church. Huntsville's black Ministerial Alliance, NAACP chapter, and traditional black leadership had all publicly opposed the demonstrations and locked the doors of the city's sanctuaries. The president of the NAACP, whose son was among the conference alumni and HA-YOU leaders, stated that local law enforcement had given the protestors "adequate protection"—even if that meant arresting them.[52]

Facing intraracial opposition, the student protestors continued to draw on the multiracial bonds forged in the Democratic Coalition. On the fourth day of the protests, HA-YOU organizers acquired "a stock" of badges emblazoned with the label "Freedom Worker," which were left over from the coalition's 1964 voter registration campaign. With these pinned to their chests, the student activists fanned out to explain the movement in person to ordinary African American adults in the community, aiming, in the words of one participant, "'to cover each block in Huntsville and every town in the county.'" At each stop, they invited their interlocutors to attend one of a series of small community meetings staged that evening in countless neighborhoods and hamlets; five to ten people attended each gathering. That evening, while the meetings were underway, Rev. Oliver again reached out to other coalition activists, who in turn made contact with officials of Dr. King's Southern Christian Leadership Conference (SCLC) in Atlanta. The venerable civil rights organization quickly added B. T. Bonner to its staff and also dispatched another veteran activist and King lieutenant. The Huntsville movement was sending shockwaves across Texas and indeed the South. Bonner arrived the following afternoon and led another mass meeting and rally outside yet another hostile church before HA-YOU again marched to the county courthouse. Under the pressure of the community meetings, some traditional black leaders reluctantly aided the youth movement. One NAACP leader served as a deacon at his church and was able to convince his minister to open the doors for Bonner's rally. But Bonner and the students rebuffed his offer and instead staged their meeting in the parking lot of a fire station across the street—a hitherto segregated public space they sought to integrate at the same time. Rev. Alfred Sampson, the SCLC Atlanta staffer, arrived the following day, July 23, as did "several white persons active in the Democratic Coalition."[53]

Sampson and the HA-YOU leadership decided to broaden the movement's base of support. On July 24, according to Goodwyn's report in the *Observer*, the SCLC staffer "walked onto the courthouse lawn, which, like any county seat in East Texas, is crowded with people on Saturday afternoon. The white whittlers and checker players were on one side of the square, the Negro whittlers and checker players on the other." Addressing the latter, Sampson contended that the city's black adults did not need to march, picket, or get arrested, but they did need to contribute financially to the movement and to pressure their ministers to support the movement. "We know you've got to support the younger brothers and sisters of the movement who are doing the marching, and we know the man has an economic hammer on you," he said. "But we are asking you not to fight the kids. . . . They're trying to make you free and they deserve your help . . . you can bake cakes, have fish fries, raise a little money to help HA-YOU." Sampson and Oliver also returned to the phones, contacting Goodwyn and other white liberals who had promised to organize white sympathizers to support the struggle. Phones rang out across Texas all night, and, by morning, about twenty-five veteran white activists were making their way to Huntsville to join the fight.[54]

The almost daily sit-ins and near nightly marches reached a climax on the afternoon of the movement's eighth public day of activity, Sunday, July 25—just ten days after the biracial student duo first touched down in East Texas. Throughout the day, the leaders of the city's Negro Chamber of Commerce, which had disavowed any connection to the demonstrations, held a special meeting to pass a resolution in support of a "cooling-off period." They then privately exchanged phone calls with a local newspaper editor and several of the county's white business leaders and negotiated a settlement aimed at ending the protests. The owners of the recalcitrant Raven Café, the strongest holdout among businesses in town, finally agreed to serve black patrons, but they maintained that they would not serve "a large group at one time." Doubtlessly patting himself on the back, the Negro Chamber's executive director went to the Raven Café and gleefully announced that the city had been integrated. Two black businessmen were served without incident, but none of the movement leaders had been consulted, and they remained unimpressed.[55]

Having been undermined by its alleged allies, the movement needed to show that it could carry its own weight, and show it did. HA-YOU planned a meeting for that afternoon at the nearby state park, and about three hundred people attended, all "dressed in their Sunday finery." Rev. Sampson gave a lively address to the crowd in which he underscored the crux of the matter: "Who speaks for the Negro?" he asked. "The same man who asks the question answers it. No longer, white man, can you pick X-amount of Negroes and put them on committees and continue the substance of segregation by slightly altering the forms. That day is over." He urged the adults to support the youth movement, and he asked the HA-YOU leaders to better include the adults in their own decision-making processes. "We're serving notice on all of the white businesses in Huntsville," he concluded, adding that they would launch boycotts until real change occurred.[56]

The white liberals also got his message. As Goodwyn, who became a participant-observer in the action, put it, "We believed that HA-YOU... represented the spirit of the overwhelming majority of the entire Negro community—from the checker players on the courthouse lawn to the maids and porters who brought food to the houses" of the movement's adult supporters. Meanwhile, the Negro Chamber, "a roster of whose directors would make clear their economic dependence on the ruling powers in Huntsville, had not known what was going on and disclaimed responsibility." The white liberals concluded that their role was simply to bring attention and legitimacy to the city's new black leadership, the students of HA-YOU.

That evening, as the after-church picnic continued in the park, twenty-six white sympathizers from six different Texas cities entered the Raven Café en masse, filling up every available booth and counter stool and forming a line to fill those that were already occupied. As the local paying customers left, white liberals from Houston, Dallas, San Antonio, Austin, Beaumont, and San Marcos took their seats, ordered a cup of coffee, and lingered. The "tactic was to create a circumstance that would force the town to ask, 'Who is HA-YOU?'," Goodwyn reported. Several versions of the same script took place. A server, then a manager, then a police officer asked a demonstrator what was going on, and the latter replied that they were all there to integrate the café. The questioner replied that it was already integrated, that two black men had eaten there that very morning, and the protestor responded that the café owner simply needed to call HA-YOU to tell them that the restaurant was open to all. And then the reply: "What is HA-YOU?" The protestor then explained that HA-YOU was the voice of the city's civil rights movement and that it alone could sanction a settlement. Accompanied by a trio of white student activists, the older white liberals provided HA-YOU's phone number and waited, repeating the exchange until they were all rounded up, put in paddy wagons, and taken to the county jail. The reaction of local law enforcement surprised Sampson and HA-YOU leaders, both of which expected some fallout but apparently could not imagine that the Dixiecrats of Deep East Texas would arrest an all-white group.[57]

Returning from the picnic at the state park, the movement leaders organized still another march to the county courthouse, which by this time was filled with their jailed allies. One black student at the University of Texas who had arrived that day commented that the fact that white people were in jail for black freedom had an "electrifying effect in the Negro community." HA-YOU activists assembled some three hundred people and began the procession in rows of three, making a column that stretched three city blocks by the time it arrived downtown. They circled the courthouse and sang freedom songs, lifting the spirits of the white liberals, who, in typical form, spent the evening writing an open letter explaining their motives—"the recognition of the right of Negroes to select their own leadership." The following morning, a black lawyer from Beaumont negotiated their release, but the local judge required each defendant to post a $200 bond secured by local property. He would not accept cash, which the white liberals could obtain. Two African Americans from surrounding Walker County put up the $5,600 bond, risking their own futures on the movement. The prisoners were released. "This has turned everything upside down," the black UT student concluded. "Whites went to jail while Negroes stayed out, and the whites were defended by a Negro lawyer and were bailed out by rural Negroes in the heart of East Texas."[58]

Thus the Huntsville movement was about far more than the integration of a few lunch counters, though the importance of that monumental feat can hardly be overstated. Rather, the struggle grew directly out of the Democratic Coalition's 1964 voter registration effort and the 1965 summer conference sponsored by the Texas AFL-CIO. When the struggle needed outside support, coalition members responded, first with educational and financial resources, then by obtaining technical expertise through the SCLC, and finally by putting their bodies on the line for the struggle. The fight to bring the Civil Rights Act to East Texas revitalized the networks behind the coalition, even if it did not directly revive the coalition structure of previous years. It also reintroduced Texas to Bonner and landed the "lone wolf" activist on the SCLC payroll, a position that would give him even more experience and influence in the years ahead. Finally, and critically, the Huntsville movement rejected the paternalism of elite-negotiated race relations and replaced it with direct action led by younger, aggressive leaders working in close collaboration with like-minded activists across the color line. While the coalition as a formal body would continue to wane, the movement validated and deepened the commitment to civil rights on the part of organized labor, white liberals, and countless organizers of all colors.

Soon after the white liberals left, HA-YOU achieved its initial goals of integrating public accommodations and winning recognition as an independent representative of black Huntsville. By August, "substantial concessions were reported," and HA-YOU had moved on to fighting for the complete integration of schools, organizing a gardening club among adults that could double as a voter registration effort, and working to have books by black authors purchased by and made available at the local library. SCLC announced that it would direct more attention to Texas, including projects in Houston and Fort Worth. The Huntsville movement continued apace, but the broad network of activists it inspired would soon come to blows over how to carry its momentum forward.[59]

"The Liberals Are Organized Again"

On August 6, 1965, President Johnson signed the Voting Rights Act into law. Neither the poll tax nor the state of Texas fell under its purview. The registration fee had already been banned in federal elections, and cases challenging its legality in local and state races were working their way through the courts. With some exceptions in East Texas, the state lacked the systematic use of "understanding tests" and other disfranchisement devices targeted by the act. Only six southern states were covered by the original legislation, and Texas would not join their ranks until the act was expanded to include language minorities in 1975 (discrimination against Mexican Americans, not African Americans, would trigger the state's inclusion). Of course, black and brown Texans were already registering and voting en masse thanks to the Democratic Coalition's Project VOTE. Yet the state's exclusion from coverage under the new law meant that no federal registrars or courts would intervene in Texas for the next decade, and the multiracial civil rights movement would still have to go it alone.[60]

In early November 1965, the group of white liberals who wanted to create a new organization to supplant the coalition planned to do just that, finally holding their founding meeting in Houston. Since the "Democratic Coalition continued to flounder around," according to one call for the meeting, it was time for all liberals to come together to enlarge it, not as separate legs but as committed individuals, each of whom should check his organizational affiliations at the door in order to create an atmosphere that welcomed all people, fostered open discussion and collaboration, and prioritized the practice of internal democracy.[61] Two diverging accounts of what happened next reveal the depth of intercultural misunderstanding buried within the convention's call—as well as the meeting's failure to live up to its own procedural and ethical standards.

A week after the meeting concluded, *Observer* editor Ronnie Dugger offered a cautiously optimistic summation of what had taken place. More than seven hundred individuals had signed registration cards at the meeting, making it the largest gathering of Texas liberals since the 1950s, he began. "There were more Negroes present proportionally than in recent times at a state liberal meeting," he added, and "there were many young people who had never been seen at such meetings before." Politicians avoided the event, except that Don Yarborough attended several sessions as a private citizen. Likewise, labor leaders Hank Brown and Roy Evans came, but only "as liberals, neither speaking." The makeup of the crowd, in short, met the expectations of conference organizers. The content likewise fulfilled the group's early goals, Dugger reported. The first evening featured a series of three "lounge" gatherings in which groups gathered according to their interests and debated the nuances of their policy areas of choice. One group tackled civil rights, while another focused on foreign policy. The following day, temporary chairman Chris Dixie ran an efficient meeting, albeit in a somewhat heavy-handed manner, and after hearing a succession of speakers, the group approved a constitution and a new name, the Texas Liberal Democrats (TLD). There was some disagreement about foreign policy, with older liberals trying to chart a middle ground on Vietnam that challenged President Johnson's escalation policy while stopping short of the full withdrawal advocated by young activists who identified with Students for a Democratic Society (SDS), the nation's leading antiwar organization. In the end, Dixie cut off debate and prevented most resolutions from being considered, proposing instead that committees be assembled to study the issues and propose solutions at the organization's planned next meeting in the spring. Dugger concluded that overall the "day was disappointing," but still, "a place was cleared where Texas liberals can meet and discuss things. After five years of broken communications, the liberals are organized again."[62]

Yet the editor's glass-half-full conclusion emphasized the activities of white liberals while downplaying the scope and significance of the black and brown civil rights movements. Dugger's statement that the meeting was the largest of Texas liberals in decades certainly would have surprised the leaders of PASO, for example, who had brought together around the same number of people for a rally on the eve of the election in Crystal City in 1963—despite the intimidating presence of the Texas Rangers. Likewise, the leaders of the TCV surely would have contested the assertion that seven hundred liberals debating policy in a ballroom at Houston's posh Rice Hotel represented a more significant achievement than their one-thousand-strong March on Austin. The assertion that the ostensibly race-neutral "liberals" were now organized "again" completely overlooked the mass black and brown civil rights movements that had represented the vanguard of the larger fight for democracy in Texas for the past half-decade.

In fact, not all participants shared Dugger's cautiously optimistic view. His report included a discussion of significant disagreements among the conference participants over the state of the civil rights movement, particularly in Huntsville, but it sandwiched these stormy and revealing exchanges between the bookends of good, diverse attendance and the "disappointing" but still important creation of a new clear "place" for (white) Texas liberals to discuss the nuances of domestic and foreign policy.

A closer look at the debate over civil rights demonstrates that many of the meeting's attendees had much more on their mind. The night before the general meeting, members of the civil rights lounge had "shared indignation" over the sentencing on "unlawful assembly" charges of ten black Huntsville teenagers to a pair of state reform schools for their participation in that city's ongoing civil rights demonstrations.

During the subsequent plenary, Dugger reports, one unnamed "young man had a resolution calling for a T.L.D. march on the Huntsville courthouse the next day" to demand the release of ten students. When presented with this proposal, chairman Dixie, the longtime liberal, replied "that demonstrators don't march on a courthouse demanding immediate release, [and] that he, Dixie, had filed with other counsel a motion designed to get them out." The courts, he said, would provide relief. Then "Moses LeRoy of Houston angrily disagreed, saying that of course demonstrators could ask that the children be freed." LeRoy, of course, had successfully done so on more than one occasion, including the 1961 march of black longshoremen and other unionists that forced Houston authorities to drop the charges against the student sit-in protestors in the Bayou City. Likewise, B. T. Bonner, identified as "a leader of the Huntsville demonstrations and staffer" of SCLC, called out the white liberals for not truly being committed to the black freedom struggle. Dugger writes that Bonner "asked if the attorneys were so smart why hadn't they done some good" [*sic*]. The conference attendees opposed such a march, he added, "because they weren't brave enough to demonstrate." Bonner noted that none of the ten students sentenced to the reform school had previous records, making it a clear case of retribution against the direct action protestors. The white liberals' failure to respond was apparently worse than the judge's sentence. He added, "of their commitment, 'This is the dirtiest deal that's ever been done to the civil rights movement.'" Dugger concluded the section by stating that the "upshot of the matter" was that the conference passed a resolution calling for the students' release. Perhaps needless to say, such words did not get them out of jail.

Late in the day, the question of race resurfaced. Kenneth Tollet, the dean of the law school at Texas Southern University in Houston, objected that there had been no black speakers. Dixie responded that the white minister Bill Oliver's speech had been " 'traumatic and inspiring' " and that NAACP regional director Clarence Laws had been scheduled to speak but was unable to attend. Dugger writes, "Still, Tollet said, the Negro continues to be 'the invisible man' even among Texas liberals."[63]

Dugger noted that many participants left the meeting frustrated, dissatisfied, disappointed, or worse. The primary cleavage centered on age, with younger activists in particular chafing at the heavy-handed manner in which Dixie had stifled rather than fostered open debate. Still, the editor concluded, the meeting was a success, and the organization's future could be bright. More important, Dugger noted that "foreign policy and civil rights tentatively became integral parts of the program of concern in Texas liberalism." It remained unclear how any subject could "tentatively" become "integral"—either something was central or it wasn't. Moreover, it was clear that the group was far from consensus on these two leading issues.[64]

Another report of the proceedings and their meaning reached a less optimistic conclusion. Writing in the *Observer* nearly two months after the meeting, Larry Goodwyn suggested that the TLD meeting had revealed deep-seeded rifts within the former Democratic Coalition and that the main fault line had to do with race, not age or procedural disagreements. Virtually all of the conference's black participants left the meeting upset, as did the legions of younger precinct activists who had joined the liberal wing of the Democratic Party throughout the 1960s. Most were "bitterly disappointed," he wrote, and some were "depressed." So too were most of the students in attendance. While all objected to the "authoritarian manner in which free discussion was suppressed," the true "liberal dilemma" centered on a tension between what Goodwyn called "the Politics of the Present" and "the Politics of the Future." Participants in the former sought to win the next election, while adherents to the latter wanted to win elections in order to destroy the larger caste system. The object of the Politics of the Future is not simply to win but "to give people the opportunity to create fundamental changes in the quality of their lives." The tension between these two political tendencies "conditioned" most moves and countermoves in Houston, Goodwyn contended. Both groups proceeded logically according to their frames, but both were trapped "by the brooding pressures of the Southern past," ultimately leading to "that most deadly of all political diseases—suspicion." Such divisions were not inevitable, Goodwyn added, and individuals could exhibit both approaches. But there were not enough activists of either persuasion to allow them to continue separately.[65]

At a more fundamental level, the problem facing the liberal movement was that black and white activists did not know how to talk to one another and shied away from candid conversations in interracial crowds. The liberal crisis "is the crisis of caste, and the fears that flow from that crisis." It is worldwide as well as domestic, as "non-white people who want to breathe, really breathe, for the first time" assert their place on the world stage. There can be no reconciliation between the two political tendencies, and the two races, based on the old ways, Goodwyn noted. "Any discussion of relationships among Texas liberals, white and black, must start with the simple statement that we have got to find ways to begin speaking our true feelings to one another." All southerners, black and white, conservative and liberal, have been conditioned to lie, and all have been shaped by racism. "We have been children of a caste system for as long as we have lived, and segregation has created half-men in both races. We think in racist ways, even when we are trying not to. . . . It is not so much that we consciously lie to one another," he wrote. "We merely utter polite banalities in order to avoid speaking difficult truths." In short, they were all guilty of lying by omission. Goodwyn believed that the breakdown of social relations and the lack of candor among black and white activists would have profound consequences. He concluded, presciently, "Sooner than most of us think, there may be no possibility of our being able to communicate in ways that have relevancy."[66]

The crux of the issue was that white activists refused to understand that African Americans could be the new leaders of the liberal movement—a struggle that whites believed they had fought, largely alone, for decades. This "barrier of righteousness" produced paternalism that led white liberals to offer direction to their black counterparts rather than supporting and learning from the African American freedom struggle. Goodwyn cited two examples from the Houston conference. First, the "radical student" who proposed the march in Huntsville did so "without once considering the views of the Negroes of Huntsville who have been enduring the most brutal repression for the past four months." For that student, as well as for many of the others at the conference who debated the issue, "Negroes seem to exist as an abstraction, but not as people. They are an idea in history." After the first confrontational resolution was presented, another conference participant—"whose author had likewise not bothered to consider how it meshed with the plans of the people in Huntsville"—offered a "liberal" alternative. The conference finally passed a third "moderate" resolution, which politely called for the students' release from reform school but "the chief merit of which seemed to be its high degree of invisibility." Hence Moses LeRoy's and B. T. Bonner's fierce objections to the proceedings. The discussion took on what Goodwyn called an "otherworldly cast" as the issue's principal protagonists remained merely objects, not people.[67]

A second example from the Houston meeting drove his point home. At the conference "a very prominent white person from a medium-sized Texas city" approached Goodwyn and complained that African Americans in his town were not joining the (white-led) liberal organization and that the blacks were "behaving in a racist way," refusing the help of whites like him even though whites in the local coalition had "given" the African Americans the idea for organizing in the first place. Regardless of the facts, the unnamed narrator's claim implied "that Negroes are incapable of making fundamental policy changes without whites' guidance." Moreover, Goodwyn wrote, his interlocutor erred in asserting that there exists "a thing called 'the Negroes.'" Just as whites disagreed, African Americans were not monolithic, and their political world was not instrumentally controlled by whites. Internal clashes characterized each group, Goodwyn contended, as they always did "when more than two human beings get together for politics." Yet many white liberals harbored similar illusions as the gentleman telling the story. Although they might have possessed tolerant attitudes on racial matters, they still "unconsciously speak of 'the Negroes' without any feeling of inconsistency." Moreover, the fact that the man confessed his frustration to Goodwyn and not in an interracial meeting or directly to the black activists in his own town suggested just how much open communication had already disappeared. "The evidence is abundant," Goodwyn added, that white liberals "do not accept, *in their daily political or private actions*, the premise that thrust for change in America comes mainly from Negro people, not white people." This remained true despite the fact that throughout the early 1960s, more and more black and brown activists had carried the struggle for civil rights into electoral organizing, making the "palefaces frequently outnumbered" on the ground in campaign after campaign. Still, "A great body of liberals, however, cannot bear to relinquish their image of themselves as the sole conscience of the forces of dissent in the South."[68]

The civil rights movement had forever changed the political scene, but until white activists realized that African Americans propelled the struggle for democracy through their own actions, and not as the protégés of whites, no further progress would be made. Whites needed to accept blacks as leaders and even as friends. In retrospect, Goodwyn argued, the most depressing result of the Houston conference was not the authoritarianism of the chair or the sharp divisions of the participants, but the white liberals' surprise at the bitterness of the other attendees. The former group's astonishment indicated just how far removed they had drifted from the true spearheads of the movement—the black civil rights struggle and, increasingly, the campus revolts led by SDS and the New Left. (One could also add the growing Chicano/a movement to that list, though Goodwyn did not.)

Still, all hope was not lost. Rather, the liberals could become relevant again by refocusing on the Politics of the Future, Goodwyn argued. They needed to address the caste system head-on by developing new goals and strategies that looked beyond the next election. Liberals must listen to and prioritize the issues of those who are struggling to become free. In rural areas, Texans could follow the lead of activists in Mississippi, who had organized around the politics of land ownership and fought for influence on federal Agriculture Stabilization Committees. "The same principle—making our politics germane to the daily lives of people in the neighborhoods where they live—would of course apply in the cities, too," he wrote. New political institutions could be created that focused on problems of urban life: jobs, housing, parks, taxation, and antipoverty programs. He urged true interracial dialogue on fair housing codes, for example, or hiring practices at City Hall, or union apprenticeship programs—"rather than the rhetorical gesturing and resolution-passing that now all too often characterizes the relationship." Political victories based on such interactions would have real meaning in changing the way people live. The struggle for white liberals in the South, Goodwyn concluded, centered on "our" ability to defeat the caste mentality, despite enduring "the loss of our illusions about ourselves."[69]

Though they were both penned by liberal white authors, Dugger's and Goodwyn's diverging accounts of the Houston meeting underscored the depth of misunderstanding, suspicion, and division that swirled among the former leaders of the Democratic Coalition by the end of 1965. White liberals formed TLD to separate themselves from the impure, pragmatic politics of labor, but in so doing, they also isolated themselves from the idealistic "Politics of the Future" that stood at the center of the black (and brown) civil rights movements. Without even knowing it, they asserted a white cultural nationalism that privileged their own experiences and contributions while slighting those of their erstwhile allies across the color line. Their effort to build a new, statewide coalition of atomized individuals failed to substantively address, let alone subsume, racial differences in the service of liberalism.

The statewide Democratic Coalition of the early 1960s would never be reborn, and not because Stokely Carmichael shouted "Black Power" at a march in Mississippi in the summer of 1966, nor because black and brown activists stormed out of interracial gatherings and organized liberation movements into the 1970s. Rather, the problem, already clear in 1965, was the unconscious assertion of white power on the part of white liberals. What had begun as a search for direction in the postassassination wilderness had produced a heightened level of interracial solidarity in Huntsville, but the challenge presented by an increasingly assertive civil rights movement tore the remnants of the coalition asunder. Whites refused to delve into their "illusions about ourselves," and coordinated multiracial action remained elusive—at least at the statewide level. In the years ahead, veteran activists of all colors would have no choice but to follow Goodwyn's formula of approaching the problem in new ways, through new issues related to caste at the local level.

Recovering from the confusion in the immediate aftermath of Kennedy's assassination, the Democratic Coalition had reached new heights. It expanded its influence into the barrios and ghettos through Operation Bootstrap and Project VOTE and succeeded in registering and turning out enough votes to carry the state's liberal Democratic leaders to victory. The 1964 campaign represented the culmination of decades of work in the trenches, a sustained effort that finally produced a social and political sea change in Texas. Veteran black activists who had helped win the right to vote and *mexicano* organizers who had cast off the shackles of bossism and organized their *raza* for the first time had each carried forward the fight for real political influence, civil rights, and economic opportunities for all. By playing a decisive role in the reelection of Johnson and Yarborough, together they had achieved those age-old goals to a remarkable degree. Journalists' observations that they now enjoyed "new power" and would no longer accept "back seats" underscored just how much had changed since the days of Jim Crow and Juan Crow. The passage of the federal Civil Rights Act of 1964 likewise represented the realization of their longtime quest to win integration as a right, through an ordinance that guaranteed the recognition of their humanity. And Title VII of the act promised to upend the endemic employment discrimination of the age of segregation, providing new opportunities and signaling a turning point for black and brown working people who had battled for decades to win improvements and equality on the job. It had been a gradual process, but there was no denying that by the 1960s the multiracial movement had irrevocably altered the landscape, even if the struggle for true democracy continued.

In a tragic turn, the very fact that the Democratic Coalition had achieved this "New Power for the Texas Minorities" proved its undoing. As African Americans continued to fight in the streets to implement the Civil Rights Act against the intransigence of local officials in places like Huntsville, and Mexican Americans struggled to build on the momentum of the victory in Crystal City, white liberals often remained focused narrowly on electoral politics and again divorced the "liberal movement" from the black and brown liberation struggles. Many whites simply refused to share power with their dark-skinned counterparts. For their part, the leaders of organized labor continued to reach out to black and brown workers in new ways, but they too deferred to the "Politics of the Present." The fight to overturn the caste system—the "Politics of the Future"—remained unfinished.

Over time, the diverse activists of the Democratic Coalition would increasingly concentrate their work at the local level, and urban multiracial coalitions would continue to break new ground in the state's major cities. With ongoing support from labor and white liberals in their own backyards, black and brown activists would work together to achieve the independent representation that they had long sought for the ghettos and barrios, in time capturing local politics and electing liberals of all colors to the state legislature. As a result, in Austin, organized labor would finally win substantial legislative gains for working people in Texas. The constituent parts of the statewide coalition would come together one last time to rally in unison for civil rights, economic justice, and electoral gains, demonstrating the ongoing potential and power of the multiracial alliance.

Epilogue
The Multiracial Marcha

The last hurrah of the statewide coalition occurred in 1966. It began in the Valley, when several hundred migrant farmworkers struck the melon harvest at La Casita Farms near Rio Grande City, in Starr County. Eugene Nelson, a Texas native who worked for the National Farm Workers Association (NFWA), the predecessor to the United Farm Workers, in California, asked permission to be reassigned to his home state and returned in March of that year. He made a tour of local unions and liberal leaders in Houston to raise a few dollars and then headed west toward the fields. There he connected with a local resident who had long sought to unionize the area's farmworkers, and, on June 1, the NFWA's new members began what they called *la huelga* (the strike). The growers responded in typical South Texas fashion: by calling in the Texas Rangers to intimidate or beat the strikers and hiring scabs from the other side of the Rio Grande.[1]

Three NFWA organizers soon arrived to help Nelson and the local workers. Dolores Huerta, the union's second in command after César Chávez, briefly joined them, as did Pancho Medrano, who had joined the staff of the UAW after Operation Bootstrap and now delivered substantial donations from the autoworkers' union to *la causa* (the cause). The farmworkers stayed out on strike, despite constant harassment and reprisals from the growers and the Rangers. One small farmer, a *mexicano*, agreed to recognize the union and was promptly blacklisted from the growers' association and cut off from its supply chains and shipping and marketing routes. To turn away the scabs, the union staged pickets on the international bridge in the small town of Roma, where they were joined by a sympathy picket staged by the Mexican Confederación de Trabajadores Mexicanos. When that failed, the organizers padlocked the bridge's gate shut, surreptitiously (and illegally) closing the port of entry for the better part of a day. Peña and other liberal *mexicanos* in San Antonio organized caravans to bring food and supplies to the farmworkers, but the strike dragged on with no signs of a resolution. When a delegation of liberal Bexar County legislators visited Rio Grande City to investigate the strikers' charges of abuse by the Rangers, Captain A. Y. Allee threatened and pushed around one of them, a seemingly ordinary *mexicano* activist who happened to be Democratic state senate-nominee and current state representative Joe Bernal.

Veteran civil rights unionist Moses LeRoy, in the center holding the microphone, speaking to a farmworkers' rally in Corpus Christi during the march from the Rio Grande Valley to Austin. LeRoy joined the Harris County PASO, a predominately Mexican American group, which sent several busloads of members to various rallies along the route. Courtesy Moses LeRoy Collection, Houston Public Library, HMRC, MSS0090-0016.

On the Fourth of July 1966, NFWA organizers and hundreds of striking workers began a march to bring attention to their protracted fight. The union planned to stage a one-day protest, but once they got underway, the organizers decided to march all the way to the capitol in Austin. They followed a circuitous route through the Valley and South Texas that allowed them to build public support for their campaign. The Houston and San Antonio Political Association of Spanish-Speaking Organizations (PASO) chapters sent delegations to join the first day of the procession, and PASO leaders in the Lower Rio Grande Valley helped coordinate rallies in each city and hamlet along the way. One PASO member who rode the bus from Houston was Moses LeRoy, the veteran black civil rights unionist. Now nearly seventy years old, LeRoy walked many legs of the five-hundred-mile march and spoke at some of the farmworkers' rallies. The strikers headed southeast down the Valley as far as Harlingen before turning north toward Corpus Christi. By the time the march arrived there, it had gained enough momentum that even Dr. Hector P. Garcia, the founder of the

The September 5, 1966, Labor Day climax to the long farmworkers' *marcha* included black civil rights and white union activists, all united in their demands for a $1.25 hourly minimum wage. B. T. Bonner's delegation from East Texas joined members of the Austin NAACP at the capitol rally, as did the Texas AFL-CIO. Courtesy *Austin American-Statesman* Photographic Morgue (AR.2014.039), Austin History Center, Austin Public Library, Texas, Image AS-66-55186-A-16a.

American G.I. Forum (AGIF) who had long opposed demonstrations and led the fight against the Teamsters partnership with PASO, joined the NFWA in the streets. A pair of Mexican American ministers from Houston and San Antonio's Father Sherrill Smith joined *la marcha*, as the strikers called the march, giving a degree of moral and religious legitimacy to the cause.

As the march wound its way toward San Antonio and eventually to Austin, the civil rights struggle in East Texas began bubbling over. In the spring of 1966, nearly a year after the Huntsville movement had taken off, B. T. Bonner returned to the city to lead a renewed fight for school integration and economic opportunity, the latter a part of the Southern Christian Leadership Conference's (SCLC) nationwide Operation Breadbasket program. In August, when local elites refused to accept the job demands of Huntsville Action for Youth (HA-YOU), Bonner called on the youth organization to stage its own protest march to the capitol. Like the Mexican Americans in the NFWA, the African Americans led by Bonner walked a circuitous route to highlight ongoing segregation and economic misery facing blacks throughout East Texas. Bonner coordinated his march along with Texas AFL-CIO leaders and arranged a rendezvous with the unionists at the capitol on Labor Day, September 5, 1966.

All three groups—blacks from East Texas, browns from South Texas, and the white leaders of organized labor—united under a common demand: the establishment of a $1.25 minimum hourly wage. Echoing calls from the 1963 demonstrations, the protestors in 1966 again demanded a meeting with Governor Connally upon the march's arrival in Austin. Their longtime nemesis again stated that he would not be bullied by demonstrators, and he refused to meet with them under duress. It appeared that the governor would simply ignore the coalition's demands. But on the last day of August, Connally jumped in his limousine and sped southward, accompanied by Attorney General Waggoner Carr and state house speaker Ben Barnes and trailed in another vehicle by Hank Brown. The governor found the marchers on the highway just outside New Braunfels, about halfway between San Antonio and Austin. Strike leaders and the state officials met briefly on the side of the road, baking under the hot sun. Connally asked them to call off the demonstration but refused to promise a minimum wage bill. The confrontation ended in stalemate, the governor returned to his Lincoln Continental, and the march continued. Hank Brown remarked to a cluster of reporters that he had "never seen as much unity among Mexican-Americans as I see at this hour in Texas."[2] And the best was still to come.

On the morning of Labor Day, a multiracial group of ten thousand protestors from across the state joined the *mexicano* strikers at St. Edward's University in South Austin, where the marchers had spent the previous night. Urged by Brown and the Texas AFL-CIO, black, brown, and white union members from across the state joined the march en masse. Even the relatively conservative Dallas labor council sent a delegation. Houston PASO chartered several more buses and brought members of that city's still vibrant local coalition. Moses LeRoy remained in the group, and he was joined by white and black activists from the Harris County Democrats (HCD). One was Barbara Jordan, the former blockworker for the Democratic Coalition, who had recently won the party's nomination for a seat in the state senate—a feat that promised to make her the first African American in that body since Reconstruction and its first ever black woman. Alfred Hernandez of Houston, the national president of the League of United Latin American Citizens (LULAC), became that group's first leader to endorse direct action protests and personally joined the march, as did other more conservative Mexican Americans. George I. Sánchez, the sagacious liberal professor, also participated, smiling from ear to ear. San Antonio sent countless activists from the West Side and likely several from the East Side. Finally, B. T. Bonner brought a group of several hundred HA-YOU members and supporters who had marched together from East Texas, adding them to a contingent from the Austin NAACP to produce a sizable African American presence at the rally.

The marchers walked three miles up Congress Avenue and arrived at the capitol in high spirits. Senator Ralph Yarborough, Congressman Henry B. Gonzalez, Barbara Jordan, Joe Bernal, four other state senators, and fourteen state representatives joined them in rallying for a minimum wage. Yarborough, the liberal standard-bearer and highest-ranking official elected by the state's multiracial coalition, electrified the crowd with his speech. "One hundred years ago, we ended physical slavery," he said, seamlessly linking the black and brown civil rights struggles. "Today we are here to end poverty and economic slavery."[3]

The state had never seen a demonstration of that size, nor had it ever seen so clearly the fruits of decades of black and brown civil rights organizing and coalition building. Jordan and Bernal announced that they would introduce a minimum wage bill and would pull out all the stops to get it passed. Thanks to the activities of local coalitions in the state's big cities and the Valley, the 1967 legislature would be the most diverse and one of the most liberal in its history. Hank Brown later recalled that it was labor's most productive session in its history, thanks to the presence of black, brown, and white liberals and his own ability to broker deals between them and Speaker Ben Barnes.[4]

Still, the strike itself failed, and the issue of farmworker unionization remained unsettled until the union went out again the next year, just as the 1967 harvest approached. Local law enforcement and Texas Rangers renewed their campaign of harassment, beating, jailing, and intimidation of the strikers and their sympathizers. In late May, the Rangers attacked a group of farmworkers union organizers, members, and supporters who picketed the MoPac Railroad in an attempt to convince the unionized train conductors and freight handlers to refuse the produce being harvested by scabs. One of the pickets was Pancho Medrano, who attempted to photograph the police brutality and was promptly arrested. On June 1, the Rangers beat two rank-and-file union leaders nearly to death. Over the course of two months that summer, hundreds of farmworkers had been jailed, roughed up, and harassed.

The police violence refocused external attention on the conflict, and the U.S. Senate Subcommittee on Migratory Labor responded by holding widely publicized hearings at the Starr County Courthouse in July. Ralph Yarborough, Edward M. "Ted" Kennedy of Massachusetts, and Harrison Williams of New Jersey called numerous witnesses to the stand, including growers, but mostly the event served as an opportunity for the abused farmworkers to finally speak their piece before a national audience. Union members and PASO activists from across South Texas flocked to the hearings, and hundreds of farmworkers packed the gallery and stood outside listening as the proceedings were broadcast on a loudspeaker outside. The crowd frequently grew raucous and interrupted the speakers with cheers and jeers, including chants of "Viva Kennedy" to thank Ted for his support of the union.

Around the same time, the Texas State Advisory Committee to the U.S. Commission on Civil Rights held a hearing on the strike and other instances of police brutality in South Texas. The state committee included several labor appointments, including a diverse group of battle-hardened former Democratic Coalition leaders. Latane Lambert had served on the committee since 1962, and Mrs. Erma LeRoy and Henry Muñoz soon joined her. Paul Montemayor of PASO and labor's Latin American Affairs Committee was a key witness. The committee published a scathing report titled "The Administration of Justice in Starr, San Patricio, and Nueces Counties," which was then forwarded to the full federal commission for review. The state body later investigated charges of employment discrimination at San Antonio's Kelly Air Force Base and other locales across the state. Muñoz recalled that he often brought the complaints that he received as director of Texas AFL-CIO Department of Equal Opportunity to the Advisory Committee, which in turn launched inquiries after receiving numerous leads from the same worksite or community.[5]

With assistance from the UAW, the farmworkers union also filed a federal court case against the Texas Rangers. The case, named *Medrano v. Allee* after its lead plaintiff and the captain of the state police force, challenged five of the state's bevy of draconian antilabor laws. A three-judge panel took nearly five years to decide the case, but in 1972 it sided wholly with the union and ordered the Rangers to refrain from strikebreaking. Two years later, the U.S. Supreme Court upheld the lower court's injunction but did not overturn the underlying antiunion state statutes. In fact, by that time three of the five measures had already been amended or repealed, Captain Allee had retired from service, and the union had died completely in Starr County. Still, the Rangers were forced to stop "engaging in the kind of brutal lawlessness of which they were found guilty," as longtime liberal lawyer Bob Hall would later write. The strike had sparked "political insurgency" across South Texas, while the case had eliminated the threat that state-sanctioned terror would be meted out against *mexicano* labor and civil rights activists. "Perhaps most important," Hall concluded, "*Medrano v. Allee* proved that even the vaunted Texas Rangers could be restrained by the law, thus stripping them of the most effective weapon of any oppressive power: the perception that resistance is hopeless and futile."[6]

Taken together, these three federal interventions, themselves the products of years of coalition organizing, collectively amounted to a sort of Third Reconstruction. While African Americans had been emancipated after the Civil War and then won basic rights in the 1960s, Mexican Americans still felt the sting of the Treaty of Guadalupe-Hidalgo of 1848 and of its frequent violations in the decades thereafter. The Civil Rights and Voting Rights Acts helped *mexicanos* in their own fight against Juan Crow, but both federal laws initially targeted blacks. Curtailing the autocratic power of the growers and the capricious violence of the Texas Rangers represented a new beginning of immeasurable significance.[7]

More generally, the strike, the minimum wage march, and the Third Reconstruction represented the high-water mark and the quiet denouement of the long, multiracial struggle for democracy in Texas. Although the strike did not revive the statewide Democratic Coalition, and it was lost by any measure, it did bring decades of underground organizing into public view, and it empowered countless ordinary people to take action for themselves. The farmworker struggle provided a shot in the arm to veteran Mexican American organizers and undergirded the rising Chicano/a youth movement. A handful of older activists like Albert Peña had long played a role in local governance, but outside of South Texas, formal politics had remained largely black and white. The strike forever changed that. It represented a public coming-out of militant Mexican American activists who were no longer willing to live in the shadows. Even more than the first revolt in Crystal City, *la marcha* announced that the state's *mexicanos* would demand and win a place at the table of Texas politics. The Latino vote, which had been born in the struggles of the 1950s and early 1960s, was now coming into its own on a much larger stage.

Remapping Urban Politics

La marcha also enhanced the ability of veteran activists to gain power at the local level through urban multiracial alliances. In the wake of the strike, black, brown, and white activists in Houston and Dallas redoubled their local coalition-building efforts, as did Peña and company in San Antonio. The results were tangible: in each city, longtime organizers finally made progress toward their decades-old goal of independent political power. Activists worked to implement the Voting Rights Act of 1965 on the ground, and many were involved in lawsuits that led to the replacement of the old at-large electoral system with single-member, "majority-minority" districts. Some activists won elections to local office, others were appointed to local boards and commissions, and still others became local government administrators. For the first time, public policy making in urban Texas included independent voices from the state's long-disenfranchised black, brown, and poor communities. And many of the barriers to economic self-improvement also came tumbling down.

In Houston, for example, a local multiracial coalition seized control of the city's delegation to the state legislature, several U.S. congressional districts, and much of municipal politics. In 1965, responding to the *Reynolds v. Sims*

Supreme Court decision, the Texas legislature reapportioned the state's electoral map, creating several new single-member districts in Harris County. The following spring, the local coalition, composed of the HCD, the Harris County Council of Organizations (HCCO), PASO, the Harris County AFL-CIO, and the Teamsters, formed a slate that included blockworker director Barbara Jordan, former sit-in demonstrator Curtis Graves, and PASO activist Lauro Cruz. The slate swept into office. Jordan was later elected to Congress. Houston PASO became the state's most vibrant chapter and continued to function into the late 1970s, as did variants of the local coalition. One of its leaders, Leonel Castillo, who had organized the Students for Civil Liberties sit-in demonstrators in San Antonio while in college, was elected as Houston City Controller and later became the director of the U.S. Immigration and Naturalization Service during the Carter administration.

At the local level, Moses LeRoy ran for a seat on the Model (Cities) Neighborhood Residents Commission, and, once elected, he became the first chairman of that body. The position gave him a platform to criticize inaction by Houston's antipoverty administrators even as he continued his neighborhood- and worksite-based organizing. Almost immediately after the passage of the Civil Rights Act of 1964, LeRoy filed a complaint that finally ended employment discrimination at the Southern Pacific Railroad and forced the integration of his workplace and his union, the Brotherhood of Steamship and Railway Clerks—winning battles that he had been fighting intermittently since the early 1940s. In 1973, LeRoy also filed a suit that challenged the city's at-large electoral system under the Voting Rights Act. Many black and Mexican American civil rights groups endorsed and funded the litigation, but LeRoy's name appeared first on the docket, and his personal commitment to the case is often credited with helping it survive years of legal wrangling. In 1979, Houston voters approved a mixed plan that created nine single-member city council districts, a change that finally allowed African Americans and *mexicanos* in the inner city to independently elect council representatives from their neighborhoods. Meanwhile, Howard Middleton of the Progressive Youth Association and the laborers union continued to work through a more moderate coalition, a strategy that resulted in his appointment as the county's first manpower commissioner and later to a post on the Houston Port Commission.[8]

In Dallas, Pancho Medrano used his position with the UAW to build a powerful neighborhood electoral machine that helped democratize Dallas politics. After his work to expand the local coalition through Operation Bootstrap, Medrano began working for his international union's Citizenship Department, a job that gave him carte blanche to travel the country assisting local civil rights struggles and political candidates "wherever it was needed." Medrano used his position to spread the gospel of community organizing, crisscrossing the country in a car filled with leaflets and a film projector and personally participating in many of the iconic protests of the 1960s. Yet Medrano also continued to organize in his own neighborhood, using it as a base for deepening and extending the local multiracial coalition. In 1964, Medrano and his family purchased a small neighborhood grocery store that doubled as a community center focused on political education. Medrano and his wife used it to work directly with countless barrio residents, while his sons helped organize the city's youth-led Chicano/a insurgency of the early 1970s and, at times, multiracial civil rights coalitions. Medrano also brought the fight for access to skilled jobs back to his old worksite, an aircraft plant in Grand Prairie outside of Dallas. Medrano worked with the Texas Employment Commission to bring over five hundred *mexicano* workers north from the Rio Grande Valley and into a new training program that finally desegregated the industry. Each of these efforts allowed Medrano and his family to build what they called "political clout." Many of Medrano's children became local leaders and elected officials in their own right. In 2010, his daughter Pauline became the city's deputy mayor pro tem, and four years later she was elected county treasurer. Remarkably, she replaced another politician with roots in the Democratic Coalition of the 1960s: Joe Wells, the son of one of the city's leading labor lawyers and white liberal activists.[9]

Finally, in San Antonio, the state's original local coalition also continued to grow deeper and more powerful. Albert Peña became a mentor and ally to younger Chicano/a activists, who fanned out across South Texas under the banner of La Raza Unida (The United People's) party. He also remained an officer and intermittent chair of PASO into the 1970s. At the local level, he helped organize the Federation for the Advancement of the Mexican American, a group that coordinated aid caravans to Valley farmworkers and helped lead the multiracial fight to desegregate employment opportunities at Kelly Air Force Base. In 1968, Peña cofounded a local intraracial alliance called the Mexican American Unity Council as well as the regional Southwest Council of La Raza, the predecessor to today's National Council of La Raza. In 1974, he joined younger Chicano activists in creating the Southwest Voter Registration and Education Project, which helped *mexicano* communities throughout the region organize politically. Peña also grew closer to organized labor, serving briefly as the director of a UAW community unionism project in the early 1970s.

Throughout the 1960s and into the 1970s, Peña and African American activists from the East Side continued to collaborate on antipoverty and community development initiatives, and to support one another in electoral politics and civil rights demonstrations. They formed a "lunch bunch" that met at least monthly to coordinate their ongoing organizing activities. As in the other cities, the local coalition produced more electoral victories. In 1972, G. J. Sutton returned to elected office by winning a seat in the state legislature. The following year, Rev. Claude Black was elected to the city council on his third try, becoming the first independent African American to serve on that body. Conservative Mexican Americans defeated both Peña and liberal state senator Joe Bernal in 1972, but the two liberals remained active in neighborhood organizing and in the local coalition. Peña later became a municipal court judge.

Mexican Americans and African Americans also gained entry into the city's labor movement. A caucus known as San Antonio Chicano Organizers (SACO) coordinated the activities of more than a dozen organizers, including the staff of Peña's UAW project, Franklin Garcia of the meat cutters, and several organizers for the International Union of Electrical, Machine, and Radio Workers who worked under the direction of Paul Javior, the Polish farmer turned organizer and the "token Anglo" of the group. In 1967, Javior recruited Clarence "C. J." Littlefield, a protégé of Black, Sutton, and Coleman who grew up in the city's civil rights movement, to serve as the city's first black union president. SACO served as another wing of the local liberal coalition, getting out the vote for independent black and brown candidates and extending the veteran activists' influence on the ground—just as the union-sponsored Operation Bootstrap had supported a wide range of community organizing and electoral projects since 1963.[10]

In sum, through local coalition organizing, veteran black, brown, and white activists made significant headway toward their longtime goals of independent political power and economic opportunity. They won unprecedented amounts of formal influence, and their delegations to Austin at times produced significant legislative improvements.

Yet they quickly realized that they had won the battles even as they lost the war. National politics turned decisively to the right by the late 1960s, eliminating many of the federal resources that had supported the Second and Third Reconstructions in Texas. At the state level, the conservative Democrats hung on much longer than the liberals had expected, and the transition to a true two-party state would not be completed until the late 1970s. The biggest blow to liberal Texas Democrats came in 1970, when conservative Lloyd Bentsen defeated Senator Ralph Yarborough in the party's primary. Labor, of course, campaigned fervently for the liberal; many unions even contributed to a "Brown pot" to target Mexican American voters. But the state's corporate elites donated much more to Bentsen's war chest, and the conservative prevailed.

Yarborough had long been the lone statewide official elected by the liberal movement, but he could not survive following the demise of the multiracial Democratic Coalition. Each of the civil rights movements likewise struggled for footing by the early 1970s, as did organized labor. White "independent" liberals still could not go it alone. More than a decade would pass before liberal activists celebrated victory in a statewide race. In an ironic twist that showed how far the liberals had fallen, the great Democratic sweep of 1982 produced a moderate governor, Mark White, and the ticket also included outspoken liberals Jim Hightower and Ann Richards. Still, Bentsen's name was at the top of the ballot.[11]

The Democratic Coalition's task remains unfinished today. Restaurants now serve African Americans, and the Texas Rangers no longer terrorize Mexican Americans. Most of the barriers to equal employment opportunity have been lifted. Yet organized labor has shrunk to its lowest level of size and influence since the Wagner Act, while business interests continue to dominate state and national politics. Durable, structural racial inequality persists by almost any measure, including income, wealth, healthcare, education, and rates of incarceration. Most whites likewise lag far behind the increasingly distant elites.

If economic justice remains far away, the struggle for political democracy is also far from complete. In each of the major cities of Texas, as in most of urban America, black and brown neighborhoods can now elect their own, independent representatives to local, state, and national governments. But having a voice has not meant that anyone else listens to what they have to say. This is the paradox of post–civil rights America. We all have the right to determine our future, but we are too disorganized to exercise it. Many of us lack the political self-respect to demand more than a superficially representative government. And many self-styled activists have failed to find the methods necessary to transcend the deep divides that separate us. This book is a step toward recovering a few tricks from the historical toolbox—in the hopes that we may find new ways to practice democracy in our own time.

Democratic Coalitions

What lessons can be gleaned from the history of multiracial coalition building in mid-twentieth-century Texas? First and foremost, the decades-long process of finding ways to collaborate was just that: a process. The stories presented above draw attention to the full meaning of the word "coalition"—a bringing together of separate, independent parts for a common cause, a term that indicates that differences preexisted and never fully disappeared. Too often "coalition" is used as a substitute for "coalescence," which instead implies a coming together that collapses differences into a unitary whole.

The partnerships among black, brown, and white labor and liberal organizers in Texas were "coalitions"—alliances built upon an explicit acknowledgment of different starting points, disparate agendas, diverse personnel, and only partially overlapping aspirations. The multiracial struggle for democracy in the Lone Star State was a many-headed beast. It was the product of years of experimentation in which mutually distrustful elements—from geographically distant neighborhoods, with unique cultures and experiences, with similar but not identical grievances, with separate organizations and distinct bases and leaders—came together out of desperation and used one another to make progress toward their divergent (if related) goals. Over time, suspicion among coalition partners gradually gave way to a sense of common purpose in which each element came to understand the need to go beyond temporary alliances and support one another's causes full time. Still, the groups did not "coalesce." They remained distinct, each prioritizing their own needs and objectives while having learned that they needed to be there for each other in order to make it to the finish line.

Thus, while it is true that African American and Mexican American civil rights activists in Texas were in fact "fighting their own battles," as one scholar recently put it, they did so by working together. Their respective struggles did not proceed along "parallel tracks" but rather traveled along routes that frequently intersected, crisscrossed one another, at times recoiled apart, and ultimately arrived at the same depot. That is the true meaning of "coalition"—as civil rights activist and "songtalker" Bernice Johnson Reagon reminds us—working together while still starting from (and returning to) separate "houses."[12]

The story of coalition building in Texas also explodes the myths of *intra*racial solidarity that dominate our understanding of what has come to be called "identity politics." Popular memory as well as scholarly studies of the civil rights movements that opened the door to black and brown participation in self-government frequently assume a degree of unity among African Americans or Mexicans Americans in the age of Jim Crow and Juan Crow that never actually existed on the ground. Take the language used to describe them: commentators of all colors refer to "the black community," and more recently, "the Hispanic community." Present-day African American political meetings are often infused with an implicit, under-the-radar declension narrative in which the good old days of segregation produced automatic unity among all blacks, who then lined up behind their traditional leaders to rise up against their common oppressors. Scholars have poked many holes in this story, yet the myth continues to thrive. The Texas story should lay to rest any misconceptions about the existence of a unitary "black community" both then and now. Working-class African Americans like Moses and Erma LeRoy, and militant activists like G. J. Sutton who partnered with them, never described their task in simple terms of black versus white. Rather, they knew that segregation was "an economic problem" and that some of the most intransigent obstacles to their quest for progress were other blacks, leaders who, in their view, "walked around with their hands out" and acted like Judas, selling out the dreams of their children and grandchildren for a few pieces of silver.

The power of such cultural nationalism similarly asserts itself in Mexican American political gatherings, though the myth of unity has never possessed the weight that it carries among African Americans. *Mexicanos* in Texas, long perceived as political pawns whose votes were always for sale, have paradoxically transitioned into being viewed as political novices who are too shortsighted and naïve to work together for a common cause. Fragmentation replaced the *patrones*. Yet such formulations twist rather than refute the myth of a unified "community." They still assume that Mexican Americans should naturally come together to combat their common oppression by Anglos, rather than bickering among themselves over the crumbs. A closer look at Mexican American history suggests an alternate interpretation. *Mexicanos* in Texas failed to unite because their common experiences of discrimination based on color and national origin were not always enough to overcome their internal differences. As with African Americans, class, ideology, and organizing strategies and tactics all mattered at least as much as did ties of race or ethnicity. For militant civil rights activists like Albert Peña, Pancho Medrano, the brothers Garcia, or Bob Sanchez, the self-proclaimed Mexican American business and community leaders often stood in the way of progress. The *vendidos*, as the activists called the Mexican American elites, had their own profits in mind, rather than the interests of the people in the barrios whom the activists sought to organize.

*Intra*racial conflict thus raged within black and brown "communities," just as it did among whites. Few white Americans expect otherwise when it comes to their own political activities. The divisions between conservatives and liberals, business and labor, and diplomacy and militant activism all seem natural enough in white neighborhoods, in the white "mainstream" media, among white elected representatives, and between ordinary white people and their self-described spokesmen. The fact that scholars and pundits often expect something different within black and brown communities—and that black and brown people do so as well—demonstrates the deeply ingrained, unconscious white supremacy that all of us, of all colors, possess.

For black, brown, and white civil rights activists, then, class, ideology, strategy, and tactics often mattered more than did appeals to automatic racial solidarity. On the ground, and in different ways, the most militant groups of black and brown civil rights activists demanded not only access but real, tangible power. The struggle was not about abstract rights but the achievement of true political democracy and equal economic opportunity. Only self-determination could accomplish these tasks; political influence that was not independent would only produce tokenism, which was plainly inadequate in their view.

Gradualism likewise sacrificed independence for expediency, as the "Politics of the Present" was no match for the "Politics of the Future" that promised to destroy the entire caste system. To be sure, the devil was often in the details. Activists fiercely debated how far to compromise in order to make gains, just as each voter internally grapples with how much he or she can sacrifice to support a less-than-ideal candidate.

To paraphrase Albert Peña, the activists concluded that they were most successful when they stayed true to their core principles and least effective when they failed to do so. From their vantage point, their decisions were different from those faced by the "Uncle Toms" and *vendidos*, who simply sold out the long-term quest for power for short-term personal gains. The activists' dilemma at every turn centered on how to best retreat from each battle and live on to fight another day. They remained obsessed with gaining autonomy, with winning independent representation for the communities they organized. And they were willing to be unruly, to get out in the streets and demonstrate, to cast aside pluralist political decorum and risk violent reprisals and public criticism to achieve their goals. In Peña's words, they cared more about "justice" than they worried about "order." They believed that their own so-called community leaders, who served as diplomats and wielded influence with white elites, had the exact opposite set of priorities. Often thwarted in their ambitions by *intra*racial opposition, black and brown civil rights activists separately looked for ways to outflank their more conservative antagonists. *Inter*racial coalition building became their primary weapon in common.

Much the same was true for the predominately white labor movement. The Texas AFL-CIO did not become a civil rights organization for altruistic or moral reasons. They did so because of intraracial conflict. The white business elites of Texas were giving it to them on the shop floor and whipping their tails in electoral politics, to use two Lone Star colloquialisms. Labor had little choice but to search for new allies as they attempted to outflank their enemies. Finding ways to collaborate with militant African American and Mexican American activists became the unionists' best path forward. Hank Brown had seen it work in San Antonio, and he brought it to the state federation, transforming the labor movement into a force for multiracial democracy.

African American and Mexican American labor struggles, the sit-ins and Viva Kennedy movements, the creation of PASO and its subsequent splintering, the election of Governor John Connally over Don Yarborough, and finally the Crystal City revolt had all helped to "separate the wheat from the chaff," as *SNAP News* put it. After all the tumult, black, brown, and white activists all clearly understood who among their separate ethnic communities was on their side and who opposed them, as well as whom they could depend upon across racial lines.

Epilogue   411

By the early 1960s, they had developed a working relationship with one another that they called the Democratic Coalition. At its core was a series of basic agreements between its diverse participants on ideology (pro-civil rights), strategy (independent, liberal electoral politics), and tactics (direct action demonstrations and broad-based community organizing). Each leg of the coalition had its own reasons for participating, and the coordinated protests, blockworker program, electoral campaigns, and organizing initiatives served the purposes of each of their separate agendas. While their opponents advocated "voluntary," gradual desegregation and conservative politics, the multiracial liberal alliance demanded integration, in Rev. Black's words, "AS A RIGHT"—along with independent political self-determination for black and brown neighborhoods, equal economic opportunity, improved wages and working conditions, and the ability to freely form unions. They made significant progress toward all of these goals, even as they fell short of their loftiest aspirations—leaving work that remains to be done today.

Future coalition builders would do well to learn from their example. In a society as racially segregated as twenty-first-century America remains, "identity politics," or ethnic-based community organizations, will of necessity remain a centerpiece of civic life. Still, they will continue to face the obstacles produced by the nationalist myths of automatic racial solidarity and the crippling declension narratives that accompany them. Nowhere is this more true than in the ostensibly race-neutral liberal organizations dominated by well-meaning whites. Like the Ralph Yarborough campaigns and the Harris County Democrats of the 1950s or the Texas Liberal Democrats of the later 1960s, these groups claim to speak for "all the people" but fail to do so because of their own unacknowledged, unconscious white supremacy. The dispute in the summer of 2015 between the Black Lives Matter movement and the insurgent presidential campaign of Senator Bernie Sanders of Vermont represents just the latest example of this tension: Sanders and his supporters maintained that fighting economic inequality would lift all boats, but they didn't think to ask the leaders of the new civil rights movement for their input. The black protestors at Sanders's campaign stops and the leading thinkers of Black Lives Matter pointed out that special attention needed to be focused on the ongoing struggle against racism, that getting a better job or reining in Wall Street meant little in communities that have been ravaged by state-sanctioned segregation, police brutality, and mass incarceration—to name just a few of the many issues they are confronting. (Sanders appeared to learn from these confrontations, leading him to roll out a position paper specifically focused on racial justice, but the damage had been done.)

The broad-based organizers of today can do as the "independent" liberals of Texas eventually did: listen to George Sánchez's admonition that "only the *mexicanos* can speak for the *mexicanos*," only the blacks can speak for the blacks, and only white workers can speak for white workers. They must acknowledge that no single group is the "custodian of liberalism," as labor leader Hank Brown put it, and instead acknowledge differences of opinion and perspective and then "put their money where their mouth is."

The 1963 Democratic Coalition's four-legged leadership structure may at first appear antiquated or even tokenistic to present-day observers, but it is clear that it did allow the alliance's four legs to embrace conflict and openly discuss diversity in ways that stymied its predecessors and successors and that would now paralyze most twenty-first-century organizations. It did so by formally recognizing the central importance of black and brown leadership as well as the limits of white paternalism.

Coalition leaders put differences on the table and talked explicitly about race. White liberals and even big labor agreed to make black and brown civil rights the group's highest priority. And they didn't do it for charity but because their own liberation was bound up in the freedom of others.

Finally, the American labor movement could learn a lot from an understudied part of its own history, looking to the innovative strategies that sprang from desperation in one of its relative backwaters. In fact, the situation confronting the Texas AFL-CIO in the 1960s was not unlike the dilemma faced by the larger movement today. Its areas of strength and overall density were rapidly eroding, its political muscle had atrophied, and most of the unorganized workers hailed from cultures they did not understand and labored under industrial relations regimes that were not conducive to organizing. Texas labor responded to these challenges by moving beyond the worksite to engage in broad-based community organizing—in coalition with representatives from the ethnic and occupational groups they hoped to reach. "Operation Bootstrap" and other community union and political education initiatives did not succeed in reversing labor's overall fortunes, but such efforts did make the Texas AFL-CIO relevant to new audiences in the most economically depressed reaches of the state, including the inner cities. Today's American labor movement writ large would do well to respond to its challenges by similarly deemphasizing the old, workplace-based struggle and focusing on building broad coalitions for human rights.

The story of black, brown, and white cooperation and conflict also transforms how we view the individual movements that made up the Democratic Coalition. The postwar black freedom struggle appears much more intimately connected to campaigns for economic opportunity and political power than is commonly assumed. Rather than being scared straight by anti-Communist repression during the early Cold War, activists like G. J. Sutton and Moses and Erma LeRoy redirected their efforts into new channels. In San Antonio,

Sutton developed a militant community group that carried the *SNAP News* to the neighborhood and used it to organize countless ordinary East Side residents for civil rights causes and political action. The LeRoys of Houston helped found the HCCO and served as diplomats that connected the city's civil rights unionists to black businessmen and students as well as white and Mexican American labor, civil rights, and political activists. And the leaders of the Texas NAACP based in Dallas emerged from being the target of a state lawsuit and injunction to rebuild the Texas Council of Voters, which then became the coordinating body for all of the state's liberal black activists. All three cases suggest that electoral politics was not a mere endgame or legacy of the civil rights struggle, or a selling out of the movement's more expansive goals. Rather, just as economic issues were always part and parcel of the movement, so too was political organizing. It was always about power and upward mobility, not just access.

Similarly, the so-called Mexican American Generation of the postwar period—often depicted as assimilationist, conservative, and obsessed with proving their whiteness and distancing themselves from blacks—in fact proved far more variegated. Certainly none of those characterizations applied to Albert Peña, or to the hundreds of labor and liberal activists who perennially reelected him to run PASO. When chided by a local columnist who urged him to hold a meeting of the few people he represented in a phone booth, Peña responded by calling a street-corner mass meeting and protest march. His desire to unite Mexican American voters did not compel him to shy away from militant tactics, and he steadfastly supported building coalitions with African Americans. He wrote a regular column in *SNAP News*, after all! And he was not alone: the professor George Sánchez and labor activists Bob Sanchez, Paul Montemayor, Henry Muñoz, Martin Garcia, Franklin and Pepper Garcia, Pancho Medrano, the leaders of Houston PASO, and others all engaged in multiracial coalitions and direct action protests and offered steadfast support for an expansively defined liberalism and civil rights for all. In fact, Peña and the others often had much in common ideologically with the youthful militants of the Chicano movement, and at times they served as direct mentors to the next cohort of activists. They did all this while facing fierce opposition from more conservative activists their own age, people like Dr. Hector P. Garcia and Ed Idar of the AGIF, who had vastly different ideas about the purpose of PASO, its political endorsements, its involvement in coalitions with labor and blacks, and the meaning of the Mexican American civil rights struggle more generally. Attention to the liberal coalition builders suggests that generational affiliation proved to be a much less important dividing line among *mexicanos* than were differences of ideology, class, and tactics.

Finally, the story of black and brown coalition builders at work indicates that the labor movement was anything but bureaucratic and self-satisfied in the decades after World War II—at least in the South and Southwest. Rather, it was constantly working to organize the unorganized, in both traditional unionization campaigns and in new, unexpected places, namely, the African American and Mexican American civil rights movements. Organizers like Mrs. LeRoy, Pancho Medrano, Franklin Garcia, and even Hank Brown all logged innumerable miles driving around the state as labor ambassadors in the fields of electoral politics and in the black and brown fights for freedom. Even when no unions or unionists were involved, these too were working-class struggles, yet too often they are pigeonholed by "historical gerrymandering" that separates the frequent overlapping of black, brown, and labor organizing in the postwar period.[13] In Texas, labor's unionization and political activities dovetailed so seamlessly with the black and brown freedom struggles that scholars cannot hope to understand any one of the coalition's four legs without also studying the others.

In fact, for many individual organizers, working across racial lines in a variety of labor, civil rights, and political settings at times became second nature, blurring but not erasing the lines between their main "house" and the other parts of the "coalition." Likewise, the separate legs of the Democratic Coalition were never entirely distinct, as many Steering Committee members inhabited more than one of the alliance's four discrete legs. Brought together by a common need for each other and a sense of common purpose, the state's multiracial liberal alliances might not have functioned at all if it were not for the work of these bridge builders, the on-the-ground activists who straddled the coalition's divides. They were the ones who every day sold the idea of "coalitioning" to countless rank-and-file participants who otherwise would not have understood why they should care about the travails of another racial or ethnic group.

Thus it was in these many day-to-day meetings and unrecorded personal conversations that the coalition was built, took shape, and had its most lasting, transformative effects. For example, as the poll tax drive hit its final stretch in January 1964, Erma LeRoy and Latane Lambert left the coalition headquarters in Austin, jumped in one of their cars, and hit the road. The two Project VOTE codirectors were working on a shoestring to continue a hastily organized "subproject" called "Students for Freedom through Voting" that would take the duo to a half-dozen all-black colleges in East and North Texas in less than a week's time. At each stop they held meetings in collaboration with leaders of student governments and other campus organizations, who were asked to turn out crowds for the events. LeRoy and Lambert then addressed the students, urged those that were old enough to pay their poll taxes, and asked all of them to call or write or travel home to get their parents to do the same. Most of the meetings occurred with little advance notice, and turnout was generally light. But the ten, twenty, or fifty students who met them at each school sat down with the two coalition veterans and learned about multiracial organizing for political change. Few of their prior experiences would have exposed them to such ideas—most of them had grown up in all-black neighborhoods, in all-black schools, and set off from and generally hostile toward the white folks who lived in newer houses and used brand-new textbooks in their schools across the tracks. And here come two women, one white, one black, driving in a seven-hundred-mile loop around Deep East Texas and armed only with their own experiences and the idea of "freedom through voting." Both Lambert and LeRoy had been in the trenches since the late 1930s; both had close ties to a wide range of labor, civil rights, and political organizations; both had spouses who joined them in the struggle; and for both, living had become nearly synonymous with community organizing. The students saw firsthand two veterans of the struggle against Jim Crow who had become close friends because of their common activities in organized labor and the Democratic Coalition and their common faith in the capacity of ordinary men and women.[14]

As the 1960s came to a close, students and other young people would launch a new phase of the struggle, building coalitions of radical black and brown organizations both on campuses and in the surrounding communities. The older, veteran labor, civil rights, and political organizers might join them at one or another unremarkable community meeting, and together they would try to figure out how to continue moving forward. On other occasions, the liberals and radicals would clash, each frustrated by the ongoing intransigence of their conservative opponents and the barriers imposed by our culture's unconscious white supremacy.

Democracy remained an elusive goal, but the many activists who built the Democratic Coalition and the thousands they recruited had themselves been transformed. They had reclaimed what theorist Sheldon Wolin calls their "birthright" of "politicalness"—that is, they had overcome a repressive political culture and were now participating fully in public life and working to shape their own destiny. They had raised their voices and won a seat at the table of Texas politics. As Rev. Black had put it at the March on Austin, "The little people of our state have located the center of authority," and they now had the tools to fight back. A half-century later, their story reminds us that the little people can in fact liberate their own minds, come together, and change the world.[15]

Looking Back to the Future

One change wrought by the Democratic Coalition's efforts was the realignment of electoral politics in Texas. Members of the coalition led by Albert Peña again challenged the seating of their conservative antagonists at the Democratic National Convention in Chicago in 1968, and, four years later, Peña joined the McGovern Commission that finally broke down the doors of the party and ensured equal access to all. It took four more years, until 1976, for the liberals to finally take control of the Texas Democratic Party, and by that time it was fast becoming an irrelevant distinction. In 1978, Bill Clements was elected as the state's first Republican governor since Reconstruction. His ascent—along with John Tower's continued reelection to the U.S. Senate and the Republican capture of a bevy of congressional, legislative, and local seats—signaled the turning point in the conservative defection to the GOP that had begun two decades earlier. A handful of conservative Democrats hung on into the 1990s, but the Establishment that had long dominated Texas politics increasingly found its home on the right side of the aisle. Only the single-term administration of liberal governor Ann Richards (1991–95) broke the unbeaten streak of conservatives from both parties. Her defeat at the hands of George W. Bush coincided with the Democratic Party's complete dismantling in the state. Moderate Bob Bullock won reelection as lieutenant governor in 1994 and served one final term in office, but he did so as the last Democrat of any ideological persuasion to hold statewide office. Rick Perry replaced him and loomed large in Texas politics for the next two decades.

The dynamic 2008 Texas two-step primary election and caucus conventions offered a glimmer of hope to the state's Democrats but ultimately failed to reverse the party's declining fortunes. Nearly 3 million Texans participated on the Democratic side of the state's open primary, more than twice the Republican draw. Yet that fall John McCain defeated Barack Obama by nearly twelve percentage points and almost a million votes, defeating the Democratic nominee by a score of roughly 4.5 million to 3.5 million. Four years later the numbers grew even worse for the Democrats.[16]

Still, pundits and prognosticators throughout the state and nation continued to speculate that the Democratic Party would soon return to relevancy. In 2010, to much fanfare, the party nominated the popular but uncharismatic mayor of Houston, Bill White, as its gubernatorial candidate. Linda Chavez-Thompson, a retired leader of the national AFL-CIO from San Antonio, served as his running mate. Yet the campaign crashed when White dodged a visit by President Obama and refused to share contacts and resources with Chavez-Thompson. Both the African American and Mexican American wings of the party's electoral alliance remained on the outside looking in.

A few months after the 2012 elections, Jeremy Bird, one of the leading staffers in President Barack Obama's reelection campaign, announced the creation of "Battleground Texas," a project aimed at rebuilding the moribund party. The initiative captured national headlines, and Bird confidently declared that he was in it for the long haul, that Battleground Texas would enjoy unprecedented financial support from the national party, and that it would build a statewide grassroots organization modeled on the Obama campaign and work for a decade, or two decades, or as long as it took until the Democrats could win. The emergence of Wendy Davis—a state senator whose filibuster against abortion restrictions, Horatio Alger biography, and superstar persona propelled her into the 2014 gubernatorial race—added new urgency, suggesting that Democrats might not need to wait that long after all. A new chairman of the Texas Democratic Party enlarged the staff from four lonely souls to more than forty operatives in the field. Hope reigned supreme, until Davis likewise collapsed after a series of campaign missteps and a failed attempt to distance herself from both the president and her own prochoice record. A dynamic Latina running mate, Leticia Van de Putte, promised to wake up what pundits continued to call the state's "sleeping giant" of *mexicanos*, but in the end, they did not turn out in high enough numbers to carry the day.

The history of the Democratic Coalition of the 1960s offers a few final insights into these more immediate concerns. First, it is clear that Davis's attempt to capture a moderate, white, suburban vote reflected a conventional wisdom that is in fact a political fantasy. The suburbs have long been fertile ground for reactionary forces, from Jack Cox's "Freedom in Action" movement to today's Tea Party. No amount of moderation will change that. Instead, present-day politicians should follow the formula laid out by the Democratic Coalition of the 1960s: the more explicitly liberal, the more committed the organization is to civil rights, the more successful it will become. No Democrats can win in Texas unless they turn out the legions of African Americans and young people who carried Obama to victory in the 2008 caucuses, nor can they win without a massive operation among Latinos in the style that carried Clinton to victory in the 2008 primary election. They likewise need the groundwork of liberal women of all races who value reproductive justice and the gay, lesbian, bisexual, and transgender Texans who have come out of the shadows since the 1960s and now enjoy the ability to marry but not the right to equal employment. They need to capture the growing number of youthful liberals and libertarians who support gay rights, oppose the War on Drugs, demand access to college and affordable housing, and above all want a decent job and standard of living in an economy that offers none of the advantages that their parents and grandparents possessed. And the Democrats must take seriously the calls of organized labor for workplace safety, equal treatment, and collective bargaining for all. The Texas AFL-CIO has long been the finger in the dike, the one organized force stopping the legislature from dismantling all public services. It is past time for Democratic leaders in Texas to embrace labor as a movement for justice for all people instead of taking it for granted while privately dismissing it as a special interest group.

Most important, the party should measure its success by its ability to organize and energize its many grassroots bases, and it should plan its campaigns accordingly. The Democratic Coalition of the 1960s transformed the Texas electorate and state politics not because of flashy messaging but because it created an "army" of blockworkers that reached deep into the inner cities and far into their rural hinterlands. It prioritized the leadership and agenda of its nonwhite members, and it did not shy away from embracing its most radical (for the time) activists. B. T. Bonner, G. J. Sutton, Moses LeRoy, and other veterans of illegal sit-in demonstrations formed the core of the coalition, alongside Albert Peña and the other architects of the Crystal City revolt. These protest movements may appear ordinary or unremarkable to present-day eyes, but at the time they were beyond the pale of respectable politics. The most militant black and brown activists deployed tactics that drew opposition from race leaders as well as white conservative opponents. They demanded immediate justice and connected direct action to the ballot box, adding urgency and moral imperative to the age-old liberal quest of expanding the franchise. And it worked.

Progressive Democrats today must similarly embrace the confrontational, impatient, and morally driven social movements of our own time. Born in the outcry surrounding the 2012 killing of Trayvon Martin and christened in the midst of the 2014 uprising in Ferguson, Missouri, the Black Lives Matter movement has captured the nation's attention and refocused the political class on the continuing significance of race and racial inequality. It has drawn on old protest traditions, created new ones, and used social media to unmask the police brutality that terrorizes urban America. It has drawn new attention to the failed War on Drugs and breathed new life into a broad-based campaign against mass incarceration. The Black Lives Matter movement has challenged even liberal whites to better understand and prioritize the problems facing African Americans and other people of color, and it now stands poised to play a major role in formal electoral politics as well.

Likewise, the struggle for immigrant rights has galvanized the nation's Latinos and has served as a "wedge issue" in reverse, separating—perhaps permanently—all but the most conservative Latinos from the nation's Republican Party. In 2006, "mega-marches" of hundreds of thousands of protestors spread across the country, led by a demonstration of as many as a half-million people in historically conservative Dallas. The momentum of the marches helped the Democratic Party sweep control of local politics, and a multiracial coalition that also includes organized labor now dominates that city. President Obama has responded to constant protests by taking executive action to help previously undocumented immigrants, even as his administration has detained and deported record numbers of their friends and relatives. Meanwhile, Republican primary elections have compelled candidates to take ever-more extreme positions against immigrants, many of which bleed into explicit xenophobia or anti-Mexican racism. The insurgent campaign of businessman Donald Trump in the Republican presidential contest added new fuel to the fire and, in the process, helped the immigrant rights movement find new footing in 2016.

Remarkably, leaders of the Democratic Party in the state and the nation have remained remarkably quiet about both struggles, and few politicians have embraced them as the engines that could drive sweeping change. In fact, Democratic Party leaders in Texas decided that, beginning in 2016, the party would no longer hold caucus conventions on the evening of the primary election, terminating the second half of the Texas two-step that had long been the driving force behind grassroots activism at the precinct level. They have failed to recruit leading African American politicians to run for statewide office, a necessary step for motivating the party's loyal black base. They have shunned outsiders with bold ideas that promised to expand their reach to new voters, most recently when the state party leadership opposed comedian Kinky Friedman's 2014 primary campaign for agriculture commissioner due to his support for the legalization of marijuana. However kooky he might be, Friedman had won nearly 12.5 percent of the vote as an independent candidate for governor in 2006, and his ongoing appeal to young people was undeniable. The state party also abandoned the 2014 race for U.S. Senate, but it did so only after assuring the defeat in the Democratic primary *runoff* of a wing nut who promised to impeach Obama once in office. Instead of reaching outward, Texas Democrats appear to be focusing their efforts narrowly on expanding the Latino vote, but so far their efforts have borne little fruit. More important, they have done so while seemingly neglecting the remaining legs of the old liberal coalition first assembled by Maury Maverick.

In this context, it is nearly impossible to imagine that the current party will raise an "army" of volunteers capable of tying formal politics to broader social movements and of physically bringing its message down to the city blocks. It is hard to conceive of the fluorescence of a new version of the Democratic Coalition or even the HCD—of an intermediate, diverse party organization forged at the grassroots. And it is all but unthinkable that the party will attach itself to the larger crusades for freedom and full citizenship being waged among African Americans, Mexican Americans, *mexicano* immigrants, LGBT communities, and other marginalized groups. Yet history suggests that this should be the exact mission of Democratic and progressive activists of all colors. They must reconnect elections to the daily lives of ordinary people by linking the exercise of the vote to the uncompromising, urgent, and morally driven insurgent civil rights movements of the twenty-first century. Only then will the quest for a truly democratic Texas be complete. Then, and only then, will we turn Texas blue.

Acknowledgments

Thank you—I can't say it enough. It may seem trite, but there is no way this book would have become a reality without the help, support, knowledge, and love of so many of my favorite people as well as the many communities and institutions that I have called home. My first and greatest debt goes to my wife, Courtney Wait, to whom this book is dedicated, and without whose love and companionship I never would have reached the finish line. Courtney taught me how to love and how to listen, how to be quiet and diplomatic when I wanted to scream and burn things, and how to see the best in all people, even my enemies. These traits have made me a better human, husband, and father, and also a better researcher: without them, I could not have learned from the many oral history interviewees who helped me make sense of the many, messy written sources strewn throughout this book. Courtney challenges me every day and makes sure that I live up to my own best self. I love you more than I could ever express.

I am likewise indebted to all of my family. Elijah and Rayna have brought immeasurable joy to my life and have served as welcome distractions to getting my work done. I hope that this book contributes to making their world a more humane and caring one than the place I describe in this text. Perhaps they will hand down some of its lessons to their own children. Their doing so would be appropriate, since this book began with the democratic inheritance bestowed upon me by my own parents. My father Nicholas Krochmal's folks, who were Yiddish Jews, raised him in the radical interracial milieu of the civil rights unionist movement of the mid-twentieth century. I grew up with vague but powerful stories about larger-than-life figures like Paul Robeson and Golda Meir visiting my dad's boyhood home, along with other tales about my grandparents' left-wing Zionism. My mom, Leslie Doukas, regaled me with stories of the New Left in which she participated, opened my eyes to its counterculture, explained the contradictions of her own father's Greek immigrant heritage and politics, took me outside into the high desert around our many houses, imbibed me with a healthy dose of working-class resentment toward my social betters, and taught me to truly love all human beings. Thanks to both of you. Thanks also to their wonderful spouses, the inimitable and big hearted Steve Howe and the passionate and patient Connie Fox, and to my mom's brilliant sisters, Dimitra Doukas and Andrea Doukas, both of whom have believed in my work since I could barely walk and have offered insightful spiritual comments all along the way. Huge thanks to my big sister Shana Naomi Krochmal, a beautiful writer, mostly willing editor, great listener, loving friend, and perfect interlocutor and companion as we have both grown in our careers as activists and intellectuals. I'm so glad that I now share you with Jessica Maxwell, a wonderful second sister who also keeps me honest. For more than a decade, Courtney's Wait family has adopted me as one of their own, and I love them all deeply for it: Tom, Tricia, Micah, Rebecca, Allie, Scott (Cassel), and the next generation—thanks for putting up with me running away from family vacations to do one more interview, visit one more archive, or edit one more chapter.

My intellectual debts are many but can be traced to a common source. A Firefox teacher for many years, my mom first introduced me to storytelling and oral history and laid the kernel of my belief that educational processes and quotidian grassroots organizing represent the core foundations of democracy, and of building effective social movements to get there. The very first book I read in the Oakes College core course at the University of California, Santa Cruz, introduced me to Myles Horton and the Highlander Folk School's model of combining experiential education, folk traditions, and on-the-ground social change. The faculty and students of the Department of Community Studies at UCSC helped me take that knowledge and run with it, a journey that took me to the banana fields of Ecuador and into the U.S. labor movement. Dana Frank taught me the ins and outs of labor history and helped me to imagine the contours of a broader working-class struggle, while Scott Morgensen taught me how to do fieldwork and avoid colonizing my subjects. I also grew alongside and in conversation with my fellow students and friends in community studies, especially Jeremy Fredericksen and Anne Shaver. And thanks especially to Paul Ortiz, who introduced me to oral history and civil rights history via the works of Larry Goodwyn, Charles Payne, Bill Chafe, and Bob Korstad—all brilliant studies that detail the relationship building, teaching, and nuts-and-bolts processes at the center of movement building as well as the critical significance of race.

Paul also steered me to attend graduate school at Duke University, where I met, befriended, and learned from these larger-than-life thinkers and activists. Paul, thank you for the many years of friendship and mentoring and for putting me on this path. Throughout my time at Duke and beyond, Bill Chafe has been an exemplary advisor and close friend, serving as my loudest cheerleader, promoting my work to the rock stars of the profession, and letting me roam as needed while still being there to hold my hand when I needed him to guide me through crises in the archive, the job market, finding a publisher, and building new programs and institutions for the long haul. Thanks, Bill, for everything. Bob Korstad has also helped me grow in countless ways and has always been there to encourage me, even when I've missed the mark. Sally Deutsch served as an unofficial second advisor, helping me learn to articulate my ill-formed arguments, teaching me how to write a decent literature review, and showing me how to respond to reviewers. Nancy MacLean and Tim Tyson both joined my committee in my final years and contributed far more to my development than they should have in such a short time. Eduardo Bonilla-Silva and Zaragoza Vargas have also offered support, friendship, and critical advice. And the late Larry Goodwyn offered deep emotional support, sage advice, and pointed criticism but refused to steer my research even after he emerged as a subject in it. I thank him and Nell for welcoming me into their home and their family and for sharing their history with me. My entire experience at Duke owed much to my fellow students there and at the school-which-shall-not-be-named down Tobacco Road. Orion Teal, Anne-Marie Angelo, Gordon Mantler, Phil Rubio, Jacob Remes, Katharine French-Fuller, Liz Shesko, Mitch Fraas, Julia Gaffield, Kelly Kennington, Reena Goldthree, Eric Weber, Eric Brandom, Paige Welch, Mike Stauch, Karlyn Forner, Jon Free, Ryan Poe, Kerry Taylor, David Cline, Seth Kotch, Josh Davis, Catherine Conner, Joey Fink, Jessie Wilkerson, and surely others who I've forgotten—thanks to all of you for your friendship, challenging dialogue, and support. Other faculty in the Triangle area also contributed to my development. Thanks to Charlie Thompson and the folks at the Center for Documentary Studies, Jacquelyn Dowd Hall and everyone at the Southern Oral History Program, David Zonderman, Jim Crisp, Kat Charron, Blair Kelley, Felicia Kornbluh, and John Herd Thompson. And thanks also to the many Triangle alumni who helped me along the way, including Wesley Hogan, Alex Byrd, Mary Ellen Curtin, Annie Valk, Leslie Brown, Christina Greene, Hasan Kwame Jeffries, Will Jones, Jeff Cowie, Dave Anderson, and the rest of the Duke/UNC mafia. Thanks also to our many close friends in Durham who made life there so good, especially Matt Sears and Ellen Beckman, Holly Jordan, and the many great teachers of Hillside High School.

The actual research for this book would not have been possible without the help of many people and institutions. George Green has been guiding me through the Texas Labor Archives for nearly a decade. This book would not be possible without the papers and interviews he collected nor his steady encouragement. José Angel Gutiérrez also helped me get started by introducing me to a few under-the-radar activists in San Antonio who in turn taught me all about that city's long tradition of multiracial coalitions. Gene Lantz and Becky Moeller have opened many doors for me in the labor movement, as did the late Arnold Flores. Maria Jimenez and Bob Hall each taught me volumes about coalition building in Houston. Thanks to all of you for your guidance. Thanks also to the many archivists and librarians who have helped me find materials, retrieved and held boxes for me, and copied countless pages of manuscripts in the days before digital photography. Thanks especially to the entire staff of the Texas Labor Archives at UT-Arlington, most of whom I now know on a first-name basis. Their present and former ranks include Brenda McClurkin, Cathy Spitzenberger, Ben Huseman, Lea Wooster, Beverly Carver, Ann Hodges, and Claire Galloway Jenkins. Thanks also to the skilled photography curators, librarians, and archivists who helped me track down and secure rights for the images that appear in the text, especially Tom Shelton of the University of Texas, San Antonio; Tim Ronk of the Houston Metropolitan Research Center; Nicole Davis of the Austin History Center; and, again, Cathy Spitzenberger. Thanks also to Robyn Reid and the Texas Christian University Library for buying me innumerable books, rare microfilm, and costly databases. Thanks to my research assistants at TCU: Beth Hessel, Mike Green, and Katherine Bynum. And thanks to the many people who opened their homes to me as I traveled to archives and interviews, especially Tom and Tricia Wait, Wade and Sharon Goodwyn, Danielle McGuire and family, and Brian Dahlk.

Thanks to the many institutions that have provided funding for this research. A departmental fellowship from the Duke History Department and the Center for Documentary Studies paid my way through graduate school. I also received the Anne Firor Scott Prize and two Duke Graduate School Summer Fellowships. I was also honored to win the Walter Rundell Prize of the Western History Association. The TCU Department of History and the AddRan College of Liberal Arts have given me a place to continue writing and provided immeasurable support since I arrived there in 2011. Thanks to Dean Andy Schoolmaster and my wonderful department chairs, Peter Worthing and Jodi Campbell. I also appreciate the support of the university's Research and Creative Activities Fund and the Junior Faculty Summer Research Program.

Thanks especially to The Summerlee Foundation of Dallas and the Clements Center for Southwest Studies at Southern Methodist University, which combined to give me a yearlong fellowship to focus on the book. The Clements Center proved to be even better than advertised, with wonderful colleagues, great support, and endless opportunities for intellectual exchange. Thanks so much to Andy Graybill, Sherrie Smith, Ruth Ann Elmore, and their expat colleague, Ben Johnson. Thanks also to my fellow fellows, Ben Francis-Fallon, Julie Reed, Neel Baumgardner, and Bill DeBuys. They all heard way more about this work than they bargained for, and they all joined the center's invaluable workshop on my manuscript. Thanks especially to Tom Sugrue and George J. Sanchez, who served as external reviewers, and to Neil Foley and John Chavez of SMU who also joined the fray and provided a warm welcome throughout my time in Dallas. Thanks also to the former fellows who have welcomed me into their ranks and have provided good counsel over the years, including Monica Perales, John Weber, Andrew Torget, and Rob Chase.

Working at TCU since 2011 has allowed me to finish this book while joining a new community of scholars and friends. Along with the people mentioned above, I've gained great wisdom, solace, and camaraderie from Becca Sharpless, Gene Smith, Todd Kerstetter, Alan Gallay, Bill Meier, Alex Hidalgo, Sean Crotty, David Colón, Sarah Robbins, Melanie Harris, Theresa Gaul, Steve Sloan, Ryan Schmitz, Jeff Ferrell, Carol Thompson, Emily Farris, and many other colleagues. I met TCU's Gregg Cantrell and UT-Arlington's Stephanie Cole early in the research process, and they have both been great friends and mentors for years and have introduced me to colleagues throughout the region via their networks and the Dallas Area Social History (DASH) working group. I also want to thank my collaborators on the TCU Civil Rights Bus Tour: Mel Gruver, Rosangela Boyd, April Brown, Darron Turner, Cynthia Goodloe-Palmer, Keith McMillan, Bill Chandler, the late Margaret Block, Hollis Watkins, Charles McLaurin, the staff of AFSCME Local 1733, Kwame Leo Lillard, and others who have contributed to this amazing program that has taught me so much. Thanks additionally to my colleagues in the *Civil Rights in Black and Brown Oral History Project*: Todd Moye, Marvin Dulaney, Maggie Rivas-Rodriguez, Jacob Brown, Mary Saffell, June Koelker, Katherine Bynum, and our many amazing graduate student research assistants and undergraduate work-studies.

Thanks also to the community of scholars around the state and nation who have contributed to this book or encouraged my scholarly development in some way: Carlos Blanton, Emilio Zamora, Beto Calderón, Chandler Davidson, Mike Botson, Tatcho Mindiola, Merline Pitre, Melissa Hield, Richard Croxdale, Glenn Scott, Joseph Abel, LaGuana Gray, Emilye Crosby, Alice Kessler-Harris, Mike Honey, Jim Green, Jim Gregory, Shel Stromquist, Ken Fones-Wolf, Leon Fink, Quintard Taylor, John Boles, Randal Hall, David Brundage, Pedro Castillo, Lorena Oropeza, Brian Behnken, Lauren Araiza, Mark Brilliant, Tom Guglielmo, Oliver Rosales, Laurie Greene, Cindy Hahamovich, Vicki Ruiz, Michael Ezra, Clayborne Carson, Clarence Lang, Michael Innis-Jimenez, Mario T. Garcia, Davíd Montejano, Steve Pitti, Erik Gellman, Jarod Roll, the late Bob Zieger, and many, many more.

Huge thanks to my editor, Brandon Proia, who read innumerable drafts of this beast with a sharp eye and endless patience and encouragement, and to my series editors, especially Heather Ann Thompson, who believed in this project before I even knew what it would become. And thanks to everyone at UNC Press who have brought this project to fruition. Thanks also to Margaretta Yarborough, who proofread the text, and to Pamela Gray, who assembled the index.

Finally, thanks to the many civil rights, labor, and political activists and movement scholars who shared their stories with me in formal oral history interviews and casual conversations, in lectures and panels on the Civil Rights Bus Tour, or over meals and drinks or even beneath picket signs. I have gained so much from your examples and hope that I have done your lives some justice in return. Perhaps this book will allow more people to understand the sacrifices you have made, the lessons you've learned, and the path you've cleared for us to move forward. Thank you.

And thanks one more time to Courtney, just because.

Notes

Abbreviations Used in Notes

Archives

BCAH	Briscoe Center for American History, University of Texas, Austin
BLAC	Benson Latin American Collection, University of Texas, Austin
COPE	Committee on Political Education, Texas AFL-CIO Papers
HCM	*Houston Chronicle* Morgue
HMRC	Houston Metropolitan Research Center, Houston Public Library
MAAC	Mexican American Affairs Committee, Texas AFL-CIO Papers
SABHC	San Antonio Black History Collection, UTSA
SAPL-VF	San Antonio Public Library Vertical Files
TAMUCC	Texas A&M University, Corpus Christi Archives
TLA-UTA	Texas Labor Archives, Special Collections, University of Texas, Arlington
TSU	Texas Southern University Archives, Houston
TV-UTA	Tejano Voices Collection, University of Texas, Arlington
UTSA	Special Collections, University of Texas, San Antonio
WRC	Woodson Research Center, Fondren Library, Rice University, Houston

Newspapers

AA	*Austin American*
AAS	*Austin American-Statesman*
AS	*Austin Statesman*
CCC	*Corpus Christi Caller*
CCCT	*Corpus Christi Caller-Times*
CCT	*Corpus Christi Times*
DE	*Dallas Express*
DMN	*Dallas Morning News*
DTH	*Dallas Times Herald*
FT	*Forward Times* (Houston)
FWST	*Fort Worth Star-Telegram*
HC	*Houston Chronicle*
HI	*Houston Informer*
HP	*Houston Post*
SAE	*San Antonio Express*
SAEN	*San Antonio Express-News*
SAL	*San Antonio Light*

SAN   San Antonio News
SAR   San Antonio Register
SNAP   SNAP News
TO   Texas Observer

Prologue

1. Ronnie Dugger, "The Austin March," *TO*, September 6, 1963, 14–16 (all quotations except "Kennedy *sí*"); "Negro Leader Calls March Anti-Connally Political Rally," *Galveston News*, August 30, 1963, 11 (remaining quotation); Jon Ford, "Texas Marchers Vow to Battle Gov. Connally," *SAE*, August 29, 1963, 1, 10-A; "Negroes Single Out Connally as Target," *DMN*, August 29, 1963, 11; "March Takes on Political Tone," *CCT*, August 29, 1963, 4; "Statement of Commissioner Albert A. Pena, Jr., As Chairman of Bexar County Democratic Coalition and State Chairman on Civil Rights March," Houston, August 25, 1963, Peña Papers, MS 37, Box 22, Folder 8, UTSA.

2. Mexican-origin people in the United States have defied easy categorization by scholars. Throughout this book, I use "Mexican American" to refer to the diverse cohort of U.S. citizen activists of Mexican extraction who were involved in public life between roughly 1930 and the mid-1960s (and were first identified by historian Mario T. Garcia, although I have reservations about the rigidity and lack of heterogeneity implied by the generational approach). The term is intended to connote the mobilization of a collective ethnic or racial identity on the part of self-identified activists. I typically use the Spanish *mexicano* and *mexicanos* to describe ordinary working people of Mexican origin, including both U.S. citizens and immigrants from Mexico living in the United States. I also use *mexicana* and *mexicanas* to refer specifically to Mexican-origin women in the United States, including both U.S. citizens and noncitizens. I do not capitalize these terms in deference to the Spanish convention. At times, I use the Spanish terms interchangeably for Mexican American in order to avoid repetition or improve readability, or I use the historic terms that are embedded in particular sources or texts. I use "Chicano" and "Chicana" sparingly in reference to the fields of Chicano/a history and Chicano/a studies, the self-styled "Chicano Movement" (there was no "a" in its early years), or in accordance with the language of primary sources. I use "Latino" and "Latinos" only in the present-day context, reflecting popular nomenclature (and leaving out "a" and "as" for readability, while recognizing the erasure of women in the catch-all term). I do not use "Hispanic." I use "Tejano" only to refer to the *mexicano* inhabitants of the border region who preceded the influx of immigrants fleeing the Mexican Revolution beginning in 1910. On the Mexican American Generation, see Mario T. Garcia, *Mexican Americans: Leadership, Ideology, & Identity, 1930–1960*. For my (overly caustic) critique of the generational model, see Krochmal, "Chicano Labor and Multiracial Politics in Post–World War II Texas," 133–76.

The naming of race or ethnicity is always risky business, but my slippage here is self-conscious and reflects and is consistent with the ways that activists themselves spoke about their ancestry: in mixed-company conversations taking place in English, the activists would call themselves "Latin," "Latin American," "Spanish," "Spanish-surnamed" or "Mexican American," but in private company they would refer to themselves as "Mexican Americans" or simply *mexicanos*. I also use "brown" as shorthand for the same group of Mexican American activists and ordinary *mexicano* people. I try to be clear when

I am discussing immigrants from Mexico who are not U.S. citizens, though they play a relatively minor role in the story. I call Americans of European descent "white" and Americans of African descent either "African American" or "black." In all cases, I recognize that the three racial groups are socially and historically constructed rather than solely reflecting biological traits. If an actor is referred to as "black," "brown," or "white" in the text, it is because that is the box in which they would have been perceived in twentieth-century Texas.

Finally, I use "race" and "ethnicity" and "racial" and "ethnic" more or less interchangeably throughout the text. I understand both to be socially and historically constructed categories, though "ethnic" and "ethnicity" do imply some ties to national or tribal origins. Despite internal differences in each group, African Americans, Mexican Americans, and whites were all constructed as distinct racial groups in twentieth-century Texas, and all were also understood to be bound by ties of similar ethnicity as well.

3. On the two-step, see for example, Brandi Grissom and Reeve Hamilton, "Democrats Keep Controversial 'Texas Two-Step,'" *Texas Tribune*, June 27, 2010, accessed September 29, 2015, http://www.texastribune.org/2010/06/27/democrats-keep-controversial-texas-two-step. For election results, see Office of the Secretary of State, "1992–Current Election History" (State of Texas), accessed September 27, 2015, http://elections.sos.state.tx.us/index.htm.

4. On Clinton's superior performance among Latinos and her work for McGovern in Texas, see Minushkin and Lopez, "The Hispanic Vote in the 2008 Democratic Presidential Primaries"; Clinton, *Living History*, 58–60. These observations were also frequent among Mexican American informants in my oral history interviews. See, for example, author's interviews with Arnold Flores, San Antonio, October 18, 2008; September 1 and 9, 2009; and March 11, 2010.

5. Among the widespread coverage of these themes, see "Texas 2020"; Edsall, "Targeting Texas" ; Parker, "Getting Texas to Go Democratic Won't Be Easy"; Fernandez, "Texas Democrats Ponder How They Will Ever Win"; Cohn, "These Eight Charts Explain Why 'Blue Texas' Won't Happen"; Theo Anderson, "Texas: The Blue Frontier"; MacLaggan, "Report: Texas Lags in Hispanic Voter Turnout." For statistical conclusions, including the 71 percent figure, see Lopez and Taylor, "Latino Voters in the 2012 Election."

6. Author's interview with Omowale Luthuli.

7. This perspective was first expounded in Dittmer, *Local People*; Payne, *I've Got the Light of Freedom*; Chafe, *Civilities and Civil Rights*. For a recent anthology that attempts to synthesize work to date and advance this approach, see Crosby, *Civil Rights History from the Ground Up*.

8. For exemplary local studies of the Chicano/a movement, see Montejano, *Quixote's Soldiers*; Chávez, *"¡Mi Raza Primero!" (My People First!)*. For overviews that include earlier struggles, see, among many others, Montejano, *Anglos and Mexicans in the Making of Texas, 1836–1986*; Ruíz, *From Out of the Shadows*. For a superb revisionist account of the mythic United Farm Workers and its charismatic leader, César Chávez, see Bardacke, *Trampling Out the Vintage*.

9. Definitive works on organized labor in the 1930s and 1940s include Cohen, *Making a New Deal*; Lichtenstein, *Labor's War at Home*.

10. For one sympathetic account of big labor's politics in the postwar period, see Boyle, *The UAW and the Heyday of American Liberalism, 1945–1968*.

11. See, most important, Behnken, *Fighting Their Own Battles*. Other notable works on black-brown relations include Vaca, *The Presumed Alliance*; Pulido, *Black, Brown, Yellow, and Left*; Brilliant, *The Color of America Has Changed*; Foley, *Quest for Equality*; Behnken, *The Struggle in Black and Brown*; Bernstein, *Bridges of Reform*; Mantler, *Power to the Poor*; Araiza, *To March for Others*; Opie, *Upsetting the Apple Cart*; Lee, *Building a Latino Civil Rights Movement*; John D. Márquez, *Black-Brown Solidarity*.

12. Jacquelyn Dowd Hall, "The Long Civil Rights Movement"; Dittmer, *Local People*. Recent works that make similar arguments on the importance of economic issues in the movement include Jones, *The March on Washington*; Honey, *Going Down Jericho Road*; Lang, *Grassroots at the Gateway*.

13. Garcia, *Mexican Americans*; Foley, "Becoming Hispanic"; Foley, "Partly Colored or Other White?" For a critical response, see Blanton, "George I. Sánchez, Ideology, and Whiteness in the Making of the Mexican American Civil Rights Movement, 1930–1960"; Blanton, "The Citizenship Sacrifice." More nuanced treatments of Mexican Americans' legal strategies include Ignacio M. García, *White but Not Equal*; Gross, *What Blood Won't Tell*; Guglielmo, "Fighting for Caucasian Rights"; Wilson, "Brown over 'Other White'"; Lisa Y. Ramos, "A Class Apart."

14. Lichtenstein, *Labor's War at Home*; Korstad and Lichtenstein, "Opportunities Found and Lost"; Lichtenstein, *State of the Union*; Lipsitz, *Rainbow at Midnight*. Other works that indicate ongoing militancy within the postwar labor movement include Fones-Wolf, *Selling Free Enterprise*; Boyle, *The UAW and the Heyday of American Liberalism, 1945–1968*.

15. Behnken, *Fighting Their Own Battles*.

16. On Reconstruction in Texas, see Moneyhon, *Texas after the Civil War*; Campbell, *Grass-Roots Reconstruction in Texas, 1865–1880*; Pitre, *Through Many Dangers, Toils and Snares*; Crouch, *The Dance of Freedom*. On Reconstruction generally, see Eric Foner, *Reconstruction: America's Unfinished Revolution, 1863–1877*; W. E. B. Du Bois, *Black Reconstruction in America*. The classic account of the Farmers' Alliance and People's Party in Texas and the nation is Goodwyn, *The Populist Moment*. More recent histories include Postel, *The Populist Vision*; and Cantrell, "'A Host of Sturdy Patriots': The Texas Populists."

17. James R. Green, *Grass-Roots Socialism*; Johnson, *Revolution in Texas*; Zamora, *The World of the Mexican Worker in Texas*. For a brief overview, see Buckingham, "The Texas Socialist Party."

18. Green and Botson, "Looking for Lefty: Liberal/Left Activism and Texas Labor, 1920s–1960s."

19. Hine, *Black Victory: The Rise and Fall of the White Primary in Texas*.

20. Alwyn Barr, *Black Texans*, 143–56. For great works on Jim Crow beyond Texas, see Chafe, Gavins, and Korstad, *Remembering Jim Crow*; Ortiz, *Emancipation Betrayed*; Brown, *Upbuilding Black Durham*; Kelley, *Right to Ride*.

21. The best overview of race and labor in South Texas history can be found in Montejano, *Anglos and Mexicans in the Making of Texas, 1836–1986*. See also Zamora, *The World of the Mexican Worker in Texas*; Vargas, *Labor Rights Are Civil Rights*.

Chapter 1

1. George Lambert, interview by George N. Green, September 9, 1971 (part 1), and February 6, 1972 (part 2), Dallas, Texas, TLA-UTA, OH19 (hereafter George Lambert

interview), part 1, 1–5; "Longtime Labor Leader George Lambert Dies," *Dallas Craftsman* 61, no. 12, August 23, 1974, 1, in George and Latane Lambert Papers, TLA-UTA (hereafter Lambert Papers), AR127, Box 4, Folder 6.

2. George Lambert interview, part 1, 5–6. On the textile strike, see Jacquelyn Dowd Hall et al., *Like a Family*.

3. George Lambert interview, part 1, 8–9. The phrase "mountain socialists" belongs to Myles Horton. See Dickinson, *Rural Life and Culture in the Upper Cumberland*, chap. 12, quotation on 216, Lambert's name appears on 224. See also Vial, "Kate Bradford Stockton."

4. George Lambert interview, part 1, 10–12.

5. George Lambert interview, part 1, 13–14, 22. On the Atlanta strike, see Fine, *Sit-Down: The General Motors Strike of 1936–1937*, 134–36.

6. George Lambert interview, part 2, 1–6 (quotation on 2); Henry M. Rabun and John McCully, "A Grim Reminder of the Terror of the Trembling Thirties: A Historic Decision—The Dallas Ford Case," *UAW Citizen* (Dallas County), Special Labor Day Edition, 1960 (hereafter, "The Dallas Ford Case"), in Texas AFL-CIO Miscellany Collection, AR413, Box 1, Folder 14, TLA-UTA, 7; George Lambert, "Dallas Tries Terror," *Nation*, October 9, 1937, 376–78. Another account of the beatings, unionization effort, and fallout can be found in George N. Green, "Discord in Dallas: Auto Workers, City Fathers, and the Ford Motor Company, 1937–1941." The article was recently reprinted as chapter 12 of the excellent anthology, *Texas Labor History*, ed. Bruce A. Glasrud and James C. Maroney.

7. George Lambert interview, part 2, 1–14; "The Dallas Ford Case."

8. "The Dallas Ford Case," 4–5, uses the terms "outside" and "inside." George Lambert interview, part 2, 11–12.

9. Quoted in Philip Sheldon Foner, *History of the Labor Movement in the United States*, 50.

10. George Lambert interview, part 2, 8; Lambert, "Dallas Tries Terror," 377.

11. Hield, "'Union-Minded': Women in the Texas ILGWU, 1933–50," 64–65; Scott and Flores, *Talkin' Union*.

12. Lambert, "Dallas Tries Terror," 376.

13. George Lambert interview, part 2, 7; "The Dallas Ford Case," 6; Lambert, "Dallas Tries Terror," 377.

14. "The Dallas Ford Case," 8, cites the seventy-eight-page NLRB decision, published in vol. 26 of "Decisions and Orders of the National Labor Relations Board." For more information, see the Ford Motor Company, Dallas, Texas Collection, AR89, TLA-UTA.

15. On both pieces of New Deal labor legislation, see Lichtenstein, *State of the Union*, 20, 25, 36–38, 110–12.

16. George Lambert interview, part 1, 2.

17. George Lambert interview, part 2, 10–11, 15; Polakoff, "The Development of the Texas State C.I.O. Council," 8, note 4; Zieger, *The CIO, 1935–1955*.

18. The next several paragraphs draw upon the following sources: Vargas, "Tejana Radical: Emma Tenayuca"; Vargas, *Labor Rights Are Civil Rights*, chap. 3; Filewood, "Tejano Revolt: The Significance of the 1938 Pecan Shellers Strike"; Blackwelder, *Women of the Depression*, chap. 8; Gower, "Unintended Consequences: The San Antonio Pecan Shellers Strike of 1938"; Shapiro, "The Pecan Shellers of San Antonio, Texas"; Scott and Flores, *Talkin' Union*; Croxdale, "Pecan-Shellers' Strike."

19. Vargas, "Tejana Radical," 559–67 (quote on 567).
20. George Lambert interview, part 2, 24–25.
21. Ibid., 25.
22. "San Antonio: The Cradle and the Coffin of Texas Liberty" (Austin: Texas Civil Liberties Union, 1938), pamphlet, Texas AFL-CIO Miscellany Collection, AR413, Box 1, Folder 16, TLA-UTA, 11 (all quotations).
23. Ibid.
24. "Pecan Plant Workers Strike," *SAL*, 31 January 1938. This article and more than a dozen additional documents are collected online in Dublin, DelValle, and Perez, "How Did Mexican Working Women Assert Their Labor and Constitutional Rights?"
25. Vargas, "Tejana Radical," 567, 573.
26. George Lambert interview, part 2, 19–24 (quotation on 24); Filewood, "Tejano Revolt," 95. See also Alberta Snid, interview by Glenn Scott and María Flores, 1979, [probably in San Antonio], OH 116N, TLA-UTA (hereafter Snid interview), 15.
27. Vargas, "Tejana Radical," 573; Filewood, "Tejano Revolt"; George Lambert interview, part 2, 29; George Lambert, "The Jersey City of the South," unpublished manuscript submitted to the *Nation*, July 4, 1938, in Lambert Papers, AR127-16-10, 4.
28. Quoted in Selden C. Menefee and Oric C. Cassmore, *The Pecan Shellers of San Antonio: The Problem of Underpaid and Unemployed Mexican Labor* (Washington, D.C.: WPA/GPO, 1940), 16–19, in Dublin, DelValle, and Perez, "How Did Mexican Working Women Assert Their Labor and Constitutional Rights?"
29. See, for example, *SAE*, February 26, 1938.
30. "Reclaman la Restitucion de los Salarios de 6 y 7 Cents. por Libra de Nuez Limpiada," *La Prensa*, February 1938, p. 1, quoted in Filewood, "Tejano Revolt," 100.
31. George Lambert interview, part 2, 15–19 (quotation on 19).
32. George Lambert interview, part 2, 23.
33. Snid interview, 1–8.
34. Snid interview, 3, 9–11, 14–16, 19–20.
35. Snid interview, 23–24.
36. "Opposition to Henderson Leadership in S.A. Pecan Strike Gains Momentum," *SAL*, February 13, 1938, quoted in Filewood, "Tejano Revolt," 87; Richard A. Garcia, *Rise of the Mexican American Middle Class: San Antonio, 1929–1941*, 63; George Lambert interview, part 2, 26–27.
37. "Pecan Strikers Return to Work," *SAL*, March 8, 1938, 6-A; "S. A. Pecan Shellers to Arbitrate Trouble," *The Weekly Dispatch*, March 18, 1938, 1; "Pecan Strikers Dance in Street on Victory," *The Daily Worker*, March 23, 1938, 3—all in Dublin, DelValle, and Perez, "How Did Mexican Working Women Assert Their Labor and Constitutional Rights?"
38. Snid interview, 23 (quotation); "San Antonio: The Cradle and the Coffin of Texas Liberty," 15; "Pecan Strikers Dance in Street on Victory," *The Daily Worker*, March 23, 1938, 3.
39. Latane Lambert [née Bartlett], interview by David Filewood, September 17, 1991, Arlington, Texas, TLA-UTA, OH 127, 1 (first three quotations), 3 (final quotation).
40. "North Carolina Girl Bride of Popular Bluefield Man," *Bluefield Daily Telegraph*, n.d. [April 1939], 4, clipping in Lambert Papers, AR127-4-6 (first quotation); "Giving Shakespeare a Boost," unknown newspaper clipping, n.d., Lambert Papers, AR127-4-6 (all remaining quotations); Latane Lambert interview by Filewood, 2.

41. "Miss Latane Bartlett Bride of George Lambert in Texas," unknown newspaper clipping, probably from Greensboro, n.d. [April 1939], Lambert Papers, AR127-4-6 (quotation); Latane Lambert interview by Filewood, 2.

42. Latane Lambert interview by Filewood, 2 (all quotations); Latane Lambert interview by Glenn Scott and María Flores, n.d. [ca. 1979], OH116M, hand-corrected unedited transcript, TLA-UTA, 3.

43. Latane Lambert interview by Filewood, 7–8; Latane Lambert interview by Scott and Flores, 4–5.

44. On Moreno and the rest of the "gang," see correspondence in Lambert Papers, AR127, Boxes 5 and 6.

45. Latane Lambert interview by Filewood, 10–11 (first and second quotations); "Miss Latane Bartlett Bride of George Lambert in Texas" (third and fourth quotations); Letter from Latane Bartlett to George Lambert, "Sunday afternoon," n.d. [July 24, 1938], in Lambert Papers, AR127-5-8 (final quotation); Latane Lambert interview by Scott and Flores, 5–6.

46. Latane Lambert interview by Filewood, 8, 11 (second quotation), 14–16 (first quotation on 16).

47. Lambert, "The Jersey City of the South," 9; Letter from George Lambert to Caroline Whiting, July 18, 1938, Lambert Papers, AR127-16-10; "San Antonio: The Cradle and the Coffin of Texas Liberty," 1; Lambert interview, part 2, 38. Lambert recalls that the TCLU used the pamphlet to raise both awareness and money for progressive causes around the state. Future congressman Bob Eckhardt drew the pamphlet's illustration, one of his first of many widely circulated political cartoons that were a mainstay of Texas labor publications for the next two decades.

48. Lambert, "The Jersey City of the South," 8; "Mexican Speaks Here," *SAL*, July 2, 1938, 1–2.

49. Paula Mitchell Marks, "Maverick, Samuel Augustus," *Handbook of Texas Online*, Texas State Historical Association, accessed July 13, 2010, http://www.tshaonline.org/handbook/online/articles/MM/fma84.html.

50. Henderson, *Maury Maverick*, 52–56.

51. "The Cradle and the Coffin of Texas Liberty," 11 (quotation); Henderson, *Maury Maverick, a Political Biography*, 48–62.

52. Henderson, "Fontaine Maury Maverick"; Henderson, *Maury Maverick*.

53. "The Cradle and the Coffin of Texas Liberty," 13.

54. Lambert interview, part 2, 38, 43.

55. Lambert, "The Jersey City of the South," 6 (first and second quotations), 7 (remaining quotations); Judith Kaaz Doyle, "Maury Maverick and Racial Politics in San Antonio, Texas, 1938–1941," 204; Granneberg, "Maury Maverick's San Antonio," para. 3.

56. "Maverick Called Eccentric By Foe," *SAE*, July 12, 1938, 7.

57. Granneberg, "Maury Maverick's San Antonio," para. 5.

58. Lambert, "The Jersey City of the South," 7 (first and second quotations), 8 (third and fourth quotations); Filewood, "Tejano Revolt," 117–18.

59. Lambert, "The Jersey City of the South," 7.

60. Joe B. Frantz, "Foreword," in Henderson, *Maury Maverick*, xx.

61. "Maverick Called Eccentric by Foe," *SAE*, July 12, 1938, 7.

62. Filewood, "Tejano Revolt," 117–18; Letter from George Lambert to Donald Henderson, August 1, 1938, Lambert Papers AR127-6-2; Letter from George Lambert to Frank [Warren], July 28, 1938, Lambert Papers, AR127-6-2.

63. Doyle, "Maverick and Racial Politics," 203; Granneberg, "Maury Maverick's San Antonio," 36.

64. Letter from George Lambert to Frank [Warren], July 28, 1938, Lambert Papers, AR127-6-2.

65. Doyle, "Maverick and Racial Politics," 203.

66. Letter from George Lambert to Latane Bartlett, July 26, 1938, in Lambert Papers, AR127-5-5.

67. Letter from George Lambert to J. E. Clayon, July 23, 1938, Lambert Papers, AR127-6-2.

68. See all of this correspondence in Lambert Papers, AR127, Box 5, Folders 5 and 8.

69. Letter from Latane Bartlett to George Lambert, "Saturday afternoon," n.d. [July 23, 1938], in Lambert Papers, AR127-5-8.

70. Letter from George Lambert to Latane Bartlett, July 24, 1938, in Lambert Papers, AR127-5-5.

71. Letter from Latane Bartlett to George Lambert, "Tuesday morning," n.d. [July 26, 1938], in Lambert Papers, AR127-5-8.

72. George's departure from UCAPAWA was a gradual process. In her oral history interview, Latane claims that George lost the job around June, but in late July George was still lobbying to remain on the union payroll, and the state organizer-in-chief Frank Warren instructed him to resume working as usual. On August 1, he wrote to Henderson and urged the union leader to continue to invest in the San Antonio struggle, and he continued to use the union's letterhead through late August. Still, the paychecks must have stopped coming, as the two Lamberts discussed their financial troubles in their correspondence. George continued to engage in other activities, and he began a more active job search by August 5. George appears in newspaper reports as a representative of the Pecan Workers Union as late as December 1938, but by then he had accepted another position and was clearly no longer a formal employee of UCAPAWA. See Latane Lambert interview by Filewood; Letters from Frank Warren to George Lambert, July 25 and 29, 1938, Lambert Papers, AR127-6-2; Letter from George Lambert to Donald Henderson, August 1, 1938, Lambert Papers, AR127-6-2; Letter from George to Latane, August 5, 1938, Lambert Papers, AR127-5-5.

73. Letter from George Lambert to Latane Bartlett, July 28, 1938, Lambert Papers, AR127-5-5.

74. Letter from George Lambert to Latane Bartlett, July 30, 1938, Lambert Papers, AR127-5-5.

75. Letter from "L. B." to "Dearest George," August 18, 1938, Lambert Papers, AR127-5-8.

76. Postcard from George Lambert to "Bartlett, babe," August 18, 1938, Lambert Papers, AR127-5-5; Letter from George Lambert to Latane, August 21, 1938, Lambert Papers, AR127-5-5; Letter from George Lambert to Frank [Warren], August 23, 1938, Lambert Papers, AR127-6-2. Lambert claimed that "Allred double-crossed" Maverick, keeping him off the ballot as an independent. See Postcard from George Lambert to "Bartlett," August 27, 1938, Lambert Papers, AR127-5-5. A subsequent write-in effort also floundered.

77. Letter from George Lambert to Latane Bartlett, July 26, 1938, Lambert Papers, AR127-5-5.

78. Letter from George Lambert to Donald Henderson, August 1, 1938, Lambert Papers, AR127-6-2.

79. Postcard from George Lambert to "Comrade Bartlett," August 6, 1938, Lambert Papers, AR127-5-5.

80. Letter from George Lambert to Latane Bartlett, July 26, 1938, Lambert Papers, AR127-5-5; Postcard from Lambert to Bartlett, July 27, 1938, Lambert Papers, AR127-5-5; Letter from Lambert to Bartlett, August 1, 1938, Lambert Papers, AR127-5-5; Letter from George Lambert to Latane, August 21, 1938, Lambert Papers, AR127-5-5, 2; Postcard from "Geo." To "Darling," August 24, 1938, Lambert Papers, AR127-5-5; Letter from "Geo." to "Latane, you mug," September 3, 1938, Lambert Papers, AR127-5-5, 3 (quotation).

81. Letter from George to "Darling," "Monday night," n.d. [September 5, 1938], Lambert Papers, AR127-5-5 (all quotations). For references to the company union drive, see Letter from Latane Bartlett to Georgle Lambert, "Saturday night," n.d. [August 27, 1938], Lambert Papers, AR127-5-8; and Letter from George Lambert to Latane Lambert, August 30, 1938, Lambert Papers, AR127-5-5.

82. Gower, "Unintended Consequences," 99; Filewood, "Tejano Revolt," 119–20.

83. Letter from George to "Darling," "Monday night," n.d. [September 5, 1938], Lambert Papers, AR127-5-5 (all quotations). See also letters from George to Latane dated "1:00 A.M. Wednesday" [September 7, 1938]; "Saturday morning" [September 10, 1938]; September 15, 1938; and "Sunday afternoon," n.d. [September 1938]—all in Lambert Papers, AR127-5-5.

84. "Soup Kitchens Serving 3000 Meals Daily," *SAL*, November 2, 1938, 1-B (first quotation from caption); "Pecan Worker Relief Sought," *SAL*, November 2, 1938, 1-B (second quotation); George Lambert interview, part 2, 43–44.

85. Gower, "Unintended Consequences," 99; Filewood, "Tejano Revolt," 119–120.

86. Granneberg, "Maury Maverick's San Antonio," para. 5.

87. Rev. Claude W. Black Jr., interview by author, San Antonio, October 27, 2008, digital audio recording in author's possession, 32:30.

88. Doyle, "Maverick and Racial Politics"; Mason, "Paternal Continuity: African Americans and Race Relations in San Antonio, Texas, 1867–1937," 169–78, 183–87, 409–11, 427–32 (quotation on 431); Henderson, *Maury Maverick*, 60, 185. Mason incorrectly describes Maverick's defeat in the congressional primary as taking place in 1936, before Charlie Bellinger's death. I borrow "upbuilding" from Brown, *Upbuilding Black Durham*.

89. Mason, "Paternal Continuity," 377, 380–81, 391–92.

90. "A Celebration of Life: Percy Ellis Sutton," February 27, 2010, copy in "Funeral Programs, San Antonio: Sp—Sw," SAPL-VF (first quotation); Jim McCrory, "The Suttons of San Antonio: From Slavery to Leadership," *SAE*, February 27, 1977, 3A (second quotation), 8A; "S. J. Sutton Is Retired from School System," *San Antonio Register*, June 6, 1941 (third quotation); "Resume of Mrs. Lillian Viola Sutton," n.d. (all in "Sutton Family," SAPL-VF).

91. Mason, "Paternal Continuity," 377, 380–81, 391–92; "Politics, Pleasure, Pathos and Crime Punctuate '39," *SAL*, December 31, 1939, 4; "Negro Health Week to End with Parade," *SAL*, April 9, 1939, 12; "Christmas Seal Sale Planned," *SAE*, October 10, 1939, 5.

92. Leonard B. Murphy, "Sutton, Garlington Jerome (G. J.) (1909–1976)," undated draft manuscript in "Sutton Family," SAPL-VF (first quotation); Roddy Stinson, "Don't Ever

Try to Make This Man Wear a Hat," *SAE*, December 3, 1975, 3-A, copy in "Sutton, G. J.," SAPL-VF (all remaining quotations); Roddy Stinson, "G. J. Sutton's Funeral: A Lot Was Left Unsaid," *SAE*, June 28, 1976, 3-A, copy in "Sutton, G. J.," SAPL-VF; Murphy, "Sutton, Garlington Jerome," *Handbook of Texas Online*. Stinson dates the Xenia incident to 1925, which is probably a typo that should have read "1935." Sutton had graduated from Wilberforce and stopped by the campus after purchasing a hearse along with his brother in January 1937. The 1930 census lists him as a "lodger" in Wilberforce, near Xenia. See Fifteenth Census of the United States, State of Ohio, County of Green, Township of Xenia, Unincorporated place of Wilberforce, Sheet No. 16B; "Wilberforce News," *The Gazette*, Xenia, Ohio, January 22, 1937, 7.

93. Mason, "Paternal Continuity," 415–17.

94. The argument that economic independence allowed G. J. greater autonomy than Samuel is my own. The quotations are found in Mason, 417–19. Mason identifies G. J. as the principal of Wheatley High School but makes no mention of the Sutton & Sutton Mortuary business. I have not verified the school claim, though G. J. clearly had ties to education, winning election to the junior college district board in 1948. Most sources from the post–World War II period identify Sutton as a mortician. For additional biographical information, see Murphy, "Sutton, Garlington Jerome."

95. The NNC was known for its ties to the Communist Party's Popular Front, connections that prompted Randolph to resign from its presidency in 1940, following the Nazi-Soviet Pact of the previous year. On the NNC, see Gellman, *Death Blow to Jim Crow*; Salter, "National Negro Congress (1935–1940s)."

96. Doyle, "Maverick and Racial Politics," 206–7; Mason, "Paternal Continuity," 417–19. Doyle misidentifies Sutton's first name throughout her piece as George instead of Garlington.

97. Mason, "Paternal Continuity," 432 (on the Texas Centennial); Doyle, "Maverick and Racial Politics," 205 (on newspaper endorsements).

98. Mason, "Paternal Continuity," 166 ("beer county" quotation); Doyle, "Maverick and Racial Politics," 205.

99. Munz, "Gunning for Maverick," 674; Sherwood Anderson, "Maury Maverick in San Antonio," 399.

100. Letter from George Lambert to Santos G. Vasquez, March 2, 1939, Lambert Papers, AR 127-6-2; Handwritten letter from Santos to George, [1939], giving names of unemployed *mexicanos*, probably pecan shellers, who could be put to work for political action, in Lambert Papers, AR127-6-2.

101. Letter from George Lambert to E. L. Oliver, May 10, 1939, Lambert Papers, AR127-6-2.

102. Richard A. Garcia, *Rise of the Mexican American Middle Class*, 214.

103. Ibid., 212–13.

104. Ibid., 213.

105. See, for example, ibid., 214.

106. "Maury Pledge City Reorganization; Steffler Gains on Helland in Recheck," *SAL*, May 10, 1939, 1 (first quotation); Richard A. Garcia, *Rise of the Mexican American Middle Class*, 214 (second quotation); Doyle, "Maverick and Racial Politics," 207, note 46 (election results).

107. Jeffers received 347 votes, or 11 percent. These numbers are based on Doyle's calculations, which are based on a precinct-by-precinct analysis. Doyle, "Maverick and Racial Politics," 207–8. She notes that Maverick only admitted receiving approximately 20 percent, a figure that was repeated by a "reliable authority" in Granneberg, "Maury Maverick's San Antonio," para. 39. But the larger number is probably more accurate.

108. Letter from George Lambert to "Darling," May 10, 1939, Lambert Papers, AR127-5-5.

109. Doyle agrees: "Maverick received more votes than he had thought. Definite cracks had appeared in the black bloc; liberal black organizations helped deliver some votes for Maverick and the Fusion ticket. The machine could no longer claim the support of all but a few dissenting blacks." Although "Maverick probably never recognized how his challenge to the machine affected San Antonio's black political development," Doyle adds, his mayoral campaigns challenged the machine and thereby "forced the disintegration of the black bloc vote. . . . The machine would retain some influence in the black community for years to come, but its control would never again be as monolithic." Doyle, "Maverick and Racial Politics," 207 (first quotation), 220 (second), 222 (third).

110. Henderson, *Maury Maverick*, 195–96, 229–30; Doyle, "Maverick and Racial Politics," 210. See also "Quin, Anderson, Ray Davis Win City Runoff Election," *SAE*, May 28, 1941, 1–2; "Health Department Gains Chief Pride of Maverick," *SAL*, June 1, 1941, 10–11.

111. Henderson, *Maury Maverick*, 196. Ironically, the money in question was part of the donation to the Maverick campaign from ILGWU international president David Dubinsky, which Maverick then gave to the local union, and Lambert helped spend through LNPL.

112. Doyle, "Maverick and Racial Politics," 209–16. See also Henderson, *Maury Maverick*, 220–25.

113. George Lambert, "Maverick Defies the Mob," 287; Henderson, *Maury Maverick*, 213–17.

114. Henderson, *Maury Maverick*, 205–8; Munz, "Gunning for Maverick," 674.

115. "Quin, Anderson, Ray Davis Win City Runoff Election," 1–2.

116. Doyle, "Maverick and Racial Politics," 216–20 (quotation on 220); Henderson, *Maury Maverick*, 227–29. See also "Run-Off Called Negro Vote Result," *SAL*, May 17, 1941, 2.

117. Emma Tenayuca, interview by Jerry Poyo, San Antonio, February 21, 1987, UTSA, 35.

Chapter 2

1. Thomas Wright, "Oldtime Black Houston Freedom Fighters Left Proud Legacy," *FT*, March 17, 1973, 9B, clipping in Moses LeRoy Collection, MSS 90, Box 1, Folder 5, HMRC (first quotation) (hereafter LeRoy Collection); Lulu B. White, quoted in Pitre, *In Struggle against Jim Crow*, 43 (second quotation).

2. Jacquelyn Dowd Hall, "The Long Civil Rights Movement," 1246 (quotation); Korstad, *Civil Rights Unionism*; Pitre, *In Struggle against Jim Crow*, 106 (membership statistics).

3. Calvert, De León, and Cantrell, *The History of Texas*, 191, 246.

4. Obadele-Starks, *Black Unionism in the Industrial South*, 3–11; De León, *Ethnicity in the Sunbelt*, 8–42.

5. George N. Green, "Introduction," in Mers, *Working the Waterfront*, ix–xviii; Obadele-Starks, *Black Unionism*, 46–47. Much of the information here comes from informal conversations between the author and retirees from ILA Local 872, Houston ILA Retirees Association meeting at the ILA Local 1351 Hall, Houston, May 19, 2010; author's voice memos on conversation with Tommy Roy, Houston, May 25, 2010, in author's possession; "Personal Telephone Directory and Local History of I. L. A. 872," ca. 1960, digital photographs in author's possession, courtesy Tommy Roy; Howard Middleton Jr., interview by author, digital audio recording in author's possession, Houston, May 5 and 31, 2010; Gilbert Mers, "Anecdotal History of Local 1273, I. L. A.," n.d. [ca. 1970], Gilbert Mers Collection, MSS 63, Box 1, Folder 9, HMRC. In many cases in Texas, the ILA also chartered a third local composed of Mexican American workers that received a small share of the work and/or the least desirable tasks. See also Montes, "Working for American Rights: Black, White, and Mexican-American Dockworkers in Texas During the Great Depression."

6. Obadele-Starks, *Black Unionism*.

7. Korstad, *Civil Rights Unionism*, chap. 8 (quotations on p. 214).

8. Obadele-Starks, *Black Unionism*; Botson, *Labor, Civil Rights, and the Hughes Tool Company*.

9. Moses LeRoy, interview by Chandler Davidson, January 25, 1979, Houston, Chandler Davidson Texas Politics Research Collection, WRC, MS 259, Box 9, Folder 6, 1–6 (first quotation on 2; second quotation on 4; third and fourth quotations on 5; fifth and sixth quotations on 6). On the riot, see Haynes, *A Night of Violence: The Houston Riot of 1917*. For its larger national context, see Lentz-Smith, *Freedom Struggles: African Americans and World War I*. For its antecedents in the multiracial world of the Texas borderlands, see Leiker, *Racial Borders: Black Soldiers Along the Rio Grande*.

10. LeRoy interview by Davidson, 7–8 (first quotation on 8); Moses LeRoy, interview by George N. Green, August 19, 1971, Houston, Texas, TLA-UTA, OH 20, 3–5 (second quotation on 5).

11. LeRoy interview by Davidson, 10; LeRoy interview by Green, 1–5 (both quotations on 1).

12. LeRoy interview by Davidson, 10–12 (quotation on 11); "A Brief History of Jack Yates Senior High School."

13. Chandler Davidson, "Notes on Interview with Mr. Leroy, Jan. 25, 1979," 2, Davidson Texas Politics Research Collection, WRC, MS 259, Box 9, Folder 7 (all quotations). The Social Security Death Index lists her birthdate in 1911, but all other sources, including the manuscript census, suggest that she was born in 1913. Sources consulted on her early years include the above and "Moses LeRoy," Salute column, *HI*, n.d. [1973], clipping in LeRoy Collection, Box 1, Folder 5; "Woman of the Year Presentation at Nobby's Corner," *FT*, August 18, 1973, 12B, clipping in LeRoy Collection, Box 1, Folder 5.

14. Ed Wendt, "Moses and Erma Leroy: A Civil Rights Love Story," *FT*, February 17, 1990, 2C (first quotation); Letter from Congressman Bob Eckhardt to Moses LeRoy, November 28, 1967, LeRoy Collection, Box 1, Folder 1 (second quotation); Letter from Walter Katz to "Dear Mose," December 2, 1967, LeRoy Collection, Box 1, Folder 1 (third quotation); Letter from Chet Brooks to Quentin Mease, December 1, 1967, LeRoy Col-

lection, Box 1, Folder 1 (fourth quotation, "helpmate"). The marriage date is cited by Craig Watkins in the *Congressional Record*, 136 Cong. Rec. E 556; 101st Cong., 2nd Session, Vol. 135, No. 21, p. E556.

15. "Phone Call from Erma LeRoy to Ruthe Winegarten," August 29, 1991, typed notes, Ruthe Winegarten Papers, 1912–2004, BCAH, 2.325, Box W70; Sixteenth Census of the United States, State of Texas, City of Houston, Harris County, Precinct 1, Block 176, Sheet No. 18, Line 50 (Washington, D.C.: Bureau of the Census: 1940).

16. LeRoy interview by Davidson, 9.

17. LeRoy interview by Green, 3.

18. LeRoy interview by Davidson, 18 (first quotation), 8 (second quotation); LeRoy interview by Green, 21 (third and fourth quotations).

19. The following paragraphs draw upon the following excellent published works: Lavergne, *Before Brown: Heman Marion Sweatt, Thurgood Marshall, and the Long Road to Justice*; Hine, *Black Victory: The Rise and Fall of the White Primary in Texas*; Pitre, *In Struggle against Jim Crow*; Pruitt, *The Other Great Migration*.

20. Quoted in Franklin Chandler Davidson, "Negro Politics and the Rise of the Civil Rights Movement in Houston, Texas," 42.

21. LeRoy interview by Davidson, 15; Pruitt, *Other Great Migration*, 163–70 (first quotation on 165; second on 170); Hales, "Grovey, Richard Randolph."

22. Pitre, *In Struggle against Jim Crow*, 29, 36.

23. Ibid., 56.

24. Ibid., 63.

25. Burns, "Durham, William J."; Gillette, "The NAACP in Texas, 1937–1957," 19–20, 30–31; W. Dulaney, "Whatever Happened to the Civil Rights Movement in Dallas, Texas?", 70–71. See also African American Museum of Dallas, "Biography of W. J. Durham," photocopy in author's possession, courtesy W. Marvin Dulaney. The author profusely thanks Marvin for his support and his sharing of his research files on Durham and the *Dallas Express*.

26. Lavergne, *Before Brown*, Loc. 841–52.

27. Ibid; Thomas Wright, "Oldtime Black Houston Freedom Fighters Left Proud Legacy," *FT*, March 17, 1973, 9B, clipping in LeRoy Collection, Box 1, Folder 5 (quotation).

28. Hine, *Black Victory*, 228–29; Lavergne, *Before Brown*, Loc. 857.

29. Moses LeRoy, interview by Marguerite Johnston Barnes, Houston, n.d. [ca. 1986], Marguerite Johnston Barnes Research Materials for *Houston, The Unknown City, 1830–1991*, WRC, MS 455, Box 2, Folder 28, 8–11 (first quotation on 10); LeRoy interview by Davidson, 16 (second quotation); Pitre, *In Struggle against Jim Crow*, 66.

30. Pitre, *In Struggle against Jim Crow*, 36, 106–7.

31. Ibid., 65.

32. Quoted in Lavergne, *Before Brown*, Loc. 905.

33. Pitre, *In Struggle against Jim Crow*, 43.

34. Lavergne, *Before Brown*, Loc. 1006; Caption of photograph "Living Founders of the Alliance in Houston," in *Twentieth Convention of the National Alliance of Postal Employees* program, August 20–24, 1951, Houston, Cook Papers, BCAH, 2.325, Box A124a, Folder 3. For more background on Sweatt and the founding of the NAPE, see Martin Mayfield Jr., "The Alliance Story: Fifty Years of Progress," 1967; "Alliance Pioneer Passes," *The Postal Alliance*, n.d. [March 1954], 23; and "Postal Employees Make Great Contributions to Civil

Rights," *The Postal Alliance*, July 1950, 1, 4–6—all collected in Cook Papers, 2.325, Box A124a, Folder 4. For an excellent history of African Americans' participation in postal unions that also locates the *Sweatt* case within the broader Houston NAPE and NAACP left, see Rubio, *There's Always Work at the Post Office*.

35. Lavergne, *Before Brown*, Loc. 763, 1185–95, 1278; Hine, "Afterword," in *Black Victory*.

36. Lavergne, *Before Brown*, Loc. 875, 1296. The analysis regarding his relative immunity from economic reprisals is my own.

37. Texas Conference of Branches, "Official Program, Eleventh Annual Meeting," September 5–7, 1947, Denison, Texas, in Cook Papers, 2.325, Box A124a, Folder 7; "Phone Call from Erma LeRoy."

38. "Phone Call from Erma LeRoy to Ruthe Winegarten"; Letter from Anne Pittman to Moses Leroy, November 26, 1946, LeRoy Collection, Box 1, Folder 1.

39. Pitre, *In Struggle against Jim Crow*, 106, 160 note 30 (quotation).

40. On Randolph, see Kersten and Lang, *Reframing Randolph*. On the FEPC and African Americans, see, among others, Reed, *Seedtime for the Modern Civil Rights Movement*; Kersten, *Race, Jobs, and the War*; Obadele-Starks, *Black Unionism*, chap. 7. On the FEPC and Mexican Americans, see Daniel, *Chicano Workers and the Politics of Fairness*; Zamora, *Claiming Rights and Righting Wrongs in Texas*.

41. Pitre, *In Struggle against Jim Crow*, 62; Obadele-Starks, *Black Unionism*, 123–27.

42. LeRoy interview by Davidson, 17; Pitre, *In Struggle against Jim Crow*, 56–69; Obadele-Starks, *Black Unionism*, 112–23.

43. LeRoy interview by Green, 1, 6–9 (quotations on 6); Jim Curran, "Moses LeRoy Says He Believes Brotherhood to Come—Some Day," *HC*, August 29, 1971, 4–4.

44. Informal conversations between author and retirees from ILA Local 872, Houston ILA Retirees Association meeting at the ILA Local 1351 hall, Houston, May 19, 2010; author's voice memos on conversation with Tommy Roy, Houston, May 25, 2010; "Personal Telephone Directory and Local History of I. L. A. 872," ca. 1960, digital photographs in author's possession, courtesy Tommy Roy; Howard Middleton Jr., interview by author, digital audio recording in author's possession, Houston, May 5 and 31, 2010.

45. *Proceedings of the 48th Convention of the Texas State Federation of Labor*, June 24–27, 1946, Houston, 200–201, TLA-UTA.

46. *Proceedings of the 49th Convention of the Texas State Federation of Labor*, June 30 to July 3, 1947, Dallas, 193–94, 221–24, TLA-UTA; Lee A. Lewis, interview by George N. Green, October 4, 1971 Houston, Texas, TLA-UTA, OH 22, 25–27. For more on Lewis and his union, the International Alliance of Theatrical and Stage Employees Local 279-A, see Obadele-Starks, "Black Texans and Theater Craft Unionism," 532–48.

47. Lewis interview, 27–29 (both quotations on 28).

48. *Proceedings of the 50th Convention of the Texas State Federation of Labor*, June 21–25, 1948, Fort Worth, 138–39 (quotation on 138), TLA-UTA.

49. Ibid., 209–11, 235. Everett was reelected in 1949 and 1950 without incident. See *Proceedings of the 51st Convention of the Texas State Federation of Labor*, June 21–25, 1949, Beaumont, Texas, 143–45, 154–55, TLA-UTA; *Proceedings of the 52nd Convention of the Texas State Federation of Labor*, June 26–29, 1950, San Antonio, 101, 136–38, TLA-UTA.

50. Letter from W. C. Jason Jr. to "Mr. Chairman," Richard Lillie, n.d. [1946], Cook Papers, 2.325, Box A124a, Folder 2; correspondence between Rannie Cook and Post

Office officials, November 23, 1945, and April 20 and 24, 1946, Cook Papers, 2.325, Box A124a, Folder 2; Letter from Rannie Cook to Mrs. Floy W. Johnson, March 19, 1947, Cook Papers, 2.325, Box A124a, Folder 2.

51. Handwritten minutes, Texas Conference of Branches Executive Committee meeting, September 3, 1948; Letter from Mabel Kilpatrick to Mrs. R. D. Cook, April 23, 1947; Letter from Lulu B. White to "Member," January 12, 1949; postcard from C. V. Adair to Rannie Cook, n.d. [1947]—all in Cook Papers, 2.325, Box A124a, Folder 7; Texas Conference of Branches, "Official Program, Eleventh Annual Meeting," 1947; and Texas N. A. A. C. P., Officers and Executive Committee, in Texas Conference of Branches, N. A. A. C. P "Official Program, Twelfth Annual Meeting," 1948—both in Cook Papers, 2.325, Box A124a, Folder 8.

52. Stamp reading "Cook's Book & Gift Shop, 3705 Lyons Ave," attached to Office of War Information, "The United Nations' Fight for the Four Freedoms," Cook Papers, 2.325, Box A124a, Folder 6. Many similar stamps could be found on printed materials and clippings throughout the collection, especially in Folder 8. Byron Cook, "Great Books," n.d., handwritten note, Cook Papers, 2.325, Box A124a, Folder 8.

53. Rannie Cook, "What We, As Women, Owe to Our Group," n.d. [ca. 1947], Cook Papers, 2.325, Box A124a, Folder 2.

54. Letter from Moses Leroy to Mrs. White, December 2, 1946, LeRoy Collection, Box 1, Folder 2.

55. LeRoy interview by Davidson, 20–21 (quotations on 20); Nelson quoted in Wright, "Oldtime Black Houston Freedom Fighters Left Proud Legacy," *FT*, March 17, 1973, 9B. "Paramilitary politics" was coined by Hahn, *A Nation Under Our Feet*. Even African Americans in the extremely repressive Mississippi Delta attempted to organize and vote en masse after *Smith*, and they publicly supported an effort to recall their white supremacist Democratic senator, Theodore Bilbo. See Dittmer, *Local People*.

56. George N. Green, *The Establishment in Texas Politics*, chaps. 3 and 8; Polakoff, "The Development of the Texas State C.I.O. Council," 23, 271–82, 304–12.

57. Lichtenstein, *State of the Union*, 114–18; Zieger, *The CIO, 1935–1955*, 245–52.

58. Reed, *Seedtime for the Modern Civil Rights Movement*; Wada, "President's Committee on Fair Employment Practice (FEPC)."

59. LeRoy interview by Davidson, 13. On the national Progressive Party campaign and Wallace, see MacDougall, *Gideon's Army*; White and Maze, *Henry A. Wallace*. For a superb history of the Communist and Progressive Parties and the civil rights unionist left in Texas, see Carleton, *Red Scare!: Right-Wing Hysteria, Fifties Fanaticism, and Their Legacy in Texas*, chap. 2.

60. Minutes of the Committee to Get Wallace on the Ballot in Texas, 1948, Cook (Byron and Rannie) Papers, 2.325, Box A124a, Folder 1. On White, see also Pitre, *In Struggle against Jim Crow*, 75–78. Pitre writes that "White denied any involvement and asked newspapers to print retractions" that she had endorsed Wallace in her official capacity on behalf of the NAACP, even as she defended her right to privately support the candidate of her choice (quotation on 77). Still, she clearly was involved in the campaign. See also Letter from Pat Lunsford to Friend, March 11, 1948, Cook Papers, Box A124a, Folder 1.

61. Minutes of the Founding Convention Held April 25, 1948, in the Music Hall, Houston, Tex., Cook Papers, 2.325, Box A124a, Folder 1.

62. LeRoy interview by Green, 32; Pitre, *In Struggle against Jim Crow*, 77; Carleton, *Red Scare!*, 52–53. See also "Rev. Stacy Adams Removed From Political Offices," *DE*, April 3, 1948, and additional coverage of the Progressive Party in *DE*.

63. Letter from Progressive Party to Dear Friend (Precinct 47), May 25, 1948; Letter from Congressman Albert Thomas to LeRoy, May 11, 1948; Letter from O. W. L. Turner, Houston Freight Handlers Lodge 6051 to Whom It May Concern, May 15, 1948—all in LeRoy Collection, Box 1, Folder 1.

64. Letter from Progressive Party to Dear Friend (Precinct 48), May 25, 1948; National Committee for Wallace Canvasser's Guide; folder labeled "BLOCKWORKER"; Letter from Pearl Fox to Mrs. Rannie Cook, August 12, 1948; partial handwritten note on blank party precinct and county delegate notary form; miscellaneous Progressive Party minutes (quotation)—all in Cook Papers, 2.325, Box A124a, Folder 1.

65. Political sociologist Chandler Davidson writes that the Democrats trounced the Progressive Party in the "key," all-black Precinct 48. I have not located returns for LeRoy's Precinct 47. Davidson, "Negro Politics and the Rise of the Civil Rights Movement in Houston, Texas," 46. Statewide numbers can be found in *Texas Almanac*, 1949–1950 (Dallas: Belo, 1949), 475, available online via *The Portal to Texas History*, http://texashistory.unt.edu/ark:/67531/metapth117167/ (accessed April 23, 2016).

66. Zieger, *CIO*, 266–77.

67. Sullivan, *Days of Hope: Race and Democracy in the New Deal Era*, Epilogue.

68. Letter from LeRoy, "Greetings," November 12, 1948, LeRoy Collection, MSS 90, Box 1, Folder 2. He recalls sending this as county chairman of the party, a post that he may have occupied in addition to coordinating his precinct. There is no evidence that corroborates or refutes his account. See Moses LeRoy, interview by Florence Coleman, Houston, October 30, 1974, OH 102, HMRC. There is no reference to barbers turned CIO organizers Grovey and Nelson among the very fragmentary Progressive Party documents preserved in the Cook and LeRoy Collection. It is probable that they followed the CIO lead and campaigned for Truman, likely helping to swing Precinct 48 into the Democratic column. Still, the LeRoys, Hasgett, White, and others all remained in Wallace's camp.

69. LeRoy interview by Davidson, 13.

70. In fact, African Americans rarely ran for office at all. NAACP leader Rev. L. H. Simpson did seek an at-large seat on the Houston city council in 1946, but he predictably lost by a wide margin. "Negro Baptist Pastor In City Council Race," *HC*, September 23, 1959 (on Simpson); "You voted Nov. 2nd Against Taft-Hartley," Bell and LeRoy campaign flyer in LeRoy Collection, Box 1, Folder 7; LeRoy interview by Davidson, 17–18; "Phone Call from Erma LeRoy," Winegarten Papers; Letter from Chandler Davidson to Ruthe Winegarten, October 1, 1991, Winegarten Papers, 2.325, Box W70; Copy of "Erma Leroy," in Helen Hunter et al., *Houston Women from Suffrage to City Hall*, 17–18, in Winegarten Papers, 2.325, Box W70; Davidson, "Negro Politics and the Rise of the Civil Rights Movement in Houston, Texas," 47–48. All secondary sources follow Davidson in assuming that this election occurred in January of 1948, but the campaign flyer definitively suggests otherwise. Moreover, Harris County held a special election on January 8, 1949, in which both a senate and house race were contested. The victors were J. Searcy Blackwell and Carlton Moore, respectively. See "J. Searcy Blackwell, Jr.," *Texas Legislators: Past & Present*, Legislative Reference Library, http://www.lrl.state.tx.us/mobile/memberDisplay

.cfm?memberID=962 (accessed January 20, 2014), footnote 1; "Bracewell, Moore Lead Harris Voting," *Abilene Reporter News*, January 9, 1949, 1.

71. Hall, "Long Civil Rights Movement," 1250.

72. "Sweatt UT Plea Upheld; States Lose on Tidelands," *Austin American*, June 6, 1950 (first quotation); "Schools to Obey Supreme Court Action," *HI*, June 17, 1950 (second quotation)—both collected online in Thomas D. Russell, ed., *Sweatt v. Painter Archive*. See also Lavergne, *Before Brown*.

Chapter 3

1. "About Us," *Harris County Council of Organizations*; author's 2012 digital photograph of cornerstone plaque posted outside the council's office at 4610 Delano Street in Houston's Third Ward, 1987, in author's possession. The plaque lists thirteen "charter members," including Moses LeRoy, Julius White, and M. Richmond, then president of LeRoy's freight handlers union. One of the four HCCO founders listed on the plaque was civil rights and labor leader F. T. Henry, a resident of the Fifth Ward that organized the Steelworkers CIO union at the Hughes Tool Company. See Rosa Henry Doyle and Etta Walker, "Henry, Forest Thomas, Sr."

2. The term "spadework" is attributed to legendary civil rights organizer Ella Baker. See, among others, Payne, *I've Got the Light of Freedom*; Ransby, *Ella Baker and the Black Freedom Movement*; Moye, *Ella Baker: Community Organizer of the Civil Rights Movement*.

3. Polakoff, "The Development of the Texas State C.I.O. Council," 141–44, 214–22 (first four quotations on 142; final quotation on 143); Carleton, *Red Scare*, 54. The national CIO ultimately paid Mandell's $5,000 invoice. The first executive secretary who suffered the breakdown was P. F. Kennedy; the second who was injured on the job was Clyde Ingram.

4. Polakoff, "The Development of the Texas State C.I.O. Council," 128, 341 (note 9), vi; George N. Green, *The Establishment in Texas Politics*, 103. See also Griffith, *The Crisis of American Labor: Operation Dixie and the Defeat of the CIO*.

5. See, among other works, Minchin, *Fighting against the Odds*; Minchin, *What Do We Need a Union For?*; Korstad, *Civil Rights Unionism*; Honey, *Southern Labor and Black Civil Rights*. Classic anthologies on southern labor that touch on the immediate postwar stories include Zieger, *Organized Labor in the Twentieth-Century South*; Zieger, *Southern Labor in Transition, 1940–1995*; Fink and Reed, *Race, Class, and Community in Southern Labor History*. On Texas oil, see Priest and Botson, "Bucking the Odds: Organized Labor in Gulf Coast Oil Refining."

6. Krochmal, "Labor, Civil Rights, and the Struggle for Democracy in Texas, 1935–1965," 119–58; Halpern, "Interracial Unionism in the Southwest,"158–82; Adedeji, "Crossing the Colorline"; Polakoff, "The Development of the Texas State C.I.O. Council," 222–39. For national studies of the UPWA, see Halpern, *Down on the Killing Floor*; Roger Horowitz, *"Negro and White, Unite and Fight!"*. See also Halpern and Horowitz's interviews with Eddie Humphries [sic] and Mary Salinas, UPWA Oral History Project, Wisconsin Historical Society; Eddie Humphrey, interview by author, Fort Worth, November 1, 2008; and Helen Wallace, interview by author, Fort Worth, September 29, 2009.

7. Lee A. Lewis, interview by George N. Green, October 4, 1971, Houston, OH 22, TLA-UTA, 56–57 (all quotations), 60–61. For a longer version of this story, see Krochmal, "Labor, Civil Rights, and the Struggle for Democracy in Texas," 105–12.

8. Green, *The Establishment*, chap. 6–7 (quotation on 90). See also Margaret Carter, "A Letter to My Daughter," part 2, *TO*, February 7, 1964, 11.

9. Polakoff, "The Development of the Texas State C.I.O. Council," 413–37 (quotation on 423).

10. Ibid., 433.

11. Ibid., chap. 11.

12. Carleton, *Red Scare!*; Green, *The Establishment*, chap. 5.

13. Green, *The Establishment*, chap. 8, 10–11.

14. *Proceedings of the Fifty-Third Convention of the Texas State Federation of Labor*, Galveston, June 25–28, 1951, TLA-UTA, 66 (original emphasis).

15. Pitre, *In Struggle against Jim Crow*, 72–78, 89–104, 112–14 (first and second quotations on 73, quoting Wesley's *Informer*; third quotation on 102).

16. Ibid., 114–18 (quotation on 118).

17. Adair tells a slightly different version of this story, but it agrees on the main points—that she started out as an assistant to White, resented the influence of Communists within the branch, and returned to the branch staff as a non-Communist alternative after White resigned in 1949. See Christia Adair, interview by Dorothy R. Robinson, *Black Women Oral History Project*, Schlesinger Library, Radcliffe College, copy in Adair Collection, MSS 109, Box 4, Folder 2, HMRC, 19.

18. Pitre, *In Struggle*, 118–26 (both quotations on 124).

19. Gillette, "The NAACP in Texas, 1937–1957," chap. 8 (quotation on 293); Pitre, *In Struggle*, 126. For details on the case, see the *State of Texas v. NAACP*, Case Records, 1911–61, BCAH. On the fallout from the case, see "Texas State Conference of NAACP Branches Defies National Board" and "Plans Made for Future NAACP," both in *DE*, May 25, 1957.

20. The following pages are based primarily on my fieldwork in May 2010, supplemented by the vertical files at TSU and various small collections at the HMRC. See also "About Us," *Harris County Council of Organizations*; "Blacks in Office to Increase in 1972 Elections," *HC*, April 16, 1972, 20, in LeRoy Collection, Box 1, Folder 5, HMRC; Moses LeRoy interview by Chandler Davidson, January 25, 1979, Houston, Texas, Chandler Davidson Texas Politics Research Collection, WRC, MS 259, Box 9, Folder 6, 22–24; Davidson, "Notes on Interview with Mr. LeRoy, Jan. 25, 1979," Davidson Texas Politics Research Collection, MS 259, Box 9, Folder 6, WRC. No comprehensive history of the HCCO exists. The best published work on black politics in Houston is Chandler Davidson, *Biracial Politics*.

21. "Black Politics: A Time for Action," *The Commercial Newsletter* (Houston), November 18, 1971, 5, LeRoy Collection, Box 1, Folder 5, HMRC (first quotation; the original erroneously reads "red hearing"); Ed Wendt, "Moses and Erma Leroy: A Civil Rights Love Story," *FT*, February 17, 1990, 2C (second quotation); Davidson, "Notes on Interview with Mr. LeRoy, Jan. 25, 1979" (fourth quotation); Moses LeRoy interview by Marguerite Johnston Barnes, Houston, n.d. [ca. 1986], Marguerite Johnston Barnes Research Materials for *Houston, The Unknown City, 1830–1991*, WRC, MS 455, Box 2, Folder 28. On the Minute Women and the list, see Pitre, *In Struggle*, 142, 172 (note 27).

22. They all had ties to the labor movement but also doubled as small businessmen, suggesting that the two endeavors remained compatible among upwardly mobile African Americans in this period. All also had ties to the NAACP. Nelson was primarily a barber but had organized for the CIO in the 1940s. Historian Merline Pitre lists Hilliard alongside

Nelson and LeRoy as one of several "labor movement advance men," but later primary and secondary sources list Hilliard as a "real estate man" and leader in the Greater Third Ward Citizens League. Henry was fired from his job at the Hughes Tool Company in 1944 and then went to work for the steelworkers union until July 1949. He ran an accounting firm on the side and was an "entrepreneur" in addition to a community and political activist. Public records suggest that the fourth founder, M. L. Ward, ran a barbecue restaurant in 1935 even as he worked as a truck driver at a machine shop in 1940. An oral history narrator in the 1970s remembered that he was "ordinary" but owned several filling stations and led the Greater Third Ward Citizens League. See "Negro Groups Plan Election Next Sunday," *HC*, January 6, 1957, microfiche in *Houston Chronicle* Morgue, HMRC (hereafter HCM-HMRC), filed under "Harris County Council of Organizations" (hereafter HCCO); Pitre, *In Struggle*, 70; Cole, *No Color Is My Kind*, 34; Doyle and Walker, "Henry, Forest Thomas, Sr."

23. In fact, LeRoy remained the council's parliamentarian for some three decades. Letter from John L. Hill to Moses LeRoy, November 5, 1976, LeRoy Collection, MSS 90, Box 1, Folder 1, HMRC.

24. Tommy Roy interview by author, Houston, December 6, 2012, digital recording in author's possession; author's voice memos on conversation with Tommy Roy, Houston, May 25, 2010, digital recording in author's possession; informal conversations between author and retirees from ILA Local 872, Houston ILA Retirees Association meeting at the ILA Local 1351 Hall, Houston, May 19, 2010; "Personal Telephone Directory and Local History of I. L. A. 872," ca. 1960, digital photographs in author's possession, courtesy Tommy Roy; Howard Middleton Jr., interview by author, Houston, May 5 and 31, 2010, digital audio recording in author's possession. On Freeman Everett and the early history of Local 18, see also *Proceedings of the Texas State Federation of Labor*: Forty-Eighth Convention June 24–27, 1946, Houston, 200–201; Forty-Ninth Convention, June 30 to July 3, 1947, Dallas, 193–94, 221–24; Fiftieth Convention, June 21–25, 1948, Fort Worth, 138–39, 209–11, 235; Fifty-First Convention, June 21–25, 1949, Beaumont, 143–45, 154–55; Fifty-Second Convention, June 26–29, 1950, San Antonio, 101, 136–38—all in TLA-UTA. See also Lewis interview by Green OH 22, 25–30, 33–34; Krochmal, "Labor, Civil Rights, and the Struggle for Democracy in Texas," 88–93, 105–11, 119, 208–9.

25. Middleton interview; "Bill Elliott Announces for Reelection as County Judge," *HP*, February 4, 1962, Adair Collection, Box 1, Folder 11, HMRC; Jim Criswell, "Merchant Starts Group to Teach Negro Voters," *HP*, December 3, 1962, Sec. 1, 16, clipping in Adair Collection, Box 3, Folder 4, HMRC.

26. Kellar, *Make Haste Slowly: Moderates, Conservatives, and School Desegregation in Houston*, 34, 67–68.

27. "Negro Groups Move to Upset Teacher Plan," *HC*, March 24, 1958, HCM-HMRC, HCCO (first, second, third, and fifth quotations); Kellar, *Make Haste Slowly*, 105 (fourth quotation).

28. Jennifer Radcliffe, "Celebrating Black History Month: Elected Official Hattie Mae White," *HC*, February 13, 2011, http://www.chron.com/disp/story.mpl/metropolitan/7425991.html (accessed May 7, 2011) (first and second quotations); "Negro Group Fight on School Bonds Growing," *HC*, May 12, 1959, HCM-HMRC, HCCO (third and fourth quotations). Radcliffe adds that Mrs. White served for nine years, until conservatives finally defeated her in 1967.

29. John Lash, "Negro Groups Charge Police with Brutality," *HC*, August 12, 1959, (all quotations); John Lash, "Cutrer May Hear Brutality Charges," *HC*, August 13, 1959—both in HCM-HMRC, HCCO.

30. "Negro Student Claims Two Cops Beat Him," *HC*, August 26, 1959 (all quotations); John Lash, "Negroes Renew Probe Demand," *HC*, August 25, 1959. The district attorney eventually replied that the HCCO's charges were without merit. "D.A. Says Cops Doing Fine Job," *HC*, September 4, 1959—all in HCM-HMRC, HCCO.

31. "Negro Baptist Pastor in City Council Race," *HC*, September 23, 1959 (both quotations); "Negro Will Be in Race for City Council," *HC*, September 22, 1959—both in HCM-HMRC, HCCO.

32. "Negro Upped As Apprentice Stockman," *HI*, January 28, 1956, in LeRoy Collection, Box 1, Folder 5, HMRC (first quotation); Moses LeRoy, interview by George N. Green, August 19, 1971, Houston, Texas, TLA-UTA, OH 20, 9, 11–13 (second quotation on 12).

33. "Negro Upped as Apprentice Stockman," *HI*, January 28, 1956, in LeRoy Collection, Box 1, Folder 5, HMRC (all quotations).

34. LeRoy interview by Green, 22–25 (last two quotations on 24, "one little wing" on 22); Gonzales, "A Lecture, Plus More on Old Houston Hospitals" (first and second quotations); "I Feel a Train a Coming, It's Coming Round the Bend"; "Image Gallery—Hospital Postcards"; Drexler, "Sunset Hospital."

35. LeRoy interview by Green, 22 (first quotation), 26 (second and third quotations).

36. LeRoy interview by Green, 20–21.

37. "Woman of the Year Presentation at Nobby's Corner," *FT*, August 18, 1973, 12B; "Many Firsts for Mrs. Erma LeRoy," *HI*, December 7, 1965—clippings of both in LeRoy Collection, Box 1, Folder 5; Wendt, "Moses and Erma Leroy: A Civil Rights Love Story," *FT*, February 17, 1990; Research Card on Erma LeRoy, October 26, 1988, Davidson Texas Politics Collection, Box 9, Folder 7; Davidson, "Notes on Interview with Mr. LeRoy, Jan. 25, 1979," 2; "Phone Call from Erma LeRoy to Ruthe Winegarten," August 29, 1991, typed notes, Ruthe Winegarten Papers, 1912–2004, BCAH, 2.325, Box W70; Long, "The Chat-An-Hour Social and Cultural Club: African American Women Readers," 459–71; Pitre, *In Struggle*, 140–41.

38. Wendt, "Moses and Erma Leroy: A Civil Rights Love Story"; 1959 City Directory for Moses LeRoy, *Ancestry.com*; "Along the N.A.A.C.P. Battlefront," *Crisis*, March 1956, 165.

39. Dulaney, "The Progressive Voters League," 34; Dulaney, "Democratic Progressive Voters League"; Sapper, "A Survey of the History of the Black People of Texas, 1930–1954," 118–20, 161–65 (first quotation on 118; second quotation on 119). Sapper paraphrases the *Waco Messenger*, August 25, 1944, 1; and *HI*, October 21, 1944, 8. On the split between the two groups and the early history of TCV, see "Progressive Voters Reaffirm Non-Partisan Stand at Meeting," *DE*, October 21, 1944; Carter Wesley, "Lesson in Politics," *DE*, November 11, 1944; "Voters League's Program Approved by Democratic State Executive Committee," *DE*, January 13, 1945; "Durham Calls Dems to Meet," *DE*, April 27, 1946; "Texas Democrats Pledge Loyalty to Organization," *DE*, May 11, 1946; Carter Wesley, "Durham Is Still Wrong," *DE*, July 13, 1946; and "Durham, Wesley, Blast Each Other," *DE*, July 20, 1946. On the Progressive Party, see "Rev. Stacy Adams Removed from Political Offices," *DE*, April 3, 1948. The author again thanks Marvin Dulaney for sharing his research notes on Durham and the *DE*.

40. See two previous notes; LeRoy interview by Green, 41–42. See also the next section below.

41. "Fair Dealers Bolt Convention: Maverick Leads Meet Break," *SAL*, May 27, 1952, 1, 6.

42. Chris Dixie, interview by Chandler Davidson, Houston, January 17, 1977; "Local Labor Lawyer Dies from Lung Cancer at 86," unidentified newspaper clipping, March 12, 2001—both in Chandler Davidson Texas Politics Research Collection, WRC, Box 1, Folder 11, 1–2 (quotation on 2).

43. Dixie interview by Davidson, 3–10 (first and second quotations on 5, third quotation on 10).

44. Dixie interview by Davidson, 10, 12.

45. Dixie interview by Davidson, 3, 8–9 (quotations), 14–15, 18–19, 33.

46. Cox, *Ralph W. Yarborough, the People's Senator*, chaps. 1–5.

47. Robert E. "Bob" Hall, interview by author, May 18, 2010, Houston, Texas, digital audio recording to be archived at Texas Christian University, 0:20, 8:55, 13:20–18:20, 1:06:30, 1:10:40. Hall worked full time in the 1952 campaign, sat out the 1954 effort, and returned again full time in 1956, when he served as Yarborough's traveling itinerary manager. By the time of the third gubernatorial race, Hall had an offer from the Dixie & Shulman labor law firm of Houston, but he took leave to work full time in electoral politics—an activity the partners strongly supported.

48. Cox, *Yarborough*, 102–3.

49. Dixie interview by Davidson, 9, 21–22 (quotation on 22), 38, 41. White union wives came in through the women's activities division or the women's auxiliaries of their husbands' unions. Most white "union women" hailed from the Communications Workers of America (they worked at the phone company) or the garment workers unions.

50. Dixie interview by Davidson, 19 (quotation); "The History of the Harris County Democrats," no author, no date [1967], Adair Collection, Box 1, Folder 2, HMRC; Christia Adair interview by Robinson, Adair Collection, Box 4, Folder 2, HMRC, iii–iv, 21; Letter from Ross Love and Billie Carr to Democratic Precinct Chair, no date [1997], Billie Carr Papers, WRC, Box 1, Folder 1. A copy of "The History of the Harris County Democrats" (1967) can also be found in the Carr Papers, Box 4, Folder 10. The best histories of the HCD are included in Davidson, *Race and Class in Texas Politics*.

51. "History of the Harris County Democrats," [1967], Adair Collection, Box 1, Folder 2, HMRC, 1; Ronnie Dugger, "Randolph, Frankie Carter," *Handbook of Texas Online*, http://www.tshaonline.org/handbook/online/articles/fra34 (accessed May 8, 2011).

52. Dixie interview by Davidson, 22–23 (quotation on 23).

53. "History of the Harris County Democrats," [1967], 1 (first quotation); Dixie interview by Davidson, 27 (second quotation); *Texas Almanac, 1956–1957* (Dallas: Belo, 1955), 431, 521–22, available online via *The Portal to Texas History*, (accessed April 23, 2016), http://texashistory.unt.edu/ark:/67531/metapth117138/.

54. Dixie interview by Davidson, 20 (third quotation), 27 (first quotation), 39 (second quotation).

55. "Elections of Texas Governors, 1845–2010." On the "Port Arthur Story," see the feature articles in *TO*, December 13 and 20, 1954; Fred Schmidt, "The 'Port Arthur Story,'" *Texas State AFL-CIO News*, October 1960, 4; and Cox, *Yarborough*, 114–17.

56. "History of the Harris County Democrats," [1967], Adair Collection, Box 1, Folder 2, HMRC, 1; "Harris Democrats Back Party Ticket," unknown newspaper clipping dated 1954, Adair Collection, Box 1, Folder 2.

57. "History of the Harris County Democrats," [1967], Adair Collection, Box 1, Folder 2, HMRC, 1.

58. Hall interview by author, May 18, 2010, 19:45; Robert E. "Bob" Hall, interview by author, May 31, 2010, Houston, Texas; Cox, *Yarborough*, chaps. 6–7, 134–35 (vitriolic quotation on 136).

59. History of the Harris County Democrats," [1967], Adair Collection, Box 1, Folder 2, HMRC, 1.

60. Kathleen Voigt and Mimi Steinart, "Let's Compare the Records," Democrats of Texas flyer [1958], Adair Collection, Box 1, Folder 2, HMRC.

61. Hall interview by author, May 18, 2010, 27:50, 33:15, 46:25, 58:15-1:03:00.

62. Hall interview by author, May 18, 2010, 47:20–52:55; Brian Spinks, "Yarborough Expands Views on Segregation," *HP*, July 18, 1954, clipping in Adair Collection, Box 1, Folder 2; Cox, *Yarborough*, 112 (first quotation). Yarborough said "forced co-mingling" at his campaign kickoff on June 1, 1956. In his first interview, Hall mistakenly recalled that Yarborough directed the "woodpile" comment against Gordon McClendon, his opponent in the 1964 U.S. Senate primary, but the rest of Hall's story establishes the place and date as the North Side of Houston in 1956. Hall later confirmed that the gaffe took place in 1956. Robert E. Hall, Voice Memo #6 of 11, attached to an e-mail from Bob Hall to author, December 3, 2012 (log of voice memos and e-mails in author's possession).

63. R. R. Grovey, "Negro Leader Tells Why He's for Shivers," July 21, 1954, clipping in unknown publication, Adair Collection, MSS 109, Box 1, Folder 5, HMRC.

64. Form letter from Mrs. R. D. Randolph, April 12, 1957; letter from H. T. Taylor to C. V. Adair, May 4, 1957—both in Adair Collection, Box 4, Folder 9; Thomas Wright, "Oldtime Black Houston Freedom Fighters Left Proud Legacy," *FT*, March 17, 1973, 9B, clipping in LeRoy Collection, Box 1, Folder 5.

65. Hall interview by author, May 18, 2010, 27:50, 33:15, 46:25, 58:15-1:03:00; Dixie interview by Davidson, 28, 33; Adair interview by Robinson, 29–30.

66. Cox, *Yarborough*, chap. 8 (quotation on 142–43); Hall interview, May 18, 2010.

67. History of the Harris County Democrats," [1967], Adair Collection, Box 1, Folder 2, HMRC, 1.

68. De León, *Ethnicity in the Sunbelt: Mexican Americans in Houston*, 98, 110, 126–42.

69. Both LULAC and the AGIF have been well chronicled. Among many other sources, see Kaplowitz, *LULAC, Mexican Americans, and National Policy*; Kreneck, *Mexican American Odyssey: Felix Tijerina, Entrepreneur and Civic Leader 1905–1965*; Márquez, *LULAC: The Evolution of a Mexican American Political Organization*; Ignacio M. García, *Hector P. García*; Henry Ramos, *The American GI Forum*. More nuanced discussions include Orozco, *No Mexicans, Women, or Dogs Allowed*; Ignacio M. García, *White but Not Equal: Mexican Americans, Jury Discrimination, and the Supreme Court*; Zamora, *Claiming Rights and Righting Wrongs in Texas*; Blanton, "The Citizenship Sacrifice: Mexican Americans, the Saunders-Leonard Report, and the Politics of Immigration, 1951–1952," 299–320; Blanton, "George I. Sánchez, 569–604; Pérez, *The Decolonial Imaginary: Writing Chicanas into History*. I have written more about this literature in other venues. See Krochmal, "Chicano Labor and Multiracial Politics in Post–World War II Texas,"

133–76; Krochmal, "San Antonio Chicano Organizers (SACO): Labor Activists and El Movimiento," 203–26. The classic work on this period in Mexican American history remains Mario T. Garcia, *Mexican Americans: Leadership, Ideology, & Identity, 1930–1960*.

70. "Resume of John J. Herrera," long version, John J. Herrera Papers, MSS 160, Box 1, Folder 3, HMRC; Lauro Cruz, "My Point of View: Mexican American Leadership in Texas," clipping from unknown bilingual newspaper, April 18, 1975, in Herrera Papers, Box 1, Folder 4; Carole E. Christian, "Herrera, John J.," *Handbook of Texas Online*, accessed May 6, 2011, http://www.tshaonline.org/handbook/online/articles/fhe63.

71. "Resume of John J. Herrera," long version, 3 (first quotation), 4 (second and third quotations), 7 (final quotation); Message from Hector P. Garcia for Herrera's testimonial dinner, September 11, 1980, Box 1, Folder 9, Herrera Papers, HMRC (fourth and fifth quotations).

72. Letter from unknown to Ed Idar, May 5, 1954, Herrera Papers, HMRC, digital images in *The Portal to Texas History*, University of North Texas Libraries, accessed January 27, 2014, http://texashistory.unt.edu/ark:/67531/metapth250484/ (both quotations); Letter from John J. Herrera to Luciano Santoscoy, May 15, 1954, Herrera Papers, HMRC, digital images in *The Portal to Texas History*, University of North Texas Libraries, accessed January 27, 2014, http://texashistory.unt.edu/ark:/67531/metapth250456/.

73. "Resume of John J. Herrera" (first and last quotations); "John J. Herrera Announces for Legislature Position No. 6," undated letter with platform, 1–2 (block quotation); "Herrera Addresses Campaign Workers," no date, 1 (next quotation on "hand-shaking"); Letter from Herrera to "Dear Friend," undated 1958 campaign (quotations on "big push" and campaign workers)—all in Herrera Papers, Box 1, Folder 23, HMRC.

74. Foley, "Becoming Hispanic: Mexican Americans and the Faustian Pact with Whiteness," 53–70.

75. Telegram and articles from Danny Olivas to Pete Tijerina, October 23, 1956, Herrera Papers, HMRC, digital images in *The Portal to Texas History*, University of North Texas Libraries, accessed January 27, 2014, http://texashistory.unt.edu/ark:/67531/metapth250568/; Draft of article by John J. Herrera, October 22, 1956, Herrera Papers, HMRC, digital images in *The Portal to Texas History*, University of North Texas Libraries, accessed January 27, 2014, http://texashistory.unt.edu/ark:/67531/metapth250569/.

76. For an example of recent scholarship that emphasizes the Tijerina faction, see Behnken, *Fighting Their Own Battles: Mexican Americans, African Americans, and the Struggle for Civil Rights in Texas*, 1. Historian Neil Foley notes that his formulation applies only to a "narrow band" of men like Tijerina, and he leaves room for other coexisting political approaches among *mexicanos* in the period. See, for example, Foley, "Partly Colored or Other White?: Mexican Americans and Their Problem with the Color Line," 123–44.

77. CAC gave way to Houston's branch of the Viva Kennedy campaign in 1960 and to the Harris County Political Association of Spanish-Speaking Organizations (PASO) that succeeded it. "Political Activity that Led to the Formation of PASO," in Al Vazquez and Al Matta, eds., *The Harris County PASO Fact Book*, 1964, 8, in Roberto P. "Bob" Sanchez Papers, Box 5, Folder 1 (all quotations on 8), BLAC; Civic Action Committee *Bulletin*, March 9, 1960, Herrera Papers, HMRC, digital images in *The Portal to Texas History*, University of North Texas Libraries, accessed January 27, 2014, http://texashistory.unt.edu/ark:/67531/metapth248713/; Harris County PASO flyer for mass meeting, August 13, 1961,

Dr. Hector P. Garcia Collection, Box 152, Folder 40, "PASO August 1961," TAMUCC; Kreneck, *Del Pueblo: A History of Houston's Hispanic Community*, 78–79; De León, *Ethnicity in the Sunbelt*, 167; Pycior, *LBJ & Mexican Americans: The Paradox of Power*, 124.

Chapter 4

   1. "Negro Wins Jr. College Race" and Don Politico, "Minorities Combine, Win," *SAL*, April 4, 1948, 1.

   2. On St. Philip's, see Mason, "Paternal Continuity: African Americans and Race Relations in San Antonio, Texas, 1867–1937," chap. 5. On African American education generally, see James D. Anderson, *The Education of Blacks in the South, 1860–1935*.

   3. Mario T. Garcia, *Mexican Americans: Leadership, Ideology, & Identity, 1930–1960*, 79.

   4. Cynthia E. Orozco, "Garcia, Gustavo C.," *Handbook of Texas Online*, accessed March 1, 2011, http://www.tshaonline.org/handbook/online/articles/fga51. For more on Garcia and his landmark cases, see Ignacio M. García, *White but Not Equal*.

   5. Don Politico, "It Appears He'll Have Another Election Opponent," *SAL*, March 7, 1948, 7-B; Don Politico, "Their Announced Aim—Force Him From Race," *SAL*, March 14, 1948, 4-B, 7-B (first and second quotations); Don Politico, "Dinero Rears Its Head—There's Plenty Ready to Ride on Hauck vs. High Sheriff," *SAL*, March 28, 1948, 4-B (third and fourth quotations); "School Districts to Elect Saturday," *SAE*, March 29, 1948, 10-A; "Negro Wins Jr. College Race" April 4, 1948, 1 (final quotation).

   6. "Negro Wins Jr. College Race" April 4, 1948, 1 (statistics); "Minorities Combine, Win," *SAL*, April 4, 1948, 1 (first, second, and third quotations), 10-A (fourth, fifth, sixth, and seventh quotations); "Sutton Takes Victory in Stride," *SAL*, April 5, 1948, 2-A. The previous college board election was held on its own and only drew 460 voters to the polls ("School Districts to Elect Saturday," *SAE*, March 29, 1948, 10-A). Supporters of Sutton's vanquished opponent pointed out that voters at two polling places in affluent Los Angeles Heights had to travel to a third site to vote in the college board race, and only a few did so. They suggested that Sutton would have lost had their supporters been able to vote in one stop. Sutton and Bellinger replied by pointing out a number of voting irregularities on the East Side. The papers concluded that this was a relatively clean election. See "L. A. Heights Setup Decides for Sutton," *SAL*, April 5, 1948, 1; "L. A. Hgts. Vote Denial Claimed," *SAL*, April 6, 1948, 1; Don Politico, "Guillermo Hensley Is Coasting Serenely But the Don Sees Tough Weather on Horizon," *SAL*, April 11, 1948, 14-A; "Official Returns," *SAL*, April 8, 1948, 9-A. After the recount, Sutton won by a scant twenty-seven votes.

   7. Garcia, *Mexican Americans*, 82; Orozco, "Garcia, Gustavo C." Garcia doesn't mention black participation in the 1948 election itself.

   8. Don Politico, "City Race Really a Fight for Power," *SAL*, May 9, 1949, 19-A (quotation); "White, 4-1 Winner, Eyes Tax Evaders," *SAL*, May 11, 1949, 1; Kemper Diehl, "Office Quiet as Callaghan Ends 2-Year Grasp of City's Reins," *SAL*, May 31, 1949, 2-A; Don Politico, "No Rest for Weary Politicians When Pledge Payments Due," *SAL*, July 3, 1949, 2-B; "Knight Halts R. B. Green Board Move," *SAL*, July 7, 1949, 1.

   9. "Negroes Win Fight To Use Park," *SAL*, May 19, 1949, 1–2.

   10. "Negroes Prepare Segregation Suit," *SAL*, September 28, 1950, 2-A (all quotations); "Negroes Start Fight for 'Equal' College," *SAL*, October 18, 1950.

11. Rosales, *The Illusion of Inclusion*, 45–50; Palmer, *Living as Equals*, 171–72. On San Antonio in the broader context of the Southwest, see Amy Bridges, *Morning Glories*.

12. Rosales, *The Illusion of Inclusion*, 50, citing John Rodgers in *TO*. The one exception to complete elite dominance at the polls was Henry B. Gonzalez, who first won a seat on the council in 1953, before the GGL was founded. Palmer, *Living as Equals*, 172.

13. Black and Matthews, *Grandpa Was a Preacher: A Letter to My Grandson*, 3–10, 23–24; Rev. Claude W. Black Jr., interview by author, San Antonio, October 27, 2008.

14. Black and Matthews, *Grandpa Was a Preacher*, 16–18 (quotation on 18).

15. Ibid., 66.

16. Ibid., 19; Black interview by author.

17. Black and Matthews, *Grandpa Was a Preacher*, 19–22 (first quotation on 20; second quotation on 21).

18. Ibid., 29–36 (both quotations on 35).

19. The Claude & ZerNona Black Foundation, "Biography," accessed March 8, 2011, http://www.claudeblack.org/biography/.

20. Black and Matthews, *Grandpa Was a Preacher*, 65–66 (quotation on 66).

21. Ibid., 74–76. "Day Care Nursery Lays Corner Stone," *SNAP News*, October 11, 1957, MS 139, Box 2, Folder 1, SABHC.

22. Black and Matthews, *Grandpa Was a Preacher*, 49–62 (first quotation on 52; second quotation on 53).

23. Black and Matthews, *Grandpa Was a Preacher*, 62–63; Eugene Coleman, interview by author, San Antonio, September 2, 2009.

24. Coleman interview by author, digital audio recording, file 1, 0:30-11:10. Coleman adds that he also organized a noncommissioned officers club at Brooks, a fact that protected him from official reprisals or dismissal.

25. Coleman interview by author, file 1, 18:30–23:15. He hoped to get a small business loan from the Reconstruction Finance Corporation, a federal government agency designed to help the country transition from war manufacturing to a peacetime economy. Coleman believed his veteran status would help him qualify for assistance, but such aid was not forthcoming. It is unclear whether his business plan or his race caused the denial, but Coleman likely believed the latter was the main issue.

26. Coleman interview, file 1, 23:15. Note that Coleman uses "poor people" and "blacks" almost interchangeably in this excerpt.

27. Coleman interview, file 1, 25:00–26:50.

28. Coleman interview, file 1, 26:50.

29. Rosales, *The Illusion of Inclusion*, 42, 50–55 (all quotations on 53).

30. José Ángel Gutiérrez, Oral History Interview with Albert Peña Jr., July 2, 1996, San Antonio, CMAS 15, TV-UTA, 8–10.

31. Ibid., 11 (both quotations); Al Heiken, "'The Only Way I Want to Win,'" *TO*, July 4, 1959, 5.

32. Albert Peña interview by Gutiérrez, 4–7. See also José Ángel Gutiérrez, Oral History Interview with Olga Peña, April 14, 1997, San Antonio, CMAS 108, TV-UTA.

33. Albert Peña interview by Gutiérrez, 7.

34. Ibid., 8.

35. Ibid., 14–16 (first quotation on 15; second and third quotations on 16). At the Lytle hearing, Peña was accompanied by his friend Willie Maldonado, head of the laborers

union and a deputy sheriff. Maldonado doubled as Peña's bodyguard when a group of whites surrounded them after the attorney's testimony. Peña feared it was a lynch mob, but in fact it was a group of white teachers who thanked him for advocating integration. Maldonado nonetheless had his hand on his service revolver, just in case.

36. Eleuterio Escobar, the leader of the School Improvement League, was "mentioned but not considered" as Garcia's replacement on the school board. A conservative businessman got the job instead. See Jon Ford, "Backstage in Politics: Bareknuckle Dem-GOP Campaigns On," *SAE*, September 7, 1952, 16 (quotation); "Ralph Cardenas Named to Garcia School Post," *SAE*, September 18, 1952, 1B; "Trustee Post Battle Looms," *SAE*, August 20, 1952, 8; "Group Greets Gus Garcia," *SAE*, February 11, 1952, 3; "Mitin En Favor De Stevenson-Sparkman," *Brownsville Herald*, October 29, 1952, 14. Garcia also resigned in protest from the Texas Council on Human Relations and state Good Neighbor Commission that year. See "Sanchez Quits Neighbor Group," *SAE*, July 3, 1952, 1.

37. Albert Peña interview by Gutiérrez, 14–16 (quotations on 16); Rosales, *Illusion of Inclusion*, 55–56. Olga Peña also cofounded the group. Other early activists in LAD included Lalo Solis and Ruben Munguia, both of whom were also the Peñas' *compadres* (godparents). See Olga Peña interview by Gutiérrez, 43, 67.

38. Albert Peña interview by Gutiérrez, 18–20.

39. Albert Peña oral history interview, quoted in Rosales, *Illusion of Inclusion*, 54.

40. Olga Peña interview by Gutiérrez, 106. See also Rosie Castro, interview by author, San Antonio, September 8, 2009, 12:39 (digital audio recording in author's possession).

41. Ruben Munguia oral history interview, quoted in Rosales, *Illusion of Inclusion*, 54.

42. Rosales, *Illusion of Inclusion*, 54.

43. "Texas New Deal Demos Call for National Presidential Primary," *SAL*, May 28, 1952, 7-A.

44. Rosales, *Illusion of Inclusion*, 56 (quotation); "8 From SA to Aid Adlai," *SAL*, October 4, 1952, 1.

45. Jon Ford, "Bexar Demos Complain of Dwindling Finances," *SAE*, October 9, 1952, 14.

46. Harrison Lilly, "75,000 Turn Out for Flip Quipper," *SAL*, October 19, 1952, 1, 15 (first "Olé" quotation); Ed Castillo, "Adelaido Doesn't Make Jokes—Even in Spanish," *SAL*, October 19, 1952, 15 ("Vivas" and summary of tourist-Spanish speech quotations); "Text of Stevenson's 2 Speeches in San Antonio," *SAL*, October 19, 1952, 15 (English speech quotations). See also Rosales, *Illusion of Inclusion*, 56–57.

47. Rosales, *Illusion of Inclusion*, 57; "Final Stevenson Coffee Monday," *SAE*, November 2, 1952.

48. In his otherwise excellent study, Rosales all but ignores this critical development, casting non-*mexicanos* either as inert objects affected by West Side politics or as negative agents who were at best fickle allies with *la raza*. Sutton appears as a more dedicated partner, but East Side activism and coalition efforts both play subordinate, supportive roles to what Rosales depicts as the main act happening on the West Side.

49. Albert Peña interview by Gutiérrez, 16.

50. Kohout, "Gonzalez, Henry Barbosa"(quotation); Eugene Rodriguez Jr., *Henry B. Gonzalez: A Political Profile*, 52–61, 68, 71.

51. "NAACP State Meet Here, Best in History," *SAR*, October 30, 1953, 1, 3; U. J. Andrews, "Good Times A-Coming," *SAR*, February 5, 1954, 2; "Register's Choices," *SAR*,

July 23, 1954, 1; "Can We Forget?" *SAR*, August 27, 1954, 1; "Texas Jim Crow Fight Law Knocked Out," *SAR*, October 29, 1954, 1, 3; "Representation for all the people," campaign flyer in Peña scrapbook, page 29, copy in author's possession, courtesy José Angel Gutiérrez; "Legislative Ticket Platform Set," Peña scrapbook, 21; Rosales, *Illusion of Inclusion*, 55.

52. Rosales, *Illusion of Inclusion*, 57–58; Ann Diver, "Auxiliary to Push Poll Tax," *SAL*, November 24, 1954, 12; "Bexar Democratic Groups Set Open House," *SAL*, March 31, 1955, 27.

53. "Vote! Elect Them, Saturday," *SAR*, July 27, 1956, 1; "More Voters Needed, Saturday," *SAR*, August 24, 1956, 1; "Trevino, Pena Winners, Daniel Nips Yarborough," *SAR*, August 31, 1956; José Angel Gutiérrez, "Dean Emeritus of Chicano Politics," 103, 107, 113.

54. In addition to the articles cited in the previous note, see "Register's Choices," *SAR*, July 23, 1954, 1; and "Turn Back the Hate Mongers!," *SAR*, April 1, 1955, 1, 4.

55. Rodriguez, *Henry B. Gonzalez: A Political Profile*, 69.

56. *SNAP News*, March 16, 1956, MS 139, Box 1, Folder 36, 4–5, SABHC; Kohout, "Gonzalez, Henry Barbosa."

57. "S.A. Chapter to Try to Void New City Law" *SAE*, June 21, 1954, 1; "Rice, Negro Leaders Set Talks on Park, Swimming Pool Segregation" *SAL*, January 17, 1955, 3.

58. Black and Matthews, *Grandpa Was a Preacher*, 105 (all quotations).

59. *SNAP News*, March 16, 1956, MS 139, Box 1, Folder 36, SABHC, 4–5. *SNAP* notes that the original pool segregation ordinance followed an earlier incident that took place in April 1954.

60. Rodriguez, *Henry B. Gonzalez: A Political Profile*, 71–72.

61. "Dedication Banquet," *SNAP News*, September 27, 1957, MS 139, Box 2, Folder 1, SABHC.

62. "Political Action Group," *SNAP News*, May 24, 1957, MS 139, Box 2, Folder 1, SABHC.

63. "Bible Study Week," *SNAP News*, January 17, 1958, MS 139, Box 2, Folder 2, SABHC.

64. "NAACP Anniversary Dinner," *SNAP News*, undated [1958] (Campanella cover); "Deserved Recognition," *SAR*, November 8, 1957, 4; "Senator Henry B. Gonzalez Honored by Local NAACP" (photo caption) *SAR*, February 21, 1958, 1; Rodriguez, *Henry B. Gonzalez: A Political Profile*, 79–83.

65. "Court Ends Discrimination," *SNAP News*, May 8, 1959, MS 139, Box 2, Folder 3, SABHC. See also the discussion above of Sutton's fight over county facilities in 1949 and "Open Doors, Negroes Say," *SAE*, April 5, 1956, 12-B.

66. "G. J. Sutton Speaks for FEPC Law," *SNAP News*, December 12, 1958, MS 139, Box 2, Folder 2 (emphasis in original quotations), SABHC; "FEPC Ordinance to be Presented City Council, Oct. 1," *SAR*, September 18, 1959, 1, 3; "Marcee Again Heads Local NAACP Branch," *SAR*, December 20, 1957, 1; "Local Branch NAACP to Install Officers Sunday," *SAR*, January 17, 1958, 1; "Effort to Put Negro on Hospital Board Fails," *SAR*, January 31, 1958, 1.

67. For more details on their activities in this period, see Krochmal, "Labor, Civil Rights, and the Struggle for Democracy in Texas, 1935–1965," 229–51.

68. Rodriguez, *Henry B. Gonzalez: A Political Profile*, 82–83, citing Ronnie Dugger, "Filibusters and Majority Rule," *The Progressive*, August 1957, 21.

69. Rodriguez, *Henry B. Gonzalez*, 85–86 (quotations on 85).

70. Ibid.

71. Dawson Duncan, "Daniel Again Vows War Against DOT," *Dallas News*, May 17, 1958; Jon Ford, "D.O.T's Power Losing Punch?," *SAE*, May 13, 1958; Neil Addington, "Liberal Democrats Take Over County Committee," *HP*, May 13, 1958; Bob Hollingsworth, "Rise of Texas Liberals: More Power at the Polls," *Dallas Herald*, May 30, 1958; Jon Ford, "DOT Seen Swamped on Saturday," *SAE*, July 26, 1958—all clippings in Texas AFL-CIO Papers, Democratic Party Organizations, TLA-UTA, AR110-26-9-3.

72. Democrats of Texas Press Release, January 12, 1957; Democrats of Texas, January Report, 1957; Minutes, Executive Board Meeting, May 18, 1957; Draft Minutes, Executive Board Meeting, June 8, 1957; Draft Minutes, Executive Board Meeting, August 10, 1957; "Reminder: To the members of the Steering Committee," September 6, 1957; Draft Minutes, Executive Board Meeting, November 23, 1957 (Report of Committee on Principles)—all in Texas AFL-CIO Papers, Democratic Party Organizations, TLA-UTA, AR110-26-8-5. Most of downtown Austin remained segregated in the late 1950s, and the Austin Hotel continued to exclude black Democratic activists through 1961. See handwritten minutes of the second full meeting of the Democratic Coalition, September 9, 1961, item #4, Texas AFL-CIO Papers, Democratic Party Organizations, TLA-UTA, AR110-26-9-4.

73. Jon Ford, "D.O.T's Power Losing Punch?" *SAE*, May 13, 1958, clipping in Texas AFL-CIO Papers, Democratic Party Organizations, TLA-UTA, AR110-26-9-3.

74. "Gonzalez May Get Blessing of DOT In Governor Race," *CCC*, May 30, 1958, clipping in Texas AFL-CIO Papers, Democratic Party Organizations, TLA-UTA, AR110-26-9-3.

75. Sam Wood, "Minority Bloc Has Candidates Ready," *AA*, May 29, 1958, 1, 15, clipping in Texas AFL-CIO Papers, Democratic Party Organizations, TLA-UTA, AR110-26-9-2.

76. "Thus We Met," *Democratic Reporter* 1:4 (June 1958), copy in Texas AFL-CIO Papers, Democratic Party Organizations, TLA-UTA, AR110-26-9-1.

77. "Report by Creekmore Fath," May 31, 1958, Texas AFL-CIO Papers, Democratic Party Organizations, TLA-UTA, AR110-26-8-5 (all quotations). As noted below, the official proceedings ("Thus We Met") omitted the section on Durham.

78. For another critique, see "Durham Scolds Texans for Failure to Endorse Gonzalez," *DE*, June 21, 1958.

79. This analysis is my own. There is a vast literature on the white legal classification of Mexican Americans and the differences in racialization between *mexicanos* and African Americans. For an introduction, see, among many others, Gross, "'The Caucasian Cloke': Mexican Americans and the Politics of Whiteness in the Twentieth Century Southwest," 337–92; Foley, *Quest for Equality: The Failed Promise of Black-Brown Solidarity*; Johnson, "The Cosmic Race in Texas: Racial Fusion, White Supremacy, and Civil Rights Politics," 404–19.

80. Cliff Lawhorne, "Nueces Group Beats Drums for Gonzalez," *CCCT*, June 1, 1958 (first and third quotations); "Party Control DOT War Song," *CCC*, June 1, 1958 (second quotation); Jimmy Banks, "Gonzalez Almost Steals Show With Talk at DOT Convention," *DMN*, June 1, 1958, sec. 1, p. 9 (all remaining quotations); "Thus We Met," *Democratic Reporter* 1:4 (June, 1958)—all in Texas AFL-CIO Papers, Democratic Party Organizations, TLA-UTA, AR110-26-9-1.

81. "Report by Creekmore Fath," May 31, 1958, AR 110-26-8-5; "Thus We Met"; "Durham Scolds Texans for Failure to Endorse Gonzalez," *DE*, June 21, 1958. On Sutton's elec-

tion, see "Party Control DOT War Song," *CCC*, June 1, 1958, clipping in Texas AFL-CIO Papers, Democratic Party Organizations, TLA-UTA, AR110-26-9-3.

82. "Why the Negro Can't," *SNAP News*, July 25, 1958, MS 139, Box 2, Folder 2, SABHC.

83. "Gonzales for Governor," display ad, *SNAP News*, July 25, 1958, MS 139, Box 2, Folder 2, SABHC.

84. Surprisingly, Bellinger and many of Sutton's typical allies in San Antonio all endorsed Commissioner Ploch, a stand that drew the ire of *SNAP*. See "Be Their Friends—With Ballots," *SAR*, July 25, 1958, 1; "For Continued Progress, Let's Re-Elect A. J. Ploch," advertisement in *SAR*, July 25, 1958, 4.

85. Gutiérrez, "Dean Emeritus of Chicano Politics," 140–42. On Gonzalez's big donors and closer ties to wealthy white liberals such as Bill Sinkin, see the lone folder on this campaign in the Henry B. Gonzalez Papers, MSS 127, Box 50, BCAH.

86. Rodriguez, *Henry B. Gonzalez: A Political Profile*, 86–87 (budget numbers on 86; quotation on 87); *Texas Almanac, 1961–1962* (Dallas: Belo, 1961), 479, available online via *The Portal to Texas History*, accessed April 23, 2016, http://texashistory.unt.edu/ark: /67531/metapth117140/.

Chapter 5

1. "1000 in Strike Parade," *SAL*, March 14, 1959, 1 (first quotation); Al Heiken, "The Strike in San Antonio," *TO*, April 4, 1959, 6 (all other quotations); "Unionists Parade," *SAL*, March 15, 1959, 12-A (photograph). See also Letter from George Eichler to All Local Unions and Lodges, n.d. [late March 1960—"fifth week" of strike], George and Latane Lambert Papers, TLA-UTA (hereafter Lambert Papers), AR127-25-7.

2. Paul Javior, interviews by author, September 4, 2009, San Antonio, and March 23, 2010, Adkins, Texas, digital recordings in author's possession. See also Palmer, *Living as Equals*, chap. 5.

3. Javior interviews by author.

4. Ledesma, "Unlikely Strikers: Mexican-American Women in Strike Activity in Texas, 1919–1974"; Ledesma, "Texas Newspapers and Chicana Workers' Activism, 1919–1974," 309–31.

5. Flores, "An Unladylike Strike Fashionably Clothed: Mexicana and Anglo Women Garment Workers Against Tex-Son, 1959–1963," 367–402.

6. Miscellaneous clippings, Lambert Papers, AR127-4-6. On George's time in the Amalgamated, see AR127, Boxes 1 and 2. On Latane's time at Commonwealth College, see Lambert Papers, AR127-4-10.

7. "'In the South. . . . We Want to Walk With Our Heads Up,'" clipping from unknown ACWA publication, n.d. [1946], copy in Lambert Papers, AR127-4-6.

8. "Longtime Labor Leader George Lambert Dies," *Dallas Craftsman*, August 23, 1974, 1, 3, copy in Lambert Papers, AR127-4-6.

9. Lambert Papers, AR127-27-2.

10. "Council Asked to Turn Down Raise in Fares," *DMN*, August 11, 1953, 1; "ADA Takes Bow for Role in Fare Row," *DMN*, September 27, 1953, 2; other articles dated August 4 and July 29, 1953; Telegram from Lambert to Thornton, Lambert Papers, AR127-27-8; U. Simpson Tate, "A Statement to the City Council of Dallas, in Opposition to Proposed Increases in Bus and Trolley Rates," August 10, 1953, Lambert Papers, AR127-27-8.

11. "NAACP Meeting Gets Under Way," *SAE*, October 24, 1953, 2.

12. Letter from A. Maceo Smith to Roy Wilkins, November 28, 1955, and reply dated December 2, 1955, both in Lambert Papers, AR127-4-5.

13. "Report of Poll Tax Committee Meeting Held on November 8, 1954," Democratic Organizing Committee, Lambert Papers, AR127-7-6. George Lambert also coordinated the Ralph Yarborough gubernatorial campaigns in Dallas and Tarrant Counties in 1954 and in Jefferson County in Southeast Texas in 1956. See Lambert Papers, AR127-30-9. On Yarborough, see below. For more on the coalition, see Letter from Otto Mullinax, November 9, 1954; and "Suggested Plans for Dallas County Democratic Organizing Committee," September 1–14, 1953—both in Texas AFL-CIO Papers, Democratic Party Organizations, TLA-UTA, AR110-26-7-6.

14. "Installation Tea Slated for DWPA," *DMN*, May 2, 1954, 2; "Democratic Women Suggest That Johnson Head Texans," *DMN*, March 17, 1956, 3.

15. "Longtime Labor Leader George Lambert Dies"; Joe Lambert, phone interview by author, May 4, 2015, digital audio recording in author's possession. The Lamberts' many studies and files confirm this. For starters, see Lambert Papers, AR127-3, Folders 2-3.

16. Ronnie Dugger, "An Idealist Bound to be Useful," *TO*, September 4, 1959, 3.

17. George Eichler to All AFL-CIO Councils and Central Labor Bodies, February 24, 1960, Lambert Papers, AR127-25-7.

18. Ronnie Dugger, "A Garment Strike," *TO*, September 4, 1959, 1–2.

19. Lambert's past primarily represented an asset to the garment workers' campaign, though in at least one instance it served as a possible liability. Paul Thompson, a conservative columnist for the *San Antonio News*, flagged Lambert's radical political sympathies and arrest record at the top of one of his editorials six months into the strike. Thompson noted that Lambert was arrested "'six or seven times' in 1938 for disturbing the peace" during the "hectic pecan shellers' strike," and he noted the organizer's ties to then-Communist strike leader Emma Tenayuca. "Police said he [Lambert] was not a member of the Communist Party," Thompson added, "although they accused him of being a fellow traveler." To his credit, Thompson also included Lambert's reply to these charges of guilt by association: Lambert told the columnist, "If anyone tries to drag a Communist red herring into this [Tex-Son] strike, I believe I can cram it down his throat." Paul Thompson, "Top of the News" column, *SAN*, August 18, 1959, in Lambert Papers, AR127-25-7.

20. Letter, George Lambert to Fred Siems, May 10, 1959, Lambert Papers, AR127-25-7; "Tex-Son Committee Meets with Chaikin," *ILGWU Union News*, November 1958, 1, copy in Lambert Papers, AR127-5-8; Flores, "An Unladylike Strike Fashionably Clothed," 378–79.

21. Flores, "An Unladylike Strike Fashionably Clothed," 378–79.

22. "Brothers Help Sister Union," *SAL*, August 14, 1959, 10 (first quotation); Dugger, "A Garment Strike," *TO*, September 4, 1959, 2 (second quotation); photographs with captions in *SAE*, August 14, 1959, 1, 3.

23. Dugger, "A Garment Strike," 2; Flores, "An Unladylike Strike Fashionably Clothed," 392; Ledesma, "Unlikely Strikers," 174.

24. Rinaldo Panetta to Sir and Brother, September 15, 1959; Panetta to All Retailers of Children's Wear, September 21, 1959; Paul Thompson, "Top of the News" column, *SAN*, August 18, 1959—all in Lambert Papers, AR127-25-7; Dugger, "A Garment Strike," 1.

25. Flores, "An Unladylike Strike Fashionably Clothed," 390–91; Memo from George Lambert to Fred Siems, "Mass Hand Billing of San Antonio Stores," February 19, 1960; Memo from Lambert to Siems, "Tex-Son Store Programs, San Antonio," March 9, 1960; Memo from Lambert to Siems, "Tex-Son Strike—Store Program," June 12, 1960; Memo from Lambert to Siems, "Tex-Son Store Program," April 23, 1960—all in Lambert Papers, AR127-25-7. Photograph of a bunch of "don't buy Tex-son" balloons with a handwritten note on the back, Records of International Ladies' Garment Workers' Union, Local 180, San Antonio, Texas, 1936–71, UTA-TLA, AR 30-1-3; Dugger, "A Garment Strike," 1.

26. Dugger, "A Garment Strike," 2 (both quotations); Memo from George Lambert to Fred Siems, "Mass Hand Billing of San Antonio Stores," February 19, 1960; Open letter from Gregoria Montalbo, September 22, 1959; Letter from Charles J. Morris to Morris P. Glushien, February 16, 1960; Letter from Lambert to Charles J. Morris, February 19, 1960; Letter from David R. Richards to Lambert, April 15, 1960; Lambert to All Local Unions, Lodges, and Auxiliaries, n.d. [February 1960]—all in Lambert Papers, AR127-25-7.

27. George Eichler to All Locals, Lodges and Auxiliaries, December 23, 1960, Lambert Papers, AR127-25-7.

28. Letter from Gregoria Montalbo to Sir & Brother, February 1, 1961, Lambert Papers, AR127-25-7.

29. Ibid.; "Council Votes Christmas Aid for Brave Tex-Son Pickets," *AFL-CIO Weekly Dispatch*, December 7, 1962, Lambert Papers, AR127-25-7.

30. Letter from Richard Peña to Morris P. Glushien, December 16, 1959, Lambert Papers, AR127-25-7.

31. Letter from Lambert to Fred Siems, November 29, 1960, 1 (both quotations; page 2 is missing from the file), Lambert Papers, AR127-12-2. Flores quotes a letter to international president David Dubinsky from about thirty self-proclaimed members of the union as evidence that the strikers had grown suspicious of Lambert and Sophie Gonzales, another organizer. Yet the full text of the letter reveals that the signers were not committee members but rank-and-file workers who were upset that their strike benefits had been reduced by 25 percent since they had begun working elsewhere. Strike committee leader Gregoria Montalbo's name does not appear among the signatories. The letter also highlights the role of Rebecca Taylor, a union organizer who had quit the staff to join the human resources department at Tex-Son, essentially defecting. Lambert and Gonzales had long distrusted Taylor and certainly weren't in bed with her after she quit. While many of the details remain murky, it is clear that at least some of the strikers had grown impatient or distrustful of the union bureaucracy. Yet both the thirty-odd members and the strike committee appealed to Dubinsky as the ultimate arbiter, thereby legitimizing his role. Flores, "An Unladylike Strike Fashionably Clothed," 396; Letter from Local 180 Members to Dubinsky, September 20, 1960, Lambert Papers, AR127-25-7.

32. Letter from Albert A. Peña Jr. to David Dubinsky, November 25, 1960, Lambert Papers, AR127-12-2. It appears that Lambert attempted to distance himself from the strike committee's action and Peña's appeal in his report to his superior, the union's regional director, Fred Siems—in all likelihood to cover his own rear end. Yet Lambert remained active in the strike for another year, and he continued to work for Peña and Gonzalez in the political arena. Latane Lambert also served alongside Peña as officers of the Bexar County Democrats, so it's unlikely that there was any bad blood. Letter from

George Lambert to Siems, November 29, 1960, Lambert Papers, AR127-12-2; Letter from Lambert to All Delegates and Guests, Texas State AFL-CIO Convention, July 30, 1961, Lambert Papers, AR127-25-7.

33. "If Tex-Son Strike Dies, Every San Antonio Union Man Dies a Little, Too," *AFL-CIO Weekly Dispatch*, December 9, 1960, 1, in Lambert Papers, AR127-25-7; Letter from Peña to Dubinsky, AR127-12-2.

34. "San Antonio Sewer Tax Hit By Bexar County Democrats," *SAEN*, December 12, 1959, 2-A; "Coalition Sweeps Convention," *SAL*, May 15, 1960, 1, 14; Memo from George Lambert to Fred Siems, "Henry Gonzalez—Runoff Election for State Senate," May 23, 1960, Lambert Papers, AR127-12-2; Letter from Henry B. Gonzalez to George and Latane Lambert, November 9, 1960, Lambert Papers, AR127-11-4; Letter from Henry B. Gonzalez to Latane Lambert, December 14, 1961, Lambert Papers, AR127-11-4; Letter (and letterhead), from Latane Lambert to Charles Roche, February 12, 1962, Lambert Papers, AR127-3-5; "Congressman Gonzalez Praises Union," Altmann Workers Union Election Spotlight, September 25, 1962, Lambert Papers, AR127-11-4.

35. "Texas Labor 1959," is the front-page feature, which also includes a third piece on "Other Strikes" around the state. "Labor Leaders at the Picket Line" includes the two biographical sketches cited in this chapter: "An Idealist Bound to be Useful," on Lambert, and "A Man Who Needs Tangible Results," on Brown. All appear to be written by Ronnie Dugger, though his initials do not appear on every individual piece. Judging by the date, all were likely included as a special Labor Day feature. See *TO*, September 4, 1959, 1–3.

36. H. S. Hank Brown, interview by author, San Antonio, March 25, 2010, digital recording in author's possession, 1:30–3:35, 5:15–6:30; Hank Brown interview by George N. Green, OH 11, Dallas, July 30, 1971, TLA-UTA, 1–3.

37. Brown interview by author, 7:55–11:05; Brown interview by Green, 4.

38. Brown interview by Green, 29–30; Brown interview by author, 13:50.

39. Brown interview by author, 14:45, 18:40, 21:50; Brown interview by Green, 5–6.

40. Brown interview by author, 17:35.

41. Brown interview by Green, 5.

42. "Texas New Deal Demos Call for National Presidential Primary," *SAL*, May 28, 1952, 7-A.

43. Brown interview by Green, 5.

44. Brown interview by author, 21:50, 22:15. See also Brown's correspondence in the Texas AFL-CIO Papers, Executive Board series, AR110-1, TLA-UTA.

45. Brown interview by author, 24:00–28:20; Ronnie Dugger, "Craftsmen Go Out," *TO*, September 4, 1959, 1–2; Ronnie Dugger, "A Man Who Needs Tangible Results," *TO*, September 4, 1959, 3; "More Crafts Join S.A. Strike," *TO*, October 2, 1959, 2.

46. There is no direct evidence that he participated in the Tex-Son struggle, though he remembered the strike clearly and probably joined their picket lines or mass demonstrations on at least one occasion. Brown interview by author, 28:20.

47. Dugger, "A Man Who Needs Tangible Results," 3.

48. Ibid. (both quotations).

49. Ibid.

50. Proceedings, Third Annual Convention, Texas State AFL-CIO, November 16–19, 1959, San Antonio, UTA-TLA, 10–18, 29.

51. Ibid., 30–31.
52. Ibid., 31–32.
53. Ibid., 32.
54. "Giant Union Drive Planned for S.A.," *SAE*, November 17, 1959, 1.
55. Brown interview by author, 24:00–28:20; "13-Week Strike Is Ended Here," *SAE*, November 4, 1959, 1.
56. Brown interview by Green, 31.

Chapter 6

1. "Longshoremen, Sit-In Leaders Arrested Here," *HC*, June 3, 1961, in *Houston Chronicle* Morgue, Houston Metropolitan Research Center (hereafter HCM-HMRC), filed under Progressive Youth Association (hereafter PYA); "500 Negroes March on City Hall; Protest Arrest of Eight at Rally," *HC*, June 7, 1961, HCM-HMRC, PYA (first quotation); Cole, *No Color Is My Kind: The Life of Eldrewey Stearns and the Integration of Houston*, 70–71 (second and third quotations). See also Howard Middleton Jr., interviews by author, Houston, May 5 and 31, 2010; Holly Hogrobrooks, phone interview by author, Houston, May 26, 2010; notes on author's fieldwork with ILA Local 872; and "Personal Telephone Directory and Local History of I.L.A. 872," ca. 1960—all in author's possession.
2. "500 Negroes March on City Hall; Protest Arrest of Eight at Rally," *HC*, June 7, 1961, HCM-HMRC, PYA.
3. In his path-breaking community study of the Greensboro movement, historian William H. Chafe writes that the sit-ins replaced the diplomacy of race leaders in the 1950s with "a new language" that "communicated a message different from that which had been heard before. A direct connection existed between style and content. In an almost visceral way, the sit-ins expressed the dissatisfaction and anger of the black community toward white indifference . . . in a manner that whites could not possibly ignore . . . ." See Chafe, *Civilities and Civil Rights*, 99.
4. Saul Friedman, "Negro Youths' Ex-Leader Says Movement is 'Dying,'" *HC*, October 2, 1961, HCM-HMRC, PYA; "Negro Student Claims Two Cops Beat Him," *HC*, August 26, 1959, HCM-HMRC, HCCO. The definitive, semiautobiographical work on Stearns is Cole, *No Color Is My Kind*. Holly Hogrobrooks, another leader of the student demonstrators, said that she was amazed by the accuracy of Stearns's memories and the veracity of Cole's narrative. Hogrobrooks interview by author.
5. Cole, *No Color Is My Kind*, chaps. 1–2; "T.S.U. Students' 'Sit-ins,'" *TO*, March 11, 1960, 1, 3.
6. Cole, *No Color Is My Kind*, chap. 2 (quotation on 61); "Youth Group Pickets Downtown Stores," *HC*, May 8, 1960, HCM-HMRC, PYA; "Houston Changes," *TO*, September 2, 1960, 8.
7. Cole, *No Color Is My Kind*, 64–75; "Negroes Refused Service at City Hall Cafeteria," *HC*, January 25, 1961; "Negro, White Students Picket Theaters Here," *HC*, February 13, 1961; "Negroes Try Union Station Café Sit-In," *HC*, February 23, 1961; "Sit-Iners Facing First Charges," *HC*, February 25, 1961; Bill Porterfield, "Gains and Losses of Houston Integration Group Are Charted," *HC*, June 28, 1961, 18—all in HCM-HMRC, PYA. See also additional articles dated January–June 1961.

8. "Council of 60 Negro Groups Backs 'Strikes,' " *HC*, March 14, 1960; "Biracial Meeting Demanded," *HC*, May 17, 1960; "Negro Group to Urge Desegregation Vote," May 23, 1960—all in HCM-HMRC, HCCO.

9. PYA letterhead for Letter from Eldrewey Stearns to Dan Cobb, May 8, 1961; Letter from Freddie Jo Ray to Bill Porterfield, June 29, 1961—both in HCM-HMRC, PYA; "N.A.A.C.P. Planning New Shift to Labor Rights," *HC*, September, 23, 1962, HCM-HMRC, NAACP; Bill Connolly, " 'Bama Protest Rally Called Here Sunday," *HC*, March, 1965 (rally took place on March 14), HCM-HMRC, NAACP; "Attorney Heads Council of 64 Civic Groups," *HC*, January 22, 1961, HCM-HMRC, HCCO; "62 Negro Groups Demand Probe of Houston Theater Pickets Arrest," *HC*, April 6, 1961, HCM-HMRC, HCCO. For an example of the protest photographs, see the third from final plate in Cole, *No Color Is My Kind*. Cole adds that LeRoy offered to launch a joint campaign cosponsored by the NAACP and PYA in May 1960, but the students declined, not wanting "to take a back seat to their elders" (53). See also "Houston Negro Youth Leader Accuses N.A.A.C.P. of Intrusion," *HC*, May 15, 1960, HCM-HMRC, NAACP, which mentions the association's national youth director, but not LeRoy. Stearns's hostility may be partially attributable to the antiauthoritarian and youth-centered ethos of the founding SNCC convention. Nonetheless, the preponderance of evidence suggests that, at the local level, older civil rights activists like LeRoy used the HCCO, NAACP, and black labor unions to offer critical support to the students, who greatly appreciated it.

10. "Negro Doctors Back Sit-In Youth Group," *HC*, February 26, 1961, HCM-HMRC, PYA. Mease served as chair and coordinator of LeRoy's 1965 retirement dinner and celebration. On Mease, see also Cole, *No Color Is My Kind*, chap. 3; and Mease, *On Equal Footing: A Memoir*.

11. They raised an additional $2,000 two weeks later to pay fines for other Union Station demonstrators. "$4000 Raised in Campaign to Free Students," *HC*, May 16, 1962; "20 Students Freed After Fines Are Paid," *HC*, May 18, 1962"; "T.S.U. Sit-in Students Pay $500 Fines," *HC*, June 1, 1962—all in HCM-HMRC, HCCO. See also "Only a Few Shots Still to Be Fired in Houston's Battle of the Sit-ins," *HC*, May 6, 1962, HCM-HMRC, PYA.

12. Middleton interviews by author; Hogrobrooks interview by author; PYA letterhead, 1961.

13. "Café May Serve Negro Policemen," *HC*, January 24, 1961; "Café Must Serve Negro Policemen," *HC*, January 24, 1961; "Negroes Refused Service at City Hall Cafeteria," *HC*, January 25, 1961—all in HCM-HMRC, PYA.

14. Letter from Ray to Porterfield, June 29, 1961, 2.

15. Friedman, "Negro Youths' Ex-Leader Says Movement is 'Dying.' "

16. "Council Opposes Bus Delay," *HC*, February 15, 1961; "Petitions for Elections Could Snag Granting of New Bus Franchise," *HC*, February 16, 1961; "Call Off the Bus Election," *HC*, April 6, 1961—all in HCM-HMRC, HCCO.

17. "Powerful Negro Group Threatens to Oppose Bonds," *HC*, January 17, 1962; "Cutrer Opposes Negro Demand on City Hiring," *HC*, January 23, 1962; "No Decision Reached on Negro City Jobs," *HC*, January 24, 1962—all in HCM-HMRC, HCCO.

18. "18 Groups Backing Stadium Bond Issue," *HC*, December 17, 1962, HCM-HMRC, HCCO. Cole adds that the same year, Quentin Mease led a group of elites that successfully negotiated the desegregation of the local baseball stadium and hotels in order to attract a

Major League team to the city. The Houston Colt .45s, later renamed the Astros, began play in front of integrated crowds in August 1962. Cole, *No Color Is My Kind*, 76–80.

19. "N.A.A.C.P. Planning New Shift to Labor Rights," *HC*, September 23, 1962 (all quotations); "N.A.A.C.P. Takes Sides Here in Labor Hearing Dispute," *HC*, October 18, 1962—both in HCM-HMRC, NAACP. The definitive work on Ivory Davis and Hughes Tool is Botson, *Labor, Civil Rights, and the Hughes Tool Company*.

20. Cole, *No Color Is My Kind*, chap. 4; Friedman, "Negro Youths' Ex-Leader Says Movement is 'Dying' "; "Pro-Integration Group Loses Backing in Feud," *HC*, January 22, 1962—both in HCM-HMRC, PYA. Erma LeRoy served on the board of the Houston Sit-in Foundation. Given the couple's history and their active support for the demonstrations, it is likely that she did so to serve as an advocate for the students, if not Stearns.

21. Joseph Luter, "The NAACP President Speaks," *SNAP*, n.d. (late August/early September, 1960—cover featuring Mr. and Mrs. Willie Lee Parker), MS 139, Box 2, Folder 4, SABHC; "S.A. Stores Integrate; White Held in Cutting," *TO*, March 18, 1960; Goldberg, "Racial Change on the Southern Periphery: The Case of San Antonio, Texas, 1960–1965," 355–57.

22. Black and Matthews, *Grandpa Was a Preacher: A Letter to My Grandson*, 107–9 (quotation on 108).

23. "Jailing, Rope-Offs, Shovings in Sit-Ins," *TO*, May 6, 1960, 3 (all quotations); "Treat Negroes Equally, Rho Beta Asks Joske's," *Rattler* (St. Mary's), May 6, 1960, 1; Rev. Claude W. Black Jr., interview by author, San Antonio, October 27, 2008, 27:40, 45:30; Goldberg, "Racial Change on the Southern Periphery," 358. See also "As Sit-ins Subside, School Issue Grows," *TO*, April 22, 1960, 8; "Sit-Ins Resume; Addison Set Back," *TO*, April 29, 1960, 7; and photograph of G. J. Sutton and unidentified woman picketing Joske's, *SNAP*, May 20, 1960, MS 139, Box 2, Folder 4, SABHC.

24. Luter, "The NAACP President Speaks." See also "Handy Andy Picketed," *TO*, September 9, 1960, 2.

25. Black and Matthews, *Grandpa Was a Preacher*, 107. See also Black interview by author, 45:30–48:00; "Handy Andy Picketed," 2.

26. NAACP Labor & Employment Committee, "Handy-Andy Picket Schedule Explained," *SNAP*, December 16, 1960, MS 139, Box 2, Folder 4, SABHC.

27. Bill Donahue, "In Our City," *SNAP*, July 14, 1961 (first and last quotations); Bill Donahue, "In Our City," *SNAP*, August 25, 1961, 4 (middle quotations); Bill Donahue, "In Our City," *SNAP*, December 1, 1961—all in SABHC, MS 139, Box 3. See also Black interview by author, 1:21:15.

28. Goldberg, "Racial Change on the Southern Periphery," 363; Bill Donahue, "In Our City," *SNAP*, June 2, 1961, SABHC, MS 139, Box 3; "Texas Cities Witness Protests," *TO*, February 18, 1961, 3; "More Sit-Ins in Texas Cities," *TO*, March 4, 1961, 3.

29. "Standers-In Instructed in Job, Orderliness Asked of Students," *Rattler*, March 10, 1961, 2. There is no byline, but given the article's specificity, it must have been written by a participant-observer. Castillo is the most likely candidate.

30. William Donahue and Perfecto Villareal, "This Is Progress," *SNAP*, July 27, 1962, MS 139, Box 3, SABHC.

31. "Stand for Stand-ins," *Rattler*, March 10, 1961, 2 (all quotations). The editorial is also unsigned, but given his dual roles, it is again likely that Castillo penned it. Moreover,

years later, when recalling this moment, Castillo mentions the importance of reading Gandhi. See Lionel Castillo [sic], interview by Jose Angel Gutiérrez, Houston, June 28, 1996, TV-UTA, 6, 12–13.

32. Bill Donahue, "In Our City" column, *SNAP*, June 2, July 14, August 11, and August 18, 1961; Donahue and Villareal, "This Is Progress," *SNAP*, July 27, 1962—all in MS 139, Box 3, SABHC.

33. Donahue and Villareal, "This Is Progress," *SNAP*, July 27, 1962, MS 139, Box 3, SABHC; Goldberg, "Racial Change on the Southern Periphery," 363.

34. "NAACP Leaders Act," *SNAP*, June 2, 1961; "NAACP News," *SNAP*, January 26, 1962; "NAACP Hosts 26th Annual Meet," *SNAP*, November 2, 1962—all in MS 139, Box 3, SABHC.

35. "Operation 'Telephone Company,'" *SNAP*, June 9, 1962, MS 139, Box 3, SABHC.

36. "Parker Fired by Joske's," and "Please Do Not Trade at Joske's," *SNAP*, June 9, 1962, MS 139, Box 3, SABHC.

37. "Please Do Not Trade at Joske's—Until They Rehire Union Employee," *SNAP*, June 15, 1962, 1, MS 139, Box 3, SABHC.

38. "Please Trade at Joske's," *SNAP*, June 29, 1962, MS 139, Box 3 SABHC.

39. "Teamsters Win," *SNAP*, June 29, 1962, 1, MS 139, Box 3 SABHC.

40. "SNAP Goes Union," *SNAP*, August 24, 1962, MS 139, Box 3 SABHC.

41. Bill Donahue, "In Our City," *SNAP*, August 18, 1961, MS 139, Box 3, SABHC.

42. "Nebraska Street Death Trap Kills Airman," *SNAP*, January 12, 1962, MS 139, Box 3, SABHC. See also other 1962 issues of *SNAP* in the same box.

43. Bill Donahue, "In Our City"; Robert Gomez, "Social Spotlight"—both in *SNAP*, February 2, 1962, MS 139, Box 3, SABHC.

44. "Council Ducks Citizens Group," *SNAP*, February 9, 1962, 1, MS 139, Box 3, SABHC.

45. "City Council Promises Elimination of 'Death Trap,'" *SNAP*, February 16, 1962, SABHC, MS 139, Box 3. For the present image, see Google Street View, looking west from 2748 Martin Luther King Dr., accessed April 11, 2016, https://goo.gl/maps/ZcBGKJ8ZsK82.

46. "The San Antonio Example," *TO*, May 6, 1960, 8. Notably, the editor parenthetically added: "(But see this week's reports on Joske's.)"

47. See, most notably, Goldberg, "Racial Change on the Southern Periphery."

48. Alexander Heiken, "'The Only Way I Want to Win,'" *TO*, July 4, 1959, 5.

49. Albert Peña, "Liberalism in Texas," *Democratic Reporter*, June 1959, 11 (reprint of speech to state convention on May 23); "Issues Committee" Report, *Democratic Reporter*, March 1960, 3—both in Texas AFL-CIO Papers, Democratic Organizations Series, AR110-26-9-1; Memorandum from Mrs. R. D. Randolph, January 22, 1960, AR110-26-8-5.

50. For a good summary of the scene in 1960, see Memorandum from Creekmore Fath to Executive Board, June 1, 1960, and enclosed *Democratic Reporter*, June 14, 1960, in Texas AFL-CIO Papers, Democratic Party Organizations, TLA-UTA, AR110-26-8-5. On liberal skepticism of Johnson, see also Robert E. (Bob) Hall interview by author.

51. Black Texans' skepticism regarding LBJ's commitment to civil rights appears in the text below. For more on the Civil Rights Act of 1957, see Caro, *Master of the Senate: The Years of Lyndon Johnson*.

52. Pycior, *LBJ & Mexican Americans*. Among the many biographies, see also Dugger, *The Politician: The Life and Times of Lyndon Johnson*.

53. "DOT Lists Issues," *TO*, February 26, 1960, 1.

54. "Grass Roots Tangled," "Aspects of the Election," and "Liberals Gain in Legislature," *TO*, May 13, 1960, 1; "LBJ Backed; Loyalists Bolt 4 Counties" and "Houston: F.I.A. Roars; Lyndon, Pledge Nixed," *TO*, May 20, 1960, 1; "A More Liberal Austin," *TO*, July 1, 1960, 1.

55. "LBJ Backed; Loyalists Bolt 4 Counties," and "Lyndon-Liberal Trade Prevails in San Antonio" (all quotations), *TO*, May 20, 1960, 1, 6; "Democratic Convention Held," *SNAP*, May 20, 1960, SABHC, MS 139, Box 2, Folder 4. On the election of Spears, Alaniz, and the liberal slate, see Willie Morris, "A Chapter in Technique: Franklin Spears and the Bexar Coalition," *TO*, July 29, 1960, 1–2. I give more credit to Alaniz and the nonwhite elements of the coalition than either Morris or Spears did. In fact, Morris approvingly quotes Spears making extremely paternalistic, white supremacist comments about his desire to have young, Anglo faces lead the ticket as well as barefoot "Latin" voters flocking to receive campaign giveaways.

56. Ronnie Dugger, "Lyndon on to L.A.," *TO*, June 17, 1960, 1–2.

57. Ibid., 2–3; "Development of the Liberals' Debacle," *TO*, June 17, 1960, 5.

58. Albert A. Peña, interview by José Ángel Gutiérrez, CMAS 15, TV-UTA, 21–22.

59. Dugger, "Lyndon on to L.A."; "Development of the Liberals' Debacle"—both in *TO*, June 17, 1960.

60. "Development of the Liberals' Debacle," *TO*, June 17, 1960, 5; "Delegates to National Demo-Convention," *SNAP*, June 24, 1960, SABHC, MS 139, Box 2, Folder 4.

61. "Delegation to L.A.," *TO*, July 1, 1960, 3.

62. "Jack Takes LBJ on Ticket" and "Daniel Says He'll Vote, That's All," *TO*, July 15, 1960, 1.

63. Peña interview by Gutiérrez, 23; "Lyndon and the Negroes," *TO*, July 22, 1960, 1.

64. Peña interview by Gutiérrez, 25; Letter from Albert Peña to Gerald Mann, August 29, 1960, and Letter from Ed Idar Jr. to Albert Peña, August 31, 1960—both in Eduardo Idar Jr. Papers (hereafter Ed Idar Papers), BLAC, Box 8, Folder 5.

65. Peña interview by Gutiérrez, 25–26; Albert Peña, "County Comment," *SNAP*, August 18, 1961, SABHC, MS 139, Box 3; "Minutes of PASO Meeting," Hamilton Hotel, Laredo, December 27, 1961, 1, copy in Ed Idar Papers, BLAC, Box 9, Folder 2.

66. Letter from Idar to Peña, August 31, 1960, Ed Idar Papers, BLAC, Box 8, Folder 5.

67. Peña interview by Gutiérrez, 26–27; De León, *Ethnicity in the Sunbelt: Mexican Americans in Houston*, 167.

68. Letter from R. P. (Bob) Sanchez to Jerry Holleman (Report No. 39), November 10, 1960, Texas AFL-CIO Papers, MAAC, AR110-7-2-1.

69. "Texas Negroes Organize for Kennedy Ticket," *Chicago Daily Defender*, October 10, 1960, 3; Metz T. P. Lochard, "Political Beat," *Chicago Daily Defender*, October 13, 1960, 5; "Texas Negroes Organize for Kennedy Ticket," *Chicago Defender* (National Edition), October 22, 1960, 9.

70. "Negro Council Endorses Kennedy, Johnson; Prefers Platform of Dems," *HC*, October 24, 1960; "Negro Clubs to Discuss Candidates," *HC*, October 13, 1960—both in HCM-HMRC, HCCO.

71. Handwritten report from Moses LeRoy "by: E. D. L." to "Attention: Mr. Jerry R. Holleman," January 6, 1960, Texas AFL-CIO Papers, Executive Board Records, TLA-UTA, AR110-1-12-1.

72. Handwritten report from Erma LeRoy to Mr. J. R. Holleman, April 11, 1960, Texas AFL-CIO Papers, Executive Board Records, TLA-UTA, AR110-1-12-1.

73. Typed "Electioneering Report" from Erma D. LeRoy to Mr. Jerry R. Holleman, May 9, 1960, Texas AFL-CIO Papers, Executive Board Records, TLA-UTA, AR110-1-12-1.

74. Typed "Presidential Campaign Report" from Erma D. LeRoy to Mr. Jerry R. Holleman, November 12, 1960, Texas AFL-CIO Papers, Executive Board Records, TLA-UTA, AR110-1-12-1.

75. "Says Snap . . . ," *SNAP*, November 4, 1960, SABHC MS 139, Box 2, Folder 4.

76. "Democratic Women Honored," "Local and National Democratic Nominees Honored," and "Candidates at Coffee," all in *SNAP*, November 4, 1960; "The Last Stop," *SNAP*, n.d. [November 11, 1960]—both in SABHC MS 139, Box 2, Folder 4. See also "Jack's Texas Jaunt" and "Texas Party Hierarchy Solid for Kennedy," *TO*, September 16, 1960, 1, 5.

77. See Calvert, De León, and Cantrell, *The History of Texas*, 4th ed., 386–87, 396–97. Interest in Nixon's narrow loss and charges of vote fraud was renewed in the aftermath of the contested Bush-Gore election of 2000. See, for example, Peter Carlson, "Another Race to the Finish," *Washington Post*, November 17, 2000, A-1.

78. Letter from Sanchez to Holleman (Report No. 39), November 10, 1960, MAAC, AR110-7-2-1.

79. All numbers cited in "Religion Helped, Not Hurt Kennedy," *TO*, November 11, 1960; Telegram from John F. Kennedy to Ed Idar, November 10, 1960, Ed Idar Papers, BLAC, Box 8, Folder 5; Peña, "County Comment," *SNAP*, August 18, 1961; Peña interview by Gutiérrez, 28; "A Letter from the Rambler," *SNAP*, November 18, 1960, SABHC, MS 139, Box 2, Folder 4.

Chapter 7

1. "Holleman Advanced," *TO*, January 14, 1961, 3.

2. See chapter 5; H. S. Hank Brown interview by author, San Antonio, March 25, 2010, digital recording; "Labor's New President," *TO*, January 28, 1961, 5.

3. Quotation in letter from Jerry Holleman to Robert P. Sanchez, April 1, 1960, 1, MAAC, AR110-7, AR110-7-2-1. See also letter from Andy McLellan to Paul Sparks, June 29, 1953, MAAC, AR110-7-1-2; Letters from Andy McLellan to Jerry R. Holleman, September 6 and 7, 1955, MAAC, AR110-7-1-3; "Rio Grande Democratic Club Training Conference, McAllen, Texas," minutes, October 30, 1955, MAAC, AR110-7-1-3; "Statement of Andrew C. McLellan . . . on HR 3822," March 21, 1955, MAAC, AR110-7-1-3. For additional background, see Juan R. Garcia, *Operation Wetback*; and Kelly Lytle Hernandez, *Migra!*

4. Letter from Andy McLellan to Jerry Holleman, October 19, 1954, MAAC, AR110-7-1-2. In 1955, McLellan took a trip to Mexico in collaboration with the CTM, the Texas AFL-CIO, and ORIT. His letters to Holleman became sporadic, and the few that came were filled with reports of trips to Guatemala and Honduras, where he had joined local anti-Communist unions in fighting the leftist revolutions that were sweeping the region. The post of Latin American Affairs advisor was effectively vacant for most of 1956 and 1957. At some point, McLellan probably became an agent for the Central Intelligence Agency. He later returned to the United States and in 1962 founded the American Institute for Free Labor Development (AIFLD), a joint venture of the labor movement, the State Department, and the Central Intelligence Agency. See additional correspondence

in Box 1, Folder 4, MAAC, AR110-7. For a recent work on the AFL-CIO, see Scipes, *AFL-CIO's Secret War against Developing Country Workers: Solidarity or Sabotage?* Historian Dana Frank is also researching the history of the AIFLD, including McLellan. (Thanks, Dana, for sharing your stories.) For background on the bracero program, see Deborah Cohen, *Braceros*.

5. "La Importancia del Poll Tax," Texas AFL-CIO Records, Committee on Political Education [COPE, AR110, Series 8], AR110-8-9-2, translations by author. The Spanish for the Sánchez quotation is: *Por sus hijos hijos, por su pueblo, por su patria—pague su poll tax. Patria* could also mean "homeland," in reference to Mexico.

6. Letter from R.P. "Bob" Sanchez to Sherman Miles, January 4, 1957, MAAC, AR110-7-1-5, quotation on 3. Hector Garcia did send a letter of congratulations to the founding convention of the Texas State AFL-CIO in late July 1957. See Proceedings of the Founding Convention of the Texas State AFL-CIO, Austin, July 30–August 1, 1957, TLA-UTA, 77–78.

7. Proceedings, 1957, 130.

8. Letter from R. P. (Bob) Sanchez to Jerry Holleman (Report No. 1), January 6, 1958, MAAC, AR110-7-1-5.

9. Proceedings, Second Annual Convention, Texas State AFL-CIO, 1958, TLA-UTA, 21, 193–95 (quotations on 194).

10. Ibid., 195. Paul Montemayor of the steelworkers in Corpus Christi suggested that the report be amended to recommend that U.S. unions in the border regions change their constitutions to permit noncitizens to join their ranks, thereby encouraging organization of immigrant workers. Montemayor's amendment passed.

11. Letter from R. P. (Bob) Sanchez to Jerry Holleman (Report No. 12), October 29, 1958, MAAC, AR110-7-1-5.

12. Proceedings, Third Annual Convention, Texas State AFL-CIO, November 16–19, 1959, San Antonio, TLA-UTA, 105–6.

13. Letter from R. P. (Bob) Sanchez to Jerry Holleman (Report No. 28), November 20, 1958, MAAC, AR110-7-1-5.

14. Letter from Jerry Holleman to R. P. (Bob) Sanchez, April 1, 1960, MAAC, AR110-7-2-1 (all quotations); Letter from R.P. (Bob) Sanchez to H.S. (Hank) Brown, February 3, 1961, MAAC, AR110-7-2-2.

15. Letter from R. P. (Bob) Sanchez to Jerry Holleman (Report No. 39), November 10, 1960, MAAC, AR110-7-2-1.

16. "Militant Resolves on All Fronts" and "Labor Breaks New Ground," *TO*, August 12, 1960, 1, 4.

17. Ronnie Dugger, "Texas Labor Reeling after Battle," *TO*, August 5, 1961; Ronnie Dugger, "Texas Labor's Internecine Battle," *TO*, August 12, 1961; Ronnie Dugger, "After Battle: What the Future Holds for Labor," *TO*, August 18, 1961. Schmidt's splinter caucus appears in "Unions Re-Shuffle," *TO*, May 27, 1961, 8. See also Hank Brown, interview by George N. Green, Dallas, July 30, 1971, OH 11, TLA-UTA; Fred Schmidt, interview by George N. Green, Fredericksburg, Texas, May 29, 1988, OH 98, TLA-UTA; "Labor's New President," *TO*, March 25, 1961, 5; "Changing Times for Texas Labor," *TO*, March 25, 1961, 9; "'An Invisible Crisis,'" *TO*, August 5, 1961, 7; and "Thoughts About Labor," *TO*, August 26, 1960, 4–5.

18. Dugger, "Texas Labor Reeling after Battle," 6.

19. "Labor's New President," 5; Brown interview by Green.

20. "Viva Kennedy-Johnson Clubs Meeting," Gunter Hotel, November 26, 1960, with handwritten committee lists, Ed Idar Papers, Box 9, Folder 2, BLAC. Bob Sanchez was also appointed to the Statement of Particulars Committee.

21. "The American of Mexican Descent: A Statement of Principle by The Viva Kennedy Texas Organization," (written by George I. Sánchez), n.d. [late 1960/early 1961], Idar Papers, BLAC, Box 9, Folder 2; Ronnie Dugger, "Political Interests of Latins United," *TO*, September 15, 1961, 1, 3. My observations on Sánchez in this and subsequent chapters overlap with those contained in Carlos Kevin Blanton's groundbreaking new biography. See Blanton, *George I. Sánchez: The Long Fight for Mexican American Integration*, chap. 11.

22. Minutes of "Viva Kennedy-Johnson Clubs Meeting at County Courthouse, Victoria, Texas," February 5, 1961, 1–3, 11–12 (quotations on 2–3), Idar Papers, Box 9, Folder 2, BLAC. Both Idar and labor activist Franklin Garcia of Dallas declined nominations to serve as the state body's first vice-chairman. Peña's assistant Albert Fuentes of San Antonio became vice-chairman for West Texas.

23. Ibid., 12. Other labor activists present included Franklin Garcia, Paul Montemayor of Corpus Christi, and Al Rodriguez of Houston. See "Texas State MAPA Mailing Labels," 4, 8, Idar Papers, Box 9, Folder 2, BLAC.

24. Letter from Carlos McCormick to Ed Idar Jr., March 16, 1961; Letter from Albert A. Peña to "Fellow Member," May 1, 1961—both in Idar Papers, Box 9, Folder 2, BLAC.

25. "Gonzalez Enters Battle for Senate," *TO*, December 9, 1960, 3 (first and second quotations); "Maverick Announces," *TO*, December 30, 1960, 8; "Gonzalez in Race to Stay," *TO*, January 28, 1961, 1. Gonzalez announced on December 3; Maverick on December 22. I borrow the left-center-right list from Willie Morris, "Conservatives to the Fore," *TO*, April 8, 1961, 1–2.

26. Letter from James C. Sewell to "Friend," January 3, 1961; Memo from Edgar Berlin et al. to "All Members, the Democratic Coalition," n.d., calling meeting for February 8, 1961—both in Texas AFL-CIO Papers, Democratic Party Organizations, AR110-26-9-4.

27. "Labor Endorses," *TO*, February 11, 1961, 3; Minutes of "Viva Kennedy-Johnson Clubs Meeting," Victoria, February 5, 1961, 11; Ronnie Dugger, "Two Men Who Filled a Vacuum," *TO*, February 25, 1961, 5; Willie Morris, "An Endorsement," *TO*, February 11, 1961, 4. The *Observer*, led by new editor Willie Morris, joined other white liberals in endorsing Maverick.

28. Bill Sherrill, "Gonzalez' Station Wagon Politrek," *TO*, March 25, 1961, 2.

29. Handwritten memorandum from Erma D. LeRoy to Fred Schmidt, March 18, 1961, Texas AFL-CIO Records, Executive Board Office Records, TLA-UTA, AR110-1-12-1, 5; "Negro Group to Back No Senate Candidate," *HC*, March 20, 1961, HCM-HMRC, HCCO; "Candidates Step Up Bid For Backing," *Lubbock Avalanche-Journal*, February 15, 1961, 1-B, 10-B. The TCV was set to meet in Waco on March 4 to select a candidate, but I have been unable to locate any record that documents the group's decision.

30. LeRoy to Schmidt, March 18, 1961 (first five quotations); LeRoy to Schmidt, March 25, 1961 (last two quotations); and LeRoy to Schmidt, April 10, 1961—all in AR110-1-12-1.

31. Letter from H. S. (Hank) Brown to R. P. (Bob) Sanchez, February 9, 1961; Letter from Sanchez to Brown, February 10, 1961; Letter from Brown to Sanchez, February 22, 1961—all in MAAC, AR110-7-2-2.

32. Morris, "Conservatives to the Fore," *TO*, April 8, 1961, 1; "Senatorial Elections and Primaries, 1906–2012," *Texas Almanac Online*, accessed July 28, 2015, http://texasalmanac.com/topics/elections/senatorial-elections-and-primaries-1906%E2%80%932008-0. The print version of the *Texas Almanac* appeared in early 1961, before the election, and the subsequent volume, published in 1963, did not report detailed election statistics. The latter includes only a narrative of Tower's election and the Republican ascendancy. See *Texas Almanac, 1964–1965* (Dallas: Belo, 1963), 495, available online via *The Portal to Texas History*, accessed April 23, 2016, http://texashistory.unt.edu/ark:/67531/metapth113807/.

33. Hector P. Garcia, "'P.A.S.O' Takes First Gigantic Step towards Its Grass Root Movement and Local Organization," release dated July 10, 1961, Idar Papers, BLAC, Box 9, Folder 2; Letter from Ed Idar Jr. to Carlos McCormick, April 18, 1961, Idar Papers, BLAC, Box 9, Folder 2; Letter from Frankie Carter Randolph to "Democratic Friends," May 16, 1961, reprinted in *SNAP*, May 26, 1961; "Who Is Blakley For?" and "THINK! Then Vote for a Thinking Man's Candidate," *SNAP*, May 26, 1961, MS 139, Box 3, SABHC; "Negro Groups Back Blakley in Runoff," *HC*, May 15, 1961, and "Negro Says Kennedy Won Blakley Backing," *HC*, May 17, 1961, HCM-HMRC, HCCO; "Demos' Dilemma in Senate Race," *TO*, April 15, 1961, 1.

34. Garcia, "PASO Takes First Gigantic Step," Idar Papers; "GOP's Triumph: New Political Era," *TO*, June 3, 1961, 1.

35. "Summary of Coalition Action," July 7, 1961, copies in Idar Papers, BLAC, Box 9, Folder 2, and Texas AFL-CIO COPE Records, AR110-8-4-12.

36. Minutes of the September 9, 1961, meeting of the Democratic Coalition, Texas AFL-CIO Papers, Democratic Party Organizations, AR110-26-9-4 (Dixie quotations); "Liberal Dems Map Plans in Austin," *HC*, September 14, 1961, clipping in AR110-26-9-4 (Brown quotations). See also "Agenda Committee Meeting," August 26, 1961; Letter from Albert Peña to Democrat," October 5, 1961; "Proposed Agenda for Democratic Coalition," October 14, 1961—all in AR110-26-9-4.

37. Willie Morris, "Crucial Questions" (editorial), *TO*, September 29, 1961, 4. Dixie and Mrs. Randolph likewise maintained that "Nobody, and no organization, is committed to anything by attendance at a Coalition meeting—except our common general desire to work for the good of the Democratic Party in Texas. In other words, we are trying to reach a concensus [sic]—trying to come up with plans and programs at which we can all work together." Letter from Chris Dixie and Mrs. R.D. Randolph to "Democrat," October 8, 1961, Idar Papers, Box 9, Folder 2, BLAC.

38. Morris, "Crucial Questions," (first quotation); Willie Morris, "Poll Taxes Sought; Wright Quizzed," *TO*, October 20, 1961, 1 (second and third quotations).

39. Democratic Coalition, "A Program to Increase the Liberal Vote in Texas in 1962," Texas AFL-CIO Papers, AR110-26-9-4. See also Letter from Brown to "Democrat," September 1, 1961; Letter from Albert Peña to "Democrat," October 5, 1961—both in Idar Papers, Box 9, Folder 2, BLAC.

40. "Liberal Dems Map Plans in Austin," *HC*, September 14, 1961; "Demos Map Vote Plans For 1962," *CCC*, October 15, 1961; "State Democrats Air Plans to Raise Vote," *FWST*, October 15, 1961; Richard M. Morehead, "Liberals in Texas Plan Drive for 1962," October 17, 1961, *DMN*–clippings of all in AR110-26-9-4.

41. Morris, "Crucial Questions" (editorial), *TO*, September 29, 1961, 4. Morris's observations show that his own appreciation for black and brown agency had evolved, in contrast to his reporting on the Bexar Coalition in 1960 in which he gave all the credit to white liberal Franklin Spears.

42. Letter from H. S. (Hank Brown) to "Democrat," September 1, 1961, and enclosed Minutes of Agenda Committee Meeting, Democratic Coalition, August 26, 1961, copies in Texas AFL-CIO COPE Records, AR110-8-4-12 and Idar Papers, Box 9, Folder 2, BLAC.

43. For just one example, see "Grassroots Democratic Survey," attached to Democratic Coalition, "A Program to Increase the Liberal Vote in Texas in 1962," Texas AFL-CIO Papers, AR110-26-9-4. The survey asks about nine "federal issues," only one of which is related to civil rights.

44. "Demo Coalition Meeting—September 9, 1961," handwritten notes, AR110-26-9-4, 2-4. I have translated and paraphrased the cursive script as faithfully as possible.

45. The exact location of *mexicanos* in Jim Crow Texas is a subject of great scholarly debate. Here I summarize my findings based on a wide range of evidence, including the sources discussed in this chapter. There is little doubt that Mexican Americans professionals could at times occupy white public spaces while also facing substantial discrimination in their private lives. On the legal contradictions, see, among many other works, Olivas, *Colored Men and Hombres Aquí: Hernandez V. Texas and the Emergence of Mexican American Lawyering*. On the understanding of race among Mexican Americans, see Johnson, "The Cosmic Race in Texas: Racial Fusion, White Supremacy, and Civil Rights Politics," 404–19. On poor *mexicanos*, see, for example, the oral testimony of F. F. "Pancho" Medrano, who recalled being barred from city swimming pools and restaurants in Dallas. Francisco Medrano, interview by José Angel Gutiérrez, Dallas, July 16, 1997, CMAS 37, TV-UTA.

46. Democratic Coalition, "A Program to Increase the Liberal Vote in Texas in 1962," Texas AFL-CIO Papers, AR110-26-9-4.

47. Memorandum from Lyman [Jones] to Hank, RE: Coalition Meeting, September 11, 1961, AR110-26-9-4.

48. Minutes of PASO Meeting Held at Hamilton Hotel, Laredo, Texas, September 24, 1961, and list of participants, Idar Papers, Box 9, Folder 2, BLAC.

49. Wayne Chastain, "Bexar's Renewed Coalition," *TO*, July 22, 1962, 6; Letter from Maury Maverick, Jr., to Ed Idar, Jr., August 11, 1961, Idar Papers, Box 9, Folder 2, BLAC.

50. All statistics and quotation in "Probing Bexar's Election Returns," *TO*, November 10, 1961, 1. On Peña, see List of LULAC Council 2 Poll Tax Committee, September 11, 1961, Albert A. Peña Jr. Papers, MS 37 [hereafter Peña Papers], Box 25, Folder 9, UTSA; "Miscellany," *SAE*, October 10, 1971, copy in Peña Papers, Box 14, Folder 3. On the Eastside, see, for example, *SNAP*, October 27, 1961, MS 139, Box 3, SABHC. On Franklin Garcia, see the Richard A. Twedell Papers, AR264-8-7, and the Samuel A. Twedell Papers, AR124, Box 9—both in TLA-UTA. On the Lamberts, see Letter from Gonzalez to Mr. and Mrs. George Lambert, November 9, 1960; Letter from Gonzalez to Latane Lambert, December 14, 1961; and Letter from George Lambert to Gonzalez, January 8, 1962—all in George and Latane Lambert Papers, TLA-UTA (hereafter Lambert Papers), AR127-11-4.

51. Letter from Chris Dixie to "Fellow Democrat," November 20, 1961, AR110-26-9-4.

52. I borrow the term "bridge leader" from Robnett, *How Long? How Long?: African American Women in the Struggle for Civil Rights*. Of course, Mrs. LeRoy was a

bridge not only between African Americans but between black, white, and Mexican American organizations—making her exemplary of an even more expansive version of the concept.

53. Letter from Ed Idar Jr. to Officers and Representatives of PASO organizations in South Texas, December 20, 1961, Idar Papers, Box 9, Folder 2, BLAC.

54. Letter from E. D. LeRoy to Hank S. Brown, December 9, 1961, AR110-26-9-4.

55. Memorandum from LeRoy to Hank Brown, December 16, 1961, AR110-26-9-4.

56. Open letter from Mrs. Erma LeRoy to "Fellow Citizen, January 8, 1962, AR110-26-9-4.

57. Report from Erma LeRoy to Hank Brown, January 5, 1962, AR110-26-9-4.

58. Gilbert Garcia, "Report #1—December 8, 1961 to December 14, 1961," addressed to Mike Levy, December 19, 1961, AR110-26-9-4.

59. Gilbert Garcia, "Report Number Two—December 16 through 22, 1961," December 22, 1961 (quotation); Gilbert Garcia, "Report #3—December 22 to December 29, 1961," December 30, 1961—both in AR110-26-9-4. On discrimination, see also the records from the PASO meeting cited in the next note.

60. Minutes of PASO Meeting, Hamilton Hotel, Laredo, December 27, 1961, Idar Papers, Box 9, Folder 2; Letter from Ed Idar Jr. to Officers and Representatives of PASO organizations in South Texas, December 20, 1961; Letter from Ed Idar Jr. to Albert Peña, with enclosure, December 28, 1961—all in Idar Papers, Box 9, Folder 2, BLAC. Garcia's Report #3 calls it the "Valley Area Meeting." Labor activists Franklin and Pepper Garcia and Bob Sanchez were among the union members on the steering committee.

61. Gilbert Garcia, "Financial Report for 3 Weeks," December 30, 1916; Gilbert Garcia, "Report No. 4—January 2–8, 1962," January 9, 1962; Letter from Gilbert Garcia to Evans and Brown "RE: Coalition Poll Tax Drive," May 31, 1962—all in AR110-26-9-4. For the original budget, see Democratic Coalition, "A Program to Increase the Liberal Vote in Texas in 1962."

62. For a good summary of the candidates, see Willie Morris, "Sweeping Choice in Governor Race," *TO*, February 9, 1962, 1. The coverage of the race in the *Observer* rarely mentioned integration, but oral testimonies and later sources confirm Don's unprecedented position on the issue. For contemporary snippets, see "Observer Notebook," *TO*, June 1, 1962, 4; Ronnie Dugger, "Solidifying Prospect: A Man to Elect," *TO*, February 23, 1962, 4. I was unable to locate any scholarly studies that paid significant attention to Don Yarborough. In addition to *TO*, journalistic treatments include "Not So Simple," *Time* 79, no. 23 (June 8, 1962): 25; Paul Burka, "Donald Yarborough, Whose Feud with John Connally Brought JFK to Texas, Reported Gravely Ill," *Burkablog* (*Texas Monthly*), September 22, 2009, accessed August 2, 2015, http://www.texasmonthly.com/burka-blog/donald-yarborough-whose-feud-john-connally-brought-jfk-texas-reported-gravely-ill; Paul Burka, "Don Yarborough's Texas," *Texas Monthly*, October 2009, accessed August 2, 2015, http://www.texasmonthly.com/story/don-yarborough%E2%80%99s-texas?fullpage=1; Mike Tolson, "Texas Politician Don Yarborough Dies at 83," *HC*, September 23, 2009, accessed August 2, 2015, http://www.chron.com/news/houston-texas/article/Texas-politician-Donald-Yarborough-dies-at-83-1736099.php; William Grimes, "Don Yarborough Dies at 83; Stirred Texas Politics," *New York Times*, September 23, 2009, accessed August 2, 2015, http://www.nytimes.com/2009/09/24/us/24yarborough.html?_r=0. See also Andrew Kopkind, "Connally's Texas," *New Republic*, November 20, 1965,

accessed August 2, 2015, http://www.newrepublic.com/article/politics/95616/john-connally-texas-conservative-democrats.

63. "Potomac Committee," n.d.; Letter from Hank Brown to Franklin Jones, September 26, 1961—both in Texas AFL-CIO Papers, Democratic Party Organizations, AR110-26-9-4.

64. Democratic Coalition Proposed Agenda, Meeting of February 8, 1962, AR110-26-9-4.

65. Ibid. The only discussion of PASO that includes the larger coalition is contained in Benjamin Márquez, *Democratizing Texas Politics: Race, Identity, and Mexican American Empowerment, 1945–2002*, chap. 3. Márquez highlights the intra-ethnic struggles that divided *mexicanos* in the 1950s and 1960s, but his generalizations about Peña and the coalition often miss the mark.

66. Don Politico, "Yarborough Nears Decision," *SAL*, January 24, 1962, 27.

67. Democratic Coalition Proposed Agenda, Meeting of February 8, 1962, AR110-26-9-4; "Political Intelligence," *TO*, February 16, 1962, 8.

68. The exchange fills most of the folder in the Idar Papers, Box 9, Folder 4, BLAC. See especially: Letter from Ed Idar Jr. to George Sánchez, January 23, 1962 (all Idar quotations); Letter from Sánchez to Idar, January 29, 1962 (all Sánchez quotations); and Letter from Sánchez to Idar, February 2, 1962.

69. Ronnie Dugger, "The Imminent Threat to Texas Liberalism," *TO*, January 19, 1962, 5. Letter from Ed Idar Jr., to Ronnie Dugger, January 25, 1962; Letter from George Sánchez to Ed Idar Jr. January 29, 1962—both in Idar Papers, Box 9, Folder 4, BLAC.

70. Albert Peña, "County Comment," *SNAP*, February 9, 1962, MS 139, Box 3, SABHC; copy also in Peña Papers, Box 22, Folder 8, UTSA.

71. "PASSO Convention" minutes, February 9–11, 1962, Idar Papers, Box 9, Folder 4, BLAC; Letter from Ed Idar Jr. to Edward Casarez, March 12, 1962, Idar Papers, Box 9, Folder 6, BLAC; "Latin Group Split on Endorsement," *TO*, February 16, 1962, 1 (Sánchez quotations); "The Gold Dust Twins," *TO*, March 16, 1962, 4.

72. Letter from Ed Idar Jr. to Albert Pena, February 21, 1962, Peña Papers, Box 22, Folder 2, UTSA (copy in Idar Papers, Box 9, Folder 6, BLAC).

73. "Political Intelligence," *TO*, February 23, 1962, 8.

74. Minutes of PASO Meeting, San Antonio, March 28, 1962, Idar Papers, Box 9, Folder 6, BLAC.

75. Ed Idar Jr. to "Friend," April 20, 1962 (quotation on 2); Idar to Friend, March 21, 1962; Letter from G.E. Coronado to Hector P. Garcia, May 22, 1962—all in Idar Papers, Box 9, Folder 6, BLAC. "Labor Supports Don Yarborough," *TO*, February 23, 1962, 1; "Bexar Coalition Backs Yarborough: Daniel Takes Most Criticism in First Weeks," *TO*, February 23, 1962, 8.

76. Jay Milner, "West Side Story—Tactics of an Election," *TO*, May 19, 1962, 1.

77. Ibid.; "Pick No Candidate," *El Paso Herald-Post*, March 5, 1962, 5; "Political Intelligence," *TO*, March 9, 1962, 8; "Negro Group Splits on Governor Endorsement," *HC*, April 9, 1962, HCM-HMRC, HCCO; "Political Intelligence," *TO*, April 14, 1962, 8.

78. *SNAP*, April 20 and 27, and May 4, 1962, MS 139, Box 3, SABHC; Letter from Mrs. Erma LeRoy to Philip Weightman, May 8, 1962, Texas AFL-CIO Papers, Executive Board Records, AR110-1-12-1.

79. "Probing The Demo Primary," *TO*, May 12, 1962; Milner, "West Side Story," 7 (quotation). Election statistics can also be found in *Texas Almanac, 1964-1965*, 497, 500-503.

80. Minutes of PASO Meeting, San Antonio, May 14, 1962; Letter from James de Anda to PASO Members and Officers, May 22, 1962—both in Idar Papers, Box 9, Folder 6, BLAC.

81. *SNAP*, June 1, 1962, SABHC; "Political Assn. Here Endorses Yarborough," *HC*, May 23, 1962, HCM-HMRC, HCCO; "How It Happened: A Narrow Victory," *TO*, June 8, 1962, 1; Minutes of PASO Meeting, San Antonio, May 14, 1962, Idar Papers, BLAC.

82. "How It Happened" (quotation); Milner, "West Side Story"; *SNAP*, June 1, 1962, SABHC.

83. Albert Peña, "County Comment," *SNAP*, July 27, 1961, MS 139, Box 3, SABHC.

84. "Latin Group Split on Endorsement," *TO*, February 16, 1962, 1; "Political Intelligence," *TO*, February 16, 1962, 8.

85. Letter from LeRoy to Weightman, May 8, 1962, AR110-1-12-1; "41-Vote Margin Favors Dowdy," *TO*, May 12, 1962, 8.

86. Peña, "County Comment," *SNAP*, July 27, 1961, MS 139, Box 3, SABHC.

87. Ibid.; Zon, "Labor in Politics," 234-51; *Texas Almanac, 1964-1965*, 499, 504-5.

88. Albert Peña, "County Comment," *SNAP*, August 31, 1962, SABHC (all quotations); "Pena and PASO's Role," *TO*, September 7, 1962, 5.

Chapter 8

1. Peña, "County Comment," *SNAP*, July 27, 1961.

2. Willie Morris, "Political Summons in Bexar," *TO*, October 5, 1962, 1, 8 (quotation on 8).

3. Quoted in ibid., 1, 8.

4. Ibid., 8.

5. "PASO Withdraws," *TO*, October 12, 1963, 1, 3 (quotation on 3).

6. "Latin Group Split on Endorsement," *TO*, February 16, 1962, 1. See also Letter from Hector P. Garcia to George I. Sanchez, May 25, 1962, and Letter from Ed Idar Jr. to Albert Pena, June 27, 1962—both in Ed Idar Papers, Box 9, Folder 2, BLAC.

7. Willie Morris, "Angry Texas Labor to Reconsider Decision," *TO*, September 21, 1962, 1; "Organized Labor Boosts Connally," *TO*, October 19, 1962, 1 (quotation).

8. "GOP Shows Gain Despite Cox' Loss," *TO*, November 9, 1962, 1 (quotation); "AFL-CIO Lays Claim to Connally's Gratitude," *TO*, November 23, 1962, 8.

9. Two *Observer* contributors reached similar conclusions immediately after the election. Larry Goodwyn, "New Shapes in Texas Politics," *TO*, December 13, 1962, 3-4; Ronnie Dugger, "Texas Now: Texas New—A Special Report," *TO*, December 27, 1962, 7-9.

10. Larry Goodwyn, "New Shapes in Texas Politics," *TO*, December 13, 1962, 3-4 (all quotations); Ronnie Dugger, "Texas Now: Texas New—A Special Report," *TO*, December 27, 1962, 7-9; Ronnie Dugger, "No Deals," *TO*, December 27, 1962, 2; Ronnie Dugger, "Texas Politics," *TO*, January 10, 1963, 14-16. See also Letter from Larry Goodwyn to Hon. Woodrow Seals, March 30, 1963, and enclosure, Democratic Coalition, "New Shapes in Texas Politics," and thirteen charts and explanation of recent trends, Judge Woodrow Seals Papers, Box 2, Folder 29, HMRC.

11. George I. Sanchez, "Hell!," in "Dialogue," *TO*, December 27, 1962, 2, 15.

12. *Democratic Newsletter*, no author [Larry Goodwyn], no date [November 1962], first issue [vol. 1, no. 1], copy in Texas AFL-CIO Democratic Party Correspondence, AR110-26-9-4. Arthur DeWitty, a leader in the NAACP and TCV, attended the meeting and was also appointed to the temporary committee.

13. Ronnie Dugger, "Texas Politics," *TO*, January 10, 1963, 14–16.

14. *Democratic Newsletter* vol. 1, no. 4, n.d. [January 1963], AR110-26-9-5.

15. The above paragraphs all draw upon a three-page proposal for the Team Program on Democratic Coalition letterhead with blue ink, no title, no author, no date [by Lawrence Goodwyn, late March or early April, 1963]. The first sentence is "The Democratic Coalition of Texas began its organizing work on January 5th, 1963, with funds provided by Texas liberals of all races and by Texas labor." I have dated it and crosschecked the events it describes using other documents in the same folder, AR110-26-9-5, most especially the "Income Statement," September 30, 1963.

16. "Texas Is Integrating—A Special Report," *TO*, June 28, 1963, 9–14.

17. See, for example, "A Dark-Skinned Throng Before the Court," *TO*, March 7, 1963, 7–8.

18. Bill Donahue, "In Our City," *SNAP*, April 14, 1961, Box 3, SABHC.

19. Robert Gomez, "Social Spotlight," *SNAP*, December 15, 1961; March 2, 1962, and March 9, 1962—all in SABHC.

20. "Town Hall Meeting," *SNAP*, April 6, 1962, SABHC.

21. "San Antonio Protest," *TO*, October 19, 1962, 2.

22. Goldberg, "Racial Change on the Southern Periphery," 365–66.

23. "'Roll Call' For Negro Candidate," *SAN*, March 18, 1963 (first, second, and third quotations); "E. Side Warning: Back Black or Else," *SAL*, March 18, 1963; James McCrory, "Officials Get East Side Challenge," *SAE*, March 18, 1963 (remaining quotations)—clippings of all in Claude and ZerNona Black Papers, 1890–2009, Trinity University Archives and Special Collections (hereafter, Black Papers), Box 19, Folder 3. See also "Campaign Organization" and Letter from G. J. Sutton and Artman Bland to Whom It May Concern, March 13, 1963, in the same folder.

24. "The Big Race" and Albert Peña, "County Comment," *SNAP*, April 12, 1963, SABHC. The "wheat from the chaff" metaphor was first attributed in inverted form to Valmo Bellinger at the "roll call" tea (see previous note), but *SNAP* used it as well in this more common order. The *SNAP* quotation is filled with errors; I have cleaned it up for improved readability.

25. Goldberg, "Racial Change on the Southern Periphery," 368–69 (including first Black quotation); Rev. Claude W. Black Jr., interview by author, San Antonio, October 27, 2008, 1:09:20 (last quotation).

26. [Bexar County] *Coalition Newsletter*, vol. 1., no. 1 (July 23, 1963), copy in Black Papers, Box 32, Folder 11. Judging from its similarity to *SNAP*, this paper was probably edited by Coleman as well.

27. Saul Friedman, "Houston, a Backwater of the Revolt," *TO*, November 15, 1963, 8–10.

28. Howard Middleton Jr., interviews by author, Houston, May 5 and 31, 2010. In 1964, Judge Elliott reciprocated by appointing Howard as the county's first manpower commissioner, a position that allowed him to shape future job training and other War on Poverty programs.

29. Chandler Davidson, field notes on Moses and Erma LeRoy, January 25, 1979, Houston, Texas, Chandler Davidson Texas Politics Research Collection, MS 259, Box 9, Folder 6, WRC.

30. Ronnie Dugger, "Governor Connally and the U.P.O.," *TO*, July 12, 1963, 3–6; Roy R. Evans, "Civil Rights in Texas—More Than a Moral Issue," Texas State AFL-CIO *Secretary's Report* v. 6, no. 12 (July 5, 1963), copy in Black Papers, Box 32, Folder 11 (all quotations); Saul Friedman, "New Unit Challenges Negro Leadership," *HC*, August 11, 1963, clipping in Black Papers, Box 32, Folder 11.

31. Ronnie Dugger, "Conservative Negroes" (editorial), *TO*, July 12, 1963, 2.

32. Among others, see Shockley, *Chicano Revolt in a Texas Town*; Navarro, *The Cristal Experiment: A Chicano Struggle for Community Control*; Gutiérrez, *The Making of a Chicano Militant: Lessons from Cristal*; and Ignacio M. García, *United We Win: The Rise and Fall of La Raza Unida Party*.

33. Marc Simon Rodriguez pays particular attention to the high school students and recent graduates involved in the Crystal City uprising and argues that the revolt laid the groundwork for the Chicano Movement's evolution among farmworkers and urban poverty warriors in Wisconsin. The organizing tradition followed the stream of migrant agricultural laborers, first as the youth traveled north, and then back again to Texas as they returned to join La Raza Unida Party in the early 1970s. Marc Simon Rodriguez, *The Tejano Diaspora: Mexican Americanism & Ethnic Politics in Texas and Wisconsin*.

34. Carlos Conde, "Crystal City Gave PASO Pilot Project It Needed," *DMN*, May 7, 1963, Section 1, 17, reprinted as part of a flyer by Bexar County PASO, 1963, 1, Albert Peña Papers, Box 1, Folder 18, UTSA. Bexar County PASO chairman Charles Albidress Jr. added a note to the flyer stating that Conde's piece was "perhaps, the only purely factual account of on the spot events in Crystal City, although obviously, the roll [sic] of one or two persons is overemphasized." For another version, see "Crystal City Story" in "What Is PASO?" leaflet, Dr. Hector P. Garcia Papers, TAMUCC, 233.12.

35. Conde, "Crystal City," 1; Letter from Albert Fuentes Jr. to Friend and Fellow PASO Member, March 14, 1963, Peña Papers, Box 22, Folder 2, UTSA.

36. Conde, "Crystal City," 1.

37. Henry Muñoz Jr. interview by George N. Green and Carr Winn, Dallas, August 12, 1971, TLA-UTA, 1–9 (quotation on 4).

38. Ibid., 9, 12–15; Bob Sherrill, "A West Side Story," *TO*, September 9, 1961; "Hoffa Launches Texas Campaign," *TO*, February 16, 1962, 1.

39. "Hoffa Launches Texas Campaign," 1 (all quotations).

40. Conde, "Crystal City," 1.

41. Muñoz interview by Green and Winn, 23.

42. Muñoz interview by Green and Winn, 24 (all Muñoz quotations); Conde, "Crystal City Gave PASO Pilot Project It Needed," 1 (all remaining quotations). Carlos Moore recently confirmed Muñoz's and Conde's accounts. Carlos Moore, interview by author, Fort Worth, July 29, 2015, digital video recording in author's possession.

43. Conde, "Crystal City," 1–2.

44. Ibid.; Muñoz interview by Green and Winn, 24; Behnken, *Fighting Their Own Battles: Mexican Americans, African Americans, and the Struggle for Civil Rights in Texas*, 89–90.

45. Conde, "Crystal City," 2.

46. PASO Financial Report, probably by Albert Fuentes, June 8, 1963, Ed Idar Papers, BLAC, Box 9, Folder 3; Letter from Fuentes to PASO Members, March 14, 1963, Peña Papers.

47. Conde, "Crystal City," 1–2 (all quotations on 2).

48. Larry Goodwyn, "Los Cinco Candidatos," *TO*, April 18, 1963, 5.

49. Muñoz interview by Green and Winn, 24–25; Conde, "Crystal City," 2.

50. Goodwyn, "Los Cinco Candidatos," 7–8.

51. Goodwyn, "Los Cinco Candidatos," 9.

52. Flyer by Bexar County PASO, 1963, signed by Charles Albidress Jr., 2, Peña Papers; "Shock Waves from Popeye Land," *TO*, May 16, 1963, 6–7; Telegram from Bob Sanchez and Dr. R. R. (Ramiro) Casso to Senator Ralph Yarborough, May 2, 1963, R. P. (Bob) Sanchez Papers, Box 5, Folder 1, BLAC.

53. Behnken, *Fighting Their Own Battles*, 92–93.

54. "History in the Making?" *CCCT*, May 19, 1963, copy in R. P. (Bob) Sanchez Papers, BLAC, Box 5, Folder 1.

55. Goodwyn, "Los Cinco Candidatos"; Ronnie Dugger, "A Comment," *TO*, April 18, 1963, 10; Hart Stilwell, "Another Comment," *TO*, May 16, 1963, 8; George I. Sanchez, "A Re-phrasing," in "Dialogue," *TO*, May 16, 1963, 13. Dugger retreated to some extent in his editorial supporting the Crystal City and coalition-friendly faction of PASO in its internal controversy that June. Ronnie Dugger, "Too Easy to Forget," *TO*, June 14, 1963, 2.

56. Goodwyn, "Los Cinco Candidatos," 8.

57. Conde, "Crystal City," 1.

58. Bob Sanchez, with Leo J. Leo, May 31, 1963, R. P. (Bob) Sanchez Papers, Box 5, Folder 1, BLAC. The archival document is a carbon copy of text signed by Leo, but it has handwritten corrections, including Leo's name being crossed off and replaced by "Bob Sanchez." The document appears to be a speech, but the exact context is unknown. It could also be a letter to the editor, the text of a radio address (Sanchez did these frequently), or something else.

59. "Resolution Blasts Pena; Sparks Fly," *SAN*, May 9, 1963, 11-A; "Pena Discounts Censure," *SAN*, May 10, 1963; clippings of both in SAPL-VF, Commissioner Albert Peña folder. Peña was referring to the percentage of registered voters, not the total population.

60. David Lopez, "Group Fears Teamster Coup at PASO Meeting," *CCCT*, June 7, 1963, clipping in Peña Papers, Box 22, Folder 2, UTSA.

61. Minutes of PASO State Convention, June 8, 1963, Ed Idar Papers, Box 9, Folder 3, BLAC.

62. David Lopez, "Pena Faction Keeps PASO Reins," *CCCT*, June 10, 1963; "Valley PASO Leaders Deny Teamsters Link," *Valley Evening Monitor*, June 10, 1963—copies of both in Ed Idar Papers, BLAC, Box 9, Folder 3. Lopez reports that the Bonillas joined Garcia's walkout, but Casso and Leo deny this in the *Valley Evening Monitor*. The official minutes suggest that the latter report is accurate.

63. "Valley PASO Leaders Deny Teamsters Link"; David Lopez, "Opposing PASO Groups to Bear Same Names," *Corpus Christi Times*, July 17, 1963, 7-C. See, for example, Letter from Hector P. Garcia to Robert F. Kennedy, June 13, 1963, Hector P. Garcia Papers, TAMUCC, 233.14.

64. Handwritten letters from Gilbert Garcia to Ed Idar Jr., June 11, 1963 and July 15, 1963; Letter from Gregorio E. Coronado to Hector P. Garcia, July 18, 1963—all in Ed Idar Papers, BLAC, Box 9, Folder 3.

65. Minutes of PASO State Convention, June 8, 1963.

66. Albert Peña, "County Comment," June 14, 1963, including excerpts of his address, typescript in Peña Papers, Box 22, Folder 8, UTSA.

67. Coalition members learned both socially and experientially. For the paradigmatic works, see Bandura, *Social Learning Theory*; Kolb, *Experiential Learning: Experience as the Source of Learning and Development*. For a great example of social learning in the context of a labor-based civil rights movement, see Korstad, *Civil Rights Unionism: Tobacco Workers and the Struggle for Democracy in the Mid-Twentieth-Century South*, chap. 5.

68. The "heated" controversy is my inference based on the available evidence and the changes reflected in subsequent drafts of the plan; see the final section of this chapter for a discussion of the revisions. The best list of the initial sixteen-man Policy Committee is in Memo from Larry Goodwyn to Mr. Ed Ball and fourteen other recipients, May 29, 1963, AR110-26-9-5. The full committee consisted of the following members: for labor, Hank Brown, Ed Ball of the Steelworkers in Houston, Marcus Loftis of the state building trades, and an unspecified fourth member (it would later be Roy Evans of the Texas AFL-CIO and UAW); for independent liberals, Chris Dixie, Herkie Bernard of the Bexar County Democratic Coalition, former Ralph Yarborough campaign staffer Bob Hall of the HCD, and Mrs. Mary Wilson of the Democratic Women; for African Americans, W. J. Durham, Francis Williams of the HCCO and TCV, Dr. Marion J. Brooks of Fort Worth, and Willie Melton of Brazoria County (and a litigant in the cases against the "Jaybird" primary that followed *Smith v. Allright*); for Mexican Americans, Albert Peña, Albert Fuentes (Peña's assistant), Bob Sanchez, and Dr. Ramiro Casso of the Hidalgo County PASO. See also Larry Goodwyn, "The Coalition, the Repeal Election, and the Current Poll Tax Drive," background section appended to Memo from Larry Goodwyn to Co-Chairmen, Democratic Coalition, November 15, 1963, Texas AFL-CIO Democratic Party Correspondence, AR110-26-9-5; Ronnie Dugger, "A Four-Group Coalition," *TO*, August 9, 1963, 3–5. George and Latane Lambert were in the process of moving from San Antonio to Dallas, which may explain Latane's omission from the initial Policy Committee, though she would be added when it expanded to thirty-two members a few months later. G. J. Sutton would also be added to the leadership in short order.

69. Agenda, Democratic Coalition, Granada Hotel, June 1, 1963, Black Papers, Box 32, Folder 11; Goodwyn, "The Coalition, the Repeal Election, and the Current Poll Tax Drive," November 15, 1963, AR110-26-9-5; Dugger, "A Four-Group Coalition," 3.

70. The preceding paragraphs all draw upon the revised proposal for the Team Program, June 1, 1963, on Democratic Coalition letterhead with blue ink, no title, no author [probably by Lawrence Goodwyn], Black Papers, Box 32, Folder 11 (all italicized portions emphasized in the original).

71. Author's conversation with Lawrence C. Goodwyn, interview by author, Durham, North Carolina, June 14, 2010 (digital audio recording in author's possession). Mexican American civil rights activists' criticisms of the lack of attention to their cause is nearly ubiquitous in their records, from Sánchez's formulation of the "forgotten people" to the militant protests against neglect by the Johnson administration in Albuquerque in 1966. See, for example, Albert Pena Jr., "Needed: A Marshall Plan for Mexican-Americans," *TO*, April 15, 1966, 1.

72. "The Democratic Coalition is a voluntary association of individuals" [Statement of Principles], mimeograph on onion skin paper, attached to Agenda, Democratic

Coalition, Granada Hotel, June 1, 1963, Black Papers, Box 32, Folder 11 (all quotations except Dugger); Dugger, "A Four-Group Coalition," 3 (remaining quotations).

73. Revised proposal for the Team Program June 1, 1963, Black Papers, Box 32, Folder 11.

Chapter 9

1. Ronnie Dugger, "A Four-Group Coalition," *TO*, August 9, 1963, 3–5 (first quotation on 4; all other quotations on 3).
2. Ibid., 4.
3. Ibid.
4. Ibid. The coalition also affirmed the membership of the permanent statewide Steering Committee—a body of one hundred individuals composed of twenty-five members from each group (which would soon be doubled in size). The July gathering also appointed an Executive Committee comprising thirty-two members, eight from each group, which would replace the sixteen-member policy committee and provide direction to the cochairs between the full Steering Committee meetings. The Executive Committee included the previous sixteen and added, notably, Roy Evans of the UAW and secretary of the Texas AFL-CIO, Ray Shafer and R. G. Miller of the Teamsters, Jack Martin of the San Antonio building trades, Roy Elizondo of Houston PASO, Crystal City organizer Martin Garcia (representing "Latins"), J. O. "Pepper" Garcia of the Dallas PASO, G. J. Sutton and Dr. Ruth Bellinger McCoy of San Antonio, civil rights unionist Moses LeRoy of Houston, and Arthur DeWitty of Austin.
5. Ibid., 4–5 (first quotation on 4; all others on 5).
6. "Connally Petitioned by Negroes," *DMN*, July 14, 1963, Sec. 2, p. 8.
7. "Ethnic 'Marriage' Key to Influence," *CCCT*, September 22, 1963, 1, copy in Texas AFL-CIO Papers, AR 110, Correspondence with Democratic Party Organizations, Series 26 (hereafter Texas AFL-CIO Democratic Party Correspondence, AR110-26), Box 9, Folder 5.
8. Form letter from H. S. Hank Brown to appointees of the Committee on Civil Rights and Equal Employment, Texas AFL-CIO Executive Board Records, AR110-1-13-4, 1.
9. Proceedings of the founding convention of the Texas State AFL-CIO, Austin, July 30–August 1, 1957, TLA-UTA, 139–40, 145, 147–48, 156.
10. "Jim Crow Wins," *TO*, July 27, 1962, 4 (all quotations); Civil Rights Committee Report (Report No. 14), 1962 Convention, copy in Texas AFL-CIO Executive Board Records, AR110-1-13-4.
11. Miscellaneous clippings provided by the Texas Press Service, July 27, 1962 (first three quotations); Letter from Clarence A. Laws to H. S. Hank Brown, August 14, 1962 (fourth quotation); Letter from Laws to Brown, November 5, 1962, and attached program for the NAACP State Conference (fifth quotation)—all in Texas AFL-CIO, AR110, Correspondence with Non-Union Organizations, Series 25, Box 8, Folder 4.
12. Form letter from H.S. Hank Brown to appointees of the Committee on Civil Rights and Equal Employment, n.d. [late June 1963], Texas AFL-CIO Executive Board Records, AR110-1-13-4, 1–2.
13. List of participants, Civil Rights Committee Meeting (Organizational), July 17, 1963, Texas AFL-CIO Executive Board Records, AR110-1-13-4.

14. Letter from Allan L. Maley Jr. to Hank Brown, June 24, 1963, Texas AFL-CIO Executive Board Records, AR110-1-13-4.

15. Anonymous letter attached to letter from Harry Hubbard Jr. to H. S. "Hank" Brown, and enclosure, August 15, 1963, Texas AFL-CIO Executive Board Records, AR110-1-13-4.

16. "Texas Labor Leaders Blame Employers for Bias on Jobs," *DMN*, July 18, 1963 (all quotations); Minutes, Texas AFL-CIO Civil Rights Committee, July 17, 1963, Texas AFL-CIO Executive Board Records, AR110-1-13-4.

17. Minutes and "A Statement of Policy," Committee on Civil Rights and Equal Employment, July 17, 1963, Texas AFL-CIO Executive Board Records, AR110-1-13-4.

18. Jon Ford, "AFL-CIO Urges Special Session of Legislature on Discrimination," *SAE*, July 18, 1963, 5-A; "Special Session Asked on Texas Civil Rights," *Valley Morning Star*, July 18, 1963, 1—both in MAAC, AR110-7-4-1.

19. Ford, "AFL-CIO Urges Special Session" (first and second quotations; statements on Velasquez); "Labor Threatens Demonstrations for Higher Pay," clipping of UPI report in unknown paper, dated July 18, 1963 (third quotation), MAAC, AR110-7-4-1.

20. "Labor Leaders Trying to Fan Racial Issues, Texas Governor Replies," clipping of UPI report in unknown publication, dated July 18, 1963 (all quotations); "Connally to Talk on Rights Today," clipping of AP report in unknown publication, dated July 19, 1963; "Statewide TV Talk Tonight," clipping of UPI report in unknown publication, dated July 19, 1963—all in MAAC, AR110-7-4-1.

21. "Connally to Talk on Rights Today" (first four quotations); Mike Raburn, "Battle Lines Drawn for Civil Rights Showdown in Texas," *Brownsville Herald*, July 21, 1963, 12-A, clipping in MAAC, AR110-7-4-1.

22. "Connally to Talk on Rights Today" (first and second quotations); Jon Ford, "Connally's Rights View Low-Rated," *SAEN*, August 4, 1963 (all other quotations); "Connally's Distinction on Rights a Valid One," clipping of editorial in unknown publication, dated July 19, 1963—all in MAAC, AR110-7-4-1.

23. "PASO Asks Session on Race Issue," clipping of UPI report in unknown publication, dated July 19, 1963 (all Peña quotations); "Connally Talk Hit by NAACP," clipping of UPI report in unknown publication, n.d. [probably July 20, 1963] (all Laws quotations)—both in MAAC, AR110-7-4-1; Raburn, "Battle Lines Drawn."

24. Ford, "Connally's Rights View Low-Rated."

25. Form letter from Hank Brown to unknown, August 5, 1963, Texas AFL-CIO Executive Board Records, AR110-1-13-4; Minutes of Civil Rights Committee Meeting (Organizational).

26. Mike Raburn, "Battle Lines Drawn for Civil Rights Showdown in Texas," *Brownsville Herald*, July 21, 1963, 12-A, clipping in MAAC, AR110-7-4-1; Ford, "Connally's Rights View Low-Rated" (quotation).

27. Booker T. Bonner, first interview by author, Houston, May 11, 2010, file 1, 0:00–26:50.

28. Ibid., 26:50–35:45.

29. Ibid., 35:45–38:50, 41:50 (last quotation); "One Man's Protest," *TO*, March 18, 1961, 3. For more on the stand-ins in Austin, see also "Students Demonstrate against Texas Theater," *TO*, December 9, 1960, 5; Ronnie Dugger, "UT Stand-Ins Will Continue," *TO*, December 30, 1960, 1–2; "Stand-Ins In Austin Reach Peak," *TO*, February 18, 1961,

1, 3; and "Austin Theaters Give In," *TO*, September 9, 1961, 1, 3. The leader of SDA was Chandler Davidson, who later became a sociologist at Rice University and an expert witness on behalf of Houston litigants who challenged the city's at-large voting system under the Voting Rights Act. One of the group's faculty mentors and participants was Sandra Cason, later known as Casey Hayden, who became a leader in SDS, SNCC, and the radical feminist movement.

30. Bonner, first interview by author, file 1, 38:50, 50:10–52:40.

31. Jon Ford, "Gov. Connally Agrees to See Negro Waiter," *SAE*, July 31, 1963, 1, 11; Jon Ford, "State Governor's Home Is Picketed," *SAE*, July 30, 1963, 1, 12; "Negro Resumes Austin Protest," *CCC*, July 30, 1963, 1–2; "Negro Sits on Floor of Texas Capitol to Gain Audience with Connally," *El Paso Herald-Post*, July 30, 1963; B. T. Bonner, interview by author, Houston, May 11, 2010, File 2, 9:25.

32. Ford, "Connally's Rights View Low-Rated" (first, second, third, and final quotations); Ford, "Governor Agrees to See Negro Waiter," 1 (all other quotations).

33. "Texas Negro Fired After Capitol Sit-in," *SAL*, August 1, 1963, 3.

34. On the Teamsters, see "Teamsters to Help Gain Valley Control," *SAEN*, June 5, 1963, 6-B; "Teamsters Surveying Starr County," clipping in unknown publication, dated July 18, 1963; "Teamsters Cooking 'Sumpun' In Starr County, But What?," clipping in unknown publication, dated July 18, 1963; "Teamsters Try To Grab Power in 2 Valley Cities," *Brownsville Herald*, July 18, 1963, 1; "'Working Quietly' But Not Underground, Says Shafer," clipping in unknown publication, n.d. [late July, 1963]—all in MAAC, AR110-7-4-1.

35. Central Labor Council of Webb County, AFL-CIO, Memorandum on the Border Wage and Job Conference, August 2–3, 1963, MAAC, AR110-7-1-1.

36. Ibid.

37. Oscar Griffin, "Laredo Union Parley to Air 'Dirty Linen,'" *HC*, undated clipping [July 31 or August 1, 1963] (first and second quotations); Oscar Griffin, "Latin Pay Fight Brews in Valley," *HC*, July 28, 1963 (remaining quotations)—both in MAAC, AR110-7-4-1.

38. Griffin, "Laredo Union Parley" (first and second quotations); David Lopez, "Aide Says Unions to Demonstrate," *CCC*, August 2, 1963, clipping in MAAC, AR110-7-4-1.

39. David Lopez, "Union Leaders Press for Action," *CCCT*, August 3, 1963, 1, clipping in MAAC, AR110-7-4-1.

40. Ibid., 15; Bulletin from Roy Evans to Members of the Permanent Latin American Affairs Committee et al., n. d. [1963], MAAC, AR110-7-5-7.

41. Jimmy Banks, "Businessmen Shun Parley," *DMN*, August 4, 1963, 4 (quotation); "Pena Urges Drive to Register Voters," *DMN*, August 4, 1963—both clippings in MAAC, AR110-7-4-1; handwritten sign-in sheet of attendees, Saturday morning meeting, August 3, 1963, MAAC, AR110-7-1-1.

42. "Pena Urges Drive to Register Voters"; "Pena Lashes Gov. Connally," *SAE*, August 4, 1963, clipping in SAPL-VF. The period for registering voters for the November 9, 1963, constitutional referenda election had ended on January 31, but registration for the following year would begin immediately afterward.

43. Central Labor Council of Webb County, AFL-CIO, "Invitacion al Publico de Laredo," MAAC, AR110-7-1-1 (first five quotations); Banks, "Businessmen Shun Parley," (last two quotations).

44. James McCrory, "'Slave Labor' Hit By Gonzalez; Brown Tells Valley Plans," *SAEN*, August 4, 1963, clipping in MAAC, AR110-7-4-1.

45. Banks, "Businessmen Shun Parley."

46. Lopez, "Union Leaders Press for Action."

47. "Negroes Ask Texas Solons to Take Stand," *SAL*, August 2, 1963 (all quotations).

48. "Negro Refuses Talk with Gov. Connally," *SAE*, August 7, 1963, 1; "Connally, Negro Fail to Hold Talk," *CCT*, August 6, 1963, 1, 12.

49. "Bonner Admits 1945 Conviction on Mail Count," *SAE*, August 8, 1963, 8-A (first two quotations); "Negro Refuses Talk with Gov. Connally" (third and fourth quotations); "Negro Lists Demands," *SAL*, August 7, 1963 (last quotation); "Connally, Negro Fail to Hold Talk"; "Demonstrators Picket in Austin," *SAE*, August 6, 1963, 1; "Pickets at Capital," *SAL*, August 6, 1963.

50. "Connally, Negro Fail To Hold Talk," 12.

51. "Sutton Says Door Barred," *SAE*, August 7, 1963, 6-D.

52. Dawson Duncan, "Integrationist Admits Record; Plans March on State Capitol," *DMN*, August 8, 1963, 6 (all quotations); "Bonner Admits 1945 Conviction on Mail Count"; "Integration Leader Keeps Record Secret," *SAL*, August 7, 1963; "Bonner Declines to Discuss Past," *CCT*, August 7, 1963, 14.

53. Duncan, "Integrationist Admits Record," 6.

54. "Negroes Picket Connally Again," *SAL*, August 10, 1963, 1.

55. "Demonstrations in Texas for Civil Rights Planned," *CCCT*, August 11, 1963, 6.

56. "City, State, D.C. Action Scheduled By S.A. NAACP," *SAE*, August 19, 1963, 4-D.

57. "Demonstrations in Texas for Civil Rights Planned"; "Two Texas Civil Rights Marches Set," *HC*, August 11, 1963, HCM-HMRC, NAACP. Closer to twenty Houstonians ended up going to each of the two marches: "23 Houston Negroes Streak into Capital," *HC*, August 28, 1963, HCM-HMRC, NAACP; Saul Friedman, "Houston, a Backwater of the Revolt," *TO*, November 15, 1963, 9–10.

58. Bexar County PASO, "Resolution," August 22, 1963 (first quotation); "Statement of Commissioner Albert A. Pena, Jr., As Chairman of Bexar County Democratic Coalition and State Chairman on Civil Rights March," Houston, August 25, 1963—both in Peña Papers, Box 22, Folder 8, UTSA.

59. "'Incident' at March Feared by Connally," *CCT*, August 27, 1963, 7; Jon Ford, "Texas Marchers Vow to Battle Gov. Connally," *SAE*, August 29, 1963, 1, 10-A.

60. Ronnie Dugger, "The Austin March," *TO*, September 6, 1963, 14–16 (all quotations except "Kennedy *sí*"); "Negro Leader Calls March Anti-Connally Political Rally," *Galveston News*, August 30, 1963, 11 (remaining quotation). See also Ford, "Texas Marchers Vow to Battle Gov. Connally"; "Negroes Single Out Connally as Target," *DMN*, August 29, 1963, 11; "March Takes on Political Tone," *CCT*, August 29, 1963, 4.

61. Ford, "Texas Marchers Vow to Battle Gov. Connally," 10-A; Dugger, "The Austin March," 16.

62. Dugger, "The Austin March," 16; "Negroes Single Out Connally as Target"; "March Takes on Political Tone." Additional quotations from Black's speech are located in Austin Civil Rights March, Speeches, and Interviews, KTSA, August 28, 1963, audiotape recording in Black Papers, Trinity University, Box 68, Item 1, and online at http://cdm16264.contentdm.oclc.org/cdm/ref/collection/p16264coll1/id/1104 (transcription by author).

63. Austin Civil Rights March, Speeches, and Interviews, KTSA, Black Papers (transcription by author).

64. Dugger, "The Austin March," 15; "Statement of Commissioner Albert A. Pena"; Ford, "Texas Marchers Vow to Battle Gov. Connally," 10-A.

65. Dugger, "The Austin March," 15 (first quotation); "March Takes on Political Tone" (second quotation); Ford, "Texas Marchers Vow to Battle Gov. Connally," 10-A (third quotation).

66. Austin Civil Rights March, Speeches, and Interviews, KTSA, Black Papers (transcription by author).

67. Dugger, "The Austin March," 15–16 (first and block quotations on 16); Ford, "Texas Marchers Vow to Battle Gov. Connally," 10-A (last two quotations).

68. "Negro Leader Calls March Anti-Connally Political Rally."

69. Jon Ford, "Texas Liberals Rattling Swords at Conservatives," *SAE*, September 2, 1963, 6-A (first three quotations); William Clayton, "Labor Speaker Hits Connally," *News Texan*, August 29, 1963, 6.

70. Ford, "Texas Liberals Rattling Swords at Conservatives" (all quotations). For additional insight about the labor convention, see "Labor Raises the Bid" and "And Don Goes All-Out," both in *TO*, September 20, 1963, 7.

71. *Democratic Newsletter*, vol. 1, no. 1, 3, copy in Texas AFL-CIO Papers, Democratic Party Correspondence, AR110-26-9-5; Lawson, *Black Ballots: Voting Rights in the South, 1944–1969*, 290.

72. "25¢ a Vote," *TO*, May 30, 1963, 6–7 (all quotations). *Democratic Newsletter*, vol. 1, no. 8, May 28, 1963; *Democratic Newsletter*, vol. 1, no. 7, n.d. [mid-April, 1963]; Larry Goodwyn, "The Repeal Election," n.d., appended to Memo from Larry Goodwyn to Co-Chairmen, Democratic Coalition, November 15, 1963—all in Texas AFL-CIO Democratic Party Correspondence, AR110-26-9-5.

73. "1963 Voter Registration Drive and Repeal-the-Poll-Tax Campaign," 1, Texas AFL-CIO COPE, AR110-8-9-3.

74. "1963 Voter Registration Drive and Repeal-the-Poll-Tax Campaign," Texas AFL-CIO COPE, AR110-8-9-3, 2 (all quotations except third and final three), 4 (final three quotations); "The Repeal Election" (third quotation) and "Budget (November 15 through January 31)"—both in Memo from Goodwyn to Co-Chairmen, November 15, 1963.

75. Budget, Statewide Blockworker Program to Repeal the Poll Tax [initial, appended to "1963 Voter Registration Drive"]; V.O.T.E. Budget October 6 through November 9 election, with handwritten notes, George and Latane Lambert Papers, TLA-UTA (hereafter Lambert Papers), AR127-30-5; Memo from Goodwyn to Co-Chairmen, November 15, 1963.

76. V.O.T.E. Budget October 6 through November 9 election; "Budget (November 15 through January 31)" in Memo from Goodwyn to Co-Chairmen, November 15, 1963; V.O.T.E. Executive Board Meeting agenda, October 19, 1963, Lambert Papers AR127- 28-1 (misfiled in archive); "Temporary Directory of Project Directors *** Blockworker Program," October 10, 1963, Texas AFL-CIO Democratic Party Correspondence, AR110-26-9-5.

77. Memo from Goodwyn to Co-Chairmen; "Outline of Program—'Repeal the Poll Tax,'" 1963, Texas AFL-CIO COPE AR110-8-9-3.

78. Martin Wiginton, Report on PASO Activities, September 26, 1963, based on his meeting with Fuentes the previous day, Texas AFL-CIO Democratic Party Correspondence, AR110-26-9-5.

79. This paragraph summarizes dozens of documents on the repeal and subsequent poll tax campaigns. For an explicit explanation of the on-the-ground tactics, see, for example, "Project Director's Guide," Texas AFL-CIO Democratic Party Correspondence, AR110-26-9-5; Letter from Martin Wiginton to "Project Officer," October 12, 1963, 2, Lambert Papers, AR127-3-6; "Urban Program," enclosure in Memo from Goodwyn to Co-Chairmen, November 15, 1963. Goodwyn and Peña joined Fuentes, DeWitty, and Texas AFL-CIO public relations director Lyman Jones at a motivational meeting in Corpus Christi that was probably a Team Program pep rally. See "Ethnic 'Marriage' Key to Influence."

80. Don Politico, "Pena Travels Lumpy Road," *SAL*, September 1, 1963; "Bexar PASO Censures County Dads," *SAL*, August 16, 1963—clippings of both in SAPL-VF.

81. "Connally's Pena Blast Stirs State," *SAN*, September 10, 1963; "Pena Hits Back At Governor," no publication, no date [September 11, 1963]—clippings in SAPL-VF.

82. "A Memo to the Democratic National Convention," 2; "So John Burns His Bridges," 8; "The Racial Reaction," 9—all in *TO*, September 20, 1963.

83. "Background," 2, enclosure in Memo from Goodwyn to Co-Chairmen, November 15, 1963.

84. Democratic Coalition, "A Message for Official Block Captains," n.d., two issues [November 1963], Texas AFL-CIO Democratic Party Correspondence, AR110-26-9-5.

85. Ronnie Dugger, "Texas Poll-Tax Vote a Defeat for Liberals: First Test of Coalition," *Washington Post*, November 17, 1963, A4.

86. Ibid. See also Ronnie Dugger, "The Dynamics of the Poll Tax Election," *TO*, November 29, 1963, 9–10. A copy of this letter can be found in Texas AFL-CIO Democratic Party Correspondence, AR110-26-9-5.

87. "Statistical Resume," enclosure in Memo from Goodwyn to Co-Chairmen, November 15, 1963. The one statistic regarding Houston comes from "The Blockworker Program of the Texas Democratic Coalition," n.d. [mid-November, 1963], Texas AFL-CIO Democratic Party Correspondence, AR110-26-9-5. Remarkably, repeal passed in Harris County by a larger margin than in the nonbinding referendum a year earlier.

88. "The Blockworker Program of the Texas Democratic Coalition."

89. "Evaluation," enclosure in letter from Goodwyn to Co-Chairmen.

90. "The Blockworker Program of the Texas Democratic Coalition."

Chapter 10

1. C. L. Mangus, "What Now?" *SNAP*, November 29, 1963, SABHC.

2. Bulletin Regarding "Operation Bootstrap" in the Lower Rio Grande Valley, n.d. [July 1963], MAAC, AR110-7-5-7. For a snapshot of the five the activities of the five PIOs, see "Meeting of the Texas AFL-CIO PIO Staff," Laredo, handwritten notes, February 26, 1964, MAAC, AR110-7-1-1. For additional details on the justification for and goals of the program, see letter from Henry Muñoz to Roy R. Evans, July 6, 1964, MAAC, AR110-7-1-1.

3. Henry Muñoz Jr., interview by George N. Green and Carr Winn, Dallas, August 12, 1971, TLA-UTA, 26 (quotation); "Munoz Gets Union Post," *SAE*, December 17, 1963, 2; Minutes of Latin American Affairs Committee Meeting, Brownsville, handwritten notes, July 13, 1964, MAAC, AR110-7-1-1; Texas AFL-CIO Latin American Affairs Committee, "An Affair of the Conscience," pamphlet circulated at convention, n.d. [1964],

MAAC, AR110-7-1-1. The phrase "Mexican-Dixon line" is often attributed to Franklin Garcia, the PASO and meat cutters union organizer who was stationed in the Lower Rio Grande Valley, where he collaborated closely with J. H. Villareal, the Operation Bootstrap PIO in the area, and Bob Sanchez. For more details on each PIO, see their reports in MAAC, Box 2. For additional news reports, see the clippings file in MAAC, AR110-7-4-1.

4. This biographical sketch draws on my book chapter: Krochmal, "Chicano Labor and Multiracial Politics in Post–World War II Texas," 133–76. Primary sources consulted include: José Angel Gutiérrez, "Oral History Interview with Francisco Medrano," Dallas, June 27, 1996, CMAS 37, TV-UTA, 55, 63–65, 75–76, 81–85, 90–92; "Interest Mounts in Effort to Abolish Poll Tax on November 9th," n.d. [1965], probably from local NAACP newsletter, Pancho Medrano Papers, TLA-UTA, AR55-1-8 (quotation); typed field notes on author's conversation on Ricardo Medrano, November 2, 2008; Letter from Clarence A. Laws to Glover Pettes, July 22, 1964, Medrano Papers, AR55-1-2; Letter from Roy Reuther to Ted Hawks, September 24, 1964, Medrano Papers, AR55-1-2; Letter from Gillespie C. Wilson to Medrano, April 10, 1969, Medrano Papers, AR55-1-2; Joe Simnacher, "Francisco Medrano Sr.: 1920–2002—Political Patriarch Mourned," *DMN*, April 5, 2002; Bob Ray Sanders, "Activist's Life Was a Fight for Justice," *FWST*, April 10, 2002; "Medrano Was Force in Dallas—He Was Political, Civil Rights Leader," *SAEN* (Associated Press), April 6, 2002; Tony Castro, "The Medranos: Family of Activists," *DTH*, November 22, 1970, C-9, copy in Medrano Papers, AR55-1-8; American G.I. Forum National Convention program (San Diego, 1966), Medrano Papers, AR55-1-1; "Excerpt from a bulletin sent out by the New Mexico chapter of the American GI Forum," 1965, Medrano Papers, AR55-1-1; "Pancho's Qualifications," Medrano Papers, AR55-1-3; "Trujillo Heads Kennedy Group," *DMN*, October 11, 1960; and scattered invitations for AGIF and LULAC meetings in Medrano Papers, AR55-1-8.

5. Pancho Medrano, interview by George N. Green and Carr Winn, TLA-UTA, 32, 34–35; Francisco Medrano, interview by Gutiérrez, CMAS 37, TV-UTA, 74, 100–102, 139; Sharon Cobler, "Unidad: Family Fights Inside Establishment," *DMN*, July 11, 1976; Krochmal, "Chicano Labor and Multiracial Politics."

6. Oral history narrators universally agree on these points. See, for example, author's interviews in San Antonio with Arnold Flores, Roy Hernandez, Paul Javior, Eddie Felán, and Hank Brown (in author's possession).

7. F. "Pancho" Medrano, Semi-Monthly Report Form, December 15–31, 1963, MAAC, AR110-7-2-3.

8. F. "Pancho" Medrano, Semi-Monthly Report Form, January 1–15, 1964; Letter from Lenora Rolla to F. Pancho Medrano, January 9, 1964; Letter from Medrano to Bill Dodds, January 17, 1964—all in MAAC, AR110-7-2-3; Medrano interview by Gutierrez, 91.

9. Medrano interview by Gutierrez, CMAS 37, TV-UTA, 56–58; Author's field notes on Ricardo Medrano, Dallas, November 2, 2008; author's interview with Robert Medrano, Dallas, September 24, 2009. Ricardo said that Julia Scott Reed wrote an article on the incident in *DE*, the black weekly, but I have not yet located it. On the middle-class Mexican American leadership that included the Martinez family, see Carolyn Barta, "New Brown Leaders Emerge," *DMN*, August 19, 1972; and Gilbert Bailon, "Quiet Effort Opened Doors for Hispanics," *DMN*, September 15, 1987.

10. Henry Muñoz Jr., Semi-Monthly Report Forms for the following dates: December 12–31, 1963; January 1–15, 1964; January 15–31, 1964; and February 1–17, 1964—all in

MAAC, AR110-7-1-1. See also "Bexar Voting Strength at Record High," unknown publication, n.d. [March 1964], clipping attached to Memorandum from Henry Muñoz Jr. to Roy R. Evans, March 7, 1964, MAAC, AR110-7-1-1.

11. Muñoz, Semi-Monthly Report Forms, February 1–17, 1964; Albert Peña, interview by José Ángel Gutiérrez.

12. Memorandum from Henry Muñoz to Roy Evans, December 27, 1963, and enclosure, "LULAC, City-Wide Committee for Job Opportunities and Manpower Development Proposals," 1963, MAAC, AR110-7-2-4; Memorandum from Muñoz to Evans, March 7, 1964, MAAC, AR110-7-1-1 (quotations).

13. Letter from Muñoz to Roy R. Evans, July 6, 1964, 2 (first and second quotations); Henry Muñoz, Semi-Monthly Report Covering September 1–15, 1964 (handwritten), 6 (remaining quotations)—both in MAAC, AR110-7-1-1. By "so-called leaders," Muñoz was referring to Charles Albidress of Bexar County PASO, for whom he had complete disregard. Muñoz added that Albidress had been vociferously attacking the Texas AFL-CIO, and that the local PASO chapter was dying. "PASO is NOT the representative of all the Mexicanos in San Antonio," he added. It is unclear if the chapter had defected from Peña's fold or if Muñoz had, but the latter is more likely. Certainly labor now buttered Muñoz's bread. Many oral history narrators call Muñoz "an opportunist," and his nickname was "the fox," after all. Author's interviews with Arnold Flores; author's notes on conversation with José Ángel Gutiérrez.

14. Handwritten minutes of the Latin American Affairs Committee meeting, Laredo, February 27, 1964, 4; "Meeting of the Texas AFL-CIO PIO Staff," Laredo, handwritten notes, February 26, 1964; "An Affair of the Conscience"—all in MAAC, AR110-7-1-1.

15. Handwritten minutes of Latin American Affairs Committee meeting, Brownsville, July 13, 1964, and committee pamphlet—both in MAAC, AR110-7-1-1; "Union Takes a Look at 'Bootstrap,'" *Brownsville Herald*, July 14, 1964, 5; "AFL-CIO Authorizes Stronger Bootstraps," *Brownsville Herald*, August 21, 1964, 1; H. S. Hank Brown, interview by author, San Antonio, March 25, 2010 (digital recording in author's possession), 1:18:00 (quotation), 1:19:15.

16. On this last point, see also "Labor Raises the Bid," *TO*, September 20, 1963, 7; Larry Goodwyn, "The Unions and the Poor," *TO*, August 20, 1965, 8; and "Can Texas Labor Help Poor?" *TO*, January 21, 1966, 8–9.

17. Letter from Goodwyn to Co-Chairmen, November 15, 1963, and enclosures, Texas AFL-CIO Papers, Correspondence with Democratic Party Organizations (hereafter Texas AFL-CIO Democratic Party Correspondence), AR110-26-9-5. The "Semi-Final" budget considered on December 28 ended up being much more modest—only $35,000, of which $10,000 would be used to pay debts from the 1963 repeal election.

18. Press release, "Austin, Dec. 8" (1963) (all quotations), and "Status Report," December 18, 1963—both in Texas AFL-CIO Democratic Party Correspondence, AR110-26-9-5.

19. "Status Report," December 18, 1963 (first three quotations); "Proposed Poll Tax Program" and "Urban Program" (last quotation), enclosures in letter from Goodwyn to Co-Chairmen, November 15, 1963, Texas AFL-CIO Democratic Party Correspondence, AR110-26-9-5.

20. Semi-Final Budget Estimate (for Submission to V.O.T.E. Executive Board), December 28, 1963, meeting in Austin, Texas AFL-CIO Democratic Party Correspondence,

AR110-26-9-5. See also *Democratic Newsletter*, vol. 2, no. 1 (January 17, 1964), copy in Texas AFL-CIO Democratic Party Correspondence, AR110-26-9-6.

21. Democratic Coalition, "A Message for Official Block Captains," n.d. [January 15, 1964], Texas AFL-CIO Democratic Party Correspondence, AR110-26-9-5.

22. "Political Intelligence," *TO*, January 24, 1964, 8.

23. Horace L. Sheffield, "The Texas Story," *Vanguard*, April, 1964, LeRoy Papers, Box 1, Folder 9 (first quotation); Latane Lambert, "Dixie," handwritten note, n.d. [1964], George and Latane Lambert Papers, TLA-UTA (hereafter Lambert Papers), AR127-4-5 (Dixie quotations); Democratic Coalition, "Road to Political Victory" leaflet ("only significant"); *Democratic Newsletter*, vol. 2, no. 2, n.d. [1964] (all remaining quotations); VOTE report by Lambert, "Where the Money Went" (free registration statistics)—all in Texas AFL-CIO Democratic Correspondence, AR110-26-9-6. See also Ronnie Dugger, "Liberals Line Up for Don," *TO*, March 20, 1964, 7–8; Letter from Martin A. Wiginton to Sherman Miles, July 8, 1964, Texas AFL-CIO Democratic Party Correspondence, AR110-26-9-6.

24. Dugger, "The Political Situation After the Assassination"; "Political Intelligence," *TO*, December 27, 1963.

25. Letter from Larry Goodwyn to Executive Board Member, February 1, 1964, Texas AFL-CIO Democratic Party Correspondence, AR110-26-9-6.

26. Ibid.; Dugger, "Liberals Line Up for Don"; "The Spring Line-Up," *TO*, February 7, 1964, 14–15; "John and Don Have at It Again with Lyndon and Allan in the Wings," *TO*, February 21, 1964, 1; Ronnie Dugger, "Albert Fuentes Makes His Case," *TO*, February 21, 1964, 3.

27. Dugger, "Liberals Line Up for Don," 8.

28. Sheffield, "The Texas Story" (first quotation); Dugger, "Liberals Line Up for Don," 7–8 (ellipses in original); "Political Intelligence," *TO*, March 6, 1964, 11.

29. Dugger, "Senator Yarborough Reads a Letter," *TO*, March 20, 1964, 9; Letter from W. J. Durham to Francis L. Williams, March 25, 1964, Lambert Papers, AR127-31-1.

30. *Democratic Newsletter*, vol. 2, no. 2, (n.d.), and vol. 2, no. 3, (n.d.) [mid-April, 1964]; Democratic Coalition, *Democratic Precinct Convention Handbook*; Democratic Coalition, "Road to Political Victory" leaflet—all in Texas AFL-CIO Democratic Party Correspondence, AR110-26-9-6.

31. "Remarks on Various Matters," *TO*, May 15, 1964, 2; "Connally's Triumph," *TO*, May 15, 1964, 4; "The Legislature Becomes More Conservative," *TO*, May 15, 1964, 7.

32. Democratic Coalition, "Road to Political Victory" leaflet, Texas AFL-CIO Democratic Party Correspondence, AR110-26-9-6; "Self-Respect Preserved," *TO*, June 26, 1964, 2.

33. On the Civil Rights Act's legislative history, see Purdum, *An Idea Whose Time Has Come*; Risen, *The Bill of the Century*. On the Mississippi party, see Dittmer, *Local People: The Struggle for Civil Rights in Mississippi*.

34. "Political Intelligence: Elections and Conventions," *TO*, June 12, 1964, 8; *Democratic Newsletter*, vol. 2, no. 2, and vol. 3, no. 1, n.d. [1964]; Letter from Wiginton to Miles—all in Texas AFL-CIO Democratic Correspondence, AR110-26-9-6; Letter from Latane Lambert to Bill Dodds, March 26, 1964, Lambert Papers, AR127-31-1.

35. *Democratic Newsletter*, vol. 3, no. 1, 2; Letter from Franklin Jones to Maury Maverick Jr., July 23, 1964—both in Texas AFL-CIO Democratic Party Correspondence, AR110-26-9-6.

36. *Democratic Newsletter*, vol. 3, no. 1, 2. Of course, Republican John Tower had served as the state's junior senator since 1961, but his ascendancy in a special election that year was often interpreted as a fluke. The party's 1962 gubernatorial nominee, Jack Cox, hailed from the extremist Freedom in Action group and thus tied the GOP to the radical right.

37. *Democratic Newsletter*, vol. 3, no. 2, n.d. [1964], Texas AFL-CIO Democratic Correspondence, AR110-26-9-6; Letter from Wiginton to Miles.

38. "New Power for the Texas Minorities," *TO*, November 13, 1964, 3–5.

39. "Coalition Reports," *TO*, December 25, 1964, 10. The coalition estimated that the combined black and brown vote for Johnson was 451,726, or 27.2 percent of his total of 1,663,185 votes, and 443,395 for Yarborough, or 30.3 percent of his total of 1,463,958. Total vote numbers are available in *Texas Almanac, 1966–1967* (Dallas: Belo, 1965), 567, available online via *The Portal to Texas History*, accessed April 23, 2016, http://texashistory.unt.edu/ark:/67531/metapth113808/.

40. Larry Goodwyn, "'Hey-You' in Huntsville," *TO*, August 6, 1965, 1.

41. T. O. L. D. Memo from Latane Lambert, December 29, 1964, Texas AFL-CIO Democratic Party Correspondence, AR110-26-9-7.

42. Ronnie Dugger, "Observations: The Texas Liberals," *TO*, April 2, 1965, 15.

43. Ronnie Dugger, "The Liberals of Texas," *TO*, July 9, 1965, 1.

44. "Yarborough Writes on the Coalition," *TO*, April 16, 1965, 12. See also reprint of letter from Sen. Ralph W. Yarborough to Franklin Jones Sr., April 2, 1965, in Texas AFL-CIO *Secretary's Report* vol. 8, no. 8 (April 6, 1965), copy in Texas AFL-CIO Democratic Party Correspondence, AR110-26-9-7.

45. Larry Goodwyn, "State Liberals to Meet In Houston on Sept. 11," *TO*, July 23, 1965, 3.

46. Letter to editor by Nate Slough, in "Dialogue," *TO*, April 30, 1965, 16; "Political Intelligence," *TO*, December 25, 1964, 10. On Fuentes, see "Political Intelligence," *TO*, July 23, 1965, 5; "Political Intelligence," *TO*, February 4, 1966, 14; "Political Intelligence," *TO*, April 1, 1966, 10–11; and "Political Intelligence," *TO*, August 19, 1966, 10. Peña's admonition also applied to U.S. representative Jim Wright of Fort Worth, a liberal Democrat on economic issues who was then considering a run against Tower in 1966, but he too had voted against the Civil Rights Act.

47. "Political Intelligence," *TO*, July 9, 1965, 5; "Political Intelligence," *TO*, February 18, 1966, 3; "Political Intelligence," *TO*, March 4, 1966, 11; "Political Intelligence," *TO*, April 1, 1966, 10–11; "Observations," *TO*, April 1, 1965, 15.

48. Larry Goodwyn, "'Hey-You' in Huntsville," *TO*, August 6, 1965, 1, 3. See also Texas AFL-CIO Summer Youth Citizenship Conference program, June 14–26, 1965, MAAC, AR110-7-2-6. Speakers included national civil rights leaders Rev. James Bevel and Bayard Rustin of the Southern Christian Leadership Conference; Democratic Coalition leaders Latane Lambert, Chris Dixie, George I. Sánchez, Arthur DeWitty, Henry Muñoz, Barbara Jordan, and Larry Goodwyn; and politicians John Tower and Henry B. Gonzalez.

49. Goodwyn, "'Hey-You' in Huntsville," 1 (first quotation), 3 (all other quotations).

50. Ibid., 3 (all quotations).

51. Ibid., 3–4.

52. Ibid., 4.

53. Ibid., 5–6 (first quotation on 5; second quotation on 6).

54. Ibid., 6.

55. Ibid., 6–7 (quotations on 6).

56. Ibid., 7.

57. Ibid., 7–9 (all quotations on 7).

58. Ibid., 8–9 (first and third quotations on 9; second quotation on 8).

59. Ibid., 9; Nan Hunt, "Dr. King Eyes Texas," *TO*, September 17, 1965, 16.

60. See, among others, Lawson, *Black Ballots: Voting Rights in the South, 1944–1969*, chap. 10–11; May, *Bending Toward Justice: The Voting Rights Act and the Transformation of American Democracy*, chap. 6–7; Chandler Davidson and Bernard Grofman, eds., *Quiet Revolution in the South: The Impact of the Voting Rights Act, 1965–1990* (Princeton: Princeton University Press, 1994). See also U.S. Department of Justice, "Jurisdictions Previously Covered by Section 5," accessed September 16, 2015, http://www.justice.gov/crt/jurisdictions-previously-covered-section-5; Nina Perales, Luis Figueroa, and Griselda G. Rivas, "Voting Rights in Texas, 1982–2006," *RenewtheVRA.org*, 3, accessed September 16, 2015, http://www.protectcivilrights.org/pdf/voting/TexasVRA.pdf. For a history of the act's evolution, see Berman, *Give Us the Ballot: The Modern Struggle for Voting Rights in America*.

61. Ronnie Dugger, "Liberals in Texas to Meet in Houston," *TO*, October 15, 1965, 1; "Observations," *TO*, October 15, 1965, 15–16.

62. Ronnie Dugger, "Texas Liberal Democrats Organize," *TO*, November 12, 1965, 10–13 (final two quotations on 13; all others on 10). Mrs. Charles E. White of the Houston school board addressed the civil rights salon. Liberal stalwart Latane Lambert chaired the only formal committee, which prepared the group's constitution.

63. Ibid., 10 (first two quotations), 12 (all other quotations). Previous calls for the conference also included Laws as a scheduled speaker. See "Political Intelligence," *TO*, October 29, 1965, 14.

64. Dugger, "Texas Liberal Democrats Organize," 12–13 (all quotations on 13).

65. Larry Goodwyn, "The Caste System and the Righteousness Barrier," *TO*, December 31, 1965, 10–15 (first six quotations on 10; remaining quotations on 11).

66. Ibid., 11 (first five quotations), 12 (remaining quotations).

67. Ibid., 12 (first quotation), 11 (remaining quotations).

68. Ibid., 12 (first quotation and last three quotations), 13 (remaining quotations).

69. Ibid., 12–15 (all quotations on 15).

Epilogue

1. The narrative in this section draws on a variety of primary and secondary sources, especially the author's oral history interviews with organizers of the NFWA's successor organization, the United Farm Workers. See Gilbert Padilla, interview by author, Fresno, California, September 12, 2009; Bill Chandler, interview by author, Jackson, Mississippi, February 5, 2010; Dolores Huerta, interview by author, Durham, North Carolina, January 17, 2010; State Senator (fmr.) Joe Bernal, interview by author, San Antonio, September 1, 2009; Booker T. Bonner, interviews by author, Houston, May 11 and 12, 2010; and DVDs of Fortieth Anniversary Reunion of Rio Grande City UFW Activists, 2006, copies in author's possession, courtesy Bill Chandler. Also see Pancho Medrano, interview by George N. Green and Carr Winn, August 4, 1971, TLA-

UTA; Francisco F. "Pancho" Medrano, interview by José Ángel Gutiérrez, July 16, 1997, TV-UTA; Henry Muñoz, interview by George N. Green and Carr Winn, August 12, 1971, TLA-UTA; Erasmo and Sally Andrade Papers, Boxes 8 and 9, BLAC; Pancho Medrano Papers, AR55, TLA-UTA; Mexican American Farm Workers Collection, AR408, TLA-UTA; Migrant Farm Workers Organizing Movement Collection, AR46, TLA-UTA; J. A. "Tony" Alvarez Collection, HMRC; Alfred J. Hernandez Papers, HMRC; John Castillo Papers, HMRC; U.S. Senate Committee on Labor, Subcommittee on Migratory Labor, *Hearings*, Rio Grande City (Washington: U.S. Government Printing Office, 1967); Texas State Advisory Committee to the U.S. Commission on Civil Rights, "The Administration of Justice in Starr, Nueces, and San Patricio Counties," 1967, copy in George and Latane Lambert Papers, TLA-UTA (hereafter Lambert Papers), AR127-28-3; *Medrano v. Allee*, Case No. 67-B-36, 347 F. Supp. 605; *Allee v. Medrano*, 416 U.S. 802 (U.S. Supreme Court, 1974); and Judge Woodrow Seals Papers, HMRC. Secondary sources include Amberson, "'Better to Die on Our Feet, than to Live on Our Knees': United Farm Workers and Strikes in the Lower Rio Grande Valley, 1966–1967," 56–103; Bowman, "From Workers to Activists: The UFW in Texas' Lower Rio Grande Valley," 87–94; Leal, "The 1966–1967 South Texas Farm Worker Strike: A Case Study of Farm Worker Powerlessness"; Acosta, "United Farm Workers Union," *Handbook of Texas Online*; Robert E. Hall, "Pickets, Politics, and Power: The Farm Worker Strike in Starr County." Hall's blog post was also published in *Texas Law Review*. Also see "The March: A Triumph, A Task," "Labor Day in Austin," "The Confrontation," and "Politicians with the March," all in *TO*, September 16, 1966; and Behnken, *Fighting Their Own Battles: Mexican Americans, African Americans, and the Struggle for Civil Rights in Texas*, 105–9, 120–26.

2. Quoted in "The Confrontation," *TO*, September 16, 1966, 11.

3. Jon Ford, "Farm Workers End March at Capitol," *SAE*, September 6, 1966, 1, 14-A (quotations on 14-A). This and the previous quotation by Brown also appear in Behnken, *Fighting Their Own Battles*, 108–9.

4. H. S. Hank Brown, interview by author, San Antonio, March 25, 2010.

5. U.S. Senate, Committee on Labor and Public Welfare, "Hearings Before the Subcommittee on Migratory Labor," part 2, June 29, 1967, hearing in Rio Grande City, Texas (Washington: U.S. Government Printing Office, 1967); U.S. Commission on Civil Rights, Texas State Advisory Committee, "The Administration of Justice in Starr, San Patricio, and Nueces Counties" (Austin: Texas Advisory Committee, 1967). Also see Lambert Papers, AR127-28-3. For more on the case at Kelly Air Force Base, see Krochmal, "Chicano Labor and Multiracial Politics in Post–World War II Texas," 133–76.

6. Hall, "Pickets, Politics, and Power: The Farm Worker Strike in Starr County."

7. On the significance of curtailing the Rangers, see Samora, Bernal, and Peña, *Gunpowder Justice: A Reassessment of the Texas Rangers*.

8. See Moses LeRoy Papers, HMRC; Moses LeRoy, interview by Chandler Davidson, Houston, January 25, 1979; John Castillo Papers, HMRC; Leonel J. Castillo Papers, HMRC; Ben T. Reyes Papers, HMRC; Bill Chandler, interview by author; Robert E. "Bob" Hall, interviews by author, Houston, May 18 and 31, 2010; Booker T. Bonner, interviews by author, Houston, May 11 and 12, 2010; Howard Middleton, interviews by author, Houston, May 5 and 31, 2010; David T. Lopez, interviews by author, Houston, May 18 and 28, 2010; State Senator Rodney Ellis, interview by author, Houston, May 27, 2010; John Castillo,

interview by José Ángel Gutiérrez, June 27, 1996, TV-UTA; Leonel Castillo, interview by José Ángel Gutiérrez, June 28, 1996, TV-UTA; Lauro Cruz, interview by José Ángel Gutiérrez, June 20, 1998, TV-UTA; John Castillo, interview by Thomas Kreneck, Houston, December 6, 1985, Oral History Collection, HMRC.

9. See Medrano Papers, TLA-UTA; Medrano interview by José Ángel Gutiérrez, TV-UTA; Medrano, interview by George Green, TLA-UTA; Ricardo Medrano, interview by author, Dallas, September 23, 2009; Robert Medrano, interview by author, Dallas, September 24, 2009; Pauline Medrano, interview by author, Dallas, September 25, 2009; Rev. Peter Johnson, interviews by author, Dallas, February 22 and 23, 2010; and virtually all of the author's other interviews with Mexican American civil rights and union activists. For a more complete version of this story, see Krochmal, "Chicano Labor and Multiracial Politics."

10. See Peña Papers, UTSA; Arnold Flores, interviews by author, San Antonio, October 18, 2008; September 1 and 9, 2009; March 11, 2010; Peña interview by José Ángel Gutiérrez, July 2, 1996, TV-UTA; Erasmo and Sally Andrade Papers, BLAC; Joe Bernal, interview by author, San Antonio, September 1, 2009; Eugene Coleman, interview by author, San Antonio, September 2, 2009; Rev. Claude Black, interview by author, San Antonio, October 27, 2009; C. J. Littlefield, interview by author, San Antonio, September 2, 2009; G. J. Sutton and Lou Nelle Sutton folders, SAPL-VF; Roberto de Leon, interview by author, San Antonio, September 3, 2009; Rosie Castro, interview by author, San Antonio, September 8, 2009; Roy Hernandez, interview by author, San Antonio, September 8, 2009; Paul Javior, interviews by author, San Antonio, September 4, 2009, and Adkins, Texas, March 23, 2010; Eddie Felan, interview by author, San Antonio, March 23, 2010; Jaime Martinez, interview by author, San Antonio, March 10, 2010; Richard A. Twedell Papers, TLA-UTA; Samuel A. Twedell Papers, TLA-UTA; Texas State Advisory Committee to the U.S. Commission on Civil Rights, "Employment Discrimination at Kelly Air Force Base," copy in Joe J. Bernal Papers, BLAC. For more, see Krochmal, "San Antonio Chicano Organizers (SACO): Labor Activists and El Movimiento," 203–26; Krochmal, "Chicano Labor and Multiracial Politics."

11. On Texas politics since the 1960s, see Davidson, *Race and Class in Texas Politics*; Cunningham, *Cowboy Conservatism: Texas and the Rise of the Modern Right*; Reid, *Let the People In: The Life and Times of Ann Richards*; Cullen and Wilkison, *The Texas Right: The Radical Roots of Lone Star Conservatism*; Thorburn, *Red State: An Insider's Story of How the GOP Came to Dominate Texas Politics*; Wuthnow, *Rough Country: How Texas Became America's Most Powerful Bible-Belt State*. There is a vast literature on the rise of conservatism in postwar America. Among the many great works, see Sugrue, *The Origins of the Urban Crisis: Race and Inequality in Postwar Detroit*; McGirr, *Suburban Warriors: The Origins of the New American Right*; Kruse, *White Flight: Atlanta and the Making of Modern Conservatism*; Lassiter, *The Silent Majority: Suburban Politics in the Sunbelt South*; Moreton, *To Serve God and Wal-Mart: The Making of Christian Free Enterprise*.

12. Behnken, *Fighting Their Own Battles* (first and second quotations); Reagon, "Coalition Politics: Turning the Century," 343–56. The author thanks Brian Behnken for his friendship, encouragement, transparency, generosity, and support—despite our interpretive disagreements.

13. I borrow the phrase "historical gerrymandering" from Juliana Barr, "How Do You Get from Jamestown to Santa Fe? A Colonial Sun Belt," 553–66 (quotation on 555).

14. "Report on Student Project," Lambert Papers, AR127-30-5.

15. Wolin, *The Presence of the Past*, chap. 8 (quotations on 140).

16. All election statistics in this section are from the Office of the Secretary of State, "Historical Election Results: 1992–Current Election History" (State of Texas), accessed September 27, 2015, http://elections.sos.state.tx.us/index.htm. For additional information on Texas elected offices, see "Elections," *Texas Almanac*, accessed September 27, 2015, http://texasalmanac.com/topics/elections/elections.

Bibliography

Oral History Interviews

By Author (digital recordings to be archived at Texas Christian University)

Charles Andrews, Jr., San Antonio, September 8, 2009
Frances Barton, Austin, December 14, 2012
Joe Bernal, San Antonio, September 1, 2009
Rev. Claude W. Black Jr., San Antonio, October 27, 2009
Booker T. Bonner, Houston, May 11 and 12, 2010
Robert Brischetto, San Antonio, December 13, 2012
H. S. Hank Brown, San Antonio, March 25, 2010
Daniel Bustamante, Houston, May 14, 2010
Rosie Castro, San Antonio, September 8, 2009
Bill Chandler, Jackson, Mississippi, February 5, 2010
Linda Chavez-Thompson, San Antonio, December 13, 2012
Eugene Coleman, San Antonio, September 2, 2009
Ernesto Cortes, Austin, February 23, 2013
Lewis Davis, Dallas, February 20, 2010
Roberto De Leon, San Antonio, September 3, 2009
Rodney Ellis, Houston, May 27, 2010
Arturo Eureste, Houston, December 4, 2012
Frances "Sissy" Farenthold, Houston, December 4, 2012
Clara Faulkner, Fort Worth, September 24, 2009
Eddie Felán, San Antonio, March 23, 2010
Arnold Flores, San Antonio, October 18, 2008; September 1 and 9, 2009; and March 11, 2010
Domingo Garcia, Dallas, October 23, 2008
Lawrence C. Goodwyn, Durham, North Carolina, June 14, 2010; and October 13, 2012
Joe Gunn, Creedmoor, Texas, December 14, 2012
Robert E. Hall, Houston, May 18 and 31, 2010
Roy Hernandez, San Antonio, September 8, 2009
Holly Hogrobrooks, Houston (by phone), May 26, 2010
Eddie Humphrey, Fort Worth, November 1, 2008
Paul Javior, San Antonio, September 4, 2009; Adkins, Texas, March 23, 2010
Howard Jefferson, Houston, June 1, 2010
Maria Jimenez, Austin, July 7, 2012
Angela Johnson, Dallas, September 30, 2009
Rev. Peter Johnson, Dallas, February 22 and 23, 2010
Rev. Ed Krueger, Edinburg, Texas, December 12, 2012

Gene Lantz, Dallas, November 12, 2008 (notes only)
Rev. William A. Lawson, Houston
Clarence J. Littlefield, San Antonio, September 2, 2009
David T. Lopez, Houston, May 18 and 28, 2010
Omowale Luthuli, Houston, December 4, 2012
Matthew "Nite" Marshall, San Antonio, September 7, 2009
Francisco Martinez, Pharr, Texas, December 9, 2012
Jaime Martínez, San Antonio, March 10, 2010
Richard McCoy, Fort Worth, October 24, 2008
Ernest McMillan, Dallas, July 19, 2012
Pauline Medrano, Dallas, September 25, 2009
Ricardo Medrano, Dallas, September 23, 2009
Robert Medrano, Dallas, September 24, 2009
Bernard Middleton, Houston, May 12, 2010
Howard Middleton Jr., Houston, May 5 and 31, 2010.
Ethel Minor, San Antonio, September 10, 2009
Carlos Moore, Fort Worth, July 29, 2015
Antonio Orendain, Pharr, Texas, December 8, 2012
Gilbert Padilla, Fresno, California, September 12, 2009
DeLoyd Parker, Houston, December 3, 2012
Bobby Phillips, Pasadena, Texas, September 17, 2010
Frumencio Reyes, Houston, December 3, 2012
Tommy Roy, Houston, December 6, 2012
David Shapiro, Austin, July 4, 2012
Richard Shaw, Houston, December 3 and 6, 2012
Oliver Sutton, Seguin, Texas, March 11, 2010
Charles Thomason, Deer Park, Texas, December 5, 2012
Katherine Thompson-Garcia, San Antonio, December 13, 2012
R. L. Timmons, Houston, December 2012
Juanita Valdez-Cox, San Juan, Texas, December 10, 2012
Helen Wallace, Fort Worth, September 29, 2009
Davis West and UAW Local 848 African American Retirees (group interview by author and Joseph Abel), Dallas, November 20, 2008

Houston Metropolitan Research Center, Houston Public Library

John Castillo
Leonel Castillo
Frances "Sissy" Farenthold
Moses LeRoy
Gilbert Mers
Frumencio Reyes

Institute of Texan Cultures Library Oral History Collection, University of Texas, San Antonio

Rev. Claude W. Black Jr.
B. T. Bonner
Harry Burns
Emma Tenayuca

Tejano Voices, University of Texas, Arlington (José Ángel Gutiérrez)

Roberto Alonzo
John Castillo
Leonel Castillo
Lauro Cruz
Anita Martinez
Francisco F. "Pancho" Medrano
Albert A. Peña Jr.
Olga Peña

Texas Labor Archives, University of Texas, Arlington (George N. Green)

Morris Akin
Hank Brown
Roy Evans
Charlotte Graham (interview by Glenn Scott, with Latane Lambert)
Liz Kimmel
Harry Koger, Mr. and Mrs.
George Lambert
Latane Lambert (interview by David Filewood)
Latane Lambert (interview by Glenn Scott and María Flores)
Moses LeRoy
Lee A. Lewis
Steve Mauser
Pancho Medrano
Gilbert Mers
Henry Muñoz Jr. (interview by George Green and Carr Winn)
Robert Oliver
Olivia Rawlston (interview by Glenn Scott)
James Henry Saunders (interview by Carr Winn)
Fred Schmidt
Hardy Scott
Alberta Snid (interview by Glenn Scott and Maria Flores)
Samuel R. Tankersley

Texas Politics Oral History Program, Fondren Library, Rice University (Chandler Davidson)

Billie Carr
Chris Dixie
Moses LeRoy
Mrs. R. D. (Frankie Carter) Randolph
J. Edwin Smith
Ralph W. Yarborough

United Packinghouse Workers of America Oral History Project, Wisconsin Historical Society

Dale Chambers
Eddie Humphrey
Mary Salinas
Frank Wallace

Manuscript Collections

Arlington, Texas
   Tejano Voices Collection, Special Collections Library, University of Texas, Arlington (TV-UTA)
   Texas Labor Archives, Special Collections Library, University of Texas, Arlington (TLA-UTA)
      Amalgamated Meat Cutters and Butcher Workmen of North America, Local 408, Houston, Texas, Records
      Dallas AFL-CIO Council Records, 1891–1970
      George F. Dull Papers
      Food, Tobacco, Agricultural, and Allied Workers Union of America, Texas Region Records
      Ford Motor Company, Dallas, Texas Collection
      Harris County AFL-CIO Council Records
      Houston Area Industrial Union Council, CIO, Minutes
      International Ladies' Garment Workers' Union Collection (AR167)
      International Ladies' Garment Workers' Union, Local 180, San Antonio, Texas, Records
      International Ladies' Garment Workers' Union, Local 214, Houston, Texas, Records
      International Longshoremen's Association, Local 851, Galveston, Texas, Minutes
      International Longshoremen's Association, Local 1273, Houston, Texas, Records
      Harry Koger Papers
      George and Latane Lambert Papers
      Lee Lewis Papers
      Steve Mauser Papers
      Pancho Medrano Papers

Oil, Chemical, and Atomic Workers Local 4-23, Records, unprocessed mss. 92-39
Oral History Interviews
Proceedings
Hardy Scott Papers
Screwmen's Benevolent Association, ILA, Local 307, Galveston, Texas, Records
Tarrant County Central Labor Council
Texas AFL-CIO Department of Human Resources (AR 278, Series 18)
Texas AFL-CIO Mexican American Affairs Committee Records (AR278, Series 11)
Texas AFL-CIO Miscellany Collection (AR 413)
Texas AFL-CIO Papers (AR110)
   Series 1, Executive Board Office Records
   Series 7, Mexican American Affairs Committee (MAAC)
   Series 8, Committee on Political Education Records (COPE)
   Series 16, Texas State CIO Council Records
   Series 17, Texas State Industrial Union Council Records
   Series 25, Correspondence with Non-Union Associations and Organizations
   Series 26, Correspondence with Democratic Party Organizations
Richard A. Twedell Papers
Samuel A. Twedell Papers
UAW Local 276 Records
UAW Local 848, unprocessed mss. 91-1
UAW Local 848 Records, 1937–94, unprocessed mss. 95-66
UAW Local 848 Records, 1941–89, unprocessed mss. 91-42
United Packinghouse, Food, and Allied Workers, District No. 5 Records

Austin, Texas
  Nettie Lee Benson Latin American Collection, University of Texas, Austin (BLAC)
    Lucy Acosta Collection
    Paul Andow Collection
    Erasmo and Sally J. Andrade Papers
    Joe J. Bernal Papers
    William D. Bonilla Collection
    Carlos E. Castañeda Papers
    José Angel Gutiérrez Papers
    Eduardo Idar Jr. Papers
    George I. Sánchez Papers
    R. P. (Bob) Sanchez Papers
    U.S. Latino & Latina WWII Oral History Project Collection
  Dolph Briscoe Center for American History, University of Texas, Austin (BCAH)
    Black Texas Women Archive
    Byron and Rannie Cook Papers
    Juanita Jewel Shanks Craft Collection
    Franklin Garcia Papers
    Henry B. Gonzalez Papers
    Labor Movement in Texas Collection
    James Leonard Jr. and Lula Peterson Farmer Papers
    Oral History of the Texas Oil Industry

  People's History in Texas Records
  State of Texas v. NAACP Case Records
  Ruthe Winegarten Papers
Corpus Christi, Texas
 Mary and Jeff Bell Library, Texas A&M University, Corpus Christi (TAMUCC)
  Dr. Hector P. Garcia Collection
Dallas, Texas
 Texas/Dallas History and Archives Division, Dallas Public Library
  Juanita Craft Collection
  Dallas Negro Chamber of Commerce Collection
Detroit, Michigan
 Walter P. Reuther Library of Labor and Urban Affairs
  American Federation of State, County and Municipal Employees
   AFSCME Communications Department Records
   AFSCME Office of the President: Jerry Wurf Collection
   AFSCME Office of the Secretary-Treasurer: William Lucy Records
  Service Employees International Union
   SEIU Executive Office: George Hardy Records
   SEIU Executive Office: David Sullivan Records
   SEIU Secretary-Treasurer's Office: Affiliate Officers Records
   SEIU Secretary-Treasurer's Office: Richard Cordtz Records
  United Auto Workers
   UAW Community Action Program (CAP) Department Records
   UAW Fair Practices and Anti-Discrimination Department Records
  United Farm Workers
   UFW Texas Records
Houston, Texas
 Houston Metropolitan Research Center, Houston Public Library (HMRC)
  Christia V. Adair Collection
  J. A. "Tony" Alvarez Collection
  John Castillo Papers
  Leonel J. Castillo Collection
  Colored Trainmen of America Papers
  Hector Garcia/Political Association of Spanish-Speaking Organizations Collection
  Alfred J. Hernandez Papers
  John J. Herrera Papers
  Houston Chronicle Morgue (HCM)
   Harris County AFL-CIO
   Harris County Council of Organizations
   International Longshoremen's Association
   National Association for the Advancement of Colored People
   Progressive Youth Association
  Houston Young Women's Christian Association Collection
  Moses Leroy Collection
  LULAC News Collection

      Gilbert Mers Collection
      Mexican-American Small Collections
      Oral History Collection
      Ben T. Reyes Papers
      Judson Robinson Sr. Family Collection
      Judge Woodrow Seals Papers
      Rev. Lee Haywood Simpson Records
      C. F. Smith Family Collection
   Texas Southern University, Department of Special Collections, Robert J. Terry Library
      Vertical Files (TSU-VF)
   University of Houston Libraries, Special Collections
      Thomas R. Cole Desegregation Papers
   Woodson Research Center, Fondren Library, Rice University (WRC)
      Marguerite Johnston Barnes Research Materials for *Houston, the Unknown City*
      Billie Carr Political Papers
      Chandler Davidson Texas Politics Research Collection (includes Texas Politics Oral History Program)
      Frankie Carter Randolph Papers
Madison, Wisconsin
   Wisconsin Historical Society
      United Packinghouse, Food, and Allied Workers, Records 1937–82, Mss. 118
      United Packinghouse Workers of America Oral History Project
San Antonio, Texas
   Institute of Texan Cultures Library
      Oral History Collection
   Special Collections, University of Texas, San Antonio, Institute of Texan Cultures (UTSA)
      Albert A. Peña Jr. Papers
      Mario Marcel Salas Papers
      San Antonio Black History Collection (SABHC)
   Texana/Genealogy Collection, San Antonio Public Library
      Vertical Files (SAPL-VF)
   Trinity University Archives and Special Collections
      Claude and ZerNona Black Papers, 1890–2009

Newspapers, Magazines, and Serial Publications

AFL-CIO News
AFL-CIO Weekly Dispatch (San Antonio)
Austin American
Austin American-Statesman
Austin Statesman
Bluefield Daily Telegraph
Brownsville Herald
Corpus Christi Caller

Corpus Christi Caller-Times
Corpus Christi Times
Crisis
Daily Worker
Dallas Craftsman
Dallas Express
Dallas Morning News
Dallas Times Herald
Democratic Newsletter
El Paso Herald-Post
El Sol (Houston)
El Sol de Texas (Dallas)
Fort Worth Star-Telegram
Galveston News
Gazette (Xenia, Ohio)
Houston Chronicle
Houston Forward Times
Houston Informer
Houston Post
La Prensa
LULAC News
Nation
New Republic
New York Times
News Texan
Papel Chicano
Postal Alliance
San Antonio Express
San Antonio Express-News
San Antonio Light
San Antonio News
San Antonio Register
SNAP News
Survey Graphic
Texas Aerospacer
Texas Almanac
Texas Observer
Texas State AFL-CIO News
Texas Tribune
UAW Citizen
UAW News
UAW Washington Report
Valley Evening Monitor
Valley Morning Star
Washington Post
Weekly Dispatch (San Antonio)

Books, Articles, Theses, Dissertations, and Websites

"About Us." *Harris County Council of Organizations.* Accessed January 23, 2014. http://harriscountycounciloforganizations.org/aboutus.htm.

Acosta, Teresa Palomo. "United Farm Workers Union." *Handbook of Texas Online.* Accessed September 29, 2015. http://www.tshaonline.org/handbook/online/articles/ocu02.

Adedeji, Moses. "Crossing the Colorline: Three Decades of the United Packinghouse Workers of America's Crusade against Racism in the Trans-Mississippi West, 1936-1968." Ph.D. diss., North Texas State University, 1978.

Amberson, Mary Margaret McAllen. "'Better to Die on Our Feet, than to Live on Our Knees': United Farm Workers and Strikes in the Lower Rio Grande Valley, 1966-1967." *Journal of South Texas* 20, no. 1 (2007): 56-103.

Anderson, James D. *The Education of Blacks in the South, 1860-1935.* Chapel Hill: University of North Carolina Press, 1988.

Anderson, Sherwood. "Maury Maverick in San Antonio." *New Republic* 102, no. 13 (March 25, 1940): 398-400.

Anderson, Theo. "Texas: The Blue Frontier." *In These Times,* December 22, 2014. http://inthesetimes.com/article/17443/texas_the_blue_frontier.

Araiza, Lauren. *To March for Others: The Black Freedom Struggle and the United Farm Workers.* Philadelphia: University of Pennsylvania Press, 2013.

Bandura, Albert. *Social Learning Theory.* Englewood Cliffs, N.J.: Prentice Hall, 1977.

Bardacke, Frank. *Trampling Out the Vintage: Cesar Chavez and the Two Souls of the United Farm Workers.* New York: Verso, 2011.

Barr, Alwyn. *Black Texans: A History of African Americans in Texas, 1528-1995.* 2nd ed. Norman: University of Oklahoma Press, 1996.

Barr, Juliana. "How Do You Get from Jamestown to Santa Fe? A Colonial Sun Belt." *Journal of Southern History* 73, no. 3 (August 2007): 553-66.

Behnken, Brian D. *Fighting Their Own Battles: Mexican Americans, African Americans, and the Struggle for Civil Rights in Texas.* Chapel Hill: University of North Carolina Press, 2011.

———, ed. *The Struggle in Black and Brown: African American and Mexican American Relations during the Civil Rights Era.* Lincoln: University of Nebraska Press, 2011.

Berman, Ari. *Give Us the Ballot: The Modern Struggle for Voting Rights in America.* New York: Farrar, Straus and Giroux, 2015.

Bernstein, Shana. *Bridges of Reform: Interracial Civil Rights Activism in Twentieth-Century Los Angeles.* New York: Oxford University Press, 2011.

Black, Claude W., and Taj I. Matthews. *Grandpa Was a Preacher: A Letter to My Grandson.* Bloomington, Ind.: AuthorHouse, 2007.

Blackwelder, Julia Kirk. *Women of the Depression: Caste and Culture in San Antonio, 1929-1939.* College Station: Texas A&M University Press, 1984.

Blanton, Carlos Kevin. "The Citizenship Sacrifice: Mexican Americans, the Saunders-Leonard Report, and the Politics of Immigration, 1951-1952." *Western Historical Quarterly* 40, no. 3 (Autumn 2009): 299-320.

———. "George I. Sánchez, Ideology, and Whiteness in the Making of the Mexican American Civil Rights Movement, 1930–1960." *Journal of Southern History* 72, no. 3 (August 2006): 569–604.

———. *George I. Sánchez: The Long Fight for Mexican American Integration*. New Haven, Conn.: Yale University Press, 2015.

Botson, Michael R. *Labor, Civil Rights, and the Hughes Tool Company*. College Station: Texas A&M University Press, 2005.

Bowman, Timothy P. "From Workers to Activists: The UFW in Texas' Lower Rio Grande Valley." *Journal of the West* 47, no. 3 (2008): 87–94.

Boyle, Kevin. *The UAW and the Heyday of American Liberalism, 1945–1968*. Ithaca, N.Y.: Cornell University Press, 1995.

Bridges, Amy. *Morning Glories: Municipal Reform in the Southwest*. Princeton, N.J.: Princeton University Press, 1997.

"A Brief History of Jack Yates Senior High School." *Houston ISD*. Accessed March 22, 2016. http://www.houstonisd.org/domain/37851.

Brilliant, Mark. *The Color of America Has Changed: How Racial Diversity Shaped Civil Rights Reform in California, 1941–1978*. New York: Oxford University Press, 2010.

Brown, Leslie. *Upbuilding Black Durham: Gender, Class, and Black Community Development in the Jim Crow South*. Chapel Hill: University of North Carolina Press, 2008.

Buckingham, Peter H. "The Texas Socialist Party." In *The Texas Left: The Radical Roots of Lone Star Liberalism*, edited by David O'Donald Cullen and Kyle G. Wilkison, 74–91. College Station: Texas A&M University Press, 2010.

Burns, Richard Allen. "Durham, William J." *Handbook of Texas Online*. Accessed June 12, 2010. https://tshaonline.org/handbook/online/articles/fdu46.

Calvert, Robert A., Arnoldo De León, and Gregg Cantrell. *The History of Texas*. 4th ed. Wheeling, Ill.: Harlan Davidson, 2007.

Campbell, Randolph B. *Grass-Roots Reconstruction in Texas, 1865–1880*. Baton Rouge: Louisiana State University Press, 1997.

Cantrell, Gregg. "'A Host of Sturdy Patriots': The Texas Populists." In *The Texas Left: The Radical Roots of Lone Star Liberalism*, edited by David O'Donald Cullen and Kyle G. Wilkison, 53–73. College Station: Texas A&M University Press, 2010.

Carleton, Don E. *Red Scare!: Right-Wing Hysteria, Fifties Fanaticism, and Their Legacy in Texas*. Austin: Texas Monthly Press, 1985.

Caro, Robert A. *Master of the Senate: The Years of Lyndon Johnson*. New York: Knopf, 2002.

Chafe, William Henry. *Civilities and Civil Rights: Greensboro, North Carolina, and the Black Struggle for Freedom*. New York: Oxford University Press, 1980.

Chafe, William H., Raymond Gavins, and Robert Korstad, eds. *Remembering Jim Crow: African Americans Tell About Life in the Segregated South*. New York: New Press, in association with Lyndhurst Books of the Center for Documentary Studies of Duke University, 2001.

Chávez, Ernesto. *"¡Mi Raza Primero!" (My People First!): Nationalism, Identity, and Insurgency in the Chicano Movement in Los Angeles, 1966–1978*. Berkeley: University of California Press, 2002.

Clinton, Hillary Rodham. *Living History*. New York: Simon and Schuster, 2004.

Cohen, Deborah. *Braceros: Migrant Citizens and Transnational Subjects in the Postwar United States and Mexico*. Chapel Hill: University of North Carolina Press, 2011.

Cohen, Lizabeth. *Making a New Deal: Industrial Workers in Chicago, 1919–1939*. Cambridge [England]: Cambridge University Press, 1990.

Cohn, Nate. "These Eight Charts Explain Why 'Blue Texas' Won't Happen." *The New Republic*, August 11, 2013. http://www.newrepublic.com/article/114145/blue-texas-eight-charts-show-why-it-wont-happen.

Cole, Thomas R. *No Color Is My Kind: The Life of Eldrewey Stearns and the Integration of Houston*. Austin: University of Texas Press, 1997.

Cox, Patrick. *Ralph W. Yarborough, the People's Senator*. Austin: University of Texas Press, 2001.

Crosby, Emilye, ed. *Civil Rights History from the Ground Up: Local Struggles, a National Movement*. Athens: University of Georgia Press, 2011.

Crouch, Barry A. *The Dance of Freedom: Texas African Americans during Reconstruction*, edited by Larry Madaras. Austin: University of Texas Press, 2007.

Croxdale, Richard. "Pecan-Shellers' Strike." *Handbook of Texas Online*. Accessed June 25, 2010. http://www.tshaonline.org/handbook/online/articles/PP/oep1.html.

Cullen, David O'Donald, and Kyle G. Wilkison, eds. *The Texas Right: The Radical Roots of Lone Star Conservatism*. College Station: Texas A&M University Press, 2014.

Cunningham, Sean P. *Cowboy Conservatism: Texas and the Rise of the Modern Right*. Lexington: University Press of Kentucky, 2010.

Daniel, Cletus E. *Chicano Workers and the Politics of Fairness: The FEPC in the Southwest, 1941–1945*. Austin: University of Texas Press, 1991.

Davidson, Chandler. *Biracial Politics: Conflict and Coalition in the Metropolitan South*. Baton Rouge: Louisiana State University Press, 1972.

———. *Race and Class in Texas Politics*. Princeton, N.J.: Princeton University Press, 1990.

Davidson, Chandler, and Bernard Grofman, eds. *Quiet Revolution in the South: The Impact of the Voting Rights Act, 1965–1990*. Princeton, N.J.: Princeton University Press, 1994.

Davidson, Franklin Chandler. "Negro Politics and the Rise of the Civil Rights Movement in Houston, Texas." Ph.D. diss., Princeton University, 1969.

De León, Arnoldo. *Ethnicity in the Sunbelt: Mexican Americans in Houston*. College Station: Texas A&M University Press, 2001.

Dickinson, W. Calvin. *Rural Life and Culture in the Upper Cumberland*. Lexington: University Press of Kentucky, 2004.

Dittmer, John. *Local People: The Struggle for Civil Rights in Mississippi*. Urbana: University of Illinois Press, 1994.

Doyle, Judith Kaaz. "Maury Maverick and Racial Politics in San Antonio, Texas, 1938–1941." *The Journal of Southern History* 53, no. 2 (May 1987): 194–224.

Doyle, Rosa Henry, and Etta Walker. "Henry, Forest Thomas, Sr." *Handbook of Texas Online*. Accessed January 24, 2014. http://www.tshaonline.org/handbook/online/articles/fhe98.

Drexler, Alethea. "Sunset Hospital." *The Black Bag: Foundations of Medicine*, January 14, 2011. http://mcgovernhrc.wordpress.com/2011/01/14/sunset-hospital/.

Dublin, Thomas, Taina DelValle, and Rosalyn Perez. "How Did Mexican Working Women Assert Their Labor and Constitutional Rights in the 1938 San Antonio

Pecan Shellers Strike?" Binghamton: State University of New York at Binghamton, 1999. *Women and Social Movements in the United States* (online database published by Alexander Street Press).

Du Bois, W. E. B. *Black Reconstruction in America: An Essay Toward a History of the Part Which Black Folk Played in the Attempt to Reconstruct Democracy in America, 1860–1880*. Edited by Daniel Levering Lewis. New York: Free Press, 1997.

Dugger, Ronnie. *The Politician: The Life and Times of Lyndon Johnson—The Drive for Power, from the Frontier to Master of the Senate*. New York: W. W. Norton & Company, 1982.

Dulaney, W. Marvin. "Democratic Progressive Voters League," June 12, 2010. http://www.tshaonline.org/handbook/online/articles/wed01.edit.

———. "The Progressive Voters League: A Political Voice for African Americans in Dallas." *Legacies: A History Journal for Dallas and North Central Texas* 3, no. 1 (Spring 1991): 27–35.

———. "Whatever Happened to the Civil Rights Movement in Dallas, Texas?" In *Essays on the American Civil Rights Movement*, edited by John Dittmer, George C. Wright, and W. Marvin Dulaney, 66–90. College Station: Texas A&M University Press, 1993.

Edsall, Thomas B. "Targeting Texas." *Opinionator*. Accessed September 29, 2015. http://opinionator.blogs.nytimes.com/2013/05/15/targeting-texas/.

Fernandez, Manny. "Texas Democrats Ponder How They Will Ever Win." *New York Times*, November 5, 2014. http://www.nytimes.com/2014/11/06/us/politics/high-hopes-dashed-texas-democrats-wonder-if-their-time-will-ever-come.html.

Filewood, David Lewis. "Tejano Revolt: The Significance of the 1938 Pecan Shellers Strike." M.A. thesis, University of Texas at Arlington, 1994.

Fine, Sidney. *Sit-Down: The General Motors Strike of 1936–1937*. Ann Arbor: University of Michigan Press, 1969.

Fink, Gary M., and Merl E. Reed, eds. *Race, Class, and Community in Southern Labor History*. Tuscaloosa: University of Alabama Press, 1994.

Flores, Lori A. "An Unladylike Strike Fashionably Clothed: Mexicana and Anglo Women Garment Workers against Tex-Son, 1959–1963." *Pacific Historical Review* 78, no. 3 (August 2009): 367–402. doi:10.1525/phr.2009.78.3.367.

Foley, Neil. "Becoming Hispanic: Mexican Americans and the Faustian Pact with Whiteness." *Reflexiones*, 1997, 53–70.

———. "Partly Colored or Other White?: Mexican Americans and Their Problem with the Color Line." In *Beyond Black & White: Race, Ethnicity, and Gender in the U.S. South and Southwest*, edited by Stephanie Cole and Alison M. Parker, 123–44. College Station: Texas A&M University Press, 2004.

———. *Quest for Equality: The Failed Promise of Black-Brown Solidarity*. Cambridge, Mass.: Harvard University Press, 2010.

Foner, Eric. *Reconstruction: America's Unfinished Revolution, 1863–1877*. New York: Harper & Row, 1988.

Foner, Philip Sheldon. *History of the Labor Movement in the United States, Vol. 2: From the Founding of the A. F. of L. to the Emergence of American Imperialism*. New York: International Publishers, 1975.

Fones-Wolf, Elizabeth A. *Selling Free Enterprise: The Business Assault on Labor and Liberalism, 1945–60*. Urbana: University of Illinois Press, 1994.

García, Ignacio M. *Hector P. García: In Relentless Pursuit of Justice*. Houston, Tex.: Arte Público Press, 2002.
———. *United We Win: The Rise and Fall of La Raza Unida Party*. Tucson: MASRC, the University of Arizona, 1989.
———. *White but Not Equal: Mexican Americans, Jury Discrimination, and the Supreme Court*. Tucson: University of Arizona Press, 2009.
Garcia, Juan R. *Operation Wetback: The Mass Deportation of Mexican Undocumented Workers in 1954*. Westport, Conn.: Praeger, 1980.
Garcia, Mario T. *Mexican Americans: Leadership, Ideology, & Identity, 1930–1960*. New Haven, Conn.: Yale University Press, 1989.
Garcia, Richard A. *Rise of the Mexican American Middle Class: San Antonio, 1929–1941*. College Station: Texas A&M University Press, 1991.
Gellman, Erik S. *Death Blow to Jim Crow: The National Negro Congress and the Rise of Militant Civil Rights*. Chapel Hill: University of North Carolina Press, 2012.
Gillette, Michael Lowery. "The NAACP in Texas, 1937–1957." Ph.D. diss., University of Texas at Austin, 1984.
Glasrud, Bruce A., and James C. Moroney, eds. *Texas Labor History*. College Station: Texas A&M University Press, 2013.
Goldberg, Robert A. "Racial Change on the Southern Periphery: The Case of San Antonio, Texas, 1960–1965." *The Journal of Southern History* 49, no. 3 (August 1983): 349–74.
Gonzales, J. R. "A Lecture, Plus More on Old Houston Hospitals." *Bayou City History*, January 28, 2011. http://blog.chron.com/bayoucityhistory/2011/01/a-lecture-plus-more-on-old-houston-hospitals/.
Goodwyn, Lawrence. *The Populist Moment: A Short History of the Agrarian Revolt in America*. New York: Oxford University Press, 1978.
Gower, Patricia E. "Unintended Consequences: The San Antonio Pecan Shellers Strike of 1938." *Journal of South Texas* 17, no. 2 (2004): 88–103.
Granneberg, Audrey. "Maury Maverick's San Antonio." *Survey Graphic: Magazine of Social Interpretation*, July 1939. Accessed July 2, 2010. http://newdeal.feri.org/survey/39a07.htm.
Green, George N. "Discord in Dallas: Auto Workers, City Fathers, and the Ford Motor Company, 1937–1941." *Labor's Heritage* 1, no. 3 (July 1989): 21–33.
———. *The Establishment in Texas Politics: The Primitive Years, 1938–1957*. Westport, Conn.: Greenwood Press, 1979.
Green, George Norris, and Michael R. Botson. "Looking for Lefty: Liberal/Left Activism and Texas Labor, 1920s–1960s." In *The Texas Left: The Radical Roots of Lone Star Liberalism*, edited by David O'Donnell Cullen and Kyle G. Wilkison, 112–32. College Station: Texas A&M University Press, 2010.
Green, James R. *Grass-Roots Socialism: Radical Movements in the Southwest, 1895–1943*. Baton Rouge: Louisiana State University Press, 1978.
Griffith, Barbara. *The Crisis of American Labor: Operation Dixie and the Defeat of the CIO*. Philadelphia: Temple University Press, 1988.
Gross, Ariela J. "'The Caucasian Cloke': Mexican Americans and the Politics of Whiteness in the Twentieth Century Southwest." *Georgetown Law Journal* 95 (2007): 337–92.

———. *What Blood Won't Tell: A History of Race on Trial in America*. Cambridge, Mass.: Harvard University Press, 2008. Kindle edition.

Guglielmo, Thomas A. "Fighting for Caucasian Rights: Mexicans, Mexican Americans, and the Transnational Struggle for Civil Rights in World War II Texas." *Journal of American History* 92, no. 4 (March 2006): 1212–37.

Gutiérrez, José Angel. "Dean Emeritus of Chicano Politics: Albert A. Peña, Jr. of San Antonio, Texas, 1917–2006." Unpublished manuscript in author's possession, fall 2013.

———. *The Making of a Chicano Militant: Lessons from Cristal*. Madison: University of Wisconsin Press, 1998.

Hahn, Steven. *A Nation Under Our Feet: Black Political Struggles in the Rural South, from Slavery to the Great Migration*. Cambridge, Mass: Belknap Press of Harvard University Press, 2003.

Hales, Douglas. "Grovey, Richard Randolph." *Handbook of Texas Online*. Accessed August 19, 2010. http://www.tshaonline.org/handbook/online/articles/GG/fgrat.html.

Hall, Jacquelyn Dowd. "The Long Civil Rights Movement and the Political Uses of the Past." *The Journal of American History* 91, no. 4 (March 2005): 1233–63.

Hall, Jacquelyn Dowd, James Leloudis, Robert Korstad, Mary Murphy, Lu Ann Jones, and Christopher B. Daly. *Like a Family: The Making of a Southern Cotton Mill World*. Chapel Hill: University of North Carolina Press, 1987.

Hall, Robert E. "Pickets, Politics, and Power: The Farm Worker Strike in Starr County." *Bob's Remonstrance*. Accessed September 29, 2015. http://bobsremonstrance.com/farmworkers-strike-in-south-texas/.

Halpern, Rick. *Down on the Killing Floor: Black and White Workers in Chicago's Packinghouses, 1904–54*. Urbana: University of Illinois Press, 1997.

———. "Interracial Unionism in the Southwest: Fort Worth's Packinghouse Workers, 1937–1954." In *Organized Labor in the Twentieth-Century South*, edited by Robert H. Zieger, 158–82. Knoxville: University of Tennessee Press, 1991.

Haynes, Robert V. *A Night of Violence: The Houston Riot of 1917*. Baton Rouge: Louisiana State University Press, 1976.

Henderson, Richard B. "Fontaine Maury Maverick." *Handbook of Texas Online*. Accessed July 13, 2010. http://www.tshaonline.org/handbook/online/articles/MM/fma83.html.

———. *Maury Maverick, a Political Biography*. Austin: University of Texas Press, 1970.

Hernandez, Kelly Lytle. *Migra!: A History of the U.S. Border Patrol*. Berkeley: University of California Press, 2010.

Hield, Melissa. "'Union-Minded': Women in the Texas ILGWU, 1933–50." *Frontiers: A Journal of Women Studies* 4, no. 2 (Summer 1979): 59–70.

Hine, Darlene Clark. *Black Victory: The Rise and Fall of the White Primary in Texas*. New ed. Columbia: University of Missouri Press, 2003.

Honey, Michael K. *Going Down Jericho Road: The Memphis Strike, Martin Luther King's Last Campaign*. New York: W.W. Norton, 2007.

———. *Southern Labor and Black Civil Rights: Organizing Memphis Workers*. Urbana: University of Illinois Press, 1993.

Horowitz, Roger. *"Negro and White, Unite and Fight!": A Social History of Industrial Unionism in Meatpacking, 1930–90*. Urbana: University of Illinois Press, 1997.

"I Feel a Train a Coming, It's Coming Round the Bend." *Texquiem*, December 13, 2012. http://texquiem.blogspot.com/2012/12/i-feel-train-coming-its-coming-round.html.

"Image Gallery—Hospital Postcards." *RailwaySurgery.org*. Accessed January 24, 2014. http://railwaysurgery.org/Hospitals.htm.

Johnson, Benjamin Heber. "The Cosmic Race in Texas: Racial Fusion, White Supremacy, and Civil Rights Politics." *Journal of American History* 98, no. 2 (September 1, 2011): 404–19. doi:10.1093/jahist/jar338.

———. *Revolution in Texas: How a Forgotten Rebellion and Its Bloody Suppression Turned Mexicans into Americans*. New Haven, Conn.: Yale University Press, 2003.

Jones, William P. *The March on Washington: Jobs, Freedom, and the Forgotten History of Civil Rights*. New York: W.W. Norton, 2013.

Kaplowitz, Craig Allan. *LULAC, Mexican Americans, and National Policy*. College Station: Texas A&M University Press, 2005.

Kellar, William Henry. *Make Haste Slowly: Moderates, Conservatives, and School Desegregation in Houston*. College Station: Texas A&M University Press, 1999.

Kelley, Blair L. M. *Right to Ride: Streetcar Boycotts and African American Citizenship in the Era of Plessy v. Ferguson*. Chapel Hill: University of North Carolina Press, 2010.

Kersten, Andrew. *Race, Jobs, and the War: The FEPC in the Midwest, 1941–46*. Urbana: University of Illinois Press, 2000.

Kersten, Andrew, and Clarence Lang, eds. *Reframing Randolph: Labor, Black Freedom, and the Legacies of A. Philip Randolph*. New York: New York University Press, 2015.

Kohout, Martin Donell. "Gonzalez, Henry Barbosa." *Handbook of Texas Online*. Accessed April 1, 2011. http://www.tshaonline.org/handbook/online/articles/fgo76.

Kolb, David A. *Experiential Learning: Experience as the Source of Learning and Development*. 1st ed.. Englewood Cliffs, N.J.: Prentice Hall, 1984.

Korstad, Robert Rodgers. *Civil Rights Unionism: Tobacco Workers and the Struggle for Democracy in the Mid-Twentieth-Century South*. Chapel Hill: University of North Carolina Press, 2003.

Korstad, Robert, and Nelson Lichtenstein. "Opportunities Found and Lost: Labor, Radicals, and the Early Civil Rights Movement." *The Journal of American History* 75, no. 3 (December 1988): 786–811.

Kreneck, Thomas H. *Del Pueblo: A History of Houston's Hispanic Community*. College Station: Texas A&M University Press, 2012.

———. *Mexican American Odyssey: Felix Tijerina, Entrepreneur and Civic Leader 1905–1965*. College Station: Texas A & M University Press, 2001.

Krochmal, Max. "Chicano Labor and Multiracial Politics in Post–World War II Texas." In *Life and Labor in the New New South*, edited by Robert H. Zieger, 133–76. Gainesville: University Press of Florida, 2012.

———. "Labor, Civil Rights, and the Struggle for Democracy in Texas, 1935–1965." Ph.D. diss., Duke University, 2011.

———. "San Antonio Chicano Organizers (SACO): Labor Activists and El Movimiento." In *The Chicano Movement: Perspectives from the Twenty-First Century*, edited by Mario T. Garcia, 203–26. New York: Routledge, 2014.

Kruse, Kevin Michael. *White Flight: Atlanta and the Making of Modern Conservatism*. Princeton, N.J: Princeton University Press, 2005.

Lang, Clarence. *Grassroots at the Gateway: Class Politics and Black Freedom Struggle in St. Louis, 1936–75.* Ann Arbor: University of Michigan Press, 2009.

Lassiter, Matthew D. *The Silent Majority: Suburban Politics in the Sunbelt South.* Princeton, N.J.: Princeton University Press, 2006.

Lavergne, Gary M. *Before Brown: Heman Marion Sweatt, Thurgood Marshall, and the Long Road to Justice.* Austin: University of Texas Press, 2010. Kindle edition.

Lawson, Steven F. *Black Ballots: Voting Rights in the South, 1944–1969.* New York: Columbia University Press, 1976.

Leal, Ray Robert. "The 1966–1967 South Texas Farm Worker Strike: A Case Study of Farm Worker Powerlessness." Ph.D. diss., Indiana University, 1983.

Ledesma, Irene. "Texas Newspapers and Chicana Workers' Activism, 1919–1974." *The Western Historical Quarterly* 26, no. 3 (Autumn 1995): 309–31.

———. "Unlikely Strikers: Mexican-American Women in Strike Activity in Texas, 1919–1974." Ph.D. diss., Ohio State University, 1992.

Lee, Sonia Song-Ha. *Building a Latino Civil Rights Movement: Puerto Ricans, African Americans, and the Pursuit of Racial Justice in New York City.* Chapel Hill: University of North Carolina Press, 2014.

Leiker, James N. *Racial Borders: Black Soldiers Along the Rio Grande.* College Station: Texas A&M University Press, 2002.

Lentz-Smith, Adriane. *Freedom Struggles: African Americans and World War I.* Cambridge, Mass.: Harvard University Press, 2009.

Lichtenstein, Nelson. *Labor's War at Home: The CIO in World War II.* New York: Cambridge University Press, 1982.

———. *State of the Union: A Century of American Labor.* Princeton, N.J: Princeton University Press, 2002.

Lipsitz, George. *Rainbow at Midnight: Labor and Culture in the 1940s.* Urbana: University of Illinois Press, 1994.

Long, Elizabeth. "The Chat-An-Hour Social and Cultural Club: African American Women Readers." In *A History of the Book in America*, edited by David Paul Nord, Joan Shelley Rubin, and Michael Schudson, 5:459–71. Chapel Hill: University of North Carolina Press, 2009.

Lopez, Mark Hugo, and Paul Taylor. "Latino Voters in the 2012 Election." *Pew Research Center's Hispanic Trends Project.* Accessed September 29, 2015. http://www.pewhispanic.org/2012/11/07/latino-voters-in-the-2012-election/.

MacDougall, Curtis Daniel. *Gideon's Army.* New York: Marzani & Munsell, 1965.

MacLaggan, Corrie. "Report: Texas Lags in Hispanic Voter Turnout." *The Texas Tribune.* Accessed September 29, 2015. http://www.texastribune.org/2014/02/26/hispanic-voters/.

Mantler, Gordon K. *Power to the Poor: Black-Brown Coalition and the Fight for Economic Justice, 1960–1974.* Chapel Hill: University of North Carolina Press, 2013.

Márquez, Benjamin. *Democratizing Texas Politics: Race, Identity, and Mexican American Empowerment, 1945–2002.* Austin: University of Texas Press, 2014.

———. *LULAC: The Evolution of a Mexican American Political Organization.* Austin: University of Texas Press, 1993.

Márquez, John D. *Black-Brown Solidarity: Racial Politics in the New Gulf South.* Austin: University of Texas Press, 2014.

Mason, Kenneth. "Paternal Continuity: African Americans and Race Relations in San Antonio, Texas, 1867–1937." Ph.D. diss., University of Texas at Austin, 1994.

May, Gary. *Bending Toward Justice: The Voting Rights Act and the Transformation of American Democracy*. New York: Basic Books, 2013.

McGirr, Lisa. *Suburban Warriors: The Origins of the New American Right*. Princeton, N.J: Princeton University Press, 2001.

Mease, Quentin R. *On Equal Footing: A Memoir*. Edited by Shannon Davies. Austin, Tex.: Eakin Press, 2001.

Mers, Gilbert. *Working the Waterfront: The Ups and Downs of a Rebel Longshoreman*. Austin: University of Texas Press, 1988.

Minchin, Timothy J. *Fighting against the Odds: A History of Southern Labor Since World War II*. Gainesville: University Press of Florida, 2006.

———. *What Do We Need a Union For?: The TWUA in the South, 1945–1955*. Chapel Hill: University of North Carolina Press, 1997.

Minushkin, Susan, and Mark Hugo Lopez. "The Hispanic Vote in the 2008 Democratic Presidential Primaries." *Pew Research Center's Hispanic Trends Project*. Accessed September 29, 2015. http://www.pewhispanic.org/2008/03/07/the-hispanic-vote-in-the-2008-democratic-presidential-primaries/.

Moneyhon, Carl H. *Texas after the Civil War: The Struggle of Reconstruction*. College Station: Texas A&M University Press, 2004.

Montejano, David. *Anglos and Mexicans in the Making of Texas, 1836–1986*. Austin: University of Texas Press, 1987.

———. *Quixote's Soldiers: A Local History of the Chicano Movement, 1966–1981*. Austin: University of Texas Press, 2010.

Montes, Rebecca Anne. "Working for American Rights: Black, White, and Mexican-American Dockworkers in Texas During the Great Depression." Ph.D. diss., University of Texas, 2005.

Moreton, Bethany. *To Serve God and Wal-Mart: The Making of Christian Free Enterprise*. Cambridge, Mass.: Harvard University Press, 2009.

Moye, J. Todd. *Ella Baker: Community Organizer of the Civil Rights Movement*. Rowman & Littlefield Publishers, 2013. Kindle edition.

Munz, Charles Curtis. "Gunning for Maverick." *Nation* 149, no. 25 (December 16, 1939): 673–74.

Murphy, Leonard B. "Sutton, Garlington Jerome." *Handbook of Texas Online*. Accessed November 11, 2009. http://www.tshaonline.org/handbook/online/articles/SS/fsu11.html.

Navarro, Armando. *The Cristal Experiment : A Chicano Struggle for Community Control*. Madison: University of Wisconsin Press, 1998.

Obadele-Starks, Ernest. "Black Texans and Theater Craft Unionism: The Struggle for Racial Equality." *Southwestern Historical Quarterly* 106, no. 4 (April 2003): 532–48.

———. *Black Unionism in the Industrial South*. College Station: Texas A&M University Press, 2000.

Olivas, Michael A., ed. *Colored Men and Hombres Aquí: Hernandez V. Texas and the Emergence of Mexican American Lawyering*. Houston, Tex.: Arte Público Press, 2006.

Opie, Frederick Douglass. *Upsetting the Apple Cart: Black-Latino Coalitions in New York City from Protest to Public Office*. New York: Columbia University Press, 2014.

Orozco, Cynthia E. "Garcia, Gustavo C." *Handbook of Texas Online.* Accessed March 1, 2011. http://www.tshaonline.org/handbook/online/articles/fga51.

———. *No Mexicans, Women, or Dogs Allowed: The Rise of the Mexican American Civil Rights Movement.* Austin: University of Texas Press, 2009.

Ortiz, Paul. *Emancipation Betrayed: The Hidden History of Black Organizing and White Violence in Florida from Reconstruction to the Bloody Election of 1920.* Berkeley: University of California Press, 2005.

Palmer, Phyllis. *Living as Equals: How Three White Communities Struggled to Make Interracial Connections During the Civil Rights Era.* Nashville, Tenn.: Vanderbilt University Press, 2008.

Parker, Richard. "Getting Texas to Go Democratic Won't Be Easy." *New York Times*, February 19, 2013. http://www.nytimes.com/2013/02/20/opinion/getting-texas-to-go-democratic.html.

Payne, Charles M. *I've Got the Light of Freedom: The Organizing Tradition and the Mississippi Freedom Struggle.* Rev. ed. Berkeley: University of California Press, 2007.

Pérez, Emma. *The Decolonial Imaginary: Writing Chicanas into History.* Bloomington: Indiana University Press, 1999.

Pitre, Merline. *In Struggle against Jim Crow: Lulu B. White and the NAACP, 1900–1957.* College Station: Texas A&M University Press, 1999.

———. *Through Many Dangers, Toils and Snares.* 2nd ed. Austin, Tex.: Eakin Press, 1997.

Polakoff, Murray. "The Development of the Texas State C.I.O. Council." Ph.D. diss., Columbia University, 1955.

Postel, Charles. *The Populist Vision.* New York: Oxford University Press, 2007.

Priest, Tyler, and Michael Botson. "Bucking the Odds: Organized Labor in Gulf Coast Oil Refining." *Journal of American History* 99, no. 1 (June 2012): 100–110.

Pruitt, Bernadette. *The Other Great Migration: The Movement of Rural African Americans to Houston, Texas, 1900–1941.* College Station: Texas A&M University Press, 2013.

Pulido, Laura. *Black, Brown, Yellow, and Left: Radical Activism in Los Angeles.* Berkeley: University of California Press, 2006.

Purdum, Todd S. *An Idea Whose Time Has Come: Two Presidents, Two Parties, and the Battle for the Civil Rights Act of 1964.* New York: Henry Holt and Co., 2014.

Pycior, Julie Leininger. *LBJ & Mexican Americans: The Paradox of Power.* Austin: University of Texas Press, 1997.

Ramos, Henry. *The American GI Forum: In Pursuit of the Dream, 1948–1983.* Houston, Tex: Arte Público Press, 1998.

Ramos, Lisa Y. "A Class Apart: Mexican Americans, Race, and Civil Rights in Texas." Ph.D. diss., Columbia University, 2008.

Ransby, Barbara. *Ella Baker and the Black Freedom Movement: A Radical Democratic Vision.* Chapel Hill: University of North Carolina Press, 2003.

Reagon, Bernice Johnson. "Coalition Politics: Turning the Century." In *Home Girls: A Black Feminist Anthology*, edited by Barbara Smith, 343–56. New Brunswick, N.J.: Rutgers University Press, 2000. First published 1983 by Kitchen Table: Women of Color Press.

Reed, Merl E. *Seedtime for the Modern Civil Rights Movement: The President's*

Committee on Fair Employment Practice, 1941–1946. Baton Rouge: Louisiana State University Press, 1991.

Reid, Jan. *Let the People In: The Life and Times of Ann Richards*. Austin: University of Texas Press, 2012.

Risen, Clay. *The Bill of the Century: The Epic Battle for the Civil Rights Act*. New York: Bloomsbury Press, 2014.

Robnett, Belinda. *How Long? How Long?: African American Women in the Struggle for Civil Rights*. New York: Oxford University Press, 1997.

Rodriguez, Eugene, Jr. *Henry B. Gonzalez: A Political Profile*. New York: Arno Press, 1976.

Rodriguez, Marc Simon. *The Tejano Diaspora: Mexican Americanism & Ethnic Politics in Texas and Wisconsin*. Chapel Hill: University of North Carolina Press, 2011.

Rosales, Rodolfo. *The Illusion of Inclusion: The Untold Political Story of San Antonio*. Austin: University of Texas Press, 2000.

Rubio, Philip F. *There's Always Work at the Post Office: African American Postal Workers and the Fight for Jobs, Justice, and Equality*. Chapel Hill: University of North Carolina Press, 2010.

Ruíz, Vicki. *From Out of the Shadows: Mexican Women in Twentieth-Century America*. New York: Oxford University Press, 1998.

Russell, Thomas D., ed. *Sweatt v. Painter Archive*. 2008. Accessed January 20, 2014. http://www.houseofrussell.com/legalhistory/sweatt/.

Salter, Daren. "National Negro Congress (1935–1940s)." *The Black Past: Remembered and Reclaimed*. Accessed July 29, 2010. http://www.blackpast.org/?q=aah/national-negro-congress.

Samora, Julian, Joe Bernal, and Albert Peña. *Gunpowder Justice: A Reassessment of the Texas Rangers*. South Bend, Ind.: University of Notre Dame Press, 1979.

Sapper, Neil Gary. "A Survey of the History of the Black People of Texas, 1930–1954." Ph.D. diss., Texas Tech University, 1972.

Scipes, Kim. *AFL-CIO's Secret War against Developing Country Workers: Solidarity or Sabotage?* Lanham, Md.: Lexington Books, 2010.

Scott, Glenn, and Maria Flores. *Talkin' Union*. Austin: People's History in Texas, Inc., 1978. Documentary film. http://www.peopleshistoryintexas.org.

"Senatorial Elections and Primaries, 1906–2012." *Texas Almanac Online*. Accessed July 28, 2015. http://texasalmanac.com/topics/elections/senatorial-elections-and-primaries-1906%E2%80%932008-0.

Shapiro, Harold A. "The Pecan Shellers of San Antonio, Texas." *Southwestern Social Science Quarterly* 32, no. 4 (1952): 229–44.

Shockley, John S. *Chicano Revolt in a Texas Town*. South Bend, Ind.: University of Notre Dame Press, 1974.

Sugrue, Thomas J. *The Origins of the Urban Crisis: Race and Inequality in Postwar Detroit*. Princeton, N.J: Princeton University Press, 1996.

Sullivan, Patricia. *Days of Hope: Race and Democracy in the New Deal Era*. Chapel Hill: University of North Carolina Press, 1996.

"Texas 2020." *NPR.org*, July 30, 2013. http://www.npr.org/series/196613711/texas-2020.

Thorburn, Wayne. *Red State: An Insider's Story of How the GOP Came to Dominate Texas Politics*. Austin: University of Texas Press, 2014.

Vaca, Nicolas C. *The Presumed Alliance: The Unspoken Conflict Between Latinos and Blacks and What It Means for America*. New York: Rayo, 2004.

Vargas, Zaragosa. *Labor Rights Are Civil Rights: Mexican American Workers in Twentieth-Century America*. Politics and Society in Twentieth-Century America. Princeton, N.J: Princeton University Press, 2005.

———. "Tejana Radical: Emma Tenayuca and the San Antonio Labor Movement During the Great Depression." *Pacific Historical Review* 66, no. 4 (1997): 553–80.

Vial, Rebecca A. "Kate Bradford Stockton." *Tennessee Encyclopedia of History and Culture*. Accessed March 16, 2016. http://tennesseeencyclopedia.net/entry.php?rec=1268.

Wada, Kayomi. "President's Committee on Fair Employment Practice (FEPC)." *The Black Past: Remembered and Reclaimed*. Accessed September 17, 2010. http://www.blackpast.org/?q=aah/presidents-committee-fair-employment-practice-fepc.

White, Graham J., and John R. Maze. *Henry A. Wallace: His Search for a New World Order*. Chapel Hill: University of North Carolina Press, 1995.

Wilson, Steven H. "Brown over 'Other White': Mexican Americans' Legal Arguments and Litigation Strategy in School Desegregation Lawsuits." *Law and History Review* 21, no. 1 (Spring 2003): 145–94.

Wolin, Sheldon. *The Presence of the Past: Essays on the State and the Constitution*. Baltimore: Johns Hopkins University Press, 1989.

Wuthnow, Robert. *Rough Country: How Texas Became America's Most Powerful Bible-Belt State*. Princeton, N.J.: Princeton University Press, 2014.

Zamora, Emilio. *Claiming Rights and Righting Wrongs in Texas: Mexican Workers and Job Politics during World War II*. College Station: Texas A&M University Press, 2009.

———. *The World of the Mexican Worker in Texas*. Texas A&M University. College Station: Texas A&M University Press, 1993.

Zieger, Robert H. *The CIO, 1935–1955*. Chapel Hill: University of North Carolina Press, 1995.

———, ed. *Organized Labor in the Twentieth-Century South*. Knoxville: University of Tennessee Press, 1991.

———, ed. *Southern Labor in Transition, 1940–1995*. Knoxville: University of Tennessee Press, 1997.

Zon, Mary Goddard. "Labor in Politics." *Law and Contemporary Problems* 27, no. 2 (Spring 1962): 234–51.

Index

Adair, Christia V., 97, 98, 107, 109, 114, 122, 123, 446 (n. 17)
AFL-CIO (American Federation of Labor-Congress of Industrial Organizations), 4, 181, 247, 351, 417; civil rights and, 252, 320, 321, 322, 323, 324, 334; labor movement, 1950s and, 171, 183; *mexicano* civil rights activism and, 336–37
African Americans: 1954 gubernatorial primary campaign and, 116; 1960 presidential election and, 216, 226–29, 230–31, 233; 1961 U.S. Senate race and, 233, 243–44, 246, 468 (n. 29); 1962 gubernatorial race and, 271–74, 275, 277–78, 279, 330–31, 473 (n. 9); 1963 Democratic Coalition and, 282, 292, 309, 311, 315–17, 331, 332, 474 (n. 12); 1964 elections and, 378, 379, 487 (n. 39); 1964 post-election Democratic Coalition and, 379–80, 382, 383, 390–91, 392–94, 401, 488 (n. 63); Austin and, 141–42, 352, 353, 372; conservatives and, 159, 230, 286, 287, 290, 292–93, 316, 327, 328, 332–33, 339–40, 345, 346–48, 378, 380; Democratic Party and, 10, 56, 65–66, 79–80, 81, 83, 443 (n. 55); Democrats of Texas (DOT) and, 118, 121, 162, 167, 228, 229, 456 (n. 77); Fort Worth labor movement and, 82, 91–92, 173; Harris County Democrats (HCD) and, 131–32, 353, 372, 378, 401; Houston, labor movement, 1930s and, 13, 58–59, 60, 61–62; Houston, labor movement, 1950s and, 99–102, 104–6, 107; Houston, labor movement, 1960s and, 200–202, 210, 226–29, 291, 292, 391; Houston, labor movement, early 1940s and, 56–57, 63–64, 71, 446–47 (n. 22); Houston, labor movement, later 1940s and, 74–79, 87, 414; Houston, police brutality against African Americans and, 103–4, 194–95, 196, 448 (n. 30); Houston, politics, 1950s and, 99–109, 112–14, 446–47 (n. 22), 447 (n. 23); Houston, politics, later 1940s and, 81–86, 89, 112, 443 (n. 60), 444 (nn. 65, 68), 444–45 (n. 70); Houston, voting rights and, 56–57, 64–67, 68–70, 78, 79–80, 85–86, 87, 103; labor movement, 1930s and, 16, 57; labor movement, 1950s and, 90–92; Mexican-American partnership and, 46, 128, 130, 133, 134–37, 139, 152–54, 157–59, 160, 167, 169, 195–96, 243–44, 454 (n. 48); *mexicano* labor movement and, 399, 400; multi-racial coalition and, 45, 250–51, 252–54, 470 (n. 43); political office and, 83–84, 87, 102–3, 104, 106, 136–37, 370, 444–45 (n. 70), 447 (n. 28), 452 (nn. 6–7); political patronage and, 250, 255–56, 265–66, 292, 380; politics, 1960s and, 250, 292; poll tax repeal possibility and, 351–58; recent political history and, 3, 4, 417–18, 419; San Antonio, 1930s and, 14, 25, 37, 43–48, 49, 50, 51–52, 55, 65, 82, 439 (n. 109); San Antonio, 1950s and, 140, 142, 144–45, 157, 159, 167, 457 (n. 84); San Antonio, early 1940s and, 53, 54; San Antonio, late 1940s and, 133, 134–39, 143, 145, 452 (n. 6); San Antonio, politics 1960s and, 230, 285–87, 288, 289–90, 474 (n. 24); voting rights and, 10, 14, 79, 107–9, 119, 327, 404, 443 (n. 55); white liberal Democrats and, 112, 119–24, 137, 280, 374, 450 (n. 62);

African Americans (*continued*)
women and, 11, 19, 83–84, 85, 102–3, 106–7; women workers and, 77–78, 209–10. *See also* Civil rights movement; Civil rights unionism; Harris County Council of Organizations (HCCO); Jim Crow; National Association for the Advancement of Colored People (NAACP); Segregation; Texas poll taxes; United Political Organization (UPO); "White primary"

Agricultural Stabilization Committees, 395

Alaniz, John, 218, 230, 465 (n. 55)

Allee, A. Y., 296–97, 298, 302, 398, 403

Allred, James V., 28–29, 36, 43, 127, 436 (n. 76)

Amalgamated Clothing Workers of America (ACWA), 42, 49, 177, 178

Amalgamated Lithographers of America Local 83, 211

Amalgamated Meat Cutters, 258, 367

Amalgamated Tin, Iron, and Steel Workers, 187–88

American Civil Liberties Union, 34

American Federation of Labor (AFL), 19, 20, 58; labor movement, 1950s and, 91, 128; labor movement, later 1940s and, 73, 75, 76; politics, 1930s and, 37, 38, 48, 53

American G.I. Forum (AGIF): civil rights activism and, 127, 130, 135, 147–48, 149, 217, 235; founding of, 126; multi-racial coalition and, 94, 95, 125, 295; PASO and, 304, 305, 306, 400, 414; politics, 1950s and, 128, 151, 154, 155, 162, 166, 167, 234; politics, 1960s and, 224, 225, 238, 241, 260, 264, 269, 277, 363, 367

American Legion, 52

"American of Mexican Descent" (Sánchez), 240–41, 267

Americans for Democratic Action (ADA), 116, 178, 179

American Student Union, 30

Anderson, M. J., 293, 333

Anti-Communism, 25, 29, 37, 53, 54, 90, 93, 94, 95–97, 114, 123, 173, 446 (n. 17)

Anti-Violence Act of 1941, 80, 89

Armour & Company, 92

Austin, 110, 111, 112, 113, 153, 293, 353, 367, 397; 1963 Democratic Coalition and, 280; African Americans and, 141–42, 352, 353, 372; civil rights activism and, 329–30, 331–34; Democrats of Texas (DOT) and, 162–64, 246; March on Austin and, 1–2, 6, 334, 339–49, 350, 374, 391, 416, 481 (n. 57); *mexicano* labor movement and, 399–404; segregation and, 43, 162, 456 (n. 72); youth leadership conference and, 380

Baer, Max, 19

Ball, Eddie, 114, 147

Barnes, Ben, 401, 402

Bartlett, Latane. *See* Lambert, Latane Bartlett

Battleground Texas, 4, 418

Bell, Virginia L., 83–84

Bellinger, Charles, 25, 44–45, 47, 48, 437 (n. 88)

Bellinger, Ruth, 272, 273, 340, 346, 366, 478 (n. 4)

Bellinger, Valmo: San Antonio, politics, 1930s and, 44–45, 48, 49, 51; San Antonio, politics, 1940s and, 53, 54, 135, 137, 145, 452 (n. 6); San Antonio, politics, 1950s and, 140, 147, 157, 159, 167, 457 (n. 84); San Antonio, politics, 1960s and, 230, 288, 290, 474 (n. 24)

Benavides, Roberto, 257, 262, 272, 304

Bentsen, Lloyd, 407, 408

Bernal, Joe, 398, 402, 407

Bernhard Altmann Company, 180

Bexar County, 35–36, 42, 48, 120, 165, 168, 218, 279, 298, 306, 378, 398

Bexar County Commissioners Court, 155–57, 304–5, 354

Bexar County Democratic Coalition, 233, 259, 288, 465 (n. 55), 470 (n. 41); 1960 presidential election and, 223, 224, 230, 231; 1961 U.S. congress race and, 257, 258; 1962 gubernatorial race and, 270, 271, 272, 280; 1963 Democratic

514   Index

Coalition and, 281, 317; civil rights activism and, 346; Crystal City revolt and, 296; Democratic Coalition of Texas and, 247, 365; founding of, 186, 219–20
Bexar County Democratic Party, 44, 150, 151, 152, 186, 459–60 (n. 32)
Bexar County Democratic Party Executive Committee, 366
Bexar County Democratic Women, 229–30
Bierner, Mike, 19
Bird, Jeremy, 418
Bishop College, 363
Black, Claude W., Jr., 140, 141–43, 272; 1963 Democratic Coalition and, 319, 366; civil rights activism, 1950s and, 144–45, 157, 158, 159; civil rights activism, 1960s and, 203, 204, 211–12, 285, 286, 287–88, 340, 344–46, 374, 416; equal rights employment and, 205, 206, 209; multi-racial coalition and, 219, 412; political office and, 288–90, 293, 407, 474 (n. 24)
Black, Claude W., Sr., 140–41, 142
Black Lives Matter, 412, 419
Blackwell, Randolph, 318
Blakley, William, 242, 243, 245–46, 256
Bonilla, William, 304, 305, 476 (n. 62)
Bonner, Booker T. "B. T.": 1964 post-election Democratic Coalition and, 391, 393–94; civil rights activism and, 329–34, 339, 340, 341–42, 348, 359, 373, 400; Huntsville movement and, 385, 386, 388, 401; March on Austin and, 342–44, 346, 347; multi-racial coalition and, 353, 374, 390, 419; political office and, 372, 375
Border Wage and Job Conference, 335–38
Bracero program, 235, 237, 267, 276, 306–7, 338
Brannin, Carl, 17
Brewery Workers union, 181, 183
Brooks, Homer, 23, 33
Brooks, Marion J. "Jack," 247, 316, 344, 477 (n. 68)

Brotherhood of Sleeping Car Porters, 47, 140
Brotherhood of Steamship and Railway Clerks (BSRC), 61–62, 74–75, 82, 104–5, 201, 227, 405
Brown, Herman, 117
Brown, H. S. "Hank," 187–91, 460 (n. 46); 1961 U.S. Senate race and, 243, 245, 246; 1962 upcoming elections and, 260, 264, 266, 269; 1963 Democratic Coalition and, 280–81, 308, 313, 315, 317, 318, 361, 365, 477 (n. 68); 1964 post-election Democratic Coalition and, 382; 1964 upcoming elections and, 372, 373, 374, 376; civil rights activism and, 209, 320, 322–24, 325, 326, 346, 411, 415; Crystal City revolt and, 299, 303; *mexicano* civil rights activism and, 334, 335, 336, 337, 338, 339; *mexicano* labor movement and, 367, 368, 401, 402; multi-racial coalition and, 151, 192–93, 215, 219–20, 222, 234, 247–50, 252–53, 255, 259, 274, 413; Texas State AFL-CIO presidency and, 233–34, 238–39
Brownsville, 362, 367
Brownsville Herald, 328
Brown v. Board decision, 98, 102, 120, 134, 158, 201, 321
BSRC Local 1534, 104
Building and Construction Trades Council of San Antonio, 188, 234
Bullock, Bob, 417
Burns, Harry V., 203, 209–10, 287, 290, 342
Bush, George H. W., 376–77
Bush, George W., 3, 417, 466 (n. 77)

California Packing plant, 296, 298, 299–300
Camp Logan Riot of 1917, 60–61
Carmichael, Stokely, 395
Carr, Waggoner, 401
Casso, Ramiro, 305, 476 (n. 62)
Castañeda, Carlos, 127
Castillo, Leonel J., 206–7, 208, 213, 405, 463 (n. 29), 463–64 (n. 31)

Index 515

Catholic Church, 28, 37, 52, 171
CBS News, 323, 335, 337
Chávez, César, 7, 398
Chavez, Dennis, 127
Chavez-Thompson, Linda, 417
Chicano movement, 294, 404, 406, 407, 414, 430–31 (n. 2), 475 (n. 33)
CIO Political Action Committee (CIO-PAC), 69, 94
Citizens Committee for Better Government (CCBG), 297
Civic Action Committee (CAC), 87–88, 130–31, 167, 225, 241, 451–52 (n. 77)
Civil Rights Act of 1957, 216
Civil Rights Act of 1964, 362, 365, 375, 376, 378, 382, 383, 388, 396, 404, 405, 487 (n. 46)
Civil rights movement, 13, 215, 259, 400, 403, 407, 409–10, 415, 421; 1963 Democratic Coalition and, 281, 284–85, 312–13, 314, 315, 316–17, 318–19, 327–28, 331, 333; 1964 Democratic Coalition and, 365, 366, 369, 373, 374; 1964 post-election Democratic Coalition and, 380, 382, 384–89; Austin and, 1–2, 6, 329–30, 331–34, 339–49, 350, 374, 391, 416, 481 (n. 57); Dallas and, 284, 292, 339, 340, 363, 364–65; equal rights employment and, 197, 200–201, 204–6, 209–10, 213, 284–85, 320, 322, 324–25, 378, 396; Huntsville movement and, 383–89, 391–92, 393, 395–96; integration and, 284–85, 319–20, 326–27, 339; multi-racial coalition and, 5, 133, 139, 203–4, 213, 251–53, 278, 279, 294, 470 (n. 43); sit-ins, Austin and, 331–32, 339; sit-ins, Houston and, 194, 195, 196–97, 198–200, 202, 214, 251, 290–91, 462 (nn. 9, 11); sit-ins, Huntsville and, 362, 385; sit-ins, San Antonio and, 203–4, 251; sit-ins and, 292, 363, 461 (n. 3); "spadework" and, 88, 445 (n. 2); stand-ins and, 206–9, 285, 329–30, 384–85, 463–64 (n. 31); white liberals and, 387–88, 389, 392. See also AFL-CIO (American Federation of Labor–Congress of Industrial Organizations); Desegregation; Houston; Kennedy, John F.; Labor movement; Mexican Americans; National Association for the Advancement of Colored People (NAACP); San Antonio; Texas State AFL-CIO
Civil rights unionism: Cold War period and, 89, 90, 92, 97, 98; HCCO and, 99, 101; Houston NAACP and, 57, 67, 69, 70, 73, 74, 78, 79, 85, 87, 98, 99, 106, 202; LeRoy, Moses and, 60, 67, 70, 74–79, 85, 87, 99, 106, 108, 195, 196, 202, 414; politics, 1930s and, 64–65; politics, later 1940s and, 80–81, 83, 84; segregation and, 70–71, 73, 74–79, 442 (n. 36)
Clements, Bill, 417
Clinton, Hillary, 3, 418, 431 (n. 4)
Cold War, 88–89, 93, 95, 98, 99, 108, 113, 131, 176, 178, 202, 413
Coleman, Eugene, 140, 143–45, 157, 159, 407, 453 (nn. 24–26); civil rights activism and, 144–45, 203, 213, 285, 342; politics, 1960s and, 229, 288, 290, 366, 474 (n. 26); underpass campaign and, 211–12
Combs, Arthur, 110–11
Committee on Fair Employment Practices (FEPC), 74, 77, 78, 80, 81, 127
Committee on Political Education (COPE), 229, 281; 1961 U.S. Senate race and, 243, 245; 1962 gubernatorial race and, 269, 270, 275, 278; 1964 upcoming elections and, 371, 373, 374; Democratic Coalition of Texas and, 247, 250, 254, 255; poll tax repeal possibility and, 351, 352; voter registration and, 108–9, 179, 371. See also Texas State AFL-CIO
Committee to Get Wallace on the Ballot in Texas, 81–82
Communist Party, 54, 81, 438 (n. 95); 1930s and, 30, 32, 39, 52, 177; CIO and, 53, 67, 90, 92, 94, 97, 114, 116, 173, 445 (n. 3); Houston NAACP and, 90, 95,

100, 112, 446 (n. 17); labor movement, 1950s and, 88–89, 92, 173, 445 (n. 3); pecan shellers strike, 1938 and, 23, 25, 26–27, 28, 33, 36, 37, 458 (n. 19). *See also* Anti-Communism

Conde, Carlos, 294, 295, 297–98, 299, 304, 475 (nn. 34, 42)

Confederación de Trabajadores Mexicanos (CTM), 34, 41, 181, 234, 335, 398, 466–67 (n. 4)

Congress of Industrial Organizations (CIO), 77, 95, 101, 128, 188, 239; 1930s and, 20, 22, 37, 38, 39, 42, 48, 51, 53, 54; 1948 presidential election and, 83, 444 (n. 68); Communist Party and, 53, 67, 90, 92, 94, 97, 114, 116, 173, 445 (n. 3); labor movement, 1940s and, 73, 80, 446–47 (n. 22); "Operation Dixie" and, 90–91, 177; segregation and, 58, 66, 68, 69

Congress of Spanish-Speaking Peoples (El Congreso de Pueblos de Habla Español), 32

Connally, John: 1962 gubernatorial race and, 265–69, 271–72, 273–74, 276, 277–79, 292, 294, 330, 411; 1964 reelection and, 375, 377, 378; 1964 upcoming elections and, 306, 348, 359, 361, 371, 372, 373, 380; civil rights and, 318, 325, 326–27, 328, 331–32, 333, 334, 337, 373, 376, 385; conservative African Americans and, 292, 293, 316, 327, 333, 340, 341, 345, 346–48, 378, 380; hospitalization and, 360, 368, 369; March on Austin and, 1, 339, 340–42, 343, 344–49; *mexicano* labor movement and, 325, 326, 334, 335, 336, 401; *mexicano* politics, 1960s and, 286, 298, 302; poll tax repeal possibility and, 350, 354–55, 356; popularity and, 360, 361, 375

Cook, Rannie, 77–78, 82, 85

Cornejo, Juan, 293–95, 296, 297, 300, 302, 303

Corpus Christi, 126, 142, 166, 235, 262, 268, 304, 336, 358, 367, 399, 467 (n. 10), 468 (n. 23), 483 (n. 79)

Cox, Jack, 217, 218, 267, 278, 418, 487 (n. 36)

"Cradle of Texas Liberty" (pamphlet, Lambert), 37

Craft, Juanita, 374

Crossland, John, 114

Cruz, Lauro, 405

Crystal City, 293–307, 311, 346, 354, 363, 374, 390, 396, 404, 411, 419, 475 (nn. 33–34, 42), 476 (nn. 55, 59), 478 (n. 4)

Cuellar, Renato, 376

Cunningham, E. Brice, 340

Cutrer, Lewis, 194, 200

Dallas, 12, 82, 110, 117, 154, 177, 242, 306, 360; 1960 presidential election and, 218, 225, 227; 1963 Democratic Coalition and, 315–19, 375; African Americans and, 107–8, 380; civil rights activism and, 284, 292, 339, 340, 363, 364–65; labor activism, 1930s and, 17–20; *mexicano* labor movement and, 363, 364; NAACP and, 67, 68, 98, 99, 108, 120, 178–79, 226, 322, 327, 363; politics, later 1960s and, 382, 405–6; poll tax repeal possibility and, 357

Dallas AFL-CIO Council, 323, 363, 401

Dallas Chamber of Commerce, 18, 19

Dallas County Council of Organizations for Political Action, 380

Dallas County Democratic Organizing Committee, 179

Dallas Craftsman, 178

Dallas Express, 364, 484 (n. 9)

Dallas Open Shop Association (DOSA), 18–19, 20

Daniel, Franz, 171

Daniel, Price: 1956 gubernatorial primary campaign and, 117, 123; 1956 presidential election and, 118, 215; 1958 gubernatorial race and, 161, 162, 164, 166, 168, 169; 1960 gubernatorial primary and, 218; 1960 presidential election and, 217, 219, 220, 223, 224, 230; 1960 state legislature elections and, 221, 222; 1961 U.S. Senate race and, 242, 246; 1962 gubernatorial race and, 265, 267, 268, 269, 270, 272, 273, 275, 277, 279

Index 517

Davis, Ivory M., 201
Davis, Wendy, 418
Davison, Gerald, 384, 385
Davison, Kermit, 383, 384
Delgado v. Bastrop ISD, 127, 137
DeLoney, Erma. *See* LeRoy, Erma
Democratic Coalition of Texas, 2, 4–6, 8, 407; 1962 gubernatorial race and, 265–74, 275; 1963 general assembly and, 9, 315–19, 322, 478 (n. 4); 1963 reorganization and, 280–85, 331, 413, 474 (nn. 12, 15); 1964 elections and, 367, 375, 376–77, 378–79, 396, 487 (n. 39); 1964 upcoming elections and, 318, 339, 348, 349, 350–52, 357–59, 361, 362, 368, 370–75, 396; Committee on Political Education (COPE) and, 247, 250, 254, 255; Crystal City revolt and, 298–99, 300, 302, 303, 306; early coalitions as forerunners of and, 45, 50, 54, 92, 94, 95, 109, 125, 151, 152–53, 159, 169, 175; founding of, 233, 259; Huntsville movement and, 383–89, 391–92, 393, 395–96; ideology and, 412, 413; Kennedy assassination and, 6, 361, 368–69, 378, 379, 396; legacy and, 397, 408–16, 417, 419; March on Austin and, 339, 340, 343, 345, 346, 347, 348; *mexicano* labor movement and, 362–68, 403, 404, 406; "Policy Committee" and, 308–10, 312, 313, 477 (n. 68); poll tax drive, 1961 and, 259–65, 306; poll tax drive, 1963–64 and, 282–84, 368, 369–71, 377, 480 (n. 42); poll tax repeal possibility and, 349–50, 351–59, 362, 371, 377, 485 (n. 17); voter registration, 1963–64 and, 314, 338, 347, 350–51, 355, 361, 362. *See also* African Americans; Civil rights movement; Democratic Party; Mexican Americans; Political Association of Spanish-Speaking Organizations (PASO); Project VOTE; Texas State AFL-CIO; White liberal Democrats

Democratic National Committee, 117, 118, 124, 160, 215, 217, 219, 222

Democratic National Convention of 1944, 93
Democratic National Convention of 1948, 94
Democratic National Convention of 1952, 151
Democratic National Convention of 1960, 216, 274
Democratic National Convention of 1964, 374–75
Democratic National Convention of 1968, 417
Democratic National Convention of 2008, 3
Democratic Newsletter, 282, 371–72, 375, 377
Democratic Party: 1938, San Antonio and, 35–39, 44; 1938 congressional Democratic primary and, 37–39, 40, 257, 436 (n. 76), 437 (n. 88); 1940 presidential election and, 53, 93; 1944 presidential election and, 93, 109; 1948 presidential election and, 81, 82–83, 85, 94, 99, 109, 147, 188, 444 (nn. 65, 68); 1952 gubernatorial primary campaign and, 112–14, 160, 449 (n. 47); 1952 presidential election and, 109, 114, 130, 151–52, 189; 1954 gubernatorial primary campaign and, 114–17, 121, 160, 234, 274, 449 (n. 47), 458 (n. 13); 1954 state legislature election and, 154–55, 161; 1956 gubernatorial primary campaign and, 117, 157, 160, 449 (n. 47), 458 (n. 13); 1956 presidential election and, 109, 118, 130, 215, 216; 1956 state legislature election and, 155, 156, 157, 160, 168; 1958 gubernatorial race and, 130–31, 160–69, 172, 215, 225, 316, 457 (n. 84); 1960 presidential election and, 195–96, 216, 217–18, 223–31, 232, 239–40, 242, 261, 377, 466 (n. 77), 468 (n. 20); 1960 state legislature election and, 186, 221, 229, 230, 242; 1962 gubernatorial race and, 233, 276–77, 278–79, 330–31, 471–72 (n. 62); 1962 upcoming elections and, 246–50, 253–54, 259–65, 469 (n. 37), 470 (n. 43); 1964 guber-

518 Index

natorial race and, 375, 377, 378; 1964 presidential election and, 369, 376, 377, 378, 379, 396, 487 (n. 39); 2008 presidential election and, 3–4, 417, 418; 2012 presidential election and, 4, 418; 2014 gubernatorial race and, 418; 2016 presidential campaign and, 420; African Americans and, 10, 56, 65–66, 79–80, 81, 83, 443 (n. 55); civil rights unionism and, 64–65, 80–81; future coalitions and, 417–21; Mexican Americans and, 127–28, 130, 147, 156, 172, 221; Mexican immigrant rights and, 419–20; *mexicanos* and, 149–52, 153; multi-racial coalition and, 186, 189, 192–93, 215, 218–24, 229–31, 234, 239, 246, 247–59, 469 (n. 37), 470 (n. 41); patronage and, 217, 265–66, 267, 268; segregation and, 147, 162–63, 456 (n. 72); social equality for all and, 420–21; "Texas two-step" and, 3, 115, 417, 420; white conservatives and, 93–94, 116–18, 152, 217, 218, 246, 256, 257, 271, 279, 285, 361, 417; "white primary" and, 44, 45, 48, 56, 64–66, 67, 68–70, 72, 73, 82, 84, 85, 107, 108, 119, 121, 226, 231; white supremacists and, 65, 80, 86, 94, 108, 195. *See also* Democratic Coalition of Texas; Democrats of Texas (DOT); Harris County Democrats (HCD); Loyal American Democrats (LAD); Texas Organization of Liberal Democrats (TOLD); U.S. Senate; White liberal Democrats

Democratic Women, 155, 164

Democrats of Texas (DOT), 111; 1958 gubernatorial race and, 160, 161, 162, 163–69; 1960 presidential election and, 216, 217–18, 219, 220–21, 222, 231, 274; 1961 U.S. Senate race and, 232, 243, 244, 245; African Americans and, 118, 121, 162, 167, 228, 229, 456 (n. 77); becoming multi-racial and, 215, 246–47, 248, 250; founding of, 118–19, 131, 158, 189; Mexican Americans and, 118, 162, 165–66, 167, 172, 191, 192, 257; white liberals and, 118, 162–63, 167, 168, 170, 216, 223, 252, 259, 310, 316, 356, 456 (n. 77). *See also* Harris County Democrats (HCD); White liberal Democrats

Desegregation, 82; armed forces and, 83, 142; buses/bus/train stations, 122, 197, 198–99, 200; Democratic Coalition of Texas and, 284–85, 318–19, 331; federal laws and, 319–20, 378, 396; higher education and, 319–20; labor movement and, 173–75, 284; movie theaters and, 207, 284, 285; public facilities and, 138, 157, 158, 200, 202, 212, 213, 327, 378, 462–63 (n. 18); restaurants and, 203, 204, 212, 284, 285, 386, 388; schools and, 98, 99, 102–3, 104, 120, 128, 284, 341; sit-ins and, 194, 195, 203; voluntary and, 342, 346. *See also* Civil rights movement; Segregation

DeWitty, Arthur, 487 (n. 48); 1963 Democratic Coalition and, 281, 282, 311–12, 316, 331, 474 (n. 12), 478 (n. 4); civil rights activism and, 328; poll tax repeal possibility and, 352, 353, 354, 483 (n. 79)

Dickens, Andrew, 294, 295

Dickie, Alex, 220, 221, 222

Dies, Martin, 93, 94, 95, 123, 124

Dixie, Christian, 118, 130, 449 (n. 47); 1952 gubernatorial primary campaign and, 113–15, 116; 1963 Democratic Coalition and, 280, 308, 313, 315, 372; 1964 post-election Democratic Coalition and, 380, 382, 390, 391, 392, 487 (n. 48); Democrats of Texas (DOT) and, 111, 131, 165, 243; Harris County Democrats (HCD) and, 111, 122, 123, 124, 131, 215, 372; labor movement, 1930s and, 110–11, 112; multi-racial coalition and, 247, 248, 249, 250, 258, 259, 469 (n. 37)

Dixie, Katie, 114

Dobie, J. Frank, 82

Donahue, William "Bill," 204–6, 208, 209, 211, 212, 213, 285–86

Dubinsky, David, 48, 185, 439 (n. 111), 459 (n. 31)

Index   519

Dugger, Ronnie: 1963 Democratic Coalition and, 312, 313, 315, 316–17, 476 (n. 55); 1964 post-election Democratic Coalition and, 381, 390–92, 395; 1964 upcoming elections and, 348, 373, 374; Crystal City revolt and, 303, 476 (n. 55); PASO and, 267, 303, 476 (n. 55); poll tax repeal possibility and, 356, 358; United Political Organization (UPO) and, 292–93, 346; U.S. Senate campaign and, 382–83
Duncan, Raymond, 101, 194–95
Durham, W. J.: 1963 Democratic Coalition and, 308, 313, 315, 316, 318, 319, 331, 348, 365, 477 (n. 68); 1964 post-election Democratic Coalition and, 379–80; 1964 upcoming elections and, 372, 376; civil rights activism and, 1, 71, 345, 346–47, 348, 373; Democrats of Texas (DOT) and, 165, 167, 456 (n. 77); NAACP and, 67–68, 98, 99, 108, 162, 164, 179, 226

Eckhardt, Bob, 124, 435 (n. 47)
Eichler, George, 180, 181, 183–84, 185–86
Eisenhower, Dwight D., 109, 114, 118, 130, 152, 215
Elizondo, Roy, 225, 478 (n. 4)
Ellinger, Don, 247, 250
Elliott, Bill, 101, 291, 474 (n. 28)
El Paso, 65, 178, 218, 294, 362
Escobar, Eleuterio, 135, 454 (n. 36)
Evans, Roy R., 239, 390; 1963 Democratic Coalition and, 477 (n. 68), 478 (n. 4); 1964 upcoming elections and, 372, 373; civil rights activism and, 322, 323, 325–26, 327, 328; *mexicano* labor movement and, 334, 335–36, 338, 366, 367, 368; poll tax repeal possibility and, 355
Everett, Freeman, 75–76, 77, 78, 93, 100–101, 442 (n. 49)
Evers, Medgar, 320, 322
Executive Order 8802, 74

Fairchild, Euretta, 141
Fair Labor Standards Act of 1938, 42

Fath, Creekmore, 112, 113, 164–65, 167, 220, 222
Federation for the Advancement of the Mexican American, 406
FEPC (Fair Employment Practices Committee). *See* Committee on Fair Employment Practices (FEPC)
Fifteenth Amendment, 64, 70, 71
Ford, Jon, 332, 333, 348, 349
Ford Motor Company, 18–20
Fort Sam Houston, 38
Fort Worth, 49, 80, 177, 243, 260, 262, 296, 316, 379, 487 (n. 46); 1960 presidential election and, 225, 231; 1962 gubernatorial race and, 271; 1964 upcoming elections and, 375; African Americans, labor movement and, 82, 91–92, 173; civil rights activism and, 344; Democratic Party and, 117–18; *mexicano* labor movement and, 363, 364; poll tax repeal possibility and, 357; segregation and, 76; United Packinghouse Workers of America (UPWA) and, 91–92, 173, 225, 323
Fourteenth Amendment, 71
Freedom in Action (FIA), 217, 218, 222, 418, 487 (n. 36)
Freedom Now Committee, 342–43
Freedom Summer, 383
Freight Handlers Local 6051 (BSRC), 104
Friedman, Kinky, 420
Friedrich Refrigerator, 173–74, 193
Fuentes, Albert, 158, 225, 468 (n. 22), 477 (n. 68); Crystal City revolt and, 297, 298–99, 300, 305; PASO and, 303, 306, 353, 372, 382; political office and, 372, 373, 375; poll tax repeal possibility and, 353–54, 483 (n. 79)

Galveston, 95, 196, 239, 358
Garcia, Franklin, 225, 258, 414, 468 (nn. 22–23); *mexicano* labor movement and, 336, 338, 367, 407, 410, 415, 483–84 (n. 3); PASO and, 256, 269, 306, 363
Garcia, Gilbert, 225, 260, 262–65, 266, 269, 283, 306

Garcia, Gustavo C. "Gus," 139, 151, 169, 170, 230; *mexicano* civil rights activism and, 127, 454 (n. 36); political office and, 133, 134, 135–37, 140, 145, 147, 149, 452 (n. 7)
Garcia, Hector P., 151, 235, 241, 467 (n. 6); 1960 presidential election and, 224, 225; *mexicano* civil rights activism and, 126, 127, 128, 147–48, 216–17, 262; *mexicano* labor movement and, 399–400; PASO and, 242, 245–46, 269, 277, 304, 305–6, 414, 476 (n. 62)
Garcia, J. O. "Pepper," 256, 257, 363, 364, 365, 410, 414, 478 (n. 4)
Garcia, Mario T., 135
Garcia, Martin, 414, 478 (n. 4); Crystal City revolt and, 295, 296, 297, 299, 300, 303, 305; PASO and, 306, 346, 352; poll tax repeal possibility and, 353, 354
Garcia, Willie, 38
Garner, John Nance, 53
G.I. Bill, 126, 147
Goldwater, Barry, 376, 377
Gomez, Robert, 212
Gonzalez, Gus, 375
Gonzalez, Henry B., 279, 288, 306, 459–60 (n. 32), 487 (n. 48); 1950 state legislature election and, 153–54, 155, 156; 1953 San Antonio city council election and, 154, 167–68, 453 (n. 12); 1955 San Antonio city council reelection and, 154, 168; 1956 state legislature election and, 155, 156, 157, 160, 168; 1958 gubernatorial race and, 130–31, 160–69, 172, 215, 225, 316, 457 (n. 84); 1960 presidential election and, 223, 226; 1960 state legislature reelection and, 186, 221, 229, 230, 242; 1961 U.S. congressional race and, 186, 257–58, 271; 1961 U.S. Senate race and, 232, 233, 242–45, 246, 257, 468 (n. 25); 1962 gubernatorial race and, 270–71, 272; 1962 U.S. congressional reelection and, 271, 278; African-American support and, 159, 160; black civil rights activism and, 157–58, 160, 170, 273, 281, 340,

341, 360; *mexicano* civil rights activism and, 240, 335, 338; *mexicano* labor movement and, 402
Good Government League (GGL): Mexican Americans and, 140, 145, 147, 150; San Antonio, 1950s and, 140, 154, 155, 453 (n. 12); San Antonio, 1960s and, 230, 246, 285, 287, 288, 289, 290, 293, 367, 372
Goodwyn, Larry, 279; 1963 Democratic Coalition and, 280, 281–82, 283, 309, 311–12, 313, 315, 346, 353, 477 (n. 68); 1964 post-election Democratic Coalition and, 381–82, 383, 392–95, 396, 487 (n. 48); 1964 upcoming elections and, 357–59, 368, 376; Crystal City revolt and, 300–301, 303; Huntsville movement and, 386, 387; poll tax repeal possibility and, 353, 354, 355, 358–59, 483 (n. 79)
Gould, Jay, 18
Grace, Charlie, 186
Graves, Curtis, 405
Great Depression, 12, 22, 27, 30, 35, 45, 66
Greater Fifth Ward Citizens League (Houston), 100
Grovey, Richard Randolph "R. R.," 65, 66, 67, 68, 69, 70, 72, 85, 121, 122, 444 (n. 68)
Grovey v. Townsend, 65, 68, 78
Gutiérrez, José Ángel, 299

Hall, Robert E. "Bob," 113, 119, 120–21, 122, 403, 449 (n. 47), 450 (n. 62)
Hall, Walter, 164
Handy Andy stores, 205–6, 209, 219, 285
Harris, Herb, 17, 19
Harris, Ruth, 174
Harris County AFL-CIO, 109, 117, 405
Harris County Council of Organizations (HCCO), 88, 99–104, 108, 115, 130, 405, 446 (n. 20), 447 (n. 23); 1960 presidential election and, 226; 1961 U.S. Senate race and, 244, 246; 1962 gubernatorial race and, 271, 272; 1963 Democratic Coalition and, 308,

Harris County Council of Organizations (HCCO) (*continued*) 319; civil rights activism and, 103, 131, 195, 196, 197, 198–99, 200–201, 202, 292, 293, 346, 448 (n. 30), 462 (n. 9); founding of, 87, 99, 100, 414, 445 (n. 1), 446–47 (n. 22); Harris County Democrats (HCD) and, 117, 121–23, 124; Mexican Americans and, 128, 129; multi-racial coalition and, 109, 125; political patronage and, 291; poll tax repeal possibility and, 356; women and, 106–7

Harris County Democrats (HCD), 87, 111, 117–18, 151, 158, 218, 412; 1954 gubernatorial primary campaign and, 114–16; 1958 gubernatorial race and, 162, 163; 1963 Democratic Coalition and, 308; African Americans and, 131–32, 353, 372, 378, 401; becoming multi-racial and, 117, 215, 247, 291; Harris County Council of Organizations (HCCO) and, 117, 121–23, 124; Mexican Americans and, 125, 128, 129, 130, 131–32, 214–15. *See also* White liberal Democrats

Harris County Negro Democratic Club, 64, 65, 66

Hasgett, Sidney, 67, 68, 69, 82, 85, 444 (n. 68)

Hasgett case, 68, 69, 72, 78

Hays, Lee, 177

Henderson, Donald, 23, 40, 436 (n. 72)

Henry, F. T., 100, 445 (n. 1), 446–47 (n. 22)

Hernandez, Alfred, 401

Hernandez v. Texas, 127, 128, 149

Herrera, John J., 124–25, 126, 127–29, 130, 131, 167, 225

"Hey you." *See* Huntsville Action for Youth (HA-YOU)

Higher education, 70, 71–73, 78, 84–85, 96, 319–20, 341

Highlander Folk School, 16

Hightower, Jim, 408

Hill, Herbert, 201

Hilliard, Sid, 100, 102, 446–47 (n. 22)

Hilton, Hollis, 210–11

Hod Carriers and Common Laborers (HCCL) Local 18, 73, 75, 76, 77, 100, 101, 193, 199, 252, 291, 321, 323

Hoffa, Jimmy, 295–96, 304

Holleman, Jerry R., 189, 224, 227, 233, 234, 235, 236–38, 251, 466–67 (n. 4)

Homestead Strike of 1892, 188

House Un-American Activities Committee (HUAC), 93, 100

Housing Act of 1949, 144

Houston, 417; 1960 presidential election and, 218, 225, 226; 1964 upcoming elections and, 370, 372; civil rights activism and, 194, 195, 196–97, 198–202, 210, 213–14, 251, 290–93, 339, 342, 463 (n. 20), 481 (n. 57); Mexican-American politics, 1950s and, 87–88, 89, 124–32, 167; Mexican-American politics, 1960s and, 241, 414, 468 (n. 23); *mexicano* labor movement and, 399, 401; *mexicanos*, 1930s and, 58; oil industry and, 57–58, 74, 111; politics, 1950s and, 109–10, 111, 112–14, 120; politics, later 1940s and, 79–80, 81–86, 89, 112; politics, later 1960s and, 404–5; poll tax repeal possibility and, 353, 356, 357, 358, 483 (n. 87); racism and, 60–61, 62, 63, 66, 78; wards and neighborhoods and, 88, 167. *See also* African Americans; Houston NAACP; Labor movement

Houston College for Negroes, 143. *See also* Texas Southern University (TSU)

Houston NAACP: civil rights activism and, 103, 109, 197, 198, 200, 292, 342, 462 (n. 9); civil rights unionism and, 57, 67, 69, 70, 73, 74, 78, 79, 85, 87, 98, 99, 106, 202; Communist Party and, 90, 95, 96–98, 100, 112, 446 (n. 17); founding of, 71, 82; growth, 1930s and, 58, 66–68; higher education segregation and, 72–73, 84; labor movement, 1940s and, 56, 446–47 (n. 22); Progressive Party and, 81–82, 83, 443 (n. 60); voting rights and, 64, 69, 72, 80; white liberal Democrats and, 114, 122, 123; women's rights and, 77, 107

Houston Port Commission, 405
Houston Ship Channel, 57–58, 125, 194
Houston Sit-in Foundation, 202, 463 (n. 20)
Hudspeth, Charles, 206
Huerta, Dolores, 398
Hughes Tool Company, 20, 201, 445 (n. 1), 446–47 (n. 22)
Humphrey, Hubert H., 376
Huntsville, 362, 383–89, 391, 393, 395, 400
Huntsville Action for Youth (HA-YOU), 384–88, 389, 400, 401
Huston-Tillotson College, 329, 333

Idar, Ed, Jr., 225, 230, 234, 235, 238, 241, 257, 262, 266–68, 269, 306, 414, 468 (n. 22)
ILA Local 872, 75, 76, 77, 100, 101
ILA Local 1273, 76
Informer, 77, 84–85, 105
Inman, John, 46, 47, 48, 82
Integration. *See* Desegregation
International Brotherhood of Electrical Workers Local 60, 360
International Ladies' Garment Workers' Union (ILGWU), 19, 258, 323; Maverick, Fontaine Maury and, 48, 53, 439 (n. 111); Tex-Son strike and, 175–76, 179–80, 182, 183, 184, 185, 186, 187, 459 (n. 31)
International Longshoremen's Association (ILA), 58, 75, 76–77, 100, 194, 440 (n. 5)
International Union of Electrical, Machine, and Radio Workers (IUE), 173–75, 193, 407
IUE Local 780, 174, 175, 193

Jack Yates High School, 62, 63
James, H. Rhett, 272, 292, 347–48, 349, 380
James, Samuel H., 290
Javior, Paul, 174, 193, 407
Jeffers, Leroy, 49, 50, 439 (n. 107)
Jim Crow, 16, 331, 340, 347, 409, 416; early twentieth century and, 10–12; federal laws and, 320, 396; Houston, 1950s and 1960s and, 107, 109, 197; Houston, early 1940s and, 56–57, 70; labor movement, 1930s and, 58–59, 60; labor movement, 1950s and, 91, 104; Mexican Americans and, 129–30, 253, 273; *mexicanos* and, 126, 253, 470 (n. 45); multi-racial coalition and, 2, 6, 8, 139, 253, 262, 313; San Antonio and, 45, 46, 134, 138–39, 145, 211; voting rights and, 65–66, 85–86, 119. *See also* African Americans; Civil rights movement; Juan Crow; Segregation
Johnson, Beverly, 204–6
Johnson, Lyndon B., 80; 1948 election to U.S. Senate and, 127, 216, 230; 1956 presidential election and, 118, 215, 216; 1960 presidential election and, 223–24, 226, 230, 233, 243; 1960 presidential primary election and, 216, 217–23, 242, 274; 1962 Connally gubernatorial race and, 265, 267, 271, 272, 273; 1964 reelection and, 369, 376, 377, 378, 379, 396, 487 (n. 39); 1964 upcoming elections and, 361, 371, 373, 375, 380; Democratic Party in Texas and, 218–23, 224, 238, 274; Mexican Americans and, 126, 216–17, 221, 258, 267; as President and, 7, 360–61, 363, 369, 375–76, 389, 390; as U.S. senator and, 123, 126, 215, 216, 243, 251; vacating U.S. Senate seat and, 232, 242
Jones, Franklin, 318, 373, 376, 377, 380, 381
Jones, Lyman, 255–56, 370–71, 483 (n. 79)
Jordan, Barbara, 84, 319, 353, 356, 370, 372, 375, 401, 402, 405, 487 (n. 48)
Joske's department stores, 182, 183, 204, 207, 209, 210, 211
Juan Crow, 12, 125, 293, 302, 396, 404, 409; multi-racial coalition and, 2, 6, 8, 139, 253, 254, 262, 313

Kazen, Abraham, 158
Kennedy, Edward M. "Ted," 402–3

Index   523

Kennedy, John F., 233, 246, 247, 250, 251, 257, 271, 273; 1960 presidential election and, 223–25, 230–31, 232, 238, 239, 377, 466 (n. 77); assassination and, 6, 359, 360, 368, 370, 378, 379, 396; civil rights and, 7, 224, 229, 244, 265, 319–20, 322, 324, 326–27, 342, 349, 360–61, 369, 375; March on Austin and, 1, 6, 344; Mexican Americans and, 156, 224–26, 229, 231, 239–40, 306, 336

Kennedy, Robert F., 225, 302

Kilday, Owen, 25–26, 28, 37, 39, 53

Kilday, Paul, 37, 38, 39, 48, 53, 257

Kilgore, Joe, 336

King, Hamah, 292

King, Martin Luther, Jr., 7, 229, 356–57, 364, 385

Knight, Jimmie, 218, 219

Koger, Harry, 82

Ku Klux Klan, 52–53, 66, 89, 197, 321

Labor League for Political Education, 188

Labor movement: 1930s and, 14–21, 110–11, 112, 435 (n. 47); 1960s and, 233–35, 238; civil rights activism and, 5, 7–8, 9, 194, 196, 198–99, 201–2, 210–11, 212–13, 281, 320–26, 327–28, 462 (n. 9); collective bargaining and, 21, 36, 58–59, 71, 91, 111, 190, 325; Communist Party and, 88–89, 92, 173, 445 (n. 3); desegregation and, 173–75, 284; equal rights employment and, 74, 105, 201, 233, 284, 320, 321, 322, 324–25, 403, 406, 408; Houston, 1930s and, 13, 20, 57, 58–59, 60, 61–62, 194–95, 196; Houston, 1950s and, 99–102, 104–6, 107, 114, 128–29, 182; Houston, 1960s and, 200–202, 210, 226–29, 291, 292, 391, 399, 401; Houston, early 1940s and, 56–57, 63–64, 71, 111–12, 446–47 (n. 22); Houston, later 1940s and, 74–79, 87, 414; multi-racial coalition and, 4–6, 8, 9, 92; right-to-work laws and, 5, 81, 89, 219, 275, 276, 349, 373; segregation, 1930s and, 58, 60, 66, 68, 69, 127; segregation, 1940s and, 71, 74–79, 111–12; segregation, 1950s and, 91–93, 96, 104–6, 172–75, 190; segregation, 1960s and, 194, 201, 405; white women and, 15, 19, 114, 248, 254–55, 449 (n. 49); women workers and, 77–78, 324–25. *See also* AFL-CIO (American Federation of Labor-Congress of Industrial Organizations); African Americans; American Federation of Labor (AFL); Civil rights unionism; Congress of Industrial Organizations (CIO); Mexican Americans; *Mexicanas*; *Mexicanos*; San Antonio; San Antonio pecan shellers; Texas State AFL-CIO; Texas State Federation of Labor (TSFL)

Labor's Non-Partisan League (LNPL), 38, 39, 48, 69, 439 (n. 111)

La Casita Farms, 398

La Liga Pro Defensor Escolar (the School Improvement League). *See* School Improvement League (La Liga Pro Defensor Escolar)

Lambert, David Lee, 177

Lambert, George P., 14–18, 19, 82, 86, 118, 178–81, 258, 337; civil rights activism and, 323, 324; labor layoffs, 1930s San Antonio and, 41–43, 48; Lambert, Latane Bartlett and, 31–34, 40, 41, 42, 49, 436 (n. 72), 477 (n. 68); multi-racial coalition and, 50, 54, 193, 220, 222; NAACP and, 120, 154, 178–79; pecan shellers strike, San Antonio and, 20–21, 23–25, 26–27, 28, 29, 34, 458 (n. 19); politics, 1930s and, 38–40, 48, 49–50, 436 (n. 76), 439 (n. 111); politics, 1950s and, 120, 458 (n. 13); Tex-Son strike and, 176–77, 179–81, 182–85, 186, 187, 193, 458 (n. 19), 459 (n. 31), 459–60 (n. 32); UCAPAWA and, 23, 32, 33, 40, 436 (n. 72); writings and, 20, 29, 34, 37, 52–53, 435 (n. 47)

Lambert, Latane Bartlett, 29–32, 39–40, 48, 86, 118; 1963 Democratic Coalition and, 280, 353, 364, 365, 415–16, 477 (n. 68); 1964 post-election Democratic Coalition and, 403, 487 (n. 48), 488

(n. 62); labor movement and, 177–78, 337; Lambert, George P. and, 31–34, 40, 41, 42, 49, 436 (n. 72), 477 (n. 68); multi-racial coalition and, 50, 54, 220, 222, 459–60 (n. 32); NAACP and, 120, 179; politics, 1960s and, 230, 258, 375, 376, 380; poll tax repeal possibility and, 353, 354, 415–16; Tex-Son strike and, 176–77, 180, 186

Landrum-Griffin Act, 182

La pasionara. See Tenayuca, Emma

La Raza Unida (The United People's) Party, 406

Laredo, 241, 256, 257, 262, 264, 272, 295, 304, 334–39, 362

Latin American Affairs Convention Committee, 235–37, 238, 295, 334, 335, 336, 338, 362, 367, 403. *See also* Texas State AFL-CIO

Laws, Clarence, 322, 327, 392

League of United Latin American Citizens (LULAC), 217, 225, 241; civil rights activism and, 127, 128, 130, 135, 148–49; conservative reputation and, 28, 48–49, 125–26, 129–30, 131; Council 2 (San Antonio) and, 149, 155, 258, 366; Council 60 (Houston) and, 125, 126, 225; *mexicano* labor movement and, 401; multi-racial coalition and, 363, 367; politics, 1950s and, 154, 234

League of Women Voters, 114, 354–55

Leal, E. P., 130

Leo, Leo J., 304, 305, 476 (nn. 58, 62)

LeRoy, Erma, 86, 100, 130, 265–66, 291, 403, 440 (n.13), 470–71 (n. 52); 1960 presidential election and, 226–29, 231, 261; 1961 U.S. Senate race and, 244, 261; 1962 gubernatorial race and, 272, 273; 1963 Democratic Coalition and, 316, 319, 374, 415–16; civil rights activism and, 198, 202, 346, 348, 378, 409, 413, 463 (n. 20); civil rights unionism and, 70, 79, 85, 99, 108, 196, 414; HCCO and, 131, 414; Houston NAACP and, 73, 77, 78, 97, 98, 106, 107, 198; LeRoy, Moses and, 62–63; multi-racial coalition and, 246, 247, 249, 252; political office and, 83–84, 87; poll tax drives, 226–29, 255, 260–62, 264, 266, 283, 369, 415–16; poll tax repeal possibility and, 353, 354; Progressive Party and, 81, 444 (n. 68); voting rights and, 80, 108–9; white liberal Democrats and, 114, 118, 120, 122–23

LeRoy, Moses, 59–64, 86, 130, 329, 462 (n. 10); 1963 Democratic Coalition and, 299, 316, 319, 331, 478 (n. 4); 1964 post-election Democratic Coalition and, 391, 393–94; 1964 upcoming elections and, 372, 374; civil rights activism and, 198–99, 201–2, 214, 253, 291–92, 321, 348, 378, 391, 409, 413, 462 (nn. 9, 11); civil rights unionism and, 60, 67, 70, 74–79, 85, 87, 99, 106, 108, 195, 196, 202, 414; HCCO and, 99–109, 131, 198, 200, 414, 445 (n. 1), 446–47 (n. 22), 447 (n. 23); Houston NAACP and, 73, 79, 98, 107, 198, 200, 462 (n. 9); labor movement, Houston, 1950s and, 104–6, 107; labor movement, Houston, 1960s and, 226–27; March on Austin and, 344, 345, 346; *mexicano* labor movement and, 399, 401; multi-racial coalition and, 247, 249, 250, 252, 253, 255, 264, 419; political office and, 79, 405; Progressive Party and, 81, 82, 83, 444 (n. 68); voting rights and, 66, 68, 69, 80, 108–9; white liberal Democrats and, 114, 118, 120, 122–23

Lewis, John L., 188, 189

Littlefield, Clarence "C. J.," 407

Logan, Rayford, 62, 63

Longoria, Felix, 126, 216

Longshoremen's Local 872, 194, 199. *See also* International Longshoremen's Association (ILA)

Lopez, David T., 306, 476 (n. 62)

Los cinco candidatos, 293–94, 297–98, 299, 300, 301–2, 303, 304, 363, 475 (n. 42)

Lower Rio Grande Valley Central Labor Council, 337

Index   525

Loyal American Democrats (LAD), 149–50, 151, 152, 153, 154, 167–68, 172, 223, 454 (n. 37)
Lucas, Albert A., 67, 69
Luter, Joseph, 203, 205–6

Maldonado, Willie, 149, 453–54 (n. 35)
Mandell, Arthur, 82, 90, 95, 97, 111, 112, 445 (n. 3)
Mangus, C. L., 360, 361
Manpower Development and Training Act (MDTA) of 1962, 366
March on Austin, 1–2, 6, 334, 339–49, 350, 374, 391, 416, 481 (n. 57)
March on Washington, 1, 334, 342, 343, 344, 348, 363, 374, 481 (n. 57)
March on Washington Movement, 74
Marshall, Thurgood, 67, 68, 69, 71
Martin, Jack, 221, 223, 236, 478 (n. 4)
Martin, Trayvon, 419
Mason, Kenneth, 46, 47
Maverick, Fontaine Maury, 46, 192; 1938 congressional Democratic primary and, 37–39, 40, 257, 436 (n. 76), 437 (n. 88); 1939 San Antonio mayoral campaign and, 43–45, 47–50, 82, 439 (nn. 107, 109, 111); 1941 San Antonio mayoral reelection campaign and, 53–54; death and, 154; Mexican Americans and, 152, 153; pecan shellers strike, 1938 and, 34, 36, 38; politics, 1950s and, 109, 113, 120, 189; San Antonio, 1930s and, 35–40, 133, 134; as San Antonio mayor and, 50–53, 54, 55, 109, 151, 439 (n. 111); white liberal Democrats and, 80, 93, 113, 120, 150, 171, 189
Maverick, Maury, Jr., 120, 171; 1950 state legislature election and, 154, 161; 1954 state legislature election and, 154–55, 161; 1960 presidential election and, 221–22; 1961 U.S. Senate race and, 232, 233, 242–45, 246, 257, 468 (n. 25); multi-racial coalition and, 247, 258, 420
Maverick, Samuel Augustus, 34–35
McAllen, 140, 235, 257, 262, 304

McAllister, W. W., 287, 289
McCain, John, 417
McCormick, Carlos, 224–25
McCoy, Ruth Bellinger. *See* Bellinger, Ruth
McGovern, George, 3, 431 (n. 4)
McGovern Commission, 417
McLellan, Andrew C., 234–35, 466–67 (n. 4)
Mease, Quentin, 199, 462 (n. 10), 462–63 (n. 18)
Medrano, Francisco F. "Pancho," 225, 256, 363–65, 367, 398, 402, 405–6, 410, 414, 415, 484 (n. 9)
Medrano, Pauline, 406
Medrano v. Allee, 403
Mexican-American Political Association (MAPA), 241–42, 243, 468 (nn. 22–23). *See also* Political Association of Spanish-Speaking Organizations (PASO)
Mexican Americans: 1954 gubernatorial primary campaign and, 116; 1958 gubernatorial race and, 160–69; 1960 presidential election and, 217, 224–26, 229, 230, 231, 233, 238, 239–40, 468 (n. 20); 1961 U.S. Senate race and, 232–33, 243; 1962 gubernatorial race and, 266–71, 273, 275, 276–77, 279, 473 (n. 9); 1962 upcoming elections and, 262–65; 1963 Democratic Coalition and, 307, 309, 311, 314, 315, 334, 338, 477 (n. 71); 1964 elections and, 378, 487 (n. 39); 1964 post-election Democratic Coalition and, 382, 383; 2008/2012 presidential elections and, 3–4; African-American support and, 46, 128, 130, 133, 134–37, 139, 152–54, 157–59, 160, 169, 243–44; black civil rights activism and, 1–2, 128, 157, 160, 170, 195, 203, 206–9, 213, 221, 224, 273, 281, 344; civil rights activism and, 7, 8–9, 125, 126, 127–28, 137, 139, 192, 216–17, 235, 236, 396, 410, 414, 430–31 (n. 2); Democratic Party and, 127–28, 130, 147, 156, 172, 221; discrimination and, 119–20, 125, 126, 129;

Houston politics, 1950s and, 87–88, 89, 124–32, 167; Houston politics, 1960s and, 241, 414, 468 (n. 23); Jim Crow and, 129–30, 253, 273; labor movement, 1950s and, 234–38, 239; labor movement, 1960s and, 295–96; middle class and, 22, 28, 48–49, 140, 302, 304, 305, 365, 407, 410; multi-racial coalition and, 250–51, 256–57, 267–68, 277, 279–80, 470 (n. 43); political office and, 128–29, 130–31, 133, 134–37, 153–54, 157, 160, 171–72, 370, 454 (n. 36); political patronage and, 250, 255–56, 265–66, 267, 268; politics, 1970s and, 3, 431 (n. 4); poll tax repeal possibility and, 351–58; Republican Party and, 4, 130, 258, 382; San Antonio, politics, 1950s and, 145–58, 161, 167–68, 454 (n. 36); San Antonio, politics, 1960s and, 239–42, 250, 258; San Antonio, politics later 1940s and, 134; Sánchez mission statement about, 240–41, 250, 266–67, 268, 280, 281, 412–13; veterans and, 94, 126; voting rights and, 128, 167, 404; as white and, 126, 129, 165–66, 253, 456 (n. 79), 470 (n. 45); white liberal Democrats and, 118, 119, 150, 151, 152, 157, 162, 165–66, 167, 170, 172, 191, 192, 257. *See also* Gonzalez, Henry B.; Juan Crow; *Mexicanos*; Political Association of Spanish-Speaking Organizations (PASO)

Mexican American Unity Council, 406

Mexicanas, 430–31 (n. 2); labor movement, 1950s and, 92, 171, 173, 174, 175–76, 180, 181, 184, 185–86, 187; labor movement, Dallas, 1930s and, 19; pecan shellers strike, 1938 and, 22–24, 27, 36

"Mexican-Dixon Line," 362, 483–84 (n. 3)

Mexican immigrants, 12, 22, 26, 27, 234, 235, 430–31 (n. 2), 467 (n. 10); Houston and, 58, 125; immigrant rights and, 419–20; Mexican "commuters" and, 236, 237, 241, 295, 307, 325–26, 334, 336, 338

Mexicanos, 86, 430–31 (n. 2), 440 (n. 5); African-American support and, 399, 400, 454 (n. 48); civil rights activism and, 127, 240, 262, 334–39, 406, 410, 454 (n. 36); Democratic Party and, 149–52, 153; Houston, 1930s and, 58; Houston, labor movement, 1960s and, 399, 401; Houston politics, 1950s and, 124–32, 451 (n. 76), 451–52 (n. 77); Jim Crow and, 126, 253, 470 (n. 45); labor movement, 1950s and, 149, 190; labor movement, 1960s and, 294–95, 299–300, 361–68, 398–404, 406, 415, 483–84 (n. 3), 485 (n. 13); migrant farmworkers and, 7, 12, 22, 23, 24, 27, 237, 295–96, 300, 334, 366, 398–404, 406, 475 (n. 33); police brutality and, 25–26, 29, 298, 301–2, 398, 402, 403, 404; politics, 1930s and, 25, 38–39, 43, 48, 49–50, 51; politics, 1960s and, 286, 293–95, 296–302, 313; San Antonio, 1930s and, 21–22, 25, 33, 34, 37, 38, 39, 40–43, 51, 55; San Antonio, 1950s and, 147, 170, 171, 173–75; San Antonio, early 1940s and, 53–54; segregated schools and, 148–49, 453–54 (n. 35); voting rights and, 12, 25, 37, 38, 167, 169. *See also* Juan Crow; Mexican Americans; San Antonio pecan shellers

Mexican Workers Confederation (CTM). *See* Confederación de Trabajadores Mexicanos (CTM)

Middleton, Howard, Jr., 199, 202, 291, 405, 474 (n. 28)

Middleton, J. E. "Jimmie," 101, 102, 199, 202, 252, 291, 323, 324

Minute Women, 95, 100

Mississippi, 320, 327, 384, 395, 443 (n. 55)

Mississippi Freedom Democratic Party, 376

Mitchell, H. L., 16

Model (Cities) Neighborhood Residents Commission, 405

Montalbo, Gregoria, 180, 184, 185, 459 (n. 31)

Montemayor, Paul, 166, 268–70, 321, 336, 367, 403, 414, 467 (n. 10), 468 (n. 23)
Montez, Eddie, 271, 272
Montgomery, Bob, 110, 111
Moon, H. A., 324, 382
Moore, Carlos, 296, 299, 363, 475 (n. 42)
Morehouse College, 17, 142
Moreno, Luisa, 32, 33
Morris, Willie, 249, 465 (n. 55), 470 (n. 41)
Mother Is On Strike (film), 180
Mullinax, Otto, 217
Munguia, Ruben, 150, 151, 155, 454 (n. 37)
Muñoz, Henry, Jr., 354; 1963 Democratic Coalition and, 365–67; 1964 post-election Democratic Coalition and, 487 (n. 48); black civil rights activism and, 345, 346; civil rights activism and, 1–2, 340, 368; Crystal City revolt and, 295–97, 299–300, 301, 303, 475 (n. 42); *mexicano* labor movement and, 362–63, 403, 414, 485 (n. 13)

NAACP Legal Defense Fund (LDF), 67, 71
Nation, 20, 29, 34, 37, 52–53
National Alliance of Postal Employees (NAPE), 71, 72–73, 77, 78, 82, 101, 138
National Association for the Advancement of Colored People (NAACP), 17, 83, 121, 332, 392; 1963 Democratic Coalition and, 281, 316, 474 (n. 12); anti-Communism and, 95, 96–97; civil rights activism, San Antonio 1950s and, 137, 138, 154, 157, 159; civil rights activism, San Antonio, 1960s and, 203–8, 209–10, 212, 286, 287–88, 290, 342; civil rights activism and, 320, 322, 327, 328, 344, 363, 383, 385, 386; Dallas and, 67, 68, 98, 99, 108, 120, 178–79, 226, 322, 327, 363; equal rights employment and, 201, 204–6, 209–10; Mexican-American partnership and, 158, 159, 160, 363, 401; San Antonio, 1930s and, 45, 46, 47; San Antonio, 1960s and, 203–8, 209–10, 212, 286, 287–88, 342; San Antonio and, 82, 137, 138, 141, 154, 157, 158, 159; school desegregation and, 98; Texas and, 97–99; voting rights and, 65, 178, 179; white liberal Democrats and, 116, 120, 162, 164, 165; women and, 77, 78. *See also* Houston NAACP; Texas State Conference of Branches of the NAACP
National Farm Workers Association (NFWA), 398, 399, 400
National Labor Relations Act of 1935. *See* Wagner Act of 1935
National Labor Relations Board (NLRB), 20, 111, 174, 201, 210
National Maritime Union (NMU), 90, 97
National Negro Congress (NNC), 47, 52, 438 (n. 95)
Nelson, Eugene, 398
Nelson, George T. "Pop," 68–69, 80, 85, 87, 100, 102, 200, 226, 444 (n. 68), 446–47 (n. 22)
New Deal, 12, 16, 17, 20, 36, 45, 65, 80, 109, 110, 216; San Antonio, 1930s and, 22, 23, 25, 28, 29, 35
Nixon, Richard, 130, 226, 230, 466 (n. 77)
North Carolina, 16, 29–32, 40, 176, 196, 197, 203, 318, 461 (n. 3)

Obama, Barack, 3–4, 417, 418, 420
O'Daniel, W. Lee "Pappy," 80, 81, 89, 93, 95, 161, 169
Oil industry, 57–58, 74, 91, 111, 114, 323
Oil Workers International Union (OWIU-CIO), 111
Oliver, William, 384, 385, 386, 392
"Operation Bootstrap," 362–68, 371, 379, 396, 398, 405, 407, 413, 483–84 (n. 3)
Operation Breadbasket, 400
"Operation Wetback," 234
Organación Regional Interamericana Trabajadores (ORIT; Inter-American Regional Workers' Organization), 235, 466–67 (n. 4)
Organized Voters League (OVL), 137, 151
Oviedo, Telesforo, 26, 28

Pan American Progressive Association (PAPA), 153, 168
Panetta, Rinaldo, 182
Parker, Arthur, 210
Peña, Albert A., Jr., 147–51; 1956 Bexar County Commissioner election and, 155–57, 160, 168; 1956 Gonzalez state legislature election and, 155, 156; 1960 presidential election and, 224–25, 226, 229, 230, 231; 1960 presidential primary election and, 218–19, 221–23, 224; 1961 Gonzalez U.S. Senate race and, 243, 246; 1962 gubernatorial race and, 266, 268, 269, 270–71, 272, 273, 275, 276–77, 278; 1962 PASO and, 266, 268, 269, 270, 271, 272, 273, 275, 276–77, 278, 294, 301; 1962 upcoming elections and, 258, 262, 264; 1963 Democratic Coalition and, 280, 281, 303, 308, 311, 313, 315, 317, 318, 365, 366, 477 (n. 68); 1964 elections and, 375, 378; 1964 upcoming elections and, 372, 376; African-American partnership and, 158, 159, 288; black civil rights activism and, 158, 170, 207, 208, 214–15, 221, 224, 327, 328, 342, 360, 453–54 (n. 35); civil rights activism and, 147–49, 155, 327, 328, 337–38, 340, 346, 349, 373, 382, 406, 410, 411, 414, 487 (n. 46); Crystal City revolt aftermath and, 306, 307, 354; Crystal City revolt and, 294, 297, 298, 302, 304–5, 419, 476 (n. 59); Democrats of Texas (DOT) and, 162, 163, 165–66, 167, 172, 215, 219, 221; labor movement, 1950s and, 171–72, 191–92; MAPA and, 240, 241, 242; *mexicano* labor movement and, 363, 398, 404, 485 (n. 13); multi-racial coalition, 1960s and, 218–19, 220, 221–23, 234, 239, 247, 249, 250, 253, 255, 256–57, 258, 259, 267, 274, 275; multi-racial coalitions, 1950s and, 152–53, 169, 175, 189; PASO and, 242, 250, 256–57, 262, 303, 304, 306, 327, 342, 348, 354, 382, 472 (n. 65); political office and, 153, 154–57, 160, 407; political patronage and, 225, 250, 265–66; politics, 1950s and, 149, 150, 153, 154–57, 161, 167–68, 189, 214–15; politics, 1960s and, 288, 289–90, 417, 468 (n. 22); poll tax repeal possibility and, 354–55, 356, 483 (n. 79); Tex-Son strike and, 176, 181, 184–86, 190, 193, 459–60 (n. 32)
Peña, Olga, 147, 150, 152, 154, 155, 167–68, 230, 454 (n. 37)
Perry, Rick, 417
Pittsburgh Courier, 74
Ploch, A. J., 138, 167, 457 (n. 84)
Plumbers and Steam Fitters' Union. *See* United Association of Plumbers and Pipefitters Local 142
Political Association of Spanish-Speaking Organizations (PASO), 232, 411, 451–52 (n. 77); 1961 U.S. Senate race and, 245, 246; 1962 gubernatorial race and, 266–67, 268–69, 270, 271, 272, 273, 275, 276–77, 278, 294, 301; 1963 Democratic Coalition and, 281, 283, 291, 307, 309, 315, 318, 319, 321, 476 (n. 55); 1964 post-election Democratic Coalition and, 382, 390, 405; 1964 upcoming elections and, 372, 373, 375, 376; black civil rights activism and, 1–2, 321, 327, 328, 342, 346, 348; civil rights activism and, 242, 278, 294, 335, 336, 337; Crystal City revolt aftermath and, 301, 303–4, 305–8, 314, 354, 476 (n. 62); Crystal City revolt and, 293, 294, 295, 296, 297, 298, 299, 300, 302–3, 346, 476 (n. 55); *mexicano* labor movement and, 334, 363, 364, 367, 399, 400, 401, 402, 403, 483–84 (n. 3), 485 (n. 13); multi-racial coalition and, 250, 256–57, 258, 259–60, 267–68, 274, 414, 472 (n. 65); poll tax drive, 1961 and, 260, 262, 264; poll tax repeal possibility and, 352, 353–54, 355. *See also* Peña, Albert A., Jr.
"Politico, Don," 135, 136–37, 266, 354
Poll taxes. *See* Texas poll taxes
Popular Front, 33, 47, 55, 438 (n. 95)
Populism, 10, 80, 119, 161

Port Arthur, 111, 116
Postal Alliance, 77
Prairie View A&M College, 62, 369
President's Committee on Equal Employment Opportunity, 233
Progressive Era, 44
Progressive Party, 81–83, 89, 90, 95, 108; 1948 presidential election and, 82–83, 84, 85, 96, 97, 99, 100, 112, 120, 444 (nn. 65, 68)
Progressive Voters League (PVL), 68, 94, 95, 107–8, 226, 229, 363
Progressive Youth Association (PYA), 194–95, 197, 198, 199–200, 202, 291, 292, 405, 462 (n. 9)
Prohibition, 48
Project VOTE, 389; 1964 upcoming elections and, 361, 362–65, 366, 367, 368, 371–72, 375, 377, 379, 380, 396; poll tax drive, 1964 and, 370, 415–16; poll tax repeal possibility and, 351–59
Public information officers (PIOs), 362–63, 365–68, 374, 483–84 (n. 3)

Quin, Charles Kennon (C. K.), 25, 36, 39, 42, 43, 48, 49, 50, 53–54

Racial discrimination: armed forces and, 143, 453 (n. 24); Houston and, 56–57, 74, 78; Mexican Americans and, 119–20, 125, 126, 129; San Antonio and, 159, 453 (n. 25). *See also* Segregation
Racial diversity, 6–7, 430–31 (n. 2)
Railroad Brotherhoods, 58, 73, 91, 94, 108
Rainey, Homer, 80, 94, 95, 112, 188
Randolph, A. Philip, 47, 74, 140, 141, 142, 438 (n. 95)
Randolph, Mrs. R. D. (Frankie Carter), 122, 123, 131, 265–66; 1958 Gonzalez gubernatorial race and, 160, 163–64; 1960 presidential primary election and, 217–18, 220–21, 222; 1961 U.S. Senate race and, 243, 245; Democratic National Committee and, 117, 118, 124, 215, 217, 219, 222; Democratic National Convention of 1956 and, 117, 118, 215; Democrats of Texas (DOT) and, 118–19, 160, 163–64, 165, 215, 243, 245; Harris County Democrats (HCD) and, 114–15, 116, 117, 118, 124, 218; multiracial coalition and, 247, 469 (n. 37)
Rattler, 207, 208, 463 (n. 29), 463–64 (n. 31)
Rayburn, Sam, 147, 215, 220, 224
Reagon, Bernice Johnson, 409
Reconstruction Finance Corporation, 35, 453 (n. 25)
Red Scare, 84, 89, 90, 95, 100, 108, 112, 113, 173
Reed, Julia Scott, 364, 365, 380, 484 (n. 9)
Republican Party, 3, 10, 52, 65, 83, 285, 349, 417, 419; 1952 presidential election and, 109, 152; 1956 presidential election and, 109, 215; 1960 presidential election and, 217, 226, 230, 231; 1961 U.S. Senate race and, 243, 245–46, 264, 469 (n. 32), 487 (n. 36); 1962 gubernatorial race and, 264, 267, 278, 279, 487 (n. 36); 1964 elections and, 361, 376–77; 2016 presidential campaign and, 420; Mexican Americans and, 4, 130, 258, 382
Reuther, Walter, 178
Reynolds v. Sims, 404–5
Richards, Ann, 3, 408, 417
Richardson, Clifton, Sr., 67
Richmond, M. J., 105
Rio Grande City, 398
Robeson, Paul, 82
Rolla, Lenora, 365, 375, 376
Roosevelt, Eleanor, 116, 178
Roosevelt, Franklin D., 12, 36, 53, 65, 74, 80, 81, 93, 109, 110, 114, 214

Sager, James, 32
Sager, Maria Solís, 32
Salinas, Mary, 92
Sampson, Alfred, 386, 387, 388
Samuel Huston College, 141–42
San Antonio, 12–13, 86; 1962 gubernatorial race and, 272, 273, 278; civil rights activism, 1960s and, 203–13,

530 Index

223, 285, 286, 287–90, 293, 340, 342; civil rights activism and, 137, 138–39, 140, 144–45, 157–58, 159, 192, 251, 339, 413–14, 455 (n. 59); labor movement, 1930s and, 29, 36; labor movement, 1950s and, 150, 171, 172–75, 179–87, 188–93, 236; labor movement, 1960s and, 210–11, 212–13, 360, 403, 407; Maverick's mayoral campaign and, 43–45, 47–50, 82, 439 (nn. 107, 109, 111); Mexican-American civil rights and, 127, 130, 135, 149–50, 192, 236; Mexican American middle classes and, 22, 28, 48–49, 140, 250; *mexicano* labor movement and, 363, 365–67, 398, 399, 401, 485 (n. 13); neighborhoods and, 146; politics, 1930s and, 25, 28–29, 34, 35–39, 43–45, 47–54, 133; politics, 1950s and, 109, 120, 139–40, 145–58, 161, 169–70, 453 (n. 12), 454 (n. 36), 457 (n. 84); politics, 1960s and, 193, 195–96, 218–19, 229, 230, 239–42, 246, 250, 258, 285–90, 372; politics, later 1940s and, 133–39, 438 (n. 94); politics, later 1960s and, 406–7; poll tax repeal possibility and, 354, 357; segregated housing and, 144–45, 146; sit-ins and, 195, 203–4, 405; stand-ins and, 206–7; white backlash, 1950s and, 95, 139–40, 453 (n. 12). *See also* African Americans; Mexican Americans; *Mexicanos*; National Association for the Advancement of Colored People (NAACP); San Antonio pecan shellers

San Antonio AFL-CIO Council, 175, 176, 180, 181, 183, 184

San Antonio *AFL-CIO Weekly Dispatch*, 185

San Antonio Chamber of Commerce, 37, 139–40, 153, 154, 169, 171, 175, 180, 191, 285

San Antonio Chicano Organizers (SACO), 407

San Antonio College, 134, 204

San Antonio Independent School District, 133, 135, 136

San Antonio Labor Council of the AFL, 150

San Antonio Mother's Service Organization, 142

San Antonio pecan shellers, 22–23, 33, 37, 38, 40–41, 49, 55, 82, 90, 120, 147; layoffs and, 41–43, 48; strike, 1938 and, 14, 20–21, 23–29, 30, 32, 34, 36, 50, 112, 126, 133, 171, 176, 180, 458 (n. 19)

San Antonio Police Department, 37, 39, 51, 52, 53; pecan shellers strike, 1930s and, 25–26, 28, 29

San Antonio Register, 145, 157, 159

San Antonio Union Junior College, 133, 134, 136, 145, 289, 438 (n. 94), 452 (n. 6)

Sánchez, George I., 351, 467 (n. 5), 468 (n. 21), 487 (n. 48); 1962 gubernatorial race and, 269, 272, 277; 1963 Democratic Coalition and, 279–80, 308, 314, 477 (n. 71); Crystal City revolt and, 299, 303; Mexican-American civil rights and, 235, 414; *mexicano* labor movement and, 401; mission statement on Mexican Americans and, 240–41, 250, 266–67, 268, 280, 281, 412–13; PASO and, 266–68, 303, 328

Sanchez, R. P. "Bob," 241, 245, 269, 410, 468 (n. 20), 476 (n. 58); 1960 presidential election and, 225–26, 230; 1963 Democratic Coalition and, 280, 477 (n. 68); Democrats of Texas (DOT) and, 162, 163, 164; *mexicano* labor movement and, 235–38, 239, 334, 414, 483–84 (n. 3); PASO and, 256, 303, 304; poll tax drive, 1961 and, 255, 262

Sanders, Bernie, 412

Schmidt, Fred, 238–39

School Improvement League (La Liga Pro Defensor Escolar), 135, 137, 149, 454 (n. 36)

Scott, Joseph, 290, 292

Scott, Julia. *See* Reed, Julia Scott

Seabrook, J. J., 333

Segregation, 12, 82, 170; boxing and, 154; civil rights unionism and, 70–71, 73, 74–79, 442 (n. 36); Democratic

Index 531

Segregation (*continued*)
Party and, 147, 162–63, 456 (n. 72); higher education and, 70, 71–73, 78, 84–85, 96, 319–20, 341; hotels and, 76, 77, 162, 244; housing and, 11, 144–45, 146, 287; Huntsville movement and, 383–89; labor movement, 1930s and, 58, 60, 66, 68, 69, 127; labor movement, 1940s and, 71, 74–79, 111–12; labor movement, 1950s and, 91–93, 96, 104–6, 172–75, 190; labor movement, 1960s and, 194, 201, 405; lunch counters and, 194, 195, 196–97, 199–200, 212; Mexican Americans and, 7, 43, 129–30, 135, 137, 147–49; *mexicanos* and, 148–49, 253, 453–54 (n. 35), 470 (n. 45); movie theaters and, 206–7, 208–9, 329–30, 384–85; private businesses and, 287–88, 290; public facilities and, 138–39, 157–58, 194, 197, 223, 253, 320, 327, 341, 342, 455 (n. 59); restaurants and, 43, 203–4, 365, 384, 385, 387; schools and, 45, 71–72, 102, 120, 134, 135, 137, 147–49, 453–54 (n. 35); sit-ins and, 194, 195, 203, 461 (n. 3); Texas laws and, 281. *See also* Civil rights movement; Desegregation

Seligmann, "King" Julius, 23, 28, 29, 41, 42

Servicemen's Readjustment Act of 1944. *See* G.I. Bill

Shafer, Ray, 210, 294, 296, 297, 298, 300, 303, 305, 478 (n. 4)

Shell Oil Refinery, 111, 114, 127

Shepperd, John Ben, 98

Shivers, Allan, 95–96, 150, 226, 246; 1952 gubernatorial primary campaign and, 112, 113; 1952 presidential election and, 109, 114, 130, 151, 152; 1954 gubernatorial primary campaign and, 115–17, 121, 274; 1956 gubernatorial primary campaign and, 117, 123; 1956 presidential election and, 109, 118, 130, 215

Simpson, L. H., 97

Slough, Nate, 382

Smith, A. Maceo, 67, 68, 99, 107

Smith, J. Edwin, 114
Smith, Lillian Viola, 45
Smith, Lonnie, 67, 69, 72
Smith, Sherrill, 171, 191, 400
Smith, Virginia, 114
Smith v. Allwright, 56, 68, 69–70, 71, 72, 78, 79, 80, 85, 108, 112, 119, 347, 443 (n. 55)

SNAP News: 1962 gubernatorial race and, 271–72, 273–74, 275; 1963 Democratic Coalition and, 314, 366; civil rights activism and, 158, 159, 192, 203, 205–6, 208, 209, 211–12, 223, 342, 455 (n. 59); founding of, 145; labor movement, 1960s and, 210, 211, 360; politics, 1950s and, 172, 457 (n. 84); politics, 1960s and, 229, 243, 246, 258, 278, 285–86, 288, 289–90, 360, 361, 411, 474 (nn. 24, 26); support for Mexican Americans and, 157, 167, 414

Snid, Alberta Zepeda, 27–28, 29

Socialist Party, 15, 16, 17, 20, 26, 30, 86, 90

Solis, Lalo, 168, 225, 271, 306, 340, 454 (n. 37)

Southern Christian Leadership Conference (SCLC), 385, 386, 388, 389, 391, 400, 487 (n. 48)

Southern Manifesto, 216

Southern Pacific Railroad, 61–62, 63, 104, 105, 405

Southern Pecan Company, 23

Southern Regional Council, 318

Southern Summer School for Workers, 40

Southern Tenant Farmers Union (STFU), 16

South Texas School of Law, 147

Southwestern Bell, 91, 209

Southwest Voter Registration and Education Project, 406

Spears, Franklin, 218, 229, 465 (n. 55), 470 (n. 41)

State Democratic Executive Committee (SDEC), 162, 163, 164

State of Texas v. NAACP, 68

States' Rights Party, 83, 94

Stearns, Eldrewey, 103, 104, 196–97, 199, 200, 202, 448 (n. 30), 462 (n. 9), 463 (n. 20)
St. Edward's University, 380, 401
Stevenson, Adlai, 109, 118, 130, 151–52, 156, 189, 219, 223
Stewart, ZerNona, 143
Stilwell, Hart, 303
St. Mary's University, 147, 203, 204, 206–7, 287, 295
Stock Handlers Union No. 59, 92
Stockton, Kate Bradford, 16
Storm, Marion, 94
St. Philip's College, 134, 141, 143, 204
Student League for Industrial Democracy, 15
Student Nonviolent Coordinating Committee (SNCC), 7, 197, 383, 462 (n. 9)
Students for a Democratic Society (SDS), 390, 394
Students for Civil Liberties (SCL), 203, 206–9, 212, 405
Students for Direct Action (SDA), 329–30, 479–80 (n. 29)
Survey Graphic, 37, 43
Sutton, Garlington Jerome (G. J.), 45–46, 86, 329, 437–38 (n. 92), 438 (n. 96); 1960 presidential election and, 229, 230, 231; 1960 presidential primary election and, 219, 221, 223, 224; 1962 gubernatorial race and, 271, 272, 273; 1963 Democratic Coalition and, 316, 317, 319, 331, 366, 477 (n. 68), 478 (n. 4); 1964 elections and, 372, 374, 378; Black-Coleman partnership and, 143, 145, 157; civil rights activism and, 138–39, 144–45, 159, 195, 213, 252, 253, 340, 341, 409, 413–14; civil rights ordinance and, 286, 288, 290; Democrats of Texas (DOT) and, 167, 215; equal rights employment and, 206, 209; Garcia partnership and, 133, 134, 135–37, 139, 169–70; labor movement, 1950s and, 172; March on Austin and, 342, 346, 348; Mexican-American partnership and, 152, 153, 154, 157, 158, 171, 258, 454 (n. 48); multi-racial coalition, 1930s and, 45, 50; multi-racial coalitions, 1950s and, 151, 159, 175, 186, 189, 192, 193; multi-racial coalitions, 1960s and, 207, 219, 221, 223, 224, 229, 234, 252, 253, 258, 288; political office and, 133, 134, 145, 244, 285–87, 289, 407, 438 (n. 94), 452 (n. 6); politics, San Antonio, 1930s and, 47, 48, 49, 50, 51, 52, 82; politics, San Antonio, 1950s and, 140, 167, 457 (n. 84); politics, San Antonio, early 1940s and, 53, 54; politics, San Antonio, later 1940s and, 137–39, 438 (n. 94), 452 (n. 6); sit-ins and, 203, 204, 214, 285, 419; underpass campaign and, 211–12
Sutton, Lou Nelle, 229–30
Sutton, Samuel J., 45, 134, 438 (n. 94)
Sutton-Taylor, Lillian W., 47
Sweatt, Heman Marion, 70–71, 72–73, 77, 84–85, 101, 138
Sweatt, James Leonard, 71, 73, 442 (n. 36)
Sweatt case, 68, 78, 84, 96, 97, 347

Taft-Hartley Act of 1947, 80–81, 89, 128, 318, 373
Tarrant County Precinct Workers' Council, 363
Taylor, Hobart, Sr., 121–22, 272
Teamsters union, 111, 210–11, 334, 340, 400, 405, 478 (n. 4); Crystal City revolt aftermath and, 304, 305, 306, 307; Crystal City revolt and, 294–96, 298, 299, 300, 302, 303, 346, 363
Tea Party, 418
Tejanos, 12, 22, 430–31 (n. 2)
Tenayuca, Emma, 22–23, 24, 25, 26–27, 33, 36, 46, 52, 54, 458 (n. 19)
Terrell Election Laws, 64
Texas: maps of regions and cities and, 11, 88, 146, 261, 263; nineteenth to early twentieth century and, 10–12, 34–35; recent political history and, 2–4, 417–21
Texas AFL-CIO. *See* Texas State AFL-CIO

Texas AFL-CIO News, 227
Texas Centennial Exposition, 47, 67
Texas Civil Liberties Union (TCLU), 34, 37, 435 (n. 47)
Texas Club of Democratic Voters, 108
Texas Communist Party, 95. *See also* Communist Party
Texas Council of Voters (TCV), 68, 162, 264, 352, 364; 1960 presidential election and, 226, 229; 1961 U.S. Senate race and, 244, 468 (n. 29); 1962 gubernatorial race and, 266, 271, 273; 1963 Democratic Coalition and, 281, 308, 315, 316, 318, 319, 331, 474 (n. 12); 1964 post-election Democratic Coalition and, 379, 390–91; 1964 upcoming elections and, 372, 373, 374, 375; civil rights activism and, 1, 328, 333, 334, 340, 344, 346, 347, 348; multi-racial coalition and, 247, 250, 258, 259; origins of, 107–8, 414
Texas Employment Commission, 337, 363, 406
Texas Farmers Union, 94, 95, 163, 220
Texas Federation Club (TFC), 76, 77
Texas Industrial Commission, 28–29, 36
Texas Liberal Democrats (TLD), 390, 391, 392, 395, 412
Texas Observer: 1961 U.S. congress race and, 257; 1961 U.S. Senate race and, 245; 1962 gubernatorial race and, 271, 281, 473 (n. 9); 1963 Democratic Coalition and, 309, 312, 313, 315, 316–17, 346; 1964 elections and, 377, 378; 1964 post-election Democratic Coalition and, 379, 381, 382, 390, 392; 1964 upcoming elections and, 372, 374; civil rights activism and, 204, 213, 284, 321, 330, 344, 348, 383, 386; Crystal City revolt and, 300–301, 303; founding of, 119; labor movement, 1960s and, 239, 321; labor movement, San Antonio, 1950s and, 171, 187, 190; multi-racial coalition and, 218–19, 220, 221, 222, 223, 248, 249, 267, 268, 279–80; politics, 1960s and, 224, 292; poll tax drives and, 248, 350, 370; poll tax repeal possibility and, 355, 356
Texas Open Shop Association, 10
Texas Organization of Liberal Democrats (TOLD), 111, 373, 376, 377, 380, 381, 382
Texas poll taxes, 192, 217; 1962 upcoming elections and, 186, 248–49, 252, 254, 257, 259–62, 273; 1964 upcoming elections and, 360, 361, 368, 415–16; African Americans, 1960s and, 246, 252, 254, 260–62, 264, 273, 285, 363, 369; African Americans and, 10, 64–65, 69, 103, 108, 119, 179, 370; call for abolition and, 276, 318; Mexican Americans, 1960s and, 238, 240, 254, 257, 259–60, 262–65, 294–95, 296, 297, 307, 362–68, 467 (n. 5); Mexican Americans and, 38, 39, 51, 128, 129, 150, 155, 235; poll tax drives and, 226–29, 243, 248–49, 255, 259–62, 264, 266, 280, 283, 306, 350, 368, 369–71, 377, 415–16; possible repeal and, 349–59, 362, 364, 371, 377, 483 (nn. 79, 87), 485 (n. 17); Voting Rights Act of 1965 and, 389
Texas Rangers, 98, 296, 298, 301–2, 307, 313, 363, 390, 398, 402, 403, 404, 408
Texas Social and Legislative Conference (TSLC), 94–95, 178, 259
Texas Southern University (TSU), 103, 196, 197, 199, 329, 392
Texas State Advisory Committee to the United States Commission on Human Rights, 403
Texas State AFL-CIO, 187, 413, 419, 466–67 (n. 4), 467 (n. 6); 1958 gubernatorial race and, 162, 163; 1960 presidential election and, 220, 223, 224, 226–27, 228; 1961 U.S. Senate race and, 245, 246; 1962 gubernatorial race and, 266, 272, 273; 1963 Democratic Coalition and, 280, 308, 315, 478 (n. 4); 1964 post-election Democratic Coalition and, 380, 382, 383, 388, 487 (n. 48); 1964 upcoming elections and, 370–71, 373–74; African Americans and, 84, 108–9, 172, 201, 226–29, 255,

260; Brown presidency and, 233–34, 238–39; civil rights activism and, 234, 238, 319, 320–26, 327–28, 346, 348–49, 354, 368, 411; Crystal City revolt and, 295, 299; equal rights employment and, 284, 368, 403; Mexican Americans and, 172, 191–92, 235–38, 239, 241, 255; *mexicano* civil rights activism and, 334–39; *mexicano* labor movement and, 361–68, 400, 401, 483–84 (n. 3), 485 (n. 13); poll tax drives and, 226–29, 255, 260–62, 264, 370–71; poll tax repeal possibility and, 352, 355, 483 (n. 79); public information officers (PIOs) and, 362–63, 365–68, 374, 483–84 (n. 3); Tex-Son strike and, 184, 191; voter registration and, 108–9, 350
Texas State Board of Education, 148
Texas State CIO Council, 90, 91, 92, 94, 178, 189, 234
Texas State Conference of Branches of the NAACP, 1, 47, 67–68, 72, 73, 77, 92, 99, 107, 154, 209, 414
Texas State Federation of Labor (TSFL), 19, 75–77, 78, 93, 94, 95–96, 188, 189, 234, 442 (n. 49)
Texas State Industrial Union Council, 382
Tex-Son strike, 175–77, 179, 180–86, 187, 190, 191, 193, 458 (n. 19), 459 (n. 31), 459–60 (n. 32), 460 (n. 46)
Third Ward Civic Club (Houston), 66
Thomas, Cline, 135
Thomas, George, 92
Thomas, Norman, 15, 30
Thurmond, Strom, 83, 94
Tijerina, Felix, 129–30, 451 (n. 76)
Toledano, Vicente Lombardo, 34
Tollet, Kenneth, 392
Tower, John, 243, 245, 246, 264, 339, 382, 417, 469 (n. 32), 487 (nn. 36, 46, 48)
Travis County Commissioners Court, 372
Treaty of Guadalupe-Hidalgo of 1848, 403–4
Trinity University, 204
Truman, Harry S., 142; 1948 presidential election and, 82–83, 109, 147, 444 (nn. 65, 68); labor legislation and, 80–81, 127
Trump, Donald, 420
Turman, James, 273
Twenty-Fourth Amendment, 349, 350, 371

United Association of Plumbers and Pipefitters Local 142, 187, 188
United Auto Workers (UAW), 18, 20, 178, 225, 373, 382, 405–6, 407, 478 (n. 4); *mexicano* labor movement and, 398, 403; Texas State AFL-CIO civil rights activism and, 323, 324, 363, 364
United Auto Workers (UAW) Local 893, 239
United Cannery, Agricultural, Packinghouse, and Allied Workers of America (UCAPAWA), 22, 27, 28, 36, 38, 41, 42, 43, 49; Lambert, George P. and, 23, 32, 33, 40, 436 (n. 72)
United Electrical Workers (UE), 173
United Farm Workers, 398
United Hatters, Cap, and Millinery Workers, AFL, 178
United Mine Workers (UMW), 15, 188
United Packinghouse Workers of America (UPWA), 91–92, 173, 225, 323
United Political Organization (UPO), 292–93, 307, 316, 327, 328, 332–33, 339–40, 341, 345, 346–48, 349, 378, 380
United Steelworkers, 373
University of North Carolina Woman's College, 30
University of Texas, 80, 94, 96, 110, 112, 113, 153, 160, 235; civil rights activism and, 331, 340, 388; integration and, 329; segregation and, 72, 84
UPI (United Press International), 323, 325, 337
U.S. Commission on Civil Rights, 403
U.S. Constitution, 52, 64, 70, 71
U.S. Department of Labor, 42, 233, 324, 366
U.S. House of Representatives, 186, 215, 243, 257–58

U.S. Immigration and Naturalization Service, 405
U.S. Senate, 80, 215, 382–83, 417, 420; 1948 elections and, 127, 216, 230; 1957 special election and, 123–24, 131, 160, 242, 450 (n. 62); 1958 elections and, 124, 129, 160, 162, 163; 1961 special election and, 232–33, 242–46, 257, 261, 264, 468 (nn. 25, 29), 469 (n. 32), 487 (n. 36); 1964 elections and, 361, 369, 373, 375, 376–77, 378, 379, 396, 487 (n. 39)
U.S. Senate Subcommittee on Migratory Labor, 402–3
U.S. State Department, 26
U.S. Supreme Court, 66, 90, 198, 336; *Brown v. Board* decision, 98, 102, 120, 134, 158, 201, 321; *Grovey v. Townsend*, 65, 68, 78; *Hernandez v. Texas*, 127, 128, 149; *Medrano v. Allee*, 403; *Reynolds v. Sims*, 404–5; *Sweatt* case, 68, 78, 84, 96, 97, 347. *See also Smith v. Allwright*

Valentine, Cora, 178
Vance, Peggy, 32
Van de Putte, Leticia, 418
Vanguard magazine, 373
Vasquez, Santos, 32, 33, 38, 49
Velasquez, Fidel, 325
Vietnam War, 390
Villareal, J. H. "Henry," 337, 483–84 (n. 3)
Villareal, Perfecto, 206–7, 208, 209
Viva Kennedy clubs, 156, 239–40, 241, 243, 259, 274, 277, 411, 468 (n. 20); 1960 presidential election and, 225–26, 229, 230, 231, 238; PASO and, 232, 256, 257, 306, 355, 363, 451–52 (n. 77)
Voigt, Kathleen, 151, 219
Voter Education Project, 318
Voters of Texas Enlist (VOTE), 318, 351, 356
Voting rights, 6, 10
Voting Rights Act of 1965, 389, 404, 405, 479–80 (n. 29)

Wagner Act of 1935, 20, 22, 80, 81, 91, 408
Wallace, Frank, 323
Wallace, George, 1, 319, 344
Wallace, Henry, 81, 82, 83, 84, 443 (n. 60), 444 (n. 68)
Ward, M. L., 102, 446–47 (n. 22)
War on Poverty, 366, 367, 474 (n. 28)
Washington, George, Jr., 292
Washington Post, 356
Webb County Central Labor Council, 336, 338
Weiss, Theo, 175, 180, 185
Welch, Louie, 194
Wells, Joe, 406
Wesley, Carter, 67, 68, 70, 96–97, 100, 105
West Virginia, 14–16
White, A. C. "Jack," 137, 154
White, Bill, 417
White, Mrs. Charles E. (Mrs. Hattie Mae), 102, 447 (n. 28), 488 (n. 62)
White, Julius, 67, 70, 87, 100, 445 (n. 1)
White, Lulu Belle Madison, 77, 90; Houston NAACP and, 67–68, 69, 70, 72, 74, 78, 85, 96–98, 99, 100, 106, 446 (n. 17); Progressive Party and, 81–82, 443 (n. 60), 444 (n. 68); Texas State Conference of Branches of the NAACP and, 73, 107; voting rights and, 70, 80
White, Mark, 408
White Citizens Councils, 98, 102, 321, 339
White liberal Democrats, 80, 87, 88; 1940s and, 93, 94; 1961 U.S. Senate race and, 232, 233, 243, 246; 1963 Democratic Coalition and, 303, 309, 310–12, 316–17; 1964 post-election Democratic Coalition and, 380, 381–83, 389–97, 488 (n. 62); African Americans and, 112, 119–24, 137, 280, 374, 450 (n. 62); civil rights activism and, 387–88, 389, 392; Mexican Americans and, 118, 119, 150, 151, 152, 157, 162, 165–66, 167, 170, 172, 191, 192, 257; multi-racial coalition and, 220, 249, 250, 251, 253, 259, 265, 465 (n. 55), 470 (n. 41); political patronage and, 251, 265–66; politics, 1950s and, 109–10, 111, 112–23, 129, 131–32,

160, 162–66, 179, 189, 214–15, 216; politics, 1960s and, 216, 217–19, 313–14, 375–76, 377; politics, 1970s and, 407–8. *See also* Democrats of Texas (DOT); Harris County Democrats (HCD)

"White primary," 44, 45, 48, 56, 64–66, 67, 68–70, 72, 73, 82, 84, 85, 107, 108, 119, 121, 226, 231

White supremacists, 54, 89, 102, 120, 410; 1963 Democratic Coalition and, 283–84, 309–11, 362; civil rights activism and, 320, 340, 356, 360; Democratic Party and, 65, 80, 86, 94, 108, 195; labor movement and, 59, 93, 96; multi-racial coalition and, 249, 255, 412, 465 (n. 55)

Wickliff, Aloysius, 103

Wiginton, Martin, 376, 377

Wilberforce College, 46, 438 (n. 92)

Wiley College, 46

Williams, Claude, 177

Williams, Francis, 200, 308, 319, 346

Williams, Harrison, 402

Wilson, Will, 243, 244, 245, 246, 271

Women's Activities Department (WAD) Committees, 254–55

Workers Alliance of America (WAA), 16, 23, 24–25, 27, 28, 41, 42, 54

Works Progress Administration (WPA), 24–25, 28, 41, 42

Wright, Herman, 82, 90, 95, 97, 112

Wright, Jim, 243, 245, 246, 487 (n. 46)

Yarborough, Don, 266, 292, 306, 390; 1962 gubernatorial race and, 265, 267, 268–70, 271, 272–74, 280, 330, 411, 471–72 (n. 62); 1964 elections and, 375; 1964 upcoming elections and, 348, 359, 370, 371, 372, 373–74, 380

Yarborough, Ralph W., 161, 226, 250, 265, 356, 381, 412; 1952 gubernatorial primary campaign and, 112–14, 160, 449 (n. 47); 1954 gubernatorial primary campaign and, 115–16, 117, 121, 160, 234, 274, 449 (n. 47), 458 (n. 13); 1956 gubernatorial primary campaign and, 117, 157, 160, 449 (n. 47), 458 (n. 13); 1957 U.S. Senate election and, 123–24, 131, 160, 242, 450 (n. 62); 1958 U.S. Senate reelection and, 124, 129, 160, 162; 1964 reelection and, 369, 375, 376–77, 378, 379, 396, 487 (n. 39); 1964 upcoming elections and, 361, 370, 371, 372, 373, 374, 380; 1970 defeat and, 407; African Americans and, 112, 119, 120–21, 122–23, 280, 374, 450 (n. 62); civil rights and, 327, 339, 360, 369, 374; Mexican Americans and, 166, 167, 267, 280, 302, 307, 374, 402; white liberal Democrats and, 117, 119, 157, 163, 164, 166, 251

Young Men's Christian Association (YMCA), 199, 316, 364

Young People's Socialist League, 15

Young Women's Christian Association (YWCA), 143; Blue Triangle Branch and, 62, 107

Zachary, H. B., 188

Zepeda, Mrs., 27, 28